The Economies of Argentina and Brazil

The Economies of Argentina and Brazil

A Comparative Perspective

Edited by

Werner Baer
Lemann Professor of Economics, University of Illinois, Urbana-Champaign, USA

David Fleischer
Representative for Southern Brazil and Uruguay, Inter-American Foundation (IAF), Arlington, Virginia, USA

With the assistance of Lawrence De Geest

Edward Elgar
Cheltenham, UK • Northampton, MA, USA

Published by
Edward Elgar Publishing Limited
The Lypiatts
15 Lansdown Road
Cheltenham
Glos GL50 2JA
UK

Edward Elgar Publishing, Inc.
William Pratt House
9 Dewey Court
Northampton
Massachusetts 01060
USA

A catalogue record for this book
is available from the British Library

Library of Congress Control Number: 2011925796

ISBN 978 1 84980 996 2

Typeset by Servis Filmsetting Ltd, Stockport, Cheshire
Printed and bound by MPG Books Group, UK

Contents

PART VIII FOREIGN TRADE AND INVESTMENT: PAST AND PRESENT

Contributors

Horacio Aguirre is a researcher on issues related to macroeconomic and monetary policy, having published articles and working papers on the subjects of monetary regimes in developing economies, monetary aggregates forecasting, and the financial position of households in Argentina, among others. He holds a BA in Economics from the University of Buenos Aires, an MA in Economics from Torcuato Di Tella University and is a doctoral candidate in Economics from San Andrés University. He is also a Lecturer at the University of Buenos Aires.

Edmund Amann is Reader in Development Economics at the University of Manchester, UK. He is also Adjunct Professor at the School for Advanced International Studies (SAIS) of the Johns Hopkins University, Baltimore, MD, USA. He is the author of many articles on economic development, with special emphasis on Brazil and technology. His books include *Economic Liberalization and Industrial Performance in Brazil* (Oxford, 2000) and *Regulating Economic Development: Lessons from Africa and Latin America* (Cheltenham, 2007).

Daniel G. Arce M. is Professor of Economics and Program Head at the University of Texas – Dallas, USA. He has published numerous articles on game theory, collective action, business ethics, (counter-) terrorism, and Latin American economies. He has won the inaugural Thomas Fellowship of Teaching Excellence at the Culverhouse College of Commerce and Business Administration (University of Alabama), the Dean's Award for Research and Creative Activity at Rhodes College and the Alumni Achievement Award at Western Michigan University. He has received two Fulbright grants for study and research in Latin America. Professor Arce is the editor of *Defense and Peace Economics* and is on the editorial board of the *The Southern Economic Journal.*

Carlos R. Azzoni is Professor of Economics at the University of São Paulo, Brazil, and was Dean of the School of Economics, Administration and Accounting there from 2006 to 2010. He was also Visiting Professor at Cornell University, Ohio State University and the University of Illinois, USA. His area of research is economic inequality in general, with a focus on regional inequality. He has chaired the Regional Planning Division of the state of São Paulo Secretariat of Planning for seven years. He has pubished seven books (in Portuguese) and over 50 papers in Brazilian and international refereed journals.

Carlos José Caetano Bacha is currently Professor of Economics at the University of São Paulo at Piracicaba (Esalq), Brazil. He has published extensively on such topics as economic development and policies concerning agriculture and forests.

Werner Baer is the Lemann Professor of Economics at the University of Illinois at Urbana-Champaign, USA. He is the author of many articles and books dealing with Latin American economic development, with special emphasis on Brazil. These include *The Brazilian Economy: Growth and Development*, 6th edition (Boulder, CO, 2008).

Alexandre Rands Barros is Professor of Economics at the Federal University of Pernambuco, Brazil. He is the author of many articles, including: 'How to make bankers richer: the Brazilian financial market with public and private banks', *The Quarterly Review of Economics and Finance*, May 2008, and 'A periodization of the business cycles in the Brazilian Economy', *Revista Brasileira de Economia*, January 1993.

Ricardo Bebczuk is Professor of Economics at the Universidad Nacional de la Plata, and Visiting Professor at the Universidad San Andres, Argentina. He is also a Senior Visiting Researcher at the Central Bank of Argentina. His book *Asymetric Information in Financial Markets: Introduction and Applications* (Cambridge, 2003) is a widely used texbook in intermediate and advanced courses in finance and banking in several countries.

César Ciappa is Associate Professor of Agricultural Finance and Economics at the Universidad de Belgrano, Argentina. He worked as a consultant on Agricultural Finance and Economics for the Inter-American Development Bank, the Corporación Andina de Fomento and the Argentine Ministries of Economics and Agriculture. He was also consultant to the Presidency of the Republic of Ecuador. He is a co-author of the book *Economic and Social Impact Evaluation of Public Policy in the Argentine Agroindustrial Chain* (La Plata, Argentina, 2007) and the author of *Agroindustrial Policy: Agroindustrial Sustainable Growth* (Buenos Aires, 2009).

Donald N. Coes is Professor Emeritus of Economics at the University of New Mexico, Albuquerque, USA. He is the author of many articles on international trade and on the Brazilian economy, including

Macroeconomic Crises, Policies, and Growth in Brazil, 1964–90 (Washington, DC, 1995).

Lawrence De Geest is a graduate student at the University of Massachusetts at Amherst, USA.

Atilio Elizagaray is Professor and Director of the Department of Economics at the National University of La Plata, Argentina. He is also the Executive Director of the Masters Program in Public Finance at that university. He was consultant to the World Bank, General Coordinator of the General Program of Technical Assistance of the Social Services Administration. He is the author of many articles on public finance.

Adolfo Figueroa is Professor Emeritus of Economics at the Pontificia Universidad Católica del Peru in Lima, and currently Researcher at the Centrum Business School of that university. He has published many books and articles in the field of economic growth and income distribution. His latest book is *A Unified Theory of Capitalist Development* (Lima, 2009).

David Fleischer is the Representative for Southern Brazil and Uruguay at the Inter-American Foundation (IAF), Arlington, Virginia, USA, and currently the Executive Director of the Brazilian Studies Association. He has a PhD in Cultural Anthropology and conducts research on environmental conservation and community-based development projects in Brazil and Mexico. His focus is on political ecology and sustainable livelihoods as well as the economic impacts of conservation on local markets.

Manuel A.R. da Fonseca is Professor of Economics and Finance at the Federal University of Rio de Janeiro, Brazil. He is currently the Head of that university's MBA program in Finance and Risk Management. He has published books on Applied Linear Algebra to Finance, Economics and Econometrics, and on Planning and Economic Development. He has worked as a consultant in macroeconomic planning and forecasting.

Andrés Gallo is Associate Professor of Economics and Director of the International Business Program at the Coggin College of Business, University of North Florida, USA. His research and teaching interests include Latin American economic development, property rights in agriculture, institutions, international economies and political economy, as well as law and economies in property rights and the internet.

Esteban Manuel Greco is a consultant in the fields of regulatory economies and competition policy, with special experience in the energy sector. He was Comissioner and Chief Economist at the National Commission of

Competition Defense (CNDC) and Deputy Manager of Performance and Economics at the National Entity of Gas Regulation (ENARGAS). He is also Professor of Economics of Regulation at the Center for the Study of Energy Regulatory Activity (CEARE) and teaches at the University of Buenos Aires Law School, Argentina.

Joaquim J.M. Guilhoto is Professor of Eonomics at the University of São Paulo (USP), Brazil. He was visiting Professor at MIT in 2010 and the Head of the Department of Economics at USP from 2005 to 2009. He is associate with the Regional Economics Application Laboratory (REAL) at the University of Illinois. For more than 20 years he specialized in the structural analysis of national and regional economies. Lately he has been focussing his research on questions related to energy, natural resources and environmental economies. He has more than 200 works published in his field of research, including books, papers and book chapters.

Geoffrey J.D. Hewings is Professor of Geography and Regional Science at the University of Illinois in Urbana-Champaign, USA, and directs the Regional Economics Application Laboratory (REAL) at that university. He has served as President of the Regional Science Association International. He has published and edited many books and articles. The books include: *Structure and Structural Change in the Brazilian Economy* – co-edited with J.M. Guilhoto – (London, 2001), *Equity Distortion in Regional Resource Allocation in Brazil* (co-edited with W. Baer) (New York, 2006) and *Structure and Structural Change in the Chilean Economy* (co-edited with P. Aroca (London, 2006)).

Daniel Heymann received his Licenciate in Economics and Physics at the Universidad de Buenos Aires, Argentina. He received his PhD in Economics at the University of California, Los Angeles, USA. He is Professor of Economics at the Universities of San Andrés, Buenos Aires and La Plata. He was Senior Economist at CEPAL, Buenos Aires.

Rodolfo Hoffmann was from 1966 to 1996 Professor of Economics at the University of São Paulo at Piracicaba, Brazil. Since 1997 he has been Professor of Economics at the Institute of Economics at the University of Campinas. He has written books on statistics for economists, econometrics, measures of inequality and poverty. His main areas of research are the analysis of income distribution, distribution of land tenure, and the modernization of Brazilian agriculture.

Andrew W. Horowitz is Professor of Economics at the Sam M. Walton College of Business at the University of Arkansas, Fayetteville, USA. He has served as analyst for the Congressional Budget Office, was a Fulbright Scholar in Brazil, consulted with the Inter-American Development bank, and accompanied and advised a US Congressional trade mission to Brazil. He has published articles in many journals, including *The American Economic Review*, *The International Economic Review* and *The Journal of Development Economics.*

Bernardo Kosacoff is Professor Titular at both the Universidad Nacional de Quilmes and the Universidad de Buenos Aires, Argentina. He was director of CEPAL-United Nations in Argentina from 2002 to 2010. He is currently the Academic Director of the Centro Empresa, Competitividad y Desarrollo (CECyD) at the Instituto Technologico de Buenos Aires – Universidad de San Andrés (ITBA–UdeSA). He is the author of 26 books and over 100 articles. He is the recipient of the Premio Konex Platino for his work in the field of development economies.

Andrés López is Director of the Centro de Investigaciones para la Transformación (CENIT), Buenos Aires, Argentina, and Head of the Department of Economics, University of Buenos Aires. He is Full Professor at the University of Buenos Aires and Invited Professor at the University of San Andrés. He has written extensively on issues related to industrial development, trade and foreign investment. He has been a consultant to several internal organizations, such as the Inter-American Development Bank, the United Nations Development Programme (UNDP), the World Intellectual Property Organization (WIPO), the International Labour Organization (ILO), the United Nations Conference on Grade and Development (UNCTAD) and the World Bank.

Joseph L. Love is Professor Emeritus of History at the University of Illinois at Urbana-Champaign, USA; he currently directs the Lemann Institute of Brazilian Studies at that university, where he was formerly Director of the Center for Latin American and Caribbean Studies. He is interested in the history of ideas, policy, and performance in Brazil and in Latin America as a whole. He is the author of *Rio Grande do Sul and Brazilian Regionalism*, *São Paulo in the Brazilian Federation* and *Crafting the Third World: Theorizing Underdevelopment in Romania and Brazil* (all from Stanford University Press). In addition, he has authored some 70 scholarly articles and essays and has co-edited four books, including *Brazil under Lula* (2009), with Werner Baer.

Sergio Petralia is an Invited Researcher at the Universidad de San Andrés, Argentina. He obtained his Master's degree at the Universidad de San Andrés and his BA degree in Economics at the Universidad de Buenos Aires.

Diego Petrecolla is the President of GPR Economia SA. He teaches at the Universidad de Buenos Aires, the Universidad Torcuato Di Tella and the Universidad de San Andrés, Argentina. He is a consultant to the IDB and the World Bank on Competition Policy. He was President of the Argentine Competition Commission and has published many articles in the field of competition policy and infrastructure regulation. He is the author of the book *Competition Policy Problems in Infrastructure in Argentina* (Buenos Aireo, 2004).

Armando Castelar Pinheiro is Senior Researcher at the Getúlio Vargas Foundation in Rio de Janeiro and Professor of Economics at the Federal University of Rio de Janeiro, Brazil. He previously worked at Gavea Investimentos, the Institute of Applied Economic Research (IPEA) and at the National Development Bank (BNDES). He also has taught in the graduate Economics Program at the Catholic University of Rio (PUC-Rio). He has monthly columns in the newspapers *Valor Economico* and *Correio Brasiliense*.

Alberto Porto is Professor of Economics at the National University of La Plata (UNLP), Argentina. He specializes in the field of Microeconomics and the Economics of the Public Sector. He is a member of the Academia Nacional de Ciencias Económicas. He has been Chairman of the Department of Economics at UNLP and President of the Asociación Argentina de Economía Política. He is the author of many books and of papers published in domestic and international journals.

Adrián Ramos is a Regional Advisor to the United Nations Economic Commission for Latin America and the Caribbean, and a Lecturer at the University of Buenos Aires, Argentina. His main research interest is development and macroeconomic policies, and he has published articles on industrial policy, business strategies and foreign investment, and macroeconomic fluctuations in the Argentine economy.

Carlos Adrián Romero is a researcher at the Instituto de Economía of the Univerdad de la Empresa (UADE), Argentina. He is specialized in the fields of energy economies, computable general equilibrium and efficiency analysis. He is associate Professor of Industrial Organization and Computational Economics at UADE.

Simão Davi Silber is Professor of International Economics at the University of São Paulo and also a researcher at the Foundation Institute of Economic Research (FIPE), São Paulo, Brazil. He has written many articles on Brazil's international economic relations.

Walter Sosa-Escudero is Associate Professor and Director of the Department of Economics at Universidad de San Andrés, Buenos Aires, Argentina. He specializes in applied econometrics, income distribution and poverty.

André Villela is Assistant Professor of Economics at the Graduate School of Economics, Fundação Getulio Vargas (EPGE/FGV) in Rio de Janeiro, Brazil. He specializes in Brazilian economic history. He has written many articles on Brazil's economic history and is the co-editor with F. Giambiagi, L. Barros de Castro and J. Hermann of *Economia Brasileira Contemporânea, 1945–2004* (Rio de Janeiro, 2005).

Introduction

Werner Baer and David Fleischer

Economists and other social scientists analyzing contemporary South America have often puzzled over the similarities and differences between the two giants of the region: Argentina and Brazil. Both countries were great agro-exporting economies in the second half of the nineteenth century and the first decade and a half of the twentieth century. However, Argentina had benefited from the prolonged boom of its grain and meat exports and from gigantic foreign investments in its infrastructure and meat packing plants to such an extent that on the eve of World War I it was viewed as being in the same league as the US, Canada and Australia as a newly emerging economic giant. Brazil's wealth, based on coffee exports and also on foreign investments in infrastructure, seemed not to have been large enough relative to its size so that it was not considered in the same league as Argentina.

However, there were a number of similarities. Both countries received a large number of European immigrants in the late nineteenth and early twentieth centuries (Brazil also receiving a large number of Japanese immigrants), and both experienced an incipient industrial growth at the time (mainly in the food and textile sectors).

After World War I both countries seemed to have prospered again from their traditional exports and during the Great Depression of the 1930s both had similar experiences in an incipient import-substitution industrialization (ISI) period – mainly as a result of declining export earnings, which lead to a decline of imports and thus provided protection to new industries.

After World War II these two countries had both similar and different experiences. In Argentina the appearance of President Perón resulted in policies which favored the urban working classes and some industrialists, while in various ways taxing the agricultural sector and adopting a nationalist stance vis-à-vis foreign investments. Although these policies paid political dividends in the short run, they ultimately led to severe economic crises which partially contributed to the end of the Perón regime, though not to Peronism as a political force. Subsequently the country underwent long periods of 'stop and go' development – some periods favoring the agro-industrial sectors and foreign investment in import-substituting sectors, followed by periods favoring the urban working classes. The economic–political cycles would last for a long time, diminishing long-term growth.

Brazil adopted import-substitution policies from the early 1950s on, encouraging foreign investments, while creating many state productive and financial entities to complement them. This led to long periods of high economic growth and structural transformations. However, overindulgence in ISI resulted in a series of problems – one of the main ones being the need to diversify exports, which was problematical owing to an inefficient, protected industrial structure.

Both countries underwent long periods of inflation, ultimately resulting in hyperinflation. Inflation was partially the result of the needs of government to provide social and economic infrastructures to a rapidly industrializing and urbanizing society, but the institutional backwardness of the tax collection systems made it difficult to finance those needs. The short-run way out of this was financing by the central banks, which led to inflation. Both countries experimented with various types of stabilization programs which were unsuccessful. Argentina seemed to finally conquer its chronic inflation with the introduction of the Currency Board in 1991 and Brazil with the introduction of the Real Plan of 1994 – the former collapsing in 2001, while the latter survived.

Both Argentina and Brazil fell victim to the debt crisis in the 1980s and experienced long periods of low growth and investment, and both finally adopted the so-called neo-liberal policies advocated by the 'Washington Consensus of the 1990s' – which included the opening of the economy and an extensive program of privatization.

During the first decade of the twenty-first century Argentina experienced the disastrous collapse of its Currency Board Plan, which brought on a few years of economic decline and a default on its external debt. However, the economy recovered after a brief period, owing in great measure to the world boom in the commodities it exported. Brazil's Real experiment lasted, and after a few years of modest growth its economy became so dynamic in the second half of the first decade of the twenty-first century that the country became part of the so-called BRICs, i.e. the four emerging countries which the world business community expected to become a significant economic and political power center. In addition, there was evidence to suggest that not only was Brazil emerging as an important world economic player, but also this was taking place with an improvement in the distribution of the gains from growth. So Brazil in the first years of the twenty-first century seemed to be taking the place of the Argentina of 100 years ago as the principal economic power of South America.

It was within this context that the Lemann Institute for Brazilian Studies of the University of Illinois organized a conference dedicated to the comparison of the two countries in some key areas: industrialization, agriculture, formal and informal service sectors, income distribution, the state and the privatization experience, regional development, inflation and stabilization policies, and foreign trade and investments. We selected these eight topics for discussion and invited Argentinean and Brazilian scholars to present an analysis for their country. The invited commentators were scholars from other countries. The conference was held on 22–23 April 2010 at the University of Illinois, and this volume contains the papers that were presented. Co-sponsors of the conference were: the Fundação Instituto de Pesquisas Econômicas (FIPE); the Faculdade de Economia, Administração e Contabilidade of the University of São Paulo, and the Center for International Business Education and Research at the University of Illinois (Illinois CIBER).

Abbreviations

ADEERA	Asociación de Distribuidores de Energía Eléctrica de la República Argentina
ALADI	Asociación Latinioamericana de Integración
BCRA	Banco Central de la República Argentina
BNB	Banco do Nordeste do Brasil
BNDES	Banco Nacional de Desenvolvimento Economico e Social
CAMMESA	Compañía Administradora del Mercado Mayorista Eléctrico SA
CEDES	Centro de Estudios de Estado y Sociedad
CEDLAS	Centro de Estudios Distributivos, Laborales y Sociales
CEER	Centro de Estudios Económicos de la Regulación del Instituto de Economía de la Universidad Argentina de la Empresa
CEFifo	Center for Economic Studies and Ifo Institute for Economic Research
CEMA	Centro de Estudios Macroeconómicos de Argentina
CENIT	Centro de Investigaciones para la Transformación
CEPAL	Comisión Económica para América Latina y el Caribe
CEPR	Centre for Economic Policy Research
CIAFA	Cámara de la Industria Argentina de Fertilizantes y Agroquímicos
CINDES	Centro de Estudos de Integração e Desenvolvimento
CIPPEC	Centro de Implementación de Politicas Públicas para la Equidad y el Crecimiento
COMTRADE	United Nations Commodity Trade Statistics Database
DIEESE	Departamento Intersindical de Estatística e Estudos Sócio-Econômicos
ECLAC	Economic Commission for Latin America and the Caribbean

EMBI	Emerging Markets Bond Index
ENARGAS	Ente Nacional Regulador del Gas
ESALQ-USP	Escola Superior de Agricultura 'Luiz de Queiroz'
FAO	United Nations Food and Agriculture Organization
FAOSTAT	United Nations Food and Agriculture Organization Corporate Statistical Database
FGV	Fundação Getúlio Vargas
FIEL	Fundación de Investigaciones Económicas Latinoamericanas
FIESP	Federação das Indústrias do Estado de São Paulo
FINEP	Financiadora de Estudos e Projetos
GTDN	Grupo de Trabalho para o Desenvolvimento do Nordeste
IADB	Inter-American Development Bank
IBGE	Instituto Brasileiro de Geografia e Estatística
IDES	Instituto de Desarrollo Económico y Social
IEDI	Instituto de Estudos para o Desenvolvimento Industrial
IERAL	Instituto de Estudios sobre la Realidad Argentina y Latinoamericana
ILPES	Instituto Latinoamericano de Planificación Económica y Social
INDEC	Instituto Nacional de Estadística y Censos
INTAL	Instituto para la Integración de América Latina y el Caribe
IPEA	Instituto de Pesquisa Econômica Aplicada
IPEADATA	Data of the Instituto de Pesquisa Económica Aplicada
KLEMS	capital, labour, energy, materials, services
LAIA	Latin American Integration Association
MDIC	Ministério do Desenvolvimento, Indústria e Comércio Exterior
NBER	National Bureau of Economic Research
NEAD	Núcleo de Estudos Agrários e Desenvolvimento Rural do Ministério do Desenvolvimento Agrário
NEIT-UNICAMP	Núcleo de Economia Industrial e da Tecnologia do Instituto de Economia da Universidade Estadual de Campinas
OECD	Organization for Economic Cooperation and Development
OSDE	Organización de Servicios Directos Empresarios
PNAD	Pesquisa Nacional por Amostras de Domicílios

PSE	Paris School of Economics
PUC-Rio	Pontifícia Universidade Católica do Rio de Janeiro
SAGPyA	Secretaría de Agricultura, Ganadería, Pesca y Alimentación
SEDLAC	Socio-Economic Database for Latin America and the Caribbean
SENAI	Serviço Nacional de Aprendizagem Industrial do Estado
UFMG	Universidade Federal de Minas Gerais
UFPE	Universidade Federal de Pernambuco
UNCTAD	United Nations Conference on Trade and Development
UNDP	United Nations Development Programme
UNLP	Universidad Nacional de La Plata
UNIREN	Unidad de Renegociación y Análisis de Contratos de Servicios Públicos

PART I

Industrialization

1. Industrial development in Argentina

Bernardo Kosacoff

1.1 INTRODUCTION

Argentina's industrialization started off in the late nineteenth century and developed alongside the dynamic agro-export model which dominated the economy until the beginning of the 1930s. At that time, industry began to occupy a favored position in the Argentine economy through the process known as import–substituting industrialization (ISI). In fact during the second phase of ISI, which began in 1958, industrial activities became the country's engine of economic growth and job creation, and its base for capital accumulation. At the same time, industry was developing technological capabilities which were remarkable for the Latin American context at that time.

However, by the mid 1970s this model of industrialization was facing a series of inherent difficulties. These included problems related to the type of industrial organization which had emerged – e.g. plants on too small a scale, the lack of subcontractors and specialized suppliers, poor international competitiveness etc. – and to the macroeconomic functioning of the Argentine economy – e.g. considerable transfers of income, balance-of-payments deficits and volatility among other problems.

Meanwhile, progress made in the more advanced industrial countries was generating a changeover to a new techno-production pattern in which the models for organizing industrial production were based on a kind of logic different from the prevailing Fordist mass-production models. One of the key factors behind such changes was the spectacular progress occurring in microelectronics – which made the transition possible from the electromechanical word to the electronic word. On the other hand, when faced by difficulties in restoring industrial growth, the local response was based not on taking advantage of the stocks of technology accumulated in the previous stage (so as to overcome the difficulties in that way), but on an effort to introduce a structural reform program linked to the opening up of the economy. However, the failure of this policy and program (in its detailed application) in the period 1976–81 ended by dislocating the production structure.

In the 1980s and 1990s another organizational model for the production of industrial goods emerged in Argentina which was very different from the substitution strategy. It was coupled to changes at the technological frontier and to the instability and uncertainty of the macroeconomic setting, and it gave rise to very substantial modifications at several levels: institutional, sectoral and microeconomic, and also in the way Argentine industry was linked into the global economy.

The goal of this chapter is to analyze the main characteristics of Argentine manufacturing industry and the development phases (going back more than a century), and, especially, to concentrate on its structural features during the 1980s, the changes that have occurred since the convertibility plan was introduced – between 1991 and 2001 – and the context after the convertibility collapse, when the manufacturing sector's recovery has been based on an effort to become once again a pillar of economic and social development. Table 1.1 presents a simplified schema.

1.2 FIRST STAGES OF ARGENTINE INDUSTRIAL DEVELOPMENT

Argentina's present industrial structure is the result of a long series of developments that started over a century ago. The ensuing industrial activities did not merely produce goods but led, at the same time, to the growth of learning processes, to the incorporation of technology, to continuous improvements in skills and training, and to the setting up of institutional and regulatory frameworks. They also led to the country developing a modified pattern of specialization within the international division of labor, to the economic organization of its markets, to linkages with other economic activities etc. Significant changes over time in each of the above factors helped in turn to shape the social organization for production of manufactured goods. As it developed, the Argentine economy came to be noted for its degree of industrialization within the Latin American context. However, if comparison is made with the economies of more advanced countries then the central features of Argentina's economy clearly identify it as a 'semi-industrialized' one.

The changes in the country's level of industrialization during the period 1900–90 can be appreciated by considering the share of gross domestic product produced by manufacturing industry. Manufacturing industry's growing and uninterrupted share in Argentina's economy went as far as the mid 1970s, at which time a process of continuous decline began. The resulting fall in its share of GDP was so great that the

Table 1.1 Argentine industrial development: simplified phases

The company and the environment	Agro-exporter with industrialization (1880–1929)	Substitutive internal market (1930–78)	Open market with restructuring and globalization (1979–90)
International scenario	Industrial consolidation British hegemony in production and finance	Fordist production American hegemony and emergence of NICs Protected markets	Flexible organization Growth in Germany, Japan and Southeast Asia Economic blocs Globalization and concentration of production Financial internation-alization
	Direct foreign investment Associated with infrastructure, financing and raw material and primary resource capture	**Direct foreign investment** Associated with the capture of the internal market and the factor's price	**Direct foreign Investment** Strong dynamism associated with globalization, concentration and privati-zation
Global framework	Agro-exporting model integrated into the world with incipient induction to industrialization Institutional consolidation Self-regulated cycle	Import-substituting industrialization Strong state participation State regulation	Permanent program of stabilization search Trade and financial opening Privatization and deregulation Productive transformation with growing heterogeneity

Table 1.1 (continued)

The company and the environment	Agro-exporter with industrialization (1880–1929)	Substitutive internal market (1930–78)	Open market with restructuring and globalization (1979–90)
Industrial	Food, textiles	Food, textiles	Steel and aluminum
1. Dynamic sectors	Other for internal consumption	Other for internal consumption	Petrochemicals Pulp and paper Oil vegetables
2. Destination	Agro-industrial exports Internal market	Internal market	Exports and internal market
3. Origin of technology	Imports	Local adaptation and development of technologies far from 'best practice'	Import and local adaptation Lower technological 'gap' in some sectors
4. Techno-productive organi-zation	Dual: Sectors with state-of-the-art technologies (for exports) and Dual: Sectors with state-of-the-art technologies (for exports) and other semicraft ones (for the local market)	Short series with some technology 'Idiosyncratic' Fordism	Heterogeneity: sectors with Fordist technologies and organi-zation Attempts at flexibility and global value chains
Leaders	National economic groups related to SMEs exports	Public companies TNC branch offices SMEs	National capital economic groups Some SMEs TNC branch offices

Table 1.1 (continued)

The company and the environment	**Agro-exporter with industrialization (1880–1929)**	**Substitutive internal market (1930–78)**	**Open market with restructuring and globalization (1979–90)**
Organization at forms	Family groups	Public companies Family companies TNCs: leaders in the local market and marginals in the world	Multicompanies

Source: Bisang et al., 1992.

degree of industrialization at the start of the 1990s was similar to that in the 1940s.

In broad terms three major periods can be identified in Argentina's industrialization process. The first one begins around 1880, when the country made a radical shift into becoming integrated with the rest of the world as an agro-export economy, and this position continued until the crisis of 1930. The second period, extending up until the late 1970s, refers to the application of the strategy of 'modelo de industrialización sustitutivo de importaciones' (ISI) within a semi-closed economy framework, and it includes, in its 5-decade span, various subperiods. The third period starts with the failure of the 1979–81 economic openness policy and the lengthy macroeconomic disruption of the country which lasted from the 1970s to the 1990s.

The Argentine agro-export model was based on specializing in the production of grains and meat through exploiting the country's abundant and competitive natural resources. Once it had got its institutional structure settled, Argentina vigorously won a place for itself in the international economy as a dynamic exporter of primary goods and as an importer of capital and manufactured goods. It operated an open economy regulated by the gold standard. Its economic fluctuations were linked to weather conditions (which affected total agricultural output) and to the British business cycle (as Britain was its main international trading partner). At the same time, conditions began to arise which were favorable for the incipient industrialization of the country. These conditions largely took the form of the 'stimuli' which Hirschman described for Latin America (Hirshman, 1968).

Among the stimuli can be mentioned the following:

1. The existence of competitive goods in the primary sector that had to be processed in some way before being exported (meat, tannin, leather, wool, flour etc.).
2. A flow of European immigrants who already possessed industrial skills.
3. The early development of generalized education and technical and professional specialization.
4. Difficulties in external supply during World War I.
5. Derived demands stemming from primary production and from infrastructure needs (e.g. agricultural machinery, large railway maintenance networks, cement etc.).
6. Transportation costs and natural protective barriers.
7. Sustained rapid growth in the size of the domestic market.

These factors all contributed to the gradual development of the most significant industrial structure in the region which, even before the crisis of the agro-export model, already produced 20 per cent of GDP and consisted of over 50,000 industrial establishments.

The end of the expansion of the agricultural frontier, together with the 1929 international crisis and the conflictive three-sided relationship between Argentina, the United Kingdom and the United States, caused the demise of the agro-export model. The imposition of foreign exchange control in 1931 and of import permits in 1933, and the splitting into two of the foreign exchange market and the raising of import tariffs (mainly for fiscal reasons) are illustrative of the new manner in which the economy operated.

The result of the closed-economy scheme was that foreign trade gradually became less and less important in terms of its share of GDP. These were, in fact, the conditions in which the first subperiod of ISI developed. The substitution process was based on the incipient industrialization already achieved in the first stage and it advanced very quickly into the 'easy' sectors of manufacturing production. Industries which produced consumer goods (food, textiles, clothing), household electrical appliances, simple machinery and straightforward metal products, as well as those industrial activities associated with construction, were the most dynamic activities during this subperiod, which continued until Perón took office in 1946.

Industrialization quickly deepened during this decade. Basically, this was due to the expansion of existing activities, the intensive utilization of labor and the broadening of the domestic market to incorporate the entire population. The state took up a very active role both in the production of basic inputs and in operating a wide range of policy instruments. The latter included administering import quotas, financing industrial activities through the Banco Industrial and the Central Bank's rediscounting facilities, promoting specific industrial sectors, and using non-tariff mechanisms. Industry had clearly specialized in producing consumer goods exclusively for the domestic market, but constraints on its dynamic further growth were found to exist as its level of technological obsolescence increased, and as the business community found itself unable – either entrepreneurially or technologically – to progress into more complex kinds of manufacturing, in a situation when continuous restrictions were imposed by the balance of payments.

In 1958 the last ISI subperiod started, which ran until the mid 1970s. The ISI was based on the petrochemical industry, the complex of metal products, and machinery industries (the motor vehicles industry was the most representative sector). This task ISI subperiod became the base for capital accumulation. The empty cells of the input–output matrix were progressively filled in, and this involved some extensive participation by subsidiaries of transnational corporations. This took place in the framework of a highly protected economy and was a response to the explicit policy goal of raising the level of national economic self-sufficiency.

These changes gave rise to a process of rapid technological development based on installing technologies which had been developed in more advanced countries and adapting them significantly to the local environment. This meant copying Fordist production line methods but incorporating a strong local component into them. However, this led to various problems: the output of these plants was generated in short production series and was exclusively oriented to the local market so that the scale of output from these plants was, on average, some ten times lower than that of similar plants operating at the technological frontier; the level of vertical integration was notably high owing to the weak development of specialized suppliers and subcontractors in a context where transaction costs were high; and the production mix was also markedly diversified. These were only some of the problems of international competitiveness affecting the Argentine industrial structure. In addition, Argentina's macroeconomic constraints were an obstacle for financing the transfer of income to industrial activities. Furthermore, it was industry's own trade deficit that restricted the possibilities of achieving industrial growth over any sustained period without engendering a balance-of-payments crisis.

The perception of these problems led to a search for policy solutions within the framework of ISI. On the one hand, programs of incentives to export manufactured goods were introduced. Their aim was simultaneously to generate scarce foreign currency, to expand the overall market (because the domestic market was showing signs of saturation), and to stimulate the overall competitiveness of industry. The results were quite appreciable: while in 1960 exports of non-traditional goods were practically nonexistent, in 1975 they represented a quarter of the country's exports. On the other hand, the attempt was made to deepen the extent of ISI by reducing the country's heavy dependence on imports of basic industrial inputs such as steel, aluminum, paper and petrochemicals. This led the government to promote some major industrial projects to produce these inputs locally. The promotion was based on (1) the amount of foreign currency savings these projects would produce and (2) the prospect that these projects would also lead to the broadening of the domestic market through the forward linkages that the new factories would have with high-value-added and employment-generating activities.[1] Meanwhile the government also continued to operate its existing promotional mechanisms, as well as utilizing the purchasing power and investment programs of public sector and state-owned enterprises as significant instruments of industrial policy throughout this subperiod.

1.3 THE BREAKDOWN OF ISI IN ARGENTINA

The economic policy launched in April 1976 by a military regime profoundly changed the guidelines and directions which industry had been following until then. The new authorities' full confidence in the resource allocation capabilities of market forces and in the state's subsidiary role were the philosophical underpinnings for a program of market liberalization followed by external openness. It aimed to eliminate the entire set of regulations, subsidies and privileges established in the past in an attempt to modernize and increase the efficiency of the economy (Canitrot, 1983; Sourrouille et al., 1985; Damill et al., 1988; Rodriguez, 1979).

In industrial policy, two distinct subperiods can be identified for which the dividing line can be placed around late 1978. The years before that date were characterized by a recovery in the production of durable consumer goods and capital goods, and were associated with increasing investment and with a regressive redistribution of income. In this period – which the authorities labeled as that of the '*sinceramiento*' of the economy (which translates roughly as 'making the economy sincere') – a start was made on reducing import tariffs (Berlinsky, 1977). In fact, strong reductions were imposed – on average 40 percentage points – so that tariffs fell from the previously prevailing average level of 90 per cent to 50 per cent. In spite of this, imports did not rise significantly during the next 3 years.

The explanation of this phenomenon is, on the one hand, that increased competitiveness had been achieved in the previous decade, which meant that considerable parts of the former tariff structure were redundant, and, on the other, that the exchange rate (in terms of local currency units per dollar) had been maintained at a high level. Furthermore, the financial reform approved in 1977 liberalized the interest rate and created a totally different mechanism for the allocation of credit.[2]

The second subperiod began in late 1978 with the detailed application of a policy based on the monetarist school's model of the open economy (i.e. the monetary approach to the balance of payments). The goal the authorities hoped to achieve through this policy was to bring down the domestic inflation rate progressively until it matched the international one. The intention was to use deliberate government control of the exchange rate variable to achieve a progressive downward adjustment of the external rate of inflation as measured in terms of local currency. A pre-established program of devaluations of the local currency against the US dollar was put in place in the form of a published timetable (the '*tablita*') which specified a steadily decreasing rate of devaluation over time, within a context of increasing economic openness to the outside world (both in the capital market and in product markets); it was based on the assumption that domestic interest and inflation rates would converge to the corresponding international rates. It was assumed – within the rationale of the passive monetary scheme – that convergence would be achieved after a transition period whose length would be determined by the different speeds at which the prices of goods would get adjusted, depending on whether they were traded in international markets or not. Then, once convergence was achieved, a new relative price structure would thus be in force and established. Such a price structure would induce resource allocation to favor the development of sectors with comparative advantages which could produce on an international scale and, combined with the tariff policy, it would also force less-efficient sectors to close down, so that the overall productivity of the economy would increase.

However, convergence was never achieved. Adjustment in the prices of tradable goods was slow and imperfect while the mechanisms envisaged as operating for non-tradable goods did not produce the expected results. In addition, the trend in level of the domestic interest rate was greatly affected by a growing premium (i.e. a surcharge) that was reflected in this rate owing to the prevailing uncertainty and the high costs of financial intermediation. As for the exchange rate, its devaluation timetable had been devised on the basis of a forecast level of inflation that was lower than the real one – thus producing a continuous overvaluation of the local currency (the peso).

This overvaluation of the peso, combined with the tariff reductions, strongly affected the trade balance and opened the door to a massive influx of imported products. Furthermore, there was also an unrestricted inflow of external capital – taking advantage of the freedoms conferred by the external financial openness of the economy. Almost all of this was short-term capital coming from a financial market characterized by both high liquidity and high domestic interest rates. This inflow of capital compensated for the current-account deficits and resulted in a significant increase in foreign indebtedness. Moreover these transactions – because of their serious impact on the balance of payments – gave early warning that a devaluation was impending in what was a highly liquid capital market given the very short-term maturity dates of deposits. In addition, fiscal policy was not sufficiently carefully designed: transfers of income that were difficult to justify continued throughout the whole period without the necessary screening or assessment. In addition, all these events were unfolding in an atmosphere in which changes in the political and economic authorities were expected. As a result, the risk premium for borrowing foreign capital rose considerably, which in turn led to even higher interest rates.

In that context, the concurrence of several negative factors produced the deepest crisis for the Argentine industrial sector in its entire history. The most important of these factors were that both domestic demand and export demand for locally produced industrial goods were low: domestic demand for these goods had been hit by the influx of competitive imported products, and export demand for them had been reduced by the exchange rate policy which had caused the peso to become greatly overvalued. At the same time, the existence of high interest rates largely cancelled out any possibility of making profits from production activity, and the fact that these interest rates were steadily rising resulted in firms acquiring levels of indebtedness that often exceeded the value of their assets.[3]

In March 1981 there was a change of authorities within the military regime. This produced a series of short-run measures aimed at resolving the most pressing problems in the production sector of the economy. Nevertheless, the stagnation of the industrial sector continued throughout this period, which was one marked by continuous devaluations of the domestic currency and the persistence of positive interest rates. The business sector centered its claims on the need to solve its critical indebtedness problems. Towards mid 1982, a medium-term financing system was established for firms based on regulated interest rates. These regulated rates, in combination with a growing inflation rate, provoked a thoroughgoing 'liquidation of the liabilities' of firms and provided a major source of relief for financial institutions. In addition, the state took over most of the private foreign debt through implementing a system of exchange-rate-risk insurance. The result brought about by these two mechanisms was to 'socialize' the losses of the business sector (i.e. to nationalize private business debts). By this time, a massive volume of foreign debt had built up. Its level was such that the interest payments required to service it far surpassed even the most optimistic trade balance forecasts. The revaluation of the exchange rate and the newly imposed restrictions on imports (brought in because of the huge foreign-debt burden) created conditions that signified renewed protection for the industrial sector. The import coefficient of the Argentine economy once again approached the levels it had been at before the economic openness policy was applied.

1.4 THE POST-DEBT-CRISIS PERIOD (1982–90)

The local macroeconomic framework was the key determinant of a great many of the transformations that occurred between 1982 and 1990 (Bonvecchi, 1992; Machinea, 1990; Carciofi, 1990; Damill et al., 1989). The application of the 'monetary approach to the balance of payments' in the late 1970s had proved to be the breaking point of the previous industrialization model, and the failure of this monetarist policy and the huge ensuing level of foreign indebtedness generated macroeconomic instability and uncertainty for the whole of the succeeding decade. The instability encompassed both fiscal and external disequilibria, plus a very fragile financial system. 'Stabilization' – which the economy needed – was not merely a constant goal of policymakers throughout this period, but actually became an utterly unavoidable priority once the economy began to suffer a series of major disturbances, of which the hyperinflationary episodes in 1989 and 1990 were the most blatant. The role of external determinants, and the need for coherent and persistent stabilization policies, as well as the contents of such policies, were of great concern to Argentine society throughout this whole period.

The 1982 foreign debt crisis reversed the sign of the net resource transfers from abroad as a consequence of the interruption of capital inflows and the increase in international interest rates. This immediately resulted in the reemergence and intensification of the structural external disequilibrium of the economy, and (making things worse) there was a simultaneous financial crisis in the public sector. These two basic disequilibria were complemented by the short-run dynamics of the economy in the sense that the high-inflation regime and financial fragility amplified and sharpened the consequences of the measures adopted specifically to correct these disequilibria. Therefore the challenge facing economic policymakers was to identify an efficient way to correct the structural imbalances while reducing inflation but without incurring excessive costs in terms of production, employment and real wages.

External disequilibrium can be characterized by the imbalance between the flow of income that a country can generate and the magnitude of the external payment commitments that its debt stock imposes. Argentina's search for large foreign-trade surpluses through devaluations of the local currency and the contraction of domestic expenditure led to increases in exports and a drastic decline in imports and investments. The impact of heavy foreign-debt-servicing payments was clearly visible in terms of the resultant deficit in the current account of the balance of payments, and in this respect the public sector was in a particularly unfavorable position owing to the steps taken to nationalize the private foreign debt. In turn, the deterioration in the terms of trade strongly eroded the export effort.

The fiscal accounts featured increasing levels of public expenditure that were not being matched by tax revenues, which were declining. The state's usual method in the past for financing such deficits (i.e. raising external and internal indebtedness and through tax by way of inflation) had been thrown out of gear by the foreign debt crisis and by the nationalization of foreign debt – at a time when the severity of the fiscal deficits was increasing.

The prevalence of persistent high inflation produced intense self-propelling inflation-propagation mechanisms and led to high and volatile inflation rates. At the same time, the precarious financial situation caused both by the demonetization process and by lack of external financing was one of the main obstacles to economic policy management. The obligation to service the foreign debt was in the hands of the public sector, and trade surpluses existed which were generated by the private sector. This posed acute difficulties to the fiscal authorities for purchasing the much-needed foreign-currency surpluses. In order to obtain such funds the public sector had no choice but to increase its own surplus, to finance itself through issuing money or making placements of internal debt, or else to fall into foreign-payment arrears. Each of these options had disadvantages and unwanted effects. The existence of these macroeconomic disequilibria produced a permanent climate of uncertainty which damaged the investment process and encouraged substantial capital flight.

Three major economic policy programs can be highlighted during this period: the Austral Plan, the Plan Primavera (the Spring Plan) and the Bunge and Born Plan. Each of these plans aimed to secure surpluses in the trade balance, and also attempted to improve control over nominal aggregate demand, to correct relative prices, and to reorient the process of expectations formation. In every case they came up against obstacles to sustaining their fiscal achievements because that proved to be incompatible with the real possibilities that were available from internal, external and monetary financing. As a consequence, it came increasingly to be understood that structural reforms were essential.

Between 1980 and 1990 the performance of the main economic indicators was not very encouraging and the adjustment process had a high social cost. Only exports moved in a positive direction, with 78 per cent growth between 1980 and 1990. The remaining indicators revealed the profound deterioration of the economy: GDP diminished by 9.4 per cent, industrial output by 24 per cent and consumption by 15.8 per cent; imports and investment went down by 58.9 per cent and 70.1 per cent, respectively; GDP per capita was reduced by 25 per cent. In turn, the rate of open unemployment doubled, while the level of industrial employment diminished by around 30 per cent and the average industrial real wage rate was 24 per cent lower in 1990 than it had been at the beginning of the 1980s. In line with this, a process of income concentration was observed which was linked to a more regressive income distribution pattern and to worsening states of extreme poverty.

These new conditions generated significant sectoral and microeconomic changes. As a result, unlike during previous stages when the industrial sector had been the engine of growth in the economy, the period 1975–90 was characterized by:

1. The stagnation of manufacturing activities (which lost more than 5 per cent of their GDP share).
2. The absence of new job creation at a time of serious structural difficulties in the labor market.
3. Investment levels that fell below the level of capital depreciation, producing decapitalization in the manufacturing sector.

However, it would not be correct to conclude that manufacturing industry at the start of the 1990s was in a stagnant, damaged state, producing goods under the same pattern of social organization that had prevailed throughout the import substitution stage. Instead, industrial activities had undergone a set of profound structural changes that, in a summary manner, can be described as having involved 'regressive restructuring' and a 'growing degree of structural heterogeneity'.

The 'regressive' character arises mainly from two aspects: the first concerns the inability shown by the economy to base the restructuring of industry on the positive aspects that had been built up in 4 decades of import substitution – during which knowledge, abilities, engineering and entrepreneurial skills, equipment, human resources etc. had all been accumulated. It is true that these aspects were also connected to the serious problems that had caused the ISI model to run out of impetus. However, a truly efficient allocation of resources would have been one that led to the overcoming of these problems while retaining the positive assets that existed within the stock of accumulated capabilities. Countless examples of how this criterion was not followed can be found in Argentina's restructuring experience at corporate and sectoral levels, and with regard to technology and human resources.

The second aspect refers to the income transfers that took place during the restructuring process. On the one hand, the new specialization pattern for Argentine industry which emerged from the process did not have a sufficiently good fit with the country's factor endowment, and nor did it provide enough scope for generating dynamic competitive advantages. On the other hand, the deterioration in public sector social policies (such as education, health, housing and infrastructure) that accompanied the country's fiscal dislocation had a serious impact on social equality and, in turn, on the economy's systemic competitiveness.

So far as 'growing heterogeneity' is concerned, this was brought about by the occurrence of strongly contrasting performances at the sectoral level and, even more so, at the firm level. The aggregate position of stagnation can be broken down into (1) a large group of firms that contracted in size or got dismantled or left behind, while, simultaneously, (2) other firms expanded and modernized their production structures. There are plenty of documented cases of successful microeconomic performance. However, the sum total of all such cases did not generate enough macroeconomic strength to establish a new path for economic growth in Argentina.

1.5 THE TRANSFORMATIONS DURING THE CONVERTIBILITY PLAN

The beginning of the 1990s was a time of significant political and economic changes, both nationally as regionally and internationally. The boost coming from external factors played a leading role, in particular the remarkable increase in international credit on offer to the so-called emerging countries and the higher prices of export products. However, the decade was mainly characterized by the domestic policy reforms performed. Throughout the 1990s, Argentina implemented a series of profound economic reforms whose axis was the stabilization of prices, the privatization or concession of public assets, the trade opening of many sectors of the local economy, the liberalization of a large part of goods production and the rendering of services, and the renegotiation of external liabilities.

The monetary policy was one of the areas with the most changes. In 1991, by the passing of a law, a convertibility plan with a fixed exchange rate between the local currency and the US dollar (1 peso = 1 dollar) was put underway. The charter of the central bank was also amended in order to adapt it to the new plan, limiting the entity's financing of the government and the granting of rediscount facilities. Also, in 1992, the national government reached an agreement with foreign creditors through which capital debt and interest in arrears with banks were replaced with secured long-term public bonds, within the framework of the so-called Brady Plan.

After the start-up of the economic program, the inflation rate showed a downward trend. This break with the inflationary past became a crucial element for the evolution of the economic activities, owing to its importance for price-forming and assets demand. The broadening of the horizon of decisions conveyed an important change in capital forming. Price stabilization was accompanied by a notable increase in credit volume, both in dollars and in convertible pesos. Sooner than expected, it was noted that the credit market functioning and more generally all contractual relations were largely based on expectations about the continuity of the exchange regime. The behavior of economic agents thus determined an increase in both the perceived and the effective costs of the eventual abandonment of the convertibility regime.

Regarding the reform of the functioning and scope of the state, a law was passed subjecting a number of public sector companies and activities to privatization. This process took place very promptly: in 1990 the phone company (ENTel) and the airline company (Aerolíneas Argentinas) went to private hands. Oil-producing areas and other oil assets followed the same path (1991 and 1992), as well as the electricity and gas companies (1992), the state-owned steel company SOMISA (1992) and the oil company YPF (1993) among other operations.

The conduct of fiscal policy throughout the 1990s is still controversial. Compared with the previous decade, fiscal management presented a notable improvement. However, the sustainability of the exchange regime demanded that the reduced deficit should not be interrupted halfway through the decade, but that efforts to enhance the public sector's solvency should be further increased. Initially, the effects of the aggregate product performance and the privatizations on public revenues resulted in increased public spending that accompanied the real revaluation of the economy. As time went by, the tax burden was concentrated on just a few taxes and the tax base began to be broadened. Subsequently, revenues were affected by structural reforms (particularly that of the social security system) and the financial crisis with its epicenter in Mexico. From then on, and even more so in the recessive context initiated halfway through 1998, there began a period characterized by growing tension between demand for public spending, drop in tax collection, and attempts to solve some of the problems of relative prices through the fiscal front.

The foreign trade policies of the 1990s had two pillars: trade opening and regional integration. The reduction in tariffs and non-tariff barriers to imports and the elimination of exports taxes changed the incentives for production and the demand for goods. The regional integration process in Mercosur went deeper in the 1990s and along with the trade opening led to a notable increase in trade flows among member countries. Trade policies and the attitude towards the integration process were seriously affected by the competitiveness problems of internationally tradable goods, particularly those arising from the Brazilian currency devaluation in early 1999.

The macroeconomic performance at the beginning of the 1990s was characterized by a remarkable increase in domestic demand, boosted by the greater local and international credit on offer. The origin of this lay in the positive expectations of future revenues resulting from the change in the economic regime, encouraging increased consumption and new investment opportunities. The reduced financial restriction showed not only in the comeback of bank credit, as a result of a growing monetization, but also in the boom of capital markets where debt securities and stock for significant amounts were issued. The increased aggregate demand spread throughout the different sectors of the economy, even though it is important to note that the high increase in the production of manufactured goods was lower than the total product. The low impact of the expansion of production on employment, as a result of the negative effects of the productive restructuring, helped to increase unemployment. The sudden rise in goods imports, added to the opposite performance of exports, gave rise to considerable negative trade balances. Likewise, the deficit in the current account of the balance of payments began to raise doubts regarding the sustainability of the macroeconomic scheme, although they were largely offset by operations in the areas of foreign investment and international credit.

In this context, in 1995, the increases in the international interest rate and Mexico's currency devaluation caused a financial crisis. This shock, resulting from a retracted credit supply, had an immediate impact on economic activity and on employment levels, and seriously affected the financial system. It is probable that the rapid resolution of the crisis, supported by improved international prices, together with higher demand from Brazil after the launch of the Plan Real and the regulatory reforms in the financial system, in fact helped strengthen the positive perceptions of revenue growth and the solvency of a macroeconomic scheme that now increased exports, savings and employment; the subsequent devaluation and change of the exchange regime in its principal trading partner, the sudden drop in the prices of the the country's exports, the persistent strength of the dollar relative to other currencies, and the public sector's continuous displacing of the private sector in domestic financing markets are the most clear examples of what took place. By the end of the 1990s, a long period dominated by recession and price deflation gave rise to growing tension and to changed expectations regarding the potential growth of the economy and the solvency of the public sector, leading to the last definitive collapse of the economic regime.

As an answer to a new configuration of the local competitive framework, strong business reconversion processes began to be displayed, in which not only strategies and the relative weight of the different activities and economic agents changed but so also did productive, technological and trade practices. In these dynamics, the different measures taken by companies produced opposite results, that might be put into two large groups of business behavior. On the one hand were the so-called 'offensive restructurings', characterized by having reached efficiency levels comparable to the best international practices and which involved a small group of around 400 companies. Although cases might be found throughout the whole business spectrum, it was activities related to natural-resource extraction and processing, basic-goods-producing branches and part of the automobile complex that predominated. On the other hand were just about 25,000 companies (not taking into account microcompanies), constituting the rest of the productive fabric and characterized by their so-called 'defensive behavior'; these, despite the progress made in terms of productivity relative to their own past, were far removed from international technical frontiers and retained certain features of the substitution stage, such as a reduced scale of production scale or low economies of specialization (Kosacoff, 2000).

We can say that the economic stabilization process put underway in the 1990s increased notably the ability to forecast the evolution of the main macroeconomic variables and implied an unmatchable advantage for the organization of productive activities. However, a new type of uncertainty emerged which may be called 'strategic', having to do with the change in the business competitive environment and with the new rules of the game determining what companies produced and how they did it. Decisions about investment in specific assets, incorporation or substitution of production lines, human resources skills in the company or the technological learning path to follow took on an elusive dimension that was difficult to evaluate in the prevailing patterns of a semi-closed economy.

One of the central aspects of the structural transformation was the reconfiguration of the business profile relative to that of the substitution process. A general view might indicate that to the departure of the state-owned companies, and also some involution in small and medium companies, we must add the reorganization of local economic conglomerates and the leadership and sustained dynamism of transnational companies. Within the milieu of productive companies, we should highlight, in the first place, the behavior of transnational companies, whose main strategies were associated with foreign direct investment (FDI) flows coming in throughout the 1990s. By the late 1980s, a recovery of FDI flows began to take place, reaching notable and growing levels in the following decade. According to official estimates, between 1990 and 2000, FDI of US$78 billion came into Argentina. From that, the amount of foreign capital grew to annual rates higher than 20 per cent, and went beyond US$80 billion in 2000 (Kulfas et al., 2002).

Foreign investment led the 1990s productive reconversion process, particularly those aspects that modernized the process, with a remarkably high correlation between the most dynamic sectors of local production and the increase in the share of foreign capital in such sectors. Even within the framework of strategies largely aimed at taking advantage of the domestic or the subregional market, affiliates made investments aimed at a more efficient use of physical and human resources and, much more selectively, at more actively joining the corporation's international structure. It is possible to identify two stages in the behavior of FDI flows into Argentina. Between 1990 and 1993, more than half of foreign investment income corresponded to public-asset privatization and concession operations. Subsequently, mergers and acquisitions of private companies acquired a key role in Argentina's foreign investments. To sum up, unlike previous periods, most FDI funds (at least 56 per cent of total flows between 1992 and 2000) were devoted to buying existing assets, both state-run and private. Companies' mergers and acquisitions processes in Argentina accumulated, between 1990 and 1999, an amount exceeding US$55 billion, of which 88per cent corresponded to payments of foreign capital companies. Transnational companies' affiliates' decisive advantage over local companies lay in their control of technological aspects, in their enhanced skills in operating in open economies, and in their ability to finance reconversion. However, the contribution of foreign-capital companies to the generation of productive linkings, to the spread of externalities and to an active incorporation into international trade dynamic networks remained weak.

The 1990s meant a change of direction for local economic conglomerates in Argentina. The new economic conditions opened numerous business opportunities in an environment of stability and growth, but at the same time they were faced with the need to respond to international competitors. On the one hand, their having been part of the state allowed them, in association with foreign investors and banks, an advantageous position in public-asset privatizations and concessions. Later on, many of these local conglomerates sold their stock to foreign investors. On the other hand, while the economic opening and deregulation meant access to international financial markets, it also significantly weakened their base for accumulating power in the local market in an exclusive and monopoly-like way. International liquidity conditions made it easier to borrow to acquire state-owned companies and diversify investments, including investments placed abroad.

Unlike in previous stages in Argentina's economic history, in the 1990s the behavior of local conglomerates' was highly heterogeneous and changing. The type of production, the degree of initial diversification, the relative size in comparison with that of international competitors, the demand of behavior, and the stage of generational change the economic group found itself in would decisively influence how different paths of adjustment were met. However, the strategies followed showed some common features: a tendency to specialization in a smaller group of activities than in the past, an expansion into other markets by means of direct investment, and the concentration of productive activities in sectors with higher natural advantages or lower tradability and little presence in the most internationally dynamic sectors based on knowledge and technological innovation.

As remarked above, a distinct element in strategic positioning by conglomerates was direct investment overseas, with an intensity and methodology rather different from that in the ISI stage. Most such investments were in Latin American countries, though there were some direct investment cases in the United States, Europe and East Asia. Local economic conglomerates led this process based on management capabilities, knowledge and the management of mature technologies, access to financial resources, the ability to operate in similar cultural environments, or the knowledge of specific conditions in some nearby markets. Certain national groups, through this kind of strategy, sought to reach worldwide or region-wide leadership in segments of specific markets. For another group of companies, internationalization through direct investment was essential for their own survival and expansion in the new economic context (Kosacoff, 1999).

There is some agreement on the fact that Argentina's small and medium companies' prevailing features in the ISI model were the centralization of management in 'an owner', little significant external insertion, prevailing defensive strategies, a wide production mix, limited specialized production, a low level of cooperation with other companies, little importance attached to innovation activities and low investment levels. These characteristics, which by and large prevailed throughout the 1990s, conditioned the responses that were applied to the structural reforms. Three groups of small and medium companies with their own specific characteristics can be identified:

1. A minority group with high competitive positioning (5 per cent of the total number) which showed productive and trade excellence and favorable prospects of adapting to the new rules of the game.
2. A high number (30 per cent) with little competitive positioning and few possibilities of surviving in the 1990s scenario.
3. Most of the small and medium companies, with 'defensive strategic behavior' which faced the challenge of reinventing themselves.

In this context, the difficulty of defining an adequate productive strategy during the economic transformation process involved every small and medium company, regardless of its productive specialization.

The new economic environment increased companies' uncertainty as well as the quantity and quality of information they had to process. Concern about the situation of small and medium companies translated into the proliferation of different government initiatives – in the areas of financing, technical assistance, information, etc. (which, by and large, had, for various reasons, great difficulty in meeting their goals), in the performance and proposals of the different business chambers, and in the claims that, from the social and political spectrum, aimed at the protection and promotion of small and medium companies.

The growing tendency to embrace product technologies from overseas with standards close to the best international practices went against local adaptation efforts. This implied a narrower gap in terms of product technologies, but a significant loss in the acquisition of domestic capabilities by means of R&D activities. However, the heavily promoted incorporation of imported machinery and equipment was necessarily accompanied by organizational changes and by greater investment in training. Also, the focus on doing away with vertically integrated production was basically supported by the incorporation of imported parts and pieces, thus reducing the possibility of establishing production networks based on local subcontracting.

Summing up, the main elements that characterized microeconomic performance in the 1990s were a decreased number of productive establishments, an increased opening of trade (with the focus on imports), an investment process based on the acquisition of imported equipment, a more concentrated and 'foreign-oriented' economy, and the sudden drop in the added-value coefficient. Also, there was a greater adoption of foreign state-of-the-art product technologies, an abandonment of most local technological efforts in the generation of new products and processes, a break in the vertical organization of activities based on the substitution of local added value in favor of foreign supplies, a decreased mix of production along with a higher complementation by foreign supply, a growing outsourcing of activities in the service sector, a higher internationalization of companies, and an increased importance of regional trade agreements in business strategies. But the most salient feature of productive organization in the 1990s was heterogeneity. No doubt all economic agents equally faced the challenge of moving from a 'workshop stage' to a 'company stage', implementing new production strategies in which local production went hand in hand with foreign supplies and finished goods, with the purpose of making full use of the new rules of the economic game.

Between 1998 and 2001, the return to an extremely volatile environment seriously affected production and investment decisions and gave rise to growing doubts about the solvency of a large number of companies. The problems of Argentina's economy generated financial and trade turmoil. The negative consequences at a business stage have already been shown, and nobody knew what the economic agents' responses to the return of high macroeconomic uncertainty would be.

By the late 1990s, the beginning of a long period of recession and deflation of prices gave rise to growing tensions and changed the expectations regarding the economy's growth potential and the public sector's solvency. Thus, a whole series of serious problems emerged: the vulnerability of the economy to external shocks; the deeper weakening of the financial system; a certain anti-competitive bias in the pricing structure; properly adjusted, with available funding, spending and investment; fiscal sustainability and its relation to a permanent fixed nominal exchange rate; the presence of endogenous forces leading to a recessive adjustment and a heterogeneous modernization of the productive organization that was insufficient to provide the economy with higher and growing productivity levels.

In this context, the crisis Argentina was going through wound up by translating into a long-lasting and profound recession; a steady growth in unemployment; poverty and extreme poverty rates; and a moderate process of deflation of prices and salaries. The fiscal situation was also very delicate, owing to the virtual impossibility of financing the imbalance without recourse to compulsion. Gradually, doubts about the ability to meet the growing public debt and the sustainability of the monetary regime and the related systems of contracts became certainties. The existence of a profound political crisis, deeper social turmoil and the virtually non-existent credibility of the successive economic policies tried out on the eve of the final collapse of the regime made the scenario much worse. Under these circumstances, there was a sudden and rapid decrease in bank deposits – simultaneously accompanied by a capital flight – which lead to the imposition of restrictions on the financial system and controls on payments destined for foreign countries. The different authorities declared a partial default on public debt and the abandonment of the currency convertibility regime and foreign-exchange parity that had been in force since 1991. The immediate consequences were a sharp increase in prices and a break in the systems of contracts. On the exchange front, after briefly keeping the currency peg to an official rate, a flotation regime with the intervention of the central bank was put in force.

In the first half of 2002 there were strong turbulences: the disappearance of local and foreign credit, the impossibility of provisioning, the higher prices of tradable supplies and the operating difficulties in the payment system came together to depress demand and supply for goods and services. However, the partial 'pesification' of foreign-exchange-denominated local banking and financial debt reduced the real value of liabilities. The drop in activity levels and the sharp depreciation of the exchange rate implied strong changes in sectors' profitability, demand configuration and income distribution. Within the framework of an intense capital flight, the real exchange rate reached levels comparable with those during the end of the hyperinflationary crisis in 1990. The balance of trade was extremely high owing to the sudden drop in imports, giving rise to a considerable surplus on current account. Investment decreased strongly, but, simultaneously, savings grew. Despite the intensity of the turmoil, the peso remained the denominator of prices and the medium of exchange. Although domestic prices grew considerably, the behavior of adaptation to a persistent context of inflation was not recorded.

1.6 THE ECONOMIC CONTEXT AFTER CONVERTIBILITY

The process associated with the abandonment of the convertibility system was marked by great turmoil, not only economic but also social and political. The costs of leaving a regime without 'escape mechanisms', and which turned out to be unsustainable, were in fact very high. However, the ensuing recovery was equally intense. The context and methodologies in which the economy performed as from the second half of 2002 laid the groundwork for a shift back to normal. From the point of view of the resource allocation process, the incentives structure implicit in the new relative prices of the economy was redefined in favor of tradable goods, labor-intensive processes and natural advantages. In the external sector, while in the 1990s one of the basic problems was the generation of sufficient exports to sustain dollar-denominated spending, after the devaluation it was domestic demand that appeared to be unusually compressed relative to exports. Nevertheless, this shift in the balance of trade produced some leeway for a notable recovery of domestic demand without the need to resort to foreign net financing and also exhibited decreased capital outflows.

Argentina's economic performance after convertibility was surprisingly positive. In macroeconomic terms, there is today a starting point totally different from what we had in the 1990s: a flexible and competitive exchange rate, a prudent fiscal policy with the best results for 50 years and a monetary policy consistent with the macroeconomic scheme. We have been able to leave convertibility behind without repudiating the use of the local currency and most of the foreign debt has been restructured, with very beneficial results for the country in terms of lower rates, pardons and maturities. In these aspects, the history of expansions that soon resulted in a solvency crisis seems to have left lessons that have been translated into more cautious attitudes and concerns about consistency.

The tendency to economic normalization allowed for the recovery of pre-crisis activity levels and the notable creation of jobs. The current accounts of the balance of payments and the balance of trade show surpluses. The recomposition of the investment process has been higher than expected and has already reached the record levels of the 1990s. This is specially notable in agriculture, tourism, mining, construction and throughout the small and medium company sector. Also, the international context of high raw material prices – related to the expansion of China and India – and the decreased interest rates have been very favorable for Argentina in the past few years, with forecasts of their remaining so in the medium term, providing the country with a window of opportunity.

Nevertheless, when we compare today's economic and social indicators with those of the 1970s we can see very clearly the enormous challenge we face in order to recover the population's welfare, equality and dignity. Among many other examples we see that GDP per inhabitant in 1974 was the same as that in 2003, which shows our stagnation; today's industrial added value per inhabitant is 20 per cent lower than three decades ago; the unemployment rate in 1970 was 4.9 per cent and underemployment 5.9 per cent; the proportion of households in Greater Buenos Aires below the poverty line moved from 5 per cent in 1974 to 42 per cent in 2003, and that of those below the extreme poverty line from 5 per cent in 1988 to 20 per cent in 2003; the difference in income of the 20 per cent of the poorest households relative to the 20 per cent of the wealthiest households moved from 8.7 times in 1974 to 17.1 times in 2000. One of the few economic indicators with an excellent performance was the growth in exports per inhabitant, which increased 15 times between 1970 and 2004. However, this dynamism of external sales is based on a shift back to a primary economy in the specialization of production, which impacted very favorably on macroeconomic accounts, but did not generate the necessary conditions for sustainable economic development with decent jobs.

1.7 INDUSTRIAL ACTIVITIES PERFORMANCE IN 2002–07

The devaluation in early 2002 gave rise to a radical change in the economy's relative prices, generating incentives diametrically opposed to those in force during the convertibility regime; sectors' profitability changed both in absolute and relative terms, favoring tradable goods production. Since then, Argentina's economy has experienced a fast recovery, at an average annual accumulative rate of 8.2 per cent between 2002 and 2006, recovering – by 2005 – the product levels prior to the recession and crisis.

At the level of the big sectors of the economy, industry has led this process of reactivation, which has been characterized by a relatively early recovery and high growth rates. Due to this tendency, the manufacturing sector accumulated a 39.5 per cent growth between 2002 and 2005, increasing its share in national GDP (from 16.2 per cent in 2002 to 17.7 per cent in 2005) and reversing the deindustrialization process relative to the past decade. However, while production surpasses the 1998 levels, it is not at the same industrial level existing then. Comparing the economic censuses of 1994 and 2004, there are clear signs that throughout these years sectors were dismantled and capabilities disappeared, a primary and disassembled structure was stressed and control by foreign capital in most of the industrial and service sectors consolidated.

In addition to the reduced number of activities characterized by strong, static-type comparative advantages or largely benefited by specific industrial policies, industry is made up today of companies that survived the double adjustment – first that of the convertibility conditions and then that of the recession – and that faced with the new relative prices conditions have reacted favorably. On the basis of each activity's competitive regime and its particular ability to react to sudden changes in relative prices, the branches of manufacturing showed various levels of recovery, dynamism and contribution to GDP growth; nevertheless, a salient characteristic of today's industrial growth is that it has been quite widespread at sector level.

Among the most dynamic branches during the current reactivation phase prevail those that have experienced the sharpest relative drop in production volumes during the crisis (textile and clothing, metal-mechanical (excluding machinery), construction materials, audio and video equipment, electric machinery and equipment, and automobiles). Nevertheless, as these activities (except the automobile sector) had already started their downsizing during the growth years in the 1990s, their recent performance has not been sufficient to recover their previous maximum production levels. All these areas of activity, leaders in industrial growth since devaluation, have faced a growing domestic and external demand and do not present supply-side bottlenecks, owing, mostly, to their abundant idle capacity at the onset of recovery and also, more towards the end of this recent period, to additional investments.

In turn, those sectors that grew the most in the 1990s and whose output dropped less than the average between 1998 and 2002 have shown sustained, albeit less pronounced, increases in output in the recent period that have gone beyond their historical maximum levels. This relatively less dynamic performance is explained, in most cases, by the fact they have been close to the saturation levels of their installed capacity, or that they require a large investment project whose start-up is not immediate. They are, generally, activities based on the use of natural resources and commodity producers (raw materials, metals, basic chemicals, paper, fuel and food), consolidated throughout the opening and deregulation process and currently showing a higher relative importance in the industrial structure. Their better relative performance during the crisis period is explained, mostly, by their high export indicator; in turn, post-devaluation relative prices have been equally favorable for them.

In this sense, while many sectors have totally or partially regained lost ground in a more favorable macroeconomic and incentives framework, the configuration of industry by sector has not changed significantly. In fact, we can state that this should have been expected given the short time since the collapse of the convertibility plan; anyway, investment trends might confirm the lack of existence, in the medium term, of a structural change in force. The disparities observed in expansion rates and some alterations at sector level in the leadership of the industrial recovery have not changed the growth pattern inherited from the structural reforms and the ensuing production adjustment.

The process of job creation in industry shows a similar pattern sector by sector. The activities that show most job creation and incorporation of labor are those that did most to eliminate it between 1998 and 2000; they are, basically, labor-intensive lines and, in turn, those mostly focused on the domestic market. The strong recovery of domestic demand since the second half of 2003, in the context of a relatively protectionist exchange rate before competitive imports, favored such performance. Instead, the job creation process has been comparatively less dynamic in the case of traditionally exporting sectors or those producing industrial commodities, which are of relatively little sensitivity to the domestic economic cycle and, because of this, were less prone to layoffs during the previous crisis. In general terms, most recent industrial employment growth is due to the evolution of certain branches with an important role in the production structure (food and beverages), and also to the strong reactivation of other labor-intensive manufacturing activities (textiles, footwear, metal-mechanical).

It is important to point out that the positive evolution of employment in every branch of industry is a characteristic feature of the post-devaluation growth profile, in comparison with the growth phases under the convertibility plan; in the earlier period, increased production was associated with high and increased unemployment and average labor productivity. The competitive conditions prevailing throughout the previous decade, mostly due to the opening of trade and a relatively appreciated, foreign exchange forced a structural adjustment process in the productive sector and important changes in the production function at a microeconomic level, focusing on the intensification of the labor process and lower employment content, with the subsequent reduction in staff. This adjustment process remained in force even during the recession and crisis phase, when the drop in employment volumes surpassed that recorded in production, which prolonged the rise in the medium productivity of labour.

Investment accompanied this economic and industrial reactivation process, reaching, in the third quarter of 2006, 22.8 per cent, higher than the previous record in early 1998. It is interesting that the investment process shows greater dynamism than in other post-crisis recovery periods in the past 25 years; we should also note that the construction component share in investment has been higher than previously, outstripping the incorporation of reproductive equipment. In fact, since 1998, the age of the installed indusrial park has been increasing gradually, generating obsolescence in some branches and companies; this situation turned out to be particularly serious during the crisis, resulting from a net disinvestment process affecting the reproduction of productive capacity and the increased age of the existing equipment. After a drop of about 85 per cent between 1998 and 2002, the imports of capital goods recovered rapidly; however, those aimed at manufacturing industry were, in 2005, 40 per cent lower than the drops recorded in 1998, without, at the same time, any significant substitution process through local production.

At least up to 2004, Argentina's industrial growth was based largely on the progressive use of idle capacity. Since then, there has been evidence of increased productive capacity; the indicators of the use of installed capacity have in general remained stable since that year, while there have been strong increases in production volumes. On the basis of available data on the investments by sector, while the industrial sector does not seem to capture a significantly higher relative proportion than in the previous decade, there occurred towards 2004 a growth rate in the amounts and projects analysed that was higher than those of that of the other activities. Investment by sector in manufacturing industry does not seem to have altered in its prevailing pattern in the past 10 or 15 years: the sectors producing food and beverages, automobiles and auto parts, oil and gas subproducts, and chemicals continue to attract around 70 per cent of total investments in manufacturing. Commodities and activities based on natural resources are the nucleus of Argentina's productive specialization and there are no signs of significant change.

It is interesting to observe the internationalization dynamic of companies from neighboring countries, particularly if it is contrasted with Argentine companies' weak international expansion process. In turn, mirroring the change of conditions for some public services, there has been a process of repurchase of some privatized assets and some foreign investors have been replaced with local groups or holdings; very probably this move, focused on segments with little technological dynamism, has already finished its cycle. As long as export prices, the exchange rate and expected internal demand growth remain at today's level, FDI flows will evolve accordingly. It is also probable that the purchase of national companies will still be high, while among such companies thinking is in terms of the 'exit' strategy rather than of a commitment to production.

A final comment must be made on income distribution trends. Devaluation caused a phenomenal transfer of incomes from wage-earners and other fixed-income sectors to the rest of the economy and laid the groundwork for an extraordinary recovery of industrial companies' operating profit margins. The data available in the research done in INDEC's *Encuesta Nacional a Grandes Empresas* show the drop in the salary mass in the total aggregate value. This feature is still sharper in the case of companies belonging to the industrial sector; on the other hand, such companies have been increasing their share in the profit mass generated in the group of the 500 largest companies in Argentina. It is important to point out that productivity has surpassed industry's real wages, increasing the average operating margin. Along with the strong growth recorded in activity levels, the very high poverty levels emerging from the crisis of convertibility and the solution applied have slowly and gradually been reduced, in favor of an increase in employment and a recovery of real wages. But equity and income distribution are still issues to be solved in the new growth regime.

NOTES

1. The implementation of these projects during the 1980s, while the ISI model was being dismantled, brought about significant structural changes, but with outcomes different from those expected.
2. From the 1930 crisis until today, the Argentine financial system has been characterized by the central bank's regulation of rediscounting facilities for the granting of credit at highly negative interest rates. Industrial firms have had favored treatment in terms of the credit allocations made under this system.
3. The very marked changes in relative prices that occurred during this period were favorable to service activities and to businesses producing nontradable goods. In contrast, the tradable industrial goods sectors suffered a profound fall in their relative prices and found themselves having to pay heavy loan-servicing charges based on high real interest rates.

REFERENCES

Berlinsky, J. (1977), *Protección arancelaria de actividades seleccionadas de la industria manufacturera argentina*, Buenos Aires: Ministerio de Economía.

Bisang, R., M. Fuchs, and B. Kosacoff (1992), 'Internacionalización de empresas industriales Argentinas', Project Volkswagen-Stiftung Ref. II/67/066, 'The Transformation of the Argentine Economic System: Industry and International Trade', Buenos Aires: ECLAC.

Bonvecchi, C. (1992), *El comercio internacional de manufacturas de la Argentina 1974–80*, Buenos Aires: CEPAL-ALADI, chs 1, 2.

Canitrot, A. (1983), *La política de apertura económica (1976-81) y sus efectos sobre el empleo y los salarios: un estudio macroeconómico*, Project PNUD/OIT, Buenos Aires: Ministerio de Trabajo.

Carciofi, R. (1990), 'La desarticulación del pacto fiscal', CEPAL Working Paper no. 36, Buenos Aires.

Damill, M., J.M. Fanelli, G. Rozenwurcel, and R.M. Frenkel (1989), 'Déficit fiscal, deuda externa y desequilibrio financiero', Buenos Aires: Editorial Tesis.

Damill, M., J.M. Fanelli, R. Frenkel, and G. Rozenwurcel (1988), *Las relaciones financieras en la economía Argentina*, Ediciones del IDES no. 15, Buenos Aires.

Hirschman, A. (1968), 'La economía política de la industrialización a través de la sustitución de importaciones', *Trimestre Económico*, **35** (140), 625–58.

Kosacoff, B. (1999), 'El caso argentino', in D. Chudnovsky, B. Kosacoff and A. López, *Las multinacionales latinoamericanas: sus estrategias en un mundo globalizado*, Buenos Aires: Fondo de Cultura Económica.

Kosacoff, B. (ed.) (2000), *Corporate strategies under structural adjustment in Argentina*, London: Macmillan Press/St Antony's Series.

Kulfas, M., F. Porta, and A. Ramos (2002), *La inversión extranjera en la Argentina*, Buenos Aires: CEPAL–United Nations.
Machinea, J.L. (1990), 'Stabilization under Alfonsin's government a frustrated attempt', CEDES Document no. 42, Buenos Aires.
Rodríguez, C. (1979), 'El plan Argentino de estabilización del 20 de diciembre', CEMA Documento de Trabajo no. 5, Buenos Aires.
Sourrouille, J.V., B. Kosacoff, and J. Lucangeli (1985), *Transnacionalización y política económica en la Argentina*, Buenos Aires: Centro Editor de América Latina.

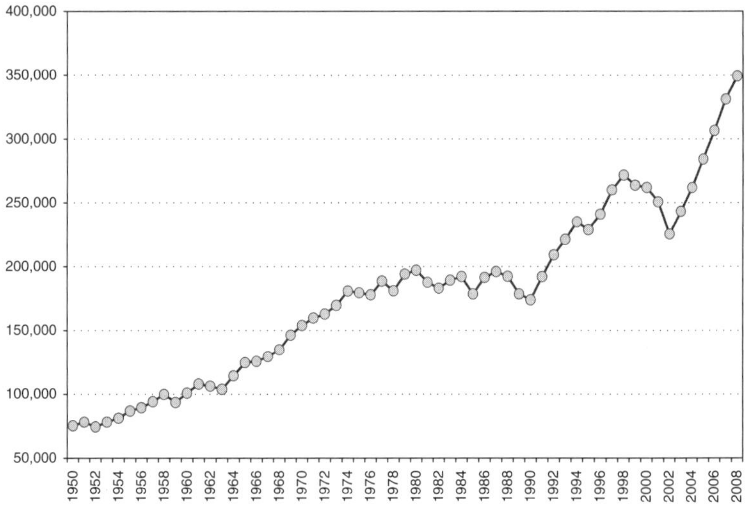

Source: ECLAC, Buenos Aires office.

Figure 1.1 Evolution of Argentine GDP (million pesos at constant 1993 prices).

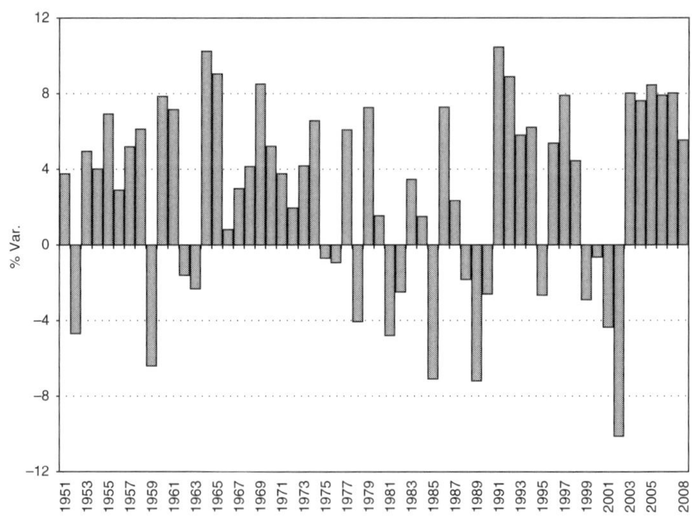

Source: ECLAC, Buenos Aires office.

Figure 1.2 Percentage change in Argentine GDP at constant 1993 prices.

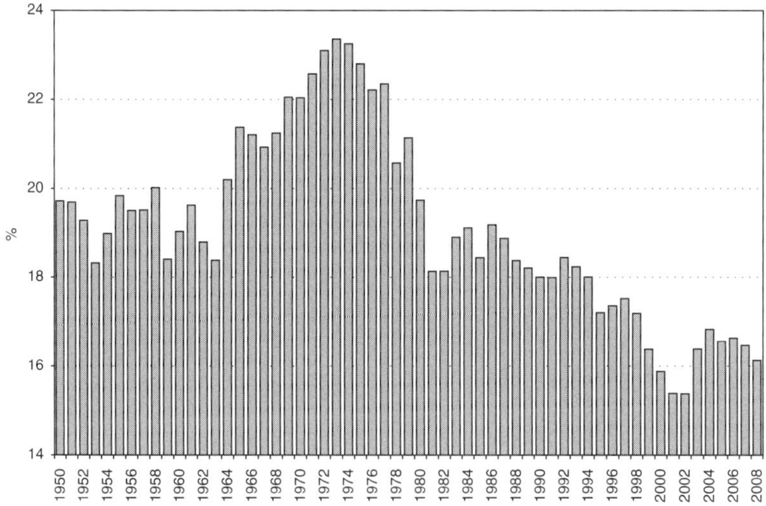

Source: ECLAC, Buenos Aires office.

Figure 1.3 Share of industrial GDP in total.

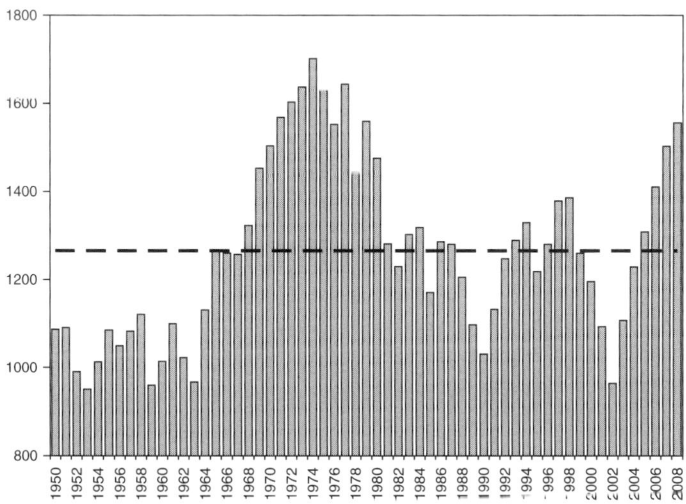

Source: ECLAC, Buenos Aires office.

Figure 1.4 Evolution of industrial GDP per capita (pesos at constant 1993 prices).

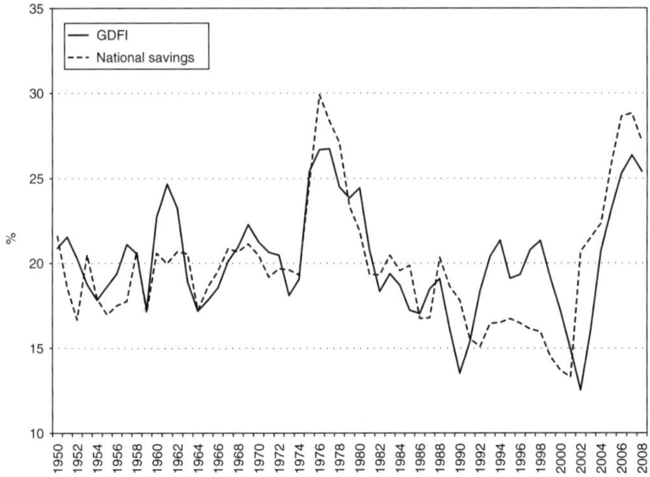

Source: ECLAC, Buenos Aires office.

Figure 1.5 Gross domestic fixed investment and national savings as a percentage of GDP at current prices.

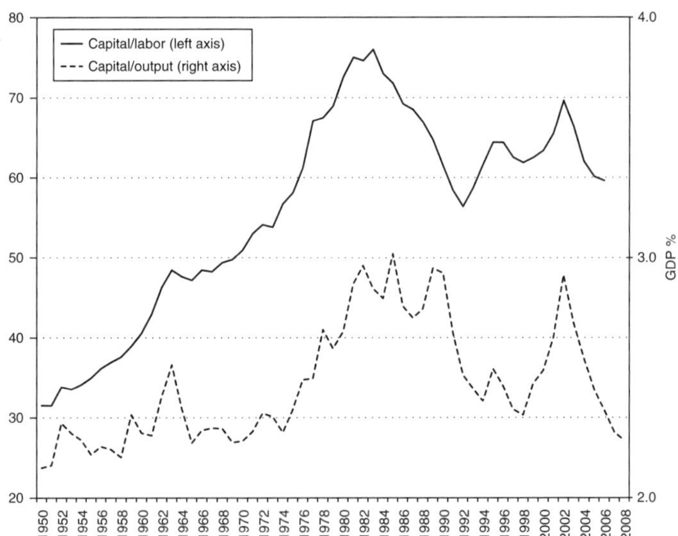

Source: ECLAC, Buenos Aires office.

Figure 1.6 Physical volume relations capital/output and capital/labor (1993 = 100).

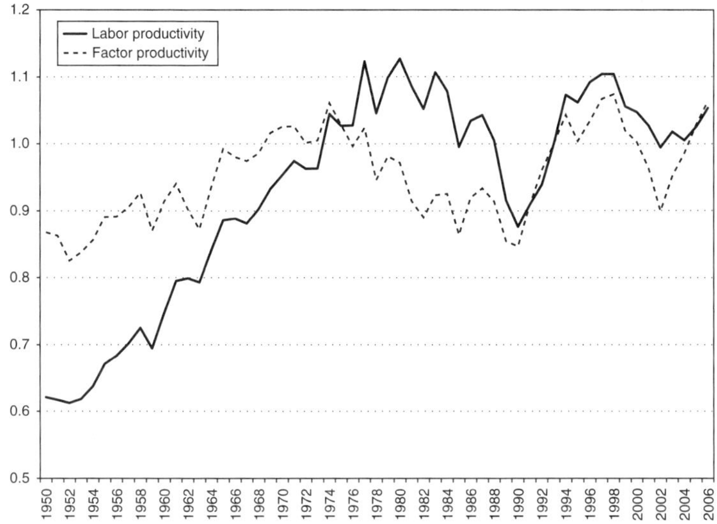

Source: ECLAC, Buenos Aires office.

Figure 1.7 Labour and factor productivity (base index 1993 = 1).

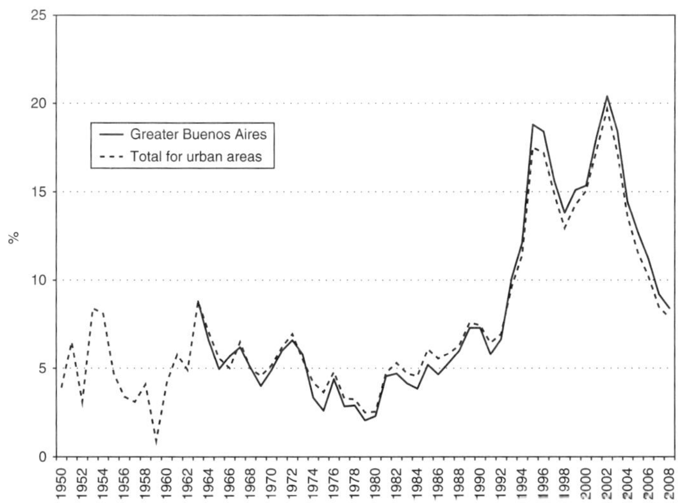

Source: ECLAC, Buenos Aires office.

Figure 1.8 Employment: unemployment rate in Greater Buenos Aires and the total for urban areas.

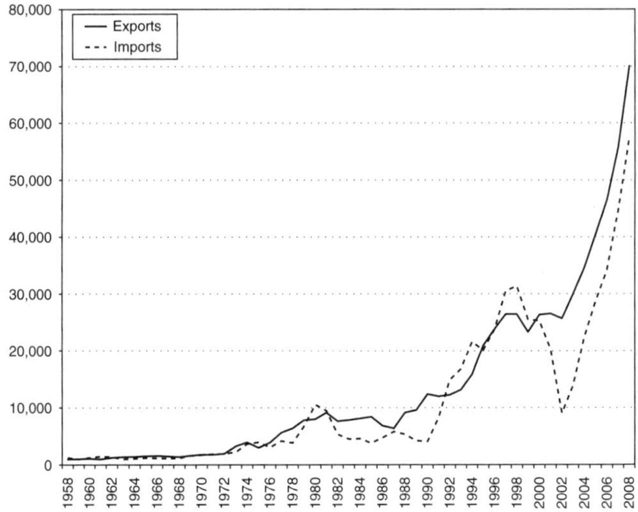

Source: ECLAC, Buenos Aires office.

Figure 1.9 *Foreign trade: exports and imports at current prices in millions of dollars.*

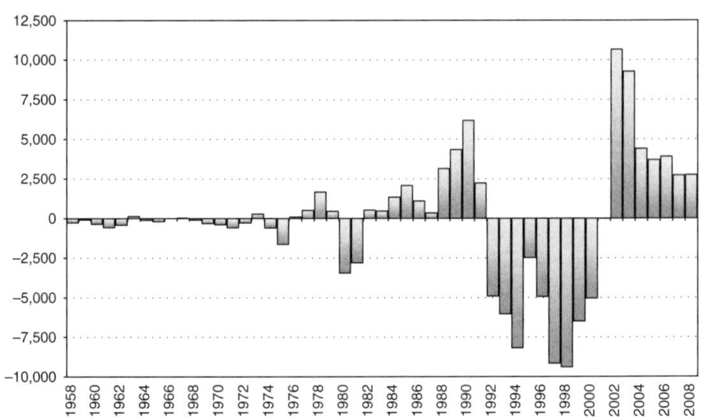

Note: [c]*Imports*: net of fuel purchases. *Exports*: excludes primary agricultural and fuel extraction.

Source: ECLAC, Buenos Aires office.

Figure 1.10 *Balance of trade in manufacturing*[c] *in millions of dollars.*

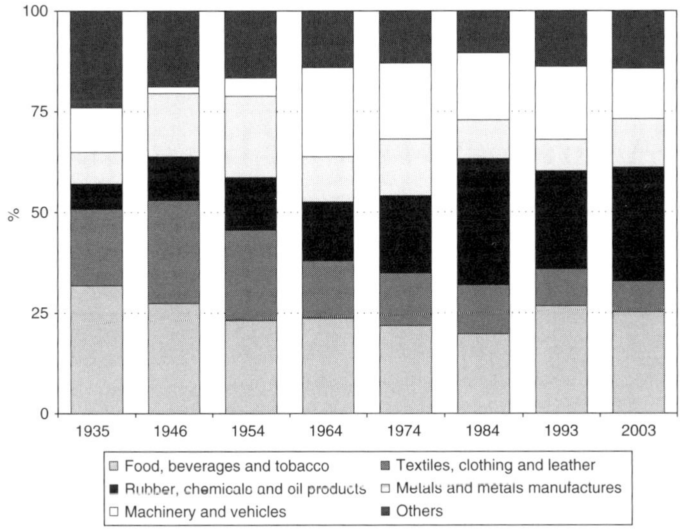

Source: ECLAC, Buenos Aires office.

Figure 1.11 Manufacturing composition by sector of activity (based on economic census).

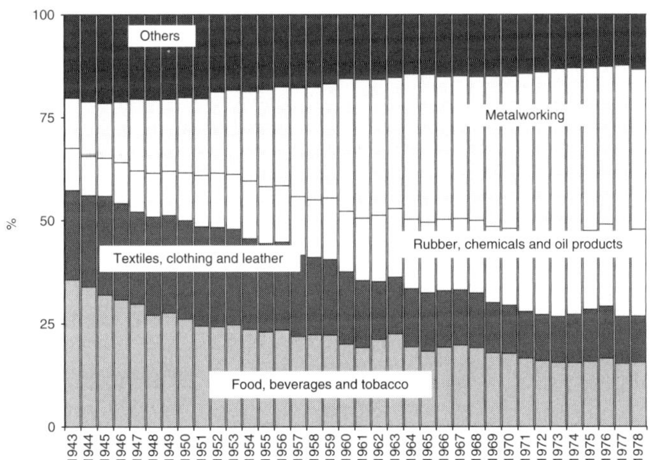

Source: ECLAC, Buenos Aires office.

Figure 1.12 Composition of the manufacturing industry by sector of activity – 1960 constant values.

2. A bird's eye view of Brazilian industrialization

André Villela

2.1 INTRODUCTION

Over the course of the twentieth century, Brazilian industry grew from a producer of, primarily, wage (non-durable consumer) goods into a diversified manufacturer of, among others, sophisticated machinery, consumer durables, telecommunication and transport equipment, and industrial inputs in general.[1] This long journey, in turn, involved three marked phases, to wit: an initial, market-driven – and export-led – 'easy' phase of industrialization; a second phase running from the early 1930s to the late 1980s, which saw the growing role of the state in fostering a modern, 'complete', industrial structure; and, finally – and following the overlap of macroeconomic disarray and trade liberalization in the late 1980s – a more market-friendly, 'globalized' period of industrial restructuring.

This chapter provides a very succinct description of the century-long history of Brazilian industrialization and is organized according to the three phases outlined above. The concluding remarks offer a more personal interpretation of this history.

2.2 OVERVIEW

From a long-term perspective, it would be hard to deny the fact that Brazil has been a success story in terms of economic growth in the past 100 years or so. Indeed, from a level of just under \$800 in 1890, GDP per capita increased sevenfold, to \$5200 in 1980, inching to \$5500 by the close of the twentieth century.[2] If one restricts the analysis to the period 1950–80, per capita income increased by a factor of four, placing the country firmly in the ranks of only 13 well-documented 'success stories of sustained, high growth', according to *The Growth Report*.[3]

Like any other nation's, this performance has involved a structural shift in the composition of output. Again, in line with international experience,

Table 2.1 Brazil 1900–2000: breakdown of GDP by sector

Year	*Shares of sectors based on 1949 prices (%)*			**Index of structural change[a] (%)**
	Agriculture	Industry	Services	
1900	44.57	11.59	43.84	0.37
1910	39.73	13.08	47.19	0.11
1920	38.09	15.72	46.19	0.17
1930	35.77	14.81	49.41	0.62
1940	29.42	18.74	51.84	0.97
1950	22.42	25.64	51.94	0.50
1960	16.91	29.85	53.25	0.14
1970	14.27	32.52	53.22	0.30
1980	9.81	34.29	55.90	0.32
1990	10.54	29.97	59.49	0.08
2000	11.04	27.74	61.22	–

Note: [a] Index of structural change calculated as the sum of the square of the differences in the shares existing in the final years of two consecutive decades.

Source: Bonelli (2006a).

at first the share of the primary sector in GDP decreased in tandem with the expansion of industry, with the service sector displaying a smaller gain in its share of total output. After reaching a peak sometime in the 1980s, industry's share of GDP receded, this time with most of the gains accruing to the service sector (Table 2.1).[4]

In what follows, Brazil's industrial history has been divided into three different periods, according to the distinct underlying development model, that is, the domestic and international setting which, ultimately, determined the nature of economic (industrial) growth in each phase. Each one of these three periods is taken up in turn.

2.3 EXPORT-LED INDUSTRIALIZATION: FROM THE MID NINETEENTH CENTURY TO THE 1930s

It could be argued that the birth of 'modern' industry in Brazil took place sometime in the mid nineteenth century, with the setting up of the first mechanized textile mills.[5] This coincided roughly with the political consolidation of the monarchy and with coffee's increasing preeminence in the

Brazilian landscape. Four decades of moderate – but positive – economic growth would ensue, leaving behind the years of political turmoil and economic stagnation which characterized independent Brazil's early history.

On the back of the expansion of coffee exports (and its production frontier), the Brazilian economy began to modernize, even if it did so within the limits of a slave-based society. Integration within the international division of labor of the Pax Britannica meant increasing commercial and financial flows, with the accompanying modernization of Brazil's cities and infrastructure. European immigrants poured in, drawn either directly or indirectly by the coffee boom. Coming on top of the abolition of slavery, in 1888, the demand for cash balances increased dramatically in the throes of the empire. In a last-ditch attempt to save the monarchy and diffuse planter discontent over abolition without compensation, the government launched a banking reform, in 1889. Through this measure it hoped to promote a substantial increase in the (gold-backed) money supply and an easing of credit conditions, a perennial source of complaint from the planter class.

Although unsuccessful in its intention to thwart regime change, the banking reform launched by the last imperial cabinet was further developed by the incoming republican administration. Under the guidance of Treasury Minister Rui Barbosa, an even bolder banking reform was put in place, allowing, this time around, for a massive increase in the supply of unconvertible paper money. This having coincided with a new, liberal, corporate law, a speculative frenzy ensued: the 'Encilhamento' had begun. Incorporation activity boomed on the Rio stock exchange, bringing with it the usual cases of malpractice and outright swindle.

Yet, despite the early literature's insistence on the excesses of the Encilhamento and the dubious character of many of the transactions it spawned, it is now widely accepted that the episode also helped fuel the first major industrial spurt in Brazil's history. The significant increase in industrial output witnessed in the early 1890s (mainly in the cotton textile sector) would constitute the first of a long list of instances of import-substituting industrialization (ISI) in Brazil.[6]

The mechanisms underlying this early instance of *unplanned* (i.e. strictly market-driven) ISI have been clearly identified by, among others, Dean (1969, 1985) and Fishlow (1972). In a nutshell, the substantial increase in the money supply following the Rui Barbosa banking reform, in conjunction with a relaxation of corporate law, allowed for credit expansion and the growth of both the number and capitalization of industrial enterprises listed on the Rio bourse.

As was the case in subsequent instances of import substitution during the First Republic (1889–1930), the exchange rate acted as the central link in a chain of events that, roughly, operated as follows: at first, through a combination of trade surpluses and capital imports, an appreciating milreis (the local currency) made imports of capital goods cheaper, thus allowing for the expansion of productive capacity (investment).[7] The subsequent decline (devaluation) in the exchange rate – resulting from balance-of-payments deficits, combined with the effects of an expansionary monetary policy – then acted as a deterrent to the imports of finished goods, thus awarding a measure of protection to the domestic manufacturing sector. As for the main actors in the early years of ISI in Brazil, Dean (1969, 1985) singles out three main groups: planter–entrepreneurs who sought to diversify their investments out of agriculture; import merchants, cognizant of the peculiarities of the local market; and immigrants in general, in their capacity either as businessmen or as part of a new, industrial, labor force, not to mention their role as consumers of manufactured wage goods.

The boom days of the early republican period faded amid political turmoil and the bursting of the Encilhamento bubble. Following a few years of muddling through, the economy finally succumbed to the stringent conditionality attached to the Rothschilds-led bailout of 1898, under the first Brazilian funding loan.[8] Severe deflation characterized most of the Campos Sales administration (1898–1902), followed by economic recovery in the early 1900s, as the new century ushered in a belle époque of strong export-led growth.

The decade preceding World War I marked the heyday of the Amazonian rubber boom which, hand in hand with the expanding coffee frontier in São Paulo and a massive inflow of foreign labor and capital, gave further impetus to the burgeoning manufacturing sector. An admittedly incomplete industrial survey carried out in 1907 counted just under 3000 manufacturing plants in Brazil, employing 136,000 workers.[9] Approximately one-third of those employees worked in the textile sector (cotton spinning and weaving, mostly), while the remainder were engaged in the sectors processing food (sugar, oil, flour mills etc.) and beverages (beer, wine, spirits) complemented by sundry non-durable consumer goods industries.[10] Both the intermediate and capital goods sectors were virtually non-existent at that early stage of Brazilian industrialization, except for a few ironworks, naval yards and repair shops for the transport sector.[11]

After a decade of robust export-led industrial growth, Brazil fell prey to the vicissitudes associated with being a peripheral, primary-exporting economy, under the rules of the classical gold standard system.[12] A collapse of the export prices of both coffee and rubber, coupled with increasing imports and capital flight associated with growing tension in Europe on the eve of World War I, led to a sudden reversal of a previously comfortable balance-of-payments position. The ensuing monetary contraction put an end to this tropical belle époque, ultimately forcing the country out of the gold standard.

Somewhat surprisingly, World War I turned out to be a blessing in disguise for Brazil's manufacturing sector. True, on the one hand, naval blockade and European warfare imposed a severe constraint on Brazil's ability to import the capital and intermediate goods necessary for further expansion of its industrial base,[13] but those very same factors acted as barriers against entry of finished products into its domestic market. Those sectors which in the previous export-led boom had managed to invest in manufacturing capacity – benefiting from a stable and appreciated exchange rate in order to increase their imports of industrial machinery from Europe and the US – were now in a position to occupy a slice of the market previously served by imports. A new round of ISI had just begun.

If, in terms of investments, the war clearly acted as a hindrance, the same cannot be said of its effects on manufacturing *output*, which did not suffer as badly. Indeed, estimates produced by Suzigan (2000) show that while it is true that the war led to a contraction in industrial production in 1914 (−8.7 per cent) and 1918 (−1.0 per cent), between 1915 and 1917 output rose by more than 30 per cent.[14] Recovery and growth in the middle years of the war responded not only to domestic but also to foreign demand for foodstuffs and manufactured consumer goods. The slowdown in 1917, followed by a contraction in industrial output in 1918, only served to show the limits of ISI under a supply shock as severe as World War I. Lack of access to inputs and industrial machinery and equipment greatly limited Brazilian industry's ability to expand productive capacity and output. This, in turn, served as a reminder to Brazilian authorities and industrialists of the need for government policies aimed at promoting industrial diversification (Suzigan, 2000, p. 61).

The 1919 census of manufactures provides a picture of the structure of the industrial sector in Brazil right after the Great War. As expected, the image that emerges is of an as yet unsophisticated industrialization, heavily biased towards low-tech consumer goods sectors mostly dedicated to the processing of locally supplied vegetable- and animal-based inputs. Local production of either consumer durables or intermediate and capital goods was negligible, with imports accounting for the bulk of domestic supply.

This situation began to change slowly in the 1920s, allowing for the emergence of a few industries not wholly dependent on the coffee sector for their inputs, machinery or demand, such as cement, rubber products, agricultural machinery, iron and steel, pulp and paper, silk and rayon textiles etc.[15] Indeed – and contrary to earlier accounts of the period – the 1920s were not that bad in terms of the history of Brazilian industrialization. As pointed out by Bonelli (1996, pp. 85–7), industrial output grew by an average of 5.4 per cent p.a. between 1919 and 1929.[16] The first major investments in the steel and cement sectors date from this period, which also witnessed important developments in the chemical, mechanical and automotive (assembly of CKD trucks) industries. Still, in the words of Fishlow (1972, p. 326), '[T]he 1920s were not very propitious from the standpoint of further propagation of the limited industrialization Brazil had attained by 1919.' A combination of fixed nominal tariffs and inflation had greatly reduced the protection enjoyed by local producers of manufactured goods. Foreign suppliers took advantage of the situation and flooded the Brazilian market with imports, which peaked in 1928.

An assessment of Brazilian manufacturing history prior to the onset of the Great Depression – that is, during an era of export-led industrial growth – shows that by the late 1920s the country had managed to achieve a certain measure of industrialization. The light consumer goods sector was firmly established, and the intermediate and capital goods industries were beginning to expand. These achievements, in turn, were to a large extent the result of private responses to opportunities opened up by the exchange rate, which either enabled imports of capital goods and industrial inputs (when the milreis appreciated) or else helped protect the local market (when the local currency was devalued). The role of the state in promoting industry had been mostly indirect and while the country boasted arguably the highest tariff levels in the world, this instrument proved to be relatively less important than the rate of exchange in shaping Brazilian imports – and hence industrialization.[17]

Prior to the seismic changes that would take place in the early 1930s (to be discussed below), industry was highly dependent on the fortunes of the coffee sector. There were two main channels through which this relationship was felt – one direct and the other indirect. In the first instance, overall demand conditions in the Brazilian economy – and hence demand for manufactured goods – were ultimately a function of the leading export sector. Plainly put, if for some reason coffee exports sagged then the economy as a whole suffered, including the consumer goods manufacturing sector. Contrariwise, when coffee boomed so did domestic demand for wage goods, which – depending on the level of the exchange rate and import tariffs – translated into a greater or lesser opportunity for local industry.

This brings us to the second, indirect, link between coffee and industry, via the rate of exchange. In this regard, one should note that if, on the one hand, a booming coffee economy afforded the domestic manufacturing sector with the labor (European immigrants), capital, imported machinery and technology necessary for industrial expansion, this very success of the export sector imparted an upward pressure (appreciation) on the rate of exchange which, ultimately, made manufacturing imports cheaper. If the government was unable to compensate this through tariff protection then industry would continue to be held hostage to the ups and downs of the coffee economy: in boom years, with an appreciating milreis, imports of machinery, and thus expansion of industrial capacity, would ensue; a collapse of the exchange rate – usually on account of falling coffee prices and reduced capital imports – would afford the protection needed for local industry to thrive amid receding imports. It thus might be said that at that stage Brazilian industry was still, literally, infantile, unable to walk on its own two feet unless aided by a fatherly coffee sector.[18]

It took the devastating crisis that hit the coffee industry in 1929 to finally allow the manufacturing sector to break loose from this relationship.[19] This crisis, in turn, not only ushered in the Great Depression but also marked the dawn of 'modern' (i.e. industry-led) economic growth in Brazil.[20]

2.4 INWARD-LOOKING INDUSTRIALIZATION: FROM THE 1930s TO 1990

It is almost a cliché to say that the 1930 revolution that brought Getulio Vargas to power marked a watershed in Brazilian political and economic history. Yet it is hard to escape that conclusion, even if one must temper it with the proviso that the ensuing gradual substitution of industry for coffee as the major driving force of economic development in Brazil was more an indirect by-product of government measures to address the coffee crisis than the result of conscious industrial policy.

The broad outlines of the historical narrative of this crucial moment in Brazilian history were laid out five decades ago in Furtado's (1959) classic account of the 'shift of the dynamic center of the Brazilian economy'. Very briefly, that author's story goes like this: the revolutionaries who came to power in 1930 were forced to act immediately to deter the downward spiral sparked by the collapse of the coffee sector. Two sets of measures formed the essence of government policy that, ultimately, rescued the Brazilian economy from the Depression and set it on a different course: on the monetary side, the decision to let Brazil off the gold standard; at the same time, an expansionary fiscal policy aimed at buying – and destroying – the fruits of excess capacity in the coffee sector. Even if unconsciously, this was Keynesianism *avant la lettre*.[21]

Ultimately, what these measures managed to achieve was to change relative prices in such a manner as to redirect the Brazilian economy partly out of coffee and, increasingly, into more profitable ventures in the manufacturing sector. In fact, the massive devaluation which resulted from Brazil abandoning gold and letting the exchange rate float promoted an expenditure shift away from the export sector and into import-competing industries. Meanwhile, deliberate, inflationary, deficit financing helped put a floor under the level of overall expenditure, and ensured that the new-found competitiveness of the domestic manufacturing sector would translate into increasing local demand.[22]

Unlike previous episodes of ISI in Brazilian history, the shifts witnessed in the 1930s steered the economy onto an altogether different development path. From then on industry – and no longer coffee – set the pace of economic growth, and for almost six decades thereafter Brazil followed the quintessential inward-looking development strategy. At first, unconsciously (and, as mentioned, as a by-product of official measures taken to rescue the floundering coffee sector), industrial growth increasingly became a matter of deliberate government policy.

Not only did the 1930s mark a break with Brazilian industrial history; they also ushered in three decades of vigorous change in the very composition of domestic output. In other words, between the early 1930s and the late 1950s the breakdown of total output between agriculture, industry and the service sector displayed the most marked shift of the century – in favor of industry, of course. Moreover, within industry itself, the 1930s saw the gradual shift away from those labor-intensive and low-tech sectors which had dominated the landscape in the earlier phase, towards a set of 'new' ones which at the time stood for modern industry – intermediate goods, mostly (Bonelli, 1996).

The impact of the Great Depression in Brazil was much less severe than in most industrial countries, largely as a result of the unconscious counter-cyclical policies pursued by the incoming Vargas administration in support of the coffee sector. Thus, after briefly dropping in 1929–31, industrial production in Brazil doubled over the course of the decade. Two main features of this industrial spurt stand out: first, its initial reliance on previously existing excess capacity, in turn a direct result of massive investment during the export-led boom of the late 1920s; second, the leadership of the new, 'modern', industrial sectors, outperforming traditional consumer goods industry.[23]

At the end of the decade, Brazilian industry displayed a structure that was more diversified than the one revealed by the 1919 census. Over the course of two decades, the share of the consumer goods sector in total manufacturing value added had decreased by 10 percentage points, a drop that occurred mostly during the 1930s. The intermediate goods sector, in turn, gained more than 7 percentage points, led by the expansion of the metals industry. However, production of capital goods and

Table 2.2 *Brazilian industrial output 1939–52: average rates of growth for selected sectors (percentages per annum)*

Sector	*1939–42*	*1942–45*	*1945–52*	**1939–52**
Nonmetallic minerals	15.1	13.1	10.4	12.1
Metallurgy	13.2	5.1	20.5	15.2
Mechanical	–	–	10.7	–
Electrical materials	–	–	22.0	–
Transport materials	−12.5	0	41.0	16.1
Furniture	9.6	–	–	–
Paper	6.2	2.0	9.2	6.8
Rubber	41.5	20.0	8.9	18.4
Leathers and hides	1.6	−6.5	4.8	1.3
Chemicals and pharmaceuticals	2.5	24.0	8.7	10.5
Textiles	1.9	9.4	3.0	4.2
Foodstuffs	0	0.3	7.7	4.1
Beverages	−1.0	16.7	10.0	8.8
Printing and publishing	−6.0	11.2	10.2	6.4
Total	3.9	9.4	9.8	8.3

Note: –: Not relevant in that year.

Source: Malan et al. (1977).

consumer durables was still in its infancy, accounting on average for less than 20 per cent of local demand. This showed the long path which still lay ahead before Brazilian industry would be 'complete', in the sense of being capable of producing not only fairly simple consumer goods but also the inputs used in most production (intermediate goods) and the necessary machinery (capital goods).

The next major event to shape the history of Brazilian industry was the outbreak of World War II. The war in many ways gave a further boost to some of the trends that had been in place since the Depression, in particular the diminishing share of imports in total supply, and the increasing role of the state as a regulator (when not a direct purveyor) of economic activity.

Brazilian industry was initially hit hard by the conflict, as imports of vital industrial inputs and machinery were hampered. Manufacturing output managed to grow at an average rate of 3.9 per cent over the years 1939–42, but increased at a hefty 9.4 per cent p.a. during the remainder of the war (Table 2.2). What these data suggest is that 1942 was a turning point as far as industrial production was concerned. Essentially, in the early years of the conflict, foreign exchange was as scarce as throughout most of the 1930s and the impact of Allied procurement policy on the Brazilian economy was yet to be felt; after 1942, on the other hand, industrial production picked up amid massive Allied purchases and some American foreign direct investment, leaving the country awash with foreign exchange. Overtly expansionary monetary and fiscal policies also played a part in this industrial recovery.

Apart from these broader trends in industrial production, the war brought a more subtle, but equally significant, change in the attitude of the Brazilian state vis-à-vis economic development, at the time usually taken to be a byword for industrialization. According to Leopoldi (2003), the process of institution-building and state modernization carried out by Vargas moved one notch up after the Estado Novo dictatorship was installed in 1937. Among the new roles the Brazilian state would be called upon to play was that of leading the way in 'strategic' sectors where private interest was found wanting, such as steel, mining, oil, energy supply and banking.[24] The creation of the first major state-owned enterprises during the war attests to this greater direct role of the Brazilian state in economic development, in contrast with earlier indirect support (via subsidies, import tariffs etc.).

As a result of the increase in exports during the war (especially after 1941–42), Brazil emerged from the conflict in a fairly comfortable balance-of-payments position – in sharp contrast to the situation which had prevailed since the onset of the coffee crisis in 1929–30.[25] Foreign exchange reserves (including gold) had increased more than tenfold since the outbreak of the War, to some $760 million, although a major share consisted of either unconvertible or blocked currencies. After a brief experiment with balance-of-payments liberalization in the early days of the Dutra administration, leading to the quick loss of convertible foreign exchange reserves, the government was forced to backtrack and reinstate severe limits on balance-of-payments operations. Subsequent measures dealing with this external constraint, by means of more or less stringent controls on the use of scarce foreign exchange, set the tone for the next 20 years or so, until Brazil could count on more abundant private capital flows. This 'given' – the foreign exchange constraint – and official policy to deal with it together constituted the single most important driver of import-substitution industrialization from the mid 1940s to the mid 1960s.

Beginning with the Dutra administration (1946–51), government policy would increasingly limit the use of scarce foreign exchange to 'essential' imports. To this end, a myriad of measures – including, among other things, the concession of import licenses, use of multiple exchange rates, foreign exchange auctions, and outright prohibition, in the 1970s – would seek to direct the use of exchange cover to designated sectors. Needless to say, business groups lobbied the government increasingly, with a view to obtaining preferential access to imports of vital inputs and machinery, while at the same time ensuring that their own sectors would be sheltered from foreign competition.

Industrialization continued apace in the 1950s, increasingly directed by the Brazilian government, and amid a permanent foreign-exchange constraint.[26] Two measures passed by the monetary authority in 1953 and 1955 were crucial for the furtherance of ISI in Brazil: SUMOC directive (Instrução) no. 70 substituted foreign exchange auctions for the (corrupt) import licensing schemes set up after the war, while Instrução no. 113 allowed foreign firms to internalize capital goods without exchange cover. In conjunction, they provided an additional boost to industrial growth in the first half of the decade, which also witnessed two major events in the history of Brazilian industrialization: the setting up in December 1950 of the Joint Brazil–United States Economic Development Commission and, as a result of its recommendations, the national development bank (BNDE) in 1952.

The commission's importance lay mostly in its identification of so-called infrastructural 'bottlenecks' in the way of economic development in Brazil. The original intention was that projects elaborated by the joint commission would be submitted to the US Eximbank and the World Bank for possible financing. However, changes in Brazil–US relations spelled an end to these hopes, although, crucially, the projects themselves later served as the basis for much of the planning leading to President Juscelino Kubitschek's Targets Plan.

To this day Kubitschek retains an almost mythical status in Brazil's collective memory, being hailed as a man of 'vision', responsible not only for the construction of a new capital (Brasilia) in the Brazilian heartland but also for promoting an ambitious industrialization drive (the Targets Plan). The latter, if not actually enabling the country to grow '50 years in the space of 5 years' (as his campaign motto would have it), clearly set it on a new, 'modern' (i.e. industrialized) course. Like most myths, this one is also true – at least in part.

To begin with, it is important to note that, contrary to generalized perception, ISI in Brazil had already advanced significantly *prior* to JK's term in office (which began in 1956). Data compiled by Malan et al. (1977, p. 405), for instance, shows that industrial production had been growing at approximately 9 per cent p.a., on average, in the first half of the 1950s. Also, imports, which had accounted for 13.5 per cent of domestic supply of manufactured goods in 1950, saw this share fall by half in 1956. Finally, manufacturing imports, having increased by 40 per cent in 1950–52 (on account of speculative stockpiling at the outbreak of the Korean War), dropped by an equivalent amount in 1952–56, in an indication of increased self-sufficiency in this area. Clearly, Brazilian industry had not remained stagnant during the Vargas and Café Filho presidencies, just waiting to be 'rescued' by Kubitschek.

Having said that, it is undeniably the case that JK's Targets Plan marked a discontinuity in the history of Brazilian industry. For one thing, it represented a significant shift in the state's attitude towards economic development. While at least since Vargas's Estado Novo regime (1937–45) the Brazilian state had been attempting to guide the private sector into certain areas of industry, and increasingly the government itself was taking charge of 'strategic' areas, with the Targets Plan economic *planning* took center stage. From then on, the private sector looked to the state to lead the development process, while counting for its own expansion on, *inter alia*, preferential access to foreign exchange, official lines of credit (through the Bank of Brazil and, increasingly, BNDE), subsidies and also, crucially, a protective umbrella which kept foreign competition at arm's length.

The plan's achievements also go some way in explaining Kubitschek's enduring legacy. The combination of private (both domestic and foreign) and public investments in sectors such as automobiles and auto parts, shipbuilding, cement, steel, electrical appliances and infrastructure moved import substitution industrialization in Brazil one further stage on. In the meantime, reliance on imports of consumer durables and a few types of capital goods had been further reduced.[27]

During Kubitschek's term in office, Brazilian GDP grew at an average rate of just over 8 per cent p.a., with population growth reaching a peak of 3 per cent p.a. In just 5 years, agriculture's share of GNP declined by 5.7 percentage points, in favor of industry. The country could boast a new, 'modern', capital and, for the first time in history, the majority of Brazilians lived in cities. Yet, in spite of these many achievements, the JK legacy must also take in growing inflation and foreign indebtedness which, together with solemn disregard for budget constraints, would cast a long and costly shadow over Brazilian society in decades to come.

Shortly after JK stepped down from office, in early 1961, the country would become increasingly engulfed in political turmoil. The tumultuous Janio Quadros and João Goulart presidencies were marked by slow growth and macroeconomic meltdown. The March 1964 coup brought to power modernizing elements among the military, who embarked on creating a new institutional edifice upon which growth would resume and, on a broader level, free-market capitalism could effectively flourish in Brazil. The PAEG Plan (Plano de Acão Econômica do Governo), implemented right after General Castelo Branco seized power, aimed at just that. A mixture of medium-term stabilization program and ambitious overhaul of the financial and tax systems, it was moderately successful in bringing inflation down from more than 100 per cent p.a. to around 40 per cent in 1967, while allowing GDP to expand by an average of 4 per cent p.a. On the microeconomic front, however, the huge reforming zeal that underpinned legislative change in a broad range of areas ultimately laid the ground for the subsequent 'economic miracle', in the darkest days of the military regime.

Between 1968 and 1973 Brazil experienced average GDP growth in the two-digit range.[28] This 'miracle', in turn, was achieved by a combination of three major elements, to wit: the liberalizing reforms undertaken by the previous administration;[29] a particularly benign international environment, characterized by rapid growth, and expanding trade and capital flows; and, finally, a change of course in macroeconomic policy in Brazil. The latter consisted, basically, of a shift away from moderately restrictive fiscal and monetary policies to expansionary ones, with a view to inducing private sector investment and consumption. On the back of massive credit expansion – facilitated by the reforms undertaken during the Castelo Branco administration – both agriculture and industry were stimulated.

Industrial growth during this period benefited, at first, from excess capacity inherited from years of macroeconomic chaos (1961–63) and stabilization efforts (1964–66). Two years of recovery convinced the private sector to invest massively in capacity expansion, which it did. At the other end, cheap credit ensured a boom in demand for consumer durables, which, together with the construction industry, would be the leading sectors throughout the 'miracle'.

By the end of the Medici government (1969–74) it was clear that the Brazilian economy was overheating, GDP having expanded by 14 per cent in 1973. As expected, imports of capital goods and oil were also peaking, only to be hit by the first oil shock in late 1973. The incoming Geisel administration, bent on carrying out a program of gradual political détente, was forced to shun the traditional, orthodox approach to the looming balance-of-payments crisis. Faced by opposition from both hardline sectors of the military and an increasingly confident civilian opposition, the president chose to react to the oil shock and the attendant balance-of-payments constraint by embarking on a bold growth-cum-debt development strategy. In other words, in order to secure backing for a policy of controlled political liberalization, the government had to ensure that economic growth would not be compromised. To this end, in December 1974 the Second National Development Plan (II PND) was launched.

The rationale for this 'positive' reaction to the first oil shock may be summarized as follows. Deeming the oil shock a temporary blip in an otherwise benign international environment, the Brazilian government took the possibilities offered by an abundant pool of foreign capital (the so-called petrodollars, recycled by European banks and offered to developing and socialist economies) and finalized its import-substitution industrialization process. The idea was for the state, in association with the private sector (domestic and foreign), to engage in a massive investment program in those areas in which the Brazilian economy was still mostly dependent on imports, such as capital and intermediate goods, as well as energy.[30] Once those projects came on stream, not only would domestic production substitute imports but, additionally, earnings from the sale overseas of part of this production would help pay for the foreign loans contracted to fund those projects. In practice, therefore, the Brazilian government was placing a bet on the possibility of buying time and 'diluting' over several years the cost of adjustment to the oil shock, thus avoiding the political fallout that would certainly follow the more obvious, recessive alternative.

In practice, the investments included in the II PND sought to 'finish' Brazil's ISI drive, by focusing on the more sophisticated areas where domestic production still lagged consumption. Even if seldom acknowledged by mentors and sympathizers in academia, the final aim was to achieve self-sufficiency, and thus free Brazil from its dependency on an inherently volatile international environment. In this respect, this 'forced march' would be the culmination of a process which had begun somewhat spontaneously during the coffee crisis of the 1930s, when the 'shift in the dynamic center' of the economy saw resources flow away from agriculture and increasingly into the manufacturing sector. From then on, an increasingly inward-looking, state-led, industrialization effort ensued. Full industrialization, it was hoped, would insure the country against the vulnerability it had been exposed to as a primary-producing economy.

Economic policy under the Geisel administration was successful in its purported aim of avoiding a recession at all costs: GDP growth, while not on a par with the 'miracle' years of 1968–73, was still a robust 6.7 per cent p.a., on average, in marked contrast with the stagflation that characterized most industrialized economies in the second half of the 1970s. Manufacturing output (capital and intermediate goods, in particular) led the way, part of which was increasingly directed to overseas markets, as Brazilian exports diversified away from primary commodities and into industrial goods. By the mid to late 1970s the more 'dynamic' industrial sectors (that is, intermediate and capital goods) accounted for two-thirds of manufacturing value added, against just over 50 per cent in 1970.[31]

Yet, despite this apparent success in carrying forward Brazil's industrialization, the growth-cum-debt strategy of the mid 1970s unleashed a host of macro and microeconomic problems that would plague the Brazilian economy for almost two decades. On the macro side, the bet implicit on the very essence of the II PND – and which in practice involved borrowing heavily overseas at variable rates of interest, with a view to repaying in the long run – subjected Brazil to sudden swings in the international economy.[32] Apart from the obvious risk posed by a possible spike in international interest rates (like the one that would eventually arise in 1979–80), the heavy accumulation of foreign debt by the Brazilian government had a counterpart in growing *domestic* debt issuance and accumulation. The transfer problem arising from this debt pile would loom large in the mid 1980s, as massive trade surpluses, combined with economic slowdown, were required to finance a growing current-account deficit. The accompanying growth in public sector borrowing needs, partly financed by money creation, in turn, would be at the root of the inflationary scourge that would dominate Brazil's economic landscape for the next 15 years.[33]

As if the macroeconomic side effects (growing foreign and domestic debt; inflation) of the growth-cum-debt strategy were not enough, its 'industrialization at all costs' ethos also brought with it serious – and negative – *micro*economic consequences. Misallocation of resources abounded in the period, as well as productive inefficiencies associated with suboptimal scales and, more generally, solemn disregard for comparative advantages when deciding many an investment. All this, arguably, may have been expected from an inward-looking industrialization strategy, where government intervention often fostered private rent-seeking practices, instead of trying to remedy specific market failures.

The combined effects of both macro and microeconomic distortions accumulated over the previous decades of inward-looking industrialization – and aggravated under the II PND – would be felt dramatically in the so-called lost decade of the 1980s, in a clear indication that the ISI strategy had reached its limits. On the macroeconomic side, the dynamism that had characterized the Brazilian economy since the end of World War II gave way to a stop-and-go-type trajectory which saw both GDP and industrial output expand by less than 20 per cent in 10 years – in practice, a decline in per capita terms. To make matters worse – and closely related to the marked slowdown in GDP growth – labor productivity dropped by approximately 10 per cent in the decade, after expanding at an average yearly rate of 4 per cent in the previous 40 years.[34] This disappointing performance, it must be stressed, took place amid successive failed attempts at stabilizing inflation, the effective fiscal collapse of the Brazilian state and the foreign debt crisis.

By the late 1980s it was becoming abundantly clear that virtual self-sufficiency – as measured for instance by the abnormally low share of imports in domestic consumption – was not necessarily good. Moreover, nominal tariffs in excess of 100 per cent for several manufactured goods[35] virtually shut off the Brazilian market from foreign competition. As a result, consumers were burdened with often low-quality and high-priced locally made products, while producers were forced to rely on the purchase of expensive capital goods. This state of affairs would only begin to change in 1988, when the country embarked on a process of trade liberalization which would see import tariffs fall from an average of 50 per cent to the 10 per cent to 15 per cent range by the mid 1990s. A new phase in Brazilian industrial history had begun.

2.5 INDUSTRY IN A GLOBALIZED WORLD: FROM 1990 TO THE PRESENT

In many respects the period of the late 1980s to the early 1990s represents a fundamental turning point in Brazilian economic history, in which three interrelated phenomena stand out. On the macroeconomic front, this period witnessed the nadir in the struggle against virtual hyperinflation, which, ultimately, lead to the successful implementation of the Real Plan, in 1994. Meanwhile, economic liberalization begun under the Collor government gained momentum in the subsequent Itamar Franco and Cardoso administrations, with new rounds of tariff reductions and an intensification of the privatization process. Taken together, stabilization, trade liberalization and privatization combined to usher a new development *model*, leaving behind 60 years or so of ISI. Globalization had finally caught up with Brazil, which embraced market-friendly reforms more out of necessity than from actual conviction as to their merits.

Two decades into this new era, results have been mixed. Looking first at the aggregate level, it is clear that economic growth in the past 20 years has fallen way short of the 7 per cent annual average which was posted between the 1950s and 1980s. At the root of this marked deceleration is a clear inflection in the rate of industrial growth, which has dropped by some two-thirds since the glory days of the ISI drive, in the postwar period. However, at same time, it would be wrong to overlook the resilience of Brazil's industrial base, as the country integrates into the world economy, and manufactured exports continue to figure prominently in foreign trade.

Starting with the first trend (the slowdown in GDP growth) there has been considerable research into its ultimate causes,[36] with two likely causes having been singled out in the literature: first, a collapse in the growth of the capital stock (caused, in turn, by an increase in the relative price of

Table 2.3 Brazilian industrial production 1992–2007 by sector: average annual rates of growth (percentages)

Sector	*1992–94*	*1995–98*	*1999–02*	*2003–07*	**1992–07**
Foodstuffs	0.82	3.88	2.23	1.53	2.16
Beverages	0.82	2.83	−1.97	4.10	1.65
Textiles	−0.21	−6.19	0.78	1.78	−0.84
Apparel	−0.13	−3.26	0.15	−3.14	−1.78
Pulp and paper	1.87	1.64	3.43	4.05	2.88
Printed material	–	–	–	2.23	2.23
Oil and alcohol refining	2.62	4.18	−0.25	1.26	1.87
Pharmaceuticals	−0.45	6.24	3.22	2.83	3.17
Other chemicals	6.62	2.11	−0.67	2.70	2.45
Rubber and plastic products	2.11	2.32	−0.52	2.23	1.54
Nonmetallic minerals	0.20	4.32	−1.14	2.39	1.58
Metallurgy	5.10	0.67	2.94	3.39	2.92
Metal products except machinery	6.85	−0.99	1.55	1.78	1.98
Machinery and equipment	10.39	−1.91	4.99	8.37	5.33
Electrical equipment	6.86	4.71	5.79	7.89	6.38
Automotive vehicles	11.18	0.91	1.79	11.49	6.36
Other transport equipment	7.25	0.13	19.6	8.21	8.86
Furniture	7.28	1.64	1.56	2.79	3.04
Total	3.94	0.80	1.58	3.98	2.56

Note: –: Insufficient data available.

Source: Adapted from Barros and Pereira (2008, Table 9.2).

investments in Brazil[37]) coupled with the state's dwindling contribution to the investment effort.[38] In other words, not only has the cost of investing increased dramatically in Brazil – partly as a result, it must be stressed, of the inward-looking industrialization model pursued until recently – but also the state has been absent from this process, as its ability to invest has all but evaporated over the past 20 years or so. The second major obstacle consists of Brazil's notoriously low level of human capital, which in conjunction with a burdensome labor code hinders both the supply and efficient use of labor in the economy.[39]

The marked slowdown in the rate of GDP growth experienced by Brazil in the past couple of decades has been in great measure the result of the collapse of the rate of growth of industrial output. Indeed, having been outperformed by both agriculture and services, the manufacturing sector, after reaching a record share of one-third of Brazilian GDP in 1980, has been losing relative ground ever since, to a current low of just over 18 per cent (see Table 2.4).[40] Although it began in the 1980s, this decline in the share of industry in the Brazilian economy gained momentum in the 1990s, in the wake of the economic downturn at the start of the decade, combined with the effects of trade liberalization on the competitiveness of the manufacturing sector.

As noted by Bonelli and Gonçalves (1998), the *relative* shrinking of Brazil's industrial sector helped in a way to correct for the 'excessive' growth experienced during the ISI phase (a point already alluded to in Section 2.4). In other words, having grown 'too much' under cover from foreign competition, Brazil's manufacturing sector was forced to adapt to a situation of greater contestability, which inevitably (especially in a recessive environment, as in the early 1990s) led to the survival of only the fittest. The result has been an industrial sector whose share in the economy has become more akin to the international norm, thus eliminating the 'industrial bias' which had persisted until the 1980s.

While this convergence toward normality (in terms of the share of the industrial sector in GDP) should be perceived as a positive trend – as it indicates a redirection of resources towards areas in which the country has greater comparative advantages – the magnitude and speed of this decline – in the order of 50 per cent between 1980 and 2000 (Table 2.4) – has raised the specter of deindustrialization in Brazil.

The issue of deindustrialization is currently hotly contested. Critics of the framework which has underpinned macroeconomic policy for over a decade now – and which gives pride of place to interest rate management in securing low inflation – have been vocal in their attacks on the perceived overvaluation of the Brazilian currency, in turn a by-product of stringent monetary policy. High rates of interest (compared with the rest of the world), according to this view, not only help keep inflation low but also increase the cost of domestic borrowing (and hence investment), and through their impact on the currency rob Brazilian industry of its international competitiveness.[41]

This line of reasoning has its merits, especially as concerns the impact of an overvalued real on the competitiveness of Brazilian industry. Yet it should be noted that the exchange rate cuts both ways; that is, while it indeed makes competing imports cheaper in the Brazilian market it also enables Brazilian manufactures to increase their purchases of industrial inputs and machinery from overseas, thus enhancing their access to improved technology. This latter effect has certainly been observed in the wake of trade liberalization, and in part helps explain the rebound in productivity growth since the 1990s, a positive trend captured by recent research.[42]

Table 2.4 Brazilian GDP: composition 1949–2007 (percentages at current prices)

Sector	*1949*	*1959*	*1970*	*1980*	*1990*	*1999*	**2007**[a]
Agriculture	**24.2**	**17.7**	**12.3**	**10.9**	**11.5**	**15.16**	**5.6**
Industry	**25.4**	**33.9**	**38.3**	**44.1**	**42.1**	**30.59**	**27.8**
Mining	*0.5*	*0.7*	*0.8*	*1.1*	*1.8*	*0.73*	*2.4*
Construction	*4.4*	*5.4*	*5.8*	*7.3*	*8.0*	*9.35*	*4.9*
Public utilities	*1.1*	*1.2*	*2.4*	*1.9*	*3.2*	*3.58*	*3.6*
Manufacturing	*19.3*	*26.7*	*29.3*	*33.7*	*29.1*	*16.75*	*17.3*
Nonmetallic minerals	1.4	1.7	1.7	1.9	1.2	1.02	0.6
Metallurgy	1.8	3.1	3.4	3.8	3.1	1.95	2.5
Mechanical	0.4	0.9	2.1	3.3	3.6	2.23	1.3
Electrical and telecom	0.3	1.1	1.6	2.4	2.5	1.1	1.0
Transport	0.4	2.0	2.5	2.7	2.2	1.43	1.5
Wood	0.8	0.9	0.7	0.9	0.4	0.28	0.4
Furniture	0.4	0.6	0.6	0.6	0.3	i.a.	i.a.
Paper and pulp	0.4	0.8	0.7	1.6	1.0	1.11	1.3
Rubber products	0.4	0.8	0.6	0.4	0.4	0.21	0.7
Leather and hides	0.3	0.3	0.2	0.2	0.2	–	–
Chemicals	1.0	2.3	3.0	4.9	3.3	2.64	2.1
Pharmaceuticals	0.5	0.7	1.0	0.6	0.6	0.72	1.0
Perfumes and soaps	0.3	0.4	0.5	0.3	0.3	i.a.	i.a.
Plastics	0.0	0.2	0.6	0.8	0.7	0.49	[b]
Textiles	3.9	3.2	2.8	2.2	1.5	0.60	0.60
Clothing and footwear	0.8	0.9	1.7	1.7	1.4	0.39	1.0
Food	4.0	4.4	3.8	3.7	3.7	2.01	2.4
Beverages	0.9	0.8	0.7	0.4	0.5	i.a.	i.a.
Tobacco	0.3	0.3	0.4	0.2	0.3	–	0.1
Printing and publishing	0.8	0.8	1.1	0.9	0.9	–	0.7
Miscellaneous	0.3	0.5	0.6	0.8	0.9	0.6	0.7
Services	**53**	**51.3**	**56.2**	**52.7**	**60.3**	**55.99**	**66.6**
Financial services	**(2.6)**	**(2.9)**	**(6.9)**	**(7.7)**	**(14)**	**(1.74)**	–
GDP at factor costs	**100**	**100**	**100**	**100**	**100**	**100**	**100**

Notes:
[a] Data for 2007 calculated at basic prices.
[b] Included in rubber products.
i.a.: Included above.
–: Insufficient data available.

Sources: Bonelli and Pinheiro (2001) and, for 2007, author's calculation, based on IBGE (2008).

Concerns over deindustrialization may also be justified in light of the massive and relatively quick decline in industry's share of Brazilian GDP.[43] Yet this result too should be interpreted with caution. For one thing, as already noted, in part this is merely the statistical effect of the fact that the price of manufacturing goods in Brazil has fallen relative to other goods. Additionally – and also stressed earlier – one could argue that the share attained by the industrial sector at its peak in the late 1970s (a third of total output) was clearly 'bloated' and therefore untenable in a competitive environment such as the one that has prevailed for the past 15–20 years in Brazil. Lastly, it should be noted that for the past decade this share has remained stable at around 18 per cent, with even a minor increase in 2006–07.[44]

To push this argument a little further, it would be wrong to assume that Brazilian industry has passively withstood the impacts arising from an appreciated currency (or globalization at large). On the contrary: after an initial period of defensive reaction to increased competition from overseas, Brazilian industry has, overall, displayed remarkable resilience and managed to remain afloat. Unsurprisingly, performance has varied enormously within individual sectors. As Table 2.3 above indicates, since 1992 sectors that one may classify as technologically more advanced have displayed rates of growth that, if not on a par with those posted in the 1950s or 1970s, were nonetheless substantial.[45]

The logical consequence of such varied performances among the different sectors over the past 15 years is a change in the *composition* of industry. As noted by Bonelli and associates, over the past two decades there has been a reduction in the relative share of traditional sectors (such as textiles, beverages, wood and furniture, and printing material), to the benefit of areas such as chemicals, electrical material and transport material.[46] This result indicates that the effects of trade liberalization on Brazil's industrial fabric are more nuanced than critics of this policy seem to suggest.

In a similar vein, Nassif (2008) and Barros and Pereira (2008) argue that instead of deindustrializing, Brazil's manufacturing sector is undergoing a process of actual restructuring. In practice, this has meant that for the past decade or more those sectors that make intensive use of natural resources (oil in particular) have gained ground at the expense of labor-intensive industries, scale-intensive industries, differentiated and science-based sectors. If this is actually the case, then perhaps it is all to the good: globalization has not only enabled the Brazilian economy to resume productivity growth but also pushed its industry into redirecting resources to those areas where it has obvious comparative advantages.

2.6 CONCLUDING REMARKS

Brazilian industry has come a long way since its infancy in the mid nineteenth century. Indeed, over the course of a century – that is, by the early 1980s – the country had moved away from a position of extreme reliance on exports of agricultural commodities and become, instead, heavily industrialized. The road taken along the way was far from smooth, however.

Beginning in the late nineteenth century the first buds of industrial development began to open. Gradually – and as a result, essentially, of market signals – resources hitherto directed to coffee began to find their way to the manufacturing sector. Brazilian industrialization at this early stage alternated between instances of import substitution and moments characterized by increased local production in tandem with foreign supply. Production was then concentrated, mostly, in the wage goods sector, although by the 1920s the manufacture of intermediate goods began to make itself felt. Reliance on the production of non-durable consumer goods, in turn, reflected both supply constraints (the low technological level) and demand conditions, associated with the growing monetization of the economy and a massive inflow of immigrants.

With the Great Depression and the ensuing 'deglobalization' of the world economy, the limits to export-led industrial growth became clear, as the country turned inwards in search of the impulses for further growth. For almost six decades, ISI would fuel economic growth and modernization of the Brazilian economy. As befits a latecomer on the industrialization trail, the state, in lieu of the market, would play a growing role in the allocation of resources, in the context of an almost permanent shortage of vital foreign exchange. At the close of this phase, in the 1980s, Brazil's industrial structure was 'completed', and ranged from the production of non-durable consumer goods to fairly sophisticated capital goods.

Contrary to contemporary expectations, the search for self-sufficiency implicit in this inward-looking model did *not* insure the Brazilian economy against mood swings in the international environment, such as the one brought on by the second oil-cum-interest-rate shocks of the early 1980s. The resultant juxtaposition of the (foreign) debt crisis, chronic inflation and fiscal disarray would help lay bare the limits of the state-led ISI strategy pursued up to that moment. Even if reluctantly, Brazil was forced by circumstances beyond its control to perform a U-turn in its development model, and face a globalized economy head-on instead.

For 20 years now a friendlier attitude towards the market mechanism and the benefits of foreign trade has prevailed in Brazil, although wholehearted embrace of globalization is generally absent from political discourse, being restricted to a few voices in academia. Despite significant gains in efficiency, results in terms of industrial growth have been far from spectacular in this latter phase, helping to reinforce opposition to further liberalization.

Having briefly reviewed Brazil's industrial history, we may ask how it compares internationally. Did it follow its own path or, did it, instead, share many of the traits of other developing economies in the course of the twentieth century?

At first glance, it appears that Brazil's manufacturing history was not too dissimilar from the experience of other latecomer countries. Indeed, starting from a very low base, industry gained ground at the expense of agriculture, although for some time it still depended on the latter for its access to foreign exchange, capital and workers. Over time – and as industry moved up towards more sophisticated sectors – the state stepped in and led the process, replacing the market as the prime allocator of resources in an increasingly closed economy. Finally – and as the limits of inward-looking industrialization became clear – the country was forced to open up and face world markets.

It therefore appears that the three phases into which the present narrative (like Brazil's industrial history) was divided conform to the general pattern followed by the international economy and most individual countries in the course of the twentieth century. If this is so, then Brazil's case would be fairly representative of the norm.

On closer inspection, however, it could be argued that Brazil constituted an *extreme* version of that norm: almost a textbook case of a latecomer industrializer. Indeed, Argentina excepted, few other developing countries bear testimony to the possibilities opened up by joining the liberal world order prevalent in the decades before the Great Depression. At the time, even as coffee continued to dominate the Brazilian economy, industrialization proceeded apace, in a clear indication that the alleged conflict between specializing in the export of primary goods and long-term economic (industrial) growth is only apparent. Structural change had been taking place even as the country appeared to be 'just another' primary producer and exporter.

Structural change, of course, was accelerated after the shocks of the 1930s and 1940s. And here again Brazil stands out as arguably the showcase of inward-looking industrialization. No other country seems to have embarked on such a path towards self-sufficiency (with the possible exception of India, but surely with much better results than that Asian country) during the decades that separate the Great Depression from the second oil shock. And this appears to have been true for both good (i.e. industrial growth and structural change) and evil, which took the form of the grave macro and microeconomic distortions resulting from that very strategy.

During the current third phase Brazil hardly appears however as a set-piece example internationally. On the contrary, it definitely stands out as a middle-of-the-road case of a country which has dropped most of the previous bias against the world economy, yet remains relatively closed to international trade. This, in turn, seems to reflect the consensus view among the bulk of relevant public opinion, from different parts of the political spectrum, which appears unconvinced of the advantages of a greater internationalization of the Brazilian economy. The apparent success achieved during the second stage of Brazil's industrial history – at least in terms of industrial growth and structural change – apparently supports this skepticism. Or perhaps this is just an extreme case of selective memory.

NOTES

1. I am indebted to Marcelo de Paiva Abreu, Regis Bonelli and participants at the Conference for valued feedback.
2. Figures in constant 1990 international dollars. See Maddison (2006).
3. See World Bank (2008).
4. From the standpoint of the system of national accounts statistics, 'industry' includes not only manufacturing industry (its largest component), but also the mining, construction and public utilities sectors.
5. See Stein (1957) for the early history of the Brazilian textile industry.
6. In practice, ISI occurs when all three of the following combine: (1) a decrease in the ratio of imports as a share of domestic supply (i.e., the sum of domestic output plus imports, net of imports); (2) a substantial increase in domestic output; and (3) the diversification of the industrial structure. Needless to say, not every instance of increase in industrial output in Brazil (or anywhere else, for that matter) can be attributed to import substitution.
7. It is worth noting that prior to the 1930s Brazil depended on imports for the bulk of its capital goods. Hence, a good proxy for fixed investment activity is provided by the value of machinery and equipment brought into Brazil in the period. For details see Suzigan (2000). For the history of the Brazilian capital goods industry see Lago et al. (1979).
8. Throughout the chapter references to the relevant political or economic policy background are kept to the strictly necessary, as the focus here is on Brazil's industrialization experience. For a more detailed discussion of short-term economic policy, the reader is referred to Villela and Suzigan (1973), Abreu (1989) and, for the post-World-War-II period, Giambiagi et al. (2005).
9. According to Dean (1985, p. 258), a truer picture of the actual size of the manufacturing sector in that year would require multiplying the figures contained in this survey by a factor of three in the case of the number of plants, and two as regards number of employees and value of output.
10. Such as sawmills, furniture, shoes, matches, apparel, tanneries, soaps, candles, hats etc.
11. Bonelli (1996, p. 83).
12. Brazil had been formally under a convertible-currency system since 1906, in an attempt to both stabilize the milreis (preventing it from appreciating any further), and impart

greater discipline on the conduct of monetary policy. For a detailed discussion of what this entailed for Brazil's policymaking capability see Fritsch (1988).

13. To which should be added a slipping milreis, after the country was forced out of the gold standard in 1913.
14. Put differently, in aggregate terms, industrial growth slowed from an average of 9.1 per cent p.a. in 1908–13 to 4.8 per cent between 1912–13 and 1918, on the basis, mostly, of the expansion of those sectors that depended on local inputs (such as cotton textiles, hats, shoes, leather goods, sugar refining, vegetable oils etc).
15. See Suzigan (2000).
16. See also Versiani (1984a, 1984b).
17. For a discussion see Fishlow (1972) and Villela (2000).
18. To these two obvious links between coffee and industry might be added a more subtle one, unveiled by recent research. In a nutshell, the argument is made that in its capacity as a price-maker in the world coffee market, Brazil could afford to maintain a high-tariff regime (which helped shelter local industry), as the greater costs deriving from this could be shifted onto foreign buyers of Brazilian coffee. For an elaboration and empirical evidence see Abreu and Fernandes (2005).
19. The origins of this crisis date back to the overexpansion of the coffee frontier (and therefore supply) in the 1920s, on the back of government-sponsored price support schemes. Successive bumper crops in the late 1920s strained to the point of collapse the capacity of the banking sector to carry on financing the stockpiling of coffee in warehouses in the interior of São Paulo State. Subsequent shipments of the product from the interior to the port of Santos swamped the market in 1929, bringing down its price, the Brazilian economy and the First Republic. For details see Fritsch (1988).
20. Note that while industry-led economic growth in Brazil would only begin in the 1930s, industrial growth had exceeded expansion of agricultural output since the early years of the twentieth century. See Table 2.1.
21. Still, as noted by Abreu (1989, p. 81), this was not the first time that the Brazilian government had acted in Keynesian fashion by accommodating a fiscal shock via an increase in deficit spending. The same pattern was seen, for instance, during the Epitacio Pessoa administration (1919–22).
22. Introduction of import controls in order to deal with a severe balance-of-payments crisis provided additional protection to domestic producers.
23. To this must be added the growth of the local capital goods industry, especially transport material.
24. Two icons of Brazilian industrial history were created in the latter years of the Estado Novo: the Companhia Siderúrgica Nacional (CSN) steelworks and the Vale do Rio Doce mining company. CHESF (Companhia Hidrelétrica do São Francisco) would be the first of a host of electricity generators and distributors controlled by the Brazilian state. Petrobras, the state-owned oil monopoly, would be created in 1953, during Vargas's second spell at the presidency. Ditto with the Banco Nacional de Desenvolvimento Econômico (BNDE) founded in 1952, which would play a decisive role in the subsequent history of Brazilian industrialization.
25. And which had led, in 1937, to a default in interest payments on its foreign debt.
26. Essentially, the country still depended greatly on coffee exports for most of its foreign exchange earnings, at a time when international capital flows were only beginning to recover from the combined shocks of the Great Depression and World War II.
27. Between 1952 and 1961, value added in the manufacturing sector grew by an average of 11.6 per cent p.a., led by consumer durables (+18.2 per cent p.a.) and capital goods (+20.3 per cent). Over the same period they each doubled their share of total manufacturing value added, from 6 per cent to 12 per cent. See Sochaczewski (1993, p. 79).
28. GDP growth averaged 11.1 per cent, with manufacturing industry growing by a staggering 13 per cent p.a., on average.
29. On the many links connecting the PAEG reforms and the Brazilian 'economic miracle' see Veloso et al. (2008).

30. It was in this context that the government directed considerable investment towards both the Proálcool program (ethanol) and research and development by Petrobras in the offshore oil fields of the Campos basin.
31. In this respect, it might be said that by the end of its ISI drive in the 1980s, Brazil's manufacturing structure was artificially (i.e. by way of government policy) skewed in favor of 'heavy' industry (non-metallic minerals, metals, electric machinery, transport equipment etc.), compared with the international 'norm' for countries of a similar level of per capita income, factor endowments and population. See Bonelli and Gonçalves (1998, 1999).
32. It is worth noting that the bulk of the threefold increase (from $14.8 billion to $40.3 billion) in Brazilian (net) foreign debt over the period 1974–78 was accounted for by state-owned enterprises, and was thus a government liability. This process of 'nationalization' of foreign debt was further compounded in 1979, as the government decided to allow private debtors to anticipate the deposit of their foreign debt commitments into the central bank before they were effectively due, thus transferring to the latter any exchange rate risk.
33. See Werneck (1986) for the fiscal origins of the macroeconomic disarray of the 1980s.
34. See Bonelli (2005a, table 12.2). Total factor productivity declined by 30 per cent in the period 1976–92, in a further indication of the limits to inward-looking development. See Gomes et al. (2003).
35. *Average* effective rates of protection for manufactured goods were somewhat lower, in the 70 per cent to 80 per cent range in 1987. See Bonelli and Pinheiro (2008).
36. For a brief survey see Bonelli (2005b). Pinheiro (2004) provides a balanced assessment of the obstacles to faster economic growth in Brazil.
37. On this point see Bacha and Bonelli (2005).
38. On this point see Carneiro and Werneck (1993). The country currently faces a fiscal cul-de-sac reflected in a relatively high tax burden (in the order of 36 per cent of GDP), necessary to sustain a state that in the words of Hausmann (2008) 'over-borrows, overtaxes and under-invests'.
39. See Bonelli (2006b) and Pinheiro et al. (2005).
40. Given that sector shares as a percentage of GDP are calculated at current prices, part of the decline in the weight of industry is due to a relative drop in the price of manufactures, a trend that intensified after the late 1980s, on account of the combined effects of trade liberalization, privatization and modernization of managerial practices among Brazilian firms. For an elaboration of this argument see Bonelli (2005a).
41. See for instance IEDI (2005).
42. See Gomes et al. (2003), Pinheiro et al. (2005), and Bonelli (2005b).
43. The extent of this decline, however, is not easy to ascertain. In the past two decades the institute responsible for compiling national accounts statistics in Brazil (IBGE) has revised its methodology on three occasions, making comparisons of sectoral shares of GDP over this period extremely hazardous.
44. Shares calculated at basic prices. For the most recent data on the composition of Brazilian GDP see IBGE (undated).
45. See the bottom five sectors in Table 2.3. This performance includes the capital goods sector, which expanded at an average annual rate of 4.6 per cent between 1992 and 2007, thus proving wrong those who feared the complete overrunning of this sector by imports, in the context of trade liberalization and an overvalued real.
46. See Bonelli and Gonçalves (1998, 1999) and Bonelli and Pinheiro (2001). Unsurprisingly, those sectors which have been gaining ground in the composition of manufacturing value added in Brazil are all high-tariff sectors. For a discussion see Abreu (2004).

REFERENCES

Abreu, Marcelo de Paiva (1989), 'Crise, crescimento e modernização autoritária: 1930–1945', in Marcelo de Paiva Abreu (ed.), *A Ordem do Progresso: Cem Anos de Política Econômica Republicana, 1889–1989*, Rio de Janeiro: Campus.

Abreu, Marcelo de Paiva (2004), 'Trade liberalization and the political economy of protection in Brazil since 1987', Inter-American Development Bank Working Paper SITI – 08b. Washington, DC.

Abreu, Marcelo de Paiva and Felipe Tâmega Fernandes (2005), 'Market power and commodity prices: Brazil, Chile and the United States, 1820s–1930', Texto para Discussão no. 511, Departamento de Economia, PUC-Rio, December.

Bacha, Edmar and Regis Bonelli (2005), 'Uma interpretação das causas da desaceleração econômica do Brasil', *Revista de Economia Política*, **25** (3), 163–89.

Barros, Octavio de and Robson Rodrigues Pereira (2008), 'Desmistificando a tese da desindustrialização: reestruturação da indústria brasileira em uma época de transformações globais', in Octavio de Barros and Fabio Giambiagi (eds), *Brasil Globalizado: O Brasil Em Um Mundo Surpreendente*, Rio de Janeiro: Campus/Elsevier, pp. 228–68.

Bonelli, Regis (1996), *Ensaios sobre Política Econômica e Industrialização no Brasil*, Rio de Janeiro: SENAI.

Bonelli, Regis (2005a), 'Industrialização e Desenvolvimento (Notas e conjecturas com foco na experiência do Brasil)', paper prepared for the seminar 'Industrialização, Desindustrialização e Desenvolvimento', jointly hosted by FIESP and IEDI, São Paulo, November.

Bonelli, Regis (2005b), 'O que causou o crescimento econômico no Brasil?', in Fabio Giambiagi, André Villela, Lavínia Barros de Castro and Jennifer Hermann (eds), *Economia Brasileira Contemporânea, 1945–2004*, Rio de Janeiro: Campus/Elsevier, pp. 307–34.

Bonelli, Regis (2006), 'Nível de atividade e mudança estrutural', in *Estatísticas do Século XX*, Rio de Janeiro: IBGE, pp. 317–412.

Bonelli, Regis and Robson R. Gonçalves (1998), 'Para onde vai a estrutura industrial brasileira?', Texto para Discussão IPEA no. 540, Rio de Janeiro, June.

Bonelli, Regis and Robson R. Gonçalves (1999), 'Padrões de desenvolvimento industrial no Brasil – 1980/95', Texto para Discussão IPEA no. 645, Rio de Janeiro, May.

Bonelli, Regis and Armando C. Pinheiro (2001), 'Desempenho Econômico e Dinâmica Industrial no Brasil', in *O Futuro da Indústria, Oportunidades e Desafios: a Reflexão da Universidade*, Brasília: MDIC.

Carneiro, Dionísio D. and Rogério L.F. Werneck (1993), 'Obstacles to investment resumption in Brazil', in Edmar L. Bacha (ed.), *Savings and Investment Requirements for Resumption of Growth in Latin America*, Washington, DC: Inter-American Development Bank.

Dean, Warren (1969), *The Industrialization of São Paulo, 1880–1945*, Austin and London: University of Texas Press.

Dean, Warren (1985), 'A industrialização durante a República Velha', in B. Fausto (ed.), *História Geral da Civilização Brasileira*, 6th edn, tome 3, vol. 1, São Paulo: Difel.

Fishlow, Albert (1972), 'Origins and consequences of import substitution in Brazil', in Luis E. di Marco (ed.), *International Economics and Development:*

Essays in Honor of Raúl Prebisch, New York and London: Academic Press.
Fritsch, Winston (1988), *External Constraints on Economic Policymaking in Brazil, 1889–1930*, London: Macmillan.
Furtado, Celso (1959), *Formação Econômica do Brasil*, Rio de Janeiro: Cia. Editora Nacional.
Giambiagi, Fabio, André Villela, Lavínia Barros de Castro and Jennifer Hermann (eds) (2005), *Economia Brasileira Contemporânea, 1945–2004*, Rio de Janeiro: Campus/Elsevier.
Gomes, Victor, Samuel Pessoa and Fernando A. Veloso (2003), 'Evolução da produtividade total dos fatores na economia brasileira: uma análise comparativa', *Pesquisa e Planejamento Econômico*, **33** (3), 389–434.
Hausmann, Ricardo (2008), 'In search of the chains that hold Brazil back', paper presented in São Paulo at a conference held at the Brazilian Center for Public Leadership, 22 August 2008.
IBGE, Diretoria de Pesquisas (2008), 'Sistema de Contas Nacionais – Brasil', Nota Metodológica no. 24 (Tabelas Comparativas), Rio de Janeiro, available at: http://www.ibge.gov.br/home/estatistica/indicadores/pib/pdf/24_tabcomparativas.pdf
IEDI (2005), 'Ocorreu uma desindustrialização no Brasil?', São Paulo: IEDI, available at: http://www.iedi.org.br/admin_ori/pdf/20051129_desindustrializacao.pdf
Lago, Luiz A. Correa do, Fernando Lopes de Almeida and Beatriz M.F. de Lima (1979), *A Indústria Brasileira de Bens de Capital: Origens, Situação Recente, Perspectivas*, Rio de Janeiro: Editora FGV.
Leopoldi, Maria Antonieta P. (2003), 'A economia política do primeiro governo Vargas (1930–1945): a política econômica em tempos de turbulência', in Jorge Ferreira and Lucilia A. Neves Delgado (eds), *O Brasil Republicano*, vol. 2: *O Tempo do Nacional-Estatismo*, Rio de Janeiro: Civilização Brasileira, pp. 241–85.
Maddison, Angus (2006), *The World Economy: A Millennial Perspective*, Paris: OECD.
Malan, Pedro S., Regis Bonelli, Marcelo de Paiva Abreu and José Eduardo de C. Pereira (1977), *Política Econômica Externa e Industrialização no Brasil (1939–52)*, Rio de Janeiro: IPEA/INPES.
Nassif, André (2008), 'Há Evidências de Desindustrialização no Brasil?', *Revista de Economia Política*, **28** (1), 72–94.
Pinheiro, Armando Castelar (2004), 'Por que o Brasil cresce pouco?', in Fabio Giambiagi, José Guilherme Reis and André Urani (eds), *Reformas no Brasil: Balanço e Agenda*, Rio de Janeiro: Nova Fronteira, pp. 25–58.
Pinheiro, Armando Castelar, Indermit S. Gill, Luís Servén and Mark Roland Thomas (2005), 'Brazilian economic growth, 1900–2000: lessons and policy implications', in Eduardo Fernández-Arias, Rodolfo Manuelli and Juan S. Blyde (eds), *Sources of Growth in Latin America: What is missing?*, Washington, DC: IADB, pp. 157–271.
Sochaczewski, Antonio Claudio (1993), *Desenvolvimento Econômico e Financeiro do Brasil: 1952–1968*, São Paulo: Trajetória Cultural.
Stein, Stanley J. (1957), *The Brazilian Cotton Manufacture: Textile Enterprise in an Underdeveloped Area, 1850–1950*, Cambridge, MA: Harvard University Press.
Suzigan, Wilson (2000), *Indústria Brasileira: origem e desenvolvimento*, new edn, São Paulo: Hucitec.

Veloso, Fernando A., André Villela and Fabio Giambiagi (2008), 'Determinantes do milagre econômico brasileiro (1968–1973): uma análise empírica', *Revista Brasileira de Economia*, **62** (2), 221–46.
Villela, André (2000), 'Tarifas de importação e câmbio na gênese da indústria brasileira, 1901–1928', *História Econômica e História de Empresas*, **3** (2), 27–46.
Villela, Annibal and Wilson Suzigan (1973), *Política do Governo e Crescimento da Economia Brasileira, 1889–1945*, Rio de Janeiro: IPEA/INPES.
Werneck, Rogério (1986), 'Poupança estatal, dívida externa e crise financeira do setor público', *Pesquisa e Planejamento Econômico*, **16** (3), 551–74.
World Bank (2008), *The Growth Report: Strategies for Sustained Growth and Inclusive Developmen*t, Washington, DC: World Bank.

3. Comments on part I

Joseph L. Love

The two studies of industrialization by Bernardo Kosacoff and André Villela show that although the two nations were simultaneously facing similar signals and impulses emanating from the developed countries, there were choices to be made. We accept Villela's definition of industrialization as a quickening expansion of output and productivity, accompanied by a structural diversification.

The periods covered by the two studies are similar – beginning in 1880 for Argentina and in 1890 for Brazil, and ending in both cases in 2007.[1] The studies cover the rise and decline of industrialization as a driving force of economic growth, but they show different paths in dealing with international opportunities and crises, reflecting different mixes of export structures and endowments on the one hand, and social and political systems on the other. In the 50 years ending in 1930, Argentina offered Latin America's classic case of successful export-driven growth based on the ideology of economic liberalism. Brazil in the same era pursued a policy of what might be called 'statist liberalism'. Although the Brazilian state had only barely begun to engage in social welfare, it famously intervened in the international market through its pursuit of coffee valorization. Brazil was also notably more protectionist than Argentina, displaying tariff levels among the highest in Latin America, though economic historians now think that protection, especially after 1930, was chiefly provided by the country's overvalued currency. Between 1870 and 1930, in any case, Brazil's high tariffs and economic growth were positively correlated.[2]

Despite these significant differences, the economic model chosen by the leaders of both nations in this early period was export-led development, including export-financed industrialization. Whereas Kosocoff offers only a quick summary of developments before 1958, Vilella treats all phases of industrialization with equal emphasis. He periodizes industrial growth in Brazil into three phases: 1913–25; 1930–61; and 1968–79. Kosacoff chooses continuous periods for Argentina: agro-exports with industrialization, 1880–1930; import-substitution industrialization (ISI), 1930–79; and market-determined industrialization, characterized by restructuring and globalization, 1979–90. Curiously, neither author periodizes developments in recent decades. Perhaps it is too early to characterize them accurately.

If import-substitution industrialization was the engine of growth in the 1930s in both countries, the process only received significant backing from the Argentine government under Perón after the end of World War II, and in Brazil under Vargas from the late 1930s. In the late 1950s in the Argentine case and during the early 1960s in the Brazilian one, the UN Economic Commission for Latin America (CEPAL) criticized the exaggerated protection and inefficient industries to which ISI had given rise. Kosacoff sees the crisis of ISI in Argentina coming in its second phrase, 1956–76, in which industrialization moved into the manufacture of durable goods. Five short stop–go cycles, a phenomenon first identified by Carlos Diaz-Alejandro, marked this period of Argentine history. Political violence led to the rise of a military government in 1976, as General Jorge Videla ousted the constitutional president, Isabel Perón. A new program based on free-market principles followed. In Brazil, by contrast, just as the military government only moderated, rather than drastically lowering, the level of Brazilian protection after the coup d'état of 1964, the oil shock of 1973 led not to state disengagement in the economy but to expanded government involvement, fueled by foreign borrowing. Despite respectable or even better levels of growth in the 1970s, Brazil joined Argentina and the rest of Latin America in suffering a decade of debt-induced stagnation during the 1980s. Inflation passed to hyperinflation during the 1980s in both countries. At the turn of the 1990s, the peronista Carlos Menem in Argentina began to get control of the inflation process, an achievement duplicated in Brazil under Itamar Franco and his minister of finance, Fernando Henrique Cardoso, in 1994.

In line with the 'Washington Consensus' between the US State Department, the World Bank and the International Monetary Fund, Argentina followed Chile in the privatizations of the 1990s, a path Brazil was less eager to tread. In both Brazil and Argentina, industry's share of GDP declined, and agriculture and services grew. In the wake of the Asian financial crisis of 1997, Argentina began the new century with a shrinking economy and a political meltdown – three heads of state resigned between December 2001 and May 2003. An economic implosion ensued, but the economy had passed its peak GDP of 1998 by 2005 and enjoyed rapid growth until the recession of 2008. Although Brazil had no comparable political crisis, its industrial and broader economic performance remained spotty through 2004. However, matters improved markedly under the Lula administration from 2005, building on the foundations of the previous government of F.H. Cardoso.

In the longer term, both countries experienced repeated macroeconomic instability in the years after 1950, but Argentina suffered more radical shifts of policy, resulting in part from its greater political instability, having to do with the exclusion and reincorporation of *peronismo* in the governing process. For better or for worse, Argentina underwent more extensive deindustrialization than Brazil in the years after 1980.

CEPAL and the broader structuralist school in the mid twentieth century had seen industrialization as the key not only to the future economic growth of Latin America, but even to the relative independence of the Latin American 'periphery' from the industrial 'center' formed by the United States and Western Europe. Examining the share of industry in Argentina and Brazil from 1949–50 to 2007–08, as revealed in the data provided by Kosacoff (Figure 1.3) and Villela (Table 2.4; Villela offers data only for census years), we see that things didn't turn out that way. Industry's contribution to GDP peaked in Argentina in 1973 at 23.5 per cent and fell to 16.0 per cent in 2008, after hitting a low of 15.5 per cent in 2002. In Brazil industry rose from 25.4 per cent of GDP in 1949 to a scarcely credible peak of 44.1 per cent in 1980, and then declined to 27.8 per cent in 2007. The enduring industries of both nations, we may surmise, will suffer a further winnowing, but the survivors can aspire to a future in which industrial exports play an increasingly important role as globalization advances.

NOTES

1. For a general overview of the history of Argentine economic policy in the last 100 years, see Gerchunoff and Llach (2005). On Brazilian industrialization, also see Baer (1965, 1970, 2008).
2. See Mata and Love (2008).

REFERENCES

Baer, Werner (1965), *Industrialization and Economic Development in Brazil*, Homewood, IL: Irwin.
Baer, Werner (1970), *The Development of the Brazilian Steel Industry*, Nashville, TN: Vanderbilt University Press.
Baer, Werner (2008), *The Brazilian Economy: Growth and Development*, 6th edn, Boulder, CO: Lynne Rienner Publishers.
Gerchunoff, Pablo and Lucas Llach (2005), *El Ciclo de la Ilusión y el Desencanto: un Siglo de Politicas Economicas Argentinas*, 2nd edn, Buenos Aires: Ariel.
Mata, Maria Eugénia and Joseph L. Love (2008), 'A reversal in the historical role of tariffs in economic growth? The cases of Brazil and Portugal', *Estudos Econômicos*, **38** (3), 461–92.

PART II

Agriculture

4. The agricultural sector in Argentina

César Ciappa and Andrés Gallo

4.1 INTRODUCTION

The agro-industrial chain (AIC) in Argentina has been historically one of the economy's most efficient and competitive sectors. However, despite the fact that agricultural exports provide most of the foreign exchange for the economy, different governments have taxed agricultural producers since the mid twentieth century.

Several studies (Krueger et al., 1991; Sturzenegger 1990, 1991; Valdés and Schaeffer, 1995; Sturzenegger and Salazni, 2007) describe the anti-agricultural policy bias that strongly discriminated against primary producers. This taxation policy was characterized by extensive use of export taxes on farm products as well as quantitative restrictions on trade. These studies agree that the policies applied to the agro-industrial chain generate different conflicts among economic agents. On one hand, agro-industrial production must satisfy the increasing local and international food demand and, accordingly, government policies should promote increases in production. On the other hand, given the characteristic of 'wage goods' of most agricultural commodities, commodities' prices will have, in the short run, an effect on real wages, poverty and indigence. As a result, this duality generates conflicts regarding economic policies for the sector.

High food prices are an incentive to production, investment and the adoption of new technologies, but they have negative impact on the local real wages on net food consumers. In the short run, price control, through taxes and other policies, can positively affect workers' incomes and poverty, but in the long run it will undermine companies' ability to expand production inducing a further pressure to increase prices. As a result, higher prices are going to have a negative impact on wages and poverty. Furthermore, price control policies hinder the ability of the agro-industrial chain to create high-paying jobs that workers in non-agricultural sectors could move to and so avoid, or mitigate, the negative impact of the increase in commodity prices.

From the 1940s onwards, export taxation was used in Argentina as an instrument to control domestic food prices, in two different scenarios: first, in the case of local currency devaluation (that increases the prices of tradable commodities in local currency); second, in the event of high food commodities prices in international markets. However policymakers subsequently claimed that the use of export taxes also served four additional non-agricultural objectives: raising fiscal revenues with few lags and low collection costs; lowering and stabilizing the prices of foods that were important wage goods; encouraging the domestic processing of farm products; and transferring income from landowners to wage-earners and producers of consumption industrial goods. Additionally, many governments financed their distributive policies and clientelistic political campaigns through taxation and redistribution of the proceeds from the interior to highly populated urban centers, where most of the votes are concentrated.

With respect to the administrative and political feasibility of imposing such export taxes, the government has two main advantages that make them a highly attractive policy instrument. On the one hand, export taxes do not need approval from the National Congress.[1] They are imposed by the federal government through executive decree, avoiding the long process required by other national taxes (income, value added, internal and others). On the other hand, export tax revenues are appropriated by the federal government, while in the case of most other taxes approximately half of the revenue is shared with provincial governments and municipalities through the regime of 'federal co-participation' (whereby a law fixes the share of tax collection going to federal, provincial and municipal governments).

This chapter discusses the effect of taxes and quantitative restrictions on the trade of agricultural products during the last 25 years on the agricultural sector (planting decisions, production, yields, prices and profits at farm level), the agro-industrial chain, local prices of wage goods, and fiscal revenues. Given the history of government intervention in the agricultural sector and the lack of a consistent plan for agricultural development, the analysis of the effects of taxation will help us to understand the possibilities and impediments for a sustained growth of Argentine agricultural exports.

4.2 THE ARGENTINE AGRO-INDUSTRIAL CHAIN (AIC)

The AIC, integrated by 41 productive activities, shows strong linkages up and down it and is a large user of inputs and productive factors (land, capital and labor) (Porto et al., 2007). The AIC contributes 18.5 per cent to the GDP. The AIC's direct and indirect use of labor represents 35.6 per cent of the total labor force (Llach et al., 2004). Based on the 41 activities and taking into account its interdependencies throughout the chain, the sector produces fiscal revenues amounting to 12.3 per cent of GDP, representing approximately 40 per cent of total tax revenue, without taking into account the subsidies to local consumption of exports commodities which are taxed (Nogués et al., 2007).

Of the total value added by the chain, 33 per cent is exported, and the rest is used for the domestic intermediate and final consumption. The AIC contributes 56 per cent of total exports and 15 per cent of imports. It therefore contributes a net foreign currency surplus of approximately US$20 billion a year. This inflow of foreign exchange helps to pay for the servicing of the external debt, and to finance imports of intermediate and capital goods.

Federal revenues from the AIC commodities export tax represent 50 per cent of total export tax collection. This is equivalent to 6.6 per cent of total federal tax collections or 1.7 per cent of GDP for the year 2008.

The four main agricultural products affected by specific taxes on exports are soybeans, cattle, corn (i.e., maize) and wheat. In current prices these products represent 60 per cent of the total value of agricultural production. Three products (wheat, corn and soybeans) are exportable goods. Live cattle have an inherent trading status as well as nontradable (dairy production). Cattle production has not shown any significant change since the 1960s. Soybeans, however, which were not produced before the 1970s, have undergone a tremendous increase in production (47 million tons in 2007), especially since the 1990s, when agricultural pricing policies, technological advances, new forms of farm organization and the impact of economic policies, together with changes in international demand for soybeans, were the main determinants of the trends. Nonetheless, the impact of those same factors was considerably smaller for wheat and corn production. Sturzenegger and Salazni (2007) consider six main factors responsible for the rate of growth of production since the 1990s: (1) the expansion of the crop frontier, which added new areas where soybeans are the main crop; (2) the intensification of land use in the pampas because of shortened crop rotations; (3) the greater application of fertilizers and of the zero tillage planting technique (*labranza cero*), and the elimination of pastures as livestock production, displaced toward more marginal lands; (4) the substantial rise in yields per hectare that followed the introduction of varieties of soybeans and corn seeds, resistant to the herbicide 'Roundup', and other advances in biotechnology; (5) the introduction of new forms of farm organization in agricultural production, professional farming, contract productions and the development of planting pools (*pool de siembra*); and (6) the introduction of economic policy reforms in the early 1990s.

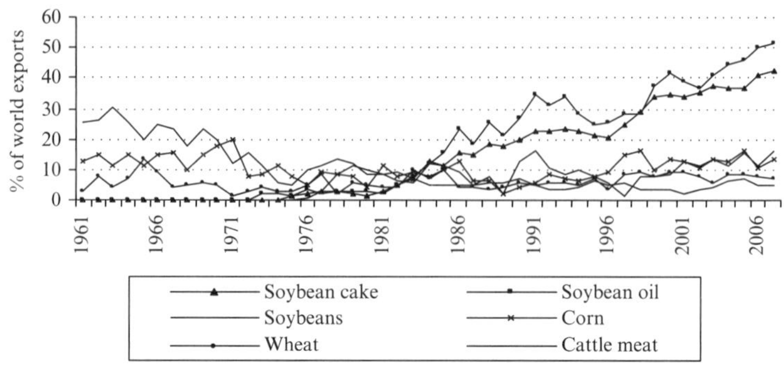

Source: FAOSTATS.

Figure 4.1 Argentine participation in world exports in commodities.

This last factor favored agricultural production by: lifting export taxes, reducing tariffs and quantitative restrictions on industrial imports, deregulating private economic activities that assisted agricultural trade, reducing financial costs, removing inefficiencies, consolidating agricultural inputs providers that incorporate frontier advances in biotechnology research, providing agricultural equipment, fertilizers, and agrochemicals, efficient storage management, handling, drying, marketing, and transportation.

4.2.1 Cattle Meat AIC

Approximately 480 processing plants make up the cattle meat processing sector, which can be divided into three segments: small processing plants or '*mataderos*' (270) that produce for small local markets (at municipal level); intermediate and large processing plants that process for local markets at provincial and national level or '*consumeros*' (90), and exporters that produce mainly boneless meat for the external markets (120). Nogués et al. (2007) indicate that there is no evidence in this AIC of market power and concentration that could affect competition in the markets. However in the export markets there are three foreign-owned firms that account for about 30 per cent of exports. Further meat production is mainly oriented to the domestic market. Figure 4.1 shows a consistent decrease in the international market share since 1970 when the country used to lead the cattle meat export market. This is the result of the slow growth of production and an increase in domestic consumption. Meat consumption in Argentina has the characteristic of being highly concentrated in beef, showing a poor diversification to other meats. The main reason is that consumers follow relative price signals which historically have favored beef over others (poultry, pork and fish).

The Basic Food Basket (BFB), a selection of the main consumption foodstuff used to measure poverty and indigence, shows the importance of beef in the Argentine diet.[2] However, policies oriented to control beef prices are still overestimating the real impact of prices on the consumers' food basket – 30.1 per cent in the (BFB), 13.9 per cent in the Basic Consumption-goods Basket (BCB) and 4.5 per cent in the CPI.[3] On the other hand, local anti-export policies, and commercial and sanitary trade barriers in the most important international markets, have lowered the local relative price of the commodity, resulting in a stronger consumer preference for beef.[4]

As a result, when the beef price rises the cost of the Basic Food Basket increases and the government is tempted to implement policies to prevent the price increase in the short run, which however worsens the problem in the long run by accentuating the anti-production cycle.

4.2.2 Wheat AIC

Wheat production in Argentina has two main uses: first as an input to the milling industry, and second as an export commodity, which is the surplus after the demand from the domestic industry is satisfied. Milling wheat demand has been steady during the last 30 years owing to stable per capita bread consumption (Nogués et al., 2007). Local wheat consumption has fluctuated between 5 and 6 million tons a year during the last 20 years. Any excess production has been sold in international markets.

There are 150 mills producing flour for Argentina's domestic consumption. They show a considerable excess capacity, hence the growth potential of the industry based on the growth of the domestic market is limited (García, 2005). The three largest firms account for 45 per cent of wheat flour production. Wheat derivatives (flour, bread, cookies, pasta etc.) represent 4.3 per cent on the CPI and 16.3 per cent and 7.5 per cent on the BFB and BCB respectively. Much as in the case of beef, price control on the wheat market correlates with the impact of price level and volatility on consumer budgets as measured by the BFB, BCB and CPI.

4.2.3 Soybean Crushing

The largest soybean crushing facilities in the world were established in Argentina in the last 30 years. This allowed not only the export of soybeans but also the export of processed subproducts (soybean oil and soybean meal). The soybean complex in Argentina had not only become the largest exporter from the AIC, but also took the leading position in international markets, representing the 42 per cent of the soybean cake (or meal) world exports market, and 52 per cent of the soybean oil market during 2007 (Figure 4.1.). Soybean crushing absorbs between 70 per cent and 80 per cent of the soybeans produced in Argentina, while the rest is exported as grain. Soybean meal and oil are not consumed in the local market, which represents just 5 per cent of total production. The CPI includes none of the soybean derivatives. One important characteristic in soybean crushing is that firms operate with very small margins. Therefore, in the presence of export taxes on the final products (oil and meal) firms are not able to absorb any tax and the tax burden falls on primary soybean producers.

4.3 IMPACT OF EXPORT TAXES AND QUANTITATIVE RESTRICTIONS ON THE AIC

The most important AICs having been briefly described in the previous section, this section will describe different aspects of the impact of export taxes and quantitative trade restrictions on primary production, poverty and indigence and also on the federal government budget.

4.3.1 Export Taxes and Quantitative Restrictions on Trade

During the last 25 years the AIC, in particular the primary producers, has suffered the effects of various regulatory interventions on the exports markets. The discrimination against the primary production sector can be analyzed from different points of view. In the following two subsections export taxes and quantitative restrictions on trade will be studied through their impact on two variables: the effective exchange rate and the gap between the local and the international price of commodities. The focus is on both the distortions in primary product markets and the impact on planting decisions, production, exports and various other productive decisions, not just by taxes but also by quantitative restrictions on the trade of exportable commodities.

4.3.2 Export Taxes and the Effective Exchange rate

The analysis of the effective exchange rate (AR$ for each US$ received by producers net of export taxes) is one of the many ways to measure the impact of export taxes on primary producers' incomes (Ciappa, 2005).[5] In

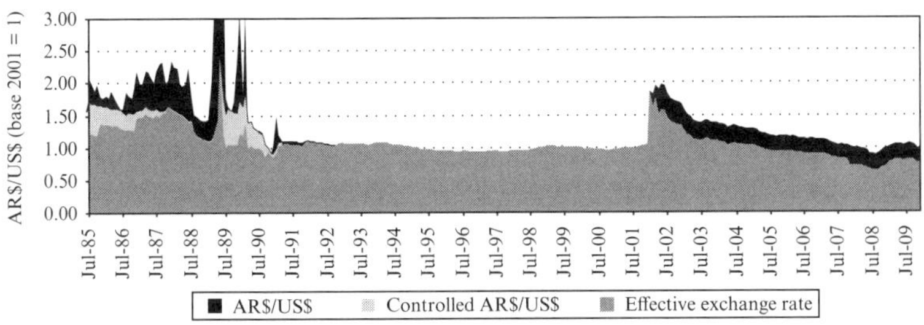

Source: Authors' elaboration based on Ciappa (2005).

Figure 4.2 Wheat effective exchange rate (1985–2009).

the last 30 years, exchange rate series show three distinctive periods. Each one is associated with a particular policy towards agricultural exports. Figure 4.2 shows the effective exchange rate for wheat exporters (the same effects can be observed on other agricultural commodities), the black area representing the discrimination between those that receive a full dollar from exports and those that suffer discriminatory policies.

Among the discriminatory policies, during the 1980s and until the implementation of the convertibility program in 1991, there were two different policies associated with agricultural exports: a differential exchange rate and export taxes on agricultural commodities. The light-gray area in Figure 4.2 represents the officially controlled exchange rate for wheat exporters. The controlled exchange rate is, of course, smaller than the free market rate (black area). Note that taxes on exports were applied in combination with the controlled exchange rate. The dark-gray area represents the effective exchange rate received by exporters. The effective exchange rate is considerably smaller than the market rate, but seems to be more stable than the market rate.

Between 1991 and 2001, during the convertibility program, the exchange rate was set at 1 to 1, in nominal terms, and export taxes were eliminated. Therefore, the effective exchange rate was the market exchange rate, showing that there was no discrimination against the sector.

With the collapse of the convertibility program, new export taxes were established and created a new gap between the market and effective exchange rates. Figure 4.3 shows how, from the beginning of 2002, the devaluation of the local currency generated a notable increase in the effective exchange rate. In February 2002 the effective exchange increased 85 per cent; however, in March of the same year export taxes were introduced. By July, when devaluation reached 200 per cent in nominal terms and 100 per cent in real terms (adjusted by Intermediate Goods Price

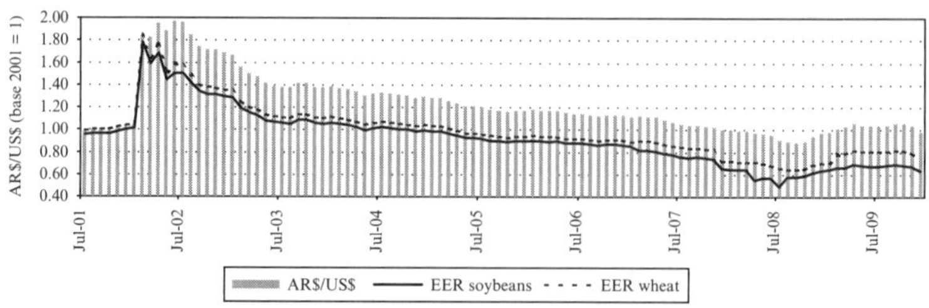

Source: Authors' elaboration based on Ciappa (2005).

Figure 4.3 Effective exchange rate 2001–09 (real terms base ICPI 2001 = 1).

Index (IGPI)), the effective exchange rate for wheat producers increased by 50 per cent. One of the main arguments in support of a large export tax was the large gains producers had received from the devaluation of the local currency. However, it can be seen in Figure 4.3 that the real gain of the devaluation was consistently undermined by the increase in domestic prices. From May 2004, for soybeans, and March of 2005, for wheat, producers obtained an effective exchange rate smaller than that received during the 1990s.

It is important to understand that historically export taxes have been implemented together with large currency devaluations in order to capture extraordinary rents from a rigid supply in the short run. At the same time these taxes mitigated the price impact of internationally traded commodities on domestic consumers. The government decreased these taxes in the medium and long run, as the local currency appreciated or when commodity prices dropped in international markets (Sturzenegger, 2007; Lema, 2008).

In recent years Argentina's government has behaved in the opposite way. Since 2002 export taxes have increased in successive phases. The first modification was in January of 2007, right after the soybean planting season when the tax for oilseeds increased from 23.5 per cent to 27.5 per cent. In November 2007 the rates were modified again, taking the oilseed rate to 35 per cent and that for wheat from 20 per cent to 28 per cent (again after the planting season). On March 2008 a new modification was introduced, imposing a mobile rate linked to the FOB price level of the commodities. In this proposed system, the tax rate would have been calculated at the export registration time. The rate was linked to the FOB price and a complicated formula that resulted in an increasing rate for higher FOB prices. The proposed system put the soybean rate up to 44 per cent and created a huge political and social opposition that ended in a revision of the system back to the flat-rate system (Ciappa, 2009a).

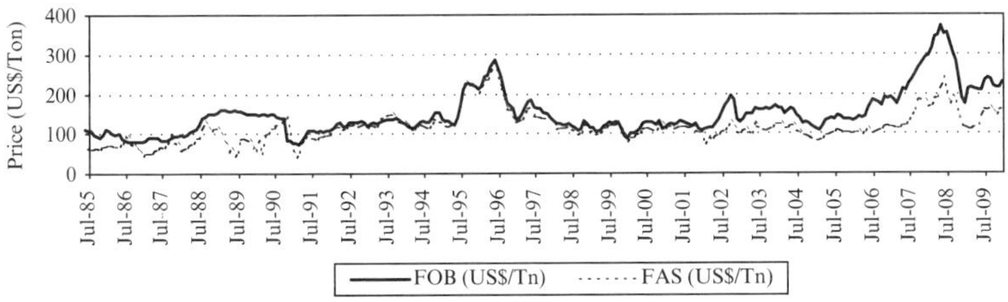

Source: Authors' elaboration based on SAGPyA and Bolsa de Cereales de Buenos Aires data.

Figure 4.4 Local and international wheat prices.

4.3.3 Export Taxes, Quantitative Restrictions on Trade and Commodity Prices

An alternative way to measure the impact of export taxes and quantitative restrictions on trade is the gap these policies generate between the international price (FOB price) and the local price that producers receive at port facilities (the FAS price).

Figure 4.4 shows the monthly FOB and FAS prices of wheat. The result of such interventionist policies can be seen in the gap between the two series. Before the 1990s and after 2002, the two series were first separated by the existence of taxes on exports.[6] However, there are a number of restrictions on trade that also affect this gap. The Argentine government has applied some of these restrictions in the wheat and beef markets in particular. For example, in May 2006 the National Office of Agricultural Marketing Control decided on the temporary suspension of export permits for wheat. The measure was taken in order to guarantee full wheat provision for the local market, given the increase in export registrations during that month. The suspension lasted just one day. However, the signal was important enough to force firms to limit their export operations. Many firms abandoned the wheat market that year, leaving local mills as the only demanders in the market. The result was a drop in local price to producers who previously had been receiving the FOB price net of export taxes. This drop in price increased the gap between local and international prices.

Figure 4.5 shows the gap between the FOB price net of taxes and the local price (FAS). This gap should be around 5 per cent (associated to fobbing expenses). In the figure it can be seen that before May 2006 the gap was on average 6.5 per cent. After the government gave the signal that it would suspend export activities when it considered this necessary, this gap increased to 16.5 per cent on average for the following 3 years.

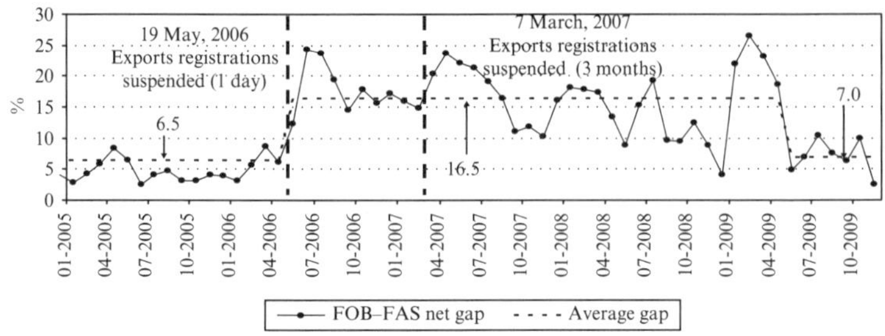

Source: Authors' elaboration based on SAGPyA data.

Figure 4.5 Net FOB–FAS wheat price gap.

This price gap is important for two reasons. First, as we can see in Figure 4.5, the gap is extremely important for producers since it represents a virtual increase of 80 per cent in the tax they were paying (the export tax during this period was 20 per cent). Second, the 20 per cent tax on exports is collected by the federal government. However, the 16.5 per cent price reduction received by the producers is not collected by the government, but represents a quasi-rent for the milling industry and for the exporters who had not bought the grain to fulfill their delivery contracts before registrations were suspended.

One possible explanation for the persistence of this gap during three crop seasons could be related to the discount exporters would obtain owing to the risks they undertake any time they buy grain in the local market and sell it on the international market while the export registry is closed. Since the commodities exports markets have large volumes and low margins, whenever the registry is closed any price increase would generate an increase in the export tax (in dollars), and this increase could be enough to eliminate any profit from the transaction.

Finally, quantitative restrictions, like the suspension of export registries, generate other distortions. These discretionary policies generate not only artificial rents among local agents, but also uncertainty in international markets about how much buyers can trust wheat-exporting firms from Argentina.

4.3.4 Impact on Grain Production

Agriculture had historically been considered as a sector with small or even null price elasticity based on evidence collected since the 1930s. On this basis, lower prices received by producers (export taxes or other policies) would not affect production and labor or other inputs demanded by the sector.

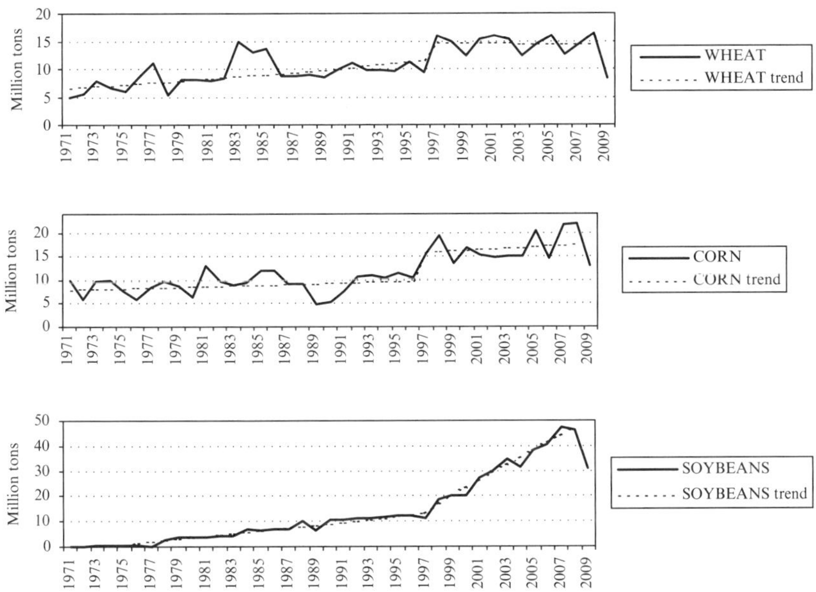

Source: Authors' elaboration based on SAGPA data.

Figure 4.6 Grain production and trends.

However, some studies (Reca, 1974; Fulginiti and Perrin, 1990) reconsidered the assumption about low price elasticity in agriculture. They proved that in the long run, agriculture has shown significant supply responses to changes in farming profits. In fact, the response of the AIC after the 1980s, and particularly during the 1990s, with the deregulation of the economy, accentuated the perception of the agro-industry as one of the most dynamic sectors in the Argentinean economy. Reca (2008) indicates that the growth of Argentina's agriculture was particularly strong from the 1990s onwards as a result of internal price stability and the openness of the economy. These factors stimulated the adoption of important levels of technology in terms of production and management. The author argues that high-quality human capital, a massive technology upgrade (zero tillage, high-tech equipment, transgenic seeds like RR soybeans, chemicals, fertilizers, irrigation etc.), as well as the incorporation of new forms of management organization, have supported a profound change in Argentina's agribusiness. Figure 4.6 shows the evolution of the three main crops. One can observe important changes in the production trend during the 1990s. Corn and wheat production underwent a strong jump, from 8 million tons of corn and 10 million tons of wheat to between 14 and 16 million tons a year in both crops.

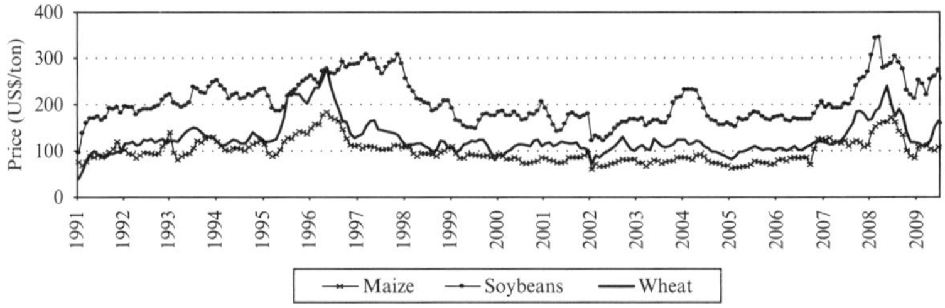

Source: Bolsa de Cereales de Buenos Aires.

Figure 4.7 Local prices of grains.

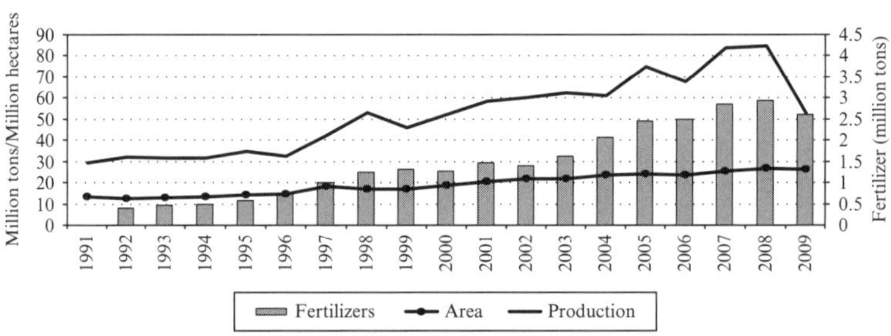

Source: Authors' elaboration based on SAGPA data and Onofri (2009).

Figure 4.8 Planted area, production and use of fertilizers.

Soybean production also underwent a change in trend during the 1990s. However, in contrast with other grains, instead of stabilizing production at a higher level, soybean production has shown continuous growth. The main reason for the trend change was the introduction of new transgenic seeds and the development of zero tillage technologies that considerably increased yields and profitability.

The other important driver of productions decisions are prices. Figure 4.7 shows that there have been two periods of high grain prices since 1991. The first was around 1996. These high prices supported the adoption of new technologies that produced the increase in the production trends of the three grains. Figure 4.8 shows that during this period there was an increase in the planting area as well as in the use of fertilizers, which generated a large increase in production from 32 million tons in 2006 to 52 million tons in 2008.

The other period of high prices was in 2007–08, which produced further increases in fertilizer use and in area planted. However, price distortions

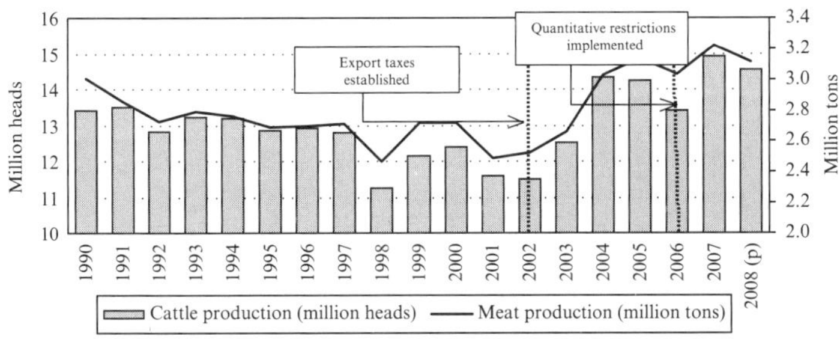

Source: Onofri (2009)

Figure 4.9 Cattle and meat production.

generated by export taxes and quantitative restrictions affected incentives for producers. The 2008–09 season is an example of such effects.

During 2008 the agricultural sector suffered government interventions that included not only a rise in export taxes, but also a number of quantitative restrictions on wheat and corn exports. This intervention, combined with a serious drought right in the middle of the growing season, produced a historic decline in grain production (38 per cent of total production). Figure 4.8 shows that part of the decline in production is explained by a drop in the use of fertilizers (12 per cent) and in the planting area (2 per cent). As mentioned above, interventions were more important in wheat and corn markets, as was clearly reflected in the planting decisions in these two commodities. Corn production declined by 40 per cent, but the drop in the planted area was 18 per cent, explaining almost half of the production decrease. In the case of wheat, production diminished by 48 per cent and planted area by 21 per cent. In contrast with these crops, the soybean planted area increased by 8 per cent and because of the drought production dropped by 33 per cent. It is important to note that the government introduces less quantitative restrictions in the soybean market than in the corn and wheat markets, but that the export tax rate on oilseeds is higher than in any other agricultural commodities.

4.3.5 Impact on Cattle Production

We observe a similar development in cattle production. Figure 4.9 shows that cattle slaughter (in million heads) and meat production (in million tons) increased during the last years, reaching the maximum level in 2007. The figure could give the wrong impression about an increase in cattle production, it appearing that export taxes and commerce restrictions had

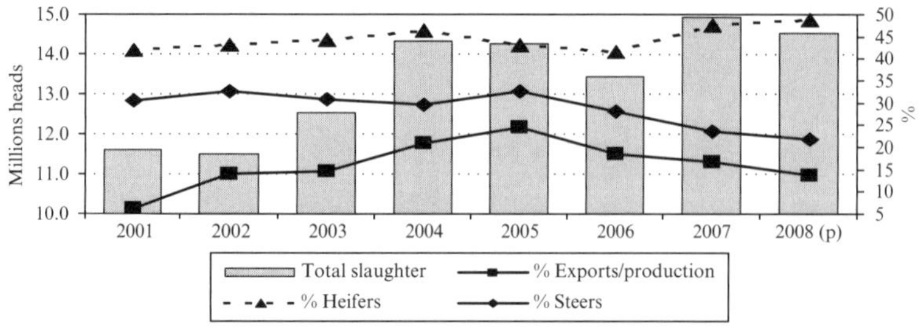

Source: Onofri (2009).

Figure 4.10 Slaughtering indicators.

improved industry conditions. However, the growth shown after 2002, even with export taxes, was generated by the increase in international demand.

Figure 4.10 shows some indicators that prove that growth was driven by exports. During 2005 exports represented 25 per cent of local production, with a decreasing trend in the slaughter of heifer cows and a growing trend in steer slaughtering. These trends were reversed in 2006 when the first interventions in meat markets appeared. Iriarte (2009) indicates that the increase in slaughter and meat production in previous years originated in an increase in the extraction rate (increase in the stock liquidation rate). In 2008 slaughters reached 48.7 per cent, the maximum level since the indicator was registered. In addition, the decreasing trend in steer slaughters is consistent with the decreasing participation of exports in total production. As in grain production, the combination of government interventions and drought during 2008 diminished the equilibrium cattle stocks, creating pressure in the intermediate and long runs on cattle supply and therefore in local consumer meat prices.

4.3.6 Effects on the AIC

Recent evidence shows that the negative effects of export taxes and quantitative restrictions on trade affect the entire productive chain. In particular there is a significant impact on those activities that sell inputs to the agricultural sector. The fall in the producer price induces farmers to adopt less intensive production practices. An example is the decrease in apparent fertilizer use. Figure 4.11 shows the use of fertilizers declining in 2008 to a level below 2004. It is interesting to observe that this drop in use generated not only a decrease in imports but also one in local production.

Similarly, one observes a decrease in the demand for agricultural

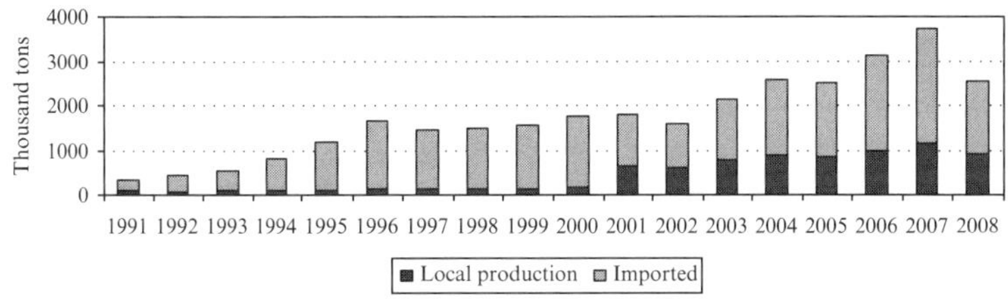

Source: CIAFA and SAGPYA.

Figure 4.11 Apparent fertilizer use.

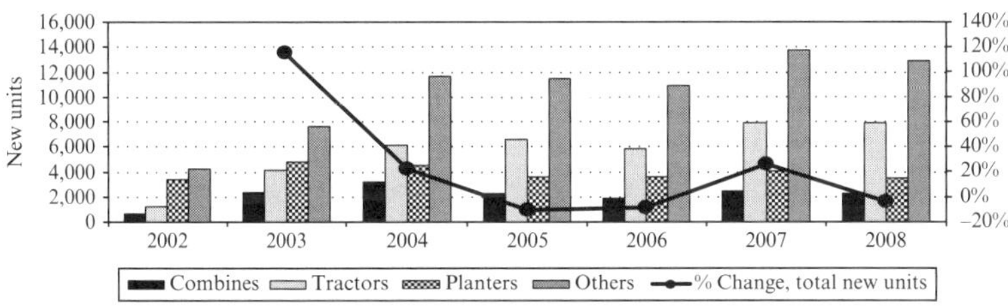

Source: INDEC.

Figure 4.12 Sales of agricultural machinery.

machinery from the end of 2007. It is clear in Figure 4.12 that in 2008 there was a decrease in every kind of machinery and the quarterly data indicate that this decrease started in the last quarter of 2007 (when export taxes were increased) and was particularly large during the first two quarters of 2008 when the conflict over Resolution 125 (mobile export tax rates) occurred (Ciappa, 2009a). The effect on local machinery producers was significant, since, according to INDEC, 20 per cent of combine harvesters and tractors, 70 per cent of other implements and 100 per cent of planters sold in Argentina are produced locally.

4.4 GENERAL EQUILIBRIUM RESULTS: GROWTH, EMPLOYMENT AND POVERTY

Anderson and Valenzuela (2007) analyze the effects of the elimination of trade barriers through the use of a multiregional general equilibrium model known as GTAP-Arg, specially designed to estimate the impact of agricultural sector policies. On the basis of this model with special calibration for Argentina, Nogués et al. (2007) determine that an elimination of export taxes and quantitative restrictions on agricultural commodities would increase agro-industrial added value by 32.6 per cent. The same study analyzes more conservative GDP growth scenarios (15 per cent, 20 per cent and 25 per cent AIC growth), and, considering the relevance of the AIC in the Argentine economy (18.5 per cent), determines that it would produce GDP growth of between 2.8 per cent and 4.6 per cent.

These figures are important in determining the impact on poverty. The link between incomes and poverty is measured by the poverty-income elasticity, which is shown at three different levels (−0.5, −1 and −1.5) depending on different evidence presented. Thus in the most conservative scenario (poverty-income elasticity of −0.5 and GDP growth of 2.8 per cent), the elimination of restrictions would take 90,000 people out of poverty (1.4 percentage points reduction). In the best scenario 450,000 people would escape from poverty (6.9 percentage points reduction).

General equilibrium results indicate that the elimination of restrictions would have a stronger impact on primary production than on the industrial sectors of the AIC. Moreover, agro-industrial expansion does not generate reductions in other industrial sectors, given the strong links between AIC and the rest of the economy, such as chemicals, agricultural machinery and transport, as well as many other services. Estimates also show that the effect on related sectors of the AIC's productive expansion would generate between 300,000 and 350,000 new jobs, particularly among low-income/low-qualifications workers, who are most likely to be unemployed and more vulnerable to poverty.

From the evidence presented in this study, it is highly probable that the elimination of export taxes and quantitative restriction will contribute to accelerate economic growth. In order to keep production expanding it is essential to sustain fiscal equilibrium and to design policies to compensate at least poor consumers while the expansion takes effect.

4.4.1 Exports Taxes and the Fiscal Sector

Export taxes were reintroduced in Argentina in 2002 and were successively modified. One reason for this was that one of the main effects of such taxes is to isolate the international and local price of commodities like food and oil, which is particularly important after large currency devaluations (Sturzenegger and Salazni, 2007). Another reason was that after large devaluations and in a recessionary environment, it is extremely difficult for governments to collect enough funds through regular taxation. Therefore taxes on exports facilitate the recovery of fiscal accounts and are

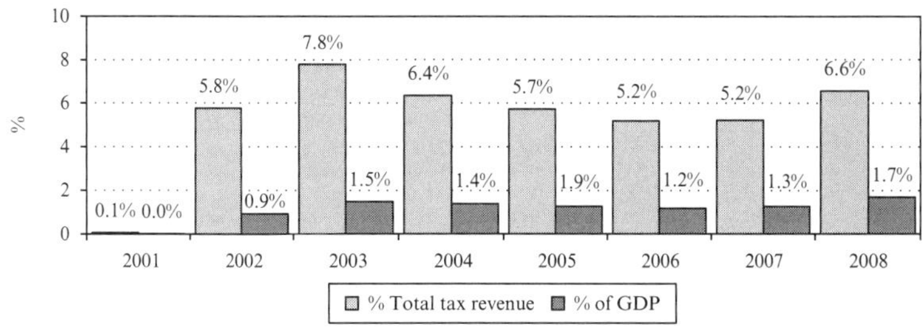

Source: Porto (2009).

Figure 4.13 Fiscal relevance of export taxes on AIC commodities.

usually accepted by exporters because of the large profit they receive from currency depreciation.

4.4.2 Fiscal Relevance

Exports taxes have been one of the main sources of fiscal revenue since the abandonment of the convertibility program in 2002. During 2008 export taxes collected amounted to $36,055 million, making them the fourth-largest source of fiscal revenues, after sale taxes ($77,300 million), income taxes ($53,600 million) and social security contributions ($51,100 million).

The AIC[7] contributed 49 per cent of export taxes collected. Figure 4.13 shows evolution of AIC export taxes as percentages of total tax collections, and their importance in terms of GDP. The contribution for 2008 represented 6.6 per cent of total tax collection, a significant increase over the 5.2 per cent for the previous year generated by the export tax rate increase of November 2007.

In terms of the GDP, export taxes represented 1.7 per cent during 2008, the highest percentage since the government reintroduced the taxes in 2002.

4.5 FISCAL EFFECTS OF THE ELIMINATION OF EXPORT TAXES

Historically, export taxes have always been reduced as the currency appreciated or when international commodity prices dropped (Sturzenegger, 2006; Lema, 2008). Even though the government has never shown any intention to reduce export taxes, some institutions have analyzed the possible consequences for the fiscal sector of the elimination of export taxes on AIC commodities. This section summarizes the results of two studies

(Nogués et al., 2007; Porto, 2009) of the effects of the elimination of such export taxes. The estimation of impacts is calculated according to the 2008 social accounting matrix (SAM) and the general tax system. The following effects can be identified:

> *Direct effect* – Loss in government tax collected due to the elimination of export taxes payable by the AIC.
> *Indirect effect 1* – Tax revenue from additional incomes in the private sector due to the elimination of export taxes payable by the AIC. This effect can be disaggregated into the higher income from export tax elimination (indirect effect 1.a) and the proceeds from the elimination of the internal consumption subsidy on the exportable commodities (indirect effect 1.b). The government, through the general tax system, has the right to collect taxes on income increases. In this way it can recover some of the funds lost by the direct effect of tax elimination.
> *Indirect effect 2* – Originates from producers' reaction to higher prices, given export tax elimination. This effect will depend on the expansion of production and on the general situation of the economy at the time of the tax elimination. The size of this effect will depend on the price elasticity of supply and the amount of resources the sector absorbs from the informal sector of the economy. Nogués et al. (2007) determine that in a conservative scenario the expansion in the added value of the economy would be around 4 per cent, applying to that expansion the average fiscal pressure for 2008.

4.5.1 Impact of the Elimination of Export Taxes on the AIC

Table 4.1 presents the detailed effect of export tax elimination on public sector revenues. Note that in Argentina the federal government has exclusive rights over export taxes. However, the general tax system presents a number of taxes which are shared by the federal government, provinces and municipalities.[8] This has resulted in a complex system of redistribution whereby taxes that in many cases are collected by the federal tax agency must be redirected to provinces though a sharing scheme.

If export taxes were eliminated, the consolidated tax revenue loss, after all the effects were computed, would be $5839 million. This is an extremely important result; it negates the assumption that the loss of the consolidated public sector would be equivalent to the full export tax revenue. As described above, there are other effects that allow the recovery of 67 per cent of the funds based on the adjustments of the economy to the new situation. From the $17,667 million revenue lost from export tax elimination, $11,828 million could be recovered through indirect effects 1.a, 1.b and

Table 4.1 Argentina: consolidated tax effect ($ million)

Effect	Tax revenues	Consolidated	Federal government	Provinces
Direct	Agricultural export tax	−17,667	−17,667	
Indirect 1.a	Income tax	4,079	2,100	1,979
	Personal assets tax	31	12	19
	Rural land tax	414		414
	Others	2,814	1,691	1,122
Indirect 1.b	Added value tax	746	409	337
	Gross incomes tax	368		368
	Others	1,959	1,432	527
Indirect 2		1,417	849	568
Consolidated		−5,839	−11,174	5,334

Source: Porto (2009).

2. The problem for the federal government (which must decide whether or not to eliminate the export tax) is that its total loss would be $11,174 million, while the provinces would receive extra revenues of $5334 million.

There is another important consideration. As is clear from the effects described above, the direct effect takes place immediately after the export taxes are eliminated, while the other effects take some time to be felt. The estimated adjustment period would be between 3 and 5 years (Nogués et al., 2007).

The consolidated loss of resources, as well as the redistribution between different government levels, requires the design of some fiscal compensation scheme. This scheme should consider at least some of the following alternatives: increase the efficiency of tax collection, increase the efficiency of government expenditures, design and implement new taxes, such as tax on farmland potential rent, tax on first sale of agricultural commodities, etc. (Porto, 2009), and finally, and the most difficult to implement, completely redesign the government–provinces relationship.

Porto (2009) presents some alternatives that include a tax on the potential rent of land, a small increase in tax collection and government expenditures, and an adjustment in the discretionary transfers to fully compensate the negative fiscal impact of the export tax elimination. In addition, the alternatives include the creation of a conditional cash transfers (CCT) program that would compensate poor consumers for the eventual increase in local food prices (as a consequence of export tax elimination). It is important to understand that local food prices impact directly on the consumer budgets of the poorest and could generate higher levels of poverty and indigence. The following section presents some results from Ciappa (2009b)[9] regarding subsidies on consumption in the case of the abandonment of export taxes and of quantitative restrictions on trade.

4.6 POVERTY AND SUBSIDIES ON FOOD CONSUMPTION

Governments usually target some policies on the price levels of food in order to mitigate the price volatility of 'wage goods' in poor consumers' budgets. They often apply direct and indirect subsidies on goods and services. These policies range from generalized subsidies related to prices to programs of cash transfers with a variety of targets and different results. One of the reasons the Argentine government argues in defense of export taxes and quantitative restrictions on trade of wheat and meat is precisely the effect these policies have on price level control.

In terms of distributive impact, if the policy target is to control the food expenses of poor consumers, the affect of policy incidence in terms of the share of the expenditure that actually goes to poor consumers should be considered. Who does or does not obtain the subsidy will depend on the goods selected, which targeting criteria are employed, and the characteristics of the distribution channels (Nogués et al., 2007). Alderman (2002) summarizes some international experience about leakage to well-off consumers (Table 4.2).

In the case of Argentina, the use of export taxes as a generalized indirect subsidy on price is an instrument with high leakage to non-poor consumers. It can be seen in Table 4.3 that only 30 per cent of bread is consumed by poor people, and 70 per cent is consumed by the well-off. Figures are very similar in the case of beef.

Targeted subsidy programs, and CCT, seem to be the best alternatives in terms of leakage and fiscal costs in order to subsidize poor consumers. Rationed subsidy policies need to be accompanied by effective targeting mechanisms, to allow the achievement of the highest impact on income distribution with the smallest possible fiscal costs.

4.6.1 Elimination of Taxes on Exports and Poverty: Alternative Compensatory Instruments

Levels of poverty and indigence are measured according to the Basic Consumption-goods Basket (BCB) and Basic Food Basket (BFB). If a household's income is not enough to buy the BCB, it is considered a poor home. If a home's income is not enough to buy the BFB, it is considered indigent.

Table 4.2 International comparison of leakage from food subsidy programs

Type of program	Country	Leakage to non-needy
Untargeted food subsidy	Egypt (early 1980s), Tunisia, Morocco and Yemen	High (60%–80%)
	Brazil	High (81%)
Untargeted food rations	India, Pakistan	High (50%–60%)
Rations shop-targeted geographically	Brazil, India	Low (5%–10%)
Self-targeted rations	Bangladesh, Pakistan	Low (10%–20%)
Food stamps targeted by income	Colombia, Sri Lanka, USA	Low–moderate (10%–30%)
Food stamps targeted by health status	Colombia, Indonesia	Low (3%–10%)

Source: Alderman (2002).

Table 4.3 Argentina: selected food consumption by income deciles

Deciles	Bread	Flour, rice and cereals	Beef	Pork	Lamb	Milk	Milk products
1 to 4	30.2%	35.0%	29.1%	17.6%	30.5%	29.6%	16.3%
5 to 10	69.8%	65.0%	70.9%	82.4%	69.5%	70.4%	83.7%

Source: Home Expenditure Survey, INDEC 1996.

Having taken this into account, Table 4.4 shows the value of the BCB and BFB per equivalent adult and the impact on the cost of both baskets if export taxes and quantitative restrictions are eliminated on the wheat and cattle meat markets. Ciappa (2009b) estimates the impact of the elimination through cattle meat and wheat AICs in order to determine the effect on consumer prices and on the costs of the BCB and BFB in April 2009.

The increase in the cost of the BCB and BFB would be $43.6. The BFB cost would increase to $281 and the BCB to $577. This would raise poverty by 2.9 percentage points (from 24.4 per cent to 27.3 per cent, or 830,000 more poor people) and indigence by 2.32 percentage points (from 7.44 per cent to 9.76 per cent, or 816,000 more indigent people).

These numbers clearly indicate that the elimination of export taxes and quantitative restrictions on trade would significantly increase poverty

Table 4.4 Argentina: impact on poverty and indigence of the elimination of export taxes and quantitative restrictions

	Current situation	Export tax elimination	Export tax elimination + $4000 transfers	Export tax elimination + $6000 transfers
Increase given elimination of export taxes and quantitative restrictions ($/ equivalent adult)		43.6		
Cost of BFB ($/ equivalent adult)	237	281		
Cost of BCB ($/ equivalent adult)	533	577		
Poverty (%)	24.40	27.30[a]	24.1	22.5
Indigence (%)	7.44	9.76	7.20	6.00

Note: [a] Equivalent to 8.5 million people.

Source: Ciappa (2009b).

and indigence levels. Therefore, the elimination of restrictions must be accompanied by the creation of some compensatory instruments for poor consumers.

The same study presented different alternatives and concluded that a CCT program with a fiscal cost of $4000 million would be enough to compensate poor consumers for the elimination of export taxes and quantitative restrictions on trade. Alternatively, a $6000 million program would reduce poverty by 1.9 percentage points and indigence by 1.4 percentage points from the current situation with export taxes. The cost of such a program was included in the fiscal adjustment alternatives presented by Porto (2009) discussed in the previous section.

4.7 CONCLUSIONS AND FINAL CONSIDERATIONS

Export taxes on agricultural commodities have a long tradition in Argentina. There are a number of justifications for export taxes in the short run, namely that they are easy to establish, have low collection costs, have positive impacts on fiscal revenues and are appropriated entirely by the federal government. In addition, they reduce the local price of exportable agricultural commodities. Since agricultural commodities are usually considered wage goods, in the short run the use of export taxes helps to improve real wages, and to control poverty and indigence.

Like export taxes, quantitative restrictions generate negative incentives on production, investment, exports etc. They generate rents for the owners of quotas or export permits, have a negative impact on producer prices without any impact on consumer prices and, finally, do not generate any fiscal revenue.

Although the use of export taxes might be acceptable in the short run, the use of quantitative restrictions on exports is the result of poor policy design. Furthermore, the excessive use of these short-term policy options has produced a vacuum in terms of long-term policies for this important economic sector.

The fiscal impact of export tax elimination is one of the arguments most used in defense of this instrument. However, elimination would not mean the loss of all the fiscal revenue. Some part would be recovered by the general tax system (because of the increase in the local price of exported and locally consumed goods), even with the same production level. Additionally, subsequent increases in production would contribute to generating extra fiscal revenues. As a result, in 3 to 5 years (depending on the agricultural supply dynamics), three-quarters of the original loss would be recovered through the general tax system.

The other argument supporting the use of export taxes and quantitative restrictions is price increases in wage goods that impact on poverty and indigence. Producer prices (given the elimination of taxes and restrictions) are partially translated into salaries depending on wage–producer-price elasticity. The effects generated on higher incomes are not instantaneous. On the contrary, they may take several years. For this reason some instrument is required to compensate consumers (especially the poor and the indigent). Depending on wage dynamics, the program should be diminished over time until the effect on income is complete.

Once adjustment is complete, the population should end up in a better situation than would be the case with export taxes, as a result of the economic growth driven by the expansion of production in the AIC, and the effect that this expansion generates among other sectors in the economy.

In the long run the following three effects should be observed:

- The highly dynamic AIC responds to price incentives with increased investment, the adoption of improved production technology and finally expanded production.

- The increased production drives an expansion in internal consumption, given the overall income increase in the population.
- The increase in exports generates the foreign currency essential to cover external debt payments and to finance inputs and capital goods imports.

NOTES

1. The National Constitution reserves for the federal government the revenues from international trade taxes. The Law 22415, art. 775, establishes that the federal government has the faculty to establish and modify taxes on export goods, allowing it not to depend on Congress resolutions regarding such taxes.
2. The CPI is based on the 1996 and 1997 Surveys of Expenditures and Consumption and the BFB is based on the 1980s Survey of Expenditure and Consumption. Since 1980 the per capita cattle meat consumption has decreased from 85kg per capita then, to 67.7kg in 2008, while poultry consumption increased from 10kg in 1980 to 26kg in 2008.
3. Basic Consumption-goods Basket (BCB) includes basic consumption goods in addition to the BFB. Homes in which incomes are not enough to buy the BCB are considered to be poor ones. In addition, if family incomes are not enough to even to buy the BFB (approximately half of the BCB) the family is considered indigent. This topic is discussed later in this chapter.
4. Cattle meat weight on the CPI in Argentina is twice as large as in Brazil, and seven times bigger than in the USA.
5. Since the exchange rate is not intended to be used as an indicator of international competitiveness, but as a measure of local purchasing power of the dollars received by producers, the current dollar price will be converted to constant prices using the IGPI (intermediate goods price index), closely associated with the production function. In this way the adjusted series represents the purchase power of inputs for each dollar received from sales of the different commodities. As such, it is independent of the international prices and it expresses the exchange policy applied to the primary producers.
6. During the 1990s the series shows a very small gap, reflecting the influence of the local factor on the wheat market. The local market absorbs a large proportion of local wheat production.
7. The agro-industrial chain (AIC) is conformed by primary agricultural producers, agricultural industry and the different components of the commercialization chain.
8. Provinces and municipalities can also collect taxes on internal activities. Under this fiscal arrangement, export taxes generate an interjurisdictional fiscal externality since it reduces the tax base of the coparticipable taxes and provincial and municipal own taxes. In this way the existence of export taxes has a negative impact on fiscal resources at these government levels.
9. Porto's (2009) and Ciappa's (2009b) studies are part of a large project on the Argentine AIC conducted at the Universidad Nacional de La Plata. Results in both papers are consistent with each other in terms of the policy recommendations and the cost of proposed instruments.

REFERENCES

Alderman, H. (2002), 'Subsidies as a social safety net: effectiveness and challenges', World Bank Social Protection Discussion Paper Series, no. 0224, Washington, DC.

Anderson K. and E. Valenzuela (2007), 'Do global trade distortions still harm developing country farmers?', *Review of World Economics*, **143** (1), 108–39.

Ciappa, C. (2005), 'Indicadores de rentabilidad en el sector agrario Argentino', Convenio Federación de Centros y Entidades Gremiales de Acopiadores de Cereales–Universidad Nacional de La Plata, Working Paper 1.

Ciappa, C. (2009a), 'Taxes on agricultural exports in Argentina: causes and consequences of a major political crisis', *Center for Latin American Studies News*, Fall 2008/ Spring 2009, p. 12.

Ciappa, C. (2009b), 'Diseño y evaluación de politicas alimentarias', in 'Política agroindustrial – fundamentos para el desarrollo sostenido y sustentable de la agroindustria', Buenos Aires: Foro de la Cadena Agroindustrial Argentina, 2009, pp. 217–47, available at: http://www.foroagroindustrial.org.ar/politicaagroindustrial.pdf

Fulginiti, L. and R. Perrin (1990), 'Argentine agricultural policy in a multiple input, multiple output framework', *American Journal of Agricultural Economics*, **72** (2), 279–88.

Garcia, M. (2005), 'Perfil descriptivo de la cadena de trigo'. Buenos Aires: Subsecretaría de Política Agropecuaria y Alimentos – Dirección Nacional de Mercados – Dirección de Mercados Agroalimentarios, available at: http://www.sagpya.mecon.gov.ar/new/0-0/programas/dma/publicaciones/perspectivas/Perfiles%20descriptivos/Cadena%20de%20trigo.pdf

Iriarte, I. (2009), 'Casi tres millones menos de terneros por la sequía', published in *La Voz del Interior* (Córdaba, Argentina), 6 March; available at: http://marcaliquida.com.ar/blog/2009/03/06/casi-tres-millones-menos-de-terneros-por-la-sequia/

Krueger, A.O., M. Schiff and A. Valdés (1991), *The Political Economy of Agricultural Pricing Policy, Volume 1: Latin America*, Baltimore, MD: Johns Hopkins University Press for the World Bank.

Lema, D. (2008), 'Política agropecuaria y crisis financiera internacional', paper presented at the seminar 'Política agropecuaria y crisis financiera internacional', at Centro para la Implementación de Políticas Públicas para la Equidad y el Crecimiento (CIPPEC), Buenos Aires, Argentina, 30 October.

Llach, J., M. Harriague and E. O'Connor (2004), *La Generación de Empleo en las Cadenas Agro-Industriales*, Buenos Aires: Fundación Producir Conservando, available at: www.producirconservando.org.ar

Nogués, J., A. Porto, C. Ciappa, L. di Gresia and A. Onofri (2007), *Estudio de Impactos Económicos y Sociales de Políticas Públicas en la Cadena Agroindustrial*, Buenos Aires: Foro de la Cadena Agroindustrial, available at: www.foroagroindustial.com.ar; see in particular the bibliography.

Onofri, A. (2009), 'Impactos económicos y sociales de la eliminación de DEX y REX en Argentina', in 'Política agroindustrial – fundamentos para el desarrollo sostenido y sustentable de la agroindustria', Buenos Aires: Foro de la Cadena Agroindustrial Argentina, 2009, pp. 185–216, available at: http://www.foroagroindustrial.org.ar/politicaagroindustrial.pdf

Porto, A., H. Piffano and L. di Gresia (2007), 'El aporte tributario de la cadena agroindustrial (CAI)', Buenos Aires: Convenio Fundación Producir Conservando, available at: http://www.producirconservando.org.ar/docs/servicios/documentos/aportetributario_info_final_pbi_resumen.pdf

Porto, A. (2009), 'Efectos fiscales sobre los impuestos a las exportaciones (retenciones)', in 'Política agroindustrial – fundamentos para el desarrollo sostenido y sustentable de la agroindustria', Buenos Aires: Foro de la Cadena Agroindustrial Argentina, 2009, pp. 145–84, available at: http://toroagroindustrial.org.ar/politicaagroindustrial.pdf/blog/2009/03/06/casi-tres-millones-menos-de-terneros-por-la-sequia/

Reca, L. (1974), 'El sector agropecuario y los incentivos económicos en torno a la experiencia de la Argentina en las últimas dos décadas." Banco Ganadero Argentino, Temas de Economía Argentina, El Sector Agropecuario 1964/73, Buenos Aires, 1974.

Reca, L. (2008), 'El conflicto por el régimen de retenciones y el futuro de la agricultura argentina', *Anales, XLIII Reunión Anual. Asociación Argentina de Economía Política, Argentina, 2009*, available at: http://www.aaep.org.ar/anales/works/works2008/reca.pdf

Sturzenegger, A. (1990), *Trade, Exchange Rate, and Agricultural Pricing Policies in Argentina*, World Bank Comparative Studies, Washington, DC.

Sturzenegger, A. (1991), 'Argentina', in Anne O. Krueger, Maurice Schiff and Alberto Valdés (eds), *Latin America*, vol. 1 of *The Political Economy of Agricultural Pricing Policy*, Baltimore: Johns Hopkins University Press and Washington, DC. World Bank, pp. 15–51.

Sturzenegger, A. (2006), 'Comentario sobre "Validez actual del impuesto a la renta neta potencial de la tierra en Argentina" de Núñez Miñana (1985)', *Económica*, **52** (1–2), 195–202.

Sturzenegger, A. and M. Salazni (2007), 'Distortions to agricultural incentives in Argentina', World Bank – Agricultural Distortions Working Paper no. 11, Washington, DC.

Valdés, A. and B. Schaeffer (1995), 'Surveillance of agricultural price and trade policies: a handbook for Argentina', World Bank Technical Paper no. 294, Washington, DC.

5. The evolution of Brazilian agriculture from 1987 to 2009

Carlos José Caetano Bacha

The goal of this chapter is to analyze the evolution of Brazilian agriculture in the period from 1987 to 2009, evaluating the agricultural stimulus policies, their evolution and the way agriculture did or did not fulfill the functions attributed to it in the process of economic development.

The existing literature on the topic evaluates mainly the changes that have occurred in the sectoral support policy of agriculture, highlighting the creation of new rural credit lending tools, together with the rise in real interest rates charged to farmers (Bacha e Silva, 2005; Gasques e Conceição, 2001), the creation of new price support programs together with the reduction in coverage of traditional programs (Del Bel Filho and Bacha, 2005; Rezende, 2001; Verde, 2001) and the reduction of public expenditures for agriculture (Barros, 1994; Gasques, 2001; Gasques et al., 2010). Even in this context of low stimulus, Brazilian agriculture grew. The works of Bacha and Rocha (1998) and Brugnaro and Bacha (2009) take note of this growth and are concerned with evaluating the factors influencing the share of agriculture in Brazil's GDP. Bacha (2004) evaluated the means by which Brazil's agriculture performed the functions normally attributed to it in the economic development of the period 1987 to 2002. The contribution of this chapter is to bring together and update the existing information in the aforementioned literature and to analyze the impacts that macroeconomic policies (especially the exchange rate and minimum wage policies) had on Brazilian agriculture.

5.1 ECONOMIC POLICIES THAT AFFECT THE PERFORMANCE OF AGRICULTURE

This section examines the six main policies that have affected agricultural performance during the last two decades: exchange rate, minimum salary, rural credit, agricultural price support, government expenditure and agricultural research policies.

5.1.1 Exchange Rate Policies

The inflationary acceleration after 1987, which lasted until the first half of 1994, and the balance-of-payments crises that lasted until the end of the 1990s led to the adoption of different exchange rate regimes between 1987 and 2009, which entailed significant exchange rate fluctuations, but tended to appreciate the currency (see Figure 5.1, below). This harmed agriculture because it reduced real income, since much of the Brazil's agricultural production is exported or is exposed to competition from imported products.

In November 1986 mini devaluations of the exchange rate were restarted, following a nominal exchange rate freeze between March and October of 1986 (during the Plano Cruzado). However, in mid June of 1987 it was recognized that, despite the mini devaluations, the exchange rate was still appreciated. A devaluation of 9.5 per cent occurred in the same month, followed by continued mini devaluations, which occurred at shorter intervals, with some periods when daily currency devaluations took place. In January 1989 the Plano Verão was instituted, with prices and the exchange rate frozen until April of the same year. From then on, there was a return to the system of mini devaluations, which became daily from July of 1989 until mid March of 1990.

In spite of the sustained mini devaluations, for most of the period between November of 1986 and February of 1990, appreciation occurred between 1987 and 1989 (see Figure 5.1). Between 1986 and 1989 the real rate of appreciation reached 36 per cent. The trend of appreciation of the national currency can be attributed to the exchange rate freezes between January and April of 1989 and to the fact that mini nominal devaluations

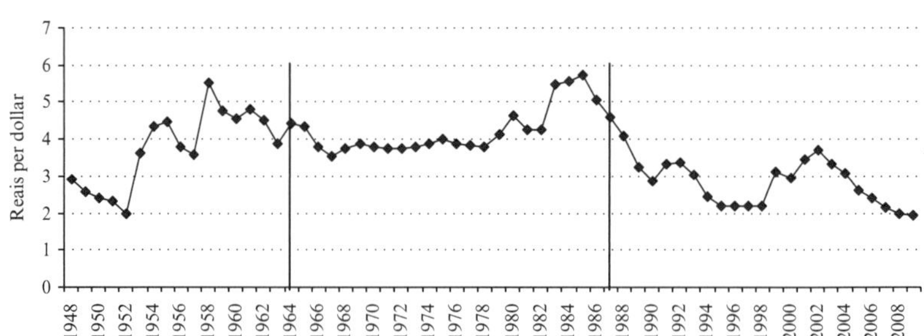

Source: IPEADATA. Deflated by PPI-USA and IGP-DI Brazil.

Figure 5.1 Exchange rate (reais per dollar) 1948–2009 (purchasing power of December 2009).

had remained below the difference between internal and external inflation rates.

From March of 1990 until June of 1994, a policy of a floating exchange rate was instituted, but the central bank intervened in the supply or demand of foreign currencies whenever it deemed that the market did not set the exchange rate in accord with the central bank's goals. This new exchange rate policy allowed for devaluation in 1991 and 1992, followed by appreciation in 1993. In this last year, the real exchange rate was 6 per cent below the same real value reached in 1989. In other words, the appreciation in 1993 offset the real currency devaluations that occurred in 1991 and 1992.

Together with Real Plan's initiation, on 1 July 1994 a flexible exchange rate was instituted. Initially, it was defined as 'broad bands' with an upper limit of R$1.00 per each dollar, but with no defined lower limit. As the inflow of foreign currency increased, the nominal exchange rate tended to decrease in the second half of 1994 and in the first two months of 1995, despite the existence of domestic inflation. On 1 July 1994 the nominal exchange rate was R$1.00 to the dollar. The average exchange rate in July was R$0.93 per dollar and that rate fell to R$0.84 in February of 1995. Only in March of 1995 did the nominal exchange rate start to rise.

From July 1995 and until December 1998, a system of 'mini exchange bands' was adopted, accompanied by mini-devaluations of these bands. These two systems (wide bands and mini bands exchange rates) caused a large currency appreciation (see Figure 5.1). Between 1993 and 1997 there was real appreciation of 28.5 per cent. The real exchange rate experienced a slight devaluation in 1998 (of 1.2 per cent in relation to 1997). This was due to the corrections of mini bands exchanges to rates above those of domestic inflation instead of considering the difference between domestic and foreign inflation rates. However, this did little to change the large valuation that already existed until then. For example, between 1993 and 1998 the bilateral real exchange rate between the real and the dollar appreciated by 28 per cent.

In 1998, the real exchange rate (R$/US$) at December 2009 purchasing power was 56 per cent below that of 1986. The real exchange rate in 1986 was R$5.06 to the dollar (at December 2009 purchasing power) and in 1998 it was R$2.21 to the dollar. This wide range of exchange rates had contradictory effects on agriculture: on the one hand, it penalized the exports of agricultural products, reducing their revenues in reais; on the other hand, it favored the purchase of agricultural equipment and inputs at lower domestic prices, because the imported products were supplied at lower prices in reais, which resulted in a decrease in the prices of inputs produced in Brazil.

Beginning in September 1996, these exports were exempted from value added tax in order to compensate for the fall in the profitability of agricultural exports (by the use of the Kandir Law[1]).

On 13 January 1999 a new exchange policy was adopted. The country returned to a floating exchange rate system. However, the financial crises and the lack of central bank reserves prevented the latter from constantly interfering in the foreign currency market until late 2002. Consequently, the bilateral real exchange rate experienced a large devaluation between 1998 and 2002, changing from R$2.21 to the dollar to R$3.69 to the dollar (December 2009 purchasing power), respectively, or in other words a real devaluation of 67 per cent, which greatly stimulated the exports of agricultural and agro-industrial products. Nevertheless, the real bilateral exchange rate in 2002 was still 27 per cent below that which existed in 1986.

Between 2003 and 2009, there was a continued appreciation of the real against the dollar. Brazil's monetary stability and high domestic interest rates caused the massive influx of foreign capital (both for direct investment and for speculative purposes), which caused the real bilateral exchange rate to fall from R$3.69 to the dollar in 2002 to R$1.93 in 2009 (all quoted at December 2009 purchasing power).

One concludes from this survey of Brazil's exchange rate policy that the period from 1987 to 2009 saw lower real exchange rates in relation to the ones existing during two previous decades (from 1965 to 1986; see Figure 5.1), with several phases of currency appreciation. Thus, the exchange rate policy was less favorable to the export segments of the agricultural and agro-industrial sectors, and resulted in an income shift to other sectors of the economy. For each dollar earned through the export of agricultural and agro-industrial products in 2009, an average of R$1.93 was obtained, compared with R$ 4.59 in 1987 (all prices in December 2009 purchasing power).

5.1.2 Minimum Salary Policy

Beginning in the mid 1990s, and especially from 2003, the federal government increased the real value of the minimum wage. The minimum wage is normally readjusted once a year, traditionally on 1 May, and the new rate goes into effect at the beginning of June. However, during the years 2007–10, the federal government moved the announcement of the new minimum wage one month earlier, and since 2010 it has been announced on 1 January, to be paid in February.

Figure 5.2 shows that the real minimum wage fell between 1987 and 1994, in large part owing to the inflationary process that corroded its value

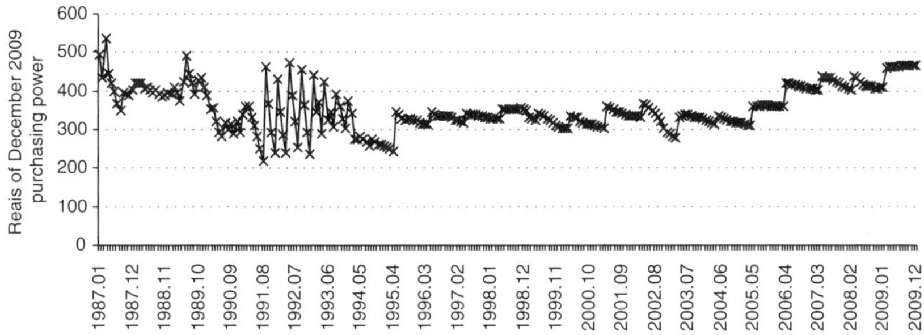

Source: IPEADATA data set.

Figure 5.2 Evolution of minimum wage in Brazil, January 1987 to December 2009.

and to the government's troubles in paying higher salaries. However, since mid 1995 its real value has recuperated. Between December 1994 and December 2009, the real minimum wage rose by 79 per cent.

The increase in the real value of the minimum wage caused a rise in the production cost of agriculture because a large percentage of the Brazilian agricultural workforce is unskilled and receives the minimum wage or a multiple thereof. To offset this, farmers sought to mechanize agricultural activities, employing less labor and thereby increasing the productivity of those who remained in the sector. Agriculture represented 24 per cent of employment in Brazil in 1999 and only 18 per cent in 2008.

Note that the two policies examined above implied, *ceteris paribus*, a reduction in agricultural profitability. The exchange policy (which leads to currency appreciation) reduces the revenue of agriculture. The labor laws (which are an incomes policy that set the minimum wage) have increased the cost of agricultural production.

5.1.3 Public Resources for Agriculture

From the beginning of 1987 the federal government's fiscal crises led to a reduction of public spending. This included a reduction of rural credit subsidies, a reduction in price guarantees, and fewer resources for agricultural research and rural extension services. Moreover, in the 1990s the state began a process of economic deregulation. It decreased many of its regulatory activities, sold or closed many state-owned businesses, and eliminated a number of public regulatory agencies. Many of these activities were linked to agriculture and protected the sector from free market conditions.

Beginning in 1987, rural credit underwent two large changes: first, the

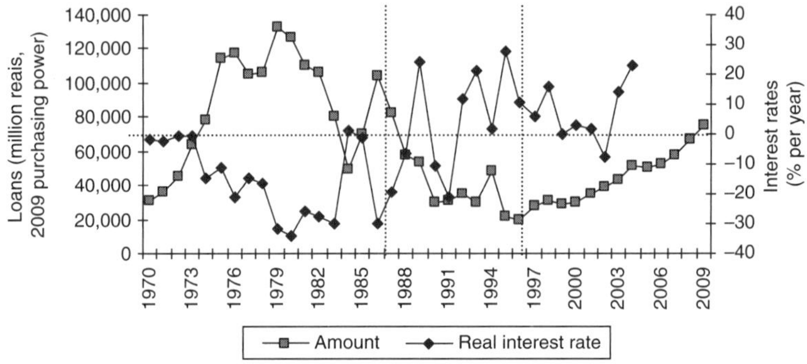

Source: Brazil's Central Bank; also Bacha et al. (2006).

Figure 5.3 Evolution of rural credit amount and real interest rates in Brazil 1970–2009.

volume of rural credit grants decreased significantly between 1986 and 1996, reaching its 1985 level again only in 2009; second, the real interest rate charged for this credit increased continuously, going from negative to positive. These changes were caused by defaults on debt owed by farmers in the second half of the 1980s, and by the government's fiscal crisis in the 1990s, which culminated in a search by the government for new private tools to finance agriculture (see Bacha and Silva, 2005). In general, the amount of credit for agriculture and its cost were less favorable from 1987 onwards than those that strengthened it from 1970 until the mid 1980s (Figure 5.3).

The fiscal crisis which affected both federal and state governments led, from the second half of the 1980s onwards, to a pronounced decline of public expenditures for agricultural activities. Table 5.1 shows that the deflated value of the federal government's expenditures on agriculture had a strong tendency to fall, with agriculture's share of total government expenditures dropping from 8.6 per cent in 1988 to 1.3 per cent in 2009. This resulted in a pronounced fall in rural extension services in the 1990s and in resources for agricultural research.

This same budgetary austerity also resulted in a decline of the effectiveness of the policy of guaranteed minimum prices (PGPM), which was administered via the acquisitions of the federal government (AGF, Aquisições do Governo Federal) and federal government loans (EGF). Barros (1995, p. 6), commenting on agricultural policy in the second half of the 1980s and the first half of the 1990s, states: 'Rare were the occasions on which the government was capable of disclosing prices in advance, providing resources at an opportune time for finance or acquisition, and manage official stocks in order to provide price stability in agricultural markets.'

Table 5.1 Brazil: federal expenditures, total and on agriculture and agrarian organization (reais with 2009 purchasing power)

Year	Total union expenditures (reais)	Union expenditures on agriculture and agrarian organization (reais)	Share of agriculture and agrarian organization in union expenditure (%)
1988	411,377,938,590	35,518,468,584	8.63
1989	968,110,233,950	18,676,907,608	1.93
1990	1,388,199,899,633	26,928,658,669	1.94
1991	573,462,383,422	25,134,676,406	4.38
1992	721,135,445,274	18,087,868,602	2.51
1993	834,498,052,087	21,160,761,503	2.54
1994	604,538,252,831	22,292,864,345	3.69
1995	525,722,785,034	27,811,876,293	5.29
1996	549,467,633,083	19,322,216,928	3.52
1997	726,976,325,417	24,794,526,791	3.41
1998	829,436,126,380	18,353,281,083	2.21
1999	784,018,482,420	19,631,362,093	2.50
2000	680,757,185,546	13,328,639,501	1.96
2001	749,766,719,228	13,320,757,267	1.78
2002	756,543,475,421	11,855,661,246	1.57
2003	692,230,375,861	11,133,803,283	1.61
2004	697,375,122,561	13,150,019,003	1.89
2005	734,573,874,474	14,603,299,874	1.99
2006	949,249,326,795	16,801,945,105	1.77
2007	1,319,622,863,214	18,040,858,856	1.37
2008	1,272,537,648,775	14,205,855,044	1.12
2009	1,423,883,440,563	18,941,739,736	1.33

Source: Gasques et al. (2010, p. 84).

Since 1997, the federal government has been using the Prime Program (Programa Prêmio Escoamento de Produto, PEP) for shifting agricultural products and the sale of options contracts for the sale of agricultural products (contratos de opção de venda de produtores agropecuários, COVPA) as tools to guarantee minimum prices. PEP does not involve costs to the producer, but it has been used in a selective manner by the federal government. COVPA involves costs to the producer, equal to the insurance premium of the selling price.

Table 5.2 shows that the use of AGF and EGF (Federal loans to farming producers) has been decreasing in the long run. From 1985 to 1989, 44.4 per cent of domestic rice production was supported through

Table 5.2 Brazilian agriculture importance of PGPM tools in some crop productions (percentages)

Crop	1985–89		1990–96		1997–2004			
	AGF	EGF	AGF	EGF	AGF	EGF	PEP	COVPA
Cotton	6.3	47.6	–	–	0.76	0	7.33	1.52
Rice	17.8	26.6	4.66	14.82	2.02	0	0	2.22
Coffee	–	–	–	–	0	0	0	1.46
Beans	6.9	4.7	–	–	0.87	0	0	0
Corn	13.9	10.5	2.1	9.47	2.29	0	0.41	2.53
Soybeans	5.1	16.4	0	4.98	0	0	0	0
Wheat	–	–	–	–	6.22	0	10.3	3.6

Notes: The percentage for a period is the mean of the percentages for the years within that period. The 2004 data set ranges until 11 November 2004.
–: No significant data available.

Sources: 1985–89: Goldin and Rezende (1993, p. 56); 1990–96: Rezende (2002); the data set for 1997–2004 was collected from the Conab webpage, http://www.conab.gov.br.

the AGF and EGF. In the period from 1990 to 1996, this percentage declined to 19.48 per cent, and fell to only 2.02 per cent between 1997 and 2004.

The 1990s witnessed profound institutional changes aimed at economic deregulation and the sale of state-owned enterprises. During the deregulation process, the following occurred:

1. The liberalization of wheat imports and sugar exports beginning in 1990.
2. The extinction of the Brazilian Enterprise for Support and Rural Extension (Embrater, in Portuguese), of the Sugar and Alcohol Institute (IAA), of the Brazilian Institute of Coffee (IBC) and of other agencies specifically supporting agricultural production.
3. During the 1990s, state-owned fertilizer producers were sold, leaving the price level for this input to be determined by the market.
4. Also during the 1990s there was a progressive decrease in the interference of state price controls on products in the production chain of sugarcane, such that in February 1999 all of the products from this chain came to have their prices determined in the market and were no longer subsidized by the state (Barros and Moraes, 2002).

5.1.4 Agricultural Research Policies

Agricultural research in Brazil is conducted by both public and private organizations. Among the first group, Embrapa (Brazilian Agricultural Research Corporation), public universities (with MSc and PhD courses) and state-funded agricultural institutes are the main players. In the second group are large multinational agro-industry firms (such as Monsanto, Syngenta, and Bunge) and farmers' organizations (such as Fundação Mato Grosso, Aprosoja and large cooperatives). However, information is only available about research results produced by public entities and especially by Embrapa. The latter has an efficient bureau to communicate its results, which leaves the erroneous impression that Embrapa is the only agency conducting agricultural research in Brazil and the only one responsible for the occupation of the Brazilian cerrado.

Embrapa was created on 7 December 1972 and began to operate in the following year. It was created as a public enterprise, which permits it to receive grants from both public and private sectors and has experimental stations in all regions of Brazil. According to Alves (2010), from 1973 to 2008, the federal government allocated around US$6 billion to Embrapa. Its success is based on several aspects, such as focusing on practical researches and spending large sums to announce results through a massive communications network. This left the impression that the agricultural expansion in the cerrado was all due to Embrapa's researches, such as recently reported by *The Economist* (2010, p. 3):

> Since 1996 Brazilian farmers have increased the amount of land under cultivation by a third, mostly in the cerrado. That is quite different from other big farm producers, whose amount of land under the plough has either been flat or (in Europe) falling. And it has increased production by ten times that amount. But the availability of farmland is in fact only a secondary reason for the extraordinary growth in Brazilian agriculture. If you want the primary reason in three words, they are Embrapa, Embrapa, Embrapa.

This is only partially true. Embrapa is an important research institution, but it is not the sole entity doing agriculture research. An important number of Embrapa's researchers got their science master and doctoral titles at public universities in Brazil, where they conducted the researches that have been attributed solely to Embrapa. Also, state-funded institutes have agreements with Embrapa for conducting research projects. Table 5.3 shows just how important are the three legs of public support for agriculture research in Brazil.

Table 5.3 Brazilian public institutions conducting agricultural researches – information for 1996

Institution	Number of units	Number of researchers	Amount received in 1996 (US$ million)
Embrapa	37 centers plus headquarters[a]	2,093	525
State institutes	19	2,341	218
Public universities		2,397[a]	

Note: [a] Equivalent researchers, based on the time that all academic staff allocate to researches.

Source: Portugal and Contini (1997).

5.2 THE PERFORMANCE OF AGRICULTURE 1987–2009

In spite of the significant reduction in agricultural stimulus (in particular that due to the fall in the real exchange rate, the growth in the value of the real minimum wage, the enlargement of real interest rates of rural credit, the decrease in the coverage of minimum price policy, and the decline of public expenditures), agriculture expanded in Brazil in the period under discussion and did so with less use of both land and labor.

Table 5.4 presents some information from the Brazilian agricultural censuses since 1970. Before analyzing these data, it should be noted that the 1995/96 agricultural census introduced changes in methodology, and comparisons between earlier and later data must be made cautiously. The main modification is a change to the reference dates for some variables. These dates are: (1) the data concerning area, employment figures, and information about machinery – 31 December 1995; (2) the data on livestock – 31 July, 1996; (3) the production data – crop year 1995/96. The other agricultural censuses since 1970 (including that of 2006) have data on area, employment figures, machinery, and livestock numbers computed for 31 December of the reference year of the census. The production data refer to the calendar year of the census.

Thus the data on area, employment figures, and equipment from the census since 1970, including the 1995/96 census, refer to the same day of the year (31 December) and may be compared with one another. The data on livestock figures and the production value from the 1995/96 census do not refer to the same data as those since 1970, including 2006, and comparisons between the two should be cautiously interpreted.

Table 5.4 Brazilian agriculture: some census indicators

Indicator	1970	1980	1985	1995–96[a]	2006
Number of agricultural establishments	4,924,019	5,159,851	5,801,809	4,859,865	5,175,489
Total farming area (thousands of hectares)	294,145	364,854	374,925	353,611	329,941
Number of employed people	17,582,089	21,163,735	23,394,919	17,930,890	16,567,544
Annual cropland (ha)	25,999,728	38,632,128	42,244,221	34,252,829	48,234,391
Permanent cropland (ha)	7,984,068	10,472,135	9,903,487	7,541,626	11,612,227
Number of cows	78,562,250	118,085,872	128,041,757	153,058,275	171,613,337
Number of pigs	31,523,640	32,628,723	30,481,278	27,811,244	31,189,339
Number of poultry	218,937,380	421,933,117	446,924,170	735,399,000	1,401,341,000
Number of tractors	165,870	545,205	665,280	803,742	820,673
Ratio of fertilizer consumption to cropland (kg/ha)[b]	29.4	85.5	61.3	110.2	350.6
Ratio of total farming area to number of tractors (thousand of hectares per each tractor)	1.77	0.67	0.56	0.44	0.402

Notes:

a Information about area, employed people and tractors refers to 31 December, 1995; information about numbers of animals refers to 31 July, 1996.

b Only nutrients are taken into consideration.

Source: Agricultural censuses of Brazil.

The data in Table 5.4 show a disappearance of 942,000 agricultural establishments in Brazil between 1985 and 1995, and the emergence of 316,000 establishments between 1995 and 2006. Consequently, the number of agricultural establishments was smaller in 2006 than in 1985. The total

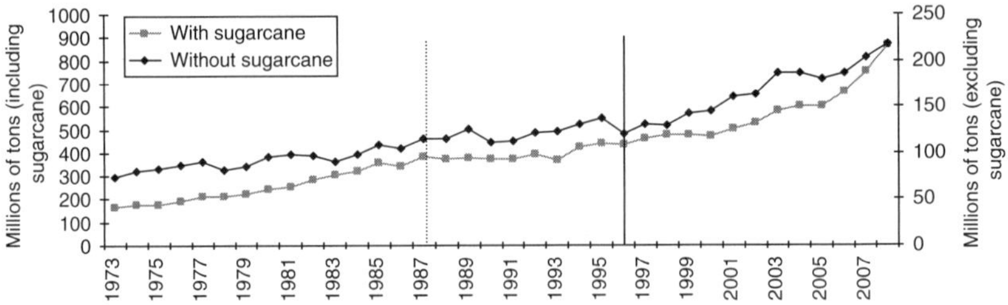

Source: Brazil's Yearbook, several issues.

Figure 5.4 Evolution of Brazilian production of main crops 1973–2008 (including and excluding sugarcane).

area of those establishments has been falling since the mid 1980s. This area was reduced by 21.3 million hectares between 1985 and 1995 and by 23.7 million between 1995 and 2006, going from 374.9 million hectares in 1985 to 329.9 million hectares in 2006. The number of people employed in agriculture went from 23.4 million in 1985 to 16.6 million in 2006.

In spite of reductions in the total area of agricultural establishments and in the number of people employed, the production of both crops and animals increased in the period of analysis (1987 to 2009). Figure 5.4 shows the evolution of production for the 37 and 38 main crops grown in Brazil.[2] Among these 38 crops is sugarcane, which was withdrawn to form the 37 principal crops grown in Brazil, because sugarcane shows the highest volume of production per hectare and its inclusion could distort the analysis.

Notice in Figure 5.4 (above) that there was an increase in crop production from 1987 on, going from 343 million tons in 1986 to 863 million tons in 2008, if you include sugarcane. By excluding this crop, we see that production rose from 104 million tons in 1987 to 218 million in 2008. This follows the pattern of growth observed since 1973. However, notice that the growth is more accentuated beginning in 2000 and is strongly associated with the booms in soybeans and sugarcane production, as will be shown later.

Figure 5.5 (opposite) shows the changes in meat production. Notice that the weight of carcasses grew from 3.8 million tons in 1986 to 19.5 million tons in 2009. Also notable is poultry production, which grew from 1.2 million tons in 1986 to 9.9 million tons in 2009, and the strong increase in pig and cattle production, beginning in 2000. Changes in meat production in the period 1987 to 2009 differ from those in the prior period. A significant part of the recent growth in Brazilian meat production, especially in the 2000s, is explained by the growth of Brazilian exports of these products.

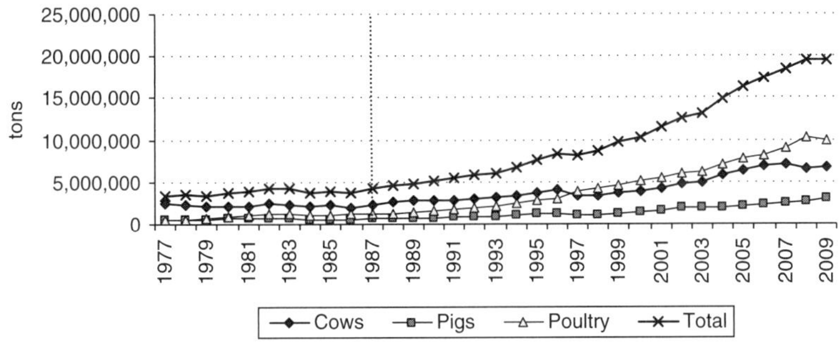

Source: IBGE.

Figure 5.5 Brazilian production of meats 1977–2009.

The growth of crop and animal production, in a context of reduced total area of agricultural establishments and total number of employed people, was only possible through increased land and labor productivity. Figure 5.6 shows the changes in production and harvested land for the 38 main crops in Brazil, including sugarcane. Figure 5.7 shows the same variables for the 37 main crops, excluding sugarcane. Notice that the curves on both graphs have the same shape, with differences only in the level of productivity, which is larger in the case in which sugarcane crops are included (see Figure 5.6, below).

Deeper examination of Figures 5.6 and 5.7 shows a reduction in area occupied by crops and a strong increase in productivity from 1987 to 1996. From 1997 on, there was a large growth in cropland, along with

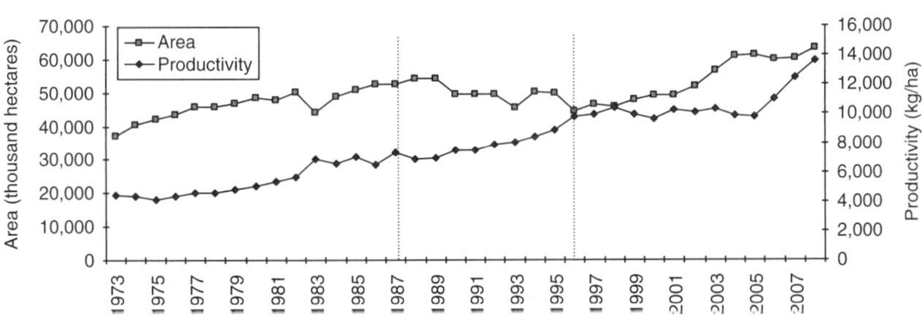

Source: Brazil's Yearbook.

Figure 5.6 Evolution of area and productivity of the 38 main crops in Brazil 1973–2008.

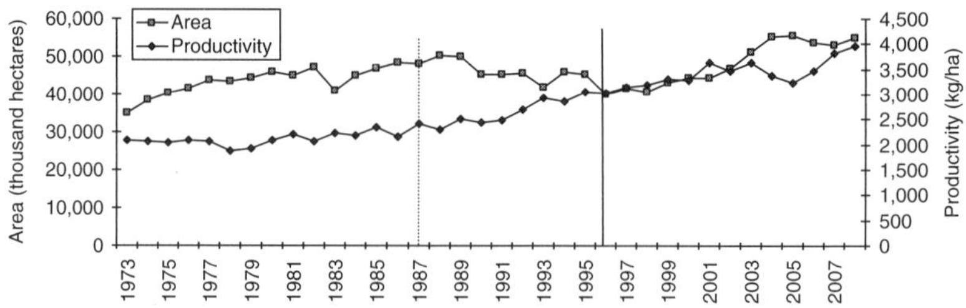

Source: Brazil's Yearbook.

Figure 5.7 Evolution of area and productivity of the 37 main crops in Brazil 1973–2008

a small growth in productivity. But how can cropland increase from 1997 on if agricultural census data indicate that the total farming area decreased between 1995 and 2006? This occurred because the production of soybeans, corn and wheat experienced large expansions during this period and these crops can occupy the same area, i.e., by planting soy in September of year *t* and harvesting it in March of year *t + 1*, then planting corn (or wheat) in April of year *t + 1* and harvesting it in August of year *t + 1*, freeing the area to be planted once again with soy in September and continuing the scheme.

The aggregate data on crops hide behavioral differences in the evolution of the harvested area and the productivity between them. Table 5.5 shows that the most dynamic crops in the foreign market (like sugarcane, oranges and soy) experienced growth in harvested area. Between 1986 and 1996, the harvested area of sugarcane grew 1.08 per cent per year, despite the fact that during these years Pró-álcool (a huge federal program to stimulate alcohol production, started in mid 1970s) was in a declining phase. The harvested area of oranges grew 2.24 per cent per year and the harvested area for soy grew 1.23 per cent per year. These were, however, geometrically much lower annual growth rates in area than those obtained in the previous time period (1964 to 1986). In the last period, the harvested areas for sugarcane, oranges and soy grew 4.35 per cent, 7.97 per cent and 16.41 per cent per year, respectively. However, the harvested area of these three crops (sugar, oranges and soy) grew from 1986 to 1996, while the harvested area of all the others (except potatoes and corn) analyzed in Table 5.5 fell, in line with the pattern of the sum of the 38 main crops planted in Brazil (see Figure 5.6). With the exception of cocoa, all of the main domestic and foreign-market-oriented crops saw great increases in land productivity.

In the period from 1996 to 2008, as we can see in Figure 5.6, there was an increase in the harvested area of the 38 main crops cultivated in Brazil.

Table 5.5 Brazil: annual geometric growth rates (per cent) of harvested area and productivity for some crops

Main destination	Crop	1964–86		1986–96		1996–2008	
		Area	Productivity	Area	Productivity	Area	Productivity
Domestic market	Rice	1.40	1.40	−4.59	3.83	−0.59	3.74
	Beans	2.40	2.40	−1.84	4.54	−0.57	3.25
	Cassava	0.83	0.83	−1.35	0.07	2.02	1.18
	Potatoes	−1.24	−1.24	0.19	2.04	−1.80	4.59
	Corn	1.61	1.61	0.03	4.03	1.33	3.50
Foreign market	Cotton	−1.06	−1.06	−11.67	4.59	4.15	9.06
	Cocoa	1.28	1.28	−1.31	−4.60	−0.98	−1.33
	Coffee	−1.32	−1.32	−4.54	2.12	1.22	−3.49
	Sugarcane	4.35	4.35	1.08	0.96	3.87	1.31
	Oranges	7.97	7.97	2.24	1.56	−1.92	2.14
	Soybeans	16.41	16.41	1.23	3.52	6.68	1.19
	Wheat	6.05	6.05	−12.32	0.29	3.93	2.36

Note: Annual geometric growth rate was calculated using the following formula: $\ln Y = a + b \cdot t$, where Y is harvested area or productivity for each crop and t is time.

Source: Rates calculated from Brazil's Yearbook data set.

One can see in Table 5.5 that cotton, coffee, sugarcane, soy, wheat, cassava and corn had the greatest expansion in harvested area. There is a sharp increase in the area of crops directed to foreign markets (except the traditional coffee and cacao crops) and a large increase in productivity of crops aimed at the domestic market.

Soy and sugarcane crops have been expanding and occupying more land in Brazil. Between 1996 and 2008, the harvested area of the 38 principal crops in Brazil expanded by 18,594 thousand hectares, 58.9 per cent of which was used for soy and 18.2 per cent for sugarcane.

Livestock (except for swine) also saw significant growth in the period under analysis. Between 31 December 1985 and 31 July 2006 the number of cattle grew by 34 per cent and the number of poultry increased by 213.6 per cent. The number of swine rose by only 2.3 per cent between these two dates.

The increase in agricultural productivity in the period of 1987 to 2008 was due in part to the rise in mechanization and use of fertilizers. Despite the reduced amount of rural credit in the first half of the period under analysis and the fact that this credit is no longer subsidized, the amount

Table 5.6 Brazilian agriculture: regional concentration indicators (percentages of whole country)

Region	Year	Gross value of production	Total farming area	Temporary cropland	Permanent cropland	Herd size			Tractors
						Cows	Pigs	Poultry	
North	1970	3.08	7.88	1.86	1.66	2.17	2.88	3.58	0.68
	1985	3.98	12.06	3.18	6.90	4.19	7.10	3.77	1.03
	1995–96	4.11	11.76	2.92	9.35	7.88	7.16	3.55	1.31
	2006	3.74	12.27	3.76	15.16	14.72	4.32	1.84	2.06
Tocantins	1985	0.73	4.63	1.42	0.55	2.81	1.30	0.49	0.78
	1995–96	0.75	4.74	0.71	0.30	3.41	0.78	0.33	0.99
	2006	0.53	4.33	1.11	0.86	3.54	0.81	0.32	1.21
Northeast	1970	18.33	25.26	24.40	49.82	17.57	22.51	17.00	4.39
	1985	24.55	17.04	23.87	42.95	17.49	25.83	17.95	6.27
	1995–96	14.74	14.05	22.47	35.13	14.92	22.86	14.40	6.90
	2006	19.76	22.91	24.15	30.24	14.76	12.63	8.59	7.60
Center-West	1970	7.46	27.78	8.69	1.80	21.96	7.96	5.67	6.23
	1985	9.75	26.44	16.12	2.39	28.21	8.36	4.63	12.96
	1995–96	14.40	30.69	18.48	3.27	33.17	8.10	5.93	14.27
	2006	13.79	31.46	23.84	6.13	33.52	11.76	12.05	15.53
Southeast	1970	37.31	23.63	28.61	27.22	34.17	18.39	41.46	49.75
	1985	38.47	19.53	23.17	38.10	27.91	18.39	33.52	35.92
	1995–96	34.59	18.12	21.38	43.37	23.49	16.17	36.54	34.84
	2006	33.34	16.44	18.94	34.78	19.85	16.78	31.20	31.30
South	1970	33.81	15.45	36.43	19.50	24.12	48.26	32.29	38.95
	1985	30.03	12.79	32.24	9.11	19.39	39.02	39.63	43.04
	1995–96	31.41	12.54	34.04	8.58	17.13	44.93	39.25	41.69
	2006	28.83	12.59	28.21	12.83	13.61	53.71	45.99	42.28

Source: Agricultural censuses of Brazil – several years.

of farming area for each tractor decreased, so that while in 1985 there was one tractor for every 560 hectares of total farming area, in 1995/96 there was one tractor for every 440 hectares. The quantity of fertilizers (considering only the nutrients) per hectare of crops was 61.3 kg in 1985 and 110.2 kg in 1995/96, jumping to 350.6 kg in 2006 (see Table 5.4).

5.2.1 Regional Distribution

From the point of view of the regional distribution of agricultural activities, it is noticeable that there is a substantial concentration in the Southeast and South, although this concentration is decreasing. Table 5.6 shows that in 1985 these two regions accounted for 32.32 per cent of total agricultural establishments, but were responsible for 68.5 per cent of the gross value produced by the country's agriculture. Both regions also accounted for 55.41 per cent of the areas for temporary crops, for 47.21 per cent for permanent crops and for 78.96 per cent of tractors. In 2006, these percentages were, respectively, 29.03 per cent, 62.17 per cent, 47.15 per cent, 47.61 per cent and 73.58 per cent. The Southeast is becoming less important for Brazilian agriculture, in large part owing to its strong urbanization, which increases the price of land and provides an incentive to convert agricultural land to urban usage. Simultaneously, the Center-West has been of increasing importance in agriculture.

There are strong connections between Southeastern and Center-Western farmers. The southerners migrated during the 1970s and 1980s to the Center-West and expanded grain crops (soy and corn, mainly) and the raising of poultry and swine. It can be observed in Table 5.6 that the Center-West held 8.69 per cent of Brazil's temporary crops in 1970, and this percentage rose to 16.12 per cent in 1985 and to 23.84 per cent in 2006. The Center-West held 4.63 per cent of the poultry population on 31 December 1985, and 12.05 per cent on 31 December 2006. These percentages for swine were, respectively, 8.36 per cent and 11.76 per cent.

In the 2000s, a new agricultural frontier has been the Northeastern cerrado. The region called MAPITO (a band of cerrado convergence of Maranhão, Piauí, and Tocantins) and the Bahian cerrado have been attracting grain-growers, especially those from the Center-West. Now, the ex-Southerners migrate to the Brazilian Northeast and make large grain plantations a part of this region (*The Economist*, 2010).

5.3 AGRICULTURAL GDP AND WORKERS' EARNINGS

The gross domestic product of agriculture in deflated values decreased between 1987 and 1993 (Figure 5.8) owing to the strong currency appreciation that occurred during these years (Figure 5.1) and to the income transfer from agriculture to other sectors. This effect more than compensated for the growth of physical agricultural production for these years (see Figures 5.4 and 5.5). Beginning in 1998, however, the larger growth in agricultural production together, at times, with increases in international agricultural and agro-industrial commodity prices surpassed the continued currency appreciation and allowed for the recovery of the agricultural GDP. Figure 5.8 shows that in 2009 the agricultural GDP was slightly lower than in 1986. This outcome shows that farmers did not see a gain

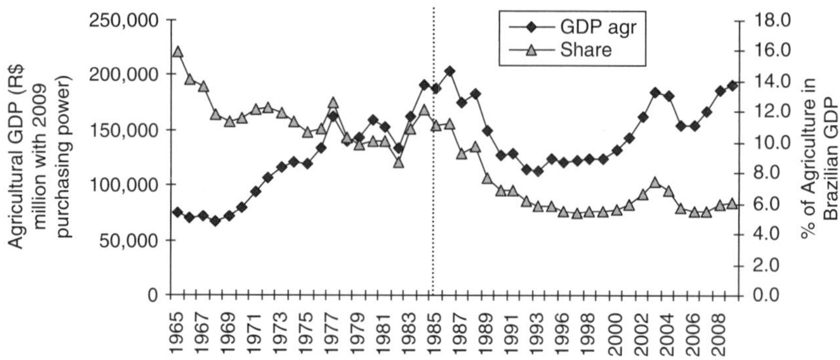

Source: Data set of IPEADATA (elaborated by the author).

Figure 5.8 Evolution of agricultural GDP and its share of Brazilian GDP 1965–2009.

in real income with the recent agricultural boom, because despite the 152 per cent increase in the physical production of agriculture between 1986 and 2008 and the 419 per cent increase in meat production from 1986 to 2009, the agricultural GDP (measured in 2009 prices) fell by 6.1 per cent between the years 1986 and 2009. This is further proof that the exchange rate policy has served to transfer income from agriculture to other sectors of the economy.

This dynamic of real agricultural GDP was accompanied by the reduced importance of the sector in total GDP. Its share fell from 11.2 per cent in 1986 to 6.1 per cent in 2009 (see Figure 5.8).

Despite the oscillation of the agricultural GDP during the last two decades, agricultural workers have seen their real salaries increase, while income inequalities among them have decreased. Table 5.7 shows average and median values of both permanent and temporary workers in agriculture and three measures of their income distribution (Gini and Theil *T* and *L* indexes). Comparing 1992 and 2008, real salaries of agricultural workers increased 73 per cent for permanent workers and 71 per cent for temporary ones. Meanwhile, the Gini index among permanent employees' income dropped by 15 per cent and among temporary workers fell 8 per cent during the same period. According to Oliveira and Hoffmann, the increase of the real value of the minimum salary (shown in Figure 5.2) answers partly for these phenomena, as the minimum salary is a reference for permanent workers receiving lower wages and for temporary workers receiving higher wages.

Table 5.7 *Brazil 1992–2008: evolution of salaries and income distribution inequality among agricultural workers*

Year	Permanent employees					Temporary employees				
	Average[a]	Median[a]	Gini index	*T* Theil	*L* Theil	Average[a]	Median[a]	Gini index	*T* Theil	*L* Theil
1992	327.8	286.5	0.3776	0.2765	0.2709	200.4	164.6	0.3773	0.2609	0.2586
1993	327.0	254.9	0.3792	0.2300	0.2786	190.0	159.2	0.3916	0.2904	0.2797
1995	363.8	273.2	0.3459	0.2492	0.2118	250.1	227.7	0.3338	0.2016	0.1965
1996	375.9	283.6	0.3506	0.2498	0.2130	275.7	226.9	0.3421	0.2099	0.2029
1997	386.7	291.2	0.3476	0.2432	0.2126	245.7	217.4	0.3156	0.1811	0.1808
1998	394.1	301.4	0.3335	0.2355	0.2006	241.2	216.6	0.3179	0.1730	0.1851
1999	389.9	318.5	0.3386	0.2779	0.2107	242.5	212.4	0.3246	0.1817	0.1884
2001	394.2	308.2	0.3290	0.2228	0.2004	224.8	184.9	0.3322	0.1937	0.2078
2002	387.8	280.4	0.3276	0.2378	0.2021	236.6	210.3	0.3361	0.1937	0.2124
2003	381.6	297.6	0.3049	0.1866	0.1721	237.8	216.0	0.3300	0.1858	0.2086
2004	416.7	328.8	0.3126	0.2094	0.1857	254.2	226.8	0.3311	0.1895	0.2073
2005	443.9	344.9	0.3182	0.2319	0.1953	264.1	215.5	0.3407	0.1981	0.2217
2006	466.8	367.0	0.3058	0.1972	0.1841	288.4	251.6	0.3445	0.1976	0.2254
2007	548.0	428.6	0.3146	0.2156	0.1926	325.4	267.9	0.3432	0.1993	0.2193
2008	567.2	420.0	0.3199	0.2128	0.1963	342.9	300.0	0.3472	0.2025	0.2342

Note: [a] Values in reais purchasing power of September–October 2008.

Source: Oliveira and Hoffmann (2010, pp. 6–11), which calculated the above values from a primary PNAD data set.

5.4 BEHAVIOR OF EXTERNAL TRANSACTIONS FOR AGRICULTURE AND AGRO-INDUSTRIAL PRODUCTS

A significant share of agricultural production expansion in the past 10 years has been destined for exports, which caused the trade balance for agricultural products to be always positive and growing.

Figure 5.9 shows that Brazilian agriculture and agro-industrial exports grew from US$9.7 billion in 1987 to US$49.9 billion in 2007. Two phenomena regarding agriculture-based export growth must be stressed: first, they became less important to Brazilian exports as a whole, although they remain very important. In 1985, agriculture and agro-industrial products represented 39.9 per cent of Brazil's global exports and in 2007 this percentage was 31.3 per cent. Second, fluctuations took place in the growth of agriculture and agro-industrial exports between 1987 and 2007. These exports fell from 1988 to 1991, grew from 1992 to 1997, and fell again from 1998 to 2000. From 2001 on there was continuous growth of agriculture and agro-industrial exports. It is interesting to note that the bilateral real exchange rate fell from 1992 to 1997 (see Figure 5.1) and tended to rise from 1998 to 2000. From 2003 on, a continuous currency appreciation has taken place. These trends in the exchange rate would lead to a decline of exports between 1992 and 1997, to a rise between 1998 and 2000, and to a fall from 2003 onwards, or in other words, the expected results caused by exchange rate trends were very different from those that actually occurred. This indicates that, in the period of analysis, the export of agricultural and agro-industrial products reacted to variables other than only the real bilateral exchange rate oscillation. One of them was the international price of agricultural

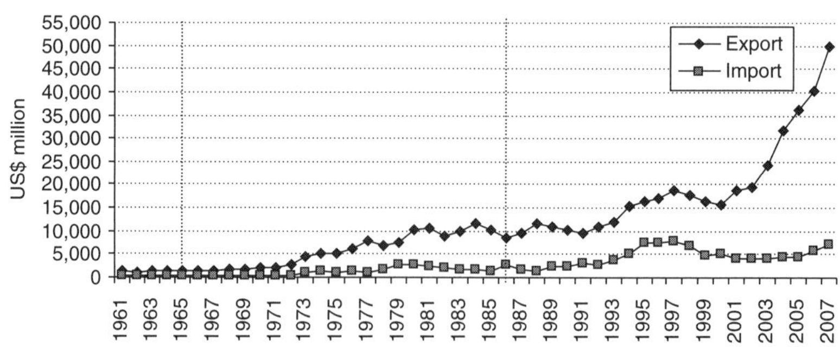

Source: FAO.

Figure 5.9 Evolution of Brazilian exports and imports of agriculture and agro-industrial products 1961–2007.

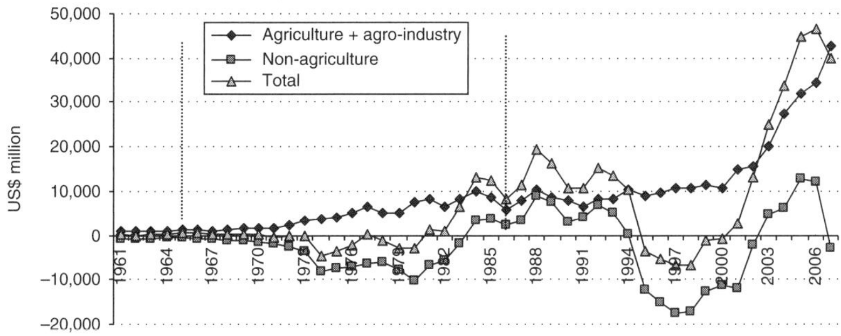

Source: FAO and IPEA.

Figure 5.10 Evolution of Brazil's trade balance 1961–2007.

commodities, which often rose during periods of currency appreciation and fell during periods of depreciation. Another element stimulating Brazilian agriculture-based exports is the expanding markets that enter into contracts which will be fulfilled regardless of changes in the exchange rate.

Figure 5.9 also shows a significant growth of Brazilian imports of agriculture and agro-industrial products from 1989 onwards, especially after 1993. In 1988, imports of these products totaled US$1.3 billion. In 1993, they were US$3.7 billion, and in 1997 they reached US$7.9 billion. With the process of real devaluation of the Brazilian currency from 1999 to 2002, these imports fell to US$3.9 billion in 2002. The gradual removal of import barriers from 1990 onwards also explains the growth of agriculture and agro-industrial imports. But in spite of the strong currency appreciation that began in 2003, the growth of agriculture and agro-industrial products was small because Brazil had become one of the world's largest exporters of agriculture and agro-industrial commodities and therefore did not need to import them, except those in which the country does not have advantages in production costs arising from soil and climatic conditions (like the case of fruits and grains typical of temperate climates).

Owing to agricultural exports growing faster than agricultural imports, these two segments of Brazilian agribusiness have been generating positive and growing balances of trade surpluses. It can be observed in Figure 5.10 that agriculture and agro-industry generated a trade surplus of US$7.9 billion in 1987 and US$42.8 billion in 2007, while there was a US$2.8 billion trade deficit of non-agricultural and agro-industrial goods in 2007. It must be concluded, therefore, that agriculture and agro-industry are the sectors that produce the positive balance of trade for Brazil.

5.5 THE ROLES OF AGRICULTURE IN THE ECONOMIC DEVELOPMENT PROCESS

Agriculture has, basically, six important functions in the process of economic development:

1. Provide food for the population.
2. Provide capital for the expansion of non-agricultural sectors.
3. Provide labor for the growth and diversification of economic activities.
4. Provide foreign currency for the purchase of inputs and capital goods necessary for national economic development.
5. Participate in the consumer market by purchasing the products of the non-agricultural sector.
6. Provide high quality raw materials at lower prices for the industrialization of the country.

In the period from 1987 to 2009, agriculture fulfilled five of these six functions, or in other words it provided food for the population, transferred income to other sectors for investment, generated foreign currency with which other sectors of the economy could import inputs and capital goods as well as consumer goods, participated in the consumer market and provided raw materials for industry. Despite continued rural–urban migration during the period under review, it is no longer necessary in the development of the non-agricultural sectors in the Brazilian economy.

The data set in Table 5.8 shows per capita production of fruits grew almost 6 per cent from 1996 to 2006 and per capita production of food and agricultural raw materials grew by 39 per cent and 25 per cent, respectively. Considering all 61 crops together, per capita production grew by 27 per cent from 1996 to 2006. So, agriculture has fulfilled its role as a food supplier.

In the period from 1987 to 2009, there was a significant process of direct income transfer from agriculture to other sectors of the Brazilian economy, especially those dependent on imported products. This was done through an exchange rate policy that caused currency appreciation. This process was only partially offset by the few times in which there were subsidies for rural credit and export incentives from VAT exception for unprocessed agricultural products from September of 1996 on.

Rural–urban migration has been ongoing in Brazil since the end of World War II, including the post-1986 period, despite the fact that these migrants are no longer needed in industry. The data in Table 5.9 shows that from 1980 to 1990 there was an annual average of 1.2 million

Table 5.8 Brazil 1996–2006 evolution of per capita production and productivity of crops

	Per capita production (kg/person)		Growth rate of per capita production		Per capita production (kg/person)		Growth rate of per capita production		Per capita production (kg/person)		Growth rate of per capita production
	1996	2006	%		1996	2006	%		1996	2006	%
Fruits				**Industrial raw materials**				**Food and beverages**			
Apples	2.63	4.62	75.82	African oil palm (fruits)	4.59	6.46	40.87	Annatto (seeds)	0.05	0.06	12.53
Avocados	0.96	0.88	−8.37	American upland cotton (seeds)	5.90	15.52	163.00	Barley (grain)	1.30	1.09	−16.22
Bananas	34.51	37.24	7.93	Castor oil bean	0.26	0.51	98.46	Beans	15.20	18.51	21.80
Figs	0.11	0.14	25.25	Creole cotton (seeds)	0.01	0.00	−75.39	Black pepper	0.20	0.43	114.66
Grapes	4.25	6.73	58.53	Jute (fiber)	0.00	0.03	737.73	Broad (fava) beans (grain)	0.13	0.08	−40.60
Guavas	1.23	1.76	43.04	Linen	0.02	0.07	327.96	Chestnuts	1.04	1.31	25.92
Kakis (or persimmons)	0.61	0.90	47.91	Mallow (fiber)	0.02	0.11	329.16	Cocoa	1.59	1.14	−28.60
Lemons	4.94	5.52	11.73	Natural latex rubber	0.55	0.94	70.15	Coconut	5.93	10.63	79.29
Mangos	3.84	6.52	69.89	Ramie (fiber)	0.03	0.01	−78.06	Coffee	16.97	13.78	−18.83
Melons	1.13	2.68	136.80	Sisal fibers	0.75	1.33	76.48	Corn (maize)	183.81	228.42	24.27

Table 5.8 (continued)

	Per capita production (kg/person)		Growth rate of per capita production		Per capita production (kg/person)		Growth rate of per capita produc-tion		Per capita production (kg/person)		Growth rate of per capita produc-tion
	1996	2006	%		1996	2006	%		1996	2006	%
Oranges	107.80	96.55	−10.44	Sugarcane	1965.66	2448.17	24.55	Garlic	0.33	0.47	44.54
Papayas	6.80	10.16	49.33	Tobacco (leaves)	2.95	4.82	63.16	Guarana	0.02	0.02	−13.80
Passion fruits	3.63	3.29	−9.14	Tung oil tree (dried fruits)	0.00	0.00	−47.66	Heart of palm	0.01	0.39	4014.78
Peaches	0.74	1.07	43.58	**Subtotal**	**1980.76**	**2477.97**	**25.10**	Cassava	109.99	142.63	29.68
Pears	0.13	0.10	−25.82					Nut	0.01	0.01	−5.77
Pineapples	7.10	9.14	28.67					Oats (grain)	1.35	2.17	61.15
Quinces	0.01	0.00	−36.04					Onions	5.62	7.21	28.22
Tangerines	5.17	6.80	31.47					Paraguay tea (green leaves)	1.33	2.33	74.90
Water-melons	7.44	10.42	40.03					Peas (grain)	0.02	0.02	28.42
Subtotal	**193.03**	**204.53**	**5.96**					Peanuts	0.96	1.34	39.92

Potatoes	14.95	16.87	12.84
Rice	53.63	61.72	15.07
Rye (grain)	0.04	0.01	−71.13
Sorghum	2.21	8.59	288.78
Soybeans	143.61	280.90	95.61
Sweet potatoes	2.57	2.78	8.11
Tea (green leaves)	0.16	0.09	−43.37
Tomatoes	16.42	18.00	9.66
Wheat (grain)	20.41	13.30	−34.82
Subtotal	**599.86**	**834.30**	**39.08**
Total	**2,773.65**	**3,516.80**	**26.79**

Source: *Statistical Yearbook of Brazil*, Rio de Janerio: IBGE.

Table 5.9 Rural–urban migration

Period	Number of migrants (thousands of persons)	Annual average of migrants (thousands of persons)	Share of migrants in relation to rural population at the beginning of the period (%)
1950–60	10,824	1,082	32.6
1960–70	11,464	1,146	29.6
1970–80	14,413	1,441	35.1
1980–90	12,135	1,213	31.5
1990–95	5,654	1,131	29.3[a]

Note: [a] This rate was calculated for 10 years in order to compare with other rates.

Source: Camarano and Abramovay (1999, p. 3).

rural–urban migrants. In the period from 1990 to 1995 this number was 1.1 million per year.

The process of migration in the 1990s occurred in the absence of strong attractive features in the cities, considering that the Brazilian economy performed poorly in the first three years of the decade. Thus, the factors of expulsion may explain much of the ongoing process of rural–urban migration. Among these factors is the lack of land to keep a significant portion of the population gainfully employed (according to Szmrecsányi, 1990, p. 91). Another factor of expulsion is the mechanization of agricultural operations, which is a strategy adopted by farmers to combat the increasing cost of labor and the reduction in revenue caused by currency appreciation.

As was evidenced in Figures 5.9 and 5.10, agriculture and agro-industry are net exporters and generate most of Brazil's balance-of-trade surplus. Therefore, these two segments of agribusiness are net suppliers of foreign currencies and allow other sectors to purchase inputs and capital goods necessary for the country's development.

Brazilian agriculture constitutes an important consumer market for inputs like fertilizers, soil correctors, veterinary medicines, agricultural machinery and production support services. The suppliers of these products and services represented, in 2008, 3 per cent of the Brazilian GDP and rely heavily on domestic demand.

The end of rural credit subsidies and the reduced amount of credit supplied had a negative impact on agriculture's demand for modern inputs. However, the drop in input prices and the need to increase agricultural activity stimulated demand.

The data from Table 5.9 illustrate that Brazilian agriculture provided food as well as drinks and other raw materials necessary to the expansion of agro-industry. In 2008 agro-industry represented 7.7 per cent of the Brazilian GDP and consumed mainly agricultural products produced in Brazil.

5.6 CONCLUSION

In the period from 1987 to 2009 Brazilian agriculture received little stimulus from economic policies, whether macroeconomic or sectoral. The highlights are that the currency appreciation reduced farmers' potential income (since the significant part of the agricultural product is exportable or suffers from competition from imports) and the recovery of the purchasing power of the minimum wage after mid 1995 raised the cost of agricultural production. Associated with this were a reduction in the amount of rural credit and/or the increase of that credit's cost to farmers, a reduction of the coverage of minimum price policies, and a reduction in government spending on agriculture. However, physical agricultural output expanded significantly, while there were reductions in both total farming area and the labor employed. This was possible owing to the large increases in land and labor productivity, themselves made possible by technology developed in or adapted for the country and to the entrepreneurial spirit of many Brazilian farmers. Of the six classic functions of agriculture in the development process, five were fulfilled in the period analyzed – or, in other words, agriculture provided food for the country's population, acquired foreign currency for the economy, transferred income to other sectors (allowing them to invest), constituted a consumer market for inputs, and supplied high quality raw materials at competitive prices to the nation's industry. Agriculture was only irrelevant in the supply of labor to urban activities. Despite the fact that rural–urban migration has continued in the period analyzed, this workforce is no longer necessary for the expansion of urban activities.

The main future risk is a greater appreciation of the real, which would decapitalize Brazilian farmers, and which would not allow agriculture to contribute further to Brazil's economic development.

NOTES

1. The Complementary Law 87/96, known as the Kandir Law, came into effect in September 1996 and relieved the VAT payment on the export of primary products and partly manufactured goods, as well as on the imports of machinery and equipment for the composition of the fixed assets. This law provided for the compensation of states that showed losses in VAT revenue due to such exemptions.

2. These 38 crops are: apple, avocado, barley, beans, cashew nut, cassava, castor, cocoa, coconut, coffee, corn, perennial cotton, upland cotton, garlic, grapes, guarana, guava, jute, lemon, mallow, mango, oats, onion, orange, passion fruit, peanuts, pepper, potatoes, rice, rye, sisal, sorghum, soybeans, sugarcane, tangerine, tobacco, tomato and wheat.

REFERENCES

Alves, E. (2010), 'Embrapa – um caso bem-sucedido de inovação institucional', *Revista de Política Agrícola*, **39** (July), pp. 65–73.

Bacha, C.J.C. (2004), *Economia e política agrícola no brasil*, São Paulo: Atlas, ch. 8.

Bacha, C.J.C. and M.T. Rocha (1998), 'O comportamento da agropecuária brasileira no período de 1987 a 1996', *Revista de Economia e Sociologia Rural*, **36** (1), 35–59.

Bacha, C.J.C. and G.S. Silva (2005), 'Os novos instrumentos de financiamento do agronegócio', *Agroanalysis* (FGV), **25** (9), 36–8.

Bacha, C.J.C., L. Danelon, and Del Bel Filho E. (2006), 'Evolução da taxa de juros real do crédito rural no Brasil – período de 1985 a 2003', *Teoria e Evidência Econômica*, Passo Fundo, RS, **14** (26), pp. 43–69.

Barros, G.S.C. (1994), 'Alocação de gastos públicos na agricultura', *Anais do XXXII Congresso Brasileiro de Economia e Sociologia Rural*, Brasília: SOBER, vol. 2, pp. 1088–1100.

Barros, G.S.C. (1995), 'A nova política agrícola brasileira', *Preços Agrícolas*, (Piracicaba), (99), pp. 4–7.

Barros, G.S.C. and M.A.F.D. Moraes (2002), 'A desregulamentação do setor sucroalcooleiro', *Revista de Economia Política*, **22** (2), 156–73.

Brazil's Yearbook, Rio de Janeiro: Brazilian Institute of Geography and Statistics (IBGE).

Brugnaro, R. and C.J.C. Bacha (2009), 'Análise da participação da agropecuária no PIB do Brasil de 1986 a 2004,' *Revista Estudos Econômicos*, **39** (1), 127–59.

Camarano, A.A. and R. Abramovay (1999), 'Êxodo rural, envelhecimento e masculinização no Brasil: panorama dos últimos 50 anos', IPEA Texto para Discussão no. 621, Rio de Janeiro, January.

Del Bel Filho, E. and C.J.C. Bacha (2005), 'Avaliação das mudanças na política de garantia de preços mínimos: período de 1997 a 2004', *Revista de Economia e Agronegócio'*, **3** (1), 51–76.

Gasques, J.G. (2001), 'Os gastos públicos na agropecuária', in J.G. Gasques and J.C.P.R. Conceição, *Transformações da Agricultura e Políticas Públicas*, Brasília: IPEA, pp. 157–90.

Gasques, J.G. and J.C.P.R. Conceição (2001), 'Financiamento da agricultura – experiências e propostas', in J.G. Gasques and J.C.P.R. Conceição, *Transformações da Agricultura e Políticas Públicas*, Brasília: IPEA, pp. 95–155.

Gasques, J.G, C.M.V. Verde and E.T. Bastos (2010), 'Gastos públicos na agricultura – uma retrospectiva', *Revista de Política Agrícola*, **19** (July), 74–92.

Goldin, I. and G.C. Rezende (1993), A agricultura brasileira na década de 80: crescimento numa economia em crise, IPEA series no. 138, Rio de Janeiro.

Oliveira, R.B and R. Hoffmann (2010), 'Desigualdade de rendimentos entre os empregados na agricultura brasileira de 1992 a 2008: o efeito do salário mínimo', in *Anais do 48º Congresso da Sociedade Brasileira de Economia, Administração e Sociologia Rural*, Campo Grande, MS, 25–28 July, pp. 1–21.

Portugal, A.D. and E Contini (1997), 'O público e o privado na pesquisa agropecuária brasileira', in *Anais do XXXV Congresso Brasileiro de Economia e Sociologia Rural*, Natal, August, pp. 8–52.

Rezende, G.C. 'A evolução da política de preços mínimos na década de 1990', in J.G. Gasques and J.C.P.R. Conceição, *Transformações da Agricultura e Políticas Públicas*, Brasília: IPEA, pp. 303–14.

Rezende, G.C. (2002), 'A politica de preços minimos e o desenvolvimento agricola da região Centro-Oeste', IPEA Working Paper no. 870, Rio de Jeneiro, April, available at http://www.ipea.gov.br/pub/td/2002/td_0870.pdf

The Economist (2010), 'Brazilian agriculture – the miracle of the cerrado', *The Economist*, 26 August. available at: http://www.economist.com/node/16886442

Verde, C.M.V (2001), Modificações recentes na política de garantia de preços mínimos', in J.G. Gasques and J.C.P.R. Conceição, *Transformações da Agricultura e Políticas Públicas*, Brasília: IPEA, pp. 315–36.

Szmrecsányi, T. (1990), *Pequena História da Agricultura no Brasil*, São Paulo, Brazil: Editora Contexto.

6. Comments on part II

Andrew W. Horowitz

In this comment I first summarize and assess the chapters sequentially, then provide a short synthesis and juxtaposition of the two articles.

ARGENTINA – CÉSAR CIAPPA AND ANDRÉS GALLO

Ciappa and Gallo have produced a broad analysis of the Argentinian agricultural sector with a focus on the potential distortionary effects of export taxation and quantitative restrictions. The analysis is well motivated and undertakes the ambitious endeavor of integrating a political–economic perspective with general equilibrium analysis. Due attention is given throughout to the citation of the relevant source literature. Section 4.1 provides a brief overview of the agro-industrial chain (AIC) and the historic incentives the federal government has had to tax the chain. Section 4.2 contains a fine introduction to some of the principal AICs in the country (cattle, wheat and soybeans) and an assessment of the impact of taxation on agricultural production, trade, poverty and the federal budget. Estimations of the direct and indirect effects of export taxes and quantitative restrictions are gathered from multiple sources to consider the impact of their elimination. The authors conclude that though export taxation is enticing to the federal government in the short run, the long-run effects are deleterious. Elimination of export taxation and quantitative controls, they argue, would yield net long-run benefits.

Ciappa and Gallo's chapter is a fine piece of scholarly work that adopts a broad political–economic perspective to build a case for the elimination of export taxation and quantitative restrictions in Argentina. Though it is straightforward to show the distortionary costs of export taxation and quantitative restriction in a neoclassical model, many important questions would need to be convincingly resolved before such sweeping policy recommendations could be implemented. The case made in this chapter depends heavily on the estimates from Porto (2009). The adjustment time estimates, on the other hand, are based on the work of Nogués et al. (2007). Estimates of the poverty and indigence effects of the policy proposal are based on Ciappa (2009). Few details of the methodology and assumptions behind these various estimates are provided and it is important to know if the modeling assumptions and data are consistent across papers. Another important question concerns the political 'costs' of tax-regime transition. Such costs, though difficult to model and measure, are acknowledged as critical in both economies and political science (Buchanan, 1987, and Patashnik, 2001, provide seminal works in each discipline). In this vein, it would be useful to have more discussion of the feasibility and cost of transition to the counter-factual tax regime. Despite these questions, this chapter constitutes an important contribution to the tax policy debate in Argentina.

BRAZIL – CARLOS JOSÉ CAETANO BACHA

Carlos Bacha provides a fine overview of the Brazilian agricultural sector from 1987 to 2009. The piece updates and expands Bacha (2004). The article endeavors to examine the impact of a number of important agricultural policies on the general process of economic development. The principal focus is upon exchange rate policies, minimum wage legislation, and changes in the availability and cost of rural credit. A number of hypotheses (detailed below) concerning the effect of government policies on the sector are proposed. Section 5.1 provides an overview of these policies and also notes the important role of both private and public research efforts on sector performance. Section 5.2 provides an excellent description of agricultural sector performance (output, area, productivity), including a discussion of regional distribution. Section 5.3 provides a brief account of the declining share of agriculture in total GDP over this period and some evidence of improving workers' earnings over the period. Section 5.4 competently recounts the explosive growth in agricultural exports since 1987 and the associated attenuation of the prior balance-of-payments and debt problems. Section 5.5 reviews the nexus between agricultural development and the broader development process.

A principal focus of the chapter is the impact of the appreciation of the real versus the dollar on agro-export competitiveness. The dollar exchange rate is clearly a critical factor over the full time horizon (1987 to 2008). However, the growing significance of the real/euro exchange rate and the growth of trade with the euro-zone are important developments over this time horizon as well. Indeed, exports to euro-zone countries increased significantly over the period analyzed. Though the importance of the real/euro exchange rate in the euro's early years is debatable, its impact in recent years is likely to prove significant. In this light it should be noted that the real has *not* shown a general trend of appreciation versus the euro (as with the dollar) over much of the last decade. Simultaneous export growth and the significant appreciation of the real versus the dollar may seem less contradictory in this light.

Another interesting question raised by Bacha in this chapter is the effect of minimum wage increases on capital intensity in agricultural production. Professor Bacha believes this effect to be significant. Contrarily, it can be argued that increased capital intensity was driven by accelerating development of the cerrado, the growth of capital-intensive crops (soya and cotton), and the decline in the *relative* share of labor-intensive crops (e.g. coffee). This is an important question that warrants careful empirical work.

SYNTHESIS

These two fine chapters have very distinct foci that reflect the idiosyncratic agricultural history and policy trajectories of the respective countries. Ciappa and Gallo focus on Argentinian export taxation while Bacha has greater concern with exchange rate and minimum wage polices in Brazil. Nevertheless, the chapters contain many subtle commonalities that reflect pervasive themes in Latin American agriculture. Both chapters argue that government policies have imposed significant costs on the sector. Both chapters suggest specific policy adjustments that would allow each country to reap the full benefits of their global comparative advantage. Finally, both chapters view the agricultural sector in the context of the broader development agenda. Nevertheless, as noted, the modes of government intervention are starkly different in these two countries. Argentina has adopted a more directly extractive stance towards the sector (through export taxation) while Brazil's exchange rate and minimum wage policies should be viewed as having collateral, rather than intentional, effects on the sector. Moreover, the costs of government policies in Brazil should be balanced with the benefits that government-sponsored and -facilitated research has yielded.

Though it is unarguable that government policies significantly affect the agricultural sector in both countries, the magnitude of the effect, relative to global market forces, is debatable. Rapid export growth in both countries has occurred despite taxation in the Argentinian case and unfavorable dollar exchange rates and increased wage costs in the Brazilian. In this commentator's opinion, the exceptional export growth in both countries is evidence that the power of comparative advantage and global markets dominates the impact of unfavorable government policies in both countries.

REFERENCES

Bacha, C.J.C. (2004), *Economia e política agrícola no Brasil*, São Paulo, Brazil: Atlas, p. 26.

Buchanan, James M. (1987), 'Tax reform as political choice', *Journal of Economic Perspectives*, **1** (1), 29–35.

Ciappa, C. (2009), 'Diseño y evaluación de politicas alimentarias', in Delia M. Ferreira Rubio (ed.), *Política agroindustrial – fundamentos para el desarrollo sostenido y sustentable de la agroindustria*, Buenos Aires: Foro de la Cadena Agroindustrial Argentina, 2009, pp. 217–47, available at: http://www.foroagroindustrial.org.ar/politicaagroindustrial.pdf

Nogués, J., A. Porto, C. Ciappa, L. Di Gresia and A. Onofri (2007), *Estudio de impactos económicos y sociales de políticas públicas en la cadena agroindustrial*, Buenos Aires: Foro de la Cadena Agroindustrial, available at: www.foroagroindustial.com.ar

Porto, A. (2009), 'Efectos fiscales sobre los impuestos a las exportaciones (retenciones),' in Delia M. Ferreira Rubio (ed.), '*Política agroindustrial – fundamentos para el desarrollo sostenido y sustentable de la agroindustria*', Buenos Aires: Foro de la Cadena Agroindustrial Argentina, 2009, pp. 145–83, available at: http://www.foroagroindustrial.org.ar/politicaagroindustrial.pdf

PART III

The service sector: formal and informal

7. General facts about the service sector in Argentina

Ricardo Bebczuk

7.1 INTRODUCTION

In economies, the services sector gets a bad rap. Services have been accused of, among other things, causing slow economic growth, poor export performance, and increasing informality and poverty. Even though the services sector's performance has been observed and studied since the 1950s, little work exists on the subject for Latin America and, to the best of our knowledge, none has focused on Argentina. This chapter aims to go over the technical arguments that lie behind this negative view, and assess their merits on the basis of statistical evidence for Argentina and selected economies around the world. The analysis has indisputable policy relevance in so far as this prejudice against the services sector – the largest productive sector in terms of output and employment around the world – may lead to flawed development strategies. In a nutshell, our review defies the usual stand on this matter by providing support to the claim that services do not jeopardize the attainment of key macroeconomic goals, including economic growth.

7.2 THE CONTRIBUTION OF SERVICES TO TOTAL OUTPUT AND EMPLOYMENT

Far from a uniform sector, the services sector is a miscellaneous collection of industries whose one common feature is that services are not part of the primary or manufacturing sector. Services can be classified into five activities:

Distribution services: Wholesale and retail trade, transport and storage, and communications (including IT).
Social services: Health and education and government administration.
Intermediation services: Real estate and financial.

Personal services: Accommodation, restaurants, cultural and recreational.
Utilities and construction services: Electricity, gas, water and construction.

Service output tends to be intangible and delivered in person at a specific location. The provision of health or education services is an example. Of course, not all services fall exactly under this paradigm. For instance, information technology – computer support and the like – now permits many services to be performed without any personal contact between suppliers and clients. Likewise, intangibility is not an attribute of all services. Construction and utility services constitute perfectly tangible services. Software programs and restaurant meals, just to name two cases, are also tangible services. However, their value arises principally from their intangible content: the human capital invested in the creation of the program and the restaurant's ambience, respectively – the disc in which the software is stored and the meal's ingredients have a negligible, or at most secondary, incidence on the market value.

This vast heterogeneity at the interior of the services sector is at the heart of several of our next findings, which make it apparent that, contrary to conventional wisdom, services are not in general associated with negative economic outcomes. In an effort to disprove this notion, we start by examining the contribution of each service subsector to total output and employment at the international level. We then do the same for Argentina.

Table 7.1 presents output composition of the services sector in the EU-15. Real estate, trade and construction are the top three industries. All sectors except trade, construction and public administration expanded their weight in total output between 1970 and 2007, which in turn explains the growing participation of services as a whole (from 57.9 per cent in 1970 to 70.9 per cent in 2007). In terms of employment as of 2007, services comprised 82.7 per cent of the total, with trade, real estate and health occupying the first places (Table 7.2).

National accounts convey similar information on the Argentine case. The preponderance of services in total GDP is even greater than in Europe. From Table 7.3, the services sector generated a stable share of 75 per cent to 78 per cent in all years during 1993–2008, implying that the sector was mostly insensitive to the drastic switch in the economic regime, and the associated turn in relative prices, since 2002. Table 7.4 shows that trade, real estate, transport and storage, education and construction are the largest subsectors (70 per cent of all services output), and again the relative participation did not change substantially over the 15 years from

Table 7.1 EU-15 countries, 1970–2007: participation in total GDP by services subsectors (percentages)

	1970	1980	1990	2000	2007
Primary sector	6.9	5.2	3.4	2.4	1.9
Manufacturing sector	35.1	32.5	30.3	28.9	27.2
Services sector	**57.9**	**62.3**	**66.3**	**68.7**	**70.9**
Real estate	9.0	10.3	13.7	16.0	16.7
Wholesale and retail trade	9.3	8.7	8.5	9.0	8.6
Construction	9.8	8.5	8.1	7.6	7.8
Transport and storage	5.2	5.6	5.4	5.7	5.7
Financial intermediation	3.1	3.8	5.0	5.2	5.7
Health	2.7	4.1	4.4	4.7	4.8
Public administration	6.6	6.3	5.4	4.9	4.6
Education	2.3	3.4	3.1	3.1	3.1
Electricity, gas and water	2.3	2.7	2.9	2.3	2.9
Communications	1.4	1.6	1.8	2.3	2.4
Hotels and restaurants	1.7	1.9	2.1	2.3	2.2
Others	4.4	5.4	5.8	5.8	6.4
Total industries	100.0	100.0	100.0	100.0	100.0

Source: Author's elaboration based on OECD KLEMS Project.

1993 to 2008, the only exceptions being those of transport and storage, which gained 4 percentage points between 1998 and 2008. In terms of labor market incidence, services account for over 77 per cent of total employment, with strong participation from public administration, trade and real estate (Table 7.5).

7.3 SERVICES AND THE LEVEL OF ECONOMIC DEVELOPMENT

Against the backdrop of the industry-driven development theories, most economies in the world have witnessed a relentless rise in the participation of the services sector in total GDP. Table 7.6 displays trends in value added by sector in 102 countries, split by income level, in 1980 and 2005. The most startling observation is that the larger the services sector, the larger is the per capita GDP.[1] In the 20 richest economies in 2005, 70.4 per cent of GDP was generated by the services sector (as against 57.9 per cent

Table 7.2 EU-15 countries, 1970–2007: participation in total employment by services subsectors (percentages)

	1970	1980	1990	2000	2007
Primary sector	6.2	4.1	3.0	2.1	1.9
Manufacturing sector	32.3	28.3	23.4	18.7	15.8
Services sector	**61.5**	**67.6**	**73.6**	**79.2**	**82.3**
Wholesale and retail trade	12.2	13.0	13.5	14.3	14.3
Real estate	4.0	5.1	7.8	11.5	13.2
Health	5.3	7.1	8.6	9.8	10.5
Public administration	7.4	8.5	8.9	8.2	7.6
Education	5.2	6.6	7.1	7.2	7.4
Construction	9.8	8.3	7.1	6.6	6.8
Hotels and restaurants	2.5	2.7	3.4	4.2	4.7
Transport and storage	4.5	4.5	4.2	4.3	4.4
Financial intermediation	2.3	3.1	3.5	3.3	3.2
Communications	1.9	2.0	2.0	1.7	1.5
Electricity, gas and water	1.1	1.1	1.0	0.7	0.7
Others	5.3	5.6	6.5	7.3	7.9
Total industries	100.0	100.0	100.0	100.0	100.0

Source: Author's elaboration based on OECD KLEMS Project.

in 1980). The overwhelming dominance of services comes at the expense of the contraction of both manufacturing (from 36 per cent to 28 per cent) and agriculture (from 6.5 per cent to just 2.1 per cent). In the poorest 20 economies, which have stagnated over the same 25-year period, services' share has fallen from 41.8 per cent to 40.6 per cent. But even there, services still exceed agriculture (about 37 per cent in both years) as the main contributing sector.

Argentina's figures are typical of other middle-income economies, with services accounting for 55 per cent of GDP in 2005 versus 52.4 per cent in 1980.[2] Despite an abundance of natural resources, the agricultural sector produced 9.4 per cent in 2005. The manufacturing sector was the only one that lost ground (from 41.2 per cent to 35.6 per cent) in the 25 years to 2005.

Kongsamut et al. (1997) list the three reasons traditionally invoked to explain the correlation between services and GDP expansion:

(1) The income elasticity of the demand for services is larger than one.
(2) Income growth encourages households and firms to contract out services previously done at home.

Table 7.3 Argentina, 1993–2008: sectoral composition of GDP (percentages)

	Agri-culture	Fishing	Mining	Manu-facturing	Services	Total	Real GDP index, 1993 = 100
1993	5.0	0.2	1.5	18.2	75.1	100.0	100.0
1994	5.1	0.2	1.6	18.0	75.2	100.0	105.8
1995	5.5	0.2	1.9	17.2	75.2	100.0	102.8
1996	5.1	0.2	1.9	17.4	75.4	100.0	108.5
1997	4.8	0.2	1.8	17.5	75.8	100.0	117.3
1998	5.0	0.2	1.6	17.2	76.0	100.0	121.8
1999	5.3	0.2	1.6	16.4	76.5	100.0	117.7
2000	5.3	0.2	1.8	15.9	76.9	100.0	116.8
2001	5.5	0.2	1.9	15.4	76.9	100.0	111.6
2002	6.1	0.2	2.1	15.4	76.2	100.0	99.5
2003	6.0	0.2	2.0	16.4	75.4	100.0	108.3
2004	5.5	0.1	1.8	16.8	75.8	100.0	118.0
2005	5.6	0.1	1.7	16.6	76.1	100.0	128.9
2006	5.2	0.2	1.6	16.6	76.4	100.0	139.8
2007	5.3	0.1	1.4	16.5	76.7	100.0	151.9
2008	4.8	0.1	1.4	16.1	77.5	100.0	162.1

Source: Author's elaboration based on Ministry of Economy Information.

Table 7.4 Argentina 1993–2008: service sector composition (percentages)

	1993	1998	2003	2008
Wholesale and retail trade	20.9	19.9	17.1	18.4
Real estate	21.0	19.9	21.5	18.1
Transport, storage and communications	9.9	11.5	12.4	15.6
Education	11.2	10.3	12.8	10.4
Construction	8.2	8.4	6.3	8.7
Others	7.9	7.6	8.1	7.9
Financial intermediation	5.7	8.4	6.0	7.5
Public administration	9.0	6.9	7.9	6.2
Electricity, gas and water	2.8	3.3	4.3	3.6
Hotels and restaurants	3.3	3.7	3.6	3.5
Total	100.0	100.0	100.0	100.0

Source: Author's elaboration based on Ministry of Economy Information.

Table 7.5 Argentina, 2006–08: participation in total employment by the services sector (percentages)

	2006	2007	2008
Agriculture	5.0	4.8	4.7
Fishing	0.2	0.2	0.2
Mining	0.6	0.7	0.7
Manufacturing sector	17.3	17.0	16.8
Services sector	76.8	77.3	77.6
Public administration	17.4	17.1	17.4
Wholesale and retail trade	14.5	14.7	15.0
Real estate	10.7	11.2	11.4
Private education, health and social services	8.8	8.6	8.5
Transport, storage and communications	6.6	6.6	6.7
Construction	5.7	6.1	5.8
Hotels and restaurants	2.9	2.9	3.0
Financial intermediation	2.4	2.4	2.4
Electricity, gas and water	0.8	0.8	0.8
Others	6.9	6.8	6.6
Private sector	82.6	82.9	82.6
Public sector	17.4	17.1	17.4

Source: Author's elaboration based on Ministry of Economy Information.

(3) Productivity growth is slower in the services sector, which means that output and employment growth must surpass that of the remaining sectors in order to meet the rising demand.

The analysis in the next section casts serious doubts upon the low-productivity argument, but this does not invalidate the other two points. Even without any productivity differential, the demand-side arguments suffice to account for the observed changes.

7.4 SERVICES AND PRODUCTIVITY GROWTH

The prevalent view is that services exhibit a lower rate of productivity growth than goods-producing sectors. One example is the hairstylist, whose productivity (the number of haircuts per hour) faces a low and well-defined upper bound, in contrast to the productivity gain potential of any typical manufacturing industry. This might be true for haircuts, but not for many other services. This premise was captured by the celebrated Baumol's

Table 7.6 102 countries, 1980 and 2005: value added by the services sector and GDP per capita

	Year	**20 lowest –income countries**	**62 middle–income countries**	**20 highest –income countries**	**Argentina**
GDP per capita	1980	924	4,410	18,528	**10,089**
(PPP constant	2005	881	6,635	32,658	**10,815**
2005 US$)	*Mean growth*	*−0.2%*	*1.6%*	*2.3%*	*0.3%*
Value added,	**1980**	**41.8**	**47.8**	**57.9**	**52.4**
services (%)	**2005**	**40.6**	**55.6**	**70.4**	**55.0**
	Change	*−1.2*	*7.8*	*12.5*	*2.6*
Value added,	1980	20.7	32.6	35.6	**41.2**
manufacturing (%)	2005	22.5	32.2	27.5	**35.6**
	Change	*1.8*	*−0.4*	*−8.1*	*−5.6*
Value added,	1980	36.9	19.6	6.5	**6.4**
agriculture (%)	2005	36.6	12.2	2.1	**9.4**
	Change	*−0.3*	*−7.4*	*−4.4*	*3.0*

Source: World Development Indicators, World Bank.

(1967) unbalanced model, which predicts that, as resources move toward slow-growing productivity sectors (such as the services sector), the aggregate productivity growth will follow accordingly.[3] Dasgupta and Singh (2006) cite Kaldor's claim that industry generates more positive spillovers than other sectors, as well as more static and dynamic economies of scale.

However, 'Baumol's Disease' – as it is known in development literature – has been scrutinized and discredited as a robust empirical finding. Oulton (1999) shows that this characterization does not fit the OECD experience over 1973–96, where manufacturing was indeed the slow-growing productivity sector in the United Kingdom, the United States, France and Germany. In the same vein, Triplett and Bosworth (2003), in looking at the post-1995 US productivity upswing, asserted that 'Baumol's disease has been cured.' Moreover, they concluded that labor's productivity acceleration in the services sector in 1995–2000, as compared with its performance in the years 1977–94, was due mostly to multifactor productivity and only partially to the contribution of IT capital, meaning that increased productivity (as opposed to increased capital intensity) was behind this result.

A simple measure of labor productivity – output per hour worked – in the EU-15 group of countries renders an accurate picture of the heterogeneity at the interior of the services sector, as portrayed in Table 7.7. On average, the services sector was below the overall average for

Table 7.7 EU-15 countries, 1970–2007: relative labor productivity by services subsectors (GDP per hour worked, index total economy = 1)

	1970	1980	1990	2000	2007
Primary sector	1.09	1.19	1.06	1.03	0.92
Manufacturing sector	1.07	1.12	1.26	1.47	1.64
Services sector	**0.95**	**0.93**	**0.91**	**0.88**	**0.87**
Electricity, gas and water	2.01	2.48	2.79	3.00	4.09
Financial intermediation	1.36	1.25	1.40	1.54	1.76
Communications	0.77	0.84	0.94	1.36	1.67
Real estate	2.25	2.02	1.73	1.39	1.24
Transport and storage	1.02	1.08	1.08	1.14	1.12
Construction	0.93	0.97	1.07	1.04	1.02
Wholesale and retail trade	0.76	0.66	0.62	0.63	0.61
Public administration	0.90	0.75	0.61	0.59	0.59
Health	0.55	0.61	0.55	0.52	0.49
Education	0.56	0.64	0.54	0.51	0.49
Hotels and restaurants	0.69	0.67	0.61	0.55	0.47
Others	0.96	1.07	0.97	0.85	0.89
Total all industries	1.00	1.00	1.00	1.00	1.00

Source: Author's elaboration based on OECD KLEMS Project.

the years 1970–2007. But this ceases to be true once we take a glimpse at the different subsectors. On one hand, some subsectors (public administration; health; education; hotels and restaurants) consistently lay at the bottom of the productivity ladder. But on the other, 6 out of the 12 subsectors exceeded aggregate average. Moreover, 3 of them (electricity, gas and water; financial intermediation; and communications) are more productive than manufacturing.

Another interesting case is India, where deindustrialization and services-led growth has captured the attention of development experts in the last decades. Table 7.8 confirms the impressive long-run performance of its services sector. Besides growing more rapidly than manufacturing, this growth came fundamentally from total factor productivity (TFP) rather than from a more intensive use of physical capital.

Returning to the Argentine case, wide labor productivity disparities are also apparent, without any definite ruling on the services-versus-industry dispute. According to Table 7.9, some services like financial intermediation and utilities rank better than manufacturing, while others lag well

Table 7.8 India 1971–97: growth accounting by sector (percentages)

	GDP growth rate	Contribution of		
		Physical capital	Labor	Total factor productivity
Agriculture	2.69	−0.23	0.61	2.31
Manufacturing	5.52	2.54	2.85	0.13
Services	**5.81**	**0.07**	**2.91**	**2.83**

Source: Verma (2006).

Table 7.9 Argentina 1993 and 2004: relative labor productivity in services subsectors (GDP per hour worked; index total economy = 1)

	1993	**2004**
Agriculture	0.62	0.74
Mining	3.59	3.83
Manufacturing sector	1.08	1.23
Services sector		
Electricity, gas and water	2.51	4.12
Financial Intermediation	2.64	2.46
Construction	0.99	0.86
Hotels and restaurants	0.79	0.73
Transport, storage and communications	0.79	0.73
Wholesale and retail trade	0.68	0.62

Source: Coremberg (2006).

behind. However, this measure suffers from the caveat that technological differences across industry may bias labor productivity in favor of the more capital-intensive industries. A more suitable approach is the use of total factor productivity. With data for 1990–2006, Table 7.10 shows that, compared with manufacturing, TFP has grown faster in 4 out of 7 services subsectors. The post-2001 crisis scenario did not substantially alter this overall conclusion in spite of the abrupt relative price change against services. If anything, the new conditions bolstered productivity gains in the agricultural sector. In regard to capital intensity, Table 7.11 contradicts the intuition that the services sector is less capital-intensive than manufacturing. It turns out that manufacturing in Argentina is as capital-intensive as agriculture (capital/output ratio of 1.8), and below the aggregate average (2.6) in 5 out of 9 services subsectors.

Table 7.10 Argentina 1990–2006: total factor productivity in economic sectors and services subsectors (index 1990 = 100)

	1990	**1998**	**2002**	**2006**	Annual change 1990–98 %	Annual change 2002–06 %
Agriculture	100.0	106.9	107.6	116.3	0.8	2.0
Fishing	100.0	89.6	86.9	83.3	−1.4	−1.1
Mining	100.0	90.9	94.2	88.9	−1.2	−1.4
Manufacturing sector	100.0	109.8	106.0	111.4	1.2	1.3
Services sector						
Electricity, gas and water	100.0	123.3	130.1	136.7	2.7	1.2
Transport, storage and communications	100.0	115.4	111.9	125.1	1.8	2.8
Financial intermediation	100.0	165.5	132.1	118.5	6.5	−2.7
Construction	100.0	119.3	101.7	114.4	2.2	3.0
Real estate	100.0	101.6	98.8	94.0	0.2	−1.2
Wholesale and retail trade	100.0	112.0	86.2	91.2	1.4	1.4
Hotels and restaurants	100.0	104.9	95.6	87.5	0.6	−2.2

Source: Coremberg (2009).

7.5 SERVICES SECTOR AND INFORMALITY

Informal economic activity, or informality, is widespread in Argentina and many other developing economies, exacting wide-ranging consequences for social well-being, tax revenues, and economic agents' behavior. That it is especially widespread in service subsectors is another accusation against them.

Two different approaches are usually employed to characterize informality. According to the productive definition, a worker is considered informal if he or she is unskilled and self-employed, is a salaried worker in a small private firm, or has zero income. The legalistic or social protection definition, in turn, labels as informal any salaried worker without the right to a pension upon retirement. Beyond this distinction, statistical measures of informality appear to yield similar values.

World Bank (2008) offers evidence of a strong and negative relationship between informality and GDP per capita. Bacchetta et al. (2009) give

Table 7.11 *Argentina and selected OECD economies, 2006: capital–output ratio in economic sectors and services subsectors*

	Argentina	Spain	Germany	Japan	UK	US
Agriculture	1.8	2.0	3.7	10.4	3.2	1.9
Manufacturing sector	1.8	2.0	1.6	2.6	1.5	1.1
Services sector:						
Real estate	6.1	20.0	16.2	12.2	17.9	9.4
Electricity, gas and water	6.0	3.4	4.7	8.4	4.3	5.1
Transport, storage and communications	4.7	1.7	4.7	6.1	2.8	2.5
Hotels and restaurants	2.7	0.8	1.5	2.8	2.0	1.7
Financial intermediation	2.4	0.9	2.0	0.8	1.3	1.5
Education and health	1.7	0.5	2.3	2.2	1.0	1.4
Wholesale and retail trade	1.3	1.6	0.9	1.3	1.3	1.1
Construction	1.2	0.8	0.6	0.6	0.5	0.6
Public administration	0.9	6.0	4.8	4.7	4.2	3.2
Total	**2.6**	**3.2**	**4.1**	**3.6**	**2.8**	**2.9**

Source: Coremberg (2009).

testimony of the widespread presence of informal workers all over the developing world. For the decade of the 2000s, labor informality was 52 per cent in Latin America, 78 per cent in Asia and 56 per cent in Africa. These values are similar to those registered in the 1990s, suggesting strong inertia.

Table 7.12 explores the link between informality and the services sector in the four largest Latin American countries, including Argentina. The proportion of informal workers in Argentina (43.6 per cent) roughly doubles that of Chile (22.5 per cent), and is 9 percentage points above the Brazilian level (34.8 per cent), but is somewhat modest compared with the 59 per cent registered in Mexico. In Argentina, the degree of informality within the manufacturing sector differs significantly between low-tech industries (50.4 per cent) and high-tech ones (28.1 per cent). As for the services sector, informality prevails especially in construction (76.8 per

Table 7.12 Argentina and other Latin American economies by subsector: informality (legalistic definition); data around 2005

	Argentina	Brazil	Chile	Mexico
Primary activities	37.8	66.8	30.0	93.4
Industry, low-tech	50.4	25.2	17.3	44.5
Industry, high-tech	28.1	18.7	17.8	21.8
Services sector:				
Construction	76.8	54.7	23.9	83.5
Trade	53.5	34.2	21.4	59.7
Utilities and transportation	45.9	22.2	20.8	60.5
Skilled services	38.8	19.0	14.5	70.5
Public administration	10.0	15.1	9.9	43.7
Education and health	21.5	18.8	14.1	27.8
Total	**43.6**	**34.8**	**22.5**	**59.0**

Source: Gasparini and Tornarolli (2007).

cent) and trade (53.5 per cent), but it is at or below the global average in the remaining subsectors. In the other countries, industry (both low- and high-tech) is below the global average, but there still exist several services subsectors that fare even better.

Wages, as shown in Table 7.13, are similar to or higher than in manufacturing in 4 out of 9 services subsectors, implying that no linear relationship can be drawn between pay and services.[4] In sum, the general picture reinforces previous findings, in that the stereotype of services creating bad jobs and manufacturing creating good ones is grossly misleading.

7.6 THE SERVICES SECTOR AND THE EXTERNAL SECTOR

Theory teaches that services cannot be traded internationally because of prohibitively high transportation costs. Hence, a larger proportion of services in total output may hold back the country's external openness and its ability to implement an export-led growth strategy.

While this is true of some services, it does not apply to them as a whole since many services can and are profitably traded across countries. The main difference between trade in merchandise and trade in services is that, in the former, productive factors remain in the exporting country while the goods produced move across borders. In contrast,

Table 7.13 Argentina: gross wage by subsector relative to average wage; data for 2008

	Gross monthly wage (AR$)
Agriculture	0.6
Fishing	1.7
Mining	3.1
Manufacturing sector	1.2
Services sector	
Electricity, gas and water	1.9
Financial intermediation	1.8
Transport, storage and communications	1.2
Public administration	1.2
Real estate	0.8
Wholesale and retail trade	0.8
Construction	0.8
Private education and health	0.7
Hotels and restaurants	0.6

Source: Author's elaboration based on Ministry of Economy.

when it comes to services, productive factors must travel to the importing country in most cases but not all. Bearing this constraint in mind, we can say that services trade may take place in four modes: across borders (transport and travel, plus services transmitted via the internet at low or no cost, including financial, information and other business services); consumption abroad (expenses in lodging, food and others by international travelers); commercial presence (when affiliates are established abroad via direct investment); and movements of people (as in some consultancy services).

In 2008, world merchandise trade was US$15.8 billion and services trade was US$3.73 billion, or about 19 per cent of world trade. Transportation and travel jointly encompassed 49 per cent of all services traded. Over 2000–08, both merchandise exports and services exports grew at an annual rate of 12 per cent.

Further proof of the independence of export performance from the share of services in total output comes from the fact that openness, like the services share, increases with GDP per capita. To demonstrate, let us say the average share of exports in GDP for the 20 richest economies in the world was 29.7 per cent in 1960–2006 and just 18.4 per cent for the 20 poorest countries, whose share of services in total output was thus much

Table 7.14 Germany: destination of domestic production (percentages of total domestic production)

	Intermediate demand	Consumption	Investment	Exports	Total
Total economy	39.0	36.0	9.3	15.6	100.0
Agriculture	66.5	21.1	3.0	9.4	100.0
Manufacturing	38.9	16.6	8.3	36.2	100.0
Construction	20.1	1.9	78.0	0.0	100.0
Other services	40.6	52.0	2.8	4.7	100.0

Source: Gordo et al. (2006) based on Eurostat.

smaller than that of the 20 richest countries. This is partly shown in Table 7.14, where Germany is taken as representing rich economies generally. Total production of each sector is devoted to consumption, investment, exports and intermediate demand by the other productive sectors. The ratio of services exported is the lowest, compared with agriculture and manufacturing. However, some 41 per cent of services produced are used as an intermediate input in more open sectors, so services may make an indirect contribution to export dynamics.

Argentina's external deficit in services is a crucial component of the current-account balance, especially before the 2001–02 crisis. As shown in Table 7.15, services exports account for about 17 per cent of total exports, in line with international figures, while Table 7.16 shows that neither merchandise nor services trade has been sensitive to the participation of services in total output, which is also consistent with international developments. Also of note is the effect of the real exchange rate (and the GDP growth rate) on the trade balance but not on the services share.

7.7 CONCLUSIONS

This chapter has for the first time evaluated the way the services sector affects a number of macroeconomic goals in Argentina and, for comparative purposes, in other countries in Latin America and elsewhere. In contradiction to the familiar prognosis that services hinder economic growth and development and promote undesirable social outcomes, after reviewing the statistical evidence we have found that the share of services within the country's productive structure bears no relationship whatsoever to national performance in terms of economic development, productivity growth, labor informality and wages, or the trade balance.

Table 7.15 Argentina, 1992–2008: balance of payments and trade in services (million US$)

	Current account	Merchandise trade balance	Exports	Imports	Services trade balance	Exports	Imports	Services exports to merchandise exports (%)
1992	−5,548	−1,396	12,399	13,795	−2,557	2,984	5,542	24.1
1998	−14,465	−3,097	26,434	29,531	−4,444	4,854	9,298	18.4
2002	**8,767**	**17,178**	25,651	8,473	−1,460	3,495	4,956	13.6
2003	**8,140**	**16,805**	29,939	13,134	−1,193	4,500	5,693	15.0
2008	**7,089**	**15,464**	70,021	54,557	−943	12,087	13,030	17.3
1992–2001 average	−8,782	4	21,595	21,591	−3,773	4,138	7,912	19.7
2002–08 average	6,756	14,716	43,271	28,555	−994	7,193	8,186	16.2

Source: Author's elaboration based on Ministry of Economy.

Table 7.16 Argentina 1992–2008: trade balance, real exchange rate and the size of the services sector

	Merchandise trade balance (US$bn)	Services trade balance (US$bn)	Real exchange rate (2001 = 1)	**Services sector (% GDP)**
1993	−2,364	−3,326	1.005	75.1
1994	−4,139	−3,779	1.189	75.2
1995	**2,357**	−3,436	1.317	75.2
1996	**1,760**	−3,547	1.369	75.4
1997	−2,123	−4,385	1.289	75.8
1998	−3,097	−4,444	1.186	76.0
1999	−795	−4,111	1.066	76.5
2000	**2,452**	−4,284	1.073	76.9
2001	**7,385**	−3,863	1.000	76.9
2002	**17,178**	−1,460	2.419	76.2
2003	**16,805**	−1,193	2.157	75.4
2004	**13,265**	−1,331	2.192	75.8
2005	**13,087**	−1,002	2.221	76.1
2006	**13,958**	−531	2.281	76.4
2007	**13,255**	−500	2.345	76.7
2008	**15,464**	−943	2.371	77.5

Source: Author's elaboration based on Ministry of Economy.

The key factor in the overturn of traditional assumptions about services comes from the mere fact that this sector defies a narrow and precise definition, once it is shown to be composed of an assorted array of subsectors with features quite disparate from each other. Hence, factor intensities, labor specialization and technological progress, among other characteristics, vary accordingly, with the end result that some subsectors are indeed relatively unproductive while at the same time others exhibit better indicators than those of manufacturing.

As the evidence runs counter to the negative bias against services in the development literature, one must wonder what the policy implications are. The central message of this study is that services are not an obstacle to healthy economic and social development and that, to the contrary, they are a necessary complement for an industry- or agriculture-based strategy, as they provide critical productive inputs. Therefore, governments should be careful before designing long-run policies lacking a solid conceptual and empirical background. The risk is that they might be forcing the economy to take a worse path, on both the economic and social fronts, than one that is intervention-free.

NOTES

1. An OLS regression of the average per capita GDP growth over 1980–2005 against the change in the services contribution to GDP in the same period delivered a positive and highly significant estimate, suggesting that a 10 percentage point change in the services share is associated with a 0.5 percentage point increase in the growth rate. Of course the elementary estimation technique and the absence of additional controls forbid us from drawing any categorical conclusion from this exercise.
2. In another OLS regression with 2005 data, with GDP per capita as the only regressor, the predicted services share for Argentina was 63.8 per cent, higher than the actual 55 per cent reported by the World Bank.
3. Baumol (1967) offers a graphical analogy resembling the example of the hairdresser by saying that 'We will always need four musicians to form a string quartet.'
4. Based on household survey microdata, Tornarolli and Conconi (2007) state that between 1998 and 2006 the ratio of income of a formal to an informal salary in Argentina jumped from 2 to 3. This in turn is explained by the relative prevalence of informality among young and unskilled workers employed in small businesses. This provides a rationale of why high-tech industries present low records of informality. However, the data also show that the relative wage in services subsectors is low in some highly informal activities (construction and trade) as well as in others that are less informal (education and health).

REFERENCES

Bacchetta, M., E. Ernst and J. Bustamante (2009), *Globalization and Informal Jobs in Developing Countries*, Geneva: International Labor Office and World Trade Organization.

Baumol, W. (1967), 'Macroeconomics of unbalanced growth: the anatomy of urban crises', *American Economic Review*, **57** (3), 415–26.

Coremberg, A. (2006), 'Productividad, costo laboral y excedente en la Argentina durante 2003 y 2004', mimeo, Buenos Aires: Ministry of Labor.

Coremberg A. (2009), 'Origen sectorial y factorial del declive de la productividad argentina', mimeo, Buenos Aires: ECLAC, November.

Dasgupta, S. and A. Singh (2006), 'Manufacturing, services and premature deindustrialization in developing countries: a Kaldorian analysis', UNU-WIDER Research Paper no. 2006/49, Helsinki, May.

Gasparini, L. and L. Tornarolli (2007), 'Labor informality in Latin America and the Caribbean: patterns and trends from household survey microdata', CEDLAS Working Paper no. 46, La Plata, Argentina, February.

Gordo, E., J. Jareño and A. Urtasun (2006), 'Radiografía del sector de servicios en España', Banco de España Documento Ocasional no. 0607, Madrid.

Kongsamut, P., S. Rebelo and D. Xie (1997), 'Beyond balanced growth', NBER Working Paper no. 6159, Combridge, MA, September.

Oulton, N. (1999), 'Must the growth rate decline? Baumol's unbalanced growth revisited', mimeo, London: Bank of England, London.

Tornarolli, L. and A. Conconi (2007), 'Informalidad y movilidad laboral: un análisis empírico para Argentina', CEDLAS Working Paper no. 59, La Plata, Argentina, October.

Tripplett, J. and B. Bosworth (2003), 'Productivity measurement issues in services industries: "Baumol's Disease" has been cured', *FRBNY Economic Policy Review*, September.

Verma, R. (2006), 'India's service sector growth – a "new" revolution', mimeo, Los Angeles: University of Southern California, June.

World Bank (2008), *The Informal Sector: What It Is, Why Do We Care, and How Do We Measure It?*, Washington, DC.

8. Size and importance of tertiary activities in Brazil[1]

Carlos R. Azzoni and Joaquim J.M. Guilhoto

8.1 INTRODUCTION

Tertiary activities – also known as services – are becoming more and more important all over the world as their share in total income increases with the level of economic activities within countries, as Figure 8.1 shows. A comparison with other countries in the same range of GDP per capita values indicates that Brazil occupies an average position, but that improved economic performance will, as the GDP growth rates in recent years indicate, tend to increase the importance of the tertiary sector in the economy. Interestingly, Brazil and Argentina are very similar as regards the importance of tertiary activities in their respective economies. With its present importance and its prospects for expansion, this sector is an interesting case study in both countries, despite its being paid relatively little attention in economic analyses to date.[2]

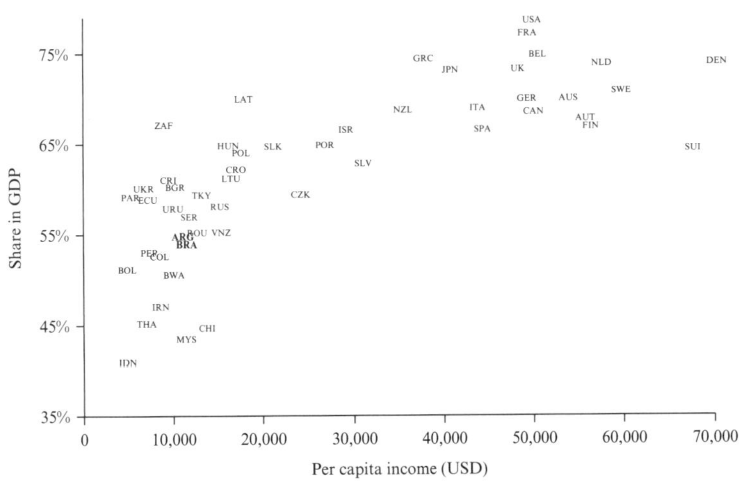

Figure 8.1 Share of tertiary activities in GDP across countries.

Given the nature of activities in the tertiary sector, their location is predominantly urban, posing particular concerns. One of these is the accelerated growth of cities. Another relates to informality. Such activities are typically offered by small establishments with little start-up capital and geographically restricted markets. Considering Brazil's urban population relative to its total population, studying these activities – especially those present in informal markets – is fundamental to understanding the economic dynamics of its cities and regions. Provision and financing of public services depends on revenue-gathering capacity, which diminishes when the share of informal activities is large. Therefore, the increasing informality that comes about with the increasing importance of tertiary activities poses important political and economic challenges.

8.2 TERTIARY AND INFORMAL ACTIVITIES: SOME DESCRIPTIVE STATISTICS

In order to analyze the tertiary sector, we disaggregate it into three subsectors: commerce, services and public administration. Their shares in national value added, portrayed in Table 8.1, are relatively stable, because the period considered is short. In 2007, the urban-located tertiary sector reached an impressive share of 66.6 per cent of total value added that year, compatible with the 81 per cent urbanization rate recorded in the 2000 population census. Between 2000 and 2007, as Table 8.1 shows, com-

Table 8.1 Brazil 2000–07: sector shares in GDP

	Total	Primary	Secondary	Tertiary			
				All	Commerce	Services	Public administration
2000	100.0	5.6	27.7	66.7	10.6	41.1	15.0
2001	100.0	6.0	26.9	67.1	10.7	40.9	15.5
2002	100.0	6.6	27.1	66.3	10.2	40.6	15.5
2003	100.0	7.4	27.8	64.8	10.6	39.1	15.1
2004	100.0	6.9	30.1	63.0	11.0	37.3	14.7
2005	100.0	5.7	29.3	65.0	11.2	38.8	15.0
2006	100.0	5.5	28.8	65.8	11.5	39.0	15.3
2007	100.0	5.6	27.8	66.6	12.1	39.0	15.5

Source: IBGE, Contas Nacionais.

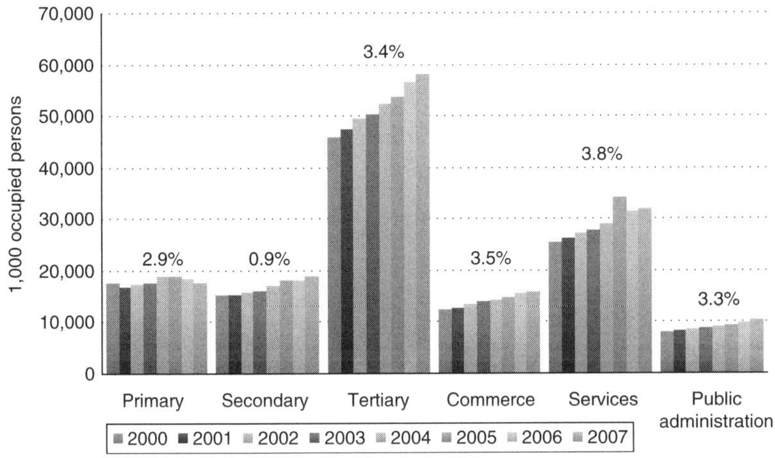

Source: Estimated from National Accounts, IBGE.

Figure 8.2 Brazil: occupation importance and growth.

merce and public administration slightly increased their importance, while services slightly decreased.

Employment in the tertiary sector was also examined. Figure 8.2 exhibits rates by major sector. The numbers above the columns indicate the average year-on-year growth rate over the period 2000–07. The share of the tertiary sector in total employment grew from 58.2 per cent in 2000 to 61.4 per cent in 2007, and the number of persons employed grew from 45.9 million in 2000 to 58.1 million in 2007. This growth occurred in the three subsectors of the tertiary, being largest in services, which grew at a yearly rate of 3.8 per cent, moving from 25.5 million employed in 2000 to 32.0 million in 2007. The primary sector share decreased from 22.3 per cent in 2000 and 18.6 per cent in 2007; the secondary sector increased from 15.4 million to 19.0 million employed persons, with a relatively constant share of around 20 per cent.

As Figure 8.3 indicates, the average year-on-year income of employed persons in the tertiary sector is comparable to that in the secondary sector (around R$12,700 in 2007), and larger than that in the primary sector (R$4900). However, the average income in the public administration sector (R$23,200) is double that in the other sectors within the tertiary (R$8600 in commerce and R$11,500 in services) and in the economy as a whole (R$11,200). In terms of growth rates, displayed above the respective blocks of columns, a general decline is evident in all sectors in the first 4 years of the period, up to the stabilization of inflation in 2004. But after

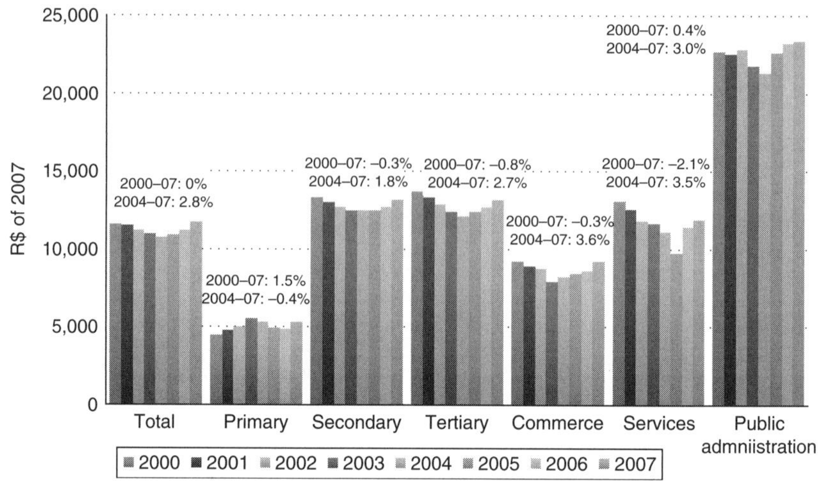

Source: Estimated from National Accounts, IBGE.

Figure 8.3 Brazil: average yearly income per occupied person.

that recovery was strong. There was a decrease of the average income of workers until 2004, following which, alongside the growth of the Brazilian economy, average incomes in the work force started to rise at a rate of 2.8 per cent per year on aggregate, and at higher rates in the tertiary sector, especially among services.

Informality in the tertiary sector was also examined. Defining formality and informality is no easy task; working definitions vary depending on the different objectives of each study (Feijó et al., 2009; Henley et al., 2009; Ulyssea, 2006). The definition used in this chapter is the one used by IBGE, which follows the International Labor Organization guidelines (Hussmanns, 2003; IBGE, 2008). The formal sector is defined as being composed of workers with an official work permit, public servants, the military and employers of formally constituted enterprises. The informal sector is composed of workers without a signed card, the self-employed, unpaid workers and informal employers (those not affiliated with formal enterprises).

As Figures 8.4 shows, agriculture is the sector with the highest level of informality, at 88.0 per cent of employment and 70.8 per cent of income. The tertiary sector has a level of informality of 51.4 per cent of its employment and 31.0 per cent of income. Within this sector, public administration presents the highest level of formality (87.6 per cent), and formal activities account for 93.0 per cent of the income generated in

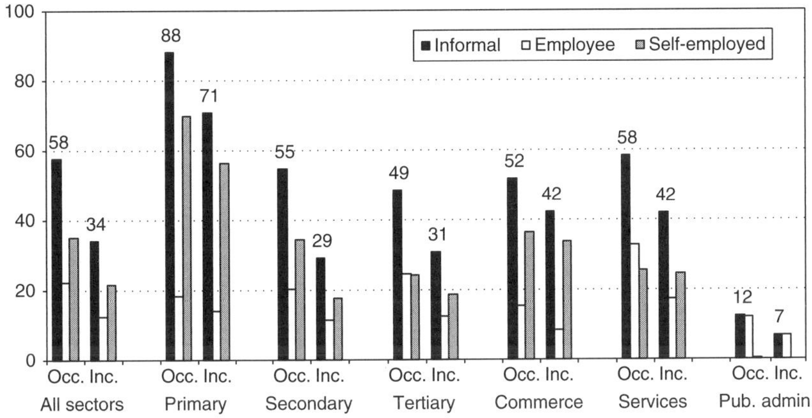

Source: Estimated from PNAD and National Accounts, IBGE.

Figure 8.4 Brazil: shares of occupied persons in occupation and income, 2006.

the subsector. Commerce's share of informality employment is 51.8 per cent and of income, 42.3 per cent, while services' share is 58.4 per cent of employment and 42.3 per cent of income. Despite the high level of informality observed in the Brazilian economy, the growth of employment in informal activities in all sectors has been more modest than the growth of formally organized activities. Another aspect is the relative share of self-employed among employment in informal markets. In agriculture and manufacturing, the share of self-employed is large, but the difference to that of the tertiary sector is negligible (24.5 per cent and 24.1 per cent, respectively), and this is granted by the subsector public administration. Within both commerce and services, the share of employees is higher than the share of self-employed. For income, the share of the self-employed is always larger than the share of employees, except, as expected, in public administration.

In short, informality is not a marginal issue; 57.6 per cent of occupation and 34.0 per cent of income are generated by informal activities. Many reasons for its existence can be found, but the difficulty of opening a business, the high tax burden, the difficulty in coping with indirect labor costs, and a poor enforcement of present regulations are the most pronounced.[3] It is not the object of this chapter to investigate the causes behind the existence of such a high level of informality within the Brazilian economy. Instead, we will try to establish its importance, quantitatively, and to reveal the sorts of connections with other activities within the economy.

8.3 INCOME DISTRIBUTION IN FORMAL AND INFORMAL ACTIVITIES

In the process of assessing the quantitative importance of tertiary activities and informality, incorporating the way they distribute income is of concern. In this section we present quantitative information in this regard.

The average yearly income for informal activities is always lower than for formal activities. The largest difference is in the primary sector, in which the average income in the formal sector is 3 times larger than in the informal sector (R$11,300 and R$3700, respectively); in the secondary sector, the ratio is 2.9 (R$18,800 and R$6400); the smallest ratio, 2.1, is found in the tertiary sector (R$16,100 and R$7600). For the economy as a whole, the ratio is 2.6 (R$16,400 and R$6200). The largest average year-on-year income comes from the public administration sector.

Figure 8.5 presents some fundamental aspects of how the sectors distribute their labor income across seven different income classes. In each sector, two blocks of columns are presented, one for formal activities and one for informal. Each column portrays the share of income, in that specific sector and formality status, assigned to people in that income bracket. We define the seven income classes boundaries, calculated in multiples of the official minimum wage value (R$350 per month in 2006), as: 0 to 1; 1 to 2; 2 to 3; 3 to 5; 5 to 10; 10 to 15; and over 15. It is clear that, in general, the share of income assigned to the first income bracket is larger in the informal activities by a multiple of at least 2.9 (agriculture); the largest differences are observed in manufacturing (4.5) and in commerce (4). This

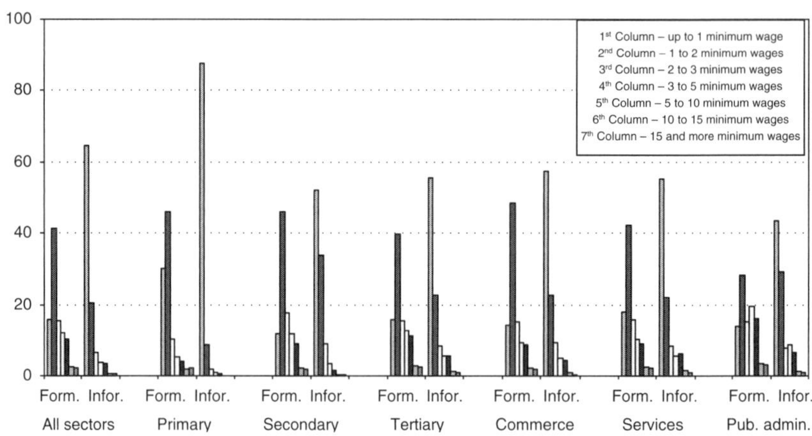

Figure 8.5 Brazil: distribution of income to different income classes, 2006.

indicates that informal activities have relatively larger shares of income among low-income workers.

Second, informal activities decrease as income grows, bar public administration, while formal activities increase until the second income bracket, and decrease in the upper income classes, with public administration again the only exception. Considering income assigned to the three lowest income brackets, the shares in informal activities are always over 85 per cent, being largest for agriculture (98 per cent) and manufacturing (95 per cent). The same shares for formal activities are always lower. Within the tertiary sector, formal commerce has 78 per cent of its income for those three lower income brackets, while informal commerce has 89 per cent. The same shares for services are 76 per cent formal and 86 per cent informal. In summary, informal activities present a more pronounced pro-poor profile overall, especially in manufacturing.

8.4 EXPECTED IMPACTS OF GROWTH ON INFORMALITY AND INCOME DISTRIBUTION

The above figures indicate that tertiary activities are a significant part of the Brazilian economy, and that informality varies across sectors. They also show that the pattern of income distribution varies across sectors and, within sectors, between their formal and informal segments. This raises questions. What would be the changes in the income inequality profile of the country? What would be the share of informal activities in the Brazilian economy as it approaches the per capital GDP of developed countries whose share of tertiary activities is higher than in Brazil? Lastly, what would be the impacts on income inequality of an increase or decrease in the degree of informality in different sectors, especially in the tertiary activities?

To try to answer such questions, a Leontief type of model is estimated. The economy is divided into 49 sectors, and an input–output matrix for the year of 2006 is utilized. Each sector is divided into formal and informal activities. Informal activities are then divided into two subcategories: persons employed without a signed card and persons self-employed. Besides the input–output relationships embedded in the input–output matrix, the model also considers the distribution of payments to factors of production, split into the seven income brackets already presented. The principal sources for such information are PNAD (Pesquisa Nacional Por Amostras de Domicílios) and the System of National Accounts, both from IBGE.

The intra-sector flows existing in a given economy, determined by both technological and economic factors, can be described by a system of simultaneous equations represented by

$$X = AX + Y, \tag{8.1}$$

where X is an $(n \times 1)$ vector of total sector output, Y is an $(n \times 1)$ vector with each sector's final demand, and A is an $(n \times n)$ matrix with the technical coefficients of production (see Leontief, 1951). The sectoral final demands are usually treated as exogenous to the system. Therefore, the output vector is uniquely determined given the final demand vector; that is,

$$X = (I - A)^{-1}, \tag{8.2}$$

where I is the $(n \times n)$ identity matrix and $(I - A)^{-1}$ is the $(n \times n)$ identity matrix with the Leontief inverse.

The model was estimated for the Brazilian economy for the year 2006, using information from the System of National Accounts, following the methodology presented in Guilhoto and Sesso Filho (2005). The 49 sectors are split between: agriculture (1); extractive (2); manufacturing (29); public utilities (1); construction (1); commerce (1); services (11); and public administration (3). In each sector, wages, salaries and payments to the self-employed are distributed to the three categories of agents: formally employed persons; employees without a signed card (informally employed); and the self-employed. In each sector and in each of these four categories income is distributed to the seven income brackets considered.

In order to assess the respective importance of informality gaps across sectors and tertiary activities in the Brazilian economy, we created scenarios in which each of the 49 sectors increased its production one at a time. We then estimated the direct and indirect impacts of the production increases on income and employment in the formal and informal economy, as well as in each of the seven income brackets. Table 8.2 presents a summary of the overall results regarding formality. For an R$1 million increase in production of each of the 49 sectors, the direct, indirect and induced effects across the other sectors of the economy were computed. The results were specific for each of the 49 sectors, which were in turn aggregated into the macro sectors displayed in the table. The original shares refer to the importance of the sector observed in 2006; the resulting shares reflect the additional employment or income resulting from the increase in production value. The last lines in each part of the table present the ratio of the two results, allowing for the assessment of the consequences of the simulated changes.

As an example, take the primary sector, in which 12 per cent of employment is formal in 2006 and 88 per cent is informal. The result-

Table 8.2 Original and resulting sectoral shares

			Primary	Secondary	Overall tertiary		
					Tertiary[a]	Commerce	Services
Employment	Original shares	Formal	12.0	45.3	51.4	48.2	41.6
		Informal	88.0	54.7	48.6	51.8	58.4
	Resulting shares	Formal	14.5	50.0	50.7	48.2	44.3
		Informal	85.5	50.0	49.3	51.8	55.7
	Change	Formal	1.21	1.10	0.99	1.00	1.06
		Informal	0.97	0.91	1.01	1.00	0.95
Income	Original shares	Formal	29.2	70.7	69.0	57.7	58.1
		Informal	70.8	29.3	31.0	42.3	41.9
	Resulting shares	Formal	35.6	69.8	62.1	58.9	55.6
		Informal	64.4	30.2	37.9	41.1	44.4
	Change	Formal	1.22	0.99	0.90	1.02	0.96
		Informal	0.91	1.03	1.22	0.97	1.06

Note: [a] Overall tertiary *less* commerce, services and public administration.

ing additional production will generate slightly different shares: the formal share increases to 14.5 per cent, and consequently the informal share is reduced to 85.5 per cent. The new formal share is 21 per cent larger than the original share, which is the largest proportional change among all sectors. The changes observed in tertiary activities are modest, with services presenting a marginal profile with larger formal participation in occupation than originally. Regarding participation in income generation, the results are different, except in the primary sector. The marginal share in income of tertiary activities presents a larger importance of informal activities than before, with services inverting the result for employment. Thus, the service sector would become more formal in terms of employment, but less formal in terms of income. Commerce, which was neutral in terms of employment, would become slightly more formal in terms of income.

Table 8.3 presents results regarding income distribution, in the same format as Table 8.2. Considering income accumulated up to the third minimum wage income level, the differences between the original shares and the resulting shares are negative for the primary and secondary sectors but positive for the tertiary. So, an increase in the size of the services sector tends to produce an improvement in income distribution, assigning more income to the three lowest income groups as compared with the 2006

Table 8.3 Original and resulting income bracket shares

		Share by minimum wage intervals							Cumulative						
		?1	1–2	2–3	3–5	5–10	10–15	?15	?1	1–2	2–3	3–5	5–10	10–15	?15
Income 2006	Primary	28.9	25.6	11.2	9.2	12.2	5.0	7.8	28.9	54.5	65.7	74.9	87.2	92.2	100.0
	Secondary	8.6	25.7	15.2	13.8	17.6	8.2	10.8	8.6	34.4	49.5	63.3	80.9	89.2	100.0
	Tertiary	8.1	17.2	11.9	15.0	23.5	10.2	14.0	8.1	25.3	37.3	52.3	75.8	86.0	100.0
	Commerce	10.0	23.3	14.3	13.1	20.1	9.2	9.9	10.0	33.3	47.6	60.7	80.9	90.1	100.0
	Services	9.8	18.5	12.4	13.1	22.1	10.4	13.7	9.8	28.3	40.7	53.8	75.9	86.3	100.0
	Public administration	4.4	11.6	9.7	19.2	27.9	10.5	16.8	4.4	15.9	25.7	44.9	72.7	83.2	100.0
Income resulting	Primary	25.4	24.7	11.6	10.0	13.7	5.9	8.6	25.4	50.1	61.7	71.7	85.4	91.4	100.0
	Secondary	9.1	21.9	14.0	14.0	19.7	9.3	12.0	9.1	31.0	45.0	59.0	78.7	88.0	100.0
	Tertiary	13.3	20.4	12.2	13.7	20.4	8.7	11.3	13.3	33.7	45.9	59.6	80.0	88.7	100.0
	Commerce	9.4	22.3	14.1	13.3	20.6	9.5	10.7	9.4	31.6	45.8	59.1	79.8	89.3	100.0
	Services	14.3	21.0	12.4	13.5	19.8	8.4	10.6	14.3	35.3	47.7	61.2	81.0	89.4	100.0
	Public administration	4.3	10.3	8.4	15.9	27.8	12.5	20.8	4.3	14.6	23.0	38.9	66.7	79.2	100.0

Employment 2006	Frimary	80.6	13.2	2.9	1.5	1.1	0.3	0.3	80.6	93.8	96.7	98.2	99.4	99.7	100.0
	Secondary	33.8	39.2	12.9	7.1	4.9	1.1	1.0	33.8	73.0	85.9	93.0	97.9	99.0	100.0
	Tertiary	35.1	31.4	12.1	9.3	8.4	2.0	1.6	35.1	66.5	78.6	87.9	96.3	98.3	100.0
	Commerce	36.6	35.1	12.1	7.2	6.4	1.6	1.0	36.6	71.8	83.8	91.0	97.4	99.0	100.0
	Services	39.8	30.6	11.4	7.5	7.3	1.9	1.5	39.8	70.3	81.7	89.3	96.6	98.5	100.0
	Fublic administration	17.7	28.4	14.4	18.3	15.1	3.1	2.8	17.7	46.1	60.5	78.8	93.9	96.9	99.7
Employment resulting	Frimary	77.4	14.6	3.6	2.0	1.6	0.4	0.4	77.4	92.1	95.6	97.6	99.2	99.6	100.0
	Secondary	41.8	31.6	11.3	7.0	5.7	1.4	1.1	41.8	73.4	84.7	91.7	97.4	98.9	100.0
	Tertiary	46.6	29.0	9.7	6.6	5.7	1.3	1.1	46.6	75.7	85.3	91.9	97.6	98.9	100.0
	Commerce	36.0	34.7	12.3	7.5	6.7	1.7	1.1	36.0	70.7	83.0	90.5	97.2	98.9	100.0
	Services	48.2	28.7	9.4	6.3	5.3	1.2	1.0	48.2	76.9	86.2	92.5	97.8	99.0	100.0
	Fublic administration	22.8	27.0	12.8	15.0	15.1	3.7	3.5	22.8	49.8	62.7	77.7	92.7	96.5	100.0

distribution of income. The same pattern is observed for the increase in employment, in which the tertiary sector would produce a more pro-poor generation of new employment.

Those differences in the share of formal activities and in the income distribution profiles are due to the distinct ways different sectors relate to each other through input–output relationships, as well as through payments to labor employed. They indicate their importance both in shaping up the share of informality as well as in potentially changing income distribution in the country.

8.5 CONCLUSIONS

The results overall show not only the importance of the tertiary sector for the Brazilian economy in terms of employment (around 61 per cent of total employment), and income generation (around 67 per cent of value added), but also the high share of the informal sector in the Brazilian economy (around 58 per cent of occupation and 34 per cent of income). The combination of these aspects results in an economy with low wages and salaries and a high concentration of income.

The simulation of increases in production in different sectors indicates that the possible growth of tertiary activities will tend to produce positive changes in income distribution, although they will also tend to increase informality. Although this is good news from a distributive point of view, it raises concerns about how to finance public services in cities, especially large ones, since informal activities generally do not pay taxes, especially local taxes.

NOTES

1. The authors would like to thank Leopoldo Millan, Denise Imori, Julio Lucchesi Moraes and Rodrigo Nishida for much-needed help with the data compilation.
2. Baer and Samuelson (1981) argue that the linkage between industrial modernization and significant service sector employment gains has not been adequately considered.
3. For a discussion see Kon (2003, 2007 and 2009), Jennequin (2008), Azzoni (2005) and Azzoni and Andrade (2005).

REFERENCES

Azzoni, C.R. (2005), 'Setor terciário e concentração regional no Brasil', in C.C. Diniz and M.B. Lemos (eds), *Economia e Território*, Belo Horizonte: Editora da UFMG, pp. 551–71.

Azzoni, C.R. and A.S. Andrade (2005), 'The tertiary sector and regional inequality in Brazil', *Région et Développement*, **21**, 155–72.
Baer, W. (1981), 'Toward a service oriented growth strategy', *World Development*, **9** (1), 499–514.
Feijo, C.A., D.B.N. Silva and A.C. Souza (2009), 'Quão heterogêneo é o setor informal Brasileiro? Uma proposta de classificação de atividades baseada na ECINF', *Revista de Economia Contemporânea*, **13** (2), 329–54.
Guilhoto, J.J.M. and U.A. Sesso Filho (2005), 'Estimação da matriz insumo-produto a partir de dados preliminares das contas nacionais', *Economia Aplicada*, **9** (2), 277–99.
Henley, A., G.R. Arabsheibani and F.G. Carneiro (2009), 'On defining and measuring the informal sector: evidence from Brazil', *World Development*, **37** (5), 992–1003.
Hussmanns, R. (2003), 'Statistical definition of informal employment: guidelines endorsed by the Seventeenth International Conference of Labour Statisticians', paper presented at the 7th Meeting of the Expert Group on Informal Sector Statistics (Delhi Group), Delhi, 2003, available at: <http://www.ilo.org/public/english/bureau/stat/download/papers/def.pdf
IBGE (2006), *Pesquisa Nacional por Amostra de Domicílios (PNAD)*, Vol. 27, Rio de Janeiro.
IBGE (2008), *Sistema de Contas Nacionais Brasil*, Relatório Metodológico no. 24, 2nd edn, Rio de Janeiro.
Jennequin, H. (2008), 'The evolution of the geographical concentration of tertiary sector activities in Europe', *The Service Industries Journal*, **28** (3), 291–306.
Kon, A. (2003), 'Labor informal conditions in Brazilian tertiary activities', available at: http://virtualbib.fgv.br/dspace/bitstream/handle/10438/1909/TD115.pdf?sequence=1
Kon, A. (2007), 'Sobre a economia política do desenvolvimento e a contribuição dos serviços', *Revista de Economia Política*, **27** (3), 130–46.
Kon, A. (2009), 'O novo regionalismo e o papel dos serviços no desenvolvimento: transformações das hierarquias econômicas regionais', *Oikos* (Rio de Janeiro), **8** (2), 4.
Leontief, W. (1951), *The Structure of the American Economy*, 2nd edn, New York: Oxford University Press.
Ulyssea, G. (2006), 'Informalidade no mercado de trabalho brasileiro: uma resenha da literatura', *Revista de Economia Política*, **26** (4), 596–618.

9. Comments on part III

Edmund Amann

Chapters 7 and 8 draw our attention to an issue which is perhaps one of the least studied elements in the development process: the role of the services sector. That the sector has been sidelined as a focus for research over the years is not surprising. It is notoriously difficult to measure productivity in parts of the services sector, added to which the existence of informality on a large scale merely compounds the problem of data accuracy and availability. Given the increasingly quantitative nature of development economies it is quite understandable that researchers have focused on sectors for which more plentiful – and reliable – data are available.

Still, seeing that by any estimate services account for the bulk of output and employment in most middle-and upper-income developing and emerging economies, it is high time more research effort was made in this direction. Chapter 7, by Ricardo Bebczuk and Chapter 8 by Carlos Azzoni and Joaquim Guilhoto make a welcome contribution. They certainly increase our – all too slender – understanding of the role of services in the ongoing economic development of Argentina and Brazil.

In studying the experience of Argentina in the international context, Bebczuk points to the relative growth of the services sector in recent years. For Argentina, the sector currently accounts for no less than 70 per cent of GDP and 82 per cent of employment. Bebczuk's analysis of Argentina is quick to highlight the role of informality. Interestingly, the data reveal that informality in services is higher than the overall national average only in one or two subsectors; in the rest it is, in fact, below average. Bebczuk also draws attention to one of the supposed nostrums of the services sector: that its productivity growth rate always lags behind that of other sectors. In fact, the chapter refutes this generalization in the Argentinean case, pointing to the sector's critical – and under-appreciated – role in the growth of total factor productivity. Bebczuk also points out the potential the sector possesses to foster improvements in trade performance; for too long services in Argentina have contributed a deficit to the current-account balance. Efforts should therefore be made to investigate what might be done to improve Argentina's track record in this key area.

Azzoni and Guilhoto concern themselves with the Brazilian experience. They are especially interested in the role services play with respect to the incidence of informality and the distribution of income. Eschewing a lengthy description of the development of the services sector of Brazil, the authors set out to model the effects of its future expansion for income distribution and informality. This is done using a Leontief-style input–output model. They find that the future growth of the services sector is likely to have the effect of evening out the interpersonal distribution of income.

However, in Brazil the expansion of the sector will probably be associated with an increase in the absolute incidence of informality. It seems to me that a number of issues are raised by these striking conclusions. If it is indeed the case that the growth of services will mean increasing numbers employed in the informal sector (though not, perhaps, an increasing share of the overall total) then clearly we face the consequences of a state, already facing important fiscal constraints, missing out on a considerable revenue stream.

Against this background it is probably worth considering what steps might be usefully taken to divert more services growth into the tax-raising formal sector. Here, one would have to acknowledge that despite the progress of Brazil in recent years (as witnessed by its spectacular growth performance and its becoming a magnet for international investment), the private sector remains afflicted with high compliance costs. These surround indirect and direct taxation regimes and labour market rules. Given the probable cautiousness of the government of Dilma Rouseff, elected in October 2010, in pressing ahead with reform here, it seems unlikely that Azzoni and Guilhoto's forecasts of the future scale of the informal sector will be too far off the mark.

In considering the role of services in the development process I would argue that it is too easy to think of service activities as being highly discrete and differentiable from manufacturing, or even from NRB (natural-resource-based) activities. In fact, to an increasing extent (especially in the case of high-valued-added capital goods) services – in the shape of technical assistance and maintenance agreements – are bundled into the sales of manufactures. In this sense alone, there is a need to move towards the view that efficient, competitive manufacturing, primary and services sectors are complementary and codependent.

Equally, it seems important to acknowledge that services – as Bebczuk highlights – can be centers for high productivity growth and, it should be stressed, innovation. It seems a pity that too little attention has been paid in the development literature to the role of services as a means of moving up the global value chain and redefining the position of an economy in the global division of labor. One only has to look at India, and its booming, export-orientated information technology and engineering services sectors, to realize how critical services activities have become in terms of addressing the external constraint and developing a skilled pool of human capital. In other words, it is high time more researchers followed the examples of the authors of Chapters 7 and 8 and delved into the linkages which connect services growth, productivity, innovation, trade performance and development.

PART IV

Income distribution

10. Anatomy of distributive changes in Argentina[1]

Walter Sosa-Escudero and Sergio Petralia

10.1 INTRODUCTION

In most regions and episodes the shapes of income distributions change slowly, a fact that led Henry Aaron (1978) to state that following them is like 'watching the grass grow'. Unlike monetary or financial indicators, poverty or inequality indexes are computed mostly on a yearly basis; moreover, comparative studies have trouble establishing the statistical and economic significance of changes in contiguous years (see Sosa-Escudero and Gasparini, 2001).

In the last 30 years Latin American countries have undergone a period of drastic changes, including episodes of marked cyclical macroeconomic performance, as well as profound changes in their economic structures associated with the globalization/privatization policies of the early 1990s. In the case of Argentina, and in contrast to Aaron's appreciations, the distribution of incomes changed rapidly and significantly during this period, to the point that the title of a song by the cult pop band The Move, 'I Can Hear The Grass Grow', seems to provide a more accurate description.

Mean income, or a related measure of central tendency, like GDP per capita, sometimes adequately serves the purpose of tracing out movements in income distribution, and performs well during episodes where its shape changes slowly. This fact may help to justify the scarcity of distributional studies before the 1990s in Argentina. The macro-dominated 1980s appropriately focused on following GDP, since most changes in the distribution of incomes during that period were macro-driven location movements, with subtle changes in other relevant aspects, as documented in Gasparini et al. (2001).

The 1990s witnessed a massive growth in the number of distributive studies for Argentina, mostly fueled by the fact that inequality and poverty have risen persistently since then. The increasing availability of micro-data, the sharp decrease in computational costs, and the development of new econometric tools, are all factors that help explain this trend. Nevertheless, the key reason inequality and poverty have received so much attention latterly is the dramatic changes experienced by the country, and the urgency of adopting sound policy measures aimed at alleviating the effects of poverty and inequality.

A relevant recent study by Leonardo Gasparini and Guillermo Cruces (2009) documents in detail the literature on inequality in Argentina, identifying historical episodes and highlighting possible explanatory factors, and serves as an important starting point for this chapter; as a matter of fact, the quote from Aaron is taken from the introduction to their paper.

Because the changes in the distribution of income in Argentina since the 1970s have been so drastic it is natural to wonder whether they can be appropriately captured by looking at just mean and/or median incomes and inequality measures. Poverty rates, the size of the middle class, and polarization indexes are examples of concepts that focus on other aspects of the distribution of income that might have worsened alongside inequality, and must be addressed as well.

The main goal of this chapter is to complement inequality and mean income analysis by looking at the *whole* of income distribution, with the purpose of providing a more detailed analysis of distributive changes in Argentina that might be overlooked in examining inequality and income trends alone. For example, as will be discussed in this chapter, the Gini coefficients for 1996 and 2006 are very similar, even though they correspond to income distributions of markedly different shapes.

Our approach is mostly descriptive. The main goal is to establish some stylized facts on the changes of the whole distribution of income, beyond its center and dispersion. We make no attempts at explaining the causes behind these changes, but try to establish similarities and differences in the evolution of alternative aspects of the income distribution, which should serve as a sound basis for further research aimed at providing causal explorations of these phenomena and, we hope, at proposing relevant policy measures.

The chapter is organized as follows. We start the next section with data description and some basic facts, focusing mostly on mean incomes and inequality. In Section 10.3 we step back and adopt a more agnostic, non-parametric approach by looking at the whole of the distribution of incomes, without any attempt to reduce it to summary measures. Section 10.4 focuses on specific regions of the distribution of income, like the bottom (poverty) or the center (middle class). Section 10.5 concludes.

10.2 THE BASIC FACTS: INCOME AND INEQUALITY IN ARGENTINA

Figure 10.1 sets the starting point for this research. It shows (in different scales) the evolution of inequality as measured by the Gini coefficient and by median income, in the period 1974 to 2006.The data from which this figure is constructed, as well as those for all the others in the chapter, are presented in Table 10.1. Figure 10.1 is eloquent about the impressions just advanced in our introductory section: median income wandered cyclically (including in periods of severe depression, more intensely than in those of recovery), but inequality rose steadily and significantly until 2002, after which clear signs of recovery are observed.

The notion of income used in the chapter is income per capita as reported to the Encuesta Permanente de Hogares (EPH), which covers mostly labor income and monetary transfers. We have deflated nominal measures using the official consumer price index. Microdata for the analysis will be the EPH for Greater Buenos Aires (GBA). The focus on a single region may sound severely restrictive at first glance, but, as Gasparini and Cruces (2009) clearly document, including all regions leaves the evolutions of aggregate distributive figures virtually unaltered. On the contrary, the costs of including other regions are prohibitive for the study of evolutions: only GBA is available for a rather long period, a key element in establishing the main point of this chapter, which requires going back in time as far as possible, using a comparable data set.

Household surveys have several limitations as a means to capture true income distribution, and a myriad of technical decisions are usually taken to deal with some of these, which include underreporting, the need to find a relevant numeraire to handle household compositions (per capita, by equivalent adults etc.) and the inability to capture alternative sources (like

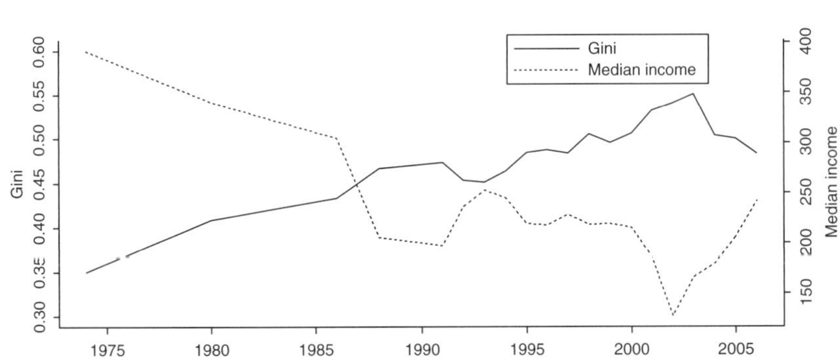

Figure 10.1 Argentina 1974–2006: inequality and income.

Table 10.1 Argentina: basic measures

Year	Gini	Atkinson (2)	Theil (0.5)	Entropy (0.5)	Mean income	Median income	90/10 Quantile	50/10 Quantile	90 Quantile	10 Quantile	Poverty (survey)	Middle class (hybrid)	Middle class (BD)
1974	0.350	0.414	0.215	0.209	475	392	4.865	2.243	849	175	0.071	0.826	0.250
1980	0.409	0.656	0.298	0.282	450	340	7.329	2.800	890	121	0.152	0.748	0.332
1986	0.433	0.493	0.332	0.322	405	305	7.619	2.857	812	107	0.215	0.684	0.403
1988	0.467	0.575	0.399	0.375	297	206	9.800	3.311	609	62	0.446	0.454	0.541
1991	0.474	0.530	0.396	0.400	297	197	8.316	2.789	589	71	0.371	0.528	0.581
1992	0.453	0.528	0.363	0.351	337	236	7.857	2.673	695	88	0.284	0.615	0.516
1993	0.451	0.548	0.368	0.350	359	252	8.583	2.991	724	84	0.250	0.650	0.465
1994	0.464	0.526	0.380	0.374	360	245	8.667	2.918	727	84	0.261	0.638	0.494
1995	0.485	0.566	0.420	0.406	333	219	9.750	3.000	712	73	0.341	0.558	0.528
1996	0.488	0.610	0.432	0.413	326	218	9.621	3.097	678	70	0.366	0.533	0.532
1997	0.484	0.590	0.427	0.403	350	228	10.780	3.234	761	71	0.318	0.582	0.492
1998	0.505	0.625	0.471	0.445	359	219	11.470	3.267	769	67	0.344	0.556	0.496
1999	0.496	0.614	0.451	0.425	339	219	11.111	3.333	731	66	0.361	0.539	0.513
2000	0.507	0.679	0.481	0.444	337	215	12.382	3.575	746	60	0.367	0.533	0.509
2001	0.532	0.697	0.541	0.493	312	186	14.583	3.889	698	48	0.432	0.468	0.507
2002	0.540	0.665	0.549	0.512	213	127	15.333	4.195	464	30	0.639	0.260	0.557
2003	0.551	0.681	0.571	0.570	295	166	12.740	3.619	583	46	0.487	0.413	0.544
2004	0.504	0.625	0.472	0.446	280	180	11.845	3.544	600	51	0.441	0.459	0.553
2005	0.500	0.606	0.459	0.442	319	206	10.915	3.394	662	61	0.372	0.527	0.531
2006	0.484	0.617	0.437	0.405	360	242	10.327	3.309	756	73	0.320	0.580	0.465

implicit rents from owned assets) among many others. These problems are important when the goal is to measure the *levels* of inequality and welfare, but are of a smaller magnitude when the focus is on their *evolutions*. For the purposes of this chapter, we favor a readily reproducible and comparable approach, for which we will stay as close as possible to official, publicly available microdata. Gasparini et al. (2001) and Gasparini and Cruces (2009) present a very detailed discussion of alternative welfare measures based on different notions of incomes. Gasparini and Gluzman (2009) compare official statistics with privately administered data. Their results support the idea that even though levels may present marked differences, evolutions behave similarly under alternative notions of income and sources.

Referring again to Figure 10.1, inequality grew steadily from 1974 onwards. The Gini measure rose almost monotonically from 0.349 in 1974 to a peak of 0.55 in 2003, after which a period of steady decline started that puts this figure at 0.48 for 2006. Alternative measures of inequality (Theil, Atkinson or an entropy-based one) reveal a similar pattern.

An alternative way to gauge the severity of the problem is to view the evolution of inequality in Argentina from a cross-sectional, comparative perspective. A Gini coefficient of 0.35 (Argentina in 1974) corresponds to the same figure for the United Kingdom in 2005, and the peak value of 0.55 in 2003 compares to inequality in Brazil or Ecuador, also in 2005. That is, in the period 1974–2003, and in terms of the performance of 2005, Argentina moved from one inequality measure of a developed country like the UK to that of Brazil and Ecuador, countries with long histories of severe distributive problems.

An important issue behind the strong and increasing trend in inequality before 2002 is the effect of early information, especially data from the first available points (1974, 1980 and 1986), which have a major effect in determining the overall, explosive positive trend. As a matter of fact, of the increase of 0.2 in the Gini coefficient between 1974 and 2003, almost half took place along these three periods. This appreciation does not cast doubt on the severity of increasing inequality in Argentina (specially in the 1990s), but does highlight the limitations of making long-run assessments when overall trends are difficult to establish. More concretely, had the analysis been conducted with the probably more reliable and comparable information starting in the late 1980s, the perception of the recovery after 2003 suggests there would have been a more drastic change in trends than would appear when we include distant years like 1974. This fact stresses the need to dig more deeply into the evolution of inequality, from a more historical, long-run perspective. Alvaredo (2008) is a clear example of the many difficulties in exploring distributive issues from a historical perspective. The *Journal of Iberian and Latin American Economic History* (2010) presents a recent collection of papers on the issue.

Another look at Figure 10.1 shows an interesting pattern. It reveals the marked counter-cyclical behavior of inequality: aggregate improvements in income (as measured by median income) are usually accompanied by improvements (decreases) in inequality. The scope of this chapter and the short temporal span of the observations prevent us from performing a meticulous time series analysis of this pattern, which would require dealing with the likely nonstationary nature of the series involved. Nevertheless, these preliminary results are strongly suggestive: in spite of the marked increasing trend in inequality, short-term movements are strongly associated to the overall performance of the economy. As a matter of fact, the correlation coefficient for the median income and the Gini measure is 0.92. This is particularly relevant for (and very likely driven by) the period after 2002, where the reversion in income trends was accompanied by a sharp decline in inequality. This is a highly relevant issue that truly deserves a more detailed econometric analysis – one, it is to be hoped, that is also causal.

To summarize the results of this section, there is clear evidence of a marked increase in inequality in the 1990s, robust to alternative ways of measuring it, and of a rapid decline after 2003. The perception of the sudden increase is magnified by its comparison with inequality at the beginning of the analysis, in 1974, where the low numbers observed are comparable to those of a developed country like the UK. The relevance of 1974 as a sound benchmark is debatable, and certainly requires more analysis. We also highlight the seldom-explored cyclical nature of inequality, that beyond its trending behavior shows a strong correlation with the cyclical evolution of median income. This is an important subject that requires more technical scrutiny.

10.3 A NON-PARAMETRIC PERSPECTIVE OF DISTRIBUTIVE CHANGES IN ARGENTINA

In 2006, following the rapid recovery after abandoning convertibility, the Argentine economy presented very similar levels of inequality (a Gini index of around 0.47) to those of 1994, that is, before the start of the crisis that climaxed in 2002. The anti-cyclical behavior suggested in the previous section, and the observed trend, hint at a stage of recovery in terms of inequality. In light of the drastic changes observed in inequality and median income in this period, we may wonder cautiously whether other aspects of the distribution changed as radically as its dispersion and center, and how this sudden recovery in terms of inequality affected the whole distribution.

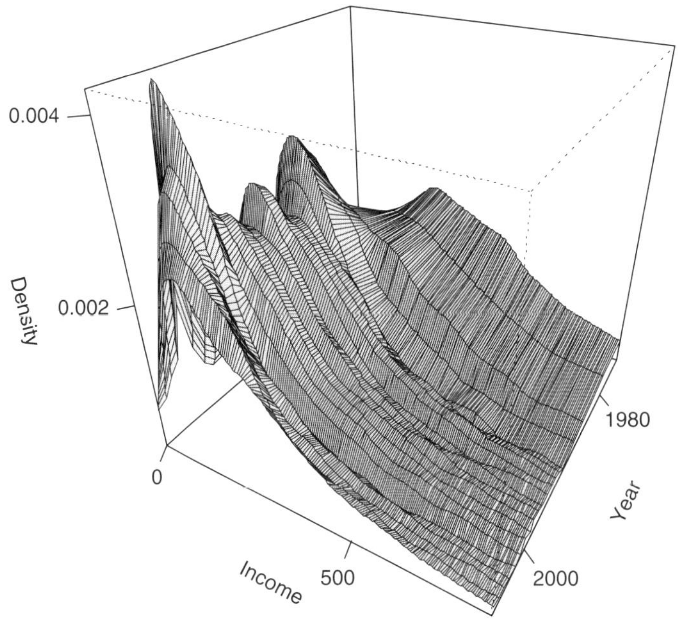

Figure 10.2 Argentina 1974–2006: evolution of income densities – three-dimensional plot.

Nonparametric techniques are powerful tools when the purpose is to reveal the shapes of relevant densities like incomes. Burkhauser et al. (1999) is one of the first studies along these lines. Botargues and Petrecolla (1999) is a very early example for Argentina. We refer to Li and Racine (2006) for a detailed discussion of these methods.

Figure 10.2 shows a three-dimensional plot of the evolution of the income densities for the period 1974–2006. The income density for each year is estimated separately using standard nonparametric kernel methods. Bandwidths are chosen using a data-driven algorithm, and the results are robust to significant variations in these values.

There are several aspects highlighted by these estimates. First, inequality increased, owing mostly to movements of the central part of the densities, to the left in the figure, with much larger intensity in the low ranges. As will be discussed in more detail in the next subsection, inequality and poverty moved synchronically in the period under study. This appreciation makes increases in inequality look even more dramatic. The deterioration in inequality is captured by a marked accumulation of values around lower levels of income – that is, a relatively flat density for 1974 contrasts strongly with the highly peaked ones of the late 1990s.

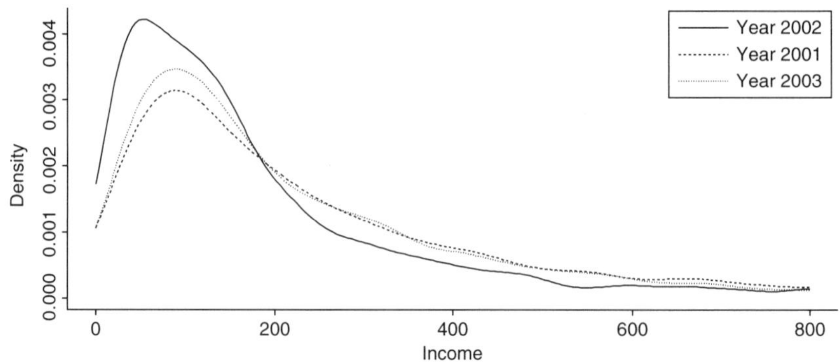

Figure 10.3 Densities during the crisis.

A relevant comment is that periods of rapid acceleration in prices (for example, the hyperinflationary episode of 1989, or the devaluation in 2002) imply drastic changes in the distribution of incomes, with a sudden accumulation in low values followed by a very rapid recovery. This pattern is highlighted in Figure 10.3, which presents densities estimated for the period covering the 2002 crisis. These sudden changes (which have a stronger impact on poverty measures) are likely driven by similar movements in the deflators used to compute real income. Consequently, years corresponding to large variations in price levels introduce significant volatility and may confound the analysis of trends. For example, in our plot in Figure 10.2, the high peaked density in 2002 looks more like an outlying observation that actually masks (and drives) the rapid recovery in the following year.

Regarding our original concern about the need to observe income distributions beyond median income and inequality, Figure 10.4 compares income densities for 1986 and 2006, which cover a period of drastic changes. The year 1986 provides a more representative starting point, free from the concerns regarding the isolated measures of the 1970s (as discussed in the previous section), right after the recovery of democracy and after the implementation of strong policy measures aimed at controlling inflation (the Plan Austral). The solid vertical line represents the poverty line (almost identical in both periods, in real terms), and median incomes are marked on the horizontal axis. The thin curve corresponds to 1986, and the thick one to 2006. Inequality is larger in 2006, but differences are not as dramatic as those implied by the years right after the crisis in 2002. Nevertheless, the shape of the density of incomes is completely different. In 1986 the poverty line lies to the left of the mode whereas in 2006 it lies to its right. The facts that the density shifted to the left and that the

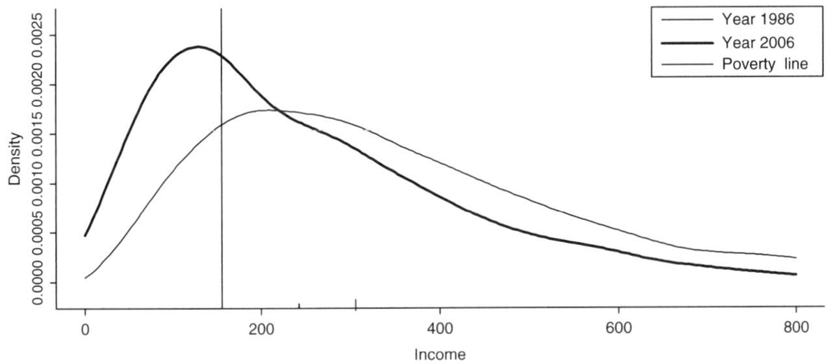

Figure 10.4 Comparative analysis 1986 and 2006.

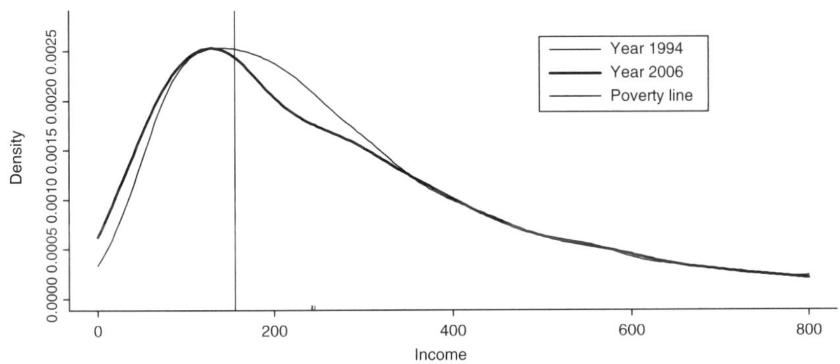

Figure 10.5 Comparative analysis 1994 and 2006.

poverty line remained constant imply that poverty in 2006 is not only higher but also much more 'stable' than in 1986. Unlike 1986, in 2006 the mode of the whole income density is also the mode of the income of the poor, whereas in 1986 the modal income of the poor is, trivially, the poverty line itself.

The results of the previous section suggest a period of rapid and significant recovery after 2003. It is interesting to observe whether this recovery implies a return to the situation in the early 1990s, right before the rapid deterioration of inequality started. Figure 10.5 compares 1994 and 2006. These two periods are interesting. The year 1994 marks the start of the process of sustained increases in inequality and poverty, but with values of inequality and median income very similar to those of 2006, the last period under analysis, and well after the decreases in inequality experienced after the crisis of 2002. Even though the centers (median and mean income) and dispersions (inequality) of these densities are almost the same, the underlying densities are different. In the comparison between these two periods, the right tail of the density remained unaltered for both distributions, whereas a substantial proportion of the center of the 1994 distribution shifted to the left.

Inequality remained unaltered in these two periods, mainly because most of the changes took place close to the left of the center of the densities. That is, more accumulation in the right tail would drive inequality up, but more concentration close to the median would drive it down. In 2006 the poverty line lies clearly to the right of the mode, unlike in 1994 where it lies very close to it. Consequently, even though in terms of inequality and median income the Argentine economy has given clear signals of recovery, the poor appear as a more homogeneous and stable grouping than in 1994.

Finally, even though the estimated densities clearly point towards a much more peaked distribution, with a stronger prevalence of the poor as a modal group, the results do not suggest obvious unambiguous clusterings based on income. Visual inspection does not reveal relevant multimodalities that would enable the classification of individuals in markedly different groups, like the extreme poor, the rich or even the middle class. A more detailed analysis of the possible presence of multimodalities is beyond the scope of this chapter, but it is an interesting research topic, which requires a more careful treatment in order to deal with the markedly asymmetric nature of the distribution of incomes, and more formal tests of these multimodalities.

To summarize, inequality increased considerably but also implied a drastic change in the center and left tail of the distribution of income, leaving the poor as a larger and more cohesive group, that now clearly contains the mode of the distribution. As a matter of fact, even after the drastic decreases in inequality in the last 5 years, the Argentine distribution of incomes is not returning to the shape it had before the sudden changes implied by the crisis in 2002.

10.4 THE POOR AND THE MIDDLE CLASS

The previous section suggests that important movements took place at the left of the distribution. Also, the lack of obvious multimodalities makes it difficult if not impossible to rely on the income distribution itself to identify groups like the poor, the rich or the middle class. That is, if these groups truly exist, they must be identified exogenously, and we must accept the fact that any disjoint, sharp partition among them should be very sensitive to the choice of the thresholds that define them.

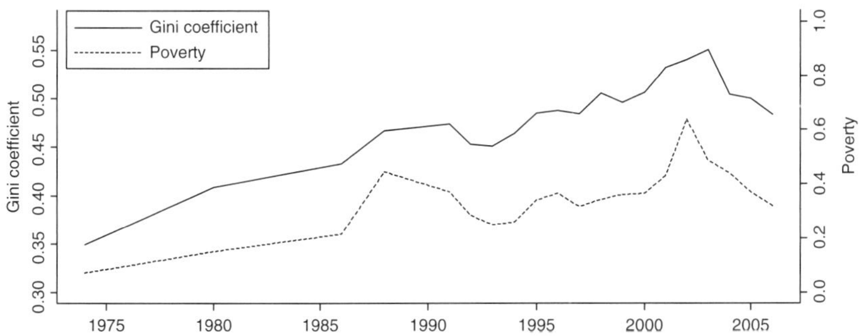

Figure 10.6 Poverty and inequality.

10.4.1 The Poor

Consider the case of the poor. If a standard poverty line criterion is adopted to identify them, then, when income becomes very concentrated close to the poverty line, classifications become erratic, as a substantial number of individuals with incomes marginally above the line are rendered as nonpoor, even though in economic terms their income is indistinguishable from that of those marginally below. Naturally, a similar comment holds for the middle class.

In periods of sudden changes in nominal and real variables, like in Argentina, this issue affects poverty considerably. Figure 10.6 shows the evolutions of inequality and poverty, the latter measured by the headcount ratio using official poverty lines. Isolated numbers are dramatic, since the range of variation covers low values in the 1980s (below 35 per cent) and figures above 60 per cent during the crisis in 2002. The long swings associated with strong accommodations of relative prices (mentioned in the previous section) are much more marked in the case of poverty than in that of inequality, which is natural, since, in computing poverty, deflators play an important role in determining income as well as the poverty line. As a matter of fact, the correlation between poverty rates and median income is negative and high (−0.84), but lower than that of inequality and median income.

An important point already stressed (Figure 10.5) is that the income of the poor in 2006 is more concentrated at lower values, so that increases in the poverty line took place in 2006 along a descending part of the density, far away from the mode, unlike 1994, when the line is very close to the modal value. Figure 10.7 explores this argument with more detail, for the whole period. The solid thick line represents the modal income, and the thin one the mean income of the poor (with a different

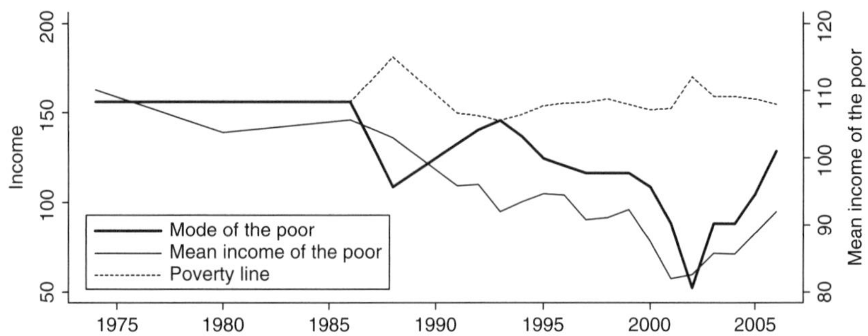

Figure 10.7 Analysis of poverty.

scale); we have also added the poverty line with a dashed line. From 1974 to 1986 the mode of the whole distribution lies to the right of the poverty line, hence the latter is (trivially) the mode of the poor. Overall, the pattern is similar to other measures: the mode departs further away (to the left) with respect to the poverty line, with a recovery after 2002. Modes represent points of high concentration of individuals, and these results clearly show that the mode of the poor has moved further to the left of the poverty line in the 1990s, but, unlike inequality, the recovery after the crisis is not enough to restore it to its initial position below the poverty line. This is the sense in which we claim that even after the clear signs of recovery in inequality terms, the poor are left behind as a more coherent group.

10.4.2 The Middle Class

It is harder to identify the middle class than it is the poor. In fact, it is relevant to remark that middle-class studies are almost nonexistent compared with those on poverty and inequality. Some very recent references for Argentina are Callorda and Caruso (2009), Olivieri (2008) and Cruces et al. (2010), the latter including a more detailed discussion of alternative measures of the middle class.

As expected, there is no well-established operational definition of the middle class. Without being too specific about details (for a lengthy discussion see Cruces et al., 2010), alternative measures favor either relative notions ('those between the 0.3 and 0.8 percentiles' as in Barro, 1999, and Easterley, 2001) or absolute ones ('those with income between 2 and 10 dollars per day', as in Banerjee and Duflo, 2007). Birdsall et al. (2000) define the middle class as those with incomes between 0.75 and 1.25 times the median income. Naturally, the Barro–Easterley measure implies a constant size of the middle class (it is always 50 per cent), so to measure its importance they focus on the mean income of this group. A second problem with this measure is that it ignores the implicit definitions of the poor in terms of poverty lines, so that in the case of Argentina in the last part of the crisis many families would be doubly classified as poor and middle class, were a standard poverty line used to identify the poor, and were the Barro–Easterly concept used to define the middle class. A similar concern affects Birdsall et al.'s measure. Banerjee and Duflo's approach is compatible with one particular definition of the poor (based on the U$S2-per-day line). Another relevant problem in identifying the sizes of the middle class is related to the well-known difficulties household surveys have in capturing rich families. This may distort severely the importance of the middle class as compared with that of those above it, since families in the latter range are either absent from surveys or appear with grossly underreported incomes.

We will consider a fourth simple strategy, which consists in defining the middle class as those above the poverty line and below the 0.9 percentile of income. Though trivial (the size of the middle class is determined by that of the poor, as its mirror image, since 'the rich' is always 10 percent), this measure is a compromise between an absolute one like Banerjee and Duflo's (but using as its lower bound the poverty line), and a relative magnitude on the right tail (like Barro and Easterley's), where there is less agreement about how to separate the rich from the rest, and in a region where missing data and underreport are very likely to occur. Two measures will be computed from our definition: the first one is simply the proportion of individuals in the middle class, which, as mentioned above, is by definition a mirror image of the poor. The second is the ratio of the size of the middle class over that of the poor, which measures the relative importance of the middle class as compared with a group well defined in absolute terms, like the poor.

Figure 10.8 presents estimates of the size of the middle class, based on the previous concepts. The thick line represents our proposed 'hybrid' criterion, and the thin line represents Banerjee and Duflo's measure (BD, henceforth). Trivially, the horizontal 0.5 line represents Barro and Easterly's measure. As expected, differences are relevant, since both measures are based on alternative thresholds. During the 1990s, both measures stay surprisingly close to the Barro–Easterley figure. When the crisis starts, our measure drops dramatically, a consequence of the sudden increase in poverty rates. The BD measure stays relatively close, mostly because it contains as middle-class many individuals rendered as poor by the standard poverty line criterion.

Figure 10.9 offers an alternative perspective. Based on our proposed

Figure 10.8 Size of the middle class.

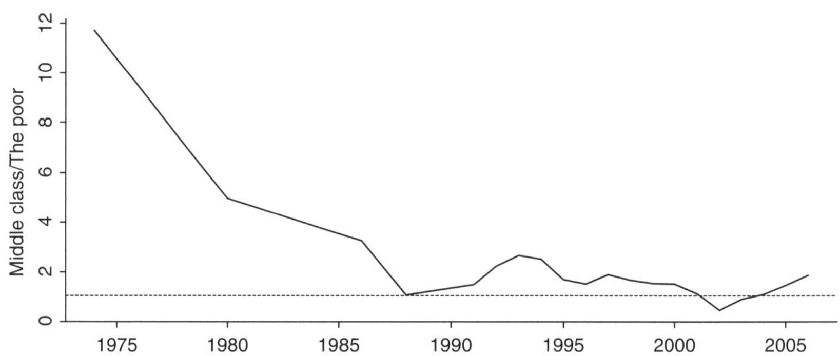

Figure 10.9 The middle class and the poor.

hybrid measure, we computed the ratio of the sizes of the middle class and the poor. This measure has a clear negative trend, more compatible with the perceived notion of deterioration of the middle class. Beyond the trending behavior described above, there is one episode where the size of the poor exceeds that of the middle class, corresponding precisely to the drastic crisis of 2002. In spite of the comments of the previous section, in terms of the volatility of poverty measures in such periods, it is important to highlight this issue: critical episodes put the poor as the largest group in the society, and in the center of the action of distributive dynamics.

Regarding the income of the middle class, Figure 10.10 presents the measures proposed by BE, BD and ourselves. The overall trends look similar to those for the sizes, but an important difference arises. When the focus is on the mean income of the middle class, the 1990s are a rather stable (though erratic) period. This may be due to a composition effect.

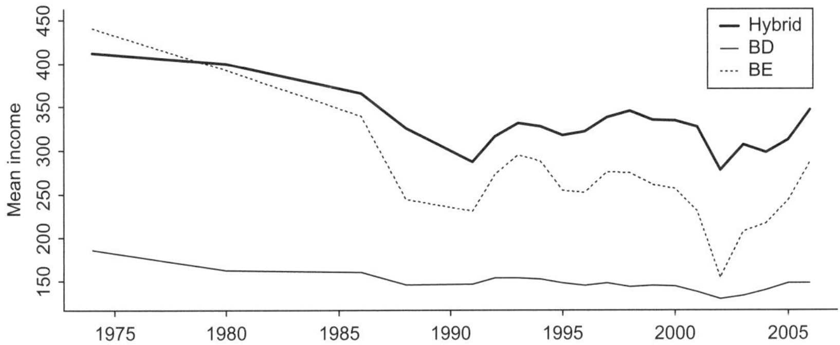

Figure 10.10 Income of the middle class.

The BD measure treats as middle-class many individuals considered as poor by standard poverty analysis (and hence out of the middle class in our hybrid definition), hence for the middle class as defined by BE the increases in median income during the 1990s are mixed with the increases in poverty (and inequality) in the same period, resulting in minor variations in the average income of the middle class as defined by BE, which includes widely heterogeneous individuals.

The results of this section suggest that the middle class is a very elusive concept if its identification is based solely in income. When defined endogenously, in relative terms, and jointly with the poor, the middle class is subject to the wide movements of the poor, and as a consequence, it decreased considerably in the 1990s, but recovered quickly after 2003. On the other hand, when defined exogenously and in absolute terms, as by Barro and Easterly, it is a much more stable unit, except in periods where median income decreases sharply, as in the crisis.

Many social actors perceive that the 1990s had a strong negative effect on the middle class. According to our results this perception is compatible with a relative notion of middle-class (like our hybrid measure), mostly reflecting the increasing importance of the poor. In connection with the results of the previous sections, the fact that in the 1990s modes occur outside most characterizations of the middle class in Argentina implies that the center of the distribution of those in the middle class is not representative of them – that is, unlike within the poor, the distribution of incomes within the middle class became flatter. Either the existence of the middle class became unrepresentative, as compared with that of the poor, or its identification should rely on alternative welfare components, that cannot be appropriately represented by income.

10.5 CONCLUDING REMARKS

From the mid 1970s onwards Argentina experienced drastic changes in its income distribution, mostly characterized by a long period of increased inequality and poverty, and a stage of recovery after 2003. Inequality and poverty figures reached dramatic levels, which justifies placing these distributive issues right at the center of the academic and policy agenda of the country.

The results in this chapter show that it is important to trace out the whole income distribution along that of inequality, especially in its lower levels. Increases in inequality are mostly driven by deterioration in the lower levels of the distribution of income. Besides increasing inequality, the 1990s left the poor as a larger and more homogeneous entity. If modal income is taken as representative of a distribution, in the 1980s it represented the division between the poor and the nonpoor, while since the crisis (and even after the recovery took place) it now represents the poor.

The middle class is an elusive group, that if defined residually from the poor evolves as the poor's mirror image. The fact that after the 1990s, the mode of the income distribution has lain within the range of the poor implies that the distribution of income inside the middle class is more homogeneous, and hence its median income less representative of its individuals, that is, the average income of the middle class represents a center of a rather flat distribution, making it a less coherent group. A dramatic result is its *relative* performance in critical periods. The results show that since the mid 1970s, and coinciding with the crises, the middle class has lost its predominance over the poor.

Other relevant results in this chapter are the strong correlation of median incomes and inequality, or poverty: crises affect inequality and poverty negatively, but recoveries quickly restore levels to less dramatic ones. We also highlight the fact that critical episodes introduce substantial instabilities in distributive figures, so those years should be handled with care.

Many aspects of this study deserve further analysis. The cyclical behavior of inequality and income (a long-standing issue in the development literature that dates back to the 'Kuznets Hypothesis') deserves more careful study. Time series analysis seems impossible owing to the limited availability of long series of distributive measures, but dynamic panel strategies may compensate the short temporal dimension with cross-sectional variability. An exploration more focused on the performance of the rich is still a difficult but highly relevant subject. Also, this study focuses strictly on monetary income. Recent trends in the literature (see the collection of papers in Kakwani and Silber, 2008) emphasize the multidimensional nature of welfare, suggesting that other dimensions should be studied alongside income in order to assess its evolution. In particular, the results in this chapter suggest that income has per se serious troubles in producing well-separated groups like the poor or the middle class, which draws attention to the relevance of adding other dimensions of welfare that may help with finding and defining such partitions. Finally, and obviously, causal studies of the determinants of these changes are as urgent as the need to design and agree on the implementation of sound policy measures which are aimed at alleviating the negative effects of the drastic distributive changes experienced by Argentina in its recent history. The results in this chapter should, we hope, help in establishing some empirical regularities that deserve deeper investigation.

NOTE

1. We are much indebted to our colleagues Leonardo Gasparini and Guillermo Cruces for their previous work, their relevant comments, and access to the SEDLAC database. Leopoldo Tornaroli and Mariana Viollaz (from CEDLAS) were very helpful with the EPH survey. As usual, we retain responsibility for any error and omission. Contact information: Walter Sosa-Escudero, Universidad de San Andres, Vito Dumas 284 (B1644BID), Buenos Aires, Argentina. Phone: (54-11) 4725-7053. wsosa@udesa.edu.ar

REFERENCES

Aaron, H. (1978), *Politics and the Professors*, Washington DC: Brookings Institution.

Alvaredo, F. (2007), 'The rich in Argentina over the twentieth century: from the Conservative Republic to the Peronist experience and beyond 1932–2004', PSE Working Paper 2007–02, Paris.

Barro, R. (1999), 'Determinants of democracy', *Journal of Political Economy*, **107** (S6), S158–29.

Banerjee, A. and E. Duflo (2007), 'What is middle class about the middle classes around the world?', MIT Department of Economics Working Paper no. 07-29, Cambridge, MA.

Birdsall, N., C. Graham and S. Pettinato (2000), 'Stuck in the tunnel: is globalization muddling the middle class?', Brookings Institution Center on Social and Economic Dynamics Working Paper no. 14, Washington, DC.

Botargues, P. and D. Petrecolla (1999), Estimaciones paramétricas y no paramétricas de la distribución del ingreso de los ocupados del GBA', Argentina 1992–1997, *Económica*, **45** (1), 13–34.

Burkhauser, R., A. Cutts, D. Crews and S. Jenkins, (1999), 'Testing the significance of income distribution changes over the 1980s business cycle: a cross-national comparison', *Journal of Applied Econometrics*, **14,** 253–72.

Callorda, F. and G. Caruso (2009), 'Does the middle-class really exist?: a cluster-analysis approach', mimeo, Universidad de San Andrés, Buenos Aires.

Cruces, G., L. Lopez-Calva and D. Battiston (2010), 'Down and out or up and in? In search of Latin America's elusive middle class', UNDP/Research for Public Policy Inclusive Development – Working Paper ID-03-2010, Washington, DC.
Easterly, W. (2001), 'The middle class consensus and economic development', *Journal of Economic Growth*, **6** (4), 317–35.
Gasparini, L. and G. Cruces (2009), 'Desigualdad en Argentina: una revisión de la evidencia empírica', *Desarrollo Economico*, **48** (192) and **49** (193).
Gasparini, L. and P. Gluzman (2009), 'Estimating income poverty and inequality from the Gallup World Poll: the case of Latin America and the Caribbean', CEDLAS Working Paper 83, La Plata, Argentina.
Gasparini, L., M. Marchionni and W. Sosa-Escudero (2001), *La Distribución del Ingreso en la Argentina*, Buenos Aires: Triunfar.
Journal of Iberian and Latin American Economic History (2010), Special Issue on Latin American Inequality, **28** (special issue 02).
Kakwani, N. and J. Silber (2008), *Quantitative Approaches to Multidimensional Poverty Measurement*, New York: Palgrave Macmillan.
Li, Q. and J. Racine (2006), *Nonparametric Econometrics: Theory and Practice*, Princeton: Princeton University Press.
Olivieri, S. (2008), 'Debilitamiento de la clase media: Gran Buenos Aires 1986–2004', unpublished MSc thesis, Facultad de Ciencias Económicas, UNLP, Buenos Aires.
Sosa-Escudero, W. and L. Gasparini (2000), 'A note on the statistical significance of changes in inequality', *Economica*, **46** (1), 111–22.

11. The evolution of income distribution in Brazil[1]

Rodolfo Hoffmann

11.1 INTRODUCTION

This chapter analyzes the evolution of income distribution in Brazil, a country known worldwide for its deep inequality. Changes in inequality are examined in more detail from 1992 onwards. Section 11.2 recalls the historical conditions of inequality in Brazil, in particular the polemics around the increase in inequality between 1960 and 1970. Section 11.3 describes the method of decomposition of the Gini index into shares related to income components, in order to identify what has caused the changes in inequality. It shows how to measure the degree in which those income components are progressive or regressive in their effect on the overall income distribution. In Section 11.4 this technique is used to analyze the evolution of the per capita household income in Brazil in the period 1995–2008. Section 11.5 studies the determining factors of the changes in income inequality among occupied persons in the period 1992–2008, fitting earnings equations for every year.

Finally, Section 11.6 presents brief conclusions.

11.2 SOME HISTORY

The wide inequality of the income distribution observed in Brazil is the result of historical conditions in which big tracts of land where originally distributed by the Portuguese king, and afterwards there was never a revolution that radically dismantled the previous power system. Ironically, even the country's independence was proclaimed, in 1822, by the son of the king. The late abolition of slavery, in 1888, was not complemented by anything that could have made easier the insertion of the new citizens into the economy and the society as new independent producers or workers with a salary.

After independence, as available land was simply occupied and cultivated on a large scale, a vigorous expansion of the so called 'economy of the *posseiros* (squatters)' took place. However, this expansion was interrupted in the middle of the nineteenth century by the Land Act of 1850, passed to forbid the occupation of land unless it was bought, to increase land prices and to organize public land sales that would provide the government with resources to bring European immigrants for agriculture (Guimarães, 1968; Vinhas de Queiroz, 1967). During that same period the US government was promoting small agricultural units: the Homestead Act of 1862 approved the free distribution of land, limited to 160 acres per family (Guimarães, 1968; Huberman, 1966). In Brazil, agricultural production in family units has had some relevance only in a few regions where a systematic colonization by European immigrants took place, in particular in some areas of the states of Santa Catarina, Rio Grande do Sul and Espírito Santo (Prado Jr, 1967; Vinhas de Queiroz, 1967; Guimarães, 1968).

At present we still find a negative correlation between the degree in inequality of land ownership and the human development index in 515 micro-regions of Brazil (Hoffmann, 2007a). There is a reasonable explanation for this relationship: the current inequality in the structure of property in land in each micro-region is a good proxy for this inequality throughout past centuries, which is historically at the origin of the overall socioeconomic structure and most of its characteristic features – including the quality and distribution of education – that still today affect infant mortality rates and life expectancy at birth.

The military coup of 1964 obviously was no revolution, even though it was called the 'redemptory revolution' by its promoters. The military government that took power had a conservative character. It systematically repressed trade unions and implemented economic policies that, in the name of fighting inflation, reduced the value of basic wages and salaries in real terms. It is revealing that the real value of the legal minimum wage in the state of São Paulo,[2] measured by its annual average, suffered a severe decline: in 1969 it was already 27 per cent lower than in 1964 and in 1974 it was 39 per cent less than in 1964.

Comparisons between the Brazilian Demographic Census of 1960 and that of 1970 lead to the conclusion that an extraordinary increase in inequality had taken place (Fishlow, 1972; Hoffmann and Duarte, 1972). Given that normal chains for political expression were closed – even the press was under censorship – such 'academic' critique of the military regime had an unusual repercussion. At first, the statistical results were questioned. An economist of the stature of Mario Henrique Simonsen, quoting the study by Hoffmann and Duarte (1972), said then that 'the debate on the increase of income concentration between 1960 and 1970 can be sustained only through a good deal of statistical carelessness' (Simonsen, 1972, p. 50).

The study by Langoni (1973), done with support of the then minister of finance, Professor Antonio Delfim Netto, was crucial in establishing a consensus over the deepening of inequality between 1960 and 1970. The controversy moved on to the interpretation of the phenomenon: while some authors emphasized the government's policy (social and economic policy, as well as the repression of any demonstration or social movement), other authors considered that the heightened dispersion of incomes reflected, at its core, a market where increased demand for qualified labor was not met by a corresponding increase of its supply in the short run. Langoni had privileged access to microdata of the census and did a competent econometric analysis. But the bias in his analysis was the absence of reference to the military and their repressive policies. Even if it is hard to include social and political phenomena in the econometric models, it is obviously no justification to ignore their existence. While analyzing the distribution of incomes in Brazil in the last two decades, there is no reason to mention any radical political change, because strictly there was no radical political change. However, this is not true for the decade of the 1960s.[3]

11.3 DATA SOURCES, METHODOLOGY FOR THE DECOMPOSITION OF THE GINI INDEX AND THE MEASUREMENT OF PROGRESSIVITY OF AN INCOME COMPONENT

The main source of data to monitor the evolution of income distribution in Brazil in the last decades is the National Household Sample Survey (PNAD in the Brazilian acronym), issued yearly by the National Census Bureau (IBGE), except in the years in which the demographic census takes place and in the year 1994.

As data are obtained through a questionnaire answered by the household member considered 'able' for the purposes of replying, it is known that data on incomes tend to be understated and that the value of production for self-consumption is explicitly omitted. The degree of understatement varies according to the type of income: it is smaller for formal payments (made or known by the government) and for regular payments, and larger for informal and/or irregular receipts.

In this section, the analysis is restricted to the period after the successful stabilization program started in 1994, the so called Plano Real. We avoid thus the periods of extremely high inflation, which tends to introduce a lot of 'noise' into income data (and, for that matter, into any economic data).

The methodology presented here allows us to determine the fractions of the Gini index that are associated with the different components of income, in order to measure, subsequently, the degree of progressivity or regressivity of a given component – that is, to evaluate the extent to which that component contributes to weakening or to strengthening the inequality of the income distribution.[4]

Let x_i be the income of the i-th person in a population of n persons. It is assumed that incomes are ordered so that the series is

$$x_1 \leq x_2 \leq \cdots \leq x_n. \tag{11.1}$$

The average income is

$$\mu = \frac{1}{n}\sum_{i=1}^{n} x_i. \tag{11.2}$$

Considering all persons from the poorest to the i-th position in the series (11.1), the cumulative proportion of the population is

$$p_i = \frac{i}{n} \tag{11.3}$$

and the respective cumulative proportion of income is

$$\Phi_i = \frac{1}{n\mu}\sum_{j=1}^{i} x_j. \tag{11.4}$$

It is known that the Lorenz curve shows how Φ_i changes as a function of p_i. Assuming that $x_i \geq 0$, and with β indicating the area between the Lorenz curve and the horizontal axis (p_i), the Gini index can be defined as

$$G = 1 - 2\beta. \tag{11.5}$$

It can be demonstrated that the same index can be obtained by

$$G = \frac{2}{n\mu}\operatorname{cov}(i, x_i). \tag{11.6}$$

Consider, then, that income x_i is the sum of k components, and thus

$$x_i = \sum_{h=1}^{k} x_{hi}, \tag{11.7}$$

where x_{hi} represents the value of the h-th component of the income of the i-th person.

The average of the h-th component is

$$\mu_h = \frac{1}{n}\sum_{i=1}^{n} x_{hi}, \tag{11.8}$$

and the accumulated proportion of the total sum of this component up to the *i*-th person in the series (11.1) is

$$\Phi_{hi} = \frac{1}{n\mu_h}\sum_{j=1}^{i} x_{hj}. \tag{11.9}$$

Analogous to the definition of the Lorenz curve, the curve that shows how Φ_{hi} will change as a function of p_i is called the 'concentration curve' of the *h*-th component. It should be noted that in building the concentration curve of x_{hi} the ordering used is of the x_i (and not of the x_{hi}, which can be different).

Assuming $x_{hi} \geq 0$, and with β_h indicating the area between the concentration curve of x_{hi} and the horizontal axis (p_i), the respective 'concentration ratio' is defined as

$$C_h = 1 - 2\beta_h. \tag{11.10}$$

Note the similarity between (11.5) and (11.10). Analogous to (11.6), it can be demonstrated that

$$C_h = \frac{2}{n\mu_h}\operatorname{cov}(i, x_{hi}). \tag{11.11}$$

And thus

$$-1 + \frac{1}{n} \leq C_h \leq 1 + \frac{1}{n}.$$

The share of the *h*-th component in total income is

$$\varphi_h = \frac{\sum_{i=1}^{n} x_{hi}}{\sum_{i=1}^{n} x_i} = \frac{\mu_h}{\mu}. \tag{11.12}$$

It can be demonstrated that the Gini index is the weighted average of the concentration ratios, as follows:

$$G = \sum_{h=1}^{k} \varphi_h C_h. \tag{11.13}$$

Since the sum of the shares $\Sigma\phi_h = 1$, it is possible to write

$$G = G - \sum_{h=1}^{k} \varphi_h (G - C_h). \tag{11.14}$$

With $\varphi_h > 0$, the sign (minus or plus) of $G - C_h$ is what determines whether the component contributes to increase or to reduce the value of the Gini index. When $C_h < G$, the component of income x_{hi} is contributing to diminish the Gini coefficient. When $C_h > G$, the component x_{hi} is contributing to increase the Gini coefficient.

For a component $x_{hi} \geq 0$ of income x_i, the progressivity measure of Lerman–Yitzhaki is defined as

$$\pi_h = G - C_h. \tag{11.15}$$

A tax (t_i) can be considered to be a negative component of the final income, that is,

$$t_i = -x_{hi}. \tag{11.16}$$

The concentration curve of a tax is constructed using the values of t_i and the respective concentration ratio can be obtained using (11.10) or (11.11). Observe that, in the latter expression, the change of sign of x_{hi} has no effect on the result, because a change in the sign of the covariance and of μ_h takes place.

According to (11.14), a tax contributes to a reduction of inequality when $C_h > G$, as the respective φ_h will be negative. Thus, if it is to include an analysis of the impact of taxes, the Lerman–Yitzhaki measure of progressivity should be defined as

$$\pi_h = (\text{sign of } \varphi_h)(G - C_h). \tag{11.17}$$

The name of this measure of progressivity is a tribute to Lerman and Yitzhaki (1985, 1995) for their pioneering work, underlining the importance of taking into account the ordering of the final incomes and demonstrating that, given a small proportional increase in x_{hi}, that is, multiplying x_{hi} by $1 + \theta$, with an arbitrarily small θ, the variation ΔG that is caused to the Gini index is such that

$$\lim_{\theta \to 0} \frac{\Delta G}{\theta} = \varphi_h (C_h - G) = -\pi_h |\varphi_h|, \tag{11.18}$$

with $|\varphi_h|$ indicating the absolute value of φ_h.

This expression shows that the elasticity of G in relation to x_{hi} is

$$\varphi_h\left(\frac{C_h}{G} - 1\right) = -\frac{\pi_h|\varphi_h|}{G}. \tag{11.19}$$

Expressions (11.18) and (11.19) show how the effect of a small proportional increase in a component x_{hi} on the Gini index depends on the degree of progressivity of the component and on the absolute value of its share in the total income. In fact, these results are the reason why expression (11.17) should be considered the adequate measure of the progressivity of the component x_{hi}.

In the same manner as the Gini index (G), the Mehran index (M) and the Piesch index (P) are associated with the area between the Lorenz curve and the line of perfect equality:

$$G = \frac{2}{n}\sum_{i=1}^{n-1}(p_i - \Phi_i), \tag{11.20}$$

$$M = \frac{6}{n}\sum_{i=1}^{n-1}(1 - p_i)(p_i - \Phi_i), \tag{11.21}$$

$$P = \frac{3}{n}\sum_{i=1}^{n-1}p_i(p_i - \Phi_i). \tag{11.22}$$

Note that in the Mehran index the difference between the ordinate of the line of perfect equality and the ordinate of the Lorenz curve is weighted by $1 - p_i$, making this index relatively more sensitive to changes in the lower end of the distribution, when compared with the Gini index. In the Piesch index the weighting factor is p_i, making it relatively more sensitive to changes in the upper end of the distribution.

Both Mehran and Piesch indexes can be decomposed into shares representing the various components of income, in a manner perfectly analogous to the decomposition of the Gini index that is shown in (11.13) (Hoffmann, 2004).

Using subscripts 1 and 2 in order to indicate two different years, it can be verified from (11.14) (Hoffmann, 2007b) that

$$\Delta G = G_2 - G_1 = \sum_{h=1}^{k}\left[(C_h^* - G^*)\,\Delta\varphi_h + \varphi_h^*\Delta C_h\right], \tag{11.23}$$

with

$$G^* = 0.5(G_1 + G_2),$$

$$C_h^* = 0.5(C_{1h} + C_{2h})$$

and

$$\varphi_h^* = 0.5(\varphi_{1h} + \varphi_{2h}).$$

Expression (11.23) allows us to quantify the contribution of each component of income in modifying the Gini index in a given time period and to distinguish, for each component, what belongs to the composition effect (due to the change in φ_h) and what belongs to the concentration effect (associated with the change in C_h).

Changes in the Mehran index and the Piesch index can be decomposed in analogous manner.

11.4 CHANGES IN INEQUALITY OF THE DISTRIBUTION OF PER CAPITA HOUSEHOLD INCOME IN BRAZIL 1995–2008

This section will show the evolution of inequality in the distribution of per capita household income in Brazil from 1995 to 2008, postponing to Section 11.5 the analysis of changes in the distribution of the labor earnings (earnings from work) of the occupied persons. Table 11.1 presents the main characteristics of both distributions according to PNAD 2008 data.

The per capita household income is obtained dividing the household income (that is, the sum of all incomes received from all sources by the persons in the household) by the number of persons in the household, excluding persons who are boarders in the house, and domestic servants and their family members residing in the employer's house. Only permanent private households with a declared household income are considered. People with declared zero household income, who constituted 0.93 per cent of the total, are included. In each household there were on average 3.28 persons.

From Table 11.1 we can see, in both distributions, that the 10 per cent richest appropriated 43 per cent of total income and the 1 per cent richest appropriated 12 per cent or more of total income.

The last line of Table 11.1 shows the value for the borderline between 'relatively rich' and 'relatively poor' – that is, the threshold of income above which an increase causes inequality to rise. When the Gini index (G) is adopted as the inequality indicator, this limit is the percentile of the order $(1 + G)/2$ (Hoffmann, 2001). For earnings of occupied persons, taken account of the understatement of incomes in replies to PNAD, this limit is compatible with the income limit below which

Table 11.1 Brazil: Distribution of earnings of occupied persons and distribution of per capita family income, according to PNAD 2008 data

	Earnings of occupied persons	Per capita household income
Number of persons (1,000s)	82,013	183,244
Gini index	0.521	0.544
Theil *T* index	0.572	0.596
Theil *L* index	0.498	–
Income (%) appropriated by		
40% poorest	12.4	10.2
50% poorest	17.6	15.4
20% richest	58.1	58.8
10% richest	42.7	42.9
5% richest	30.4	30.2
1% richest	12.3	12.0
Observed values[a]		
Average	1,036.1	589.8
1st quartile	415.0	181.0
Median	600.0	346.0
3rd quartile	1,000.0	635.0
90th percentile	2,000.0	1,215.0
95th percentile	3,100.0	1,880.0
99th percentile	8,000.0	4,333.3
Rich–poor borderline[b]	1,080.0	680.0

Notes:

[a] In reais (the Brazilian currency) of September–October 2008. Recall that there is an understatement of about 30 per cent to 40 per cent.

[b] Any increase in incomes over this limit leads to a rise in the Gini index.

people are exempt from paying income tax in Brazil. In 2008 that legal limit for exemption was the annual income of R$16,473.72, or R$1372.81 per month.

To examine the evolution of inequality in Brazil since 1995, we have to exclude the rural areas of the states of Rondônia, Acre, Amazonas, Roraima, Pará and Amapá (the old North region), as they were not covered by PNAD before 2004.

Table 11.2 and Figure 11.1 show the behavior of several measures of inequality of the distribution of per capita household income from 1995 to 2008.[5]

From Figure 11.1 it is clear that inequality remains rather stable from 1995 to 1998 and diminishes systematically starting in 2001.

Table 11.2 Brazil, 1995–2008: measures of inequality in per capita household income; Gini (G), Theil T (T), Mehran (M), Piesch (P) indexes, percentage of income appropriated by the 10 per cent richest (10^+), the 5 per cent richest (5^+), the 1 per cent richest (1^+) and the 50 per cent poorest (50^-)

	G	*T*	*M*	*P*	10^+	5^+	1^+	50^-
1995	0.599	0.727	0.730	0.533	47.7	34.0	13.7	12.5
1996	0.600	0.726	0.735	0.533	47.3	33.6	13.4	12.2
1997	0.600	0.731	0.734	0.533	47.5	33.8	13.6	12.2
1998	0.598	0.728	0.730	0.532	47.6	34.0	13.8	12.4
1999	0.592	0.706	0.724	0.526	47.1	33.4	13.1	12.8
2001	0.594	0.720	0.726	0.528	47.2	33.8	13.8	12.7
2002	0.587	0.705	0.718	0.522	46.8	33.5	13.4	13.1
2003	0.581	0.680	0.713	0.515	46.0	32.7	13.0	13.3
2004	0.569	0.656	0.700	0.503	45.0	31.9	12.8	14.0
2005	0.566	0.651	0.697	0.501	45.0	32.0	12.9	14.2
2006	0.560	0.635	0.690	0.495	44.5	31.6	12.6	14.6
2007	0.552	0.614	0.684	0.486	43.6	30.8	12.3	14.9
2008	0.543	0.594	0.674	0.477	42.8	30.2	12.0	15.5

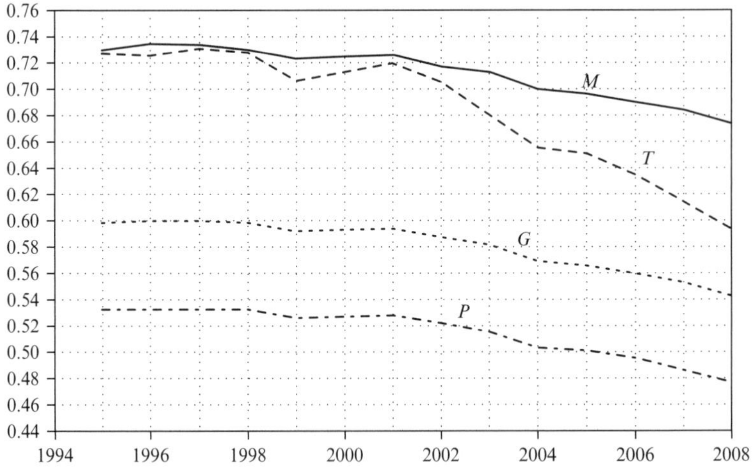

Figure 11.1 Brazil 1995–2008: evolution of Gini (G), Mehran (M), Piesch (P) and Theil T (T) indexes of inequality in the distribution of per capita household income.

Per capita household income can be divided into nine components, described as follows:

1 – CSM: earnings of civil servants and military personnel.
2 – EMP: earnings of other employees.
3 – SLF: earnings of self-employed workers.
4 – YER: earnings of employers.
5 – PE1: official pensions, paid by the official social security (INSS) or by government overall.
6 – PE2: other pensions.
7 – DON: donations of other households.
8 – RNT: rents.
9 – IBF: interest, the Bolsa Familia income transfer program and other incomes.

Obviously it would be more helpful to separate, in the last component, what is the result of financial investment and what represents public transfers. However, the value is derived from a single question in the PNAD questionnaire. Some authors have tried to separate the data, distinguishing the values typical of transfer programs (Soares et al., 2007; Barros et al., 2007).

On the basis of the overall conditions in the country, it is reasonable to admit that no striking changes affected incomes from interests and dividends after 1995. Thus, the strong alterations in the aggregate IBF (interests, the Bolsa Família transfer program and other incomes) are essentially due to the expansion of public transfers, in particular the so-called Bolsa Família (family stipendium program) and BPC (a benefit to very poor elderly and people with deficiencies).

The BPC benefit was included in the 1988 Federal Constitution of Brazil, establishing a monthly transfer of one minimum wage to elderly people (more than 65 years old) and to people with deficiencies living in families with per capita income below a quarter of the legal minimum wage. It stipulated that the benefit would be conceded even if no previous contributions to social security were made by the beneficiary. The implementation of the BPC benefit started in 1996, as the government started to set into practice the Organic Law of Social Assistance (Lei Orgânica da Assistência Social or LOAS) (Soares et al., 2007; Rocha, 2008).

In the mid 1990s some municipalities created income transfer programs with conditionality, designated the Bolsa Escola (school stipendium for the family, conditional on the family's children being at school). In 1997 the federal government started partnerships with the municipalities, by which it covered 50 per cent of the expenditures with those transfers. In 2001, the federal government began to cover 100 per cent of the value of the benefit of Bolsa Escola. In 2003, the first year of the new government, Bolsa Escola and other transfer programs for poor families were unified with the name of Bolsa Família (family stipendium) (Rocha, 2008; Soares et al., 2007). With the increase granted by the government in September 2009, when the national minimum wage was equal to R$465.00, the average amount transferred per family became R$95.00, with a maximum amount of R$200.00 (depending on the per capita family income and the number of children and teenagers in the family).

Formally, the incomes received through the BPC program should be included in the last question of the questionnaire of the sample survey PNAD, together with interests, dividends, Bolsa Família and other incomes. However, Soares et al. (2007) note that a significant part of the BPC transfer is perhaps being captured in the question about retirement benefits and pensions.

Table 11.3 shows the proportion of each of the nine components in the total household income, from 1995 to 2008, and Table 11.4 shows the respective concentration ratios.

From Table 11.4, it can be observed that CSM (earnings of civil servants and military personnel), YER (earnings of employers) and RNT (rents) are always regressive, that is, their concentration ratios are higher than the Gini index. In contrast, the components EMP (earnings of other employees), SLF (earnings of self-employed workers) and DON (donations from other households) are always progressive.

The concentration ratio of PE1 (official pensions and retirement benefits) diminishes more slowly than the Gini index, and thus this component changes from being slightly progressive in the period 1995–97 to become slightly regressive from 1999 on. Note that, because of the 'official' and formal nature of this component of income, it is less likely to be understated, and thus its participation in total income as well as its concentration ratio is likely to be overestimated.

Note also in Table 11.4 the extraordinary reduction of the concentration ratio of the component IBF (interests, the Bolsa Família transfer program and other incomes), which goes from being regressive until 1999 to become the most progressive of all nine components starting in 2003, reflecting the expansion of income transfer programs towards the poorest families.

The results presented in Table 11.3 and Table 11.4 can be used to calculate, for each year, the contribution of each component to the Gini index, according to equation (11.13). The percentage share of the h-th component to the Gini index is

$$100\frac{\varphi_h C_h}{G}.$$

Table 11.3 Brazil 1995–2008: share (φ_h) of each component of the household income in total household income

	1–CSM	2–EMP	3–SLF	4–YER	5–PE1	6–PE2	7–DON	8–RNT	9–IBF
1995	0.1010	0.3986	0.1895	0.1314	0.1334	0.0091	0.0058	0.0225	0.0088
1996	0.0974	0.3973	0.1985	0.1237	0.1346	0.0107	0.0051	0.0236	0.0089
1997	0.0965	0.3989	0.1882	0.1306	0.1414	0.0110	0.0057	0.0216	0.0061
1998	0.0990	0.3961	0.1758	0.1225	0.1547	0.0124	0.0069	0.0240	0.0087
1999	0.1018	0.3855	0.1775	0.1199	0.1657	0.0126	0.0070	0.0218	0.0083
2001	0.0997	0.3975	0.1647	0.1174	0.1712	0.0143	0.0067	0.0193	0.0091
2002	0.0994	0.3976	0.1576	0.1191	0.1722	0.0144	0.0076	0.0191	0.0129
2003	0.1003	0.3915	0.1583	0.1166	0.1848	0.0135	0.0071	0.0174	0.0105
2004	0.1017	0.3975	0.1521	0.1120	0.1813	0.0147	0.0074	0.0174	0.0160
2005	0.0989	0.4012	0.1457	0.1131	0.1817	0.0162	0.0071	0.0182	0.0178
2006	0.1070	0.3926	0.1401	0.1193	0.1798	0.0152	0.0071	0.0173	0.0216
2007	0.1093	0.4050	0.1545	0.1008	0.1797	0.0145	0.0055	0.0149	0.0159
2008	0.1094	0.4115	0.1350	0.1094	0.1821	0.0130	0.0050	0.0168	0.0178

Table 11.4 Brazil 1995–2008: concentration ratios (C_h) relative to the Gini index for nine components of per capita household income

	1–CSM	2–EMP	3–SLF	4–YER	5–PE1	6–PE2	7–DON	8–RNT	9–IBF
1995	0.7337	0.5075	0.5164	0.8629	0.5817	0.6491	0.3992	0.8130	0.7891
1996	0.7219	0.5020	0.5533	0.8713	0.5748	0.6513	0.4356	0.8020	0.8148
1997	0.7292	0.5083	0.5359	0.8650	0.5794	0.6598	0.3803	0.7960	0.7692
1998	0.7338	0.5096	0.5094	0.8618	0.5953	0.6413	0.4128	0.8033	0.7638
1999	0.7332	0.4981	0.5044	0.8567	0.6024	0.6118	0.3546	0.8032	0.6945
2001	0.7388	0.4987	0.5232	0.8600	0.6010	0.6261	0.3951	0.7975	0.5379
2002	0.7415	0.4951	0.5010	0.8565	0.5929	0.5869	0.4292	0.8033	0.5106
2003	0.7336	0.4842	0.5041	0.8599	0.5938	0.5702	0.4028	0.8012	0.3372
2004	0.7336	0.4694	0.4993	0.8551	0.5964	0.5685	0.4617	0.7868	0.1571
2005	0.7361	0.4697	0.4858	0.8531	0.5852	0.6141	0.4120	0.7891	0.2352
2006	0.7461	0.4528	0.4854	0.8563	0.5764	0.5812	0.4409	0.7908	0.1206
2007	0.7442	0.4498	0.5157	0.8515	0.5623	0.5522	0.4162	0.7896	0.0104
2008	0.7406	0.4400	0.4764	0.8370	0.5649	0.4919	0.4330	0.7983	0.0115

Table 11.5 Brazil, 2008: decomposition of the Gini index of the distribution of per capita household income, considering its nine components

Component	$\varphi_h C_h$	%
1 – CSM	0.0810	14.92
2 – EMP	0.1810	33.34
3 – SLF	0.0643	11.84
4 – YER	0.0916	16.86
5 – PE1	0.1029	18.94
6 – PE2	0.0064	1.18
7 – DON	0.0022	0.40
8 – RNT	0.0134	2.47
9 – IBF	0.0002	0.04
Total	0.5430	100.00

Table 11.5 presents such decomposition in the year 2008.

A regressive component, such as YER (earnings of employers), has a percentage contribution (16.86 per cent) to the Gini index higher than its share in total income (φ_h = 10.94 per cent in 2008). In contrast, a progressive component such as IBF (interests, the Bolsa Família transfer program and other incomes) has a percentage contribution (0.04 per cent) far lower than its share in total income (φ_h = 1.15 per cent in 2008).

Of course the results are different when the Mehran index or the Piesch index is used instead of the Gini index, but the evolution of the contribution of the components over the long run tends to be similar.

As inequality remained practically unchanged in the period 1995–98, the analysis that follows will focus on the period 1998–2008. The results of the decomposition of the change in the Gini index ($\Delta G = -0.0554$) in this period are in Table 11.6.

We should note first of all the contribution of EMP (earnings of other employees, i.e. employees who are not members of the military or civil servants), higher than 53 per cent and substantially larger than its share in total income, which has remained near 40 per cent during the whole period since 1995, with perhaps some slight expansion in the boom year 2008 (as can be verified from Table 11.3). This contribution to the decline in the Gini index is due essentially to the concentration effect: the concentration ratio of EMP went down from 0.51 in 1998 to 0.44 in 2008 (see Table 11.4). In Section 11.5 we examine some of the determinant factors in this reduction.

The second call on our attention comes from the component IBF

Table 11.6 Brazil 1998–2008: decomposition of the change in the Gini index ($\Delta G = -0.0554$) of the distribution of per capita household income

Component	Total effect % of ΔG	Concentration effect % of ΔG	Composition effect per cent of ΔG
1 – CSM	–4.41	–1.28	–3.13
2 – EMP	53.38	50.71	2.66
3 – SLF	3.54	9.27	–5.73
4 – YER	11.78	5.19	6.59
5 – PE1	8.79	9.25	–0.47
6 – PE2	3.43	3.43	0.00
7 – DON	–0.71	–0.22	–0.49
8 – RNT	3.17	0.19	2.99
9 – IBF	21.02	17.99	3.03
Total	100.00	94.54	5.46

(interests, the Bolsa Família transfer program and other incomes). Considering its tiny participation in total income (going from less than 1 per cent in 1998 to 1.8 per cent in 2008), the contribution of the component IBF to the reduction of the Gini index (21 per cent) is really extraordinary.

The contribution of YER (the earnings of employers) to the reduction of the Gini index is basically due to the decline of the share of this regressive component in total income – it fell from 12.2 per cent in 1998 to 10.9 per cent in 2008. This fall is explained at least partly by the gradual replacement of individual or family enterprises by corporations managed by executives who certainly classify themselves as employees of the company.

In the period from 1998 onwards, the component PE1 (official pensions and retirement benefits) also contributes to reducing inequality, through a lowering of its concentration ratio. Since the lowest level of pension benefits changes officially with the minimum wage, in order to have a better understanding of what happened, one should separate PE1 into two parts: one part with those pensions and retirement benefits equal to or lower than one legal minimum wage[6] and the other part with the remainder. The contribution of the former equals 9.68 per cent of ΔG, with concentration effect –9.87 per cent and composition effect 19.55 per cent. For the remaining higher pensions and retirement benefits the total contribution is –0.89 per cent, with concentration effect 0.72 per cent and composition effect –1.61 per cent. Thus, practically the whole contribution of PE1 to the reduction of inequality derives from the rise in the official minimum wage: the real value of the minimum wage was 58 per cent higher in 2008 than it was in the comparable month in 1998 (comparing the month of reference of both PNAD surveys).

The contribution of CSM, the earnings of members of the military and statutory civil servants, is –4.41 per cent of ΔG, that is, the changes in this component contributed to increase the Gini index. Distinguishing between the earnings of military personnel and the earnings of the statutory civil servants, it can be verified that the contribution of the former is 0.59 per cent (positive) and that of the latter –5.00 per cent, with a concentration effect of –1.08 per cent and a composition effect of –3.92 per cent. The earnings of statutory civil servants are a regressive component of total income ($C = 0.736$ in 1998 and $C = 0.742$ in 2008). Thus, the increase of that share in total income ($\varphi = 9.2\%$ in 1998 and $\varphi = 10.5\%$ in 2008) meant that its contribution was towards an increase in the Gini index.

The contribution of the various components of household income towards the change of the Gini index varies considerably, depending on the period examined. Table 11.7 shows the impact of each component, distinguishing between two subperiods: 1998–2003 and 2003–08. The contribution of the earnings of military personnel and statutory civil servants (CSM) is near zero in the period 1998–2003, but is substantial in the

Table 11.7 Brazil 1998–2003 and 2003–08: decomposition of the change in the Gini index of the distribution of per capita household income

Component	Period 1998–2003 $\Delta G = -0.0174$			Period 2003–08 $\Delta G = -0.0380$		
	Total effect % of ΔG	Concentration effect % of ΔG	Composition effect % of ΔG	Total effect % of ΔG	Concentration effect % of ΔG	Composition effect % of ΔG
1 – CSM	–0.96	0.13	–1.10	–6.13	–1.94	–4.19
2 – EMP	54.93	57.39	–2.46	51.98	46.72	5.26
3 – SLF	–3.20	5.14	–8.34	6.29	10.69	–4.40
4 – YER	10.48	1.28	9.21	12.24	6.82	5.42
5 – PE1	0.69	1.53	–0.84	14.07	13.94	0.13
6 – PE2	5.20	5.29	–0.10	2.69	2.73	–0.04
7 – DON	0.63	0.40	0.23	–1.26	–0.48	–0.78
8 – RNT	8.31	0.25	8.06	0.50	0.13	0.37
9 – IBF	23.93	23.51	0.42	19.62	12.15	7.46
Total	100.00	94.93	5.07	100.00	90.76	9.24

period 2003–08, in fact restricting a more rapid decline in inequality. The contribution of other employees (EMP) represents 52 per cent or more of ΔG in both subperiods. Official pensions and retirement benefits (PE1) have virtually no impact in the first subperiod but contribute substantially to the decline in inequality in the second.

The contribution of interests, the Bolsa Família transfer program and other incomes (IBF) presents an expressive decline, from almost 24 per cent in the period 1998–2003 to less than 20 per cent in the period 2003–08. However, we should note that the absolute reduction in the Gini index associated with IBF is larger in the second subperiod ($\Delta G = -0.0075$) than in the first ($\Delta G = -0.0042$).

11.5 EVOLUTION OF THE EARNINGS OF OCCUPIED PERSONS AND ITS DETERMINANTS

This section covers the evolution of inequality in the distribution of earnings from all work of occupied persons in Brazil, from 1992 until 2008. Basic data are from PNAD and occupied persons declaring zero earnings are excluded. Recall that the PNAD survey did not take place in 1994 and 2000.

As it is intended to subsequently use the same sample in order to adjust earnings equations, we excluded those observations that do not contain information about any of the variables included in those equations. We excluded as well persons who had a working time per week equal to or less than 14 hours or more than 98 hours, and those persons classified as indigenous. Despite these restrictions, the sample included 114,565 persons in 1992 and 157,860 persons in 2008.

Table 11.8 presents the values of the main inequality indicators. Figure 11.2 shows how some of these measures changed in the period: the Gini index (G), the Theil T index, the Theil L index, and the share of income appropriated by the 10 per cent richest (10^+). Figure 11.3 shows the contrasting evolution of the income share appropriated by the 50 per cent poorest (50^-) and the income share appropriated by the 1 per cent richest (1^+): at the beginning of the period these shares were similar, and at the end of the period the former one (50^-) was 50 per cent larger than the second one (1^+).

Note that the inequality in this distribution has a clear declining trend since 1993, in contrast with the inequality in the distribution of per capita household income, which only begins to decline substantially from 2001 on.

Table 11.8 Brazil 1992–2008: inequality measures of the distribution of earnings of occupied persons with positive income: Gini (G), Theil T and Theil L indexes, and percentage of total income appropriated by the 10 per cent richest (10^+), the 5 per cent richest (5^+), the 1 per cent richest (1^+) and the 50 per cent poorest (50^-)

	G	*T*	*L*	10^+	5^+	1^+	50^-
1992	0.566	0.662	0.607	44.8	31.9	13.0	14.3
1993	0.596	0.777	0.676	48.7	35.6	15.4	13.1
1995	0.581	0.687	0.616	46.8	33.3	13.2	13.5
1996	0.576	0.677	0.603	46.5	33.0	13.0	13.8
1997	0.576	0.680	0.607	46.4	32.9	13.1	13.9
1998	0.571	0.665	0.589	46.2	32.8	13.1	14.3
1999	0.562	0.637	0.570	45.4	32.1	12.3	14.7
2001	0.560	0.652	0.568	45.8	32.7	13.1	15.1
2002	0.557	0.642	0.562	45.7	32.5	12.7	15.3
2003	0.548	0.622	0.544	44.9	32.1	12.6	15.9
2004	0.541	0.610	0.527	44.2	31.4	12.5	16.3
2005	0.537	0.610	0.521	44.4	31.7	12.8	16.7
2006	0.534	0.602	0.514	44.1	31.3	12.7	17.0
2007	0.522	0.572	0.490	42.9	30.4	12.2	17.5
2008	0.514	0.557	0.473	42.4	30.1	12.1	18.1

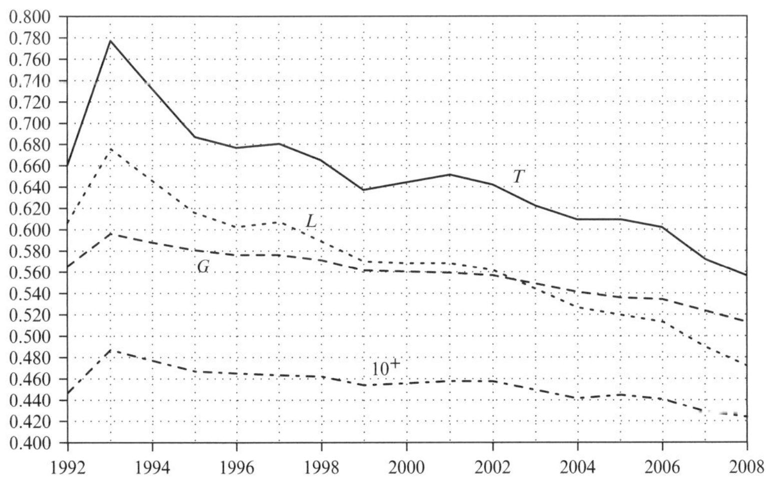

Figure 11.2 Brazil 1992–2008: evolution of the inequality in the distribution of earnings of occupied persons.

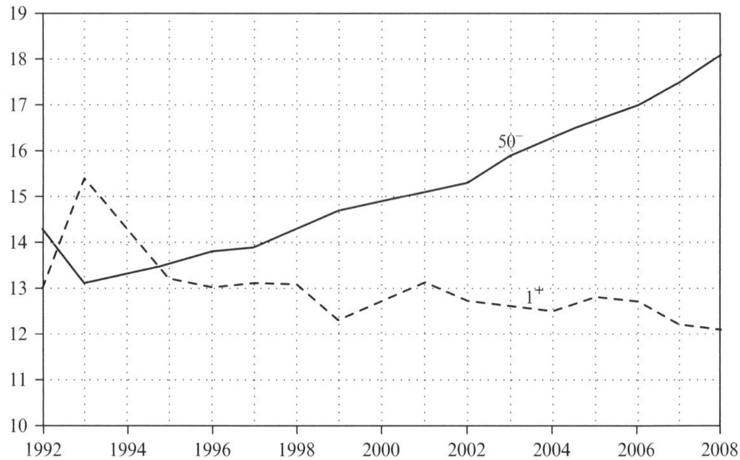

Figure 11.3 *Brazil 1992–2008: growth in the share of the 50 per cent poorest in total income (50^-) compared with reduction in the share of the 1 per cent richest (1^+) in the distribution of earnings of occupied persons.*

With the aim of evaluating which factors determined the change in the inequality of earnings of occupied persons, an earnings equation for each year will be estimated. Further, the variation of each regression coefficient will be analyzed along the 1992–2008 period.

The dependent variable is the natural logarithm of labor earnings per occupied person. The explanatory variables are characteristics of the person, of the occupation and of the geographical localization, as now described.

1. Schooling of the person (E), varying from 0 to 17. Values 0 to 14 correspond to the level of schooling achieved by the person, and the value 17 is attributed to persons with 15 years or more of schooling. Rates of return for schooling show a very substantial change around 10 years of schooling. Because of that, a binary variable Z was created, with $Z = 0$ for $E \leq 10$ and $Z = 1$ for $E > 10$. The model for the earnings equation includes terms $\beta_1 E$ and $\beta_2 Z(E - 10)$, corresponding to a polygonal[7] with vertex at $E = 10$, declivity β_1 for $E \leq 10$ and declivity $\beta_1 + \beta_2$ for $E > 10$.

   With b_1 and b_2 indicating the respective estimates of β_1 and β_2, the estimate of the rate of return for schooling is $100[\exp(b_1) - 1]$ for $E \leq 10$, and is $100[\exp(b_1 + b_2) - 1]$ for $E > 10$.

2. The logarithm of weekly hours of work. The coefficient of this variable is the income elasticity relative to the number of hours worked per week.
3. A binary variable with value 1 for women and value 0 for men.
4. The age of the person, measured in decades, and the square of such number of decades. Age is measured in decades only to avoid extremely small coefficients. Denominating as c_1 and c_2, respectively, the estimates of the coefficients for age and for the square of age, the estimate of the age in which earnings reach their maximum value is $-10c_1/(2c_2)$ years.
5. Four binary variables to distinguish five positions in occupation: military or statutory civil servants, domestic servants, other employees, self-employed, and employers. The third category (other employees) is taken as the basis.
6. Three binary variables to distinguish between four categories of skin color, according to what the interviewed person in PNAD declared: white (the category adopted as the basis), black, yellow, and mulatto or mixed.
7. Five binary variables to distinguish six regions of the country: North; Northeast (taken as the basis); the grouping of the three states of Minas Gerais, Espírito Santo and Rio de Janeiro; the state of São Paulo; the South; and the Midwest.
8. A binary variable of value equal to 1 when the person is occupied in the agricultural sector and equal to 0 for the remaining economic sectors, i.e. the, nonagricultural sector.
9. Finally, a binary variable equal to 1 when the person is a resident of the rural area and equal to 0 when she is in the urban area. Account has to be taken of the fact that the delimitation of urban areas was expanded in the 2000 census. Thus, when analyzing the meaning of the corresponding coefficient and its evolution it is necessary to take into account this change in coverage of the variable between the 1999 PNAD and the 2001 PNAD.

The estimation of the coefficients in each year was made by using weighted least squares, taking into account the latest actualization of the expansion factors for the sample obtained from the National Statistical Office (IBGE).

Table 11.9 shows the main results of the estimation of earnings equations.

The coefficient of determination (R^2) of the regression is usually between 57 per cent and 60 per cent.

The evolution of rates of return for education (in fact, rates of return for

Table 11.9 Brazil 1992–2008: earnings equations for occupied persons

	R^2	Return to schooling[a]		Hours of work[b]	Women[c]	Age[d]	Age squared[d]	Age of maximum earnings
		Up to 10	Over 10					
1992	0.556	9.1	13.4	0.5722	–35.1	0.8107	–0.0842	48.1
1993	0.572	9.5	14.7	0.6416	–35.5	0.8066	–0.0815	49.5
1995	0.600	8.2	15.8	0.5839	–34.9	0.7366	–0.0750	49.1
1996	0.578	7.9	15.6	0.5462	–33.7	0.7323	–0.0746	49.1
1997	0.601	8.1	15.4	0.5833	–33.5	0.7413	–0.0751	49.3
1998	0.603	7.7	16.0	0.5461	–32.6	0.7302	–0.0734	49.8
1999	0.597	7.5	16.1	0.5596	–31.8	0.7335	–0.0736	49.8
2001	0.582	7.2	16.4	0.5574	–30.6	0.7234	–0.0713	50.8
2002	0.586	6.9	17.1	0.5666	–30.8	0.7131	–0.0701	50.9
2003	0.577	6.7	16.4	0.6128	–30.5	0.7014	–0.0681	51.5
2004	0.573	6.5	16.3	0.6030	–30.3	0.7097	–0.0696	51.0
2005	0.572	6.4	15.9	0.6054	–29.2	0.6771	–0.0651	52.0
2006	0.575	6.2	15.6	0.5964	–29.3	0.6892	–0.0670	51.4
2007	0.554	5.9	15.0	0.6114	–28.5	0.6421	–0.0618	52.0
2008	0.547	5.4	14.6	0.6078	–29.2	0.6278	–0.0615	51.0

	Position in occupation[e]				Color		
	Military or civil servant	Domestic servant	Self-employed	Employer	Black	Yellow	Mulatto
1992	7.8	–33.6	–5.2	80.7	–10.5	13.2	–10.1
1993	9.9	–31.1	1.2	96.6	–10.3	14.6	–11.3
1995	12.7	–22.0	4.6	116.9	–11.7	11.8	–11.0
1996	12.6	–19.8	7.2	110.3	–13.4	19.7	–11.7
1997	13.9	–21.9	–0.6	109.0	–11.5	19.3	–11.3
1998	20.5	–22.5	–3.6	97.8	–10.8	15.3	–11.1
1999	22.1	–22.1	–3.3	99.8	–13.8	5.2	–11.7
2001	24.6	–22.3	–8.0	90.7	–11.4	21.5	–12.3
2002	27.6	–21.5	–9.1	95.0	–11.4	–0.8	–11.0
2003	26.9	–21.4	–11.6	88.9	–12.6	12.7	–12.0
2004	25.7	–22.8	–12.1	90.3	–10.3	7.7	–11.6
2005	26.0	–23.6	–15.0	89.3	–9.4	9.7	–10.3
2006	29.5	–23.2	–14.1	88.3	–9.4	1.8	–10.7
2007	29.1	–23.4	–9.9	90.7	–10.2	3.6	–9.9
2008	30.1	–24.0	–11.9	87.0	–10.0	4.0	–10.9

Table 11.9 (continued)

	Region[e]					Agricultural sector[e]	Rural area[e]
	North	MG + ES + RJ	S. Paulo	South	Midwest		
1992	27.0	38.4	82.1	51.0	41.7	–24.6	–14.6
1993	45.2	36.0	87.6	64.7	63.1	–22.4	–14.9
1995	28.7	29.1	79.5	39.3	38.4	–28.1	–16.3
1996	27.5	32.0	81.7	39.9	41.9	–29.7	–14.2
1997	28.1	34.2	85.0	45.0	44.1	–31.8	–13.5
1998	20.5	32.1	75.1	38.2	39.1	–30.8	–12.7
1999	21.6	31.7	72.9	36.5	38.1	–27.8	–11.0
2001	26.8	31.7	68.1	38.1	44.1	–27.6	–13.4
2002	28.9	35.1	69.7	44.6	48.9	–24.7	–12.2
2003	29.5	34.3	67.0	46.6	51.4	–23.0	–9.3
2004	33.6	36.4	64.6	48.5	55.2	–21.3	–8.4
2005	33.2	35.5	61.5	49.2	53.3	–22.0	–10.5
2006	29.8	34.4	57.3	46.2	51.6	–23.5	–11.0
2007	30.9	37.5	61.7	49.5	54.9	–22.5	–11.5
2008	25.8	35.2	56.1	45.4	49.7	–21.3	–12.3

Notes:

[a] Percentage increase in expected earnings for each year of additional schooling with change in the rate at the threshold of 10 years of schooling.
[b] The coefficient is the income elasticity in relation to hours worked per week, since the logarithm of the number of hours worked per week was used.
[c] Percentage difference in relation to the category taken as basis, namely men.
[d] The variable age is measured in decades.
[e] Percentage difference in relation to the category taken as basis (employee who is not military or statutory civil servant or domestic servant); white color; Northeast region; nonagricultural sector; and urban area.

years of schooling below and above the threshold of 10 years) is presented in columns 3 and 4 of Table 11.9 and illustrated in Figure 11.4. Rates of return for schooling up to 10 years have a clear declining trend. Rates of return for schooling above 10 years reach a peak in 2002, in the same manner as the rate of return for 'higher education' in Barros et al. (2009, figure 6.2). These authors study as well the evolution in the dispersion of schooling (measured by its standard deviation), which declines systematically from 2001 on, the year in which average schooling reaches 7 years.[8] Through counterfactual simulations, Barros et al. (2009) show that, in the period 2001–07, 'education was responsible for 50 per cent of the recent decline in labor earnings inequality, and for almost 30 per cent of the decline in family per capita income inequality'. They continue by observing that

> the breakdown of this contribution reveals that the reduction in the steepness of the relation between labor earnings and education (*price effect*) was by far the most important factor. It constituted 35 per cent of the decline in labor earnings inequality and 23 per cent of the decline in per capita income inequality.

The direct contribution of changes in the distribution of education (*quantity effect*) was smaller, representing 11 per cent of the decline in earnings inequality and only 3 per cent of the decline in per capita income inequality.

Beyond the rates of return to schooling, Table 11.9 shows other coefficients that have an evolution favoring the reduction in inequality. In 2008, the expected value of the earnings of a woman is still almost 30 per cent less than the earnings of a man with the same characteristics, but the absolute value of such difference fell from over 35 per cent in 1992 and 1993 to around 29 per cent in the last years of the period examined.

The differential between the state of São Paulo and the Northeast, still seen as the poorest region in the country, diminished from over 79 per cent in the years 1992–97 to less than 62 per cent in the last 4 years of the period.[9]

There is also a declining trend in the earnings differential in favor of the category of yellow (persons of Japanese and other Asiatic origin), compared with white.

On the other hand, there is a clear trend of a growing differential in favor of civil servants and the military, coherent with the results presented in Tables 11.6 and 11.7, which show how the share of CSM (earnings of military personnel and statutory civil servants) in total per capita family income contributed to restrain the decline in inequality.[10]

Table 11.10 *Brazil 1992–2008: distribution of labor earnings per occupied person with positive income*

Year	Average earnings	1st decile	1st quartile (Q_1)	Median (Q_2)	3rd quartile (Q_3)	9th decile	$Q_3 - Q_1$	% $\frac{Q_3 - Q_1}{Q_2}$	Real minimum wage
1992	848.2	117.6	294.0	451.5	881.9	1,763.8	587.9	130	307.0
1993	890.0	113.7	273.1	426.4	852.8	1,847.8	579.8	136	273.1
1995	1,077.3	195.2	244.0	512.3	1,097.8	2,439.5	853.8	167	244.0
1996	1,113.3	217.0	282.1	542.6	1,085.1	2,387.3	803.0	148	243.1
1997	1,103.4	187.2	291.2	582.4	1,114.9	2,392.1	823.7	141	249.6
1998	1,094.8	201.8	302.7	565.1	1,109.9	2,421.7	807.2	143	262.4
1999	1,014.4	189.6	284.4	544.2	1,042.8	2,180.5	758.4	139	257.9
2001	1,003.2	165.1	297.2	520.1	990.8	1,981.5	693.5	133	297.2
2002	978.8	180.3	300.4	525.8	946.4	2,103.1	646.0	123	300.4
2003	911.7	167.2	308.6	514.3	900.1	1,928.7	591.5	115	308.6
2004	910.6	182.2	315.9	486.0	947.6	1,822.4	631.8	130	315.9
2005	951.3	184.8	346.4	519.6	923.8	1,905.4	577.4	111	346.4
2006	1,021.3	219.1	393.2	561.7	1,011.1	2,190.7	617.9	110	393.2
2007	1,048.9	214.3	407.2	589.3	1,071.5	2,143.0	664.3	113	407.2
2008	1,064.8	240.0	415.0	600.0	1,037.0	2,000.0	622.0	104	415.0

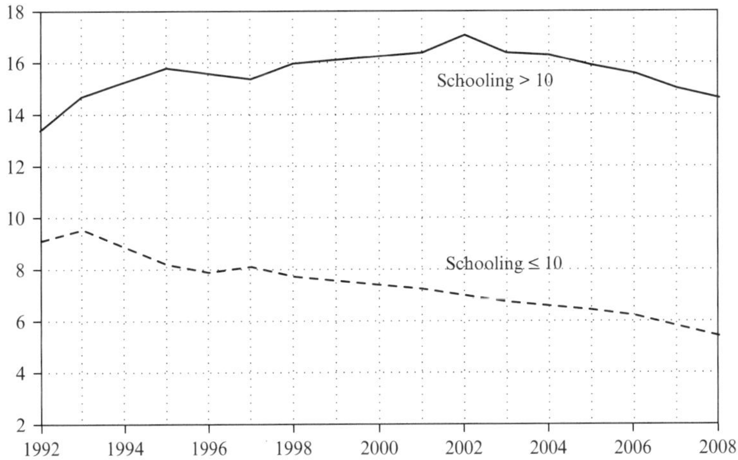

Figure 11.4 *Brazil 1992–2008: percentage increase in expected earnings with each additional year of schooling, considering that the rate of return changes at the threshold of 10 years of schooling.*

In Brazil, the legal minimum wage is an important factor of the changes in the inequality of income distribution (see Hoffmann, 1998). To allow us to examine this phenomenon in the period 1992–2008, Table 11.10 presents the evolution of the minimum wage, in real terms, and various statistical measures of position in the income distribution by occupied persons. Figure 11.5 illustrates the evolution of the real minimum wage, as well as the average, the quartiles and the first decile of that distribution. Note that the minimum wage rises substantially from 1996 onwards. From September–October 1996 to September–October 1998, the real minimum wage jumped 70.7 per cent. Note, as well, that the first quartile coincides with the minimum wage during the years 2001–08. In the period 2001–04 the median and the third quartile suffer a decline in their real values, but the first quartile grows, accompanying the value of the minimum wage, diminishing the dispersion (and the inequality) of incomes. Further, Table 11.10 shows that the difference between the third and first quartiles goes down from over R$800 in the period 1995–98 to less than R$670 after 2002. Indicating the three quartiles by Q_1, Q_2 and Q_3, we have the following measure of inequality:

$$\frac{Q_3 - Q_1}{Q_2} \times 100.$$

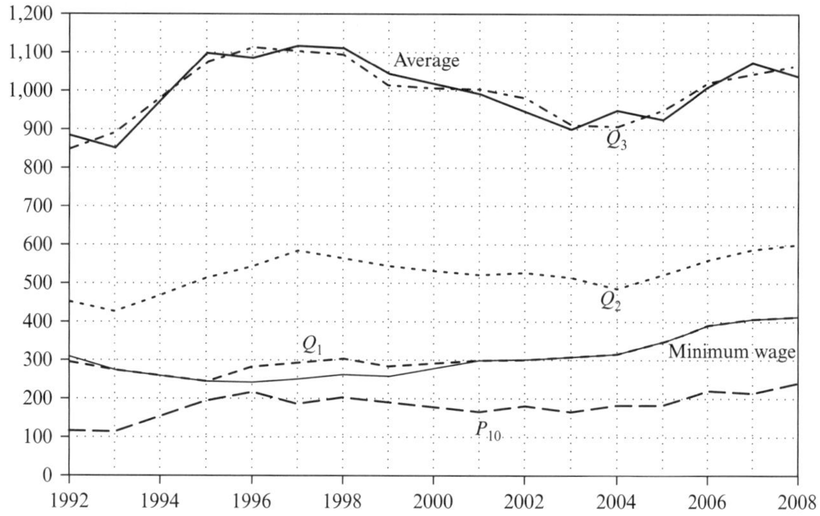

Figure 11.5 Brazil 1992–2008: evolution of the real minimum wage, the average, the quartiles and the first decile (P_{10}) of the distribution of earnings per occupied person.

This expresses the interquartile range as a percentage of the median. Note, in Table 11.10, that this inequality measure is higher than 140 per cent in the period 1995–98 and becomes less than 114 per cent from 2005 on.[11]

The importance of the minimum wage is stressed in a recent publication (IPEA, 2009). Using the technique of decomposing the Gini index into shares related to components of the per capita family income, this paper shows that, for the period 2001–08, incomes equal to the minimum wage contributed in 28 per cent towards the decline in inequality, of which 19 per cent had effect through the labor market and 9 per cent through pensions and retirement benefits.

11.6 CONCLUSION

The degree of inequality in the income distribution of Brazil is notoriously high. And the country was also noted in the literature for the strong rise in inequality between 1960 and 1970, a phenomenon that is in part explainable by changes in the labor market, but that cannot be dissociated from the government's repressive character in the years after the military coup of 1964.

Available data show that, from 2001 on, there has been a systematic decline in the inequality of the distribution of per capita household income. Inequality in the distribution of the labor earnings of occupied persons has clearly had a declining trend already since 1993.

Several statistical techniques can be used to measure the effect of various factors, helping to understand the reduction process of that inequality. Here we have privileged the method of decomposition of the Gini index, though this method can be used, in a totally analogous manner, to decompose the Mehran and Piesch indexes.

The relative importance of factors affecting Brazilian income distribution varies according to the period examined, as measured in detail. The quantitative results were described and commented on in the previous sections. Here, only the main factors are pointed out:

1. The programs of income transfer, such as the Bolsa Família (family stipendium) and the BPC (benefit to very poor elderly and people with deficiencies) were crucial, but their contribution to the decline in inequality in the period 1998–2008 was around 21 per cent. Nevertheless, the impact of the Bolsa Família income transfer program is of special relevance when its tiny share in total incomes is taken into account.
2. Over 50 per cent of the reduction in inequality is associated with earnings obtained in the labor market. They are the consequence of changes in the rate of return to schooling, combined with changes in the level and the distribution of schooling. However, the influence of the rise of the real minimum wage, from 1996 on, should not be forgotten.
3. According to the PNAD data, official pensions and retirement benefits are a regressive component of the family per capita income since 1999, given that since then its concentration ratio has remained slightly higher than the Gini index. Nevertheless, thanks to the more rapid rise of the floor of those benefits, which by statute follow the minimum wage, they contributed 9 per cent to the reduction of the overall inequality in the period 1998–2008.
4. Changes in the total amount and in the level of wages paid to statutory civil servants contributed to increase the Gini index. This effect became even stronger in the period 2003–08.

Of course, as one should not forget, the impacts of economic variables depend on the political and institutional environment. Obviously the real impact of an increase in the legal minimum wage, for instance, depends on due inspections of the Ministry of Labor, on the publicity of reports about illegal working conditions, and so on. Isn't it likely that the political opening and the popular movement that fought for direct elections helped to bring about the political and institutional conditions responsible for the expansion of transfer programs such as the Bolsa Escola and the Bolsa Família?

NOTES

1. The author is grateful for the support of the national research council CNPq. He also acknowledges the indispensable help of Helga Hoffmann.
2. Real values using as deflator the cost of living index of DIEESE; the annual average was calculated including the thirteenth wage (one extra month of wages given to each formally registered worker near Christmas).
3. Such lack of historical perspective can be sometimes observed even in studies of competent analysts of income distribution in recent Brazil. See, for instance: 'In the sixties inequality increased substantially in Brazil; this generated great concern. Langoni . . . showed that a large fraction of the increase in inequality was a natural consequence of the educational system's inability to provide a prompt response to the demands of a fast economic growth process' (Barros et al., 2009). Neither before, nor after, does there appear any mention of the 1964 coup.
4. This presentation reproduces to a large extent section 1 of Hoffmann (2009).
5. Year-by-year measures of inequality since 1977 can be found in Barros et al. (2009) and Barros et al. (2006).
6. The limit adopted was, for every year, a value 9.5 per cent above the current minimum wage.
7. See Hoffmann and Ney (2004) and Hoffmann and Simão (2005). Barros et al. (2009), while analyzing the relationship between 'labor earnings' and 'years of schooling' in Brazil in 2007, state that 'the relationship is initially concave then becomes convex'. A careful examination of their figure 6.1, however, shows that the observed points for years of schooling from 0 to 10 are virtually on a straight line. The supposed concave format is an imposition of the model applied (apparently a third-degree polynomial).
8. The average schooling of occupied persons has been growing continuously, from 5.9 years in 1992 to 8.6 years in 2008. The mean absolute difference (a measure of dispersion) of years of schooling increased from 5.17 in 1992 to 5.35 in 2001–03, and then decreased continuously to 5.26 in 2008. Schooling inequality, measured by the Gini index or by the coefficient of variation, decreases continuously from 1992 to 2008. Note that the earnings equation relates income inequality directly to schooling dispersion (and not to schooling inequality).
9. It can be verified that the income inequality between the 27 Brazilian Federation Units shows a clear decreasing trend in the 1996–2008 period. This decreasing trend is stronger than the one observed in overall inequality, so that the participation of the inequality between the 27 Federation Units in the Theil *T* index of the distribution of per capita household income decreases from 10.9 per cent in 1996 to 8.6 per cent in 2008.
10. For details about the evolution of the differences in pay between governmental and private employees, see Vaz and Hoffmann (2007).
11. Oliveira (2009) shows the impact of the minimum wage on the pay of those employed in the Brazilian agriculture in period 1995–2007.

REFERENCES

Barros, R.P., M. Carvalho and S.Franco (2007), 'O papel das transferências públicas na queda recente da desigualdade de renda brasileira', in R.P. Barros, M.N. Foguel and G. Ulyssea (eds), *Desigualdade de Renda no Brasil: uma Análise da Queda Recente*, vol. 2, Brasília: IPEA, pp. 41–86.

Barros, R.P., M.N. Foguel and G. Ulyssea (eds) (2006), *Desigualdade de Renda no Brasil: uma Análise da Queda Recente*, vol. 1. Brasília: IPEA.

Barros, R., M. Carvalho, S. Franco and R. Mendonça (2009), *Markets, the State and the Dynamics of Inequality: Brazil's case study*. Available at www.undp.org/latinoamerica/inequality (accessed December 2009).

Fishlow, Albert (1972), 'Brazilian size distribution of income', *American Economic Review*, **62** (2), 391–402.

Guimarães, Alberto Passos (1968), *Quatro Séculos de Latifúndio*, Rio de Janeiro: Editora Paz e Terra.

Hoffmann, Rodolfo (1998), 'Desigualdade e pobreza no Brasil no período 1979–97 e a influência da inflação e do salário mínimo', *Economia e Sociedade* (Campinas), (11), 199–221.

Hoffmann, Rodolfo (2001), 'Effect of the rise of a person's income on inequality', *Brazilian Review of Econometrics*, **21** (2), 237–62.

Hoffmann, Rodolfo (2004), 'Decomposition of Mehran and Piesch inequality measures by factor components and their application to the distribution of per capita household income in Brazil', *Brazilian Review of Econometrics*, **24** (1), 149–71.

Hoffmann, Rodolfo (2007a), 'Distribuição da renda e da posse da terra no Brasil', in P. Ramos (ed.), *Dimensões do Agronegócio Brasileiro: Políticas, Instituições e Perspectivas*, Brasília, MDA: NEAD Estudos no. 15.

Hoffmann, Rodolfo (2007b), 'Transferências de renda e redução da desigualdade no Brasil e em cinco regiões, entre 1997 e 2005', in R.P.Barros, M.N. Foguel and G. Ulyssea (eds), *Desigualdade de Renda no Brasil: uma Análise da Queda Recente*, vol 2, Brasília: IPEA, pp. 17–40.

Hoffmann, Rodolfo (2009), 'Desigualdade da distribuição da renda no Brasil: a contribuição de aposentadorias e pensões e de outras parcelas do rendimento domiciliar per capita', *Economia e Sociedade* (Campinas), **18** (1), 213–31.

Hoffmann, Rodolfo and João Carlos Duarte (1972), 'A distribuição da renda no Brasil', *Revista de Administração de Empresas*, **12** (2), 46–66.

Hoffmann, Rodolfo and Marlon G. Ney (2004), 'Desigualdade, escolaridade e rendimentos na agricultura, indústria e serviços, de 1992 a 2002', *Economia e Sociedade* (Campinas), **13** (2), 51–79.

Hoffmann, Rodolfo and Rosycler C.S. Simão (2005), 'Determinantes do rendimento das pessoas ocupadas em Minas Gerais em 2000: o limiar no efeito da escolaridade e as diferenças entre mesorregiões. Belo Horizonte', *Nova Economia*, **15** (2), 35–62.

Huberman, Leo (1966), *Nós, o Povo*, São Paulo: Editora Brasiliense.

Ipea (2009), 'PNAD 2008: primeiras análises', Brasília: Instituto de Pesquisa Econômica Aplicada, Comunicado da Presidência no. 30, September.

Langoni, Carlos Geraldo (1973), *Distribuição da Renda e Desenvolvimento Econômico do Brasil*, Rio de Janeiro: Editora Expressão e Cultura.

Lerman, R.I. and S. Yitzhaki (1985), 'Income inequality effects by income source: a new approach and applications to the United States', *Review of Economics and Statistics*, **67** (1), pp. 151–6.

Lerman, R.I. and S. Yitzhaki (1995), 'Changing ranks and the inequality impacts of taxes and transfers', *National Tax Journal*, **48** (1), 45–59.

Oliveira, Fabíola C.R. (2009), 'Ocupação, emprego e remuneração na cana-de-açúcar e em outras atividades agropecuárias no Brasil, de 1992 a 2007', MSc dissertation, Escola Superior de Agricultura 'Luiz de Queiroz', Piracicaba, Brazil; available at: www.esalq.usp.br/gemt

Prado Jr, Caio (1967), *História Econômica do Brasil*, 10th edn, São Paulo: Editora Brasiliense.

Rocha, Sonia (2008), 'Transferências de renda focalizadas nos pobres: o BPC versus o Bolsa Família', *Sinais Sociais*, **3** (8), 150–86.

Simonsen, Mário Henrique (1972), *Brasil 2002*, Rio de Janeiro: APEC/Bloch.

Soares, Fábio V. et al. (2007), 'Programas de transferência de renda no Brasil: impactos sobre a desigualdade', in R.P. Barros, M.N. Foguel and G. Ulyssea, (eds). *Desigualdade de Renda no Brasil: uma Análise da Queda Recente*, vol. 2, Brasília: IPEA, pp. 87–129.

Vaz, Daniela V. and Rodolfo Hoffmann (2007), 'Remuneração nos serviços no Brasil: o contraste entre funcionários públicos e privados', *Economia e Sociedade* (Campinas), **16** (2), 199–232.

Vinhas de Queiroz, Maurício (1967), 'Notas sobre o processo de modernização no Brasil', Separata da Revista do Instituto de Ciências Sociais da Universidade Federal do Rio de Janeiro.

12. Comments on part IV[1]

Adolfo Figueroa

Chapters 10 and 11 are both descriptive. As their data base, both studies utilize the national household surveys conducted by the official statistical institutes. The periods covered are 1974–2006 for Argentina and 1992–2008 for Brazil. Both chapters present Gini coefficients for the period under examination, which indicate changes in the degree of inequality.

The two chapters differ in the method of statistical analysis utilized. The Argentinean study analyzes inequality changes by examining the changes in the entire frequency distribution. The Brazilian study does it by using the method of decomposition of the Gini coefficient and by regression analysis. On decomposition, because the standard view is that the Gini coefficient is not meaningfully decomposable, this type of analysis is usually made using the Theil index; however, the author presents a theorem that justifies the use of this method of decomposition.

The two chapters claim some empirical findings that can be summarized as follows. In Argentina, or more precisely in Greater Buenos Aires, inequality increased until 2003 and declined afterwards. An interesting empirical finding is that inequality is counter cyclical: it increases in recessions and declines in recoveries; that is, inequality has declined in the recovery period of 2003–06. Another finding is that changes in Gini coefficients come mostly from shifts in the lower tail of the distribution, which implies that the poor have become a larger social group and more homogeneous as well. We all know that the Gini coefficient is a summary measure and that a change in its value is consistent with different shifts in the distribution, so it is nice to see this principle in action in this study.

In Brazil, inequality remained almost constant in the period 1998–2001 and declined continuously thereafter. The most important single factor responsible for this decline was the workings of the labor market, including here the role of minimum wage policy. Programs of public transfers appear among the factors of second order of importance.

SOME COMMENTS ON THE CALCULATIONS

Both chapters rely mostly on household survey data alone. The consequence is that macro variables are not presented or discussed or utilized to pursue the micro–macro consistency, which could check their conclusions.

Conceptually, what is the aggregate income that is captured through household surveys? The sum of wages, self-employment incomes, interest, rents, and profits (net of depreciation) represents national income. But this is not the measure obtained in household surveys. The main problem is the calculation of profits, which in a household survey refer, at most, to distributed profits only. Then aggregate household income could, at most, be equal to 'personal income' in national accounts, and inequality could refer to the distribution of this income category. If government intervention were included, as taxes and transfers, then the aggregate would correspond to 'disposable personal income' in national accounts. The micro data analyst must tell us which one is the corresponding income aggregate that has been captured in the surveys; moreover, the authors ought to tell us the biases (under- and overestimation) that can be identified in the information collected in the surveys.

It appears that in both chapters the household income under measurement refers basically to 'labor income'. Wages and salaries and income from self-employment are the basic statistical categories captured in the household surveys. The category 'earnings of employers' possibly refers mostly to self-employment (small businesses with some workers); certainly, it could hardly refer to distributed profits of firms. The very wealthy are usually excluded from household surveys.

It is well known that national accounts data show that profits constitute a large share of national income in every Latin American country; it is also known that these profits are appropriated by a very small group of people. Household surveys do not miss households; they do miss incomes. They are representative of the national population, not of the national income. The magnitude involved in missing the very wealthy can be deduced from the figure shown for the case of Peru (a country known to have a Gini of around 0.60), where the top 1 per cent receives around 30 per cent of national income, whereas according to the chapter on Brazil, the top 1 per cent there receives around 12 per cent of household income (see Table 11.1).

Therefore, including profits and other incomes of the very wealthy in the calculations of inequality measures would possibly tell a different story, not only about levels of inequality, but also about changes in inequality in Argentina and Brazil. Both chapters should then be read more precisely as the study of labor-income inequality and its changes. From these studies, one cannot draw conclusions about changes in income inequality in either society. The Argentina chapter has the additional limitation that it refers to Greater Buenos Aires only.

Both studies seek to connect inequality to growth or economic cycles. In order to do this, the chapters need to inform us about the level of national income or national income per capita calculated from national accounts. This exogenous information is absent from both chapters. In Argentina, the cyclical behavior of inequality is found from within the data set: the correlation found is between median income and inequality of household income. In macroeconomic terms, one may ask, would there be a correlation between the inequality calculated from household surveys and GDP?

In Brazil, if labor markets play a role in inequality changes, do the household survey data coincide, for instance, with the wage rate, the wage bill, the employment level data estimated by the method of national accounts? The Brazilian study implies that both the relative wage rate and the employment level for the unskilled have increased relative to the skilled workers in the aggregate. A test of this relationship could have served to confirm the hypothesis that inequality in the labor market is the single most important factor in explaining the fall in labor-income inequality.

The micro–macro data consistency reclaimed here does not imply that national accounts data are fine and that survey data are not. Both methods have shortcomings. The idea is that the measurement of economic variables can be improved by studying that consistency of both methods.

SOME SPECIFIC COMMENTS

In the case of Argentina, the calculations of Gini coefficients are, according to the authors, more meaningful for the period 1986–2006 only. The data base before 1986 seems less reliable or comparable. Were that the case, then the cyclical characteristic of labor-income inequality would still hold true, but changes in inequality would not be as dramatic as shown in the chapter. One can hardly find in the literature any changes of Gini coefficients as dramatic as those reported in the chapter, even for labor incomes: from 0.35 in 1975 up to 0.55 in 2002 – that is, a change of 25 percentage points. The empirical literature generally shows a kind of viscosity in the changes in the degree of inequality over time (cf. Li et al., 1998).

In the case of Brazil, the introduction of public transfers creates some problems. Conceptually, as shown above, income inequality can be measured either before or after public net transfers (transfers minus taxes). But it is problematic to interpret the concept of inequality when the study introduces into the calculation of labor income just one category of transfer, such as the Bolsa Familia. The inclusion of this transfer is appropriate for the study of poverty, but not for that of inequality. There is therefore a downward bias in the calculation of inequality.

ADDITIONAL COMMENTS ON EPISTEMOLOGY

'Science is measurement' is an accepted principle. Economics needs to take this principle seriously. Empirical studies like the ones commented on here are certainly important contributions in that direction.

But science is more than measurement. Science is explanation. Unfortunately there is no direct route from measurement to explanation. No matter how hard researchers try, data cannot speak for themselves. Recourse to theory is unavoidable in providing explanation. Data collection is indeed influenced by theory, either explicitly or implicitly.

For example, according to the classical theory, income inequality is related to inequality in the asset endowments in society (physical capital, human capital, land, and political entitlements). Data should then be ordered by social classes (not by individuals) and their mean incomes should be measured and then utilized to refute the theory statistically. The sequence goes from theory to the derived hypotheses, to measurement, and to econometric analysis, because what is under attack is the theory.

According to the estimates of the degree of inequality in the distribution of national income in the decades of the 1960s and 1970s, Argentina and Costa Rica were relatively less unequal (Gini coefficients of the order of 0.45) compared with Brazil and Peru (Gini coefficients of the order of 0.60) (Weiskoff and Figueroa, 1976). How can these differences be explained by the classical theory? The colonial legacy of Brazil and Peru generated an initial inequality in the distribution of assets that is of higher degree than in Argentina and Costa Rica. These initial inequalities in the concentration of economic and political power did not change much in the long-run process of economic growth. In the short run, changes in the distribution of national income may vary with the economic cycle, but these changes will move around the long-run value of inequality. Certainly, other economic theories will generate empirical predictions that are contrary to those predictions derived from classical theory.

Individual income distribution is the approach followed in the two chapters. In the case of Argentina, there is an attempt to study changes in the distribution by social classes, the poor and the middle class. However these classes are defined quantitatively within the same distribution; social class is a qualitative concept, and if it is defined exogenously then all the distributions of income and their changes could have been analyzed as composed of distributions by classes. The Brazilian chapter in turn discusses, in the initial section, the colonial legacy of inequality, but it does not pursue this any further.

As the authors themselves recognize, some further research is needed on what they have now produced. Future researchers may want to consider connecting their empirical work with a theory and to seek to refute it with the use of the set of measurements they have produced. Scientific advance implies submitting theories to the refutation process; thus, from the funeral of one theory to the next, science makes progress. This approach applies to economies as well. Then, and only then, those economic studies will be able to generate science-based public policies.

NOTE

1. Comments presented at the session on income distribution at the seminar, 'A Comparative Analysis of Growth and Development: Argentina and Brazil', organized by the Lemann Institute for Brazilian Studies and the Center for Latin American and Caribbean Studies, University of Illinois, Urbana-Champaign, 22–23 April, 2010.

REFERENCES

Li, H., L. Squire and H. Zou (1998), 'Explaining international and intertemporal variations in income inequality', *Economic Journal*, **108** (1), 26–43.

Weisskoff, R. and A. Figueroa (1976), 'Traversing the social pyramid: a comparative review of income distribution in Latin America', *Latin American Research Review*, **11** (2), 71–112.

PART V

The state and the privatization experience

13. Argentina's gas and electricity reform

Esteban Manuel Greco, Diego Petrecolla and Carlos Adrián Romero

13.1 INTRODUCTION

Since the start of the 1990s, Argentina has instituted reforms in its energy sector. Among them was the implementation of a more decentralized system to encourage greater private participation. As a result of this process, key economic variables were positively affected, including the following: a higher number of agents participating in the market on the supply and demand sides; a growth in networks and the number of users served; improvements in the quality of the service; fewer energy losses; a wholesale electricity price decrease as a result of competition; and the incorporation of modern equipment. However, in the years following privatization, regulatory aspects and market mechanism design issues began to appear as well.

Most apparent were structural problems. There was the lack of competition in the gas upstream; the failure of the system to make electricity transport investments; and the deregulation in the marketing segment. Structural problems already existed before the 2002 crisis[1] even though their ramifications did not appear until after the crisis; for instance, the lack of energy planning, which contributed to gas supply–demand imbalances that began in 2004 and affected the electricity sector's development as well. The outbreak of the 2002 crisis was significant not only for changes in the exchange rate regime but also in the energy sector. In particular, the crisis revealed the structural problems previously mentioned and generated new ones.

This chapter focuses on selected issues which help to identify the 'stylized facts' of the energy sector regulation considering both the structural problems that were present before the 2002 crisis and the problems created by the crisis.

13.2 PRIVATIZATION AND REGULATION

In Argentina's privatization process of its energy sector, efficiency and competition were regarded as key goals. This allowed for more consistent regulatory frameworks. Options for the regulation of the industrial structure were incorporated and autarkic regulatory agents were set.

13.2.1 Gas Sector

Prior to privatization, the gas industry was composed primarily of two state enterprises. The first, Gas del Estado, was responsible for the purchase, transportation, distribution and marketing of gas. The second, YPF, was in charge of production. In December 1992 the industry was restructured. Gas del Estado's activities in transmission and distribution were broken up.[2] The companies resulting from this process were concessioned through international tenders.[3] Thus, the structure of Gas del Estado was two transporters to whom existing pipelines were assigned and nine distributors that served users.

The privatization of YPF was conducted in 1993 with the sale of 59 per cent of the company's shares. At the same time, gas prices at the point of entry into the transportation system were deregulated and the supply and demand transactions of gas were freed within the guidelines of the industry's operation as introduced by the regulatory framework.

After the deregulation of gas prices a wholesale market of natural gas began to develop. Distributors bought gas for resale to sell to users. Then, demand began to diversify with the access of large users (mainly industries and power plants) in the wholesale market. Large users could purchase gas directly from producers or indirectly through marketers. In the second half of the 1990s, another demand segment became involved: exports, which arose from the development of advanced infrastructure.

Figure 13.1 shows the pattern of transactions of the Argentinian gas wholesale market between 1992 and 2001.

Transactions in the wholesale market could be made in the contract or the spot market. Even in the presence of policies encouraging the operations in the spot market,[4] this market did not have a significant share in total transactions until at least 2004.

The provision of gas transport and the distribution of public services are subject to the following principles:

- Transporters and distributors are obliged to allow third-party access to the capacity of their systems in a non-discriminatory way ('open access').

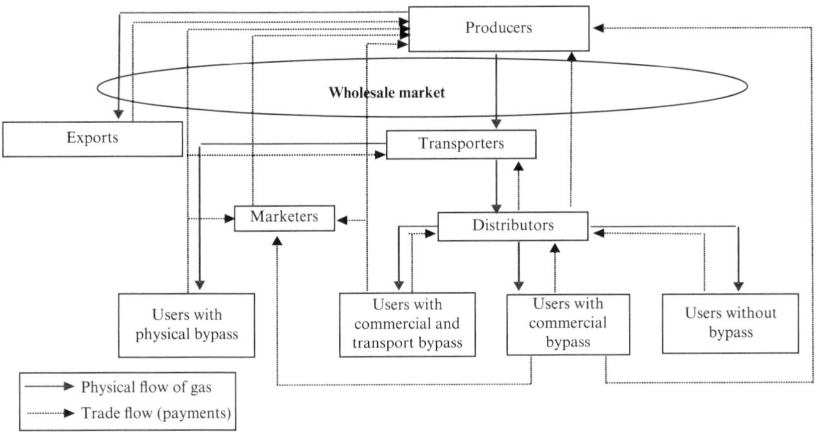

Source: Authors' elaboration.

Figure 13.1 Argentine gas wholesale market.

- Transporters and distributors must take precautions to ensure the provision of uninterruptable services.
- Transporters are not required to expand their facilities beyond the mandatory investments under the license but must allow the construction of connection and measurement facilities which ENARGAS determines at a third applicant exclusive cost.
- Distributors must meet all reasonable demands for service and prioritize the extension of the distribution network.
- Transporters and distributors must maintain their facilities to ensure a regular and continuous service without endangering public safety.
- No provider is required to maintain the supply to a user who does not meet obligations.

With respect to remuneration, the regulatory system is a hybrid. The transfer of the most significant costs, such as gas, is according to the following principles:

- The tariff for the end user consists of: the price of gas at the point of entry to the transport system plus transport tariffs and distribution tariffs ($P = G + T + D$).
- Maximum tariffs must be revised every 5 years.
- The regulation 'price-cap' is guided by the following general formula:

$$PPI - X + K,$$

where *PPI* is the United States producer price; *X* is the 'X factor' or 'efficiency factor' which decreases the tariffs in order to transfer the benefit of the productivity gains of regulated companies to users;[5] the K-factor or 'investment factor' reflects the necessary tariff increase to fund desirable investment projects, which are not profitable at the original rate.

- The 'pass-through' mechanism applies for highly costly tariffs (such as the purchase price of gas and taxes) to mitigate firms' risks and reduce their capital costs. Similarly, the 'pass-through' mechanism originates from an approach wherein the deregulated market is competitive and the agreed price is an efficient signal and an exogenous cost to the distributor.
- Tariffs are calculated in US dollars and converted to local currency under the convertibility law.
- The transmission and distribution tariffs are adjusted every 6 months according to the producer price index for industrial goods.[6]
- The tariffs reflect the differences that may exist between different types of services (mode of delivery, geographical location, relative distance to the mines, etc.).
- Tariffs should ensure the minimum cost to consumers and be consistent with the security of supply.
- Cross-subsidies are prohibited. Tariff subsidies should be explicit in the national budget.
- Companies which operate in an economically and prudent manner have the opportunity to (1) recover all reasonable operating costs that are applicable to the service, taxes and depreciation, and (2) obtain a reasonable return.

13.2.2 Electricity Sector

In 1989 the preparation for the privatization of the electricity sector[7] was initiated nationwide. The starting point was the privatization of the electricity company in the area of Buenos Aires (SEGBA) in 1992. The company had previously separated vertically and horizontally from different business units. After this, the privatization of the generating plants of companies with assets within the country (Agua y Energía Eléctrica and HIDRONOR) followed. The privatization process continued until 2001, mainly through the transfers of provincial distribution companies.[8]

The method in the case of thermal generation was the sale of assets, the concession with an obligation to pay royalties to the provinces for hydroelectric power and the concession for a period of 95 years[9] for the transmission and distribution segments.

Once the regulatory process had begun, the Electricity Energy Law was enacted. This law introduced the basic legal framework for the sector. The implementing agency was the Energy Secretariat, which establishes rules for the system's nationwide operation. The law created the regulatory body at the national level[10] and stipulated its functions. In turn, each provincial jurisdiction created its own legislation along the national lines and their own regulation entities.

Before privatization, the industry was vertically broken down into four stages: generation, transmission, distribution and marketing. Each had its distinct market structure.

Technological changes have meant that traditionally registered indivisibilities in generation are currently much lower, allowing for production schemes under competitive conditions at the level of the generating plants. In turn, the existence of multiple generators integrated into the system – combined with network reliability restrictions and the high social costs of the outage – led to the creation of institutional mechanisms for the coordination of the agents' activities, establishing an order of merit for entry into production based on 6-month declarations of variable production costs.[11]

Like the gas sector, the wholesale electricity market has a spot and a futures market. In the futures market, supply contracts for quantities, prices and conditions (point of delivery, guarantees, penalties for non-compliance, etc.) are freely set by the parties; only minimum information is necessary for their administration and minimum duration periods are imposed by the wholesale electricity market (MEM) regulation. In the spot market, the energy and power not commercialized through the futures market are sold. This includes the surpluses and shortages of energy and power required to cover contracts in the futures market.

The spot pricing in the wholesale market is carried out hourly based on the cost of generating an additional megawatt to meet the system's demand at that moment. The price of electricity at each node linked to the market equals the market price minus the marginal value of losses due to the transport of energy.[12] Under this rule, lower-cost generators obtain a rent originating in the fact that they are paid at the marginal cost of the last machine dispatched. In addition, generators are also paid for the power they make available; this is a way to reward the need for reserves in the system.

To promote competition in the wholesale market, the regulatory framework permits large consumers to purchase electricity directly from producers or marketers and utilize transportation directly from transporters.[13]

Given the practical difficulty of developing a final user tariff based on a purchase price in the wholesale market (which varies on an hourly basis), the model implemented includes the creation of a stable or seasonal price

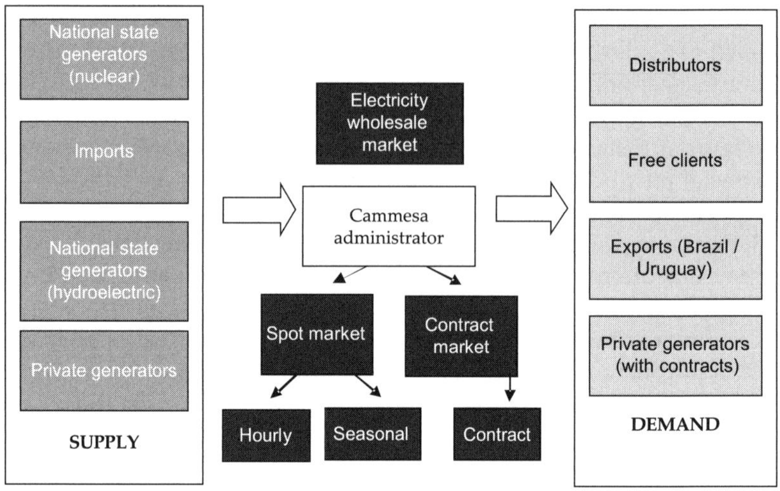

Source: Authors' elaboration.

Figure 13.2 The Argentine wholesale electricity market.

system. Every 3 months the implementing authority sanctions the seasonal price of energy to govern the period. This is the price at which distribution companies and large users buy in the spot market and represents the expected average spot price for that quarter. The differences between purchases at seasonal prices (determined by distributors and large users)[14] and sales at the spot price (determined by generators) in the hourly market are deposited in a stabilization fund whose balance is incorporated into the calculation of the following quarter's seasonal price.

The operation of MEM, its participating agents and its prices are summarized in Figure 13.2.

The electricity transmission activity links generators with distributors and large users.[15] It is treated as a public service by the legislation. It has two types of transporters: those who cover long distances (high-voltage transport) and regional networks operating with medium-voltage lines (core distribution).

The high-voltage transmission in the wholesale electricity market was granted to one enterprise in order to exploit economies of scale, while regional monopolies were created for the core distribution. To prevent abuse from such monopolies, a regulated payment system was designed for the transport service through a maximum income recalculated every 5 years. Additionally, these firms are forbidden to buy and sell electricity, and the principle of open access to the transport network is established.

The transporter cannot deny agents access to the network if they pay the non-discriminatory charges.

The electric energy distribution linking the transportation system, plant generation and end users is carried out through the distribution (low-voltage) of electricity and its marketing. This activity has been a concession as a public[16] service and a legal monopoly, granted by a concession contract in relation to the exclusive use of the monopoly's networks.[17]

The modality chosen in Buenos Aires for the distributors' remuneration is the setting of a price cap as $RPI - X + Y$, where RPI in the Argentine case is a mix of US wholesale and retail prices; X represents the efficiency factor transposable to tariffs; and Y is the cost of energy and power in the wholesale market, plus the cost of transport to the distributor node.

13.3 PERFORMANCE

Since privatization there have been improvements in key variables. However, the 2002 macroeconomic crisis negatively affected these improvements. There has been a recovery in their performance in recent years. Note that in some cases key variables, like the lack of investment, began to decelerate before 2002.

The following subsection describes the performance and evolution of the energy sector. We will first present gas and second electricity and show that gas is the most important input in electricity production.

13.3.1 Gas Sector Performance

The evolution of the sector is described by the indicators shown in Table 13.1. The nominal capacity of transportation has increased 89 per cent since privatization. From this trend, we can see that a growth in capacity stopped during the period 2001–04, owing to deferred investment plans and contract renegotiations initiated by the National Executive Power after the 2002 devaluation. Since 2005, we have seen an increase in transport capacity, fostered by the national government trust fund programs.

Distribution capacity was expanded by 49,000/km after privatization (to 2005; December 1992 stock was 67,000/km). Of note is the recuperation of the construction of new networks from the minimum value observed in 2003.

With regard to the number of users, this variable has increased annually. After the slowdown in the growth rate in 2002, we can see a change in direction that can be justified by the decrease in relative prices of gas with respect to its substitutes.

Table 13.1 Argentine gas sector 1993–2008: development indicators chosen

Indicator[a]	1993	1994	1995	1996	1997	1998	1999	2000	2001	2002	2003	2004	2005	2006	2007	2008
Nominal transport capacity (MM m^3/day)[b]	72	83	87	92	98	103	109	117	121	121	121	121	127	132	135	136
Distribution stock network (thousand km)[c]	75.6	82.0	86.7	89.2	92.4	96.8	101.6	103.0	108.5	111.8	113.4	115.1	117.3	–	–	–
Users (thousands)	4740	4947	5076	5239	5399	5597	5761	5910	6019	6061	6212	6387	6572	6769	6997	7244
Type of commercialization (%)																
Commercial by pass	1.5	6.1	12.4	20.7	27.6	26.1	25.3	30.7	33.0	34.1	35.3	34.4	36.8	53.1	52.1	52.2
Physical by pass	1.4	2.5	2.1	2.6	4.2	4.8	7.6	8.3	9.4	10.0	9.8	9.9	10.6	11.5	11.4	12.9
Total injected gas (thousand MM m^3/day)[d]	64.3	65.6	72.4	78.2	79.2	84.0	94.0	98.0	92.3	91.2	103.6	111.6	115.0	117.9	118.7	115.8

Notes:
[a] At 31 December.
[b] Capacity at 31 December. Includes regional transport pipelines and export pipelines; it doesn't include wellhead consumption.
[c] Plumbing stocks at 31 December from licensees information (norm 102).
[d] Injected gas to the transport system. Includes exports. Does not include consumption at wellhead.
–: No significant information available.

Source: Authors' own elaboration based on Energy Secretariat's and ENARGAS's databases.

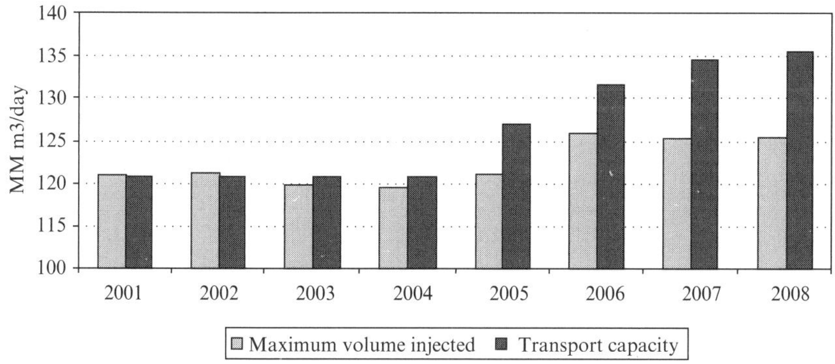

Source: Authors' elaboration based on ENARGAS's database.

Figure 13.3 Volume injected into the daily maximum demand compared with available transport capacity.

One way the regulatory framework promotes competition is by increasing the number of large users who buy gas directly from producers or marketers. The participation of consumers with commercial bypass in national gas demand grew from 1.5 per cent in 1993 to 52.2 per cent in 2008 and the participation of those with physical bypass went from 1.4 per cent to 12.9 per cent. A greater share of this type of commercialization in demand has been evident since 2005 because of the 'unbundling'. This forced large users, who had previously been given the bypass option, to buy gas directly from the producers.[18]

Besides the increasing trend in gas injection shown in Table 13.1 above, the gas sector has been unable to meet the demands of the domestic market and its export commitments since 2004. What has to be considered here is that the provision restrictions of 2004 did not reflect those seen in previous years because the cause of the problem was the lack of gas and not the transport capacity. This description is accurate when analyzing the injection of gas into the transport system. Figure 13.3 shows that the available transport capacity was superior to the volume of gas injected into the daily maximum consumption during winter between 2003 and 2007.

The Argentine reserves/production ratio has been decreasing steadily since 1995. The evolution of reserves, whose reduction is at the root of the problem of gas shortage, could have been affected by several factors. Among these are long-run investment decisions in exploration, the methodology to estimate them and the exploitation of fields. Figure 13.4 shows the reserves/production ratio since privatization.

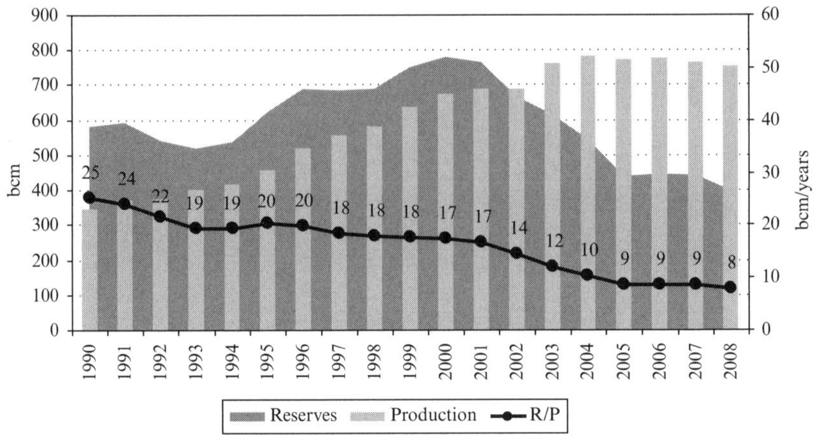

Note: bcm: Billions of m^3.

Source: Authors' elaboration based on Energy Secretariat data.

Figure 13.4 Reserves/production evolution.

During the period 1970–2010, the average exploration of wells after 1998 was 61 per cent lower than the average of the 28 previous years. The overestimation in their registration could also explain the fall in reserves.

The post-privatization wellhead prices did not show decreasing rates before the macroeconomic crisis. This development can be justified by the high concentration in supply. From 2002 we can see a major segmentation of the market with regard to price determination, a permanent growth in prices and an increase in the share of demand that these growths affected after the significant real reduction following the crisis.[19]

In 2002, the average reduction in domestic wellhead prices was about 40 per cent. Segmentation began with Decree 689/02, which dollarized export prices and led to a 249 per cent increase in export prices (measured in local currency at the December 2002 exchange rate).

In May 2002 gas prices increased. The average increase was in the order of 10 per cent and applied to all distributor users. In early 2004, Decrees 180 and 181/04 and Resolution MPFIPyS 208/04 were issued, establishing a schedule of increases in gas prices for large users who still bought gas from distributors for power plants; supply volumes were set for the domestic market. After finishing the schedule of gas price increases, the Energy Secretariat issued Resolution SE 752/05, by which it determined that large users that still bought from distributors would have to begin arranging

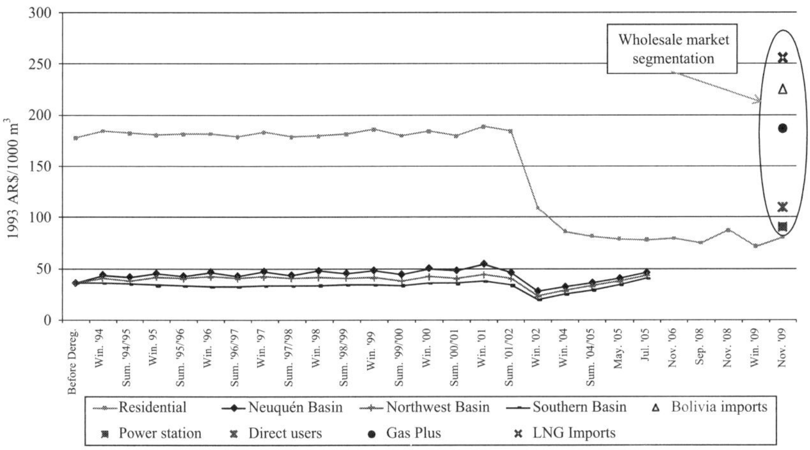

Figure 13.5 Real wholesale gas prices and residential tariffs.

their own accounts from September 2005. Since then, substantial price increases have been recorded for these 'new direct users'.

Since the agreement approved by Resolution MPFIPyS 208/04 expired in December 2006, a subsequent agreement was signed, approved by Resolution SE 599/07, which extended the supply commitments to the domestic market until 2011 and set guidelines for price increases. These guidelines were supplemented by an agreement ratified by Resolution SE 1.070/08. In 2008 adjustments in the wellhead price were established to fix the tariffs of residential users.[20]

In turn, 'Gas Plus' was created. This program aimed to boost the production of gas (Resolution SE 24/08), whereby new sources, as well as those characterized as 'Tight Gas', would not be subject to the guidelines in the price agreement approved by Resolution SE 599/07 and could receive significantly higher prices (see Figure 13.5).

In this context, the market shows different wellhead pricing patterns. 2010 prices for the bulk of domestic demand were well above the pre-2002 level and also exceeded the maximum projected long-term contracts signed in the late 1990s, while prices for residential users were particularly low.

Transport and distribution tariffs did not reflect the same trend as wholesale prices. The cost of transport to users has not changed since July 2001. However, while the cost of transport included in the price has remained constant since that date, the ultimate cost to larger firm users (e.g. SGP3, SGG, FD, FT, GNC) was increased from April 2005 because of the application of the denominated 'gas trust charge'[21] destined to finance the transport capacity expansions.

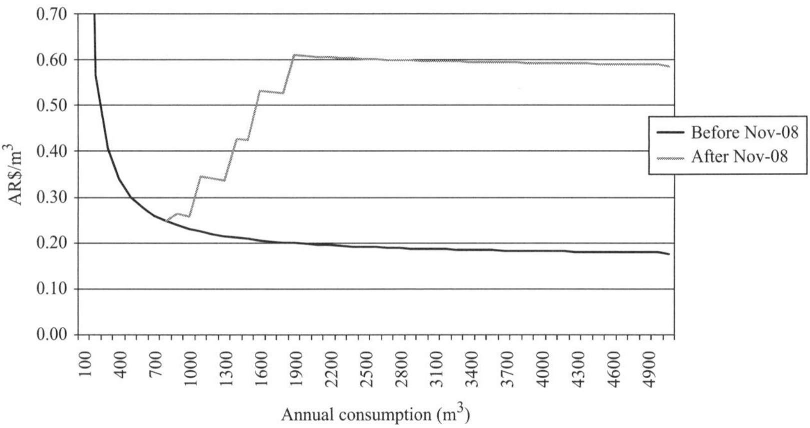

Figure 13.6 Change in natural gas residential tariff structure: average value according to consumption level.[25]

Transitory increases in distribution margins of almost 30 per cent were established in agreements reached between government and some firms, with the firms committed to conduct integral tariff review processes and public hearings.[22] As of now, many of these transitory increases have still not been implemented.[23]

Figure 13.5 presents the evolution of real[24] wholesale gas prices and residential tariffs.

Finally, let us mention two points about prices and tariffs. First, because of the above-mentioned problems to satisfy domestic gas demand, imports were necessary. The price of these imports was considerably higher than domestic ones. For example, imported gas from Bolivia reached US$10.35 per MMBTU at the fourth trimester of 2008, although it decreased to US$6.16 per MMBTU by the end of 2009. Liquefied natural gas (LNG), a substitute, was also imported; however, this was registered at even higher prices. Second, as was mentioned, tariff increases were not the same for the different demand segments. Major segmentation has been seen in final tariffs in relation to wholesale prices.

Residential customers have been paying two-part tariffs since privatization (a fixed charge and a consumption charge), which implied an average tariff declining together with consumption. As Figure 13.6 shows, a major change in the residential tariff structure was approved in November 2008, with significant increases for high consumption due to an additional charge aimed to cover imported gas.

The main tariff increases reached consumption exceeding 1000 m³/year[26] and ranged from 55 per cent to 235 per cent. The new charge, challenged by consumers and Congress, was suspended during the winter of 2009, demonstrating the sustainability, efficiency and equity issues that need to be dealt with and which are analyzed in Section 13.4.

13.3.2 Electricity Sector Performance

With regard to transport investment, high voltage rose by 30 per cent of its kilometers and core distribution by 70 per cent. In addition to these improvements, we can see that some years showed no extension improvements, even in the core distribution before the 2002 macroeconomic crisis.

The growth trend in the number of agents participating in the wholesale market in the early years of privatization has not continued. Table 13.2 shows that the number of generation firms has increased from 24 in 1993 to 44 in 1997, only to decrease after 2005. In the case of large users, the number rose only until 2002.

A continuous reduction in thermal unavailability occurred until 1997, dropping from 41.2 per cent to 23.4 per cent, followed by years with unavailability oscillating around the 1997 percentage. Total capacity, measured in installed nominal power generation, shows a decrease in the growth rate after the 2002 crisis. However, we can see a recovery in 2006.

Except for the decline in 2002, increases in production have been seen every year. By 2006, annual production had increased by more than 100 per cent since privatization.

From the year 1993, as a result of the increased transport capacity of the pipeline, gas for power stations became more available, replacing the use of liquid fuel (especially in winter). This, together with the greater thermal availability from improvements in the privatized plants and the incorporation of more efficient thermal equipment, explains the significant reduction in wholesale prices during the early years of the privatization process.

After the convertibility regime was abandoned, seasonal prices did not totally follow the evolution of the spot prices and were only adjusted on some occasions. As a result, the difference registered between the remuneration to producers (wholesale monomic spot prices in Figure 13.7) and prices paid by distributors (seasonal prices in Figure 13.7) was initially absorbed by the stabilization fund, but this fund was depleted in June 2003, increasing the subsidy required by the electricity sector.

Consequently, it was impossible to cancel all the debts of the producer agents because of their participation in the spot market, generating debts that favored them, which were partially cancelled by national state funds in the form of loans to the sector.

As in the gas sector, demand segmentation developed. From February 2004, seasonal prices changed progressively in a differentiated manner,

Table 13.2 Argentine electricity sector 1993–2008: development indicators chosen

Indicator[a]	1993	1994	1995	1996	1997	1998	1999	2000	2001	2002	2003	2004	2005	2006	2007	2008
Transport extention (thousand km)																
High voltage	7.4	7.7	7.7	8.3	8.3	8.3	8.4	9.7	9.7	9.7	9.7	9.7	9.7	10.0	10.0	10.0
Core distribution	9.9	10.4	10.7	10.7	11.3	11.4	11.7	11.9	12.4	12.5	12.5	12.7	12.9	15.8	16.3	16.7
Number of generation firms	24	31	37	43	44	44	44	43	44	43	43	43	41	40	–	–
Number of large users	18	80	415	724	1147	1894	1983	1893	2269	2336	1369	1524	2614	2107	–	–
Total thermal unavailability (%)	41.2	38.7	28.3	27.5	23.2	25.0	27.2	29.4	24.1	21.7	18.3	22.6	25.8	26.1	–	–
Installed nominal power (GW)	14.0	15.4	16.3	17.1	18.2	18.9	19.5	20.7	22.3	22.8	23.0	23.0	23.3	24.0	24.4	26.2
Production (thousand GWh)	51.6	55.3	56.9	60.5	65.7	69.0	72.9	80.0	81.3	76.7	81.8	88.7	94.0	104.3	108.5	112.4

Notes:
[a] At 31 December.
–: No significant information available.

Source: Authors' elaboration based on Cammesa's, Energy Secretariat's and ADEERA's databases.

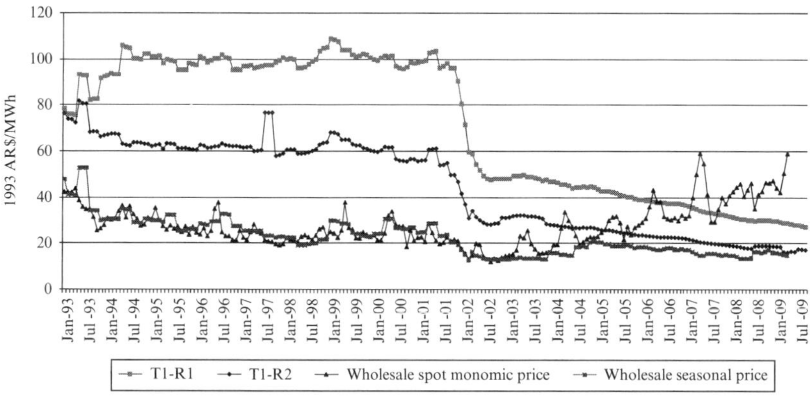

Source: Authors' elaboration based on Cammesa's database.

Figure 13.7 Real wholesale electricity prices and residential tariffs.

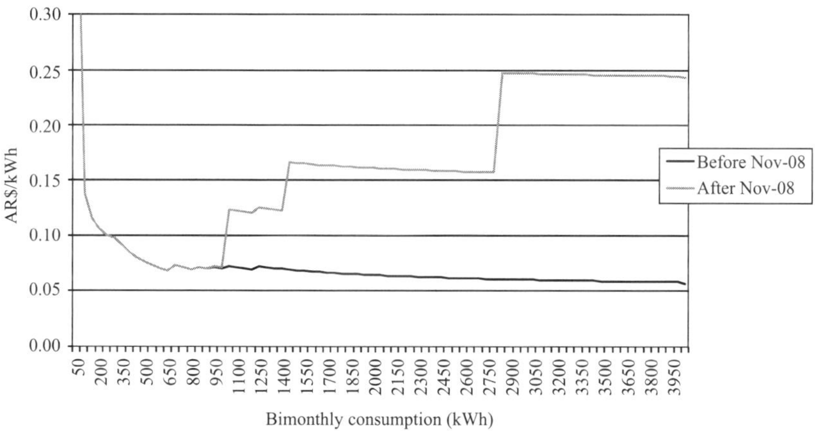

Figure 13.8 Change in electricity residential tariff structure: average value according to consumption level.

increasing purchasing values for those segments that had recovered overall as a result of sustained increases in economic activity. These changes were greater in the largest demands, allowing the value set to cover the average costs of the market. Residential and small-demand tariffs remained low in Greater Buenos Aires (see lines T1-R1 and T1-R2 in Figure 13.7). In November 2008, Resolution SE 1169/08 modified seasonal prices including residential demand, producing a significant change in tariff structure, as seen in Figure 13.8.

Residential customers faced decreasing non-linear tariffs[27] until 2008. As in the gas sector, after November 2008, there was a substantial change in the residential tariff structure, with large increases for high consumption, aimed at reducing subsidies.

Tariff increases were targeted to users with bimonthly consumption exceeding 1000 kW h[28] and ranged from 85 per cent to 350 per cent. Also, as in the gas sector, tariff increases were suspended during the winter of 2009 owing to opposition arising in a pre-electoral period.

13.4 STRUCTURAL PROBLEMS AND THE 2002 CRISIS

Before the 2002 crisis, discussions began on the possibility of revising the reforms of Argentina's energy sector, in terms of maintaining their achievements but unlocking restrictions which had not allowed certain factors to progress. Moreover, the 2002 crisis also changed the conditions in which businesses operated. This section analyzes the structural problems present before the 2002 crisis and the problems triggered by the crisis.

13.4.1 Structural Problems

Structural issues were already under discussion during the 1990s; then the 2002 crisis revealed certain structural aspects that had not been well considered. Some targeted the energy sector as a whole, while others only applied specifically to the gas or electricity sectors.

In the gas sector, with deregulation and YPF's high market share (more than 60 per cent) and its contract scheme with other producers, the privatization generated a concentration of supply that hindered the development of potential competition. This somewhat contradicted the rest of the gas structural reforms (and electricity reforms), which broke up the industry to promote competition.

Another problem observed in the gas production segment was the lack of investment in exploration and exploitation due to, among other factors, a fall in international prices by the end of the 1990s and the international diversification strategy of the firms.

High levels of gas exports were inconsistent with post-crisis levels of supply and the reduction in reserves. Supply–demand imbalances revealed problems with the energy planning. Also, the electricity sector had made significant investments in the 1990s (Romero, 2000), principally in thermal gas generators. However, this seems to have been a problem because it generated a dependence on a scarce input.

Regarding the high-tension transportation in the electricity sector, the main failure was the lack of incentives to invest in networks. The law stipulated that investments in the electricity transmission network should be decided and financed by the private sector.

In the distribution and marketing segments, for both gas and electricity, the inclusion of competitive mechanisms on the demand side exerted pressure on competitive pricing. Competition was partially limited to large users.

The effects of the deregulation of retail marketing can be grouped into two types: those affecting the sector's functioning directly and those influencing the welfare of the different segments of the population. To analyze the suitability of introducing competition, the cost–benefit relationship of these two aspects has to be evaluated (Petrecolla and Romero, 2005). Given the international experience, one would think that the net benefit of the project would be positive. However, high implementation costs draw attention to the benefits that can be obtained from deregulation on such a broad scale (the option value), particularly for developing countries.

Competition in the marketing segment depends on open access, one of the aspects imposed by regulatory schemes in the energy sector. Because of the vertical integration of distribution and the marketing segment and the possibility of distribution companies increasing their revenue by increasing their participation in the deregulated segment, firms will have incentives to discriminate access to transport services in order to exclude rivals in the competing section.[29]

So there are reasons to revise the tariff structure in order to promote competition. On the one hand, transparent mechanisms to determine access charges should be imposed. These would help identify the price of the unregulated commercialization service and avoid exclusionary practices. Also, it would be fitting to set tariffs that reflect the cost of service, with the objective of sustainable competition.

The necessity to implement a social tariff mechanism was another structural problem. Although this problem was present before the 2002 crisis, it became particularly serious owing to the decrease in households' purchasing power.

Social issues were not exclusively about tariff affordability but about access to service, too. Poor residential gas consumers need gas provision. At issue is whether to provide them with natural gas or LPG.

There were structural problems regarding the pass through of the productive efficiency gains to consumers in regulated segments. On the one hand, in the case of electricity distribution, the regulatory period was too long (10 years). On the other hand, in the case of gas distribution and transportation, although the revision period was shorter (5 years), the methodology did not make it possible to significantly transfer the productivity gains to consumers.

Finally, institutions matter. Gas and electricity national regulatory agencies presented relative advantages, compared with other sectors, concerning institutional design (Gerchunoff et al., 2003): both institutions were enacted by law before privatization. The competitive appointment of directors and congressional approval are necessary. Their budget needs congressional approval too, but funding comes from annual fees paid by regulated firms (unlike charges included in tariffs) and public hearings have to be called for main decisions. Some of these characteristics limit the capture risk of the agencies from regulated firms (congressional approval for directors' appointments and public hearings), but appointment procedures have not been fulfilled in recent years. Delays in the appointment processes began before the 2002 crises, and executive government intervention has increased since then, both designating officials and concentrating main regulatory decisions.

Policies for competition were not considered either in institutional design or in regulatory practice. Initially, from privatization to 1999, the sector's regulators were involved in antitrust issues.[30] After the enactment of a new Competition Law in 1999, all attributions went to the Competition Agency. But in any given period there was a lack of coordination on the analytical approach to common issues like mergers and acquisitions in regulated sectors, competitive advocacy, and third-party access regulation. Poor coordination between regulatory and competition policy is a notorious structural problem, taking into account the allegedly competitive goals of the 1990s liberalization policies.

13.4.2 The 2002 Crisis and the Ongoing Transition

Since the enactment of Law 25,561 'Public Emergency and Exchange Rate Regime Reform' of 6 January 2002, which eliminated convertibility, the Argentine market (1) faced frozen tariffs for gas and electricity sold in the domestic market and (2) experienced difficulties accessing financial markets, which, in turn, hindered the financing of investment projects.

Petrecolla and Romero (2003) suggest that measures to solve problems occurring during a macroeconomic crisis should be treated in a transition period, given the difficulty of making appropriate decisions in a highly uncertain environment. However, in practice, some measures, like contractual renegotiation, have not yet been fully achieved today.

Contract renegotiation was necessary owing to the change in the economic regime. Regarding the renegotiation process in regulated energy sectors (gas and electricity transportation and distribution), different measures have been implemented and a specific agency was created and committed to conduct the process.[31] By 2010, 8 years after the crisis, even though several renegotiation agreements had been signed, no integral tariff revision had been completed. Periodic tariff adjustment methodology and asset valuation criteria were the main uncertain outcomes of the renegotiation process (Greco and Stanley, 2004). Despite the delay in contract renegotiation, firms had managed to maintain their operations, some by renegotiating their debts (in particular, holding debts in dollars).

Renegotiation requires a discussion on tariffs. Increases in tariffs would have limited residential reach. Two main schemes have emerged: sustainable tariffs and social tariffs. These are related and require a consistent solution. The poorest sectors generally face serious problems accessing and maintaining the service and companies confronting a scenario of frozen tariffs may find it difficult to continue to expand their services.

Social tariffs have more to do with structural problems. However, this became particularly serious because of the crisis, which decreased household purchasing power. The principal objective of a social tariff is to act as a mechanism that allows the poor access to infrastructure services. There were existing mechanisms prior to the 2002 crisis.

For the electricity sector, a compensation tariff fund – FCT – financed by an overcharge on the wholesale price existed before the 2002 crisis. This fund was distributed between jurisdictions to offset the differences in the supply costs of electricity. The result was that small provinces received a higher percentage of resources that had nothing to do with poverty indicators. In addition, provinces had ample discretion in the way they could allocate the resources. Several jurisdictions had not used their resources transparently, and others had even diverted funds to the administration's overhead. This showed how necessary it is to standardize their use and create systems to target subsidies to lower-income families, such as those living in the provinces of Salta and Chaco.

With regard to gas consumption, a subsidy exists in Patagonia which is financed by an overcharge of gas at the wellhead. As in the case of the FCT, this subsidy is justified by territorial integration considerations – particularly the desire to compensate the local residents for the high cost of heating relative to the rest of the country. In this sense, the subsidy has nothing to do with purchasing power. In fact, Patagonia contains no more than 5 per cent of the country's poor. In 2002, the subsidy had a 70 per cent inclusion error and a 4 per cent exclusion error.

Although Argentina spends money on social policies in infrastructure sectors, it is not the same as a coherent social policy framework which warrants a basic level of access and equitability for the most vulnerable households (Foster and CEER, 2003). A new social policy framework has not yet been developed.

An alternative or complement to the social tariff is the implementation of cross-subsidies. Theoretically, cross-subsidies should be avoided. However, during crises like the ones that occurred in Argentina, efficiency objectives could be relaxed, giving priority to equity considerations.

Network expansion funding is another issue that arose after the 2002 crisis owing to the lack of regulatory reforms and tariff revisions. The government dealt with this issue with trust funds and public investment dedicated to pay for the new assets. Even when new capacity finally became available, there were significant efficiency problems. For example, the expansion costs in the gas sector were too high. So were charges to users. Questions of transparency surfaced and excess capacity showed resource allocation problems (see Figure 13.3).

Solving these problems does not imply a renouncement of public policy. Greco (2004) suggests that government intervention in investment funding may be desirable when private and social project evaluations differ. So, there is a social role for expansions oriented to granting the poor access. Additionally, the government could play an important role by generating funding mechanisms when firms find it difficult to access credit.

In the gas sector, several factors contributed to the rise of the 2004 supply shortage: the previously noted reduced investment in exploration; the lack of public planning; the fluctuations in relative prices; demand increase; and regulatory uncertainty related to national and provincial jurisdiction over the hydrocarbon concessions. Policies intended to alleviate this imbalance were: restrictions on gas exports; making national demand a priority; policies for the rational use of gas; increases in wholesale prices; and policies fostering production like the Gas Plus program, which permitted free price arrangements for gas coming from new gas fields.

Shortages in the gas sector also affected the electricity sector because it was the prior input in electricity generation. Programs for the rational use of electricity energy were imposed and the 'Fund for Necessary Investment to Boost Electricity Supply in the MEM' (FONINVEMEM) was established. Resolution 1866/2005 established a transitory tariff paid by all agents in the MEM – except residential consumers – to finance this fund.

Regarding the electricity sector, in many situations and depending on the thermal dispatch, the costs of generation could surpass the spot price. Because of Cammesa sanctions MEM's spot prices used a declared or maximum value recognized for each generated unit production variable cost (CVP), thermal machines operating with costs over the established cap (120$/MWh set by Resolution 240/2003) would be remunerated for their recognized costs and the difference be collected.

The functioning of this price formation system called for national state subsidies, whose causes could be distinguished in the way they affected different demand segments. On the one hand, the seasonal prices paid by distributors in recent years have increased slowly and have been inferior to spot prices. Currently, seasonal prices differ among the distinct demand segments, whereby residential and small-demand users pay lower prices than larger users. That difference between the seasonal and the spot prices is one of the main sources of the subsidy that was necessary for electricity generation activity. On the other hand, even users who obtained energy in the wholesale market and paid the spot prices have been subsidized. Differences in fuel costs made it necessary to generate enough electricity to meet the demand requirements and the implicit cost in the sanctioned spot price – which is limited by Resolution SE 204/03 – constitutes the other important source of the subsidy required to support the electricity generation sector.

In this context, a major transition issue which remains unsolved is the path toward new market equilibrium with reduced and socially targeted subsidies. Accumulated regulations and supply restrictions seem to indicate that this will be the 'second-best path'. Energy supply adjustments take place in the medium to long term and do not react solely to price conditions. So, a complete and sudden liberalization is unadvisable in a market with supply restrictions because it could generate excessive price increases in the short run that would inhibit medium- to long-term market equilibrium.

However, a gradual adjustment could give rise to arbitrage between market segments[32] and incentive problems if medium-term commitments are not credible but offer the opportunity to plan and adapt decisions to the new equilibrium.

Argentina has begun to differentiate pricing for 'old' and 'new' energy. Gas Plus, Energy Plus and complementary rulings[33] are taking this direction. Even when such policies could be criticized on grounds of efficiency (e.g. breaking local price laws), there are noteworthy precedents. The US Natural Gas Policy Act of 1978 established a complex pricing scheme for old and new gas and a 7-year transition period. Then there are the recent reforms in Brazil's electricity sector which divided up bids for old and new generation capacity.

Nevertheless, the implementation process revealed ad hoc decisions, lack of transparency, and uncertainty about medium- and long-term goals. What seems to be clear is the need for a convergence between policies to deal with transition and structural problems. This is still a pending issue.

13.5 CONCLUSIONS

The scope of the reforms in the utilities services in Argentina at the beginning of the 1990s was new to a developing country. Structural regulation in the energy sector was relatively better-designed than in other infrastructure sectors considering efficiency goals. The analysis of the original reforms and performance may offer useful lessons when restructuring the sector in other developing countries.

Sector evolution after the reforms exhibited several improvements. There was an increase in the number of agents participating in the market; an expansion and extension of networks; an increase in the number of users; an improvement in the quality of the services; a decrease in energy losses; and a significant decrease in the wholesale electricity price. However, 17 years after the privatization took place, the energy sector still faces challenges regarding its short-term equilibrium and long-term policies. Even when the 2000s brought general (2002) and specific (2004) crises affecting the sector, some of the relevant issues to be dealt with were rooted in existing structural problems.

Structural issues coming from the initial post-privatization years included the concentration of the gas supply and the YPF privatization, the reduced upstream gas exploration activity, the ill-designed incentive mechanisms for electricity transmission and capacity expansions, weak tariff review methodology to allow consumers to benefit from efficiency gains, the lack of competition in the marketing activity and the related third-party access regulation, poor institutional coordination between regulatory and competition policies, and the lack of planning given the *ex post* outcomes.

Access and affordability for the poor, which had not been adequately considered in the original reforms, became an obvious need after the 2002 crisis.

The Argentine case has also shown that both the country's firms and its regulatory framework – the latter designed to enhance convertibility commitment – were extremely vulnerable to macroeconomic shocks. The 2002 crisis made it necessary to renegotiate contracts on tariff adjustment rules and valuation methods. The role of the government in infrastructure expansion needs to be evaluated as well. In the gas and electricity markets, pricing and market segmentation are pending issues. Although prices in the wholesale markets have been increasing, large subsidies are still in place. Resource allocation signals need improvement.

Currently, the sector faces an opportunity for reform that goes beyond a mere return to the original rules and deregulation, but that still guards achievements. Dealing with structural problems requires a forward-looking approach, which improves regulation, promotes sustainable competition when possible and strengthens public involvement in energy planning and social policy design, as well as funding and environmental issues. The transition to these structural goals involves a second-best way to trade off short-term allocative efficiency for equity and sustainable long-term development and thus avoid orthodox fundamentalism.

NOTES

1. Ten years after implementing a fixed-exchange-rate regime (convertibility), Argentina moved to a flexible-exchange-rate system with a hyper-devaluation of 67 per cent (the exchange rate increased from 1 to 3 pesos for each dollar). The increase in the exchange rate impacted financial and real costs via rising input costs, imported and tradable goods, and debt services.
2. The regulatory framework was established by Law 24,076 (Ley del Gas).
3. Total revenue from the privatization of Gas del Estado was US$2.077 million, of which US$680 million was paid in cash and the remainder in securities of domestic and external debt.
4. Decree 1020/95.
5. Upon review, the regulator determines the efficiency factor X and, consequently, the reduction the tariffs will have in real terms. In this sense, once X is known, the firm has strong incentives to improve productivity in order to achieve greater profitability.
6. Since 2000 the licensee has ceased to receive the adjustment of its tariffs for changes in the United States wholesale price index as Law 24,076 authorized owing to a court order obtained at the request of the Ombudsman's Office, returning to the nominal values of July 1999.
7. State Reform Law 23,696.
8. Total revenue was approximately US$3.6 million, consisting of cash and government bonds (at nominal value).
9. This period is divided into management periods: the first for the distributors lasts 15 years and the following lasts 10 years. Six months before the end of the period of administration Ente Regulador de la Electricidad (ENRE) should call for a Public International Competition for the tender of the core package. The concessionaire delivers a sealed envelope containing the valuation of the business unit. If the rest of the offers are less than or equal to this amount, the concessionaire continues in business. In contrast, a higher offer sets the purchase value of the company payable to the concessionaire in activity.
10. The jurisdiction of ENRE covers the entire country for the generation and transmission and covers the area of Buenos Aires for distribution (concession area companies Edenor, Edesur and Edelap).
11. This coordination activity is conducted by a private company, Cammesa, that must fully adhere to the technical procedures set out in the regulations. More precisely, the task of the coordinator is to indicate, from the information provided by the agents and the procedures established by public authority, what the production levels are for each one. These amounts arise as a result of the minimization of the system's costs subject to technological and reliability constraints. From them, prices are determined in each network node.
12. The market price is the value of energy at the load center (Buenos Aires).
13. Large users purchasing energy in the wholesale market are those who make the so-called 'commercial bypass'. The bypass can also be 'physical' if the users also connect directly to the transport system with their own branches, thus avoiding the use of the distributor's facilities.

14. Gumas (larger demanders in the large user category), self-generators (when they act as demanders) and generators (to cover what lacks in the futures market contracts) purchase electricity in the wholesale market at the spot price.
15. Argentina has two major interconnected markets: the wholesale electricity market (MEM), and the wholesale electricity market of the Patagonian system (MEM-P).
16. The characterization of the distribution of electricity as a public service (Law 24,065, art. 1) is used to ensure that 'distributors satisfy all the required demand for electricity' (art. 21), 'being forced to indiscriminate access to third parties to the transport capacity' (art. 22) and cannot 'grant or provide benefits or preferences in access to its facilities' (art. 23).
17. This is not so in marketing as users with certain consumption characteristics might contract generators directly, a measure that introduces competition into that market.
18. Resolutions SE 752/05 and 2020/05.
19. See Figure 13.5.
20. Residential users who faced this increase were those whose consumption surpassed 800 m^3/year, representing approximately 80 per cent of the volume.
21. Cargo Fideicomiso de Gas.
22. The agreement also included transitory adjustment mechanisms to take into account cost variations.
23. Gas Natural Ban has received a 33 per cent increase in the distribution margin in November 2006: 27 per cent was due to the initially agreed increase and 6 per cent was due to cost variation.
24. Deflated with the wholesale price index (IPIM).
25. Tariffs for Greater Buenos Aires.
26. These are not increasing block tariffs (with increasing marginal prices), but 'volume differentiated tariffs', where all consumers pay the higher price once the threshold has been exceeded. This scheme gives rise to substantial changes in bills with small changes in consumption.
27. T1-R1 tariff for bimonthly consumption below 300 kWh and T1-R2 for higher consumption levels. T1R1 had a lower fixed charge and a higher variable charge, compared with T1-R2. This tariff structure was equivalent to a declining two-block tariff: with the same fixed charge as T1-R1, two consumption blocks with a 300 kWh bimonthly threshold, and marginal prices equal to T1-R1 and T1-R2 variable charges, respectively.
28. As in the gas sector, these are not increasing block tariffs but 'volume differentiated tariffs'.
29. See Laffont and Tirole (1994); Armstrong et al. (1995, ch.5).
30. Gas regulation was explicit about procedures for dominant position abuses (Decree 1738/92, art. 23).
31. Decree 293/2002 created the Commission for the Renegotiation of Works and Public Services to conduct the renegotiations of transporter and distributor concession contracts. In June 2003, with the initial deadline and an extension for the process already passed, Decree 311/2003 was sanctioned which dissolved the Renegotiation Commission and created the UNIREN in its place.
32. Speculation in production between periods could arise in the case of gas. Given a fixed stock (reserves), if the present value of the price increase is positive, there will be incentives to postpone production.
33. See Resolutions 220/07 and 599/07 issued by the Energy Secretariat.

REFERENCES

Armstrong, M., S. Cowan and J. Vickers (1995), *Regulatory Reform, Economic Analysis and British Experience*, Cambridge, MA: MIT Press.

Beato, P. (2000), 'Cross subsidies in public services: some issues', Sustainable Development Department Technical Papers Series, Washington, DC: IFM Publications, Inter-American Development Bank.
Chisari, O., P. Dal-Bo and C. Romero (2001), 'High-tension electricity network expansions in Argentina: decision mechanisms and willingness-to-pay revelation', *Energy Economics*, **23** (6), 697–715.
Chisari, O., A. Estache, G. Lambardi and C. Romero (2003), 'Devaluation and public services: trade-offs and remedial policies – a CGE model for Argentina', paper presented at EcoMod 2003, International Conference on Policy Modeling, Istambul, 3–5 July.
Chisari, O., A. Estache and C. Romero (1999), 'Winners and losers from utility privatization in Argentina: lessons from a general equilibrium model', *World Bank Economic Review*, **13** (2), 357–78.
Foster, V. and CEER (2003), 'Hacia una política social para los sectores de infraestructura en Argentina: evaluando el pasado y explorando el futuro', World Bank Office for Argentina, Chile, Paraguay and Uruguay – Working Paper no. 10/2003, Buenos Aires.
Gerchunoff, P., E. Greco and D. Bondorevsky (2003), 'Comienzos diversos, distintas trayectorias y final abierto: más de una década de privatizaciones en Argentina, 1990–2002', Serie Gestión Pública no. 34, Santiago de Chile: CEPAL/ILPES.
Greco, E. (2004), 'Regulación y competencia en la industria del gas: las condiciones de acceso a los servicios de transporte y distribución', in *Problemas de Defensa de la Competencia en Sectores de Infraestructura en la Argentina*, D. Petrecolla and C. Ruzzier (eds), Buenos Aires: Editorial Temas.
Greco, E. and Stanley, L. (2004), 'Valuación de activos, tarifas e incentivos: la base de capital en las empresas reguladas y la renegociación contractual', UADE-CEER Discussion Text no. 55, Buenos Aires; available at: http://www.uade.edu.ar/paginas/InstEconomiaIDE.aspx
Joskow, P. and Tirole, J. (2003), 'Merchant transmission investment', CMI EP Working Paper no. 24, Cambridge–MIT Institute, May; available at: http://www.econ.cam.ac.uk/electricity/publications/wp/index.htm
Laffont, J.J. and J. Tirole (1994), *A Theory of Incentives in Procurement and Regulation*, Cambridge, MA: MIT Press.
Petrecolla, D. and C. Romero (2003), 'Desempeño, crisis y reformas en el sector eléctrico argentino: lecciones para países en desarrollo', *Revista de Economía Mundial* (9), 23–48.
Petrecolla, D. and C. Romero (2005), 'Concentración horizontal en un ambiente regulado: el caso de la distribución de electricidad en el Gran Buenos Aires', *Revista de la Competencia y la Propiedad Intelectual*, **1** (1), 127–52.
Romero, C. (1998), 'Regulación e inversiones en el sector eléctrico argentino', work prepared for the project 'Crecimiento, empleo y equidad: América Latina en los años noventa' (HOL/97/6034), http://www.uade.edu.ar/paginas/InstEconomiaIDE.aspx
Romero, C. (2000), 'Regulación de las inversiones en el sector eléctrico argentino', in D. Heymann and B. Kosacoff (eds), *La Argentina de los Noventa: Desempeño Económico en un Contexto de Reformas*, Buenos Aires: Eudeba.

14. Two decades of privatization in Brazil

Armando Castelar Pinheiro

14.1 INTRODUCTION

For political scientists, the many privatization programs around the world in the late twentieth century can be grouped into three categories: systemic, tactical and pragmatic.[1] Initiatives in the first group have deep, ample objectives, being intended to reshape economic and political institutions, as was the case in Chile, the United Kingdom and New Zealand. Tactical cases are those in which privatization is aimed at the short-term objectives of political actors, such as political parties and interest groups. Pragmatic privatization, in turn, tends to suffer less influence from ideology or politics, being only one of a number of alternatives the bureaucracy deems adequate to further social objectives.

It is not straightforward to say in which category Brazilian privatization fits best. Sprawling over two decades, with total revenues of close to US$83 billion and almost 170 state-owned enterprises transferred to the private sector, it is undeniable that privatization has substantially changed the country's economic and political landscapes. In 1996–98, in particular, when ports, railways, roads, telecommunications and electricity were transferred to private hands, the state substantially reduced its weight in the economy, allowing for the establishment of new national and foreign players, with deep implications for the way product, labor and political markets operate.

Yet, as we argued elsewhere (Pinheiro and Giambiagi, 1999), privatization in Brazil was above all a pragmatic response to short-term macroeconomic problems, arising mainly from the state of disarray of the country's fiscal accounts. It did not, in this sense, differ much from the process of nationalization of the economy in the period after World War II, when state-owned enterprises were seen as a means to boost investment in certain sectors. Ideology and the pursuit of structural adjustment were motivations espoused by only a fraction of those in charge of taking the process forward (Velasco, 1997a, 1997b). In fact, various opinion polls showed that throughout these two decades a substantial share of the electorate opposed privatization. In many instances, the reason it was tolerated was the perception, correct in our view, that privatization was instrumental in achieving macroeconomic stability and allowing for a recovery in investment.

Pragmatic privatizations, even when widespread as was the case of Brazil, risk being less durable than those that reflect profound changes in society's view about the role of the state. Looking at privatizations worldwide, Feigenbaum et al. (1999, p. 173) conclude:

> Much of what has occurred to date has been shaped by pragmatic and tactical motives, and . . . may prove to be self-limiting, as the constituency for a backslash strengthens. The coalition that has carried privatization forward is more diverse and disunited in motive and interest than the rhetoric of the privatization revolution acknowledges.

Velasco (1997a, 1997b) makes a similar assessment for the Brazilian case, highlighting the underlying tensions in the coalition that has managed Brazilian privatization. In the same vein, Baer and McDonald (1998) note that in Brazil many of the sectors now being privatized were nationalized in the past, and stress the sensitivity of the status quo to volatile political mood, asking whether the future will see the pendulum swing back in the direction of an economic model with a strong presence of the state in the economy. This indeed took place in the last 2 years of the Lula government and more will come under President Dilma Roussef.

The object of study of this chapter is this swinging pendulum. In particular, we analyze the forces that made it swing in the past, both towards greater state intervention and later in the direction of privatization. Building on this analysis, we discuss in which way we should expect the pendulum to move in the future. In Section 14.2 we briefly review the reasons that led to the establishment of state-owned enterprises (SOEs) in several sectors of the Brazilian economy, and discuss the first movements in favor of privatization. In Section 14.3 we argue that privatization in Brazil met the imperative needs of the stabilization effort, more than it resulted from an ideological conversion process (although these two were not the only motives). Section 14.4 discusses the quality of regulation in public services after privatization. A final section considers the question of how durable we may expect privatization in Brazil to be.

14.2 NATIONALIZATION AND PRIVATIZATION IN BRAZIL

State-owned enterprises (SOEs) have existed in Brazil since colonial times, but state intervention in the economy, by creation of SOEs or otherwise, was relatively limited until Getúlio Vargas came to power in 1930. With the establishment of Vargas's Estado Novo (Nem State), the liberalism of Brazil's First Republic gave way to economic nationalism, protectionism, high public investments in infrastructure and basic input sectors, and the creation of public monopolies for products such as sugar, coffee, mate tea etc. In the subsequent decades, SOE presence in the economy grew steadily, as the result of several different processes:

1. Developmentism, especially the decision to install a diversified industrial sector in Brazil, with the creation of SOEs in areas in which the private sector lacked the interest or the financial muscle to invest. A typical case was steel. The same kind of motivation was behind public investments in infrastructure, as in highways.
2. Concern for 'national security', whose vague mantle covered three main areas: concerns with shortages of some important products during World War II; the desire to keep industries which were considered to be strategic under government control; and the decision to limit the participation of foreign companies in the Brazilian economy. Companies such as Fábrica Nacional de Motores, Álcalis, Lloyd, Serviço de Navegação da Bacia do Prata and Embraer were created, or nationalized, for this reason. Economic nationalism, as reflected in the concern to keep exploitation of the subsoil in Brazilian hands, determined the creation of both CVRD and Petrobrás, respectively the largest mining and oil companies in the country.
3. Nationalization of foreign companies in areas in which regulation failed to attract the levels of investment required by Brazil's high economic growth – as with communications and electricity, for instance.[2] This movement, however, also met the needs of the 'national security' argument, put forward by groups who feared control of these sectors by foreign companies.
4. Regulatory failure of the opposite kind (i.e. excessive protection to investors) followed by nationalization. This occurred when regulation obliged large transfers of public funds to foreign companies, a process that faced great political opposition. This was the case of the railways nationalized in the late nineteenth and early twentieth centuries. The problem then consisted of the creation of contingent fiscal liabilities through the concession of public guarantees of a minimum return to

investors, with the state absorbing much of the risk involved in operating the concession.[3]

5. Verticalization and diversification of the activities of large state-owned enterprises (SOEs), motivated by the objectives of occupying 'empty spaces', a central element of the import substitution strategy, and of increasing SOE profitability, with the creation of subsidiaries in sectors with high rates of return. This process, facilitated by the high self-financing capacity of SOEs, led to a rapid rise in public sector participation in sectors such as pulp and paper, petrochemicals, aluminum and transportation. The 1967 administrative reform (Decree Law no. 200) and the increase in SOE tariffs in the late 1960s intensified this process, by giving those companies the freedom and means to expand.
6. Nationalization of bankrupt companies – most of them large debtors of public banks – operating in sectors which were naturally alien to public administration, such as hotels, sugar mills, publishing companies etc. These firms subsequently showed a remarkable resistance to returning to private hands. Of the 268 federal SOEs that existed in 1979, 76 came under state control this way, compared with a total of 40 created by law.

There is no consensus in the literature as to whether the rapid growth of the Brazilian state sector was the result of an ideology of state intervention or whether it was caused by superimposed although disconnected movements. For several authors, although economic policy began to be more interventionist with the Estado Novo, the rapid postwar growth in the number of SOEs (there were only 20 federal SOEs in 1940) was neither a planned phenomenon nor the result of a nationalizing ideology (Baer et al., 1973; Cardoso, 1973).[4] For Martins (1977, pp. 26–7), however:

> [T]here was always an ideology of state intervention (whether in the form of *statism, nationalism*, or *developmentism*), in which the point of reference was the concept of the nation . . . This was why, on the ideological plane, these three 'isms' often appeared in an intermingled form, as interchangeable concepts . . . It is historically inexact, however, to state, as is now frequently stated, that the business activities of the state emerged in Brazil almost accidentally and without any link to any defined political project.

Quite apart from this controversy, however, the rapid expansion of the state sector did not cause any significant concern before, at least, the end of the so-called 'economic miracle', which lasted from 1968 to 1973. In a paper written in the early 1970s, Baer et al. (1973, p. 281) asserted that:

> The continuous growth in the participation of the state in economic activities in Brazil in the last three decades was almost inevitable. The Brazilian private sector is still relatively small and does not have the capacity to play an important role in the country's enormous needs for infrastructure or in the industries which use more sophisticated technology, which are also the most dynamic – petrochemicals, steel, transportation equipment, etc. Soon, the growth of the state will no longer be considered as a threat to Brazilian private companies.

But like the 'Brazilian miracle', this harmonious coexistence between private and state capital was at the time already coming to an end. With the deterioration in economic conditions, and the decision of the government that took office in March 1974 to reduce the influence of the private sector in deciding how to allocate public savings, the first objections against the excessive state participation in the economy would soon arise. Eugênio Gudin, a known liberal elected 'Man of the Year' by the magazine *Visão* in 1974, stated at the award ceremony: 'We live, in principle, in a capitalist system. But Brazilian capitalism is more controlled by the state than in any other country, except for those under communist regimes.' Gudin's speech was to be followed by a series of articles under the joint title (Os Caminhos da Estatização (The Directions of Nationalization) published in early 1975 by the influential *O Estado de São Paulo* newspaper, and by the 'Campaign against Nationalization' mounted by private-sector businessmen.[5]

A proper reading of the businessmen's arguments, however, shows that this was above all a movement against deprivatization, even if partial, of the state. Thus, the businessmen's exclusion from decision-making forums was a particularly important element behind their dissatisfaction – starting from the composition of the Conselho de Desenvolvimento Econômico (CDE; Economic Development Council), on which only the president and some ministers would have seats from 1974 onwards. In particular, private sector businessmen wanted to be 'heard throughout the whole process of decision on the national economy, helping to establish criteria for the activity of the state and the private sector, orienting the use of the SOEs and controlling their expansion, deciding directions for the investment of their savings, etc'. (Pessanha, 1981, p. 154).

Among their principal suggestions to reverse the process of nationalization, Pessanha (1981, pp. 95–96) mentions

> the suppression of some privileges enjoyed by the public companies, such as the freedom to invest funds and exemption from some taxes, limitation of their capacity to create subsidiaries, through control of diversification, prohibition of use of funds arising from compulsory savings and other tax incentives.

The sale of SOEs, although mentioned, was accompanied by so many misgivings or doubts on its effectiveness and on the issue of in what sectors it could happen, that it finished up playing only a symbolic role in the overall body of the businessmen's proposals.[6] Privatization was not a priority for businessmen.[7]

The government's reply came in the proposal to strengthen national private companies through tax and credit subsidies.[8] On the issue of SOE privatization, Pessanha (1981, p.133) noted:

> [T]he reply contained in the document admits that it is clear that the return to the private sector 'should take place in the specific cases identified, to characterize a political orientation'. However, 'that is not where the essence of the problem is', since to assure a nationalizing trend for the country is to give 'strength and vitality' to Brazilian companies, 'which, above all, need capitalization', since the problem of 'empty spaces' is frequently 'an expression of the lack of risk funding in the hands of the national private sector'. But *'the transfer to the private sector of companies which – especially those in infrastructure (Petrobrás, Eletrobrás and its system, Telebrás and its system, CVRD, Usiminas, CSN, Cosipa, etc.) – are within the areas defined by the II National Development Plan (II PND) as being the public sector's social responsibility, has never been considered nor could be considered.* [Author's emphasis]

To go beyond these measures was seen as contrary to the country's best interest. In other words, the government continued to perceive that it was urgent to industrialize the country, 'occupying' sectors regarded as 'strategic', and that while national private companies were not equipped to do so, it was not desirable, from the point of view of 'national security', that this should be done by foreign firms. Severo Gomes, then trade and industry minister, commented at the occasion on the subject of the Campaign Against Nationalization, that 'to privatize, today, would be to de-nationalize'. In the same vein, Mário Henrique Simonsen, the Finance Minister and a well-known liberal, remarked in response to Gudin's statement that 'any discussion on privatization will always be innocuous, if one is to leave empty spaces'. He added that the origin of the state company in Brazil was linked to the objective of 'filling empty spaces', and not to ideological motives (Pessanha, 1981, p. 122).

At the end of the 1970s, the country's macroeconomic situation again worsened, making control of inflation and external balance top priorities, to the detriment of short-term growth. The rapid expansion of the state business sector was inconsistent with the objective of stabilization, and even the idea of privatization began to permeate government discourse, although with a lack of practical consequence. In a message to his cabinet shortly after taking power, in March 1979, President Figueiredo recommended adoption of the measures necessary 'for privatization of the

SOEs and services that are not strictly essential to correction of market imperfections or for meeting the needs of national security' (Palatnik and Orenstein, 1979, p. 52).

Still in 1979, the government decided to curb the growth of SOEs, with the creation of the National De-Bureaucratization Program and the Special Secretariat for Control of SOEs (SEST). The reasons behind that decision were different from those which would later lead to the sale of those companies, and this explains the emphasis on the creation of control agencies, and the very small importance given to the agencies responsible for selling state assets. The point in question at that time was not the inefficiency of SOEs but the need to decelerate expansion of the state business sector, so as to control aggregate demand, a difficult task given the almost complete lack of control of these companies by federal authorities. The predominant view was well reflected by Rezende (1980), who, after rejecting, 'the hypothesis that private sector production is intrinsically more efficient than public sector production' (p. 35), observed that (p. 37):

> In fact, the whole debate on the need to limit the increase in the functions of the state reflects the incapacity of the public administration to control the actions of government companies, whose decisions to expand escape the control exercised during the periodic analysis of the budget. . .to the extent that the decisions to invest in certain sectors by private enterprises are subordinated to public credit and/or fiscal incentive schemes, control of the decisions of the privately controlled companies is greater than the control of the decisions of the public companies, whose capacity to mobilize funds gives them a certain independence in relation to the central power.

Thus, it was not an ideological about-turn on the developmental role of the state, but rather a change in the emphasis of economic policy, imposed by changes which were up to a certain point outside government control. The priority was no longer growth and import substitution, but control of inflation and, principally, overcoming the foreign exchange crisis. Since the SOEs were responsible for a considerable portion of domestic investment and consumption, it would be almost impossible to stabilize the economy without some form of control over their expenditures and without eliminating or at least reducing their deficits (Werneck, 1987).

The macroeconomic imperatives – in particular, the foreign exchange crisis – were to have two additional effects on the SOEs. Before the foreign debt crisis (1982), the SOEs were led to contract foreign loans beyond their needs, as a means of financing the country's growing current-account deficit. With their external obligations considerably increased, these companies were seriously harmed by the increase in international interest rates, starting in 1979, and the significant currency devaluation after 1983. Further, since 1975 the prices of goods and services produced by the SOEs had been reduced in real terms, initially to control inflation and then, after 1982, to subsidize manufacture exports. Thus, the use of these companies as instruments of macroeconomic policy – with limits on their investments, increases in their debt, reductions in the real prices of their output, and indeed a loss of focus on their business objectives – would lead to a gradual but continuous deterioration in their performance, with the expansion of pent-up demand and loss of quality in their services.

It was not until 1981, though, that privatization was actually put on the economic policy agenda. In July of that year, a presidential decree created the Comissão Especial de Desestatização (Special Privatization Committee) and set 'rules for the transfer, transformation and divestiture of companies controlled by the federal government'. The main objectives of the committee were to strengthen the private sector, limit the creation of new SOEs, and close or transfer to the private sector those SOEs whose control by the public sector was no longer necessary or justifiable.

Once set up, the committee identified 140 SOEs ready to be privatized in the short term. Of these, 50 were initially put on the list for sale. However, the actual balance of this first attempt at privatization was not to reach even this number: a total of 20 companies were sold to private investors, 1 was leased, and 8 were incorporated into other public institutions. In this same period, however, 6 companies in a bankrupt situation were incorporated by the BNDES, through what were then called 'hospital operations'. The companies sold in this period were, in general, cases of reprivatization, and their list did not include any of the major SOEs.

The 20 companies privatized in 1981–84 totaled assets of only US$274 million and employed a total of less than 5000 workers, while their sale produced total proceeds of only US$190 million. The highest revenue, US$77.5 million, came from the sale of a group of companies linked to Riocell (wood pulp), and the lowest, from the sale of Fiação e Tecelagem Lutfala, was only US$2000.

The speed of privatization in the Sarney administration (March 1985 to March 1990) was similar to that in its predecessor, in spite of the more aggressive rhetoric, as reflected in the series of presidential decrees and draft bills restructuring and enlarging the privatization program. In all, 18 companies valued at US$533 million were sold, with a similar number transferred to the state governments, 2 merged into other federal institutions, and 4 closed down. Most of them were small and medium companies in sectors where the private sector was dominant, and whose privatization was decided as a means to improve the financial health of their owner, BNDESPAR, the subsidiary of BNDES responsible for capital market operations. Their combined assets mounted to US$2.5 billion, and together they employed 27,600 people.

On assessing the Brazilian privatization experience in the 1980s, the World Bank (1989) concluded that 'Brazil's first flirtation with privatization was a "classic example of failure"'. Indeed, in terms of both speed and scope, the sale of SOEs in the 1980s fell far short of the level promised by government rhetoric. Further, most of the sales were made by the BNDES, whose motivation for privatizing was more related to its need to free itself of problematic, loss-making companies than to a favorable perception about privatization on the part of the government.[9] Privatization was not a priority for the public sector.

It could thus be argued that the privatizations achieved in the 1980s were those that were possible under the circumstances, three of them being particularly relevant in limiting the breath and depth of Brazilian privatization in its first decade:

1. Until the middle of the decade, SOEs continued to show a relatively good operational performance, reducing the scope for productivity gains in the event of their transfer to the private sector. This, for one, constrained public support for privatization, and, for another, reduced the interest of private investors in buying those companies.
2. The 'protective mantle of "national security"' continued to be laid over the SOEs for most of the decade, in such a way that it would have been virtually impossible to sell large SOEs while the military maintained their influence in the federal government.
3. As was well characterized by the 1988 Constitution, a large segment of Brazilian society, from the military to leftist parties, continued, like Severo Gomes 10 years earlier, to see privatization as a code word for the denationalization of the economy, with multinational companies seen as the only ones able to buy the major Brazilian SOEs. And an enlargement of the presence of foreign investors in the economy was perceived to be against the national interest.

14.3 BRAZILIAN-STYLE PRIVATIZATION: PRAGMATISM OR IDEOLOGY?

The previous section showed that perception on the role of the state in the Brazilian economy began to change during the mid to late 1970s, and that it was not a coincidence that by then Brazil's growth engine started to rattle, bringing to an end the long cycle of growth begun in the 1940s. The continuous deterioration of the economy – and in particular the fiscal crisis that emerged in the early 1980s – helped to provide support for privatization in subsequent years. Even so, years of rhetoric and privatization efforts produced only modest results, with only a marginal effect on the state's presence in the economy. Only small companies, in sectors the state should never have entered, were privatized. More important, perhaps, is that there was no firm political commitment to privatization. In 1989, Congress rejected Provisional Measure 26, which would have made all SOEs subject to privatization, except for those that could not be sold owing to constitutional restrictions. Indeed, the 1988 Constitution was clearly a nationalizing one, establishing public monopolies in telecommunications, oil and distribution of gas, and setting up barriers to foreign ownership in mining and electricity.

Yet, less than 2 years after the promulgation of the new constitution, the Collor administration launched the Programa Nacional de Desestatização (PND; Brazilian Privatization Program), significantly enlarging the scope of privatization. What were the causes of this shift in the official view of the role of the state in the Brazilian economy? The answers to this question include changes in the domestic and international political scenarios, the reorientation of the economic development strategy, a worsening of SOE performance, and the needs of macroeconomic policy.

A notable aspect of the discussion on privatization is how the issue of national security and, on a smaller scale and with a slight lag, the argument that privatization would lead to the denationalization of the economy lost importance in the public debate. Instead, in the 1990s opponents of privatization criticized the minimum sale prices set for the SOEs, argued that the risks of transferring companies with market power to the private sector were too big, and doubted the benefits of privatization, particularly with regard to its impact on the quality of services offered. But little was said about the risk of denationalization of the economy and even less about threats to national security – this in spite of the high participation of foreign capital in the process since 1995.

To a large extent, this change can be credited to the process of democratization, with the gradual move from military to civilian rule; together with an international environment characterized by the end of the cold war. The strong influence of the military in the creation of SOEs dated back to the Vargas period, and it was not by chance that elsewhere in Latin America privatization also made significant progress with democratization. The fact that President Collor was elected by popular vote, in contrast to the negotiated transition that allowed the rise of Sarney to the presidency, was thus important in legitimizing this change of direction. The end of the East–West conflict also helped to reduce pressures to keep strategic sectors (such as telecoms, oil and electricity) under state and national control. The same process was seen in the OECD countries, especially in Western Europe (Nestor and Mahboodi, 1999). In this regard, it is probable that the 1988 Constitution would have had a less nationalizing and xenophobic bias had it been written after the fall of the Berlin Wall and in an environment of weaker military influence.

The main feature of the change in development models in the early 1990s was the shift from a strategy focused exclusively on the process of accumulation – presented as a concern to 'occupy empty spaces' – to one more concerned with efficiency and productivity growth. Consequently, the very existence of a state company as an instrument of economic policy seemed no longer to make sense, for if it served to accumulate capital then it did so at the cost of a high burden on efficiency. Thus it was no mere coincidence that the PND was launched simultaneously with trade liberalization and the significant deregulation of the domestic economy, together with the ending of public monopolies in sectors such as sugar, ethanol, coffee, wheat etc.

Moreover, at the beginning of the 1990s it became clear, or so it looked, that the state had exhausted its capacity to lead the process of accumulation, since it was not capable either of generating a fiscal surplus or of borrowing abroad. Finance to SOEs also disappeared for another less obvious reason: virtually all long-term credit in Brazil was (and mostly still is) extended by public banks. Because these could not execute the collateral given by SOEs, for political and legal motives, SOEs did not bother to pay back.[10] So in the mid 1980s public banks were forbidden to lend to SOEs, cutting their last source of finance. Privatization became then the only way public banks could finance the sectors in which SOE presence was massive – being private, these companies could credibly pledge their assets as collateral.

This was the common ground that allowed a tactical coalition between those who believed the state should permanently exit commercial activities and those who saw privatization as a necessary evil. The deterioration in the performance of the SOEs in the 1980s also contributed to raise support for privatization. In the second half of the 1980s, a large number of management positions were filled by political appointees with scarce management skills, who usually remained in their posts for only a short period. They were rarely de facto subordinated to their line minister, and even more rarely were they compensated on the basis of the economic financial performance of the companies they managed. In addition, with the relaxation of fiscal constraints, vis-à-vis the early 1980s, SOEs were back on operating with soft budgets, with the federal government coming to their rescue when necessary. Investment was the only type of spending kept under control. As a result, SOEs developed new vices, without recovering their old virtues, vices which were made all the more evident by the process of trade liberalization, which revealed inefficiencies previously hidden by SOE monopoly positions.[11]

Nonetheless, the main driving force in overcoming inertia and widening the scope of privatization was the poor performance of the economy in the late 1980s (Pinheiro and Giambiagi, 1999) – one, because it reduced the degrees of freedom for state intervention, forcing the government to adopt more market-oriented policies; two, because it increased the need to control the spending of the SOEs, at a time when these companies needed massive investment to modernize and expand output capacity.

Foremost, though, was the role privatization was expected to play in the stabilization program launched at the beginning of the Collor government, which explains the government's decision to privatize rapidly and independently of the unstable macroeconomic situation of the time. On the one hand, fiscal revenue was increased with the creation of privatization certificates, a security acquired under government pressure by financial intermediaries and that could be used only to buy SOE shares. On the other hand, and even more important, the government expected to drastically reduce the public debt by accepting public debt securities as privatization currencies, thus cutting the fiscal deficit and consolidating price stability. Foremost among these privatization currencies were the tens of billions of dollars in private savings, denominated in new cruzados, the old currency, which were temporarily frozen at the central bank as part of the stabilization program launched simultaneously with the PND.

These frozen savings, due to be returned in 12 installments, starting in November 1991, were expected, in turn, to guarantee a high demand for SOE shares.[12] The symbiosis between stabilization and privatization was to fail because of problems in both programs. Privatization began with very optimistic targets in terms of revenue and timetable, which turned out to be impossible to fulfill because of the bad financial situation of the SOEs and the complexity of these companies' stockholders' agreements.[13] The SOEs were not ready for sale: they needed a long process of preparation before they could be privatized. As is known, it was only at the end of 1991 that the first company was sold under the PND. Since at that time the new cruzados were beginning to return to private investors, regaining their liquidity, their use as a privatization currency turned out to be almost nil. Thus, even though privatization revenues continued to be used to reduce the public debt, the original logic of the PND had to be changed, to the extent that the new privatization currencies were liabilities with relatively low liquidity. That is to say, the impact of privatization on the profile of the public debt was to be much less positive than initially projected.

As the failure of the Collor government's first stabilization plan became increasingly evident, the government started to rely on the PND as a proof of its commitment to structural change. This caused the program to continue, even after Collor´s impeachment and the rise to office of a president who had previously voiced publicly his opposition to privatization. However, rising inflation and low growth reduced the already compressed levels of domestic and foreign investment, severely limiting the scope of privatization. Thus, until 1996 the role of privatization in Brazil's macroeconomic policy was essentially that of signaling the commitment to reducing the size of the state and implementing structural reforms. In fact, even the policy of using privatization revenues exclusively to retire public debt was strongly questioned by sectors of the government itself, and was indeed partially abandoned in some cases.

All in all, 33 companies were privatized during the Collor and Franco governments (1990–94), for total revenues of US$8.6 billion, and the transfer to the private sector of US$3.3 billion in debt (Table 14.1). Almost all the companies were in manufacturing, with revenues concentrated in the steel, petrochemical and fertilizer sectors. The companies selected for sale had in common that they belonged to relatively competitive sectors or to ones for which trade liberalization would create a competitive environment. Included in this profile were: (1) the small private companies absorbed by the state; (2) the subsidiaries established after the 1967 reform, with the vertical integration and diversification of the major SOEs; and (3) the state steel companies, for which there was a reasonable consensus that the presence of the state was no longer necessary. The privatization of the state monopolies was not even considered at the time.

Starting in 1995, the scope of privatization was greatly widened by two almost simultaneous movements: the determination to end the public sector monopolies in infrastructure, and the decision of the local state governments to develop their own privatization programs (Table 14.1). In all, the 80 privatizations in the period 1995–98 provided total revenues of US$60.1 billion and transfer of debt to the private sector amounting to US$13.3 billion.

Several factors contributed to these two movements. First, the repeated failures of successive governments to control inflation had limited their ability to follow a more aggressive privatization program. The success of the Real Plan in achieving stabilization gave the government the political leverage required to get the necessary constitutional amendments through Congress, so as to extend privatization to the telecom and gas sectors and to facilitate its progress in mining and electricity. Second, to sustain price stability the government needed to achieve fiscal discipline, and this limited its ability to carry out the high levels of investment necessary to increase supply at the pace required by the recovery in economic growth.

Table 14.1 Brazilian privatization results 1991–2000: proceeds and debt transferred (US$ million, up to November 2000)

	1991	1992	1993	1994	1995	1996	1997	1998	1999	2000	Grand total		
											Proceeds	Debt transferred	Total
Total	1610	2401	2627	1966	1004	5486	22,616	30,975	3202	10,201	82,088	18,076	100,164
1. Federal	1610	2401	2627	1966	1004	4080	8999	23,478	554	7635	54,354	11,326	65,680
Steel	1470	921	2250	917							5558	2626	8184
Petrochemicals		1266	172	445	604	212					2699	1003	3702
Fertilizers		202	205	11							418	75	493
Mining				6			3299				3305	3559	6864
Railroad						1477	15	205			1697		1697
Ports							251	149	21		421		421
Electricity					400	2358	270	880	1		3909	1670	5579
Oil and gas										4032	4032		4032
Financial							240			3595	3835		3835
Telecom							4734	21,823	421		26,978	2125	29,103
Minority stakes				395		33	190	421	62	8	1109		1109
Other	140	12		192					49		393	268	661

Table 14.1 (continued)

	1991	1992	1993	1994	1995	1996	1997	1998	1999	2000	Grand total		
											Proceeds	Debt transferred	Total
2. Local state						1406	13,617	7497	2648	2566	27,734	6750	34,484
Telecom								1018			1018	822	1840
Financial							401	647	147	869	2064		2064
Gas							576		1131	298	2005	88	2093
Electricity						587	9945	5166	1370	1293	18,361	5840	24,201
Water and sewerage										106	106		106
Railroad						25		240			265		265
Other							307	96			403		403
Minority stakes						794	2388	330			3512		3512
Number of SOEs	4	14	6	9	8	18	36	18	11	6			130
Federal	4	14	6	9	8	16	21	7	6	1			92
Local state						2	15	11	5	5			38

Source: BNDES.

Also for fiscal reasons, economic policy limited the access of SOEs to domestic and external financing.

Third, the states saw in privatization an important source of funding, which would allow them to reduce their debt (both registered and non-registered) and, in some cases, expand spending. Moreover, in the debt-restructuring contracts between the states and the federal government the latter included clauses that required the states to amortize part of the principal, which could be done only through the sale of their assets, i.e. through privatization (Pinheiro and Giambiagi, 1999). An additional stimulus was provided by the contracts of the states with the BNDES, which made it possible to borrow against future privatization revenue. Fourth, stability itself, and the change in the perceptions of the risk and of the growth potential of the Brazilian market – reflected, for example, in the high growth in foreign direct investment flows – helped to increase the value of these companies, making privatization more interesting both for the public sector and for private investors.[14]

Fifth, the success of the privatizations carried out in 1991–94, evidenced by the companies' increased efficiency and investment, helped to widen political support for the program. Pinheiro (1996) shows that privatization substantially improved the performance of the former SOEs, with significant increases in real sales, sales per employee, net profit, stockholders' equity, investment, fixed assets and the ratio of investment to sales. Efficiency practically doubled when measured in terms of sales per employee, increasing 83 per cent when gauged by labor productivity. Profitability went from negative to positive, shareholders' equity multiplied by almost five, while debt diminished and liquidity increased. The median investment also increased almost by a factor of five, rising more than four times as a proportion of sales and more than doubling in relation to fixed assets. Sales per employee went up in 92 per cent of the companies, net profit in 78 per cent of them, investment in 93 per cent and labor productivity in all of them.

Of all the factors contributing to expand privatization in Cardoso's first term, the most important was the role played by privatization in sustaining his stabilization program, the Real Plan. With the large sales of 1997–98, Brazil attracted sizable volumes of foreign direct investment, which helped to finance the country's high current-account deficit – in 1997–2000, the ratio between FDI inflows associated with privatization and the current-account deficit averaged almost 25 per cent. Privatization was also instrumental in averting an explosion in public debt, in spite of the growing fiscal deficit posted since 1995. Carvalho (2001) shows that thanks to the predominant use of privatization to redeem public debt, in December 1999 this was 8.4 per cent of GDP lower than it would have been without privatization.

14.4 FROM PRIVATIZATION TO REGULATORY REFORM

Starting in the second half of the 1990s, all of Brazil's infrastructure sectors were subjected to some form of privatization, but with substantial cross-sector variation in the quality of regulation. The sale of assets was complete in the telecom and railroad sectors. In the electricity industry, 63 per cent of distribution was transferred to private investors. Also, cargo that enters and leaves the country is now mostly handled in private port terminals, while all the main highways are in the hands of private operators. Only in water and sewerage services has privatization not reached an important degree, although it encompassed some relevant operations in some medium-sized cities.

The importance of good regulation for the success of privatization was recognized in all the sectors. With varying degrees of success, an effort was made to decide the regulations before privatization and, when this did not happen, concession contracts contained several regulatory clauses. There has also been, in general, a concern to introduce competition in the sectors being privatized, through the setting up of a nonmonopolistic industry structure, at least on a nationwide scale, with several SOEs being separated both horizontally and vertically before privatization. Examples of horizontal separation include the railroad, electricity and telecom sectors, and examples of vertical breakups were telecom and electricity. In addition, limits were imposed on the participation of individual investors in different markets, regional and national, and even on the ownership structure of some companies (such as CVRD and the railroads). Also, by law, each privatization sale is subject to approval by the competition agency.

The most successful case of privatization-cum-regulatory-reform is, undoubtedly, telecommunications.[15] The process began with the approval of the so-called 'Minimum Law', which enabled the B-Band cellular telephony concessions to be auctioned.[16] This was followed by a significant tariff rebalancing in 1996 and 1997, then by the approval of the General Telecommunications Law in 1997, by the creation of the Brazilian Telecommunications Agency (Anatel), the sector regulator, in the same year, and finally by the privatization of Telebrás, the public monopoly company, in 1998. Thus, when privatization took place, the entire regulatory structure had already been established and the regulatory agency responsible for the sector was functioning at full steam. Indeed, telecom companies signed concession contracts in which the new regulatory environment was embedded while they were still state-owned, so that the new owners knew exactly what rules would be in force after privatization.

Telecom was also the sector with the most ambitious targets for investment and for competition. The concession contracts required expansion of the number of fixed lines from 15.3 million to 50 million, and the number of cellular lines from 4.0 million to 26.2 million in the period of 10 years, a growth of 226 per cent and 550 per cent, respectively. Two years after privatization, the number of fixed lines had reached 35.0 million and that of cellular phones 21.5 million, almost doubling the number of lines. By 2008, Brazil had 41.3 million fixed lines and 150.6 million cell phones. Competition has been gradually increased in a number of ways:

- Telebrás was divided into 13 companies, of which one was the long-distance carrier, 3 were fixed-line and 9 were mobile-phone companies. These 9 companies corresponded essentially to the areas previously auctioned for the B-Band, so that when privatization occurred there was a 'duopoly' in cellular telephony in each concession area.
- Restrictions were also placed on a single investor having stockholdings in more than one area or more than one service.
- In 1999, Anatel auctioned concessions for fixed-line operation in each area, so that currently these are also duopolies. The same happened in the long-distance segment.
- The fixed-line companies were allowed to compete with the long-distance companies within their own concession areas beginning in 1999.
- Entry in the market was totally deregulated starting in 2002, but existing operators were allowed to enter other markets only after they had fulfilled all Anatel's supply and quality targets before that date.

The coordination between regulation and privatization in the electricity sector was less well executed than in telecommunications. For example, Aneel, the sector regulator, was created only in 1997, two years after privatization in the sector had begun. The Mercado Atacadista de Energia (MAE; Energy Wholesale Market) and the Operador Nacional do Sistema (ONS; National System Operator), two central elements in the new regulatory model, were created only on 30 September 1998, when a large portion of distribution was already in private hands.

Indeed, because of the lack of progress in defining the regulatory rules for the sector (which, we note in passing, began to be debated as early as 1992), just going ahead with the sale of SOEs turned out to be a way to force decisions on regulation. This perverse order of events also tended to limit the capacity of the regulatory agency to operate, and as a result limited its prestige in the eyes of the public at large. Moreover, electricity regulation continues to lack a clear separation between the functions of the various agencies involved (Aneel, ONS, the Mining and Energy Ministry and Eletrobrás, the federal electricity holding company), restricting the accountability of the various institutions.

Even so, electricity reform has also been characterized by a concern with the introduction of competition and the gradual deregulation of contracting among different players. The first element of this strategy was the concern with both vertical (generation, transmission and distribution) and horizontal separation of SOEs, at the federal and state levels. Second, limits were set on market concentration, at national and regional levels, for distribution, generation, and the sum of the two.[17] Third, a timeframe was established allowing an increasing number of consumers to choose freely from which company to buy electricity, with a gradual reduction in the minimum level of demand necessary for a consumer to have such freedom. Also, an increasing flexibility was given to generators and distributors to contract between them, with complete deregulation to be in place 9 years after privatization.

In transportation, the quality of regulation varies among the different segments. Privatization of highways was closely based on the franchise bidding, or concession auction, model proposed by Demsetz (1968) and others as an alternative to economic regulation. In federal privatization auctions, a minimum set of investments was defined, including rehabilitation and expansion of the existing network, and the concession was given to the bidder that offered to charge the lowest toll rate. Once this was decided, regulation was limited to inspection of investment and operation activities and the annual tariff adjustments – that is, regulation has been mostly technical. The states, which as a group privatized more than the federal government, followed a similar model, but some of them charged a fixed positive price for the right to explore the concession.

In the privatization of ports, the emphasis has fallen on container terminals, since private terminals already handled the great majority of bulk and liquid cargo. Container terminals in all Brazil's major ports were privatized. The evidence so far is that these privatizations made possible a considerable increase in investment and productivity, but that a minor part of this rise in productivity was transferred to consumers by way of lower prices. The explanation for this appears to be the absence then of significant competition, which in turn resulted from two factors: the high concentration of traffic in the port of Santos (above 40 per cent) and the low efficiency of the railroads.

The railroads privatized included the RFFSA (the former federal railroad network), Fepasa, Ferroeste and the railroads from CVRD (the latter were sold with the rest of the company). Before the RFFSA was sold it was split horizontally into six networks. This was the privatization in which the greatest responsibility was given to competition, in this case inter-modal competition, as an instrument of self-regulation. The result has in general been positive, owing to the predominance of highway freight haulage in Brazil, with large increases in productivity, admittedly from a very low base, but there have been some cases of abuses of captive consumers and price discrimination (see for instance Estache et al., 2000). In this way, although a 20 per cent cap was set for the shareholdings of each investor in each network, railway concessions were mostly awarded to consortia formed by large customers, who were in a position to harm their competitors by discriminating against them in the supply of railroad services. Further, several companies have not met the contractual targets for production and reduction in the number of accidents without sanctions having been imposed.

The sector in which least progress has been made, both in regulation and in privatization, is water and sewerage services. Although there have been privatizations in several municipalities, some initiatives were aborted and none of the large state companies has yet been sold. There is an enormous regulatory imbroglio in this sector, with both states and municipalities claiming the right to award (i.e. sell) concessions. Eventually, however, some agreement may be reached, since the investment needs and the possible gains in efficiency in this sector are gigantic.

The rhetoric on privatization would change from neutral to negative in late 2002, when the Partido dos Trabalhadores (PT), which historically opposed the program, won the presidential elections. Yet, the Lula government refrained from reversing SOE sales or taking any measure that would make any operation unfeasible. On the other hand, it attacked fiercely the regulatory model adopted in infrastructure and the oil and gas sector. In particular, it greatly weakened the regulatory agencies, in practice transferring back to line ministries the final decision of some critical aspects of regulation. This new wave of regulatory reform was more explicit in the electricity sector, where new legislation was approved establishing a new regulatory model in which the state played a more important role in setting prices and controlling supply. All in all, though, the basic regulatory structure established in the 1990s survived, together with private ownership in infrastructure. Moreover, the Lula government continued the process of privatization in the highway sector and initiated the discussion on the privatization of airports.

14.5 FINAL OBSERVATIONS

In 1991–2000, Brazil privatized 130 SOEs, generating revenues of US$82.1 billion and transferring debts of US$18.1 billion to the private sector. These figures make the Brazilian privatization one of the largest in the world. But it is not only the scale of the companies involved that makes the program noteworthy. Equally important is the fact that in only 4 years the state greatly reduced its participation in sectors in which for several decades it was the single producer. Ironically, the participation of SOEs in the Brazilian economy in 2000 was not much different from that a century before. Thus private investors now control the telecom and railway sectors, the country's largest ports, most of the main highways, two-thirds of the distribution and a fifth of the generation of electricity, together with a small share of sewage and water services. Some large public banks have been privatized, while the oil and gas sectors are open to private investment. In the early 1990s, few would have foreseen such remarkable transformation.

Our look at the history of privatization has shown how its frontiers expanded over time, from a simple helping hand to private firms, to control of SOE growth, and finally to the sale of large and traditional state companies. Overall, privatization in Brazil resulted essentially from three factors: changes in politics, with foreign ownership of infrastructure and basic input sectors no longer seen as a threat to 'national security'; a shift in the focus of development policies towards efficiency and away from the mere accumulation of capital; and a close relationship between privatization and macroeconomic policy. We have argued that the macroeconomic policy connection was the most important factor of the three. In this respect, the chapter has shown that it was not by chance that the first attacks on SOE expansion occurred in the mid 1970s, when the growth cycle that started in the 1940s showed the first signs of exhaustion. From then onwards, until the 1990s, Brazil's failure to stabilize its economy and resume sustained growth served as the main motive for privatization to reach sectors which some years before were not seen as privatizable. On the other hand, we have also stressed the importance of the virtuous circle between privatization and stabilization, in which the latter created the political conditions for expanding the process, while privatization was instrumental in sustaining stability. This was the case in 1996–98, in particular, when the dynamics of privatization were closely linked to the needs of the price stabilization program.

It should not come as a surprise, then, that the priority ascribed to privatization declined in 1999–2000, when fiscal adjustment and exchange rate devaluation put the Real Plan on a sounder footing. The primary fiscal balance turned from a deficit of 0.9 per cent of GDP in 1997 into a surplus of 3.2 per cent of GDP in 1999 (3.5 per cent of GDP in 2000). Meanwhile, the current-account deficit came down, while inflows of non-privatization-related FDI went up, reducing the importance of privatization for the finance of the external deficit. Moreover, the stagnation of output, the rise in unemployment and the decline in real incomes in 1998–99 hurt the government's popularity, reducing its political degrees of freedom. So, after the record results of 1997–98, proceeds dropped substantially, with a considerable slowdown in the privatization of electricity generation and water and sanitation.

This slowdown also resulted from a change in the focus of privatization. Fiscal discipline and a floating exchange rate lightened the burden carried by monetary policy since 1994, allowing for a reduction in interest rates. With this, the opportunity cost of using privatization for ends other than not maximizing the amount of public debt redeemed with the sale of SOEs also declined, encouraging a shift in priorities towards using privatization to strengthen the stock market, through the use of large flotations as a means to sell SOE shares. This alternative, although foreseen when the PND was established, had been used before only in a few cases and on a small scale. In contrast, in the sale of Petrobrás shares, in August 2000, 337,000 individuals bought shares, possibly a record in the history of the Brazilian stock market.

To the extent that Brazilian privatization (as had been the case in the past with the process of nationalization) was the result more of pragmatism than of an ideological change, it was not a major surprise when the Lula government, despite all the previous political opposition to the program, did not reverse the process or any single operation, nor moved in that direction. On the contrary, it furthered the privatization of Brazilian's main highways and started paving the way for doing the same with the largest airports.

The same was not true, though, of the regulatory apparatus put in place to control private operators in infrastructure. In particular, although the basic structure of such a model was maintained, the regulatory agencies were weakened and power partially transferred to line ministries, which were more subject to political intervention. In the second Lula administration, state intervention in the economy increased substantially. This consisted, in one form, of attempts to establish new SOEs to carry government programs in sectors in which the private sector is well prepared to operate – the manufacture of drugs and fertilizers and the provision of broadband internet services, for instance. Another form was to greatly expand lending by public banks and to allocate these loans in more interventionist ways. The BNDES, in particular, sponsored the merger of large companies – for instance, in paper pulp, petrochemicals, telecom and food processing – with the stated objective of creating 'national champions'. This second strand of intervention was originally justified as a means to compensate for the recessionary effects of the international crisis, but was kept intact when the economy recovered strongly in the second half of 2009.

What are we to expect from the Dilma Roussef administration – pragmatic privatization or more state intervention? Most likely, some of each. The political preference for expanding current expenditures has consistently restrained public investment in infrastructure and will likely continue to encourage the government to transfer such responsibility to private investors. In some cases, such as highways and airports, this will likely involve transferring the operation of existing facilities to private firms. On the other hand, both frontrunner candidates have in the past defended different forms of industrial policies and these are likely to continue being part of the policies in place.

More than at any other time in the last two decades, however, the result of the 2010 elections will have an important impact on the degree of state intervention in the economy in the next decade or so. In particular, the emphasis given in this chapter to the economic motivations of privatization does not mean that we expect its future to depend exclusively or mostly on economic arguments. In the medium to long term, the role played by the state in the economy will depend on political factors as well, notably now that the tactical alliance formed to foster privatization in the 1990s, motivated by the need to eliminate the excesses of the import substitution model and the lack of fiscal instruments to back a more intrusive industrial policy, has weakened with the consolidation of macro stability and the increase in tax revenues. As Feigenbaum et al. (1999, p. 172) note:

> [A]n exclusive focus on economic forces obscures the intensely political nature of the privatization movement. Privatization initiatives are political because they redistribute costs and benefits among diverse and competing groups. And portraying privatization as a necessary adaptation to fiscal constraints fails to acknowledge the considerable range of alternative responses open to governmental actors and the extent to which selection of policies within that range may reflect partisan tactics and pressure from mobilized interest groups.

Is there any concrete possibility that the pendulum will swing to the extent of reversing privatization sales and giving the state a presence in commercial activities similar to what it had until the 1980s? Highly unlikely. The one risk would be in infrastructure, in which poor regulation can lead to insufficient investment and growth bottlenecks, but the success of privatization in improving quality of services and supply has been so great that only a deep ideological shift could lead to such a move. Furthermore, privatization, like other reforms, created parties interested in maintaining the new status quo. That is to say, the pendulum does not swing back automatically, like in a clock; it needs to be pushed, overcoming the opposing forces of inertia and established interests, something which history has shown to be a slow process, particularly while privatization succeeds in fostering growth. This is a key lesson of the Brazilian experience: development models last for as long as they are capable of producing economic growth, and are replaced when it becomes clear that they are no longer able to do so.

NOTES

1. See, for instance, Scheneider (1990b) and Feigenbaum et al. (1999).
2. For a recent discussion on this process in the electricity sector, see Baer and McDonald (1998).
3. 'To attract foreign capital in the 19th century the Brazilian government made use of legislation which guaranteed a minimum rate of return, ranging from 6 to 7 per cent, for a period of 60 years. Railways and sugar processing plants were the sectors that most benefited from these incentives. The rate of return guarantee " . . . meant that a major difficulty faced by foreign capital invested in an economy outside the gold standard was partly circumvented, as the actual rate of return did not vary with fluctuations in the exchange rate" (Abreu, 1996, p. 9). Toward the end of the century these guarantees became a political and economic liability to the government, resulting in the gradual nationalization of the railways' (Baer and McDonald, 1998, p. 505).
4. Cardoso (1973, p.143), for example, argues that '[t]hat policy orientation [concentrated on strengthening the role of the state as investor], as has now been well documented, was more a short term response to practical problems than a coherent set of projections based on a nationalist ideology'.
5. Considering the success of the intervention strategy begun at the end of the 1930s, it was to be expected that continuation of this process, as provocatively imagined by Baer et al. (1973, p. 282), would be a cause for concern to the Brazilian private-sector business community: 'The recent activities of gigantic companies such as Petrobrás and CVRD, entering into related sectors through the creation of subsidiaries, raises questions. Petrobrás, for example, is now expanding into several areas of petrochemicals. It would not be entirely impossible for Petrobrás, one day, to expand into overnight hotels, restaurants and/or food distribution establishments.'
6. Ironically, this was due to, of all things, the criticism of the for-profit nature of SOEs. As noted by Pessanha (1981, p. 84), 'some SOEs are accused of running in contrast to their goals (operating in pioneering and basic activities, but of low profitability and with a long-time horizon for return), seeking operations in industry directed specifically at making a profit, such as the case of CVRD, which "always refused to participate in doomed projects, which even recently occurred in the case of the Caraíba copper project in Bahia state" (*O Estado de São Paulo*, 22 March 1975)'.
7. In the businessmen's view, one of the reasons why privatization was not a solution was their lack of funds and the concentration of credit in public banks. In a document produced by business leaders, this issue is expressed as follows (Pessanha, 1981, p.105):

'Either the private-sector company acquires state-controlled companies from the government, "*with funds from the public sector itself*"[author's emphasis], an option which will make it extremely difficult to choose the new owners without falling into paternalism, or the already scarce funds of the private sector will be absorbed in buying existing undertakings, leading the government to fill up the newly-formed "empty spaces" with these funds.' Experience was later to show the importance of providing financing to domestic buyers to make privatization viable. This happened in the 1980s with financing from the BNDES (Brazilian Development Bank), and later through financial instruments created using 'privatization currencies', and, later still, once again through financing from the BNDES and even the Treasury itself.

8. The rationale behind this position was presented in the document 'Action for Domestic Private-Sector Companies, the Government and the Market Economy', prepared by the Economic Development Council, Brasilia, and published on 15 June 1976.
9. Márcio Fortes (1994), president of the BNDES at the end of the Sarney government, and a central figure in moving privatization forward at a time in which the process faced little to no support, put the issue in the following way: 'Privatization, in reality, was not such a central policy. It was the need which the BNDES had, primarily, to generate funds from within its own equity holdings, second, to obtain liquidity for its normal activities, and, third, because its own internal management was greatly weakened by the buildup of necessary management activities in its day-to-day routine. It was, after all, owner or controlling stockholder of more than 25 highly complex companies.'
10. In fact, SOEs failed to pay not only the public banks but also their SOE suppliers: the steel company would not pay its electricity supplier, which would not pay the power generator, which would not pay the oil company that supplied its fuel and so on. And there was little that creditors could do beyond exerting political pressure, not the least because legally a creditor cannot ask for an SOE bankruptcy. As arrears built up, these multiple defaults were 'solved' by transferring debts to the Treasury, with the taxpayers picking up the tab.
11. The opening to imports also helped to increase the support of business for privatization. While the economy was closed, all companies were equally harmed, for example, by the low supply and bad quality of telecommunications, so this was not an important differential between their respective capacities to compete. With trade liberalization, the bad quality of public services became a barrier to competitiveness for the private sector, giving rise to the expression 'Brazil cost'.
12. This question is discussed in greater detail by Pinheiro and Giambiagi (1999).
13. When the PND was launched, in the first half of 1990, the government promised rapid and significant results. In early May 1990, the government forecasted revenues of US$9 billion for the whole of the year. This forecast fell to US$7 billion at the end of that month, and to US$4 billion at the end of July. Around mid year, the target for proceeds of the program in its first two and a half years was US$17 billion, with the sale of one state company per month in the second half of 1990 (Schneider, 1990a, pp.17–18).
14. Economic instability was also the main reason (though not the only one) for the lack of interest of foreign investors in Brazilian privatization until 1994 – in this period foreigners participated with less than 1 per cent of total revenues. Currently this share amounts to 46 per cent.
15. Detailed descriptions of privatization and of the regulations for the telecom, electricity, transport and water services sectors can be found in Pinheiro and Fukasaku (1999). For more information on telecom, see also Pires (1999).
16. The B-band companies are private sector firms operating in a range of the spectrum different from the one used by former SOE operators, this being called A-band.
17. Of the market in the North, Northeast and Center-West, 35 per cent; in the South and Southeast, 25 per cent; and in the national market as a whole, 20 per cent. For generation and distribution together, the limit is 30 per cent of the national market.

REFERENCES

Abreu, M.P. (1996), 'British business in Brazil, 1850–1950', mimeo, Rio de Janeiro: Departamento de Economia, Pontificia Universidade Católica.

Baer, W., I. Kerstenetzky and A. Villela (1973), 'The changing role of the state in the Brazilian economy', *World Development*, **11** (1), 23–34.

Baer, W. and C. McDonald (1998), 'A return to the past? Brazil's privatization of public utilities: the case of the electric power sector', *Quarterly Review of Economics and Finance*, **38** (3), 503–23.

Cardoso, F.H. (1973), 'Associated-dependent development: theoretical and practical implications', in Alfred Stepan (ed.), *Authoritarian Brazil: Origins, Policies and Future*, New Haven, CT: Yale University Press.

Carvalho, M.A. (2001), 'Privatização: aspectos fiscais e dívida pública, MSc dissertation, Getúlio Vargas Foundation, Rio de Janerio.

Demsetz, H. (1968), 'Why regulate utilities?', *Journal of Law and Economics*, **11** (1), 55–68.

Estache, A., A. Goldstein and R. Pittman (2000), 'Privatization and regulatory reform in Brazil: the case of freight railways', Antitrust Division, US Department of Justice, Discussion Paper 00-5, Washington, DC.

Feigenbaum, H., J. Henig and C. Hamnett (1999), *Shrinking the State*, Cambridge: Cambridge University Press.

Fortes, M. (1994), 'Integração competitiva e privatização', *Folha de São Paulo*, 19 October.

Martins, L. (1977), 'Expansão recente do Estado no Brasil: seus problemas e seus atores', mimeo, Rio de Janeiro: FINEP.

Nestor, S. and L. Mahboodi (1999), 'Privatization of public utilities: the OECD experience', in A.C Pinheiro and K. Fukasaku (eds), *Privatization in Brazil: The Case of Public Utilities*, Rio de Janeiro: BNDES-OECD, pp. 103–44.

Palatnik, B. and L. Orenstein (1979), 'Perspectivas do processo de privatização no Brasil', in *Encontros com a Civilização Brasileira*, Rio de Janeiro: Editora Civilização Brasileira, pp. 43–62.

Pessanha, C.F. (1981), 'Estado e economia no Brasil: a campanha contra a estatização', doctoral thesis, Instituto Universitário de Pesquisas do Rio de Janeiro.

Pinheiro, A.C. (1996), 'Impactos microeconômicos da privatização', *Pesquisa e Planejamento Econômico*, **26** (3), 357–98.

Pinheiro, A.C. and K. Fukasaku (eds) (1999), *Privatization in Brazil: The Case of Public Utilities*, Rio de Janeiro: BNDES-OECD.

Pinheiro, A. and F. Giambiagi (1999), 'The macroeconomic background and institutional framework of Brazilian privatization', in A.C. Pinheiro and K. Fukasaku (eds), *Privatization in Brazil: the Case of Public Utilities*, Rio de Janeiro: BNDES-OECD, pp. 13–44.

Pires, J.C.L. (1999), 'A reestruturação do setor de telecomunicações no Brasil', *Revista do BNDES*, (11), pp. 1–34.

Rezende, F. (1980), 'A empresa pública e a intervenção do estado na economia: ação suplementar à iniciativa privada – perspectivas em face da conjuntural atual', in IPEA, *A Empresa Pública no Brasil: uma Abordagem Multidisciplinar*, Brasilia.

Schneider, B.R. (1990a), 'Brazil under Collor: anatomy of a crisis', *World Policy Journal*, **8** (2), 321–47.

Schneider, B.R. (1990b), 'Privatization in Brazil and Mexico: variations on a statist theme', in E. Suleiman and J. Waterbury (eds), *The Political Economy of Public Sector Reform and Privatization*, Boulder, CO: Westview, pp. 319–45.
Velasco, L. (1997a), 'A economia política das políticas públicas: fatores que favoreceram as privatizações no período 1985/94', Texto para Discussão no. 54, Rio de Janeiro: BNDES.
Velasco, L. (1997b), 'A economia política das políticas públicas: as privatizações e a reforma do estado', Texto para Discussão no. 55, Rio de Janeiro: BNDES.
Werneck, R. (1987), *Empresas Estatais e Política Macroeconômica*, Rio de Janeiro: Ed. Campus.
World Bank (1989), 'Brazil: prospects for privatization', mimeo, Washington, DC.

15. Comments on part V

Werner Baer

The growth of the state in Argentina's and Brazil's economies was an important part of these countries' industrialization processes. Public firms were established either in fields where the private domestic or foreign sectors were not capable of or interested in making investments, or else in fields which for political reasons were closed to them. Public utilities, which previously had been dominated by private foreign groups, were nationalized; heavy industries, such as steel, were public from their beginning; exploitation of natural resources, especially oil and certain minerals, were declared a monopoly of the state; and for various reasons state financial institutions were created to help finance the industrialization process or provide credit where the private financial sector had no interest.

Of course, the specific history of the growth of the state differs between the two countries. In Argentina the state sector grew rapidly with the appearance of Perón, who nationalized the railroads and who confiscated German firms, after the country had joined the Allies in the last week of World War II, and established the state-owned conglomerate Fabricaciones Militares. In Brazil, the railroad system was nationalized at an earlier period, and, as Armando Castelar shows, the growth of the state in such sectors as steel, public utilities and finance was part of the determination of the country's policy-makers to lead the country through a period of import-substitution industrialization.

In both countries the state had an important role in contributing to the latter. Some have claimed that for a while the interaction between the public and private sectors was positive, i.e. that the presence of the state had a 'crowding-in' effect with regard to the private sector (providing crucial inputs and finance to the latter). However, as mentioned in Castelar's review of the Brazilian case, the state sector entered into decadence (the same can be said of the case of Argentina) as state enterprises were forced to over-employ and were used as instruments of macroeconomic policies, and as many state firms suffered from corrupt practices. The foreign debt crisis of the 1980s and the continuous deterioration of government finances gradually led to stabilization programs in both countries, which included privatization. The policies adopted were called 'neo-liberal'. I believe that these programs were partially imposed on both countries, as a result of ongoing debt renegotiations throughout the 1980s.

One of the aims of both privatization programs was the raising of revenues for the government to deal with its debt and to make fiscal adjustments. The privatization process of Argentina was characterized by its speed and scale. In a short period of time it privatized every public service managed by the state – electricity, postal services, telecommunications, television, railways, water and sewerage, petroleum and gas, highways, steel etc. Prior to the privatization of public utilities through concession contracts, tariffs were raised substantially in order to make them attractive to the private domestic and foreign sectors. After the 2001–01 crisis, a renegotiation of all privatized concessions began, and in many cases this process led to cancellation of existing concession contacts, which resulted in either in renationalization or else in new privatization.

Greco et al. present an excellent Argentinean case study of the complexities involved in regulating the privatized (through concession contracts) gas and electricity sectors. Especially noteworthy are the complex income distributional problems the regulators have faced in rate making and in determining the sources of investment funds.

Castelar's review of Brazil's privatization process provides an interesting contrast to that of Argentina. Brazil's privatization process developed more slowly, lasting almost a decade. The slower pace resulted in a well-thought-through regulatory structure which seems to have worked well in most sectors.

Although privatization has improved the efficiency of many sectors in both Argentina and Brazil, and some of the worst abuses of the presence of the state have been eliminated, some doubts remain concerning the privatized system which emerged in both countries:

1. What has been the impact of privatization in the distribution of wealth and income? Privatization did not result in the mass participation of shareholders in former state firms (although some workers' retirement funds acquired some shares), as was the case in the UK. In the case of Brazil, although the distribution of salary/wage income has slightly improved, is this the case with wealth ownership?
2. With a large and intricate regulatory framework, how is the trade-off between equity and efficiency handled? What is the influence of politics and lobbying groups?

3. What is the influence of the state in allocating investment finance? In the case of Brazil the state development bank (BNDES) seems to be a major force in the allocation of investment resources and thus some could claim that it is still the state that 'picks the winners' rather than the market. How do most investment resources get allocated in Argentina – is the market more involved than in Brazil?

PART VI

Regional development

16. Regional development, regional disparities and public policies in Argentina: a long-run view[1]

Alberto Porto and Atilio Elizagaray

16.1 INTRODUCTION

Regional disparities, between and within countries, are an important issue for economic theory and also for economic policy. Within countries, fiscal equalization transfers are commonplace,[2] while between countries there are also territorial transfers.[3] Among international organizations the terms of loans (amounts, interest rates and maturity) change according to the economic and social conditions of the recipient countries.

In this chapter, aspects of the regional development and territorial imbalances in Argentina are examined. For a long time this territorial disequilibrium has been a relevant issue on the Argentine public agenda.[4] For instance, Bunge (1940) asserts that: 'in this way . . . [the country] . . . is shaped like a fan, with population density, economic capacity, cultural level and the standard of life constantly decreasing as you move farther away from the capital.' Bunge believes that the main responsibility for this outcome relies on the economic policies which were geared more toward foreign trade and less toward the underdeveloped regions of the interior of the country. He concludes that consistent and sustainable policies could, during the time span of a generation, reduce these economic, social and cultural gaps.

Economic policies have not had much success in achieving convergence in per capita gross domestic output. Nonetheless, they did achieve convergence in social indicators and began to reduce population concentration in the Buenos Aires Metropolitan Area. The set of economic policies implemented have been rather inconsistent and variable throughout time. Consequently, they have incurred large efficiency costs and have been unable to achieve the regional equalization goals established in the 1853 Constitution. The design of efficient regional policies is, even today, a controversial subject.

16.2 THE INITIAL SITUATION

We start with a simple model of two regions $i = 1, 2$. We define their production functions to be $f_i(L_i, K_i, G_i, N_i)$ where L_i is the number of workers, K_i is private capital,[5] G_i is provincial expenditures[6] and N_i represents natural resources. All the factors, except for L_i, are immobile among regions. The marginal productivities of labor are positive and decreasing. All factors are remunerated according to their marginal productivities. It is assumed that $K_1 > K_2$, $G_1 > G_2$, and $N_1 > N_2$, such that marginal productivity of labor is higher in region 1, that is $f_{L1} > f_{L2}$. The total amount of labor is assumed to be constant ($L = L_1 + L_2$). This situation is depicted in Figure 16.1.

The initial point is A with population OA in region 1 and AB in region 2 ($OA > AB$). In A, marginal productivity of labor (equal to wages), and total and per capita output are all higher in region 1. If local public expenditure depends positively on income and negatively on the level of taxation (which we assumed to be determined by population), the total utility of residents in region 1 will be higher than that of residents in region 2 owing to higher salaries and lower prices of public goods. Differences in salaries and utilities create incentives for migration from the less to the more favored region.

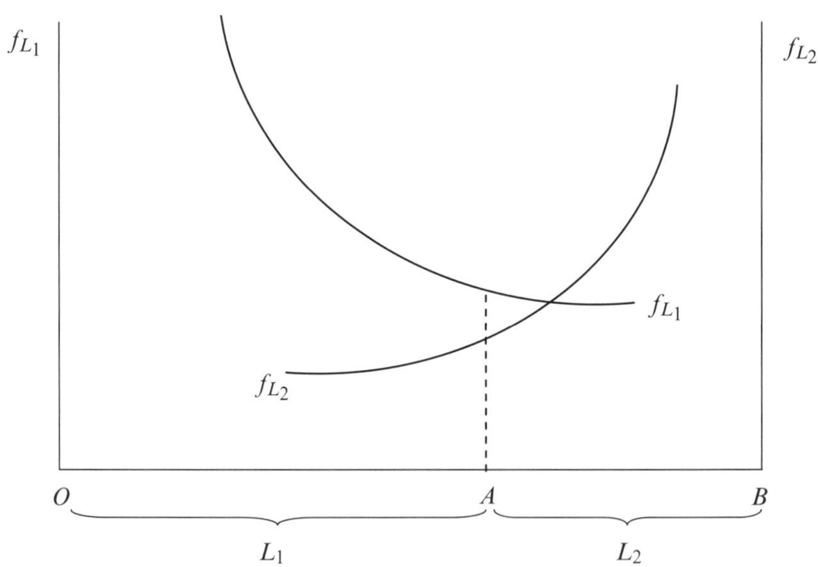

Figure 16.1 Two-regions model – initial situation.

Social and demographic indicators illustrate the situation:

1. The highest per capita economic capacity index[7] (being the Federal Capital plus the province of Buenos Aires = 100) in 1937 was observed in the Federal Capital (106.3) and Buenos Aires (96.4) and the lowest in Catamarca (9.5) and Santiago del Estero (9.8). The average for the country was 73.9.
2. The illiterate rate of the adult population (14 years and above), according to the 1914 census, was on average 35.9 per cent, with a minimum of 21.2 per cent for the Federal Capital and a maximum of 67.2 per cent for the province of Jujuy.
3. The number of university graduates in relation to the total population, according to the 1914 census, was on average 0.34 per cent, with a maximum of 0.69 per cent for the Federal Capital and of 0.4 per cent for Santa Cruz, and with a minimum of 0.1 per cent for Catamarca and for Santiago del Estero.
4. Infant mortality rate (for every thousand live births), according to the 1914 census, on average was 160.4, with a minimum for Santa Cruz (102) and a maximum for Jujuy (298).
5. The average monthly wage of public employees (civil servants and teachers) was \$178 at the federal level, \$140 in the province of Buenos Aires, \$139 in Mendoza, \$119 in Santa Fe, \$93 in Jujuy, \$92 in Entre Rios, \$90 in Santiago del Estero, \$87 in La Rioja, \$81 in Catamarca and \$76 in Corrientes. In the city of Buenos Aires (only civil servants) the average wage was \$119 (Bunge, 1917).
6. Per capita provincial public expenditures varied a lot among provinces. In 1916, the highest values were those of Mendoza, the Federal Capital and Buenos Aires (44 per cent, 26 per cent and 19 per cent higher, respectively, than the national average); the lowest values were those of La Rioja, Catamarca and Santiago del Estero (69 per cent, 67 per cent and 58 per cent, respectively, lower than the national average). The working of federalism, with regional inequalities and without equalization transfers, made the budget restriction binding, and as a consequence, each province had to adjust expenditures to available resources (Porto, 1990). The result was that each province supplied a different level of local public goods.

16.3 MIGRATIONS

A later situation is depicted by Figure 16.2, which shows the interactions between demographic changes and economic variables.[8] The migration

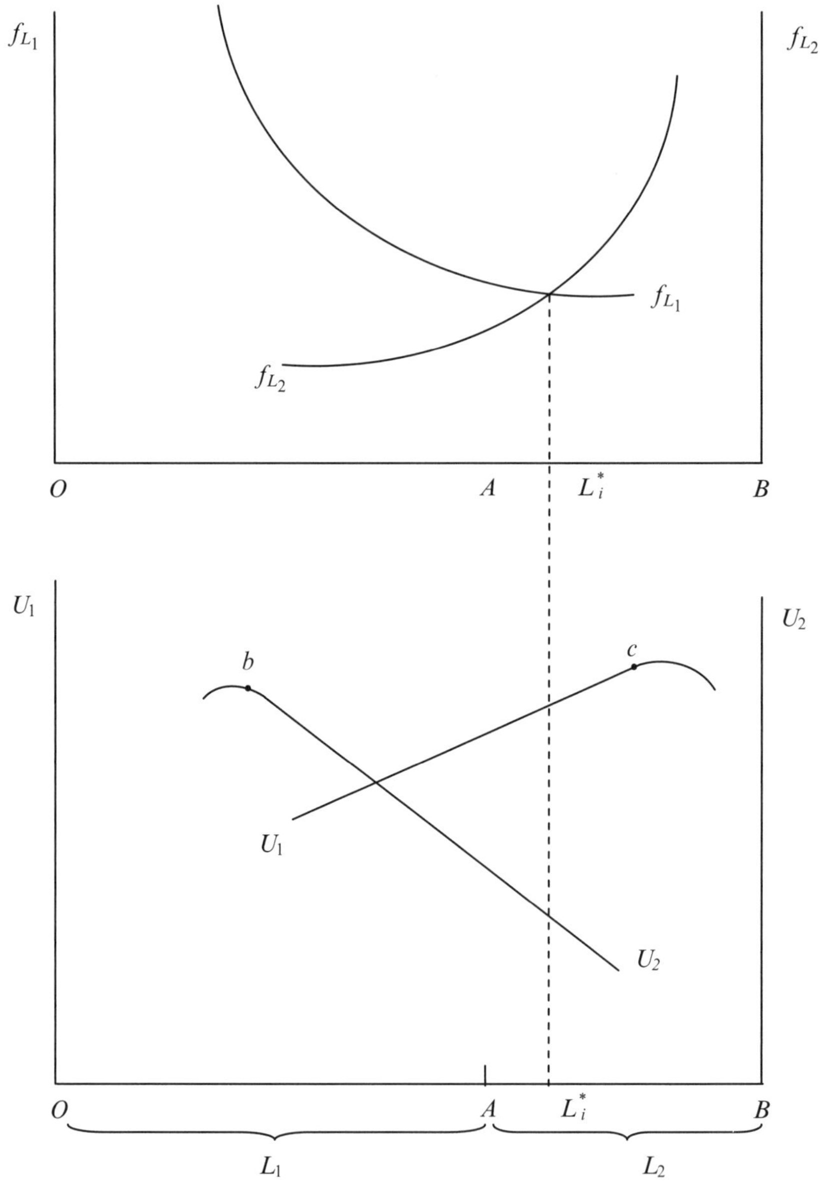

Figure 16.2 Two regions model – later.

process has moved point *A* to point L_i^* (or to a nearby one) where the equality between the marginal productivity of labor in both regions holds (upper part of the figure).[9] For this distribution of population, utilities differ between regions, as shown in the lower part of the figure. *Ceteris paribus*, utilities go up with *L* owing to several factors. The larger population in region 1 results in public goods becoming cheaper because fixed costs are distributed among a larger number of people,[10] and also, results in a greater variety of public goods; this is what Oates (1988) called the 'zoo effect'.

Something similar happens with private goods. First, with increasing returns to scale,[11] the price of goods falls as population increases, and second, more people make a larger supply of goods possible (the zoo effect again), via outlets such as supermarkets, sports, theaters and cultural activities. For all these reasons, region 1 has a higher utility than region 2. Different utilities, despite wage equality,[12] generate incentives for migration from region 2 to region 1.[13] As population increases (points *b* and *c* in Figure 16.2) utility may begin to decrease if the lower tax, as a consequence of one more taxpayer, is lower than the increase in congestion costs and the reduction in the marginal productivity of labor. It may also be the case that the population finds a limit in a particular region because of a finite or fixed number of houses (Ennis et al., 2006).

In Tables 16.1 and 16.2 the migration process can be observed. The result of migration was Bunge's '*país abanico*' ('fan country'). Migrations during 1947–60 show the process clearly (Figure 16.3). Population in the Metropolitan Area represented 29.7 per cent of the national total in 1947 and 33.7 per cent in 1960. In the remaining regions, population decreased or remained more or less constant. This process continued until 1970, except in the Patagonian region.

16.4 PUBLIC POLICIES

Since the mid twentieth century, several governments have faced the challenge of regional inequalities and have implemented the following public policies in efforts to improve them:

1. Changes in the political and institutional organization of the country consisting of: (a) larger representation in the National Congress of provinces with a reduced population;[14] (b) giving 'voice' (Hirschman, 1970) in the National Congress to the 'federal districts' ('national territories' under the political and financial authority of the national government),[15] which under the 1853 Constitution did not have representation; and (c) changing the status of those 'national territories'

Table 16.1 Argentina: total and provincial population 1914–2001

	1914	**1947**	**1960**	**1970**	**1980**	**1991**	**2001**
Buenos Aires	2,066,948	4,273,874	6,766,108	8,774,529	10,865,408	12,594,974	13,827,203
Capital Federal	1,575,814	2,981,043	2,966,634	2,972,453	2,922,829	2,965,403	2,776,138
Santa Fe	899,640	1,702,975	1,884,918	2,135,583	2,465,546	2,798,422	3,000,701
Córdoba	735,472	1,497,987	1,753,840	2,060,065	2,407,754	2,766,683	3,066,801
Mendoza	277,535	588,231	824,036	973,075	1,196,228	1,412,481	1,579,651
Tucumán	332,933	593,371	773,972	765,962	972,655	1,142,105	1,338,523
Entre Ríos	425,373	787,362	805,357	811,691	908,313	1,020,257	1,158,147
Chaco	46,274	430,555	543,331	566,613	701,392	839,677	984,446
Salta	142,156	290,826	412,854	509,803	662,870	866,153	1,079,051
Corrientes	347,055	525,463	533,201	564,147	661,454	795,594	930,991
Santiago del Estero	261,678	479,473	476,503	495,419	594,920	671,988	804,457
Misiones	53,563	246,396	361,440	443,020	588,977	788,915	965,522
San Juan	119,252	261,229	352,387	384,284	465,976	528,715	620,023
Jujuy	77,511	166,700	241,462	302,436	410,008	512,329	611,888

Río Negro	42,242	134,350	193,292	262,622	383,354	506,772	552,822
Formosa	19,281	113,790	178,526	234,075	295,887	398,413	486,559
Chubut	23,065	92,456	142,412	189,920	263,116	357,189	413,237
Neuquén	28,866	86,836	109,890	154,570	243,850	388,833	474,155
San Luis	116,266	165,546	174,316	183,460	214,416	286,458	367,933
La Pampa	101,338	169,480	158,746	172,029	208,260	259,996	299,294
Catamarca	100,769	147,213	168,231	172,323	207,717	264,234	334,568
La Rioja	79,754	110,746	128,220	136,237	164,217	220,729	289,983
Santa Cruz	9,948	42,880	52,908	84,457	114,941	159,839	196,958
Tierra del Fuego	2,504	5,045	11,209	15,658	29,392	69,369	101,079
Sin Determinar	18,425	–	–	–	–	–	–
Total	**7,903,662**	**15,893,827**	**20,013,793**	**23,364,431**	**27,949,480**	**32,615,528**	**36,260,130**

Source: National censuses of population.

Table 16.2 Argentina: regional distribution of population 1869–2001[a] (percentages)

	1869	1895	1914	1947	1960	1970	1980	1991	2001
Metropolitana	13.2	19.8	25.8	29.7	33.7	35.8	34.9	33.5	31.6
Pampeana	40.2	47.3	47.8	42.1	38.0	36.7	35.8	35.2	34.9
Cuyo	10.4	7.0	6.5	6.4	6.7	6.6	6.7	6.8	7.1
Nordeste	7.4	7.3	5.9	8.3	8.1	7.7	8.0	8.7	9.3
Noroeste	28.8	17.9	12.6	11.3	11.0	10.2	10.8	11.3	12.3
Patagonia	–	0.7	1.4	2.3	2.5	3.0	3.7	4.5	4.8
Total	**100.0**	**100.0**	**100.0**	**100.0**	**100.0**	**100.0**	**100.0**	**100.0**	**100.0**

Note: [a] Regions are defined as follows. Metropolitana: Capital Federal and 19 municipalities of the Province of Buenos Aires; Pampeana: the rest of Buenos Aires, Santa Fe, Entre Rios, Córdoba and La Pampa; Cuyo: Mendoza, San Juan and San Luis; Nordeste: Corrientes, Chaco, Formosa and Misiones; Noroeste: Salta, Juuy, La Rioja, Catamarca, Tucuman and Santiago del Estero and Patagonia: Neuquén, Rio Negro, Chubut, Santa Cruz and Tierra del Fuego.

Source: National censuses of population.

which became provinces, a process which was completed with Tierra del Fuego (in 1991) and with the city of Buenos Aires which became an autonomous entity in 1994. From a total of 13 provinces at the beginning of the twentieth century, Argentina has had 24 autonomous political jurisdictions since 1994.

2. Since 1935, transfers of resources to provinces have increased through the implementation and modification of the revenue-sharing regime between the central government and the provinces.[16] The primary distribution of this regime has changed in favor of the provinces, allowing an increasing supply of provincial public goods.
3. Generalization of the fiscal equalization transfers, which were established under the 1853 Constitution, had never been implemented before as part of a revenue-sharing regime. Since 1935, frequent changes in secondary distribution among provinces have always favored the poorest provinces. By the 1960s, these changes had leveled the large differences prevalent in per capita provincial expenditures, and since then have reversed the situation.[17]
4. With funds from the national budget, the supply of social services throughout the country increased as a consequence of changes in the regional distribution of political power in the National Congress. Besides transfers through the revenue-sharing system, the federal budget was used to make transfers from the richest provinces to

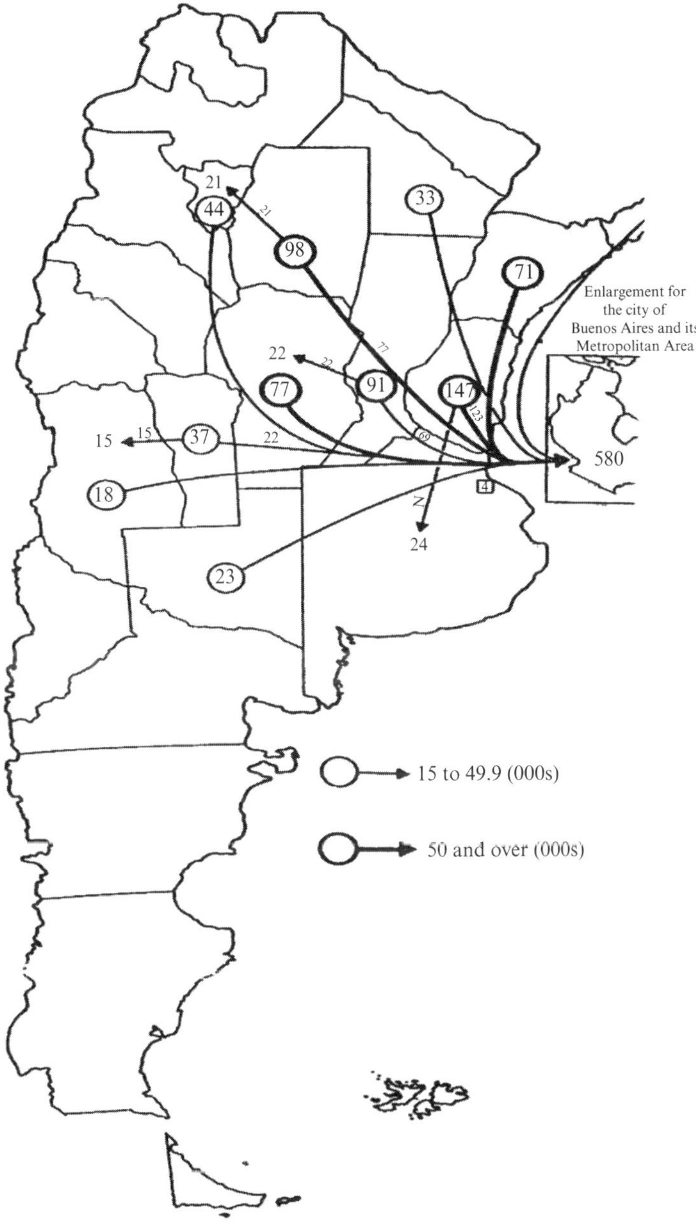

Source: Recchini de Lattes and Lattes (1969).

Figure 16.3 Argentina 1947–60: population migration trends.

the poorest and to the less populated ones.[18] Also, since 1970, the supply of university education has spread throughout the entire country.

5. Subsidies to families and firms in region 1, through prices and tariffs of public enterprises,[19] were so large between 1945 to 1955 that, in real terms, those values were down by 48 per cent. The consequences of such policies were the capital obsolescence and the requirement of huge funds transfers (paid for by taxes) by those firms. For several years the needs of funds by public enterprises was higher than investment, and from 1965 to 1987 it amounted to $50 billion. The large redistribution of resources via such subsidies were, no doubt, of much larger impact on region 1 than the impact of some enterprises' activities on region 2.[20]

Policies (1) to (4) were intended to move U_1 down and to move U_2 up (Figure 16.2), and thus reduce or reverse the incentives to the migration mentioned before. Policy (5) was in the opposite direction.

These policies in mind, we consider now the question: should public policy focus on the regional distribution of income, the personal distribution of income, or both?[21] Theoretically, one supposes personal distribution of income to be of greater concern because the arguments included in the welfare function are individuals' utilities. Moreover, it could be that regional distribution could generate the unwanted result of poor people from rich provinces subsidizing rich people from poor provinces. Such a proposition has been subject to challenge, theoretically and empirically.[22] On the empirical side, the evidence points to the existence of a significant impact of subnational governments' budgets on regional distribution of income, mainly through the revenue-sharing system. Furthermore, federal and provincial constitutions alike declare regional income redistribution an important goal.[23] In the case of Argentina, there is evidence that shows how the regional redistribution of resources, through provincial budgets and their financing with national transfers, has a positive impact on personal distribution of income for all provinces (Cont et al., 2009).

Apart from policies (1) to (4), others were implemented which also made significant impacts. The two most important were:

6. The design and implementation of sectoral and regional policies aimed at regional economic growth.
7. The protection of economic activities in region 1 through trade barriers and export tax distortions in region 2. Impacts on marginal productivities of labor, net of taxes and subsidies, are the direct opposite of those of the policies mentioned in (6).[24]

Among those policies is the creation of funds to reduce regional disparities, including the Fondo de Integracion Territorial (Fund for Regional Integration) and the Fondo de Desarrollo Regional (Fund for Regional Development). There also emerged specific policies to promote growth in some provinces. One such was the industrial promotion law, whose goal was to promote industrial investment and industrial localization in the interior of the country, particularly in four provinces: San Juan, San Luis, Catamarca and La Rioja. In addition, there were funds designed specifically to promote regional growth (Tierra del Fuego, Patagonia) and sectoral growth (wine, tobacco, sugar, forests, and yerba mate).[25] In these cases, regional growth was promoted by subsidizing economic activities in region 2, with the costs falling on region 1 such that marginal productivity of labor and net taxes in region 1 fell.

We are reminded here of two related works worth mentioning. The first is a paper by Galiani et al. (2005) on the effects of public policies on the regional labor markets in Argentina. This paper presents evidence of the impact of changes in policies such as those described in policies (6) and (7) above. The authors find that regional unemployment is not persistent and that changes in its territorial composition are explained by public policies such as differences in labor taxes, trade liberalization, privatization of state-owned enterprises, deregulation of markets and openness to foreign investment. It is also shown that regional unemployment is not persistent to regional shocks because the regional unemployment elasticity of regional pay is high. The second work is a book by Padovano (2007), which suggests that fiscal equalization transfers could have interfered with the normal processes of convergence that characterize economic growth.

Some of the policies mentioned in this chapter have been reinstituted in recent years. Between 2002 and 2009, a long tariff freeze was imposed on public utilities, particularly transportation, electricity, liquid fuels, gas and water. Since the firms were private, they received large subsidies from the federal budget, subsidies that to a large extent went to people located in the Buenos Aires Metropolitan Area. At the same time, high taxes and trade barriers were imposed on agricultural exports. These policies had a negative impact on economic activities located further away from the Metropolitan Area. Since the beginning of the 1990s, an important difference from past policies became evident: the federal government began to concentrate more and more resources unto itself, significantly weakening the financial autonomy of local governments.

16.5 OUTCOMES OF ECONOMIC POLICIES: POSITIVE AND NEGATIVE

In terms of long-run GDP per capita growth, Table 16.3 shows that there has been no convergence among Argentine regions.[26] In terms of social indicators, however, a different picture emerges (Figures 16.4 to 16.6). Over time, gaps in illiteracy rates and infant and total mortality rates consistently shrank (Ingram, 1994; G.G. Porto, 1995). A similar picture emerges from the observation of a development-gap indicator.[27] In the

Table 16.3 Argentina: provincial gross domestic product 1953–2004 (per capita – country mean = 100)

	1953	**1959**	**1965**	**1968**	**1970**	**1980**	**1993**	**2004**
Buenos Aires	96	64	107	104	88	78	93	85
Catamarca	35	41	34	36	38	52	64	129
Córdoba	72	83	85	87	74	86	76	92
Corrientes	46	49	50	57	57	63	77	43
Chaco	65	59	63	50	41	50	30	43
Chubut	145	146	117	122	139	188	168	162
Entre Ríos	63	65	59	61	73	73	78	61
Formosa	58	44	37	38	44	33	34	36
Jujuy	75	75	52	53	59	68	61	47
La Pampa	105	136	128	105	102	128	117	106
La Rioja	40	42	35	36	38	42	73	52
Mendoza	99	95	93	97	99	96	68	98
Misiones	48	34	43	44	42	46	49	44
Neuquén	68	62	62	72	104	182	177	191
Río Negro	101	86	92	115	90	88	108	82
Salta	59	59	56	62	57	55	52	51
San Juan	66	71	69	59	51	55	60	47
San Luis	50	59	64	58	70	80	249	95
Santa Cruz	173	202	293	280	155	156	161	282
Santa Fe	90	99	100	93	95	102	93	94
Santiago Del Estero	40	34	31	29	40	41	32	39
Tucumán	65	62	41	44	66	75	64	45
Capital Federal	175	200	182	194	222	270	250	258
Tierra del Fuego	212	218	202	216	126	246	405	220
Mean	**100**	**100**	**100**	**100**	**100**	**100**	**100**	**100**
Standard deviation	**47**	**54**	**62**	**62**	**44**	**65**	**88**	**72**

Source: Calculations based on Porto (1990) and updates.

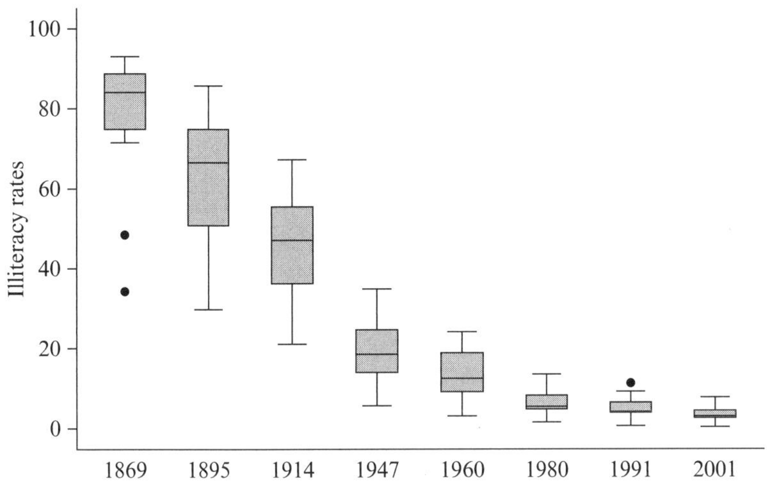

Source: Calculations based on national censuses of population.

Figure 16.4 Social indicators: illiteracy rates (percentages of adult population).

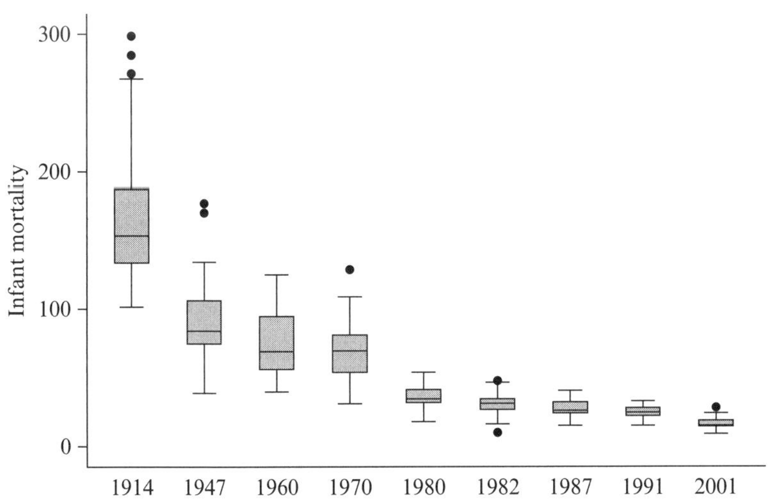

Sources: Calculations are based on data from publications by the Ministries of Health and of Domestic Affairs and from national censuses.

Figure 16.5 Social indicators: infant mortality rates (per thousand children born).

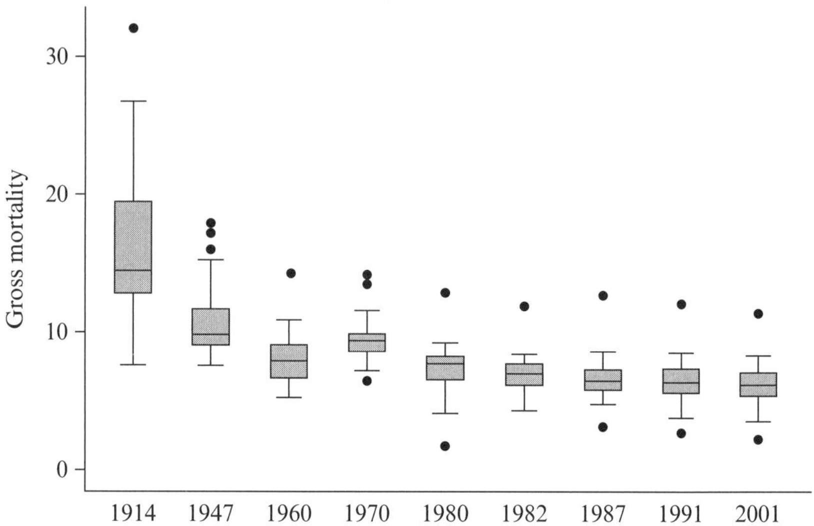

Sources: Calculations based on data from national censuses and from the Ministry of Health.

Figure 16.6 Social indicators: gross mortality rates (per thousand in total population).

same direction, data on the distribution of population show that concentration in the Buenos Aires Metropolitan Area either has been stopped or has been reversed (see Table 16.4).[28]

Regional economic policies have had significant costs in the past and will increase in the future unless radical changes occur. It can be said that there has been some sort of reversion due to the policy of giving small provinces a voice in the National Congress; the underrepresented provinces of the past are currently being overrepresented, and vice versa. This change in the distribution of territorial political power has had a powerful impact on the design of public policies. The outcome has been an increasing flow of funds to those overrepresented provinces, thereby increasing public expenditures. The real GDP growth during the 1970s was 61.4 per cent for the less-developed provinces, 50.3 per cent for the intermediate-level provinces and 75.7 per cent for the low-population-density jurisdictions. More than a quarter of this growth is explained by public expenditure growth: 30 per cent in less-developed provinces, 27 per cent in the intermediate-level ones and 19.3 per cent in the low-population-density provinces.[29]

Regional and sectoral economic policies have had large costs in terms

Table 16.4 *Argentina: total and provincial population growth 1947–80 and 1980–2001 (percentages)*

	1947–1980	1980–2001
Buenos Aires	154.2	27.3
Capital Federal	−2.0	−5.0
Santa Fe	44.8	21.7
Córdoba	60.7	27.4
Mendoza	103.4	32.1
Tucumán	63.9	37.6
Entre Ríos	15.4	27.5
Chaco	62.9	40.4
Salta	127.9	62.8
Corrientes	25.9	40.7
Santiago del Estero	24.1	35.2
Misiones	139.0	63.9
San Juan	78.4	33.1
Jujuy	146.0	49.2
Río Negro	185.3	44.2
Formosa	160.0	64.4
Chubut	184.6	57.1
Neuquén	180.8	94.4
San Luis	29.5	71.6
La Pampa	22.9	43.7
Catamarca	41.1	61.1
La Rioja	48.3	76.6
Santa Cruz	168.1	71.4
Tierra del Fuego	482.6	243.9
Total	75.9	29.7

Note: Shaded figures correspond to provinces with a rate of population growth above average.

of efficiency and in terms of tax expenditures. The estimates calculated by Artana (1989) for the 1987 fiscal year showed that tax expenditure costs amounted to 3.4 per cent of GDP, and that efficiency costs were between 1 per cent and 2 per cent of GDP.

It can be concluded that the economic policies were not consistent. Some of the policies were intended to stop migrations while others promoted them; see policies (1) to (4) versus (5), and policy (6) versus (7) in Section 16.3.

16.6 SUMMARY AND CONCLUSIONS

In this chapter we have studied the main aspects of regional development in Argentina, characterized by strong territorial imbalances. A simple analytical scheme is used to study the interactions among public policies and workers' mobility. Beginning with a description of stylized facts during the early twentieth century, the chapter examined the main set of public policies aimed at the reduction of territorial disparities and their subsequent outcomes.

The efforts by federal and local governments to bridge historically wide regional disparities in Argentina ushered in a great variety of fiscal policies and institutional changes, such as giving a voice in the National Congress to regions which had not previously had one and increasing the representation of poor and underpopulated provinces.

Yet public policy over time was not consistent and in some cases was plainly contradictory. Results have been mixed. On the one hand, achievements have been poor; and on the other hand, efficiency costs have been significant. It has been found that there is convergence in terms of social indicators, but there is no evidence of economic convergence among provinces throughout the twentieth century. Estimates for the 1970s have shown that, except for the developed jurisdictions, at least a quarter of the per capita GDP provincial growth is the result of public sector output growth, due to the increasing flow of transfers from the central government. A positive impact of regional policies was the reduction of overpopulation in the Buenos Aires Metropolitan Area. This was reflected in the population movements over two periods: 1947–80 and 1980–2001. Finally, and on the negative side, regional policies have had significant efficiency costs.

From all of the above, it can be concluded that the implementation of efficient and effective regional policies is a controversial subject in Argentina. Nowadays, the debate on large subsidies for fuels and public utilities, and taxes on agricultural exports is a new and amplified version of the same old problem.

NOTES

1. An earlier version of this chapter was presented as a paper at the conference 'A Comparative Analysis of Growth and Development: Argentina and Brazil', held at the University of Illinois at Urbana-Champaign in April 2010. We highly appreciate comments by participants and in particular those by Professor G. Hewings (see Chapter 18). We also thank Laura Carella for her collaboration in an early version of this chapter.
2. For instance, the process of fiscal equalization transfers has had an increasing

importance throughout Argentine history, which concludes in the 1994 National Constitution: '(distribution from the revenue sharing regime has to take into consideration) . . . equity, solidarity and give priority to the achievement of an equivalent degree of economic development, of standard of life, and of equality of opportunities in the whole country.' Canada's Constitution Act 1982 says: 'Parliament and the Government of Canada are committed to the principle of making equalization payments to ensure that provincial governments have sufficient revenues to provide reasonably comparable levels of public services at reasonably comparable levels of taxation.' Similar mandates are imposed, in some form or another, in most countries in the world.

3. For instance, by the 1990s the General Budget of the European Community made significant territorial redistributions, with Denmark, Greece, Ireland, Netherlands, Portugal, and Spain as net recipients of funds and Belgium, France, Germany, Italy, Luxemburg and the United Kingdom as net contributing countries. The Maastricht Treaty moved in a similar direction when in 1993 it established the Cohesion Fund aimed at programs to achieve economic convergence, benefiting 'cohesion countries' (Greece, Ireland, Portugal and Spain). In the European Union Constitution project, policies for regional cohesion had a central role owing to the fact that large disparities were present not only among states but also, and above all, among its 250 regions. This document says: 'Depending upon the place where they live, Europeans will not have the same means, or the same opportunities to overcome the challenges of globalization. This is what the European cohesion policy intends to fix' (European Community, 2004).
4. Regional disparities were the main obstacle to national unity by the time of the 1853 National Constitution. Buenos Aires, the wealthiest region, did not want to join the 13 poorer provinces in the country's interior, which were pejoratively referred to as 'ranchos' (rural houses).
5. It includes skilled workers.
6. Representing the level of social and economic infrastructure provided by the provincial government.
7. Calculated as the average of the value of total production, the value of industrial production, capital invested in industry and the numbers of cars, all in per capita terms (Bunge, 1940).
8. For the interplay between demographic changes and fiscal policies, see Wildasin (2003).
9. For simplicity, it is assumed that there are no migration costs.
10. Local public goods are mainly financed with their own resources. In a Henry George type model, provision is larger in the region with higher retribution to the immobile factor. In a different model, in which the rent of the immobile factor is personal income of the residents in each region, it depends upon the form of the production function whether the per capita income will be higher in region 1. Yet, even with wage equality in both regions, the local public good will be cheaper in the more populated region (Flatters et al., 1974).
11. Increasing returns to scale may result from diminishing transaction costs for firms (mainly transportation costs), and/or (positive) externalities from the demand side, where the utility of a good or service depends upon the numbers of consumers. Krugman (1992) also considers the importance of other factors such as the existence of specialized labor markets in the generation of increasing returns to scale.
12. The same result is obtained with some lower salaries in region 2.
13. From L_i^*, migrations produce two opposite effects: as L_1 increases, the marginal productivity of labor goes down, and the public good becomes cheaper; the opposite happens when L_2 diminishes.
14. In the 1949 National Constitution, abolished in 1955. A larger political representation of these provinces was reestablished in 1958.
15. From the 1951 Electoral Law.
16. In Argentina, tax collection is largely conducted by the central government. Revenue-sharing laws specify the distribution between the federal government and the provinces

(primary distribution) on the one side, and the distribution among provinces (secondary distribution) on the other.

17. Equalization transfers instruments to reduce regional disparities have been prevalent in Argentina since 1935. They first appeared in the 1853 Constitution as a way for the National Congress 'to give subsidies from the National Treasury to Provinces whose revenues were not enough, according to their budgets, to finance their current expenditures'. In those days, subsidies were small. With its own funding as the only source of revenue, each province had to make do. Consequently, since regional disparities were pronounced, the provision of local public goods was very unequal among provinces. The redistribution process increased throughout time, up to the point that the 1994 National Constitution explicitly includes in its text the revenue-sharing system and fiscal equalization transfers (see note 2 above).
18. For decades the Federal Capital (currently known as the Autonomous City of Buenos Aires) received significant subsidies from the national budget through the net incidence of taxes and expenditures, and from the revenue-sharing regime, comparing the origin and allocation (destination) of taxes. From the 1960s on, transfer of services (from the national government to the Federal Capital), in addition to several modifications of the revenue-sharing regime, reversed that process. Several authors (Cavallo and Zapata, 1986; Ministry of Economics of the Province of Buenos Aires, 1996; Artana and Moskovits, 1999) show that those subsidies were no longer in effect, or were reversed. It must be pointed out that the regional distribution of the national budget (comparing taxes and expenditures in each region) shows both similarities to and differences from the distribution of the revenue-sharing regime. One similarity is that, in both cases, most of the resources come from the most developed provinces, in particular the province of Buenos Aires; and a difference is that the distribution among provinces fluctuates a lot and takes place following the discretion of the national government.
19. There were also subsidies for families (e.g. for foods and housing rents) all over the country. Since it is assumed that the impact on different regions was similar, those subsidies are not taken into consideration in the present article.
20. Núñez Minana and Porto (1976, 1982) and Porto (1992). Public enterprises provide, besides other goods, liquid fuels and gas, communications, transportation, water and sanitation.
21. During the conference, this point was raised by A. Figueroa.
22. Pauly (1973), Bird (1995) and Tresch (2002). Tresch set up a hierarchically nested structure of welfare functions to argue that 'it is no longer true that redistributions among people at the national level are the "preferred alternative" as Oates had claimed before. In the alternative model presented here, only the lowest level of government redistributes among people. The higher government uses grants in aid to other governments exclusively in their redistributions (p. 851).'
23. See note 2, pp. 300–301.
24. Porto (1991).
25. See, among others, Díaz Alejandro (1971, 1975), Reca (2007, 2008) and Cortes Conde (2005).
26. The economic theory of convergence, based on the neoclassical theory of growth, predicts that if factor endowments of all regions are equal then their GDP per capita will equalize (Baumol et al., 1994). This is due to the initial difference in the stock of capital between rich and poor regions. In the poor regions, with a reduced stock of capital, its marginal productivity is higher. Thus, capital will move to those regions up to the point of equalization of marginal productivities and GDP per capita. Empirical studies for Argentina (among others, Elias, 1995; G.G. Porto, 1995, 1996; Wellington, 1998), using not very reliable data on geographic GDP, conclude that there is no absolute convergence. These results may be due to differences in the stationary state among provinces. In this case the way to get convergence is by controlling for those differences due to differences in regional characteristics (quantity and/or quality in factor endowments) or

due to economic policies (different levels of public expenditures and/or governmental transfers). Those studies conclude that when controlling for regional disparities the lack of conditional convergence still holds. On the contrary, they do find convergence controlling for economic policies (Porto, G.G., 1995, 1996) and/or for human capital (Elias, 1995).

27. In 1972, H. Nuñez Miñana computed a complex indicator to measure, at a point in time, the level of economic development for Argentine provinces. The index is an average of three variables: the quality of housing, the number of cars in per capita terms and the quality of human resources. This indicator was used to compute a 'development gap' criterion for the revenue-sharing law which ruled intergovernmental financial relations in Argentina from 1973 to 1984. The relationship between the highest and the lowest value of that gap was 8.32 in 1970, 4.56 in 1980 and 4.46 in 1991. Much as with social indicators, the trend in the development gap, defined in the way abovementioned, suggests convergence among Argentine provinces.
28. The Metropolitan Area – the Federal Capital and the 19 municipalities of the province of Buenos Aires (which surround the metropolitan area) – had an increase in its share of the total population between the census of 1869 (13.2 per cent) and that of 1970 (35.8 per cent), which was reversed when it went down to 34.9 per cent in 1980, 33.5 per cent in 1991 and 31.6 per cent in 2001. Population in the border municipalities of the Metropolitan Area has grown very fast in recent years. Even including them in it does not change the trend: the participation in the total population decreases from 34.8 per cent in 1991 to 33.3 per cent in 2001.
29. Nuñez Miñana y Porto (1983). There are no data available for other periods.

REFERENCES

Artana, D. (1989), 'La promoción económica en la Argentina: introducción y síntesis de los principales resultados', in Porto (1991), pp. 13–25.

Artana, D. and C. Moskovits (1999), 'Efectos de la política fiscal nacional sobre la distribución regional y personal del ingreso', in FIEL (1995), *La Distribución del Ingreso en la Argentina*, Buenos Aires.

Baumol, W.L., R.R. Nelson and E.N. Wolf (eds) (1994), *Convergence of Productivity*, Oxford: Oxford University Press.

Bird, R. (1995), 'Fiscal federalism and fiscal finance', *Anales de las 28as Jornadas de Finanzas Públicas*, Universidad Nacional de Córdoba, Argentina.

Bunge, A. (1917), *Riqueza y Renta en la Argentina, su Distribución y su Capacidad Contributiva*, Buenos Aires: Agencia Central de Librerías y Publicaciones.

Bunge, A. (1940), *La Nueva Argentina*, Buenos Aires: Kraft.

Cavallo D. and J. Zapata (1986), *El Desafío Federal*, Buenos Aires: Ed. Sudamericana-Planeta.

Cont, W., C. Peluffo and A. Porto (2009), 'Personal and regional redistribution through public finance. The case of provincial governments in Argentina', available at: www.aaep.org.ar/Anales

Cortés Conde, R. (2005), *La Economía Política de la Argentina en el Siglo XX*, Buenos Aires: Edhasa.

Díaz Alejandro, C.F. (1971), 'The Argentine state and economic growth: a historical review', in G. Rannis (ed.), *Government and Economic Development*, Yale University Press.

Díaz Alejandro, C.F. (1975), *Ensayos Sobre la Historia Económica Argentina*, Buenos Aires: Amorrortu Eds.

Elías, V. (1995), *Regional Economic Convergence: The Case of Latin American Economies*, Estudios de Economía, Chile, no. 2, pp. 159–76, Facultad de Ciencias Económicas y Administrativas de la Universidad de Chile, Santiago de Chile.
Ennis, H.M., S. Pinto and A. Porto (2006), 'Choosing a place to live and a workplace', *Económica*, Número Especial, January to December.
European Community (2004), *Una Constitución para Europa*, Brussels.
Flatters, F., V. Henderson and P. Mieszkowski (1974), 'Public goods, efficiency and regional fiscal equalization', *Journal of Public Economics*, **3** (2), 99–112.
Galiani, S., C. Lamarche, A. Porto and W. Sosa-Escudero (2005), 'Persistent and regional disparities in unemployment (Argentina 1980–1997)', *Regional Science and Urban Economics*, **35** (4), 375–94.
Hirschman, A.O. (1970), *Exit, Voice and Loyalty: Responses to Decline in Firms, Organizations, and States*, Cambridge, MA: Harvard University Press.
Ingram, G.K. (1994), 'Social indicators and productivity convergence in developing countries', in Baumol et al. (1994), pp. 316–33.
Krugman, P. (1992), *Geografía y comercio*, Barcelona: A. Bosch.
Ministry of Economics of the Province of Buenos Aires (1996), *Estudio de las Finanzas Provinciales y el Sistema de Coparticipación Federal de Impuestos*, Cuadernos de Economía no. 15, La Plata, Argentina.
Nuñez Miñana, H. (1972), 'Indicadores de desarrollo regional en la República Argentina', Documento Interno no. 10, Instituto de Investigaciones Económicas, Facultad de Ciencias Económicas, Universidad Nacional de La Plata.
Nuñez Miñana, H. and A. Porto (1976), 'Análisis de la evolución de los precios de empresas públicas en la Argentina', *Desarrollo Económico*, **16** (63), 307–32.
Nuñez Miñana, H. and A. Porto (1982), 'Inflación y tarifas públicas: Argentina 1945–1980', *Desarrollo Económico*, **17** (66), 347–52.
Nuñez Miñana, H. and A. Porto (1983), 'Aportes del Gobierno Nacional a la Provincia de Buenos Aires. Análisis y propuestas', Convenio Ministerio de Economía de la Pcia. de Buenos Aires–Facultad de Ciencias Económicas de la Universidad Nacional de La Plata.
Oates, W.E. (1988), 'On the measurement of congestion in the provision of local public goods', *Journal of Urban Economics*, **24** (1), 85–94.
Padovano, F. (2007), *The Politics and Economics of Regional Transfers: Decentralization, Interregional Redistribution and Income Convergence*, Cheltenham, UK: Edward Elgar Publishing.
Pauly (1973), 'Income distribution as a local public good', *Journal of Public Economics*, **2** (2), 35–58.
Porto, A. (1990), *Federalismo Fiscal: el Caso Argentino*, Buenos Aires: Instituto Torcuato Di Tella.
Porto, A. (ed.) (1991), *Regulación de Actividades Económicas y Financieras*, Buenos Aires: Instituto Di Tella.
Porto, A. (1992), 'Una revisión crítica de las empresas públicas en la Argentina', in P. Gerchunoff (ed.), *Las Privatizaciones en la Argentina*, Buenos Aires: Instituto Torcuato Di Tella.
Porto, G.G. (1995), *Las Economías Regionales en la Argentina*, Buenos Aires: Fundación Arcor, Nuevo hacer Grupo Editor Latinoamericano.
Porto, G.G. (1996), 'On positive feedbacks in Argentina: a test of increasing returns based on migration evidence', Seminario no. 13, Instituto y Universidad Torcuato Di Tella.

Reca, L. (2007), 'Cambios en el sector agropecuario argentino: 1950–2005', in Navarro (2007).
Reca, L. (2008), 'El conflicto por el régimen de retenciones y el futuro de la agricultura argentina', available at: www.aaep.org.ar/Anales
Recchini de Lattes, Z.L. and A.E. Lattes (1969), *Migraciones en la Argentina. Estudio de las Migraciones Internas e Internacionales Basado en Datos Censales: 1869–1960*, Buenos Aires: Centro de Investigaciones Sociales, Instituto Torcuato Di Tella, Editorial del Instituto.
Tresh (2002), *Public Finance: A Normative Theory*, San Diego, CA: Academic Press.
Wellington, C.M. (1998), 'Un análisis empírico del crecimiento regional en Argentina', IERAL Documento de Trabajo no. 14, Córdoba, Argentina: Fundación Mediterránea.
Wildasin, D.E. (2003), 'Liberalization and the spatial allocation of population in developing and transition countries', in J. Martinez-Vazquez and J. Alm (eds), *Public Finance in Developing and Transitional Countries*, Cheltenham, UK: Edward Elgar Publishing, pp. 63–100.

17. The regional question in Brazil: nature, causes and policies

Alexandre Rands Barros

17.1 INTRODUCTION

Brazil is the fifth country in the world in area, with the particularity that most of it is suitable for human life and economic activities, unlike other big countries such as Russia and Canada. Even the Amazon forest, which takes up almost half the country, can easily be occupied economically, although most of it is only lightly populated at present. The drought areas of the Northeastern Sertão are also suitable for human settlements, as its historical occupation has shown, although life can be hard in those parts of the planet. Under such circumstances, it is reasonable to expect that regional disparities could emerge.

Regional gross domestic product (GDP) per capita and most economic and social development indicators have shown that regional disparity is a reality in Brazil. The Northeast and North regions, whose populations together make up 36.2 per cent of the total population,[1] are relatively very poor. Their per capita GDP in 2007 was only 35 per cent and 47 per cent, respectively, of the average GDP per capita in the Southeast, the most developed region, according to the latest available data from IBGE.[2] These spatial inequalities have acquired a huge literature on them in the last 50 years, which is still growing, as this is a very complex phenomenon and many of its causes and consequences are still unrevealed or subject to diverse interpretations.

Such disparities have lasted a long time, although only since the 1950s have they been the object of more intensive economic and social studies. Before that time, there existed only a few statistics to indicate the existence of such disparities and the idea that any government intervention should be required to reduce this problem was not widespread.

17.2 EXTENT AND NATURE OF REGIONAL INEQUALITIES

Brazil is normally divided into five geographical regions, which are shown in Figure 17.1. Table 17.1 contains some basic statistics for each of these regions. They clearly indicate that the Northeast and the North are the most backward regions of the country, while the Southeast and the South are the most prosperous. Poverty indicators, as well as educational achievements, GDP per capita, and life expectancy all show the same reality as regards regional inequalities in the country.

The inequality is even more serious when states are considered, as every

Figure 17.1 Brazilian geographical regions.

Table 17.1 Brazilian regions: basic statistics

Statistics	North	Northeast	Center-West	Southeast	South
Population (millions of inhabitants)[1]	15.08	52.94	13.57	79.11	27.33
GDP per capita (R$ 2007)[2]	9,134.62	6,748.81	17,844.46	19,277.26	16,564.00
Share of population (%)[1]	8.0	28.2	7.2	42.1	14.5
Share of households with per capita income under poverty line in 2008 (%)[a,1]	33.6	43.0	19.0	14.5	13.5
Illiteracy rate of population over 14 years old in 2008 (%)[1]	21.5	38.8	16.4	11.6	10.9
Average schooling years of population over 14 years old in 2008[1]	7.0	6.2	7.7	8.1	7.8
Life expectancy in 2005 (years)[3]	71.0	69.0	73.2	73.5	74.2

Note: [a] Poverty line established at half minimum wage per capita in the household.

Sources: [1] IBGE, PNAD 2008; [2] IBGE, Contas Regionais, 2009; [3] IBGE, Indicadores Sociodemográficos e de Saúde no Brasil 2009.

region has inequalities among its own states. Although GDP per capita in the Northeast in 2007 was only 35 per cent of that in the Southeast, if the same comparison is made between Brazil's richest state, namely São Paulo,[3] and Piauí, the poorest state in the Northeast, the figure is 20.6 per cent. Such comparisons show that spatial disparities in Brazil are even more serious than they appear when large, geographical units are compared, although they can already be alarming at the more aggregated level.

Regional inequality in Brazil, as in all countries, could have two different origins. First, regions could have individuals with different attributes, so that their average income could differ because of these differences in attributes. For example, the population of a specific region could have a higher average educational attainment than that of another. If the return to education is exactly the same in the two regions, their per capita income would differ because of these differences in endowments. In this case regional disparities would arise even were welfare levels to be equalized among regions for individuals with the same endowment, as is assumed by most recent urban studies.[4]

The second source of regional inequalities would be that the same attributes or endowments could have different returns in the two regions. For example, the same person's expected income, given their endowments and attributes, could differ depending on which of the two regions they were in. The returns could be nominal or in real terms, given differences in local prices. Were this second source to be in real terms, then the idea of welfare equalization would not be satisfied.

Although the decomposition of the inequality between these two components may seem simple, it is not. The existence of (1) nontradable goods and services and (2) transport costs means the differences in cost of living and prices combine these two sources in a way that makes it very difficult to identify their relative roles, given the data currently available. Therefore, there is no consensus as yet on the relevance of each of these sources to the regional inequalities in Brazil.

In a study (Barros, 2010a) I relied on two simple assumptions from economic theory to see how far the disparities are from what orthodox economic theory can explain. My results shed some light on the nature of regional inequalities. These will be briefly reviewed. The first basic assumption is that there is arbitrage in the labor market, so that workers will migrate to regions which pay more in real terms for their skills. Although there are non-negligible migrating costs, this hypothesis could prevail in the long run, as there is free movement of labor across the regional frontiers in Brazil. The second hypothesis is that the production function in each region can be closely represented by a Lucas (1988) type Cobb–Douglas production function.[5]

On the basis of these hypotheses, I used county data for 2000, the last Brazilian census year, to decompose the regional inequality between the Southeast and the Northeast, the two most populous regions in the country and also the two extremes in the spectrum of GDP per capita. Some cross-section regressions were run with data for education, schooling years, a proxy for quality of education, proxies for production and living costs and preferences towards working, measured by the proportion of working hours to total working hours available for the population of working age. Several alternative econometric methods were tried, but all indicated that this set of indicators was sufficient to explain all the regional inequalities found in Brazil. Therefore, educational achievements, costs of production, cost of living, and preferences towards working are enough to explain the regional inequalities in Brazil. Educational achievements

Table 17.2 *Brazil: role of each source of regional inequality between Northeast and Southeast*

Model	**Regional sources of counties included in estimations**	***Regional dummies***	**Role of human capital (%)**	**Role of productive effort (%)**	**Role of price and cost differences (%)**
Weighted GMM	Brazil	No	101.49	5.48	−6.98
Weighted OLS	Brazil	No	101.26	5.19	−6.45
Weighted LAD	Brazil	No	102.02	4.16	−6.19
Weighted GMM	Brazil	Yes	97.46	5.41	−2.87
Weighted OLS	Brazil	Yes	95.91	5.79	−1.70
Weighted LAD	Brazil	Yes	97.56	4.48	−2.03

Note: The way these decompositions are formed they do not add up to 100 per cent. LAD means least absolute deviations, GMM is generalized method of moments and OLS is ordinary least square.

Source: Barros (2010).

account for more than 95 per cent and possibly as much as 100 per cent of total inequalities between Northeast and Southeast. Working preferences (productive effort) account for something around 5 per cent of total disparities and production costs had negative contribution. Table 17.2 shows the share of each group of variables in the total regional inequality in the many estimated models. In spite of all the imprecision of these estimations, a major conclusion already emerges from this decomposition, which is that no violation of the basic hypotheses of standard theory is necessary to explain Brazil's regional inequalities, as has been assumed by many of the pioneer researches on this subject.[6]

A second relevant conclusion that can be obtained from such an exercise is that regional disparities in Brazil do not necessarily emerge from any market failure, but only from differences in human capital employment, preferences towards work or leisure and living and production costs. If this conclusion is correct, it should be expected that the role of differences between the incomes of two persons with the same attributes, but living in different regions, is small. Therefore, differences in the regional distribu-

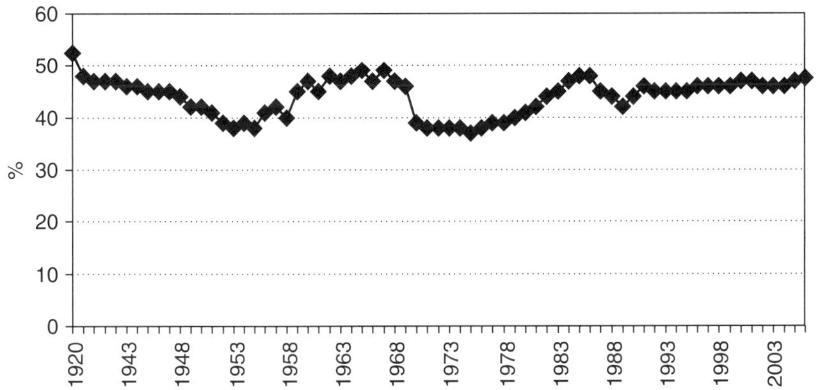

Source: IPEADATA, based on data from IBGE.

Figure 17.2 Proportion of per capita GDP in the Northeast to the national average, 1920–2006.

tion of individual attributes and endowments would be the major sources of regional inequalities in Brazil. Studies with Mincerian estimations of individual income determination normally challenge this conclusion, but they do not correct for differences in cost of living, so that they are not able to challenge it successfully.

17.2.1 Dynamics of Regional Inequality

A second striking feature of Brazil's regional inequality is its long-term dynamic behavior. The major statistic normally used to measure this inequality and that is comparable over time, namely GDP per capita in regions or states, seems to indicate that it is reasonably stable. Figure 17.2 compares this rate in the Northeast with the national average from 1920 to 2006, the first and last years with available data. The series shows that this rate is quite stable over time, although it has had some variation. Nevertheless, there is no relevant convergence, although most empirical studies investigating this particular problem have identified some which are statistically significant.[7]

Thus, any theory to explain Brazil's regional inequalities has to also explain why there is no convergence in income per capita among regions within the country. Neither changes in the productive structure of the Brazilian economy nor migrations of factors of production were sizable enough to eliminate the disparities or even to lead to a reasonable rate of their disappearance.

17.3 MAJOR EXPLANATIONS FOR THE REGIONAL IMBALANCES IN BRAZIL

There are several explanations for the existence of regional disparities in Brazil. A few of them are well organized, but most of them are loosely presented without much rigor in their arguments. The most organized and best-known hypothesis is the one presented by Furtado (1959). The others are less elaborate, as normally they are not fully developed, although often they play an important role on policy designs and discussions of the subject. This section presents a summary of Furtado's hypothesis and a brief description of other arguments and hypotheses found in the literature.

17.3.1 Furtado's Hypothesis

Furtado's hypothesis was originally presented in the document *Uma politica de desenvolvimento para o Nordeste* (GTDN, 1959), produced by a working group which had him as the head and intellectual leader. It is based on the center–periphery model originally proposed by Prebisch (1949 [1986]). The model violates three basic hypotheses of standard orthodox theory. The first stresses that there is increasing return to scale in some sectors, especially in industry.[8] The second hypothesis is that there are non-negligible transport costs. The third is that those markets in which there are increasing returns to scale are not perfectly competitive. In more rigorous terms, and within a modern version of this model presented by the New Economic Geography, it is assumed that there is monopolistic competition.[9]

According to Furtado, the Brazilian economy, as a primary exporter, had expansion cycles determined by market conditions for some of its exports. Sugar was the country's first major export product. Gold and other minerals constituted the next major export commodities. When the domestic market was large enough and there was access to industrial technologies at the end of the nineteenth century and the beginning of the twentieth, Brazil's major primary export was coffee, which was produced in the Southeast, mainly in the state of São Paulo. Thus, the inhabitants of this region had the necessary capital and access to a market that could justify industrialization, which did in fact begin in that region. Inhabitants of the Northeast and the North had neither the capital nor access to a market that would provide the necessary production scale for industrial activities.

The development of the Southeast's industries was such that this region started to export manufactured goods to other regions. Transport costs were not enough to offset the cost reductions arising from scale effects. Consequently, incipient industries in other regions were destroyed by the competition of imports from the Southeast. The other regions specialized in the production of goods whose technologies were subject to decreasing return to scale; these were mainly primary commodities.

In Prebisch's and Furtado's models, information did not flow so freely among regions or countries. Therefore, there was no perfect arbitrage of capital among the spatially separated markets. Consequently, those economies that had higher saving rates and accumulated more capital could grow faster. Therefore, both introduced a mechanism that would explain the relative loss of saving ability in the periphery. This was the deterioration of terms of trade, under the assumption that there is a relationship between the average propensity to save and income. As this happens, the population in the periphery would become relatively poorer and could save less proportionately. This would reduce the growing ability of this region or country.

In the particular context of Brazilian regional disparities, the mechanism envisaged by Furtado was that when the Southeast started to industrialize, there was a protectionist policy for the new industries. This forced the inhabitants of the Northeast and the North to buy industrial goods from the protected industry. Because of the still low scale of the infant industry in the Southeast, compared with what was found in Europe, the US and other developed nations, prices were higher. Therefore, whatever new industrial goods were produced in the Southeast would start to be exported to the Northeast and the North and they would be sold for higher prices than the similar previously imported goods from abroad. This would bring a deterioration of the terms of trade of these regions, as they would have to pay more for their bundles of imports while there was no reason to increase the prices of the bundles of their exports.

Therefore, the cause of the regional disparities according to Furtado is that historical accident made the Southeast region industrialize first and faster. This generated a relative productivity gain in that region, which left other regions behind, with the exception of the South. This last region was highly integrated with the Southeast from the beginning of its industrialization and could benefit from that. This inequality was then accentuated by the regional deterioration of the terms of trade and the consequent relatively falling ability to accumulate capital in the Northeast.

17.3.2 Other Hypotheses

Many alternative hypotheses have already been put forward – most of them, however, not fully developed. Perhaps the most popular, at least in non-academic environments, is that nature was less kind to the Northeast and the North. The drought areas in the Northeast and the hard-to-control forest in the North forced these regions to lag behind, as they would need more effort to reach the same result as would be possible in the Southeast and the South, which had good land easily usable for economic purposes.

An old-fashioned but still valid hypothesis in some social environments is that the Southeast and South regions have populations with fewer African and Native Indian ethnical influences. Although this hypothesis is not explicitly forwarded any longer, as it is politically incorrect, many arguments about this topic still have their roots in this idea. It cannot therefore be neglected as a relevant hypothesis.

Recent emphasis on the role of human capital in development, which was influenced by the seminal paper by Lucas (1988), made many researchers point to its uneven availability as the source of regional disparities in Brazil. The decomposition of its sources made by Barros (2010) gives support to this hypothesis. Nevertheless, these results still leave the argument far from an alternative explanation for the existence of regional inequality in Brazil. It is necessary to explain why these differences emerged and why market forces did not eliminate them and thus why regional inequalities in Brazil have persisted since the last quarter of the nineteenth century.[10]

It has also been stressed in the literature that the institutional environment in the Northeast is less stimulating for economic growth. This is in line with the recent emphasis on the role of institutions in economic growth and development.[11] The existence of such political and social phenomena as *coronelismo* created uncertainties for investments in the most backward regions. As a consequence, growth was slower.

17.3.3 An Alternative Hypothesis

Recently a more elaborate hypothesis was made by the present author (Barros, 2011). The idea is quite simple, as it only puts together a set of standard assumptions of economic theory, most of them quite mainstream on their concerns. This hypothesis substantially reduces reliance on market failures or non-orthodox assumptions, although it does not fully discard their relevance. The first crucial assumption that is stressed is that many goods and services can be produced in any region. This recognition is important in understanding regional disparities, although it is common in economic theory to introduce the simplifying assumption of only one good in each region.

Each good is produced through a standard production function such as

$$y_i = f(k_i, h_i, l_i),$$

where y_i is the good or service i, and k_i, h_i and l_i are the amounts of capital, human capital and labor used in the production process, respectively. y_i and k_i, are measured in a standard commodity, as defined by Sraffa (1960),[12] while l_i is measured in hours of labor spent. The amount of human capital h_i is measured by a combined index of hours spent in acquiring qualification and working experience. The exact way this combination is made is not relevant to the argument, given the level of detail presented here. The function $f(.)$ results in the total output y_i, given any combination of the factors of production.

With the previous assumptions, it is possible to define an aggregated production function for each regional space that is defined as

$$Y = F(K, H, L),$$

where Y, K, H and L are aggregations of individual variables for all firms, with capital letters being aggregation of the many individual lowercase letters for all local firms. In this aggregated production function $F(.)$, it is possible to define well-behaved differentials for each argument of the production function, so that the first derivatives are all positive and the second ones for the same argument are all negative.

There is a reasonably good arbitrage of factors of production across regions, so that their prices, when costs of living are taken into account, are not much different. Differences obviously exist because there are costs of migration, but in the long term they are not high enough to explain the existing regional disparities. Brazil is a country in which there is much labor mobility across regional borders.

Although there are also costs for trading among regions, these are also small enough not to represent barriers that would justify the incapacity of regions to adjust their relative prices of tradable goods, so that specializations can be made according to the local comparative advantages. A region with a relatively higher availability of a specific factor of production could specialize in goods intensive in its use. Nevertheless, this hypothesis does not eliminate the existence of a reasonable share of goods in each economy that are nontradable. These goods and services generate differences in the costs of living among geographical areas.

The accumulation of human capital is not fully determined by market forces only, as other social features also have a relevant role to play. There are many sources, but the major ones are: (1) the existence of externalities of education;[13] (2) the existence of credit constraint and nonconvexities in the production function for education;[14] (3) an institutional framework determining public support to education, such as access to schools and policies influencing their quality;[15] and (4) the non-trivial role of personal familiar relationships.[16] A consequence of all these market failures or other factors is that the relative human capital levels in any pair of societies tend to have a high time persistence even in the long run. If a specific region has higher human capital than another in one decade, it will tend also to have higher scores for this variable in the next decades.

These hypotheses together imply that if by any chance a region is initially populated by individuals with higher human capital, it tends to have a higher income per capita, as the returns to factors of production tend to be the same in all regions, by arbitrage. More simply, this idea can be grasped through the assumption that there are two types of labor, skilled and unskilled. If two regions have different supplies of these two types of labor, the production functions of the goods and services produced in them will adjust to absorb these different proportions of factors. Skilled workers have a higher income than others, as they earn a return to their labor, similar to the one for unskilled labor, plus an additional return to their human capital. Therefore, the per capita income of the region with more skilled labor will be higher.

More formally, this idea can be seen from the Euler equation for a homogeneous production function of first degree. This equation assures that:

$$\frac{Y}{L} = r\frac{K}{L} + w + \rho\frac{H}{L},$$

where r, w and ρ are the returns to capital, labor (the wage rate) and human capital, respectively, and the other variables are as previously defined. If all these rates are the same in all regions, this output per capita (Y/L) will be higher in the region that will have higher (H/L) and (K/L). It is possible to show that when (H/L) is exogenously higher, market forces will not make (K/L) to offset it, so that (Y/L) will be higher.

My study (Barros, 2011) starts from this idea to explain regional inequalities and draws on the historical origins of colonization in the many regions in the country to explain the current regional inequality. Thus, the adversities in the colonial occupation of the North and the Northeast were such that the most efficient technologies were intensive in unskilled labor and less intensive in human capital, having slaves as the major source of labor. In the large-scale occupation of the Southeast and the South, which had already taken place in the nineteenth century, urbanization was already higher, a fact related to the nature of mining activities and the migration of the Portuguese aristocracy to Brazil in the Napoleonic era

(1808). Therefore, the relative prices of more skilled labor fell, as the risks in migration to Brazil were lower. As a consequence, the technologies in these productive expansions in the Southeast and the South regions were more intensive in human capital. These last regions, then, started from a labor supply arising from their initial higher share of skilled labor, which has persisted to give its higher intensity today.

The only market failure demanded by this hypothesis to explain regional disparities in Brazil are those that are associated with human capital accumulation, which are standard results in economies, so this idea is theoretically robust. Besides this, it has support from recent empirical researches that have stressed the role of differences in human capital in the composition of regional inequalities in Brazil. Further, it is more consistent with the existence of inequalities at the beginning of the 1870s, which were similar to the levels found at the beginning of the twentieth century.

17.4 PUBLIC POLICIES TO REDUCE REGIONAL DISPARITIES

Before the 1950s there were concerns with regional development, but they were mostly directed to particular sectors or problems.[17] In 1909 an institution was created whose aim was to develop actions that could relieve the perverse social impact of the droughts in the Northeast.[18] In 1945 this body became the Departamento Nacional de Obras Contra a Seca (DNOCS), whose focus was similar: to build infrastructure that could reduce the impact of droughts on the local population and to generate income for that population when droughts occurred. In 1933 the Instituto do Açúcar e do Álcool (IAA) was created to foster sugar production in the Northeast and to avoid the economically and socially perverse impacts of price fluctuations in the world market of this commodity. In 1942 the Banco de Crédito da Borracha was created to promote the production of natural rubber in the North region and to reduce the perverse economic and social impacts on the region of price fluctuations in the world market. In 1942 this bank became the Banco de Crédito da Amazônia, expanding its scope to other activities unrelated to rubber production. In 1948 the Comissão do Vale do São Francisco (CVSF) was created, whose purpose was to develop economic activities in the region of the São Francisco Valley. Later on, it became the Superintendência do Vale do São Franscisco (SUVALE) and in 1974 the current Companhia de Desenvolvimento do Vale do São Franscisco (CODEVASF). In 1952 the Banco do Nordeste, a development bank to work in the Northeast, was created.

Since the 1950s regional disparities have become a major political concern, despite localized focus on the problem having existed since the nineteenth century. The difference was that in that decade the idea emerged that relative backwardness necessitated more general regional policies. Specific policies to correct particular problems were the major strategy no longer. Regional policies started to become part of the political agenda, in spite of some few, specific, isolated and normally sporadic previous experiences. Because of the size of its population and its historical importance, the Northeast became the major target of regional policies.

There were already four major institutions working in the region that were concerned with its development, namely the Departamento Nacional de Obras Contra a Seca (DNOCS), formally established in 1945, but having evolved from previous institutions, as reported above; the Companhia Hidrelétrica do Vale do São Francisco (CHESF), founded in 1945, but with its first hydro-electric plant starting production in 1954; the Companhia de Desenvolvimento do Vale do São Francisco (CODEVASF), founded in its first version in 1948; and the Banco do Nordeste (founded in 1952). The first-mentioned had as its target to plan and execute actions to combat the perverse impacts of the periodic Northeastern droughts, while the second had as its target hydro-electric power generation from the waterfalls of the São Francisco Valley. The third had as its major target to develop the region around the São Francisco River. The fourth was a development bank whose investment financing should foster regional development in the Northeast. These four policy instruments together embodied the initial strategy to try to overcome a regional backwardness of an important region in Brazil.

All the discussions around the regional question in the 1950s and 1960s generated a new conception on regional policy, which is well stated in the document mentioned above, *Uma política de desenvolvimento para o Nordeste* (GTDN, 1959). The policy had the following major targets:

1. To promote industrialization in the Northeast through various types of investment incentives.
2. To promote the planning of activities that could be led by government, such as mining and agriculture, where the public sector could provide information and other types of support.
3. To promote migration in the region, so as to reduce population in areas with inadequate environmental conditions and increase it in others with more promising natural support (from Sertão to the hinterlands on Maranhão).
4. To give priority to the regional consequences of national policies, such as education and health policies.

To implement such a broad policy, a federal institution was created, the Superintendência do Desenvolvimento do Nordeste (SUDENE). This institution was afterwards replicated in other regions, e.g. the Superintendência do Desenvolvimento do Norte (SUDAM) for the North region and the Superintendência do Desenvolvimento do Centro-Oeste (SUDECO). The North got also a development bank called the Banco da Amazônia SA (BASA).

Notwithstanding their more diversified original goals, SUDENE and SUDAM became institutions that each had two major purposes. The first and the most important was to supply local regional markets with investment credit more cheaply than it was possible to get it in the Brazilian financial market. Nevertheless, access to these credits was decided discretionarily by civil servants from these institutions and was influenced by 64 state governments, as they had to be approved by a council formed by all the state governors of the region.[19] Therefore, their working logic was an incentive for corruption, which in the end reduced its social support and led to substantial falls in the resources allocated by this instrument in the 1980s. At the end of the century this mechanism was discontinued.

A second instrument widely used by both SUDENE and SUDAM, and which had a nonnegligible impact on the development of the regions that they had as targets, was the generation of economically useful information about these regions. This went from simple calculations such as GDP by state to estimations of mineral reserves and the needs and costs of investments in sanitation. This substantially reduced the costs and risk of investments in the regions. Many of these initiatives collapsed, however, owing to budget cuts.

In addition to the resources allocated to finance private sector activities through SUDENE and SUDAM, there were financial resources allocated through the Banco do Nordeste and BASA, which also were lent at special rates. Nevertheless, these resources were not always lent at costs lower than those of BNDES, the National Development Bank, and were often offset by BNDES's unfavorable bias in its lending to the Northeast.

In the 1980s and 1990s, regional policies became a second priority because the focus was on macroeconomic stabilization. Regional policies faced a collapse as the federal government was mainly concerned with fiscal adjustments. The idea of regional planning was abandoned. As a consequence, the Banco do Nordeste and BASA became the major instruments of regional policies, as their actions did not require planning interventions.[20] Nevertheless, even these institutions faced a decline in their available resources, as the public sector was in disarray.

After the Real Plan in 1994, there was also a change in regional policies. The priority of the federal government was to redefine many of the institutional frameworks of public policies with a spatial impact. Local governments (at both state and county levels) were forced to reorganize their operating mechanisms. The focus of spatial policies moved from economic development to social policies.[21] There was thus a full redefinition of the modus operandi of the latter. Most of them got a nationally unified framework aiming to reduce the discretionary role of local government that used to prevail and the consequent distortions that could arise. Such unification of policy frameworks covered health policies, with the Serviço Único de Saúde as the major instrument, and education, with the unification of teachers' salaries, Fundo de Desenvolvimento do Ensino Fundamental (FUNDEF) and national exams as the main means, and had gone as far as labor policies, with the Plano Nacional de Formação Profissional (PLANFOR) and the setup on a common basis of the Sistema Nacional de Emprego (SINE) and unemployment insurance as the leading ploys.

After the Lula government began, in 2003, there was initially a conflict between the two models of regional policies that had prevailed hitherto. There were some economists and politicians in the politically victorious alliance that defended a return to development policies as the major instrument of regional policies. The revivals of SUDENE and SUDAM were seen as major targets, together with the creation of a new financial fund with resources from the federal government budget that could be used to finance local investments and infrastructure. Nevertheless, other economists and politicians felt that such policies could bring back with them the corrupt apparatus that existed to allocate these resources. They argued that expanding and giving efficiency in social policies could be a better way to promote regional convergence.

Both models were tried, but the expansion and rationalization of social policies prevailed. The other model failed to get consensus on its format and did not get the necessary social support to take off. SUDENE and SUDAM were refounded and the Fundo de Desenvolvimento do Nordeste (FDNE) was established. Nonetheless, their institutional operating mechanisms were not well established, as the old-fashioned conceptions took over their settlements and they did not have the necessary social support to become a relevant mechanism. As a result, the resources made available were used to increase the federal budget surplus.

To offset this failure, the federal government's plan, the Plano de Aceleração do Crescimento (PAC), provides a share of investment in the Northeast that is higher than its share on Brazilian GDP, with the aim of some spatial dispersive impact on economic activities. Nevertheless, there is always a difference between planned and actual investments, so the impact remains to be seen.

17.5 AN EVALUATION OF CURRENT AND PAST POLICIES

In sum, it is possible to say that regional policies in Brazil have had three major concepts supporting them. The first is that markets do not work properly, so that there are several market failures that demand relative price distortions, especially in the case of credit risks to expand activities that could be economically efficient in regional development. Under this first hypothesis, economic activities fostered could favor both big and small enterprises, with periodical biases for each of these extremes. This concept prevailed from the 1960s to the 1980s.

The second concept is that markets work reasonably well to allocate resources, but generate social distortions because they are not able to include all individuals in their generated development path. Therefore, those individuals who lag behind should be protected by public policies, which are social policies. These, however, should be directed either to promote human capital formation or else to alleviate poverty. This hypothesis prevailed during the Lula presidential term (2003–10), although it was also an important component of the shaping of regional policies under President Cardoso (1995–2002).

The third concept is that markets work properly, but can become inefficient at generating welfare if institutions are not created properly. Therefore, a crucial regional policy is to adjust institutions to generate economic efficiency. This third hypothesis played an important role during the Cardoso presidency, although it was not the only foundation of regional policies in that period.

A closer look at Figure 17.2 shows that the proportion of the Northeastern per capita GDP in the Brazilian total did not change much in the period in which regional policies were more important, mainly after the 1960s. It is therefore difficult to identify any real impact by such policies on regional inequalities in Brazil. With so little fluctuation in the major measure of regional inequality, it is difficult to evaluate the relative impact of the alternative policies. Nevertheless, my study (Barros, 2011) made a simple simulation that indicates the potential role of social policies to regional inequalities. If Brazil had a Gini coefficient similar to the one prevailing in the United States, which could be reached through adequate social policies, the Northeastern per capita GDP could rise from 35 per cent of the Southeastern per capital GDP to 65 per cent, substantially reducing Brazil's regional inequalities.

Figure 17.3 shows that regional policies after the 1960s increased the role of government in the Northeast, but that its presence did not change much in the North. This happened because the federal government always had a strong

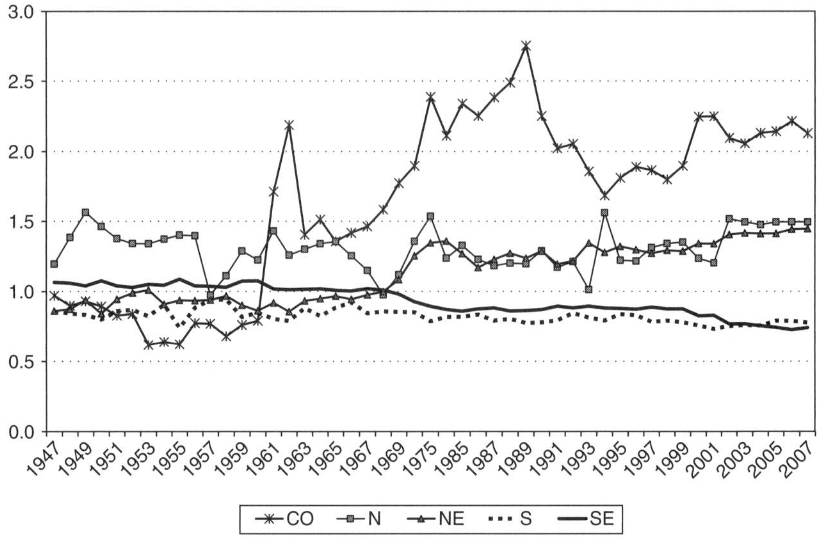

Note: The index of public sector relevance in the region is defined as the proportion of two other indexes. The first one is the share of the regional GDP of public administration in the national total. The second is the share of the total regional GDP also in the national total. More precisely, define Y_i as the total GDP for region i (for all sectors) and Y_{PAi} as the GDP of public administration only, but also for region i. Therefore, it is possible to define two shares:

$$S_{Yi} = \frac{Y_i}{\sum_{i=1}^{n} Y_i} \text{ and } S_{YPAi} = \frac{Y_{PAi}}{\sum_{i=1}^{n} Y_{PAi}},$$

where n is the number of regions in Brazil, which is 5. The index of public sector relevance for region i, which appears in the figure, is defined as

$$I_{PSR} = \frac{S_{YPAi}}{S_{Yi}}.$$

Figure 17.3 Proportion between two regional shares on the national totals: (i) GDP generated by public administration and (ii) total GDP.

presence in the economy of that region for security reasons. When it started to have a stronger presence because of regional policies, it could offset other actions in the region, culminating with the end of central government direct administration of specific territories (Acre, Rondônia, Rorsima and Amapá).

There still exists no evaluation of the relative efficiency of policies based on each of these concepts, as the data to make such a study are difficult to gather and a proper method of isolating the impact of other cyclical features of the Brazilian economy on the regional balance is not simple. Nevertheless, it is possible to make some observations regarding the consistency of such policies in the light of the observed experience. Some of them are as follows:

1. Subsidies to capital through preferential interest rates do not seem to be a policy with a relevant impact. My estimates (Barros, 2010a) indicate that inequalities in human capital availability seem to be the major source of regional disparities, so that resource allocation and the arbitrage of prices of factors among regions have been working properly. Therefore, it is not necessary to create a special capital market for the poor regions in the country. Furthermore, the economies of scale associated with the period in which the Brazilian economy was ready to develop industry do not seem to be a relevant determinant of regional inequalities, as studies have pointed to the emergence of these inequalities at the beginning of the nineteenth century, well before the first industrial upsurge in the Brazilian economy.
2. The redesign of institutions to eliminate their role in economic inefficiencies does not by itself seem to be sufficient to overcome regional inequalities, unless the institutions work to reduce differences in human capital availability. Therefore, any policy to reshape institutions has to be implemented together with other policies or else to be very specific, so that it can reduce differences in the availability of human capital.

17.6 CONCLUSIONS

This chapter has presented an overview of the regional question in Brazil. It began with some statistics that indicate that there is a pronounced regional inequality within the country, with the North and the Northeast as the poorest regions. This can be seen in data on GDP per capita, but it is also evident in most social statistics, such as average schooling years and the proportion of the population living in households below the poverty line.

The chapter also discussed the sources of these inequalities–differences in income between individuals with the same attributes but living in distinct regions, or uneven spatial distribution of individuals with more valuable attributes, parallel to a reasonable spatial arbitrage of income generated by specific attributes. The study of the relative role of these two components in Brazil's regional inequality is still at a very early stage.

Nevertheless, the little evidence existing so far seems to show that most inequality arises from the uneven distribution of individuals owning the most valuable attributes.

The major hypotheses to explain the regional inequalities in Brazil were also briefly reviewed. It was seen that the evidence hitherto indicates that there is an obvious failure of the major hypothesis put forward by Celso Furtado to fit the facts. New hypotheses are now under construction. A special emphasis was given to my own hypothesis, which is further developed in another text. Nevertheless, there is a major consensus among the most recent studies on this subject, which is that it is not possible to ignore the role of human capital to explain inequalities. Therefore, the major question that remains and that I tried to overcome is how to explain the huge differences in human capital employment in the regions.

A brief review of the policies implemented and their underlying hypotheses on the source of inequalities was also presented. It was seen that there already existed at least three major policy strategies. The first was to reduce costs for capital investments in the poorest regions. The second was to promote social policies targeting the poorest strata of the population, which would represent a major contribution to alleviate the perverse impact of regional inequalities and would increase income in the poorest regions. The third strategy was to promote institutional redesign in the poorest regions, which could allow them to pursue a convergent development path with the richest regions in the country.

There are not enough studies comparing the relative efficiency of these policies. Nevertheless, the oldest policy, i.e. the subsidies to capital investments, seems to have performed poorly. The evidence on the dynamics of regional inequalities to some extent challenges its foundations. Furthermore, as the oldest policy, it has been around for some time and it has not been able to change much the regional inequalities within Brazil.

NOTES

1. Data for 2008 from PNAD-IBGE.
2. IBGE, Contas Regionais, 2009.
3. Distrito Federal is not a state.
4. See for example Glaeser and Gottlieb (2009) and Roback (1982).
5. This function is $Y = AK^{\alpha}(HL)^{1-\alpha}$, where Y is output, K and L are stock of capital and the amount of labor employed and A is a productivity parameter. The letter α is a parameter such that $0 < \alpha < 1$.
6. See for example Furtado (1959) and Singer (1954).
7. Similar dichotomy between statistical results and effective relevance also exists in the US, as argued by Glaeser and Gottlieb (2009). Examples of studies that found convergence in Brazil are Azzoni (2000) and Azzoni et al. (2000).

8. Mainstream economies normally works with decreasing returns to scale of all factors of production.
9. See Fujita et al. (1999, ch. 5).
10. Barros (2010b) suggests that these inequalities already existed in that last quarter and at magnitudes very close to the one found nowadays.
11. See Acemoglu et al. (2001, 2005) for seminal contributions on this idea. See also Rodrik et al. (2004).
12. It is necessary to introduce this nonintuitive unit to make the quantities of these goods or services invariants to the rate of return of capital when there are no changes in the resources used in their production.
13. Lucas (1988) is the seminal paper stressing such particularity of education.
14. Galor and Zeira (1993).
15. Alexopoulos and Cavalcanti (2010) and Ferreira (2000) are examples of models that explain why social conflicts lead to failures of the institutional framework to generate efficiency in educational supply.
16. Barros and Mesquita (2008) show that what they call family-built human capital plays a major role on income determination in Brazil.
17. Oliveira and Vianna (2005, ch. 3) has a more detailed discussion of this change in policy approach to the regional problem in Brazil.
18. Most of the information on the history of institutional creations has been taken from Gomes (2010).
19. A share of it could have a market base definition of its allocation, the so-called ninth amendment (*artigo nono*). Nevertheless, the prevailing discounts involved on such operations were so high that they shocked the fairness notions of the ruling economic sectors, which imposed heavy restrictions on this mechanism of resource allocation.
20. Worldwide liberal ideologies also played a major role on this collapse of regional planning and specific development policies.
21. The previous development policies, with their emphasis on public sector actions to promote private sector economic activities, had as their underlying theoretical background the idea that market failures were the major cause of restriction in economic growth. This was not a popular view among economists any longer. The new prevailing ideas were that rent-seeking was the major obstacle to local development and that market forces generated losers, who should be compensated by public policies.

REFERENCES

Acemoglu, D., S. Johnson and J. Robinson (2001), 'The colonial origins of comparative development: an empirical investigation', *American Economic Review*, **91** (5), 1369–1401.

Acemoglu, D., S. Johnson and J. Robinson (2005), 'Institutions as the fundamental cause of long run growth', in P. Aghion and S. Durlauf (eds), *Handbook of Economic Growth*, London: Elsevier.

Alexopoulos, J. and T. Cavalcanti (2010), 'Cheap goods and persistent inequality', *Journal of Economic Theory*, **45** (3), 417–51.

Azzoni, C.R. (2000), 'Geografia e convergência de renda entre os estados brasileiros', in R. Henriques (ed.), *Desigualdade e Pobreza*, Rio de Janeiro: IPEA.

Azzoni, C., N. Menezes-Filho, T. Menezes and R. Silveira Neto (2000), 'Geography and income convergence among Brazilian states', Inter-American Development Bank Research Network – Working Paper 3096, Washington, DC, May.

Barros, A. (2010), 'Decomposição das desigualdades regionais brasileiras em seus principais determinantes', mimeo, Recife: Department of Economics, UFPE.
Barros, A. (2011), *Desigualdades Regionais no Brasil: Natureza, Causas, Origens e Solução*, Rio de Janeiro: Campus-Elsevier.
Barros, A. and C. Mesquita (2008), 'The role of social capital in individual incomes in Brazil', paper presented to the Annual Meeting of the Latin American and Caribbean Economic Association, Rio de Janeiro, November.
Ferreira, F. (2000), 'Os determinantes da desigualdade de renda no Brasil: luta de classes ou heterogeneidade educacional?', in R. Henriques (ed.), *Desigualdade e Pobreza*, Rio de Janeiro: IPEA.
Fujita, M., P. Krugman and A. Venables (1999), *The Spatial Economy*, Cambridge, MA: MIT Press.
Furtado, C. (1959), 'A operação Nordeste', Rio de Janeiro: Instituto Superior de Estudos Brasileiros.
Galor, O. and J. Zeira (1993), 'Income distribution and macroeconomics', *Review of Economics Studies*, **60** (1), 35–52.
Glaeser, E. and J. Gottlieb (2009), 'The wealth of cities: agglomeration economies and spatial equilibrium in the United States', *Journal of Economic Literature*, **47** (4), 983–1028.
Gomes, G.M. (2010), Conflito e conciliação: políticas de desenvolvimento regional no mundo contemporâneo', mimeo, Fortaleza: Banco do Nordeste.
Grupo de Trabalho para o Desenvolvimento do Nordeste (GTDN) (1959), 'Uma política de desenvolvimento para o Nordeste', manus., Recife.
Lucas, R. (1988), 'On the mechanics of economic development', *Journal of Monetary Economics*, **22** (1), 3–42.
Oliveira, C. and P. Vianna (2005), *Desenvolvimento Regional: 50 Anos do BNB*, Fortaleza: BNB.
Prebisch, R. (1949 [1986]), 'El dasarrollo económico en America Latina y algunos de sus principales problemas', 1949, reprinted in *Desarrollo Económico*, **26** (103), 479–502.
Roback, J. (1982), 'Wages, rents and the quality of life', *Journal of Political Economy*, **90** (6), 1257–78.
Rodrik, D., A. Subramanian and F. Trebbi (2004), 'Institutions rule: the primacy of institutions over geography and integration in economic development', *Journal of Economic Growth*, **9** (2), 131–65.
Singer, H. (1962), *Estudo sobre o Desenvolvimento Econômico do Nordeste*, Recife: Comissão de Desenvolvimento Econômico de Pernambuco.
Sraffa, P. (1960), *Production of Commodities by Means of Commodities: Prelude to a Critique of Economic Theory*, Cambridge: Cambridge University Press.

18. Comments on part VI

Geoffrey J.D. Hewings

GENERAL PERSPECTIVES

In his seminal paper, Williamson (1965) proposed a stylized model to explain the process of regional disparities over time. From his work came the now well-known inverted U-shape (Figure 18.1) that reveals very clearly the 'location' of countries over time. Those with low levels of per capita income tend to be associated with low levels of regional disparities. Concomitantly, the same is true for countries with high levels of per capita income. In between, we find a cluster of countries – mainly in Latin America – with medium levels of per capita income but high levels of regional disparities. Williamson was able to explain the *growth of disparities* by appealing to notions of comparative advantage enjoyed by some regions, as well as the processes of circular and cumulative causation (Myrdal, 1953; Kuznets, 1968). Now, the evidence from the new growth

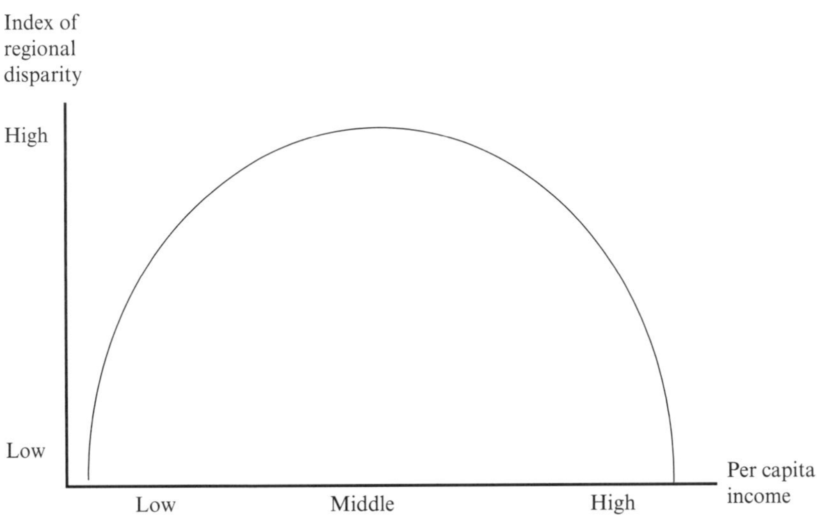

Figure 18.1 Regional disparities and per capita income.

theory and new economic geography offers additional explanations – the role of scale economies, agglomeration economies, path dependence and the critical role of transportation costs. However, none of these approaches/theories provided a convincing explanation for the *processes towards convergence*. Now, well over 100 articles in the last decade on regional disparities, convergence, convergence clubs etc. have been published using a variety of techniques (stimulated in part by the work of Barro and Sala-i-Martin (1991, 1992)), including new developments in spatial econometrics. The most recent work has focused on places other than the US, Japan or Europe, with considerable interest in India and China. Brazil and Argentina offer some interesting challenges and these two chapters provide some new perspectives.

PORTO AND ELIZAGARAY CHAPTER

In an earlier paper (Galiani et al., 2005) on unemployment in Argentina, the issues addressed were:

- First, what determines equilibrium unemployment at the local level?
- Second, how persistent are regional unemployment shocks?

The authors found a lack of persistence – even during periods when unemployment was trending upward – and they explored adjustment mechanisms by appealing to some current thinking on labor market behavior (Blanchard, 2006; Blanchflower and Oswald, 1995; Layard et al., 1991, 2005) to which one should add the work of Nobel laureate (2010) Pissarides (2000). The results suggested that the industry mix, the labor force participation rate and the differences in the regional domestic gross product per capita were important in explaining the changes in regional unemployment. Further, they indicated that trade liberalization and privatization may have affected the outcomes. One of the reasons why regional unemployment shocks display low persistence on local unemployment is that the regional unemployment elasticity of regional pay in Argentina is high and comparable to the one estimated in the literature for the US and UK. Chapter 16 presents Argentina as a country characterized by large geographical disparities between the Buenos Aires metro area and the rest of the provinces. In the twentieth century these disparities produced a huge volume of out-migration from peripheral regions to Buenos Aires. The chapter evaluates the efficiency of several fiscal policies designed to reduce the regional disparities and improve the economic conditions of the poorer provinces in Argentina.

The authors of the chapter analyzed the results achieved by regional policies designed to modify the incentives to migrate: (1) increasing the public transfers to poor provinces; (2) equalizing the geographical distribution of social services; and (3) enhancing the political participation of the peripheral regions in the national parliament. They also studied the effects of the policies that tried to reallocate production factors geographically through subsidies and protection to some specific industries. Thereafter, they evaluated the impact of these policies by examining the temporal evolution of several socioeconomic indicators such as the illiteracy rate, child mortality, GDP per capita etc.

This long-run analysis shows that some of these social indicators have a tendency to converge but that significant disparities in GDP per capita and the high concentration of population in the metropolitan area of the capital city remain prominent features at the beginning of the twenty-first century. The authors claim that a main reason can be traced in the inefficient design of fiscal policies, since some of these policies just neutralized the effects of the others. For example, the national government designed a development plan for region 2 and simultaneously the regional authorities in region 1 subsidized one industry against the competitive advantage of the same industry in region 2. The authors have estimated that the cost of this inefficiency as somewhere between 1 per cent and 2 per cent of national GDP (though no details about how this number is obtained are provided). The final recommendation of the authors is to design more efficient regional policies by more coordination between the provincial and federal authorities.

In evaluating Chapter 16, it is clear that Argentina provides a picture different from that of Brazil. However, it is difficult to estimate the impacts of policies without some more formal assessment; partial equilibrium analysis of one or two policies may not provide the comprehensive picture needed. In particular, there may be important spillover or feedback effects that may serve to either accentuate or reduce the impacts of any regional policy. Finally, as is the case in many countries with a dominant primate city, the hegemony of Buenos Aires may make effective regional policy difficult to enact.

RANDS BARROS CHAPTER

The focus here is on Brazilian inequalities – their persistence is well known and has been the subject of increasing attention in the regional science literature. The chapter proposes the development of an alternative theory to the ones usually employed; the approach is provocative but comes with several assumptions that may be challenged – and one of the tasks of a discussant is to do just that!

Ultimately, the chapter focuses on labor, and in particular on human capital; at one point we are advised that there is 'much labor mobility across regional borders'. In what sense? The assumption that there are negligible migration costs may be challenged in several ways. For the individual, there may be a wealth effect that limits migration; there may be an option value of waiting effect where the trigger to finally move may be generated by differences in wages or the accumulation of resources to facilitate migration. For the country, there are significant externalities in having accumulations of migrants with marginal attachment to the formal labor force living in less than attractive physical conditions. Further, migration is likely to be selective, with higher mobility among those with greater human capital – their outmigration from places like the Northeast generates a dynamic that exacerbates the disparity problem.

The focus on human capital is to be applauded, but there needs to be consideration of the temporal dimension. Recent work in the US (using a Mincerian framework) has suggested that return to investment in education provides a more attractive alternative development strategy and further that returns to investment in lower income/less-educated groups yields the highest returns. Barros's model needs to accommodate a longer-run perspective and to consider both the supply and demand sides of the human capital component. Greater thought needs to be given to the human capital variable, h: currently, it is a combined index of acquired qualifications and working experience but the way it is combined does matter. For example, those in the Northeast of Brazil may not see the value of investment in education if there are few opportunities to use those skills; on the other hand, firms may be reluctant to locate there because the labor skills are not as high as those in the Southeast. Thus, we have a dynamic (temporal) general equilibrium problem that an aggregate production function approach cannot embrace.

In addition, the structural differences between the Northeast and the Southeast can only be partially explained by differences in tradability, competitive advantages and the asymmetric impacts of trade liberalization. For example, the Northeast is much more dependent on the rest of Brazil than vice versa in terms of individual sector production functions; the Northeast has a structure different from the rest of Brazil's that can be explained by differences in specialization, products produced and differences in technology. It is also clear that imperfections in the spatial market in Brazil have been accentuated by high transport costs.

Barros's model hinges on the statement that 'the only market failure this hypothesis needs to explain relates to regional disparities that are linked to human capital accumulation'. This may be true, but then we need to explore how this can be expanded and disaggregated (by skill level, location, occupation, income) to provide a more comprehensive picture of the way the Northeast's economy works. Then it will be possible to conduct simulations on various policy outcomes that are nicely discussed in the chapter.

FINAL THOUGHTS

It may be premature to explore more policy options at the present time; more attention needs to be directed to understanding, in greater detail, how the regional economies of Argentina and Brazil function – how they respond to macro shocks (such as business cycles, trade liberalization and interregional trade). To accomplish this would require more expansive regional and interregional models – with much more attention to the functioning of the regional labor markets, migration and the provision of investment in human capital. These two countries are not alone; a great deal of regional development policy in the rest of the world has been crafted on platforms of knowledge about the underlying economies that are woefully inadequate.

REFERENCES

Barro, R. and Xavier Sala-i-Martin (1991), 'Convergence across states and regions', Brookings Papers on Economic Activity 1991, no. 1, pp. 107–82.

Barro, R. and Xavier Sala-i-Martin (1992), 'Convergence', *Journal of Political Economy*, **100** (2), 223–51.

Blanchard, Olivier (2006), 'European unemployment: the evolution of facts and ideas', *Economic Policy,* **45** (2), 5–47.

Blanchflower, David G. and Andrew J. Oswald (1995), 'The wage curve', *Journal of Economic Perspectives*, **9** (3), 153–67.

Galiania, S., C. Lamarcheb, A. Portoc and W. Sosa-Escudero (2005), 'Persistence and regional disparities in unemployment (Argentina 1980–1997)', *Regional Science and Urban Economics*, **35** (4), 375–94.

Kuznets, S. (1968), *Toward a Theory of Economic Growth*, New York: Norton.

Layard, Richard, Stephen Nickell and Richard Jackman (1991, 2005), *Unemployment: Macroeconomic Performance and the Labour Market*, Oxford: Oxford University Press.

Myrdal, G. (1953), *The Political Element in the Development of Economic Theory*, London: Routledge.

Pissarides, Christopher A. (2000), *Equilibrium Unemployment Theory*, 2nd edn, Cambridge, MA and London: MIT Press.

Williamson, Jeffrey G. (1965), 'Regional inequality and the process of national development: a description of the patterns', *Economic Development and Cultural Change,* **13** (4), 1–84.

PART VII

Inflation and stabilization policies

19. Inflation and macroeconomic policies in post-convertibility Argentina

Daniel Heymann, Adrián Ramos and Horacio Aguirre

19.1 INTRODUCTION

The history of inflation in Argentina over the past decades covers a very wide range of situations, from deflation to hyperinflation, reflecting large swings in economic policies, private behaviors and the external environment. Between 1945 and 1974, the annual (CPI) inflation rate was lower than 10 per cent only in 3 years, but remained below 100 per cent (with a single exception in 1959). The macroeconomic and political crisis in 1975–76 defined a transition to a period of very high and variable inflation which lasted 15 years, with inflation rates well over 100 per cent (except in 2 years), and dramatic episodes of hyperinflation in 1989 and 1990. The public perception of the large social costs of such instability supported the introduction in 1991 of a currency board system with a hard peg to the dollar, and tight constraints on monetary policies.

After a substantial price drift, the inflation rate converged to international levels, or even less. But the 'convertibility regime' eventually proved unsustainable, and collapsed in 2001 in a deep crisis of historic proportions, which included the declaration of default on public debt and massive redefinitions of private financial contracts. However, even in the context of a disturbance with very severe social and political consequences, as well as economic effects which included a sharp depreciation, the response of domestic prices was quite moderate and a spike in the inflation rate did not become entrenched. Thus, contrary to many previous fears, the end of the convertibility rule did not imply a relapse into high inflation (see Figure 19.1).

Still, the economy did not settle into a definite low-inflation regime. With real output growing fast between 2003 and 2008, CPI inflation apparently escalated over time to an annual rate around 20 per cent,[1] under a

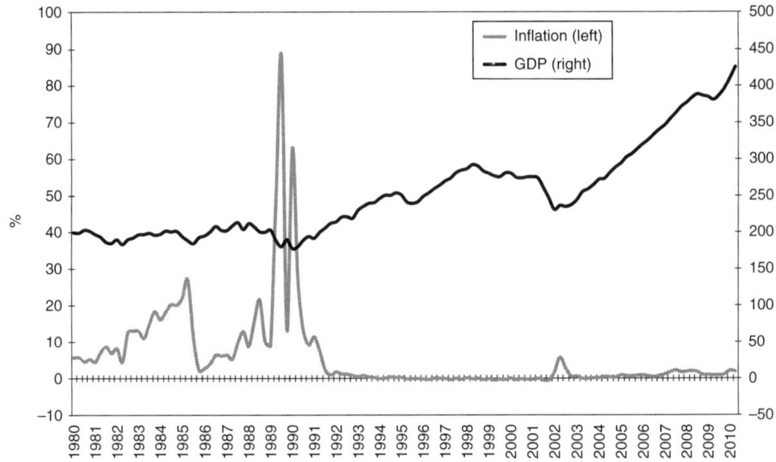

Figure 19.1 Argentine GDP at constant prices and CPI inflation rates (billions of pesos of 1993 and monthly rates of change).

monetary policy which did not commit to explicit price or exchange rate targets, while it kept de facto the movements of the dollar exchange rate within a small range, and sterilized a good part of the monetary effect of large central-bank purchases of foreign exchange. These trends lasted until 2008 when the private sector generated a substantial capital outflow, in an environment influenced by the repercussions of the international crisis and domestic conflicts over the design and implementation of economic policies. A fall in international export prices and a bad agricultural crop contributed to the recession that the economy underwent in 2009. However, this took place without strong disruptions in the financial sector and in foreign currency markets. Inflation decelerated, but remained sizable. At the beginning of 2010, with a real recovery under way and inflation returning to its pre-recession levels, the behavior and the institutional status of monetary policies became the subject of strong controversies. The episode signaled vividly that basic characteristics of the setup and implementation of macroeconomic policies remained in debate.

We propose to analyze the post-convertibility macroeconomic experience focusing mainly on inflation and the associated policies and behaviors. After a rapid review of the rise and breakdown of the convertibility regime, Section 19.2 sketches briefly the macroeconomic evolution of the post-crisis period, and discusses features of the interaction between private and policy decisions. In section 19.3 we then consider in more detail the behavior of monetary policies, with comments about the characteristics of price changes, especially in terms of the magnitude and persistence of inflation rates, and about the 'reaction function' of the central bank. Finally Section 19.4 includes a discussion of tradeoffs involved in the choice of macroeconomic policies and institutions for Argentina.

One of the themes running through the discussion is that the memory of very diverse past experiences, including episodes of prosperity and others of extreme economic instability, has left traces in behaviors, beliefs and attitudes towards policies. The eventful history brought about learning by private and government agents, but it also produced open-ended controversies and conflicts. The macroeconomic performance after the convertibility crisis was remarkable for the increase in real activity together with current-account and (until recently) fiscal surpluses. However, the search for a macroeconomic regime that would broaden decision horizons to support a robust growth trend did not converge to policy criteria that were well-defined, and generally agreed upon. In this sense, the post-crisis period represented an unfinished transition in terms of the behavior of private agents and both the political economy and the 'technical' aspects of policy choices (see Gerchunoff and Aguirre, 2005). The reappearance of inflation as a widespread concern was a prominent symptom of these conditions.

19.2 MACRO DEVELOPMENTS: CRISIS, RECOVERY, TRENDS AND UNCERTAINTIES

19.2.1 Convertibility: High Expectations and Collapse

The introduction of the convertibility monetary regime in 1991 was a key element of a package of comprehensive policy reforms which included trade and financial liberalizations and large-scale privatizations. The monetary system established as a fixed nominal anchor the exchange rate with the US dollar, a highly visible variable which had become a standard reference for denominating contracts, and even for setting some prices, while establishing a set of tight rules that restricted discretion and flexibility in monetary management, and were meant to discipline fiscal policies by cutting their access to central-bank finance. Fixing the external parity for the indefinite future signaled the intention of bringing inflation down to international levels through a once-and-for-all institutional change without an 'exit strategy'.

The first years of the system were marked by a sharp growth in real activity and (even more) in domestic demand, which supported a considerable increase in domestic prices. Despite this substantial shift in the price level, residual inflation did not persist, but steadily declined over

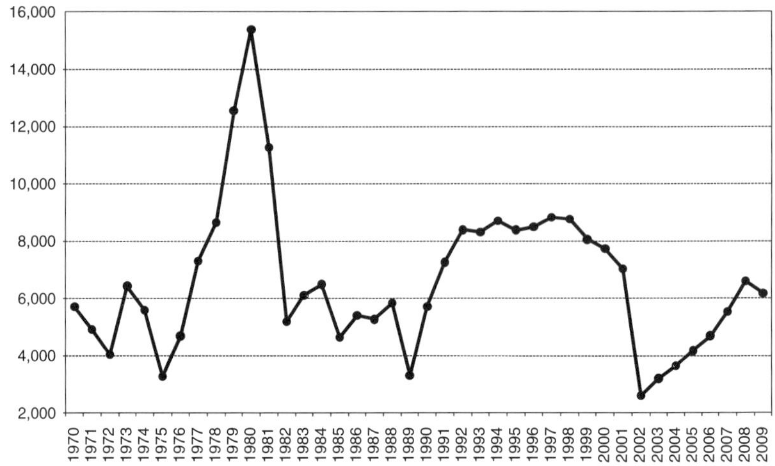

Figure 19.2 Argentine GDP per capita at constant prices (dollars of 2000).

time to practically complete stability after about 3 years. In any case, the accumulated real exchange rate revaluation pushed the dollar value of aggregate incomes and expenditures to historically high levels (although not as extraordinarily high as in the early 1980s, before the debt crisis of that decade – Figure 19.2). The sharp rise in domestic spending, supported by a rapid credit expansion, was associated with the emergence of current-account deficits. Higher tax (and privatization) revenues contributed to a large decline in budget deficits, and the government restructured its debts after a decade of non-performance. However, after a while the public sector started to demand considerable volumes of financing, in a context where government bond issues were often considered optimistically as a sign of confidence by creditors.

Although peso–dollar interest rate differentials did not indicate strong fears about the short-run sustainability of the exchange rate peg, most of the new financial obligations, as well as key contracts in different areas of the economy, ranging from privatized utilities to rents, were denominated in US dollars. Credit was offered at rates which certainly carried risk premiums, but the observed willingness to lend and to borrow seemed to respond to expectations that future levels of 'permanent income' in terms of the dollar would satisfy the conditions for overall solvency of debtors, private and public. This meant an implicit trust in a strong performance of the supply of tradable goods and favorable international conditions, which would make sustainable the level of the real exchange rate (Galiani et al., 2003). In addition, the mass of dollar debts endogenously raised the social costs of a real depreciation, whether through a rise of the nominal exchange rate or through price deflation.

Between 1993 and 1998 the value of exports doubled, an impulse derived from a remarkable improvement of agricultural productivity, good external prices and a strong demand from Brazil which was reflected especially in industrial exports. After a dramatic but short pause triggered by the international financial turmoil following the 1994 Mexican devaluation, growth restarted. But the levels of foreign and domestic debts also kept increasing. When, by the end of the decade, exports stagnated (influenced by the Brazilian depreciation and lower commodity prices) and the supply of foreign credit contracted, serious issues of sustainability emerged, and gained prominence over time. The economy was locked into a situation where external adjustment through recession and deflation, apart from their painful effects, threatened to reveal the existence of widespread solvency problems, while a 'preemptive' ending of convertibility would have implied, at a stroke, not only a requirement to redefine the whole set of economic policies after a strong shock to expectations, but also the need to process the effects of that frustration on incomes, solvency positions and the feasibility to fulfill public and private obligations. Some influential opinions carried the fear of devaluation to the point of proposing outright dollarization. But giving up the very existence of a national currency could hardly have solved the problems of external adjustment and made debtors able to honor their dollar obligations. In practice, after quite a long period (about 3 years) of economic decline and growing financial and fiscal deterioration (which included the issue of quasi-moneys by provincial governments), the convertibility regime ended with a bang in December 2001, in the midst of a run against bank deposits and the foreign reserves, a sharp recession, public unrest and a political crisis.

19.2.2 Financial Breakdown, but No Hyperinflation

The exit from convertibility immediately posed the problem of dealing with outstanding financial contracts. The government declared default on its bonds, and decided to redenominate in pesos the existing dollarized bank loans and deposits (at different conversion rates: 1 and 1.4, respectively). This brought about a considerable real reduction in the debts of firms and individuals. The application of dollar clauses in utility prices was suspended. Most non-bank obligations (including the external debts of many firms) were opened for renegotiation. Thus, practically the whole structure of assets and liabilities of the economy was formally put

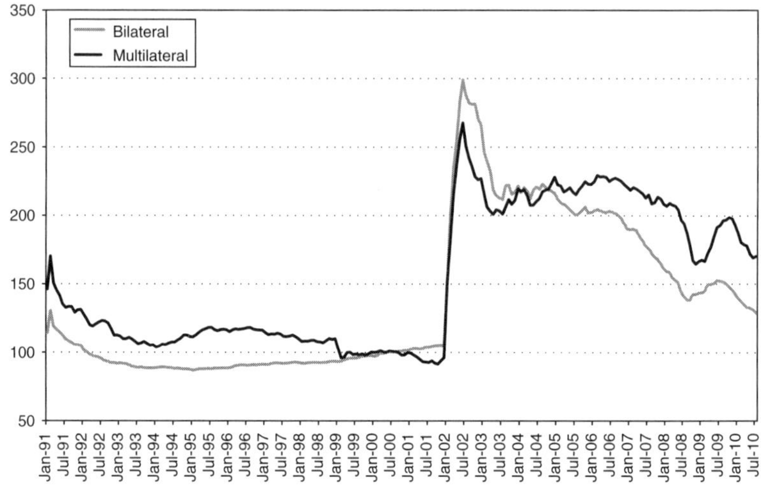

Figure 19.3 Argentina: multilateral and dollar real exchange rate (indices 2000 = 100).

into question. Naturally, this was associated with loud controversies and strong uncertainties.

The rush of the public to buy foreign exchange, only partially limited by the restrictions imposed on the withdrawal of deposits from the banks, was reflected in a steep depreciation once the central bank stopped defending the one-to-one dollar parity. By June 2002, the exchange rate reached a level of about 4 pesos per dollar. Considering the inflationary experience of the previous decades, the moderation of the price response to such a shock was quite striking. The inflation rate over the whole of 2002 was 40 per cent, with a monthly peak of 10 per cent in April, and a noticeable slowdown in the second part of the year. Thus, the real depreciation was of a very large magnitude (Figure 19.3).

In a situation of extreme social tension and economic disruption, the first reactions of people engaging in everyday transactions after the collapse of the currency board were still characterized by a general use of the local currency as the unit of account of prices for current consumption goods, and as the means of payment. The absence of those symptoms of flight from money was possibly a sign that, despite the state of deep distrust in economic policies and the reluctance to hold domestic assets, the memory of the recent experience of price stability carried more weight in the routine exchanges in goods and labor markets than the recollections of past episodes of high inflation. Such a response implied that nominal wage and price decisions were dominated by the depression in the demand

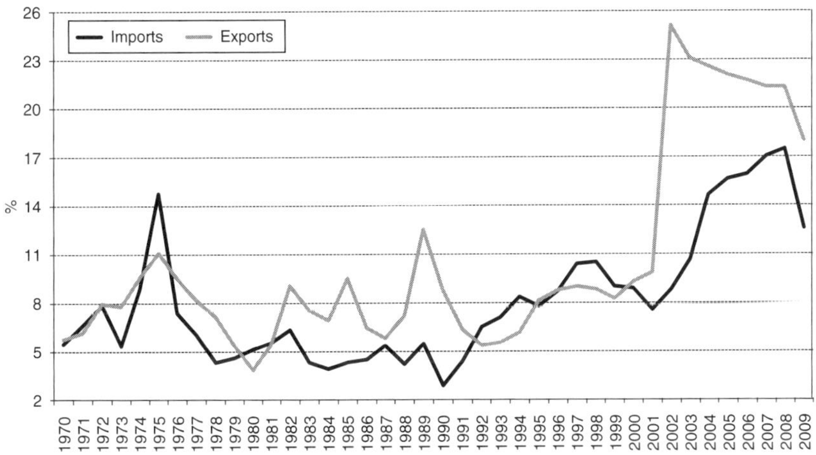

Figure 19.4 Argentine export and import coefficients at current prices (percentages of GDP).

for goods and labor: no strong pressures emerged to revise nominal wages and, even if the rise in the cost of imported goods and the incentives to build up precautionary margins over costs operated on price decisions, the response of inflation was not immediate, but showed some delay.

These behaviors provided some, even if narrow, room for maneuver for economic policies to act. The vivid fear, felt across the political spectrum, of a 'perfect storm' with a hyperinflation as well as a financial collapse was a strong incentive to avoid fiscal deficits which would require monetary financing for a government which had definitely lost its access to voluntary credit.

The sharp rise in the real exchange rate implied a jump in the domestic purchasing power of exports, and it also revalued the substantial mass of foreign assets held by residents (Figures 19.4 and 19.5). This had effects on both public and private finances. From the government's perspective, large changes in the structure of income and expenditure flows at current prices also modified the relative magnitude of potential tax bases. After some time, export taxes were introduced; along with the drop in the value of real public spending (mainly through a fall in real wages in the public sector; see Figure 19.6), this allowed cash revenues and expenditures to (precariously) balance each other. Exporters were required to liquidate foreign exchange with small delays; the supply of foreign currencies through the large trade surplus and through official interventions stopped the depreciation despite the still large size of the capital flight. From the perspective of private behaviors, consumption and investment decisions of high-income groups came to be noticeably influenced by the revaluation of

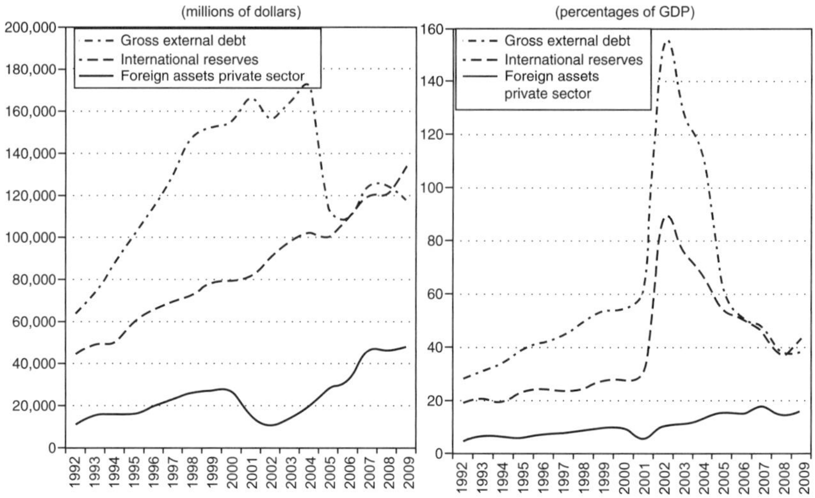

Figure 19.5 Argentine foreign assets and liabilities.

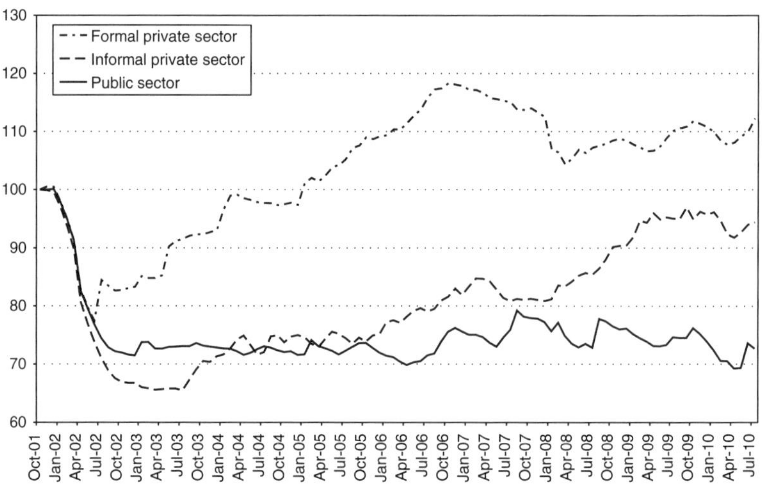

Figure 19.6 Argentine real wages (indices IV 2001 = 100).

foreign assets they held abroad, which generated a mass of available and liquid purchasing power that could self-finance spending in an economy where credit had frozen.

Once it became apparent that a runaway depreciation was unlikely, expectations of a complete crash abated, and the potential propaga-

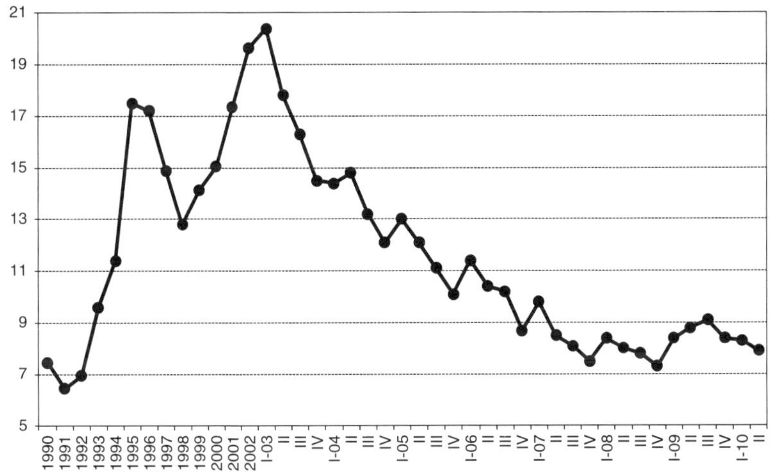

Figure 19.7 Argentine urban unemployment rate (percentages).

tion mechanisms of recent price increases did not become active. By the end of 2002, real GDP had fallen by about 20 per cent from its peak; its dollar purchasing power had been reduced to around a third of its previous values; the unemployment rate reached 25 per cent (Figure 19.7), poverty levels had shot up to around 50 per cent of the population, but the conditions for a recovery were emerging.

19.2.3 A Recovery with Unusual Features

The depression of domestic demand in the first half of 2002 resulted from a combination of effects which included a complete standstill of credit, a monetary circulation disturbed by frequent banking holidays decided by the authorities in order to deal with the threat of runs (although few financial institutions actually went bankrupt), and by restrictions on the availability of cash out of deposits; a drastic fall in real wages; and an attitude of strong precaution on the part of agents with liquid assets, which fueled the private capital flight. At the same time, a revival of expectations, however doubtful or tenuous, which induced some spending out of dollar incomes or asset holdings, was apt to have a strong real impact at the prevailing relative prices. When the movement started, the incipient symptoms of normalization (in a still very disturbed economy) became self-reinforcing. As real activity started to recover, so did tax revenues on domestic activities. Growing primary surpluses in the public sector strengthened the perception that the depreciation of the currency had

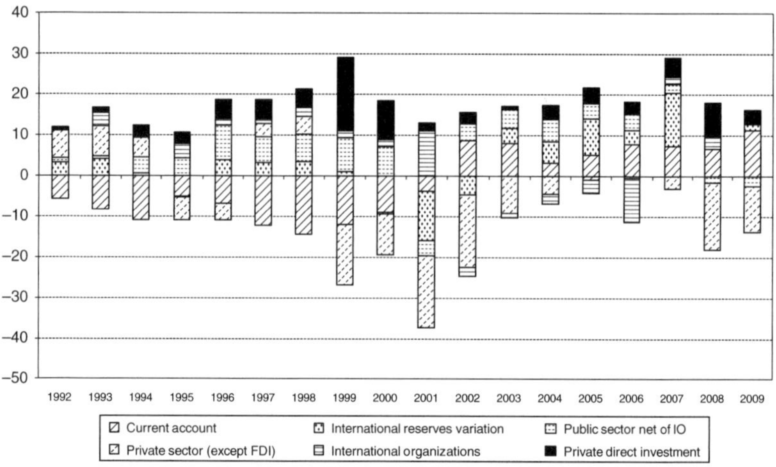

Figure 19.8 Argentine current account and capital flows (billions of dollars).

gone beyond sustainable levels. A strong excess supply of foreign currencies developed in some time. This started a long period during which the external constraint was not operative as a brake on the economy (Figures 19.4 and 19.8), a feature that sharply contrasted with the pattern observed in past phases of economic growth.

The expansion of real activity following the crisis was not an ordinary rebound in a stop–go cycle. Contrary to many expectations,[2] the growth phase was unusually sharp and long-lived and, after accounting for the recovery effect, it resulted in a peak-to-peak (1998–2008) average rate of increase of GDP of about 3 per cent per year. A noticeable feature of the period was the positive sign of the current-account balance, reflecting sizable trade surpluses, and smaller services on foreign debts resulting from renegotiations. In particular, the public sector performed in 2005 an operation of restructuring, with substantial reductions in capital or interest rates, which was accepted by the holders of about three-quarters of the bonds previously in circulation; the (not complete but very significant) normalization of the status of the debt was reflected in a sharp fall in the 'country risk' interest rate differentials (Figures 19.9 and 19.10), although the government's access to credit remained restricted.

The value of exports more than doubled in an interval of 6 years (2002–08). The very favorable evolution of international prices made a large contribution (Figure 19.11), but there were also sizable increases in the volumes of exports of agricultural and industrial goods. Production of grains reached a peak in the 2007/08 campaign, about 50 per cent above

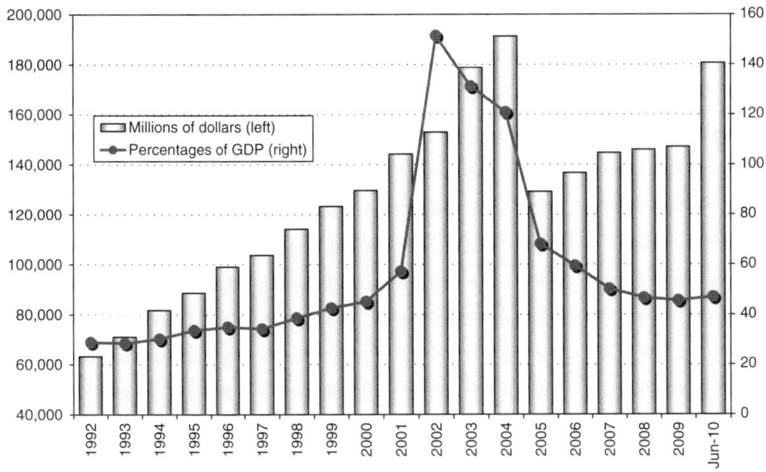

Figure 19.9 *Argentine national public sector debt (millions of dollars and percentages of GDP).*

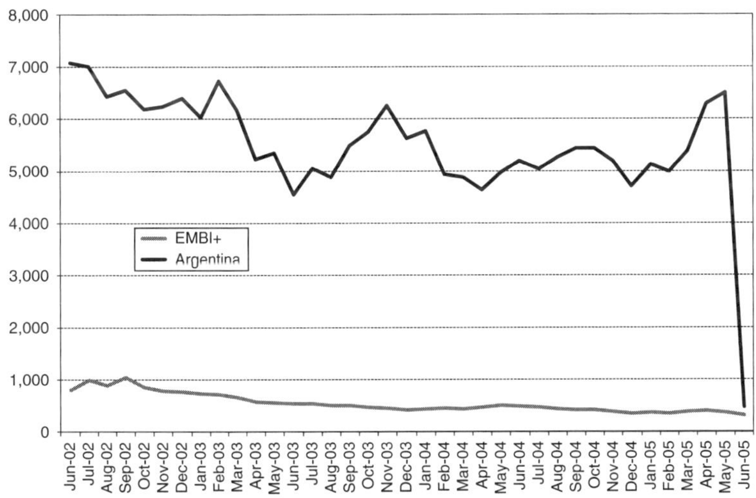

Figure 19.10 *Interest rate spreads on Argentine government bonds (basis points) June 2002 to June 2005.*

the output recorded 5 years earlier. Much higher international terms of trade, after a sharp rise in the weight of exports in GDP, had a considerable impact on the purchasing power of domestic incomes, which rose even faster than real output. Comparatively high domestic savings amply

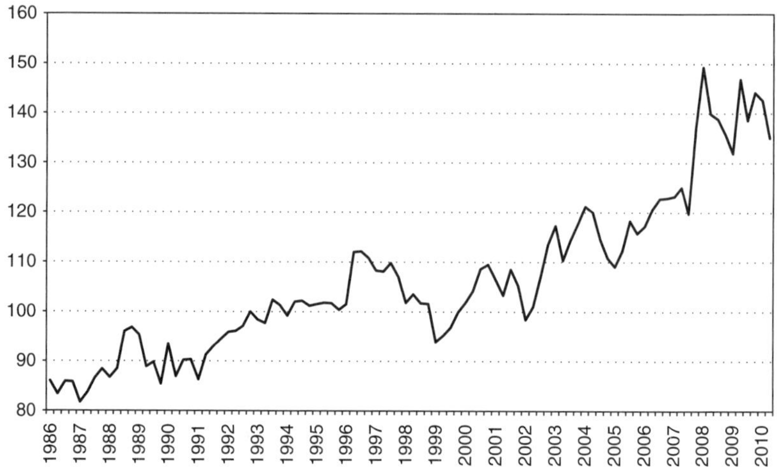

Figure 19.11 *Argentina: international terms of trade (indices 1993 = 100).*

exceeded investment (Figure 19.12), which rose sharply from very low values to levels (about 23 per cent of GDP at constant prices in 2008) higher than the maxima of the previous decade. The growth rate of the capital stock recovered noticeably (from negative levels in the crisis), but remained smaller than the rise in aggregate output. Thus, by 2008, the capital/output ratio was lower than in the cyclical peak 10 years earlier (Figure 19.13).

On the fiscal front, the rapid evolution of tax revenues allowed the government to maintain budget surpluses between 2003 and 2008, despite the strong increase in expenditures (Figures 19.14, 19.15; see also Figure 19.24). Consolidated primary public spending as a share of GDP rose 8.1 points in that period (after a fall of about 5 points in the crisis) and an additional 3.2 points in 2009, reaching historical highs. From the point of view of the incentives perceived by the government, maintaining a slack in its budget constraint seemed an important consideration because it reduced the influence of the potentially unfriendly moods and attitudes in international financial markets, and because it generated political leverage from the availability of resources to manage and to distribute. However, in the last years of the decade, the fiscal balance declined, and the government showed increasing interest in reopening international markets for its debt, in particular through a new debt swap implemented in 2010 with bonds that had not been included in the previous restructuring.

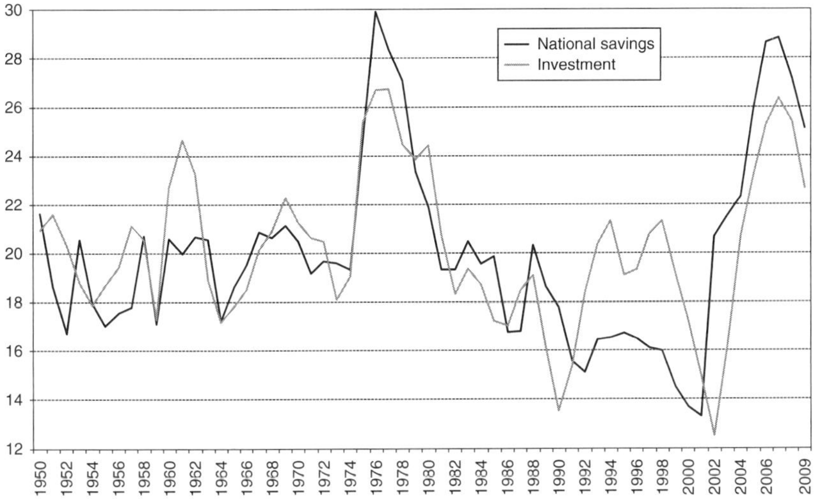

Source: Coremberg et al. (2007).

Figure 19.12 Argentine national savings and investment at current prices (percentages of GDP).

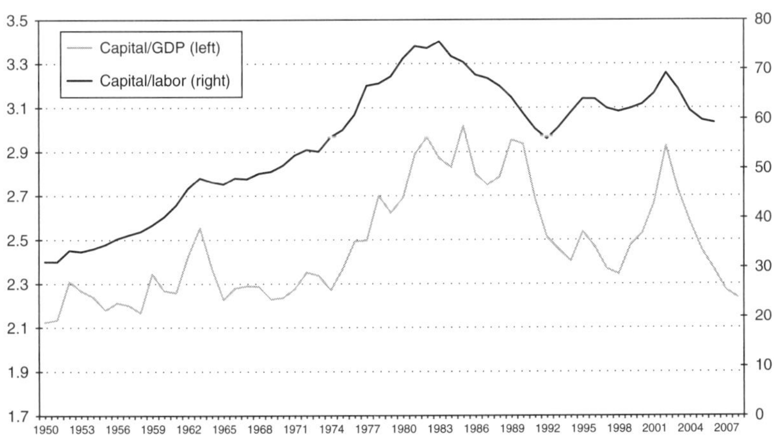

Source: Coremberg et al. (2007).

Figure 19.13 Argentine capital /GDP and capital / labor ratios (units of GDP and pesos of 1993 per worker).

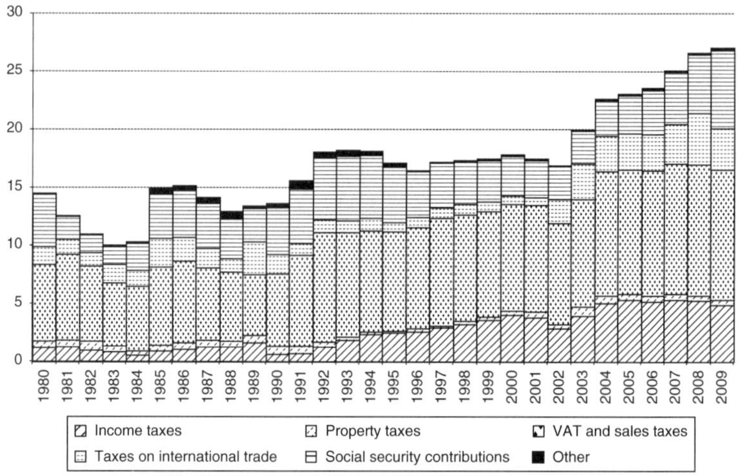

Figure 19.14 Argentine national tax revenues (percentages of GDP).

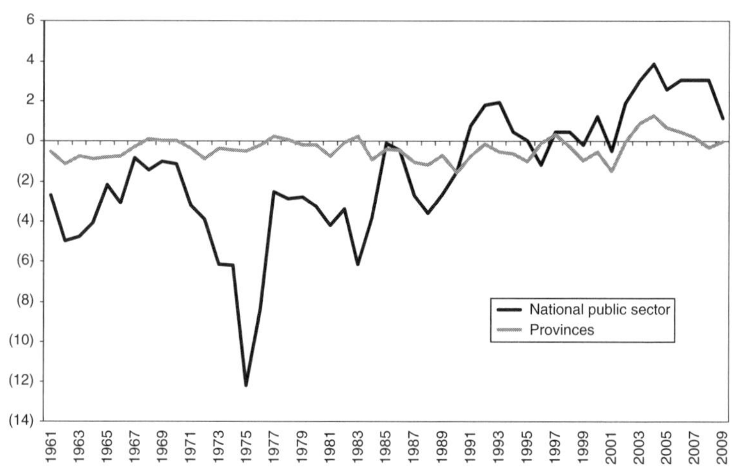

Figure 19.15 Primary budget balance – Argentine public sector (percentages of GDP).

19.2.4 Monetary Policies After the Crisis

The collapse of the convertibility regime left a strong imprint in attitudes regarding the design and implementation of macroeconomic policies, with a marked shift against tight rules and presumably unconditional pre-commitments. The dramatic ending of a period of foreign deficits in a resounding default made it hard to maintain that monetary policies should be unconcerned with current-account sustainability, and concentrate only on the management of nominal prices. The experience also led to a marked concern for avoiding real overvaluations of the currency and to an emphasis on the real exchange rate as an instrument for economic growth (see for example Frenkel and Rapetti, 2009; Rodrik, 2008). As was the case in other economies, the role of foreign reserves as self-insurance against shocks was highlighted (see Bastourre et al., 2009), with particular strength because of the unfavorable perception of the behavior of the IMF before and during the crisis, and the perspective of a tightly constrained supply of private external credit.

Monetary policies after the crisis were based on an analysis which stressed that foreign exchange rate variability (especially downwards) should be kept within relatively narrow bounds, and that the uncertainties about the transmission mechanisms of monetary policies with a small and still fragile financial sector would greatly complicate the administration of an interest-rate-based monetary policy. The central bank implemented a 'managed floating' of the dollar exchange rate, which, after being allowed to fall to around 2.8 pesos in 2003 was left to oscillate for several years near a value of 3. The authorities did not make formal announcements on the exchange rate, and their monetary programs tended to have relatively low public visibility. This marked a strong difference from the convertibility system, which was meant to act as a central economic institution with high prominence in public perceptions. However, the notion that the central bank was in a position to regulate the dollar parity, and would prevent substantial drifts, became established as an element of private decisions. Until 2008, the exchange rate policy was associated with large purchases of foreign currencies by the central bank. The monetary effect of that intervention was sterilized to a significant extent by a contraction in lending to the government, by the cancellation of credits granted to the financial sector (rediscounts and swaps) and by the sale of central-bank promissory notes, which reached a particularly large volume in 2005 and 2006 (Figure 19.16).

Monetary expansion was considerable, although it did not result from the financing of budget deficits. The real demand for liquid assets was raised by the sharp growth of real activity and by a gradual revival of the willingness of the public to hold bank deposits, after the dramatic shock to confidence due to the crisis. In the immediate aftermath of the crisis, this process of remonetization was reflected in an increase of the ratios between monetary aggregates and GDP, a pattern also observed in the aftermath of other episodes of financial disturbance (Carrera and Lanteri, 2007). Subsequently, money growth rates were more or less matched by those

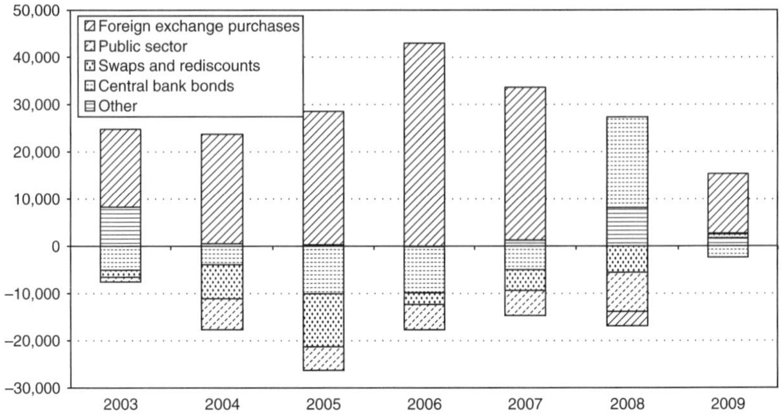

Figure 19.16 Determinants of changes in the Argentine monetary base (millions of pesos).

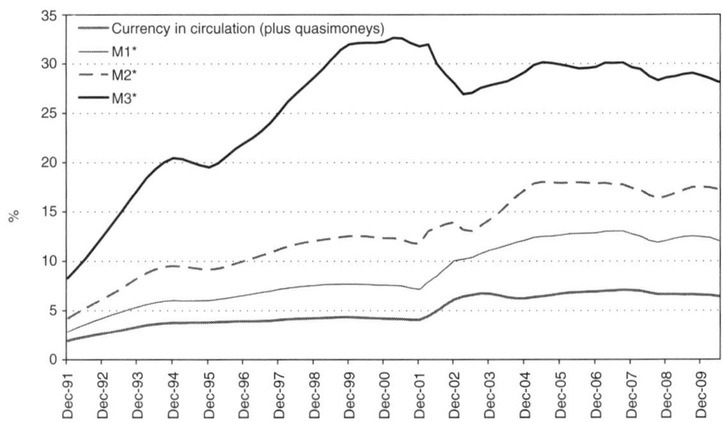

Note: Aggregates defined as follows. M1* = currency plus current accounts; M2* = M1* plus savings accounts; M3* = M2* plus time deposits and others. Holdings of private and public sectors, pesos and US dollars (denoted by *).

Figure 19.17 Argentine monetary aggregates (percentages of GDP, four-quarter moving averages).

of nominal GDP, until the emergence of financial tensions by the end of the decade, shown in some reductions in liquidity ratios (Figure 19.17). Overall, seignorage represented a nontrivial volume of resources (with maxima of about 4.5 per cent of GDP in 2003 and 3 per cent in 2006);

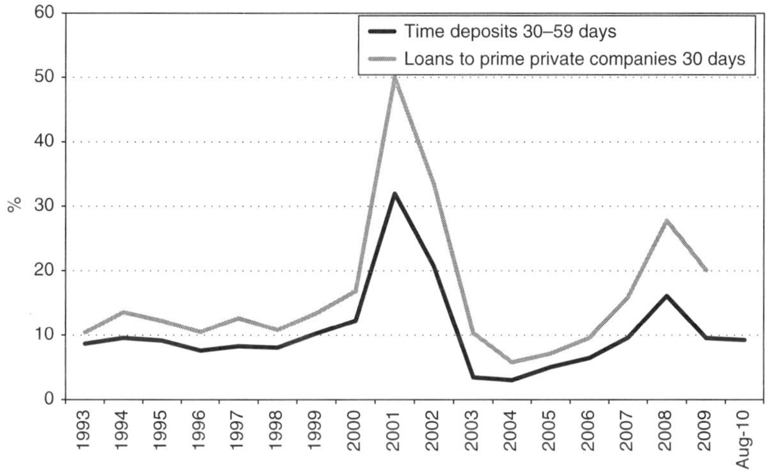

Figure 19.18 Peso interest rates end of year (percentages).

the 'inflation tax' on the monetary base reached sizable levels in 2007–09 (about 2 per cent of GDP on average). However, until 2008 most of the profits of the central bank were capitalized, and the resources derived from money creation used in the accumulation of reserves.

The large growth in production and demand after the crisis was self-financed to a good extent. The mobilization of large hoards of foreign currencies accumulated by the private sector was an important element in the initial revival of spending and, over time, in the expansion of activities such as construction. The financing requirements of firms were limited by debt reductions, and by the increases in unit margins as prices grew well above costs (especially those of labor) in the crisis. The volume of bank loans recovered sharply over the years, but to quite low levels relative to GDP (only about 12.5 per cent in 2008), and despite the growth of other credit vehicles (trust funds, in particular) the financial sector as a whole remained very small. However, there was no surge of excess demand for credit and, overall, no pressure on interest rates. As an indicator of this behavior, after 2003 the returns on time deposits (Figure 19.18) remained below the inflation rate.

19.2.5 Rising Inflation After a Slow Start

The expansion in real activity began in 2002 from a state of widespread and large sub-utilization of resources[3] (see Figures 19.6 and 19.11), and with prices generally set with high markups over costs; in addition, the

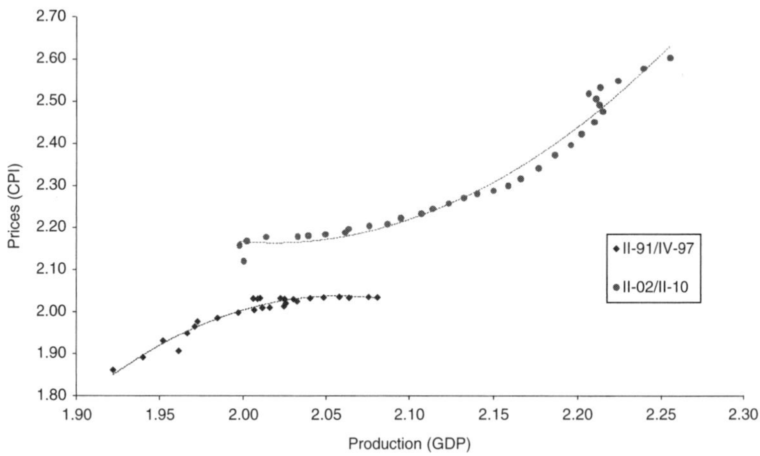

Figure 19.19 Argentine prices (CPI) and production (GDP) (log indices 1993 = 100 and polynomial trends).

exchange rate declined in nominal terms after its initial jump, and expectations did not include another round of depreciation. These conditions favored an elastic quantity response as aggregate spending recovered. Actually, taking as the origin the moment where the nominal exchange rate stopped rising in 2002, the economic response in the first phase of this expansion showed a less steep price–quantity schedule than in the analogous stage of the convertibility program, beginning in 1991(Figure 19.19). In 2003, the annual CPI inflation rate stayed below 4 per cent. The realization of such a low inflation shortly after the breakdown of the monetary system which was often perceived in its time as the barrier between stability and hyperinflation was a remarkable feature of economic performance. However, the rates of price increases grew gradually but noticeably in the following years, reaching about 20 per cent in 2007–10 (Figure 19.20).

The configuration of relative prices emerging from the crisis, with a very high real exchange rate and low real wages, left much room for a recovery of the dollar purchasing power of domestic prices and wages. At a more or less constant nominal exchange rate, kept from falling through the intervention of the central bank, the rise in internal demand stimulated internal price and wage adjustments. Wages in the formal private sector rose by around 20 per cent annually between 2005 and 2008; in the first 2 of those years, that implied a sizable increase in their purchasing power (see Figure 19.6).

The CPI grew over 12 per cent in 2005, suggesting that prices were

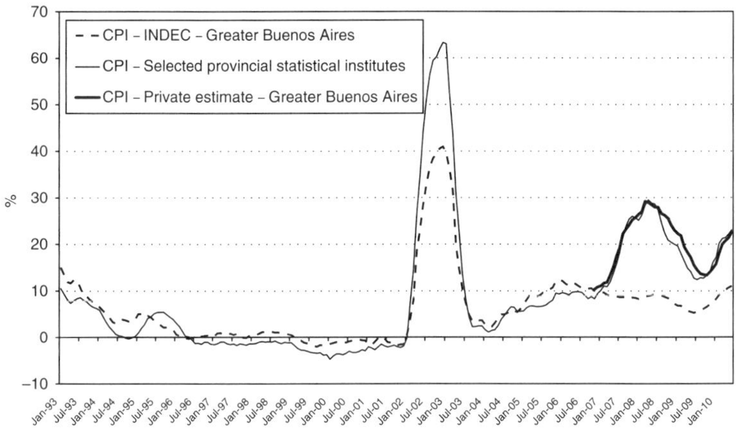

Notes: Selected provincial institutes include Chubut, Entre Ríos, La Pampa, Misiones, Neuquén, Salta and San Luis. Private estimates from Buenos Aires City – Finance and Economics (at www.bsas-city.com.ar).

Figure 19.20 Argentine inflation rates (year-on-year changes in selected indices).

becoming more sensitive to upward impulses, and raising questions about the possibility that inflation could gather momentum. The setting of a floor for the nominal appreciation of the currency was a particularly crucial choice in the aftermath of the 2002 crisis; the new decision node concerned the role of monetary and fiscal policies in the regulation of aggregate demand and the evolution of the price level. Policy discussions contemplated the possibility of using those instruments to moderate the steep rise in aggregate spending (Figure 19.21), and to favor a convergence to a somewhat slower expansion of real activity, considering that this would be in line with a likely trend after a period of steep recovery. The authorities decided against this alternative, with the view that a strong increase in demand would induce a corresponding response of investment and supply, and contribute to keep the economy growing at the very high growth rates achieved so far, implying that no deceleration was advisable. The underlying analysis seemed to be that, given the slow movements in the exchange rate and the surpluses in the fiscal accounts, aggregate inflation should be treated as a collection of individual price increases, without being much influenced by actual or expected demand. In addition to suggesting informal wage guidelines, the government then chose to act through measures intended to operate directly on the behavior of price-setters and, in the case of exportable wage goods, to redirect their

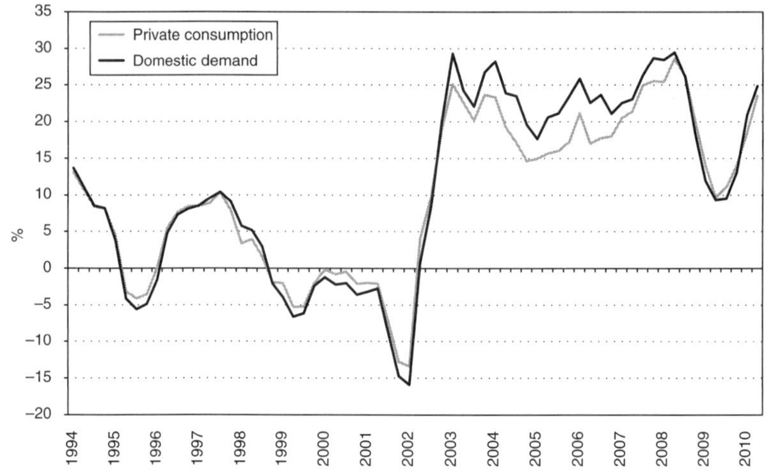

Figure 19.21 Argentina: private consumption and total domestic demand at current prices (annual rates of change).

supply to the domestic market. Large firms or business associations were exhorted to contain price rises and reduce profit margins, and export restrictions were applied on goods such as beef and wheat. In addition, the government granted subsidies, particularly to public utilities, mainly transportation and electricity (a sector where there had been signs of strains in satisfying the demand), and to various food-producing activities. Over time, such subsidies reached a considerable volume (around 3 per cent of GDP).

Along with a growth of GDP which again approached 9 per cent, the inflation rate fell some points in 2006, to around 10 per cent. By the end of the year, however, prices were accelerating again, with signs of a new push at the start of 2007. At this point, the government modified the procedures used in calculating the CPI.

Until 2007, the measurement of macroeconomic indicators and particularly the consumer price index had not emerged as an issue in public debates. It later became a matter of high visibility, with political as well as economic connotations. The government made changes in the personnel of the statistical institute (INDEC) and in the methods used in gathering and processing the data, in order to revise what they considered exaggerated estimates of inflation. (Some statements attributed potential overestimates to purposeful maneuvers in order to favor creditors on indexed financial instruments, particularly government bonds; others pointed to a presumed 'plutocratic bias' in CPI measurement, that overrepresented high-and middle-income consumption items in the goods basket used in the index). The official data showed a slowdown of inflation to 8.5 per cent in 2007 (including such striking features as an absolute drop of 11 per cent in the prices of tourism services over the year). Calculations made by official statistical agencies of some provinces, as well as by private institutions, showed much larger figures (see Figure 19.20). Discrepancies persisted in the following years, when the official national estimates remained well below those of alternative sources. According to INDEC, the total increase of the CPI between 2006 and 2009 was just over 25 per cent (averaging 8 per cent per year); in private measurements which tried to mimic the pre-2007 methodologies, the analogous variation was near 80 per cent (21 per cent per annum).[4] Naturally, those differences impinged on the estimates of indicators like the real exchange rate and measures of the purchasing power of incomes.

From the point of view of the methodological consistency and the economic significance of the information, the INDEC data under question appear as lacking reliability (see Academia Nacional de Ciencias Económicas, 2009). For the purposes of macroeconomic analysis it would seem preferable to use alternative measures, even when these are produced without the resources and the infrastructure of a national statistics institution. As for the behavior of economic agents, distrust in the official calculations, especially those related to inflation and real incomes, became widespread. In particular, no reference to the official price figures was used in wage negotiations, either on the labor or on the business side; even the government, when trying to influence the order of magnitude of wage increases, did not argue on the basis of the standard CPI series.

19.2.6 Conflicts, Shocks and Uncertainties, but No Crisis

The macroeconomic evolution in the last years of the decade was marked by successive shocks, of external and domestic origin. Its discussion thus requires using relatively short timeframes in order to describe the observed changes in behavior.

In a rapidly expanding economy, the inflation rate in 2007 probably reached over 20 per cent. The adjustments in the exchange rate and in public utility prices were of much smaller magnitude. The rise in the international price of exports, which had been a feature of the period since the crisis, accelerated sharply in that year and in the first part of the next one. The repercussions of the jump in world agricultural and food prices, felt as an inflationary factor in numerous economies, took a particular form in Argentina, where it triggered a deep political controversy about the appropriation of the income effect of the improvement in the terms

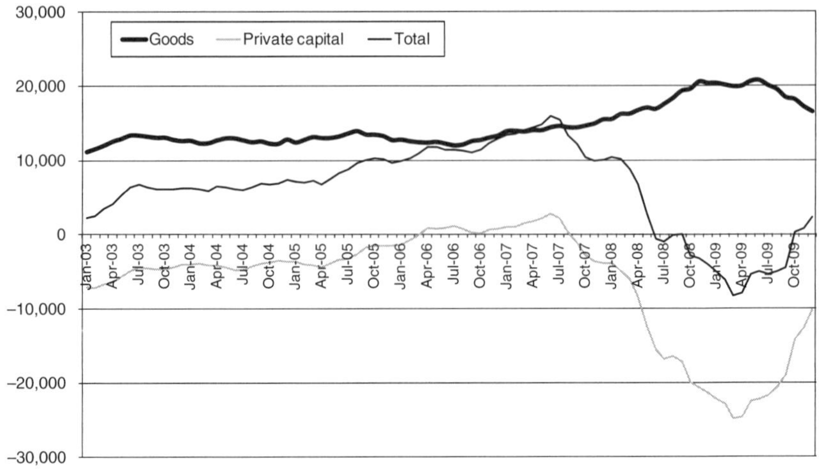

Figure 19.22 Net foreign exchange transactions – Argentine private sector (millions of dollars over 12-month periods).

of trade. In March 2008, the government decided to implement a mobile scale (contingent on international prices) of export duties for soybeans (previously set at a 35 per cent rate), which raised the levels of taxation on the main agricultural commodity, and opened the possibility of further tax increases. The measure provoked a strong reaction from farmers, and also from urban groups who perceived that their incomes were dependent on the expenditures of the agricultural sector. Eventually, the tax schedule went for parliamentary ratification, which was refused in a dramatic vote.

In 2007, the international financial crisis was felt in Argentina with a short-lived episode of stress in the banking system, and it probably had an influence in the accumulation of foreign assets by the private sector[5] (Figure 19.22). By mid 2008, the international shock was combined with the internal political and economic uncertainty caused by the conflict between the government and the farmers. This strengthened the private capital outflow, and led at some moments to net withdrawals of deposits from the banks. The central bank reacted, providing liquidity to the financial sector, particularly by redeeming large volumes of its promissory notes (see Figure 19.16), and it used reserves to satisfy the demand for foreign currencies; as a show of strength, it actually induced a fall in the exchange rate. Later in the year, however, with the worsening of the international situation associated with the Lehman episode, and the large devaluations of currencies like the Brazilian real, the exchange rate with the dollar was allowed to increase substantially, although always under a strong actual or potential intervention of the central bank in order to smooth the process of depreciation and its financial repercussions.

In the course of 2008 the fall in international commodity prices caused a fall in the terms of trade index from its recent peaks, although it still maintained historically high levels (see Figure 19.11). Domestic demand and real activity also weakened. In this setting, the government decided to increase its revenues by nationalizing the private pension system. Although the pension funds already held a good part of their portfolio (about 60 per cent) in public debt instruments, this measure implied that the government got direct access to a flow of funds of around 1 per cent of GDP, and received the transfer of a substantial stock of private and foreign assets, against its acquisition of new contingent obligations. The return to a state-managed pay-as-you-go system was not an unpopular action, and received parliamentary support. However, the measure caused fears in asset-holders, and led to another episode of financial stress.

The Argentine banking system reached the time of the international crisis with substantial levels of liquidity and without significant repayment difficulties on a mass of loans which was small relative to macroeconomic aggregates. The central bank had accumulated a large volume of foreign reserves. The fall in international demand and a steep decline in agricultural production (the result of reduced expectations of farmers and a severe drought) were reflected in a considerable drop in exports in 2009. The private sector continued to manifest a strong demand for foreign assets (Figure 19.22). However, the trade balance still showed a large surplus, as imports declined; the central bank could manage the foreign exchange market without much loss in reserves, and remained able to regulate the movements in the exchange rate. The perception that the depreciation of the currency would be kept within narrow bounds contributed to reducing the incentive for capital outflows in the course of the year. Thus, even if there was a noticeable slowdown in credit, and the banking system and the foreign currency markets went through periods of tension, these did not amount to crisis-like disruptions.

In any case, the economy experienced a recession in 2009 (Figure 19.23), with a somewhat lower inflation rate (about 15 per cent). The central bank slowed the depreciation with respect to the dollar, but the strengthening of other currencies meant that the multilateral exchange rate increased significantly. Tax collection was affected by the lower levels of domestic activity and foreign trade, while public spending kept rising fast. In spite of the addition to public revenues of the social security contributions previously paid into the pension funds and the inclusion as government receipts of items like an IMF allocation of SDRs and dividends transferred to the government by the central bank out of nominal gains on its

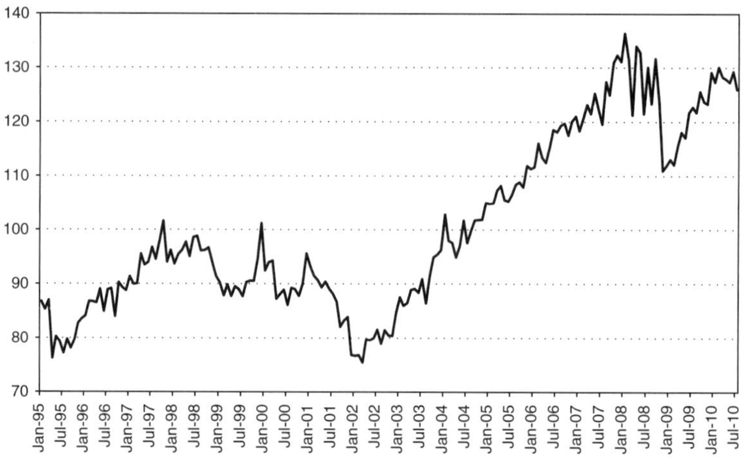

Source: FIEL, Indicadores de Coyuntura.

Figure 19.23 Argentine industrial production (indices 2004 = 100).

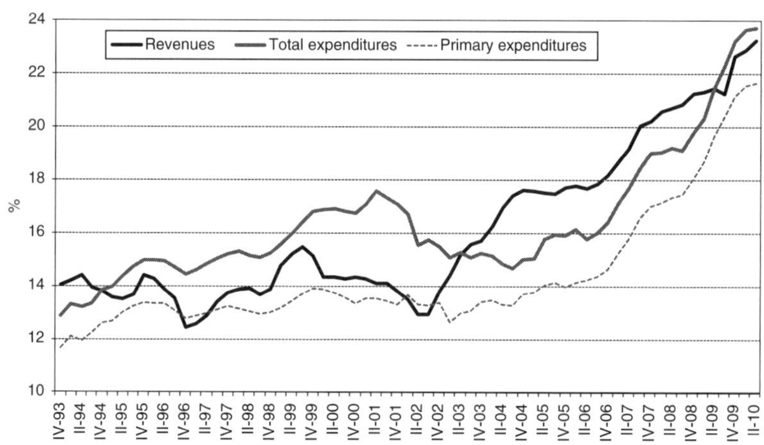

Figure 19.24 Revenues and expenditures – Argentine national public sector (percentages of GDP).

asset portfolio, the primary surplus dropped to about 1 per cent of GDP (Figures 19.24 and 19.25). There was certainly a sizable cyclical element in that fall; still, the trends of public finances were uncertain, particularly on the expenditure side. The 'country risk' differentials of returns on bonds (Figure 19.26), although much smaller than the high peaks in 2008,

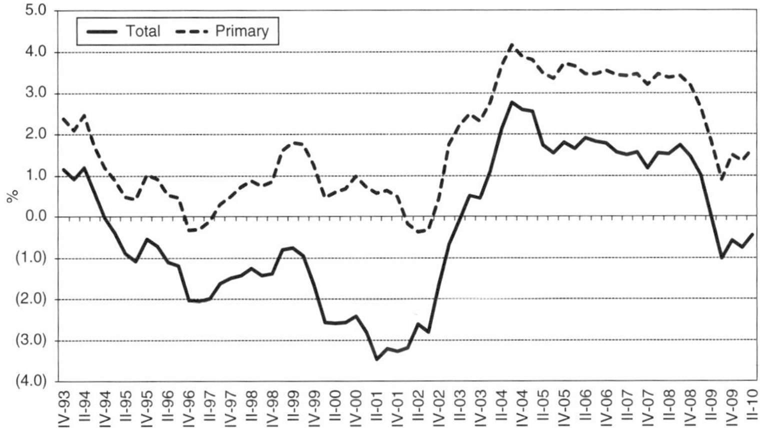

Figure 19.25 Budget balances – Argentine national public sector (percentages of GDP).

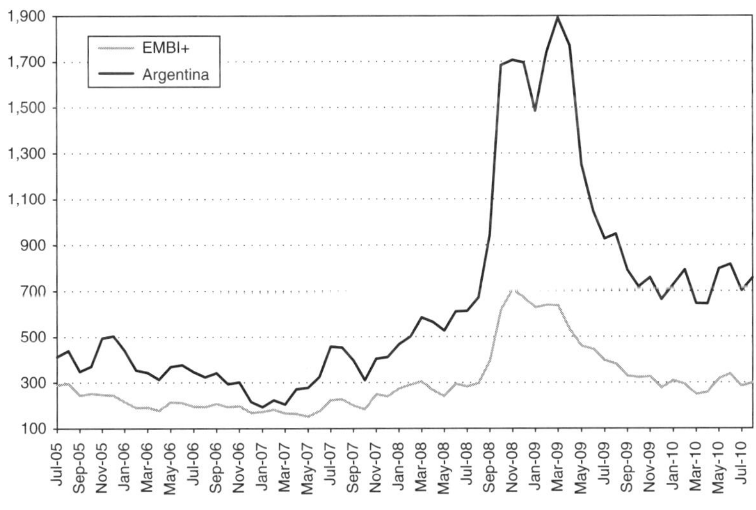

Figure 19.26 Interest rate spreads on Argentine government bonds (basis points) July 2005 to August 2010.

showed a reluctance of asset-holders to buy Argentine debt and, in practice, international credit markets were closed to the government. These conditions created the potential of funding problems for the public sector, given the significant volume of amortizations due in 2010. As a response, the government decided to indicate its intention to meet those payments by announcing the offer of a bond swap for the pre-crisis debt that had not been part of the 2005 restructuring operation ('holdouts') and decided to use central-bank reserves to constitute a fund that would guarantee debt services in 2010.

19.2.7 Economic Recovery, Higher Inflation, Monetary Institutions in Debate

The constitution of the debt-servicing fund drawn from central-bank reserves had economic and institutional implications. The government argued that those reserves had reached excessive levels for their precautionary purpose, and would be better used to reduce high-cost liabilities. In a moment where the fiscal position was perceived to be weakening, the proposed application of reserves as an urgent measure, in an international situation which did not show other countries facing tight liquidity constraints, could be interpreted either as an effective signaling device or as an emergency reaction of a financially stressed government. In the event, news about the debt swap and the availability of reserves for debt servicing raised the prices of government bonds. Yet the decree ordering the transfer of reserves from the central bank to the treasury raised legal issues, which generated political and judiciary controversies; the same happened with the removal of the president of the central bank, who opposed that transfer of funds.

Real activity recovered sharply in 2010, with several expansionary effects acting in conjunction. Better climate conditions favored an improved grain harvest (especially that of soybeans), which faced a sustained international demand. The economic growth of Brazil and other trade partners stimulated industrial exports. Domestic demand increased because of both the rapid rise in government expenditures and the sharp reaction of private spending. The trade surplus was reduced by the jump in imports, but remained sizable. The central bank managed the dollar exchange rate with a slow upward drift, at a rate much below expected inflation, and meanwhile accumulated reserves. The cyclical upswing, and the anticipation of a modest depreciation of the currency discouraged capital outflows, and made the perceived returns on the standard financial assets (dollar holdings, bank deposits) substantially negative in real terms, which fueled the demand for goods. Public finances were reinforced by quite larger tax revenues, although transfers from the central bank also reached a considerable volume.

The start of 2010 was marked by an acceleration of price increases, especially strong in foodstuffs such as beef (an item in short supply, as disincentives to livestock production had led to reductions in the size of the herd), but also reaching across the spectrum of goods. The possibility that inflation could take off, with higher volatility and a shortening of the periods of price and wage revisions, became a matter of public discussion and concern. With the exchange rate serving as a brake for price increases, the inflation rate evolved in 2010 with an order of magnitude of about 20 per cent, while expectations for the following year seemed to be set at somewhat higher levels.

19.3 PATTERNS OF PRICE PERFORMANCE AND MONETARY POLICIES

19.3.1 Changing Average Rates and Variability of Inflation; Persistence

The post-crisis experience we have reviewed shows, as two noticeable characteristics, that (1) the abrupt depreciation of the currency had a relatively small and transitory impact on the rate of price increase, so that the fears of relapse into a high inflation regime were far from realized, and (2) the post-depreciation response ended up not merely being a price level adjustment at gradually declining rates of increase, but rather taking the form of a low initial inflation, which rose over time to an inflation well into the two-digit range. Several empirical studies have analyzed the performance of prices after the collapse of convertibility and the initial shock of devaluation, and compared it with past episodes. In general terms, these works (which use data covering up to 2007, approximately – that is, do not include observations corresponding to the higher, end-of-decade inflation) tend to find that the price process had broad characteristics of a moderate or low inflation, but also some particularities that distinguished it from the previous period of extremely small or negative price changes.

In an analysis that considers the evolution of prices between 1980 and the first months of 2007, D'Amato et al. (2007) find that the data for the whole interval, going from stabilization under the currency board to the end of the series in the mid 2000s, 'belong together statistically' when compared with those for the rest of the period. These observations (which match with the visual impression in Figure 19.1) point to continuities in behavior before and after the crisis. This seems also the case with money – inflation correlations, which are similar in the convertibility regime and in the managed floating system, and of smaller magnitude at short lags than under high inflation (Basco et al., 2009). However, a look at the time series properties of inflation indicates that (leaving aside the 'abnormal' data for 2002), the rates of price increase were more autocorrelated after the breakdown of convertibility than before, while average inflation showed an upward drift (D'Amato et al., 2007).

Table 19.1 Argentina: inflation average and volatility in selected periods

	Monthly inflation	
	Mean	Standard deviation
1993:1–2001:12	0.00088	0.00403
2002:1–2002:9	0.03810	0.02616
2002:10–2006:12	0.00619	0.00420
2007:1–2010:6	0.01606	0.00664

In what follows, we update some of the results of these studies, with a view to complementing the analysis of the preceding section. When considering average inflation rates, the period since the mid 1990s can be decomposed in several distinct intervals: the about-zero-inflation period under convertibility, the devaluation shock in 2002, a period of price increases at moderate rates that lasted some years and, since 2007, an acceleration to levels around 20 per cent per annum. The variability of the inflation rate shows, as could be expected, an especially large amplitude in the post-devaluation transition; in addition, the rise in the inflation rate at the end of the sample came together with an increase in its standard deviation (Table 19.1).

Concerning inflation persistence, a naive first-order autoregressive equation estimated for monthly data over the whole period 1993–2010 has the following form (heteroskedasticity- and autocorrelation-consistent standard errors shown in parenthesis):[6]

$$\pi_t = \underset{(0.000640)}{0.001945} + \underset{(0.081089)}{0.716292}\pi_{t-1} + \varepsilon_t. \tag{19.1}$$

In a recursive estimation of the autoregressive coefficient (Figure 19.27), the parameter after the devaluation shock has a value higher than in the convertibility period. This is also shown in equation (19.2), which provides estimates of the coefficient for different subperiods, and indicates a stronger link between current and past inflation rates in the more recent observations.

$$\begin{aligned}\pi_t = \underset{(0.000462)}{0.001518} &+ \underset{(0.102957)}{0.241336}\pi_{t-1} + \underset{(0.134739)}{0.377577}\pi_{t-1}d2 \\ &+ \underset{(0.113186)}{0.582271}\pi_{t-1}d3 + \underset{(0.009112)}{0.027769}\,d1 + \varepsilon_t.\end{aligned} \tag{19.2}$$

However, the previous equations assume that, if inflation does not diverge, it moves back to a constant mean. This does not correspond to the evidence of the period under consideration. The specification shown in equation (19.3) allows for an error-correction behavior of the current

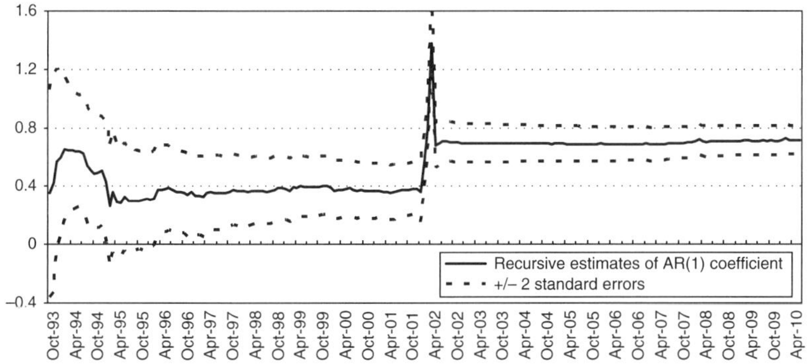

Note: dummy variables are defined as follows: *d*1, 2002:1–2002:9; *d*2, 2002:10–2006:12; *d*3: 2007:1–2010:6.

Figure 19.27 Argentina: recursive estimates of the autoregressive coefficient of inflation.

Table 19.2 Argentina: lagged inflation estimated parameters in selected periods

	Persistence estimates (equation 19.3)			
	Constant mean inflation		Variable mean inflation	
	ρ	Standard error (HAC)*	ρ	Standard error (HAC)*
1993:1–2010:6	0.84	0.078	0.24	0.119
1993:1–2001:12	0.39	0.171	0.36	0.158
2003:1–2010:6	0.93	0.054	0.42	0.107

Note: *HAC denotes standard errors robust to heteroskedasticity and autocorrelation.

inflation rate from its mean μ, whether constant or changing. If the equation is estimated (for the whole period: 1993: 1–2010: 6) while maintaining the assumption of a constant average inflation, the 'persistence' coefficient ρ indicates a value around 0.8, similar to that found in equation (19.1). Breaking the period in two parts shows a distinctly higher coefficient in the post-crisis times (Table 19.2).

$$\pi_t - \mu = \sum_{i=1}^{p-1} \varphi_i \Delta(\pi_{t-i} - \mu) + \rho(\pi_{t-1} - \mu) + \eta_t. \qquad (19.3)$$

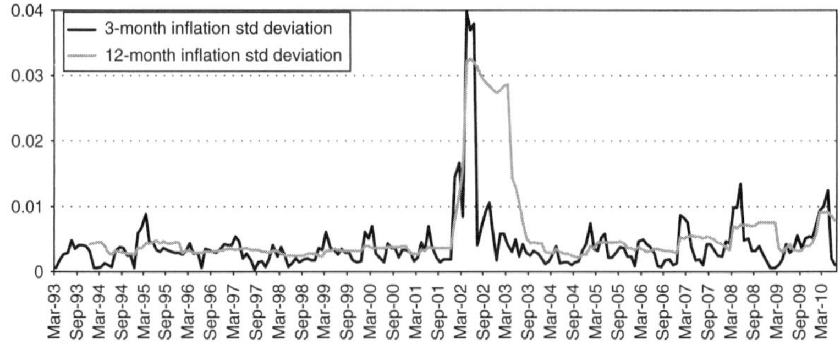

Figure 19.28 Argentina: inflation variability: 3- and 12-month windows.

In contrast, when the estimates distinguish between periods with different average inflation rates, the degree of persistence looks substantially smaller, reaching hardly more than 0.2 for the whole sample (Table 19.2). Thus, what seemed like a slower rate of decline of the effects of eventually transitory shocks may be interpreted as derived from shifts in the average value of inflation, while the observed 'return to the changing mean' now looks quite rapid. Nonetheless, this measure of persistence still shows a somewhat higher value when estimated only for the post-convertibility period.

The variability of inflation (measured with 3-month and 12-month windows) is depicted in Figure 19.28. It can be seen that, after the devaluation shock, the series went through a period of low volatility, but later showed spikes in the standard deviation of monthly rates, reaching about 1 percentage point (in the 12-month indicator) in 2008 and early 2010 (Figure 19.28).

This changing variability can be taken into consideration by estimating a GARCH model analogous to equation (19.2), once again for the whole convertibility and post-convertibility period:[7]

$$\pi_t = \underset{(0.000420)}{0.000993} + \underset{(0.124911)}{0.649487}\pi_{t-1} + \underset{(0.123132)}{0.264640}\pi_{t-1}d3 + \underset{(0.008161)}{0.032323}\,d1 + \varepsilon_t,$$

$$h_t = \underset{(2.34E-06)}{8.24E-06} + \underset{(0.159368)}{0.481017}\varepsilon^2_{t-1} + \underset{(0.121145)}{0.321306}h_{t-1}. \qquad (19.4)$$

Note: dummy variables are defined as follows: $d1$, 2002:1–2002:9; $d3$: 2007:1–2010:6.

This specification indicates both the increasing persistence and the higher variability of inflation since 2007. While the estimated autoregressive coefficient for the whole sample indicates a sizable degree of inflation being 'carried over' to the next period (just slightly below that found in the simple equation (19.1)), the interaction term $\pi_{t-1}d3$ shows an escalation of the effect toward the end of the sample; by contrast, the marginal effect of lagged inflation in the period 2003–06 is not found to be significant. In addition, in the post-crisis period the variance of inflation is positively influenced by the size of shocks to the level of the variable, while the estimated conditional variance grows noticeably over the period 2003–10. This suggests a connection between levels of inflation and diminishing precisions of forecasts (or, in this case, of measurements themselves).

19.3.2 Comovements of CPI Components

Using disaggregated CPI series that reach until 2006, Castagnino and D'Amato (2008) report that the whole period since the early 1990s shares (in comparison with the high inflation past) smaller comovements between the price changes of the different components of the CPI, while the aggregate rate of price growth (measured as the principal component of sectoral price increases) correlates more with the inflation rate of nontradable goods than with that of tradables (which was not the case in the high-inflation period of the 1980s). In the context of the macroeconomic evolution of the times, that feature marks a link, in both the convertibility and the immediate post-crisis periods, between inflation and real exchange rate appreciation, which may be interpreted as a nominal price-level adjustment to a relative price shift in systems with administered exchange rates. Still, there appear to be differences between the currency board and the managed floating regime: post-crisis data show more relative price variability (especially at higher frequencies), and a higher correlation between short-run relative price variability and inflation.

19.3.3 Simple Price Equations

Estimates of Phillips curves with the usual specification (including effects of past and expected inflation together with exchange rate and output gap factors) have found that both the 'backward-looking' inflation coefficient and that of the 'forward-looking' variable (proxied by the observed inflation rate in month $t + 1$) were higher under the managed floating exchange system than under the currency board, with a smaller parameter for the contemporaneous output gap in the later period (D'Amato and Garegnani, 2009). This would point towards a shift in persistence (which propagates the effect of the activity and exchange rate variables); the interpretation of the substantial 'expected inflation' term is less obvious, particularly given the way it is measured in the estimated equation.

In the calculations we have made extending the sample period to

Table 19.3 Phillips curve estimates (dependent variable: monthly inflation rate)

	1993:1–2010:6		1993:1–2001:12		2003:1–2010:6	
	Coefficient	Std error	Coefficient	Std error	Coefficient	Std error
Lagged inflation ($t-1$)	0.451628	0.049394	0.009794	0.044192	0.493032	0.057562
Expected inflation ($t+1$)	0.364043	0.060269	−0.135026	0.042508	0.479278	0.048462
Output gap	0.001346	0.000375	0.002327	0.000159	0.000585	0.000256
Lagged output gap ($t-1$)	−0.001224	0.000363	−0.002471	0.000161	-0.000543	0.000255
Nominal exchange rate depreciation, currency basket ($t-1$)	0.051241	0.011677	0.183197	0.016436	-0.008603	0.008562
Foreign inflation ($t-1$)	0.032594	0.011984	0.212624	0.021212	0.017513	0.072629
J-statistic	26,8477		22,4066		19,6506	

Note: Generalized method of moments estimation; instruments include lagged variables of regressors up to the twelfth lag. Variance–covariance matrix estimates are obtained using the Newey–West procedure (Bartlett kernel, fixed bandwith, 1 update of the weighting matrix). Output gap measured using the production function methodology.

incorporate recent data, the backward-and forward-looking components of the equation for the whole 1993–2010 interval add to a value of about 0.85; as found in other studies in Argentina and elsewhere, the estimated effect of the 'output gap' on inflation is relatively small (but positive), while the parameters of nominal depreciation and foreign inflation (both measured in trade-weighted terms vis-à-vis Argentina's trading partners) have the expected positive signs. Estimates look quite different in the convertibility and the post-convertibility (and post-shock) periods. Both the coefficients of past and future inflation are considerably higher, and significant, in 2003–10 than in 1993–2001 (Table 19.3). This suggests a 'trend-like' behavior of inflation in recent times, consistent with the previous narrative and with the findings in Subsection 19.3.1: in effect, a weighted average, with a unit sum of coefficients, of the values at $t-1$ and $t+1$ of a variable represents the value at t of a variable that increases linearly in time.

An alternative specification, with monthly growth rates of GDP used as regressors instead of the hard-to-measure output gap, shows no distinct connection with the inflation rate during the convertibility period, but a positive one in the post-crisis time interval (for the sample as a whole, the 'growth effect' on inflation practically vanishes if one includes dummy

Table 19.4 Phillips curve estimates, alternate specification – GDP growth (dependent variable: monthly inflation rate)

	1993:1–2010:6		1993:1–2001:12		2003:1–2010:6	
	Coefficient	Std error	Coefficient	Std error	Coefficient	Std error
Lagged inflation ($t-1$)	0.428181	0.039950	0.203153	0.043875	0.544691	0.048675
Expected inflation ($t+1$)	0.380357	0.049639	0.119560	0.021497	0.446325	0.037648
Growth	0.072170	0.031747	−0.019026	0.016034	0.041275	0.021084
Nominal exchange rate depreciation, currency basket ($t-1$)	0.052393	0.011285	0.052501	0.009304	−0.005358	0.012427
Foreign inflation ($t-1$)	0.051283	0.012449	0.070659	0.009134	−0.070171	0.103618
J-statistic	27,8324		22,6335		18,6509	

Note: Generalized method of moments estimation; instruments include lagged variables of regressors up to the twelfth lag. Variance–covariance matrix estimates are obtained using the Newey–West procedure (Bartlett kernel, fixed bandwith, 1 update of the weighting matrix).

variables for 2002). These observations (Table 19.4) seem to correspond with the image suggested by the rising steepness of the price–quantity curve in Figure 19.19.

Given the ambiguity of the interpretation of the future inflation term (which, as was mentioned, could stand for the presence of a trend), a specification with only the backward-looking effect can be of interest. Table 19.5 shows the results of an estimation for the post-crisis period, showing a large value of the auto-correlation parameters, and sizable weights of the nominal depreciation of the peso–US-dollar exchange rate, with also an influence of both current and lagged rates of real growth.

19.3.4 Monetary Policies and their Reaction Functions

Post-crisis monetary policies, as mentioned before, stressed considerations of sustainability and the ability to absorb shocks, and were reluctant to allow large exchange rate movements. In addition, the interest rate channel of transmission was judged unreliable after the financial crisis, while banks were felt to be vulnerable to interest rate variability (Balzarotti, 2007). The objectives of the central bank featured exchange rate stabilization (but without a peg, either formal or informal) and reserve accumulation as a precautionary instrument (Bastourre et al., 2009). Operations in domestic

Table 19.5 Phillips curve estimates, alternate specification – lagged inflation only, GDP growth (dependent variable: monthly inflation rate)

	2003:1–2010:6	
	Coefficient	Std error
Lagged inflation ($t-1$)	0.852883	0.024611
Growth	0.122567	0.019729
Lagged Growth (−1)	0.077069	0.022208
Nominal exchange rate depreciation, AR$/US$($t-1$)	0.146932	0.010871
US inflation, CPI ($t-1$)	−0.014228	0.046101
J-statistic	18,7909	

Note: Generalized method of moments estimation; instruments include lagged variables of regressors up to the twelfth lag. Variance–covariance matrix estimates are obtained using the Newey–West procedure (Bartlett kernel, fixed bandwith, weighting matrix updated through iteration to convergence).

assets were used to seek quantitative monetary targets and to offset the monetary effect of balance-of-payments flows.

In a cross-country analysis of monetary policies in recent years, which compares estimates of 'Taylor rules' (interest rates as functions of inflation, the exchange rate and the output gap), Sturzenegger and Talvi (2008) suggest that Latin American policymakers showed more 'fear of floating' (a stronger response to the exchange rate) than their counterparts in other developing economies or in developed countries, but on the whole reacted strongly to changes in the inflation rate. Within this picture, Argentina appears as particularly focused on the exchange rate, and less responsive to inflation.

A rule based exclusively on feedback from inflation to interest rates, without intervention in the foreign exchange market, need not be the only alternative to regulate inflation; for example, Chang (2008) has argued that the policies of Latin American 'inflation targeters' differ from the standard pure floating exchange rate approach.

In a similar vein, Aguirre and Burdisso (2008) suggest that, especially in developing economies, less-flexible exchange rate arrangements may be associated with lower inflation. In an analysis applied specifically to Argentina, Escudé (2009) estimates/calibrates a DSGE model for the period 2002–07 equipped with reaction functions for both the interest rate and the exchange rate (where this variable depends on inflation, the output gap, international reserves, the trade balance and measures of the real rate). He concludes that the exchange rate remained a central concern for monetary policy in Argentina in the post-convertibility period, and that the authorities paid attention to the multilateral real exchange rate, but made the rate of depreciation respond also to inflation (negatively) and to the output gap; in this system of 'multiple policy feedback rules', the model does show convergent dynamics despite a low-intensity reaction of interest rates to inflation. In turn, Aguirre and Grosman (2009) use a smaller-scale model (with aggregate demand and Phillips curve equations, a Taylor rule and a policy function that defines foreign exchange interventions to smooth the nominal exchange rate). They compare the actual performance under the observed (estimated) shocks and reaction functions with counterfactuals under different policies, and suggest that additional output and inflation volatility may have resulted in a pure floating exchange rate or a strictly pegged one.

As a whole, these results confirm the importance that the exchange rate had in Argentina both as a target and as an instrument of monetary management, and identify policy responses to the inflation rate. They also suggest that a welfare analysis of policy alternatives may depend on nontrivial considerations regarding the (uncertain) economic mechanisms at play, and the weights placed on different macroeconomic objectives. Still, inflation grew over time to become a salient problem.

19.4 CONCLUSIONS

The recovery from the crisis of the convertibility regime and the adjustment to the overshooting of the real exchange rate in an expanding economy implied a drift in the price level, given the policy choice of avoiding large nominal appreciations, with the (understandable) fear that nominal, and real, exchange volatility could create disturbances after the recent traumatic shock, and revive behaviors which had led to much macroeconomic instability in the past. This choice by itself ruled out policies (like the theoretical standard of inflation targeting with floating exchange rates) focusing narrowly on price stability, but it did not exclude a convergence to low inflation, after the price level transition. However, over the course of a remarkable phase of economic expansion, the process of price changes seemed to turn into an entrenched inflation.

This process remained very far from the old-fashioned high-inflation regime that the Argentine economy suffered in previous periods. The fuel of large-scale monetized deficits was lacking: although the 'inflation tax' reached nontrivial values, and seigniorage made significant contributions to the public sector's access to resources, over much of the period these funds were used in the accumulation of foreign reserves. Moreover, the large trade surplus and the volume of foreign reserves allowed the central bank to keep the evolution of the exchange rate under control. The demand for transactions money stayed high and did not show perturbations despite the presence of international shocks and political uncertainties.

Why bother about an inflation rate which, by the country's standards, remained at moderate levels and, over much of the period could be viewed as the other side of high growth? Except in the midst of the dramatic disruption in 2002, the standard reference to annual inflation rates suggested that the public did not perceive much price uncertainty over time spans of that length. Anticipations of changes in the aggregate price level did not seem to play a substantial role in everyday decisions until late in the decade. No significant 'demand for stability' emerged in public opinion, in the sense of a revealed willingness to approve policies that might reduce inflation with some current sacrifice in terms of real objectives.

This social tolerance towards inflation may have been related to the lack of longer-run references left by the crisis: in a case like that of Argentina, price instability of not too high intensity may prevent potentially welfare-enhancing changes to take place but, in contrast with countries with less extreme macroeconomic experiences, it need not disturb greatly the actual functioning of an economy in transition where, as one of the by-products of a recent crisis, short-termism was not likely to fade away rapidly as a behavioral feature. Thus, inflation did not take away a well-established economic predictability to which agents might have become accustomed. However, it probably discouraged the lengthening of economic horizons, and from that perspective it did appear costly in the search for a growth trend (Heymann, 2006).

Beyond the comparatively mild distortions of anticipated inflation at moderate rates (the inflation tax, with its certainly relevant distributive implications, the changes in relative prices associated with non-synchronic adjustments), the main problems caused by price instability derive from the noise that it introduces into economic decisions, and in the progressive reduction of the time period for which agents can make meaningful and more or less mutually consistent price forecasts (Heymann and Leijonhufvud, 1995). This affects investment and financial decisions at the 'long end' of the time scale (with a varying specification of that scale according to the nature of the inflationary process, going to the limit of a few days in hyperinflation).

The country's experience of the 1990s showed vividly the problems of using foreign currencies as units of denomination. In the post-crisis period, formal indexing (which remained subject to some legal constraints) did not arise as a widespread alternative, even before the public started to distrust the official price indexes. The absence of more or less reliable parameters to anticipate future price trends restricted the development of nominal contracting beyond the short run. The comparatively small and 'shallow' financial sector showed itself resilient to the impacts of international and domestic shocks. But, with a forward view, the special conditions of the first period of the phase of expansion which had reduced the importance of intermediated credit for the financing of production and investment (large volumes of under-utilized capital, high profit margins) could hardly be extrapolated to the future. An extension of the time period for which aggregate prices could be considered predictable thus appeared as an important element for growth purposes.

The government did not show much concern about inflation. Rather, over time it strengthened the signals that it privileged the growth of aggregate demand, more or less independently of the evolution of nominal variables. After some 4 years of inflation in the region of 20 per cent, sustained price increases of that order of magnitude had become built into expectations, and economic agents did not discard the likelihood of further accelerations. By 2010, attention was increasingly focused on the evolution of monthly inflation rates, although the immediate perspective of slow rates of depreciation functioned as a short-run anchor for expectations.

Over the decades, Argentina had experimented unsuccessfully with extreme forms in the design and the institutional framework of macroeconomic policies. As the limit case of monetary–fiscal symbiosis and absolute policy flexibility, the hyperinflationary episodes showed the great disruptions associated with regimes where, overall, the central bank operates like an agency for the monetary financing of a government which acts on a day-to-day basis responding to various pressures and demands. Symmetrically, the convertibility experiment indicated the problems of single-objective schemes based on tight rules which rendered policies unable to process errors and mistakes, and under which 'exit costs' were allowed, or desired, to become so high that the capacity for policy management could only be regained after an economic collapse. Financial crises and deep recessions, like the one which marked the end of convertibility, and the recent international crash, highlight the relevance of maintaining policy flexibility to prevent or handle shocks, and stress the fact that, ultimately, macroeconomic policies have multiple objectives and act in conjunction, beyond the procedural provisions that may be defined to induce a division of labor and areas of responsibility between agencies and instruments (see Basco et al., 2007).

The 'divine coincidence' propositions which tried to provide analytical support to monetary systems strictly and singly committed to inflation targets, on the argument that price stabilization would lead by itself to real output stabilization, hold only in special cases (for a discussion which remains within the framework of general-equilibrium models with frictions see for example Blanchard and Galí, 2005; also Blanchard et al., 2010). There is no presumption that monetary policies should be unconcerned with the levels and volatilities of real variables (output, interest rates, exchange rates) and with their tradeoffs with inflation, or even less should disregard the sustainability of wealth valuations and debt positions which act upon financial stability. In a period marked by a strong international crisis, these more or less commonsensical arguments seem to have gained wide circulation. But, at the same time, a policy which intends to be exclusively focused on real objectives lacks well-defined nominal anchors (with the mundane meaning of variables which will be allowed to lag in real terms for the sake of acting on inflation), and can readily become self-defeating.

In order to allow flexibility in 'spreading' the task of regulating inflation among several variables while avoiding price instability (and its real costs), the design and administration of systems with multiple anchors seem to require both a subtle management of tradeoffs (between real targets, in order to avoid inconsistencies, and between inflation and other objectives) and the means to communicate effectively the policy criteria and thus guide expectations. A system that seeks to facilitate decisions over more or less long horizons needs definite feedbacks from inflation to policy variables in order to dampen deviations from some long-run objective trend so that, irrespective of its precise numerical values, and of allowances made for the short-run management of shocks, agents may trust that inflation would be 'mean-reverting' and act in consequence. In the Argentine policy transitions of the 2000s, those feedback mechanisms (à la Taylor rule, but not necessarily in the form and with the instruments of that policy scheme) were not developed, or they lacked strength. A slowly varying exchange rate, monetary sterilization and fiscal surpluses (together with wage guidelines, subsidies, and interventions on price determination) were not sufficient to determine a macroeconomic regime generating a predictable price path.

The setup of macroeconomic policy decisions implied that no single or collective agency 'took specific responsibility' for inflation. The central bank, as discussed, saw its mission as a multitask activity that placed great weight on smoothing volatilities in the exchange and credit markets. By 2010, the views of the monetary authorities emphasized more strongly the objectives of sustaining demand and providing stimulus to the expansion of credit for investment. Fiscal policies maintained sizable surpluses until 2009, but real and nominal government spending grew at very high rates, and the also very rapid increase in tax collection did not much restrict the rise in private expenditures. The rapid growth in domestic demand was also a prominent policy objective, clearly signaled (before the international crisis) in the arguments that the economy could and should be stimulated in order to maintain 'Chinese growth rates', in a commonly used expression. In fact, the policies of the executive branch in the second half of the decade were influenced by views that minimized the importance of demand effects on inflation, or attributed them to the opportunistic behaviors of oligopolists, which should be addressed case by case by direct regulation or government–firm negotiations. Another influential proposition was that the preferable way to deal with inflation was by increasing supply, and therefore investment, which required the incentives of strong demand and the ample availability of credit, through monetary expansion if necessary. These arguments were used in their rejection of monetarism.

Detecting behavioral patterns for analytical or practical purposes is especially difficult in economies in transition after structural breaks, owing to the brevity of the period for which available data provide presumably relevant information.[8] This holds for Argentina, and specifically for the analysis of price dynamics sketched in the previous section. In any case, although the time series data do not show strong contemporaneous links between activity and inflation (as indicated, in particular, by the coefficient in a price equation of the current output gap, with all its conceptual and measurement issues), nevertheless the cumulative effects of demand pressures, the propagation of past price increases, both through backward looking adjustments and through anticipations that demand would accommodate further rises, were certainly important factors in establishing an inflationary trend. The slowdown of price increases in 2009 and the following rebound seemed to be associated with the oscillations of spending (and of international prices). Apart from the uncertainties about the specific mechanisms of aggregate price determination and about the transmission of policy instruments, it would seem more or less uncontroversial that the nature of the inflationary regime depends strongly on the setup and performance of macroeconomic policies which regulate the evolution of aggregate demand.

At some moments during the convertibility regime, particularly in its declining phase, it was common to find claims that there should be an urgent implementation of 'structural reforms' in order to send immediate signals to financial markets. In a very different context, the country saw in recent years several policy changes with institutional impact, decided and implemented in haste. The debates which emerged in the first months of 2010 regarding the governance and the functioning of the central bank were symptoms of current problems in the management of monetary and fiscal policies, while at the same time they also showed the existence of unsolved debates about the desirable configuration of macroeconomic institutions.

The organization of the central bank inherited from the charter voted in 1992, shortly after the establishment of the convertibility system (and with many of its provisions still nominally in effect at the beginning of 2010), was based on the notions of a strict separation between monetary and fiscal policies, and of central-bank independence, embodied in the prescriptions that restricted the removal of its president for policy reasons. In its origin, this formal structure, linked as it was to the currency board system, was meant to establish a leadership of the tightly constrained monetary policy over other macroeconomic policies. By contrast, at the end of the 2000s, the approach seemed to have been displaced towards the other end of full monetary flexibility, close interaction with other policies (possibly tending to accommodation of fiscal demands) and not much regard for nominal objectives. The former system was unable to bend, and it broke; this one was liable to show an inflationary bias.

The large potential supply of foreign currencies derived from the trade surplus and the stock of foreign reserves provided an insurance against a big market-induced depreciation, and thus weakened a crucial mechanism of inflationary accelerations. However, inflation had emerged as a visible macroeconomic issue, which would have to be addressed at some moment, and which in one way or another motivated a reconsideration of the institutional framework of macroeconomic policies.

Although matters of diagnosis and policy design are certainly crucial, and subject to debate (especially in Argentina, as has been seen), dealing with processes of price instability is not merely a 'technical' question. Inflation is at the same time a symptom and a cause of conflicts and behavioral inconsistencies, manifested in pressures on fiscal and monetary policies and in spirals of 'price increases chasing price increases chasing money injections chasing price increases'. In some way, the conflicts and inconsistencies underlying inflation have to be confronted: stabilization can be seen as a 'social investment' project, requiring the support of groups who value the future benefits to be obtained, and are willing to back a concrete set of policies that may coordinate effectively individual behaviors, and implement decisions about macroeconomic relative prices, the configuration of fiscal policies, and the rules and management procedures of the monetary system. From this perspective, the treatment of inflation in Argentina, looked at as part of a renewed search for a macroeconomic setup, may contribute to establishing a path of sustained growth, after a period of transition which combined quite novel features with issues that have been traditional in the country's economic history.

NOTES

1. The imprecision in the wording derives from the substantial discrepancy between the official price statistics and those of alternative sources, which have emerged since the beginning of 2007. The figure in the text refers to private estimates which try to follow the methods and procedures used in calculating the official data before that date.
2. For example, at an early stage, the recovery was described by a high IMF official as 'the bounce of a dead cat' (see Damill et al., 2005, for a discussion of the role of the IMF in the crisis). Indeed, macroeconomic analysts were often pessimistic about the immediate prospects of the economy following the crisis, as indicated for example in some of the statements gathered by Coiteux (2003).
3. Opinions warning that the economy was approaching its 'potential output' emerged relatively soon in the recovery. However, given the extraordinary rate of unemployment, and the high levels of the capital/output ratio, assuming that the destruction of capacity in the crisis had not gone very much beyond the standard depreciation rates, it would have followed that, for quite a while, the evolution of demand rather than supply constraints would be the main determinant of real activity. This picture evolved substantially during the expansion, as idle resources were absorbed.
4. See, for instance, http://www.bsas-city.com.ar//
5. In a period of rapidly rising incomes, and particularly of sharp increases in export prices, this behavior need not be interpreted simply as a symptom of 'flight to quality', but may have had a component of savings out of transitory receipt, in some sense analogous to the use made by governments of the increments in export earnings in countries where the public sector produces and sells exportable commodities.
6. We use INDEC data until the start of 2007, and an average of private estimates for the later period.
7. Quasi-maximum-likelihood estimates; Bollerslev–Wooldridge robust standard errors shown in brackets.
8. See Weitzman (2009) for an analysis of fundamental issues related to the bounded and possibly small size of the 'relevant sample' of data used to form expectations in systems subject to structural change. In particular, Weitzman argues that, in such a setting, the weight of prior beliefs in forecasts may never vanish, because that sample size does not 'go to infinity' as more observations are added.

REFERENCES

Academia Nacional de Ciencias Económicas (2009), *Sistemas Estadísticos: Aportes para una Estrategia*, Buenos Aires, available at: http: www.anceargentina.org

Aguirre, H. and N. Grosman (2010), 'A note on managed floating in a small economic model', proceedings of the 45th meeting of the Asociación Argentina de Economía Política, Buenos Aires.

Aguirre, H. and T. Burdisso (2008), 'Dangerous liaisons? An empirical assessment of inflation targeting and exchange rate regimes', Banco Central de la República Argentina (BCRA) Working Paper no. 39, Buenos Aires.

Basco, E., T. Castagnino, S. Katz and S. Vargas (2007), 'Política monetaria en contextos de incertidumbre, cambio de régimen y volatilidad pronunciada', Serie Estudios BCRA (Banco Central de la República Argentina) no. 25, Buenos Aires.

Basco, E., L. D'Amato, and L. Garegnani (2009), 'Understanding the money–

prices relationship under low and high inflation regimes: Argentina 1977–2006', *Journal of International Money and Finance*, **28** (7), 1182–203.

Balzarotti, V. (2007), 'Riesgo por tasa de interés real en el sistema bancario argentino: un modelo de medición', *Ensayos Económicos*, 46, Buenos Aires, pp. 7–61.

Bastourre, D., J. Carrera and J. Ibarlucia (2009), 'What is driving reserve accumulation: a dynamic panel data approach', *Review of International Economics*, **17** (4), 861–77.

Blanchard, O. and J. Galí (2007), 'Real wage rigidities and the new Keynesian model', *Journal of Money, Credit and Banking*, **39** (s1), 35–65.

Blanchard, O., G. Dell'Ariccia and P. Mauro (2010), 'Rethinking macroeconomic policy', IMF Staff Position Paper, Washington, DC.

Carrera, J. and L. Lanteri (2007), 'Shocks macroeconómicos y vulnerabilidad financiera', *Ensayos Económicos*, 48, 13–71.

Castagnino, T. and L. D'Amato (2008), 'Regime dependence, common shocks and the inflation-relative price variability relation', BCRA (Banco Central de la República Argentina) Working Paper no. 38, Buenos Aires.

Chang, R. (2008), 'Inflation targeting, reserve accumulation, and exchange rate management in Latin America', Borradores de Economía no. 487, Bogotá: Banco de la República de Colombia.

Coiteux, M. (2003), *Para Entender Diez Años de Convertibilidad en la Argentina*, Montreal: HEC and Buenos Aires: ECLAC (CD-ROM edition).

Coremberg, A., P. Goldszier, D. Heymann and A. Ramos (2007), 'Patrones de la inversión y el ahorro en la Argentina', CEPAL Working Paper, Serie Macroeconomía del Desarrollo, 63, Santiago de Chile.

D'Amato, L. and L. Garegnani (2009), 'Studying the short-run dynamics of inflation: estimating a hybrid New-Keynesian Phillips curve for Argentina (1993–2007)', BCRA (Banco Central de la República Argentina) Working Paper no. 40, Buenos Aires.

D'Amato, L., L. Garegnani and J. Sotes (2007), 'Dinámica inflacionaria y persistencia: implicancias para la política monetaria', *Ensayos Económicos*, 50, Buenos Aires, pp. 127–67.

Damill, M., R. Frenkel and M. Rapetti (2005), 'The Argentine Debt: History, Default, Renegotiation', *Economia-Revista da ANPEC*, **6** (3), 29–90.

Escudé, G. (2009), 'ARGEMmy: An intermediate DSGE calibrated/estimated model for Argentina: two rules are often better than one', BCRA (Banco Central de la República Argentina) Working Paper no. 42, Buenos Aires.

Frenkel, R. and M. Rapetti (2009), 'Flexibilidad cambiaria y acumulación de reservas en América Latina', CEDES Working Paper, Buenos Aires.

Galiani, S., D. Heymann and M. Tommasi (2003), 'Great expectations and hard times: the Argentine convertibility plan', *Economia*, **3** (2), 109–60.

Gerchunoff, P. and H. Aguirre (2005), 'Retórica política y política económica: la administración de Kirchner', en C. Alvarez (ed.), *El desarrollo económico de la Argentina en el mediano y largo plazo*, Buenos Aires: Prometeo.

Heymann, D. (2006), 'Buscando la tendencia: crisis y recuperación en la Argentina', CEPAL Buenos Aires Working Paper, Serie Estudios y Perspectivas no. 31.

Heymann, D. and A. Leijonhufvud (1995), *High Inflation*, Oxford: Oxford University Press.

Rodrik, D. (2008), 'The real exchange rate and economic growth', *Brookings Papers on Economic Activity*, Fall, pp. 365–412.

Sturzenegger, F. and E. Talvi (2008), 'Unveiling monetary policy in Latin America', paper prepared for the Chief Economists' Meeting, Washington, DC, 8–9 May.

Weitzman, M. (2009), 'Subjective expectations and asset-return puzzles', *American Economic Review*, **97** (4), 1102–30.

20. Inflation and stabilization in Brazil[1]

Manuel A.R. da Fonseca

20.1 INTRODUCTION

The economic history of Brazil since – at least – the middle of the twentieth century has been marked by very high and often growing inflation rates. In brief periods at the end of the 1980s and the beginning of the 1990s, price increases reached hyperinflationary levels. From the available information, covering several decades and reflecting virtually every possibility for stabilization policies and programs, one is led to the conclusion that the main cause of Brazilian inflation is the continued government drive to spend far beyond what could be financed by tax revenues. Further, in historical perspective, the country's capital market has been very limited and could not provide the resources necessary to finance fiscal deficits under favorable conditions – that is, in contrast with more mature economies, the market for treasury bonds has been characterized by very high real interest rates and very short maturities. Therefore, given the deficiencies of Brazil's capital market, the financing of fiscal deficits has become a major source of additional spending, higher deficits and stronger inflationary pressures.

To some extent, relatively high inflation and fiscal deficits are the necessary by-products of the government effort to push forward economic development in an essentially poor society – especially the pursuit of high rates of economic growth. The economic record of the 1950s and, in particular, of the period known as the 'economic miracle' (the end of the 1960s and beginning of the 1970s) are in conformity with this evaluation of higher inflation granting higher economic growth. However, the deterioration of the mechanisms of deficit financing and the parallel upsurge of inflation rates have led to a different state of affairs – very high and increasing inflation being one of the main factors obstructing economic growth and development. This seems the best characterization of the final years of the 1980s and the first ones of the 1990s.

Another conclusion to be drawn from Brazil's experience is that no stabilization program implemented since the 1960s can be considered entirely successful – not to mention, of course, the stabilization failures of the 1980s and 1990s, based heavily on wage and price freezes. In relation to this point, it should be mentioned that the PAEG Plan (the Plano de Ação Econômica do Governo, the orthodox stabilization program initiated by the military government the came to power in 1964), with its emphasis on fiscal discipline and monetary control, is in sharp contrast to the acclaimed Real Plan (started in 1994), which was initially based on an exchange rate anchor and later on inflation targeting. In the first case, inflation remained at a very high level, but it seems quite clear that the PAEG contributed decisively to the strong growth of the economic-miracle period. On the other hand, one of the conclusions of this chapter is that the distortions introduced by the Real Plan – especially the overvaluation of the real and the extremely high real interest rates – have impaired the possibilities of higher economic growth, leading to a stagnating economic environment for the most part of the last decade and a half. Therefore, contrary to the predominantly optimistic evaluations of the Brazilian economy in the post-Real-Plan period, the arguments developed below lead to the conclusion that the plan will probably not be the last act in Brazil's inflationary drama, for the simple reason that economic stability cannot be permanently based on major inflows of foreign capital necessary to equilibrate the balance of payments, attracted by extremely high interest rates, and leading to currency overvaluation, higher public deficit and debt, and poor economic growth.

20.2 BRAZIL'S INCIPIENT CAPITAL MARKET: A HISTORICAL PERSPECTIVE

In historical perspective, several factors explain the weakness of Brazil's capital market. One of them is the Lei da Usura (usury law), enacted in 1933,[2] which forbade interest rates above 12 per cent per annum – in *nominal* terms. Considering that, since that period, annual inflation has been below this level on very few occasions, one can infer the immense distortions in financial markets caused by this measure. In the long run, the Lei da Usura coupled with the chronic and increasing inflation of the 1950s and early 1960s worked as a powerful deterrent to private saving. This trend is illustrated in Table 20.1, which presents some financial indicators for this period. These data show that time deposits and the supply of credit by banks were deeply affected by the combination of interest rate regulation and rising inflation, leading to an overall reduction of the role of financial institutions throughout the period.[3]

The effects of the usury law lasted until 1964 when, as part of the

Table 20.1 Brazilian banks 1951–66: consolidated balance sheet[a]

	Assets (loans to the private sector)			Liabilities			Inflation rate IGP-DI
	Commercial banks	Banco do Brasil	Total	Cash deposits	Time deposits	Total	
1951	17.5	7.1	24.5	15.0	4.8	19.8	12.3
1952	16.6	8.4	24.9	14.7	4.1	18.8	12.7
1953	16.3	8.3	24.6	14.6	3.6	18.2	20.6
1954	14.1	8.5	22.7	12.6	3.0	15.7	25.8
1955	13.1	8.0	21.0	12.6	2.4	15.0	12.2
1956	12.6	7.3	19.9	12.3	2.0	14.4	24.5
1957	13.0	7.3	20.4	14.1	1.9	16.0	7.0
1958	12.6	7.5	20.0	13.9	1.7	15.6	24.4
1959	11.5	5.8	17.3	13.9	1.3	15.2	39.4
1960	12.0	5.7	17.8	13.8	1.5	15.3	30.5
1961	10.8	6.0	16.8	13.1	1.2	14.3	47.8
1962	11.2	6.4	17.7	13.9	0.8	14.7	51.6
1963	9.0	5.5	14.5	12.7	0.7	13.4	79.9
1964	8.5	4.9	13.4	11.7	0.6	12.3	92.1
1965	9.2	3.7	12.9	13.6	0.6	14.2	34.3
1966	7.8	4.0	11.7	10.2	1.1	11.3	39.1

Note: [a] Selected items, % of GDP.

Source: Ministério do Planejamento e Coordenação Econômica, *Situação Monetária, Creditícia e do Mercado de Capitais – Diagnóstico Preliminar* (Rio de Janeiro, 1966); Contas Nacionais (see Table 20.3); *Conjuntura Econômica*, Rio de Janeiro: Fundação Getúlio Vargas, several issues.

measures included in the PAEG program adopted in that year, several laws were enacted creating bonds and notes subjected to legal clauses that differentiated effective interest from the correction of values due to inflation. These notes – the most important was the Obrigação Reajustável do Tesouro Nacional (ORTN) – promised the payment of interest on top of inflation that eventually occurred since they were issued. This mechanism became known as 'monetary correction' (*correção monetária*). Later on this inflation correction mechanism gradually spread out to the labor market and to the markets of most goods and services, becoming an important cause of price increases – that is, an important inertial component of the inflationary process was set in motion.

Table 20.2 Brazil: inflation[a] averages in selected periods (%)

1948–57	1958–67	1968–77	1978–87	1988–94	1995–02	2003–09
14.6	44.9	26.0	138.2	1252.2	12.3	5.7

Note: [a] Índice Geral de Preços (IGP-DI).

Source: *Conjuntura Econômica*, Rio de Janeiro: Fundação Getúlio Vargas, several issues.

Several other initiatives were also included in the PAEG, aiming at the modernization of the financial system: the country's central bank was created, specific legislation was introduced for investment banks and for institutions specialized in real-state financing, and the Banco Nacional da Habitação (BNH) – until 1986, the major state bank providing credit for housing – was created.[4] Moreover a major readjustment of the fiscal budget was implemented, with an overhaul of the tax system and a restructuring of expenses, which for the most part solved the chronic fiscal imbalances of the previous decades.[5] Although inflation remained high afterwards – see Tables 20.1 and 20.2 – considering the strong economic growth that occurred in the late 1960s and early 1970s there is some basis to conclude that the PAEG was a successful stabilization program. As will be seen in Section 20.3, the positive experience of the PAEG in equilibrating the fiscal budget and contributing to a period of solid economic growth is in sharp contrast with the celebrated Real Plan.

Despite all changes brought about since 1964 to promote the development of Brazil's capital market, it seems fair to say that long-term credit remained unavailable either to Brazilian private firms or to individuals. In 1994, at the start of the Real Plan, 65.6 per cent of the total supply of credit by financial institutions was provided by commercial banks. In comparison, the share of the federal and regional development banks – which provide longer-term loans – was 5.9 per cent.[6] Given this chronic deficiency in the country's capital market, most Brazilian firms have traditionally been able to finance investment projects through retained profits. However, this alternative was basically available to large corporations, which often operate in highly concentrated markets.[7] Moreover the major limitations of Brazil's capital market are undoubtedly linked to the pattern of extremely high real interest rates that has predominated since the 1980s.[8] Since 1991, and in particular after the agreement reached in 1992 with international creditors on the country's foreign debt, Brazilian corporations have increasingly obtained longer-term financing abroad. On the other hand, institutional investors – pension funds, insurance companies and mutual funds – have gradually become more active in Brazil's financial system, following the trend prevailing in major international markets, but – at least, until the first half of the 2000s – this did not contribute in a significant way to reduce the shortage of long-term credit.[9]

20.3 THE REAL PLAN: ITS ORIGINS AND LATER DEVELOPMENTS

20.3.1 The Failed Stabilization Schemes of the 1980s and 1990s

From 1985 onwards, several government initiatives contributed to push inflation to ever higher levels: major increases in spending (especially with wages and interest payments), a moratorium on the external debt (which virtually eliminated foreign capital inflows) and, most important, unorthodox stabilization programs based on wage and price freezes. These programs ultimately led individuals and businessmen to adopt defensive strategies to minimize financial losses in anticipation of the start of a new plan – like the acquisition of real assets and preventive price increases. The deterioration of the government budget, observed since the early 1980s and aggravated from 1985 onwards, led to increasing government deficits. Furthermore, given the deficiencies of the country's capital market, it was ever more difficult to properly finance these deficits. As a consequence, an important trend was observed since the middle of the 1980s that made a major contribution to the upsurge of inflation – the monetization of the public debt. This trend mainly resulted from the increasing role of the central bank as a financial agent of the Treasury. Gradually the monetary authority engaged in rolling over the public debt by providing guarantees to financial institutions through repurchase agreements – the central bank would automatically buy back treasury bills if some institution were short on reserves – and this was done on a daily basis.[10]

In the second half of the 1980s, after two decades of military rule, there was strong opposition to any proposal perceived as conservative, especially those viewed as originating from international financial institutions, particularly the IMF – the so-called Washington Consensus.[11] Therefore any initiative in the direction of reducing the fiscal deficit and promoting monetary discipline met strong opposition. Echoing this rebellious mood, a new line of economic thinking emerged that became very popular among Brazilian economists and, in fact, in several other Latin American countries. The main proposition that, in general terms, was shared by the so-called unorthodox economists was that fiscal and monetary policies were useless in promoting stability and that, in order to curb inflation, it was only necessary to eliminate its so-called 'inertial component' – that is, the indexation of wages and prices.[12] Based on these ideas, several unorthodox stabilization programs were implemented in Brazil from 1986 to 1991 centered on wage and price freezes. Their final result was to push price increases to near hyperinflationary levels: as a rule, at the end of each plan, inflation rates were higher than at the start.[13] Moreover, in the case of the Collor Plan, which began in March 1990, government intervention reached unprecedented levels – the major part of the treasury bonds in the domestic market and the bank deposits that backed these bonds were confiscated.[14]

One important aspect that helps in understanding the failure of the pre-Real-Plan stabilization programs is the effect of the exchange rate freeze on the balance of payments. In each plan, with the overvaluation of the domestic currency in real terms, there were significant reductions of trade balances, and deficits in the current account emerged – with the exception of the Summer Plan (Plano Verão), there were current-account deficits in every year when an unorthodox plan was introduced. Given that international financial markets were, for the most part, closed to Brazilian companies and institutions, these deficits brought considerable pressures on the administration of international reserves. In other words, the external debt default of 1987 made it almost impossible to maintain current-account deficits for relatively longer periods. This situation changed radically in 1992 after the renegotiation of the country's external debt and, as it will be argued below, this was one of the major factors behind the success of the Real Plan.

20.3.2 Fundamentals of the Real Plan: Nominal Anchor Based on the Exchange Rate

After a long series of failed stabilization attempts, all of them based on ideas proposed by Brazil's unorthodox economists, monthly inflation reached almost 50 per cent in June 1994, immediately before the Real Plan was launched. The plan implemented one of the ideas suggested a decade earlier by two exponents of the unorthodox school: the introduction of an indexed currency to curb high inflation rates.[15] The origin of the plan was the executive law (*medida provisória*) no. 434, enacted on 28 February 1994, which introduced a new index – the Unidade Real de Valor (URV), linked to the dollar, whose main goal was to facilitate the coordinated change from a fast-depreciating currency (the cruzeiro real) to a new currency (the real) that was initially pegged to the dollar at a one-to-one parity. Later on there was a fixed maximum exchange rate that the central bank committed itself to. The URV was used compulsorily to adjust prices in government-controlled markets, especially the labor market. This index was, in reality, the official real–dollar exchange rate and was fixed daily by the central bank. The practical effect was to make prices that followed the URV change according to the dollar exchange rate. The initial goal was to link most domestic prices to the dollar and, when the URV was finally transformed into the new currency, it was hoped that the latter would keep a constant value in relation to the American currency, thus reducing inflation to near zero.[16] Therefore, at its origin, the Real Plan was consolidated on a nominal anchor based on the dollar exchange rate.

The backbone of the plan was the elimination of indexation mechanisms and the de facto freezing of prices in markets controlled by the government: the exchange rate, the labor market, public-utility prices – including oil and gasoline – and some generally used contracts – especially those applying to rents, private schools and medical insurance. After July 1994,[17] wages, public-utility prices, and prices settled by legal contracts could no longer be raised according to previous inflation, at least in shorter periods: any increase occurring before a 1-year interval was prohibited. Despite statements made by government officials that a balanced budget needed to be achieved, no significant fiscal adjustment was implemented. There were some initiatives in the direction of reducing the government deficit, but these were very limited and did not alter in any fundamental way the items of the 1988 Constitution that caused major increases in government expenses[18] – in particular, the rates of major federal taxes were raised, especially income tax rates. Another measure that augmented the revenues at the federal level was the reduction, approved by Congress, of the funds transferred by the national administration to states and municipalities by 15 per cent. As mentioned in Section 20.2, the limitation of the Real Plan on the fiscal front makes it essentially different from the stabilization program of the 1960s, the PAEG.

The real was initially pegged to the dollar; in fact, in the first months of the plan, the Central Bank allowed the real to float and it appreciated in relation to the dollar owing to large influxes of foreign capital (Figure 20.1). This trend mainly resulted from the very high levels of domestic interest rates. By the end of September 1994, the dollar exchange rate had fallen 15 per cent in relation to 1 July. In the same period, the country's most followed price index (the IGP-DI) increased by 31 per cent, given that inflation did not fall instantaneously. Thus the real became strongly overvalued. Another factor that contributed to the reduction of inflation was the process of opening the Brazilian economy – the so-called '*abertura*' – that started in 1990. Import tariffs were reduced considerably and virtually all industrial sectors were exposed to foreign competition. Also, a major agreement was reached in 1992 with international creditors on

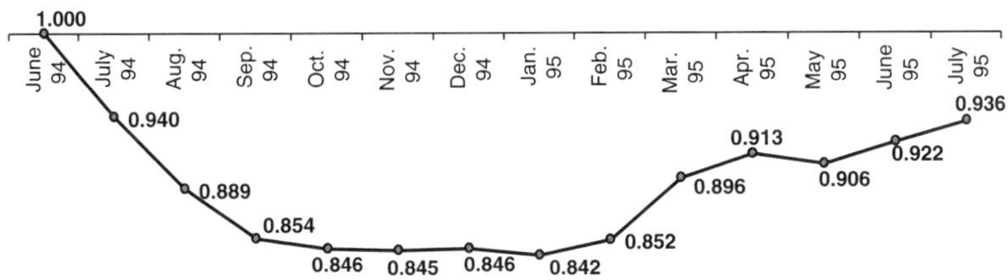

Source: Brazil's central bank, *Boletim Mensal*, several issues.

Figure 20.1 Dollar–real exchange rates: figures for the last day of the month.

the country's external debt, which made it possible for large Brazilian companies to raise money in international financial markets. Until 1992, the country was in default on its debt payments, which made practically impossible the raising of money abroad. Moreover the privatization of large state-controlled companies – a process initiated in 1990 with the Collor administration and that gained momentum after the start of the Real Plan – contributed in a major way to attract foreign capital.

Until 1996, the exchange rate, especially in relation to the dollar, appreciated strongly, reaching less than half the level in real terms of the years 1983–85 – a period marked by the appearance of very large trade surpluses, which later on became a common feature of the Brazilian economy. In response to the profound changes in the exchange rate policy introduced by the Real Plan, the current account started to show overwhelming annual deficits: over US$20 billion from 1996 to 2001, and over US$30 billion in 1997 and 1998.[19] However, following the significant exchange rate devaluation that occurred in 2002, this situation gradually reverted and, until 2007, there were once again trade surpluses. In the labor market, the maintenance of very high inflation rates at the initial stages of the Real Plan led to important losses in the share of wages in GDP, which contributed to the stagnation of demand that prevailed in several sectors – especially those that depended on domestic markets.

As argued in the previous paragraphs, the instruments of the Real Plan, in much the same way as its predecessors, affected almost exclusively the cost components of inflation – especially the exchange rate – leaving the financial disequilibrium of the public sector not significantly different from the situation before the plan. As will be seen below, especially in Section 20.4, the consequences of this disequilibrium are more clearly perceived in the monetary and capital markets, in the impressive growth of the public debt until the beginning of the 2000s, and also in the firm stance of the government pursuing, and obtaining, frequent increases in tax revenue.

20.3.3 Stabilization Strategy in the Post-1998 Period: Inflation Targeting

The exchange rate crisis that affected the major emerging-market countries in 1998 had dramatic consequences for the Brazilian economy, since the very foundations of the then prevailing stabilization strategy had collapsed – the dollar exchange rate increased from R$1.21 at the end of December 1998 to R$1.98 in January 1999. One of the first initiatives of the government to deal with the crisis was to request an emergency loan from the IMF – which was approved in an unusually brief period – that provided important relief to international reserves, which were fast declining. As had happened in several major countries,[20] the Brazilian authorities introduced a new stabilization strategy centered on inflation targeting – a movement led by the central bank's board of directors. According to the official discourse, the macroeconomic policy introduced in 1999 and that has been in effect for more than a decade, is based on inflation targeting, a floating exchange rate, and explicit goals of *primary* – that is, excluding interest payments – budget surpluses, expressed as percentages of GDP. The decision by the central bank on the level of the benchmark interest rate (the Selic rate), which applies to the treasury bond market, has as its main goal the accomplishment of the inflation target previously announced by the monetary authority – something that, however, has often not occurred.[21]

The predominant economic argument among Brazilian economists – that is, those who support the status quo – is that the relative price stability of the post-Real period is the result of three factors: monetary discipline, fiscal responsibility and the financial equilibrium of the state. However there are major reasons to doubt this evaluation. In relation to monetary discipline, data for money supply (M1) show that, in relation to GDP, the money stock doubled in comparison with the position at the start of the Real Plan (Table 20.3). Further, in relation to GDP, the public debt more than doubled.[22] These combined trends could hardly be considered consistent with what most economists would call monetary discipline. In relation to the debt, its growth has also been determined by the strong inflow of foreign capital, especially in 2007 and again in 2009 – the surpluses in the capital account were, respectively, $89.1 billion and $70.6 billion. The central bank has bought considerable amounts of dollars trying to reduce its downfall – international reserves in 2009 were 177.9 per cent higher than in 2006, reaching $238.5 billion in December – and, clearly, part of the growth of the public debt in this period was due to this major increase of reserves.

Further, in relation to GDP, current expenses of the government were virtually stable at considerably high levels. Therefore the 'fiscal

Table 20.3 Brazilian macroeconomic data, 1995–2009: annual averages in periods

	Cardoso		Lula da Silva	
	1995–98	**1999–02**	**2003–06**	**2007–09**
Real rate of change(%)[a]				
GDP at market prices	2.5	2.1	3.5	3.7
Industrial GDP	1.8	1.1	3.4	3.2
Agricultural GDP	3.2	5.5	3.2	3.6
Exchange rate, R$/US$ (PPP, using IPA-Br and PPI-US)	−5.8	15.1	−11.7	−5.2
Share of GDP – data in real terms (%)[a]				
Government revenue[b]	28.6	32.7	34.0	–
Government current consumption	20.2	20.2	20.0	19.3
Aggregate investment	18.9	17.4	16.0	18.8
Exports	8.7	10.9	14.4	–
Imports	12.8	11.6	11.5	–
Profits (surplus)[b]	32.9	33.9	35.2	–
Wages and autonomous income[b]	54.3	51.7	49.6	–
M1[b,c]	3.7	5.3	5.7	7.5
Public debt in domestic market[b,c]	20.9	42.1	41.3	42.6
Labor force (%)				
Unemployment rate	–	11.7	10.9	8.6
Annual rate of change (%)				
IGP-DI	8.2	16.4	6.1	5.1
IPCA	9.4	8.8	6.4	4.9
Interest rates (%)				
Selic (effective rate)	33.1	19.8	18.4	17.6
Commercial credit	97.5	54.9	43.8	62.9

Notes:
[a] Includes estimates for 2009.
[b] Current values.
[c] Averages of stocks in each year were used.
–: Not available

Sources: Original data from *Contas Nacionais* and *PIB Trimestral*, available on www.ibge.gov.br, and from *Boletim do Banco Central*, on www.bcb.gov.br. The data used in the table come from the database of www.planejamento.org

responsibility' argument is, in fact, a euphemism for a brutal increase of the tax burden observed throughout the post-Real period – taking into account the level of tax revenues just before the start of the plan, this increase exceeds 10 per cent of GDP. In relation to this point, it is important to take into account the major weight of interest payments on the fiscal budget. As shown in Table 20.3, real interest on treasury bonds was above 10 per cent per year during virtually all the post-Real-Plan period (using as deflator the official price index, the IPCA). During the first term of President Cardoso, real interest based on the Selic rate surpassed 20 per cent per year. Given that the share of the public debt in GDP has moved up to above 40 per cent, simple arithmetic reveals that the value of the interest payments alone corresponds to more than 4 per cent of GDP in real terms. In other words, monetary policy after the Real Plan has caused large interest payments by the government – a value greater than one-fifth of the expenditures with wages and all other current spending items – which means that the Brazilian government has systematically transferred large shares of national income to investors, both nationals and foreigners, who own treasury bonds.[23]

20.4 OVERALL MACROECONOMIC TRENDS OF THE POST-REAL-PLAN PERIOD

20.4.1 Economic Stagnation and 'Deindustrialization'

Brazil's macroeconomic data – see Table 20.3 – show that the post-Real-Plan period has been marked by very low rates of economic growth – much lower than those observed in major emerging-market countries.[24] Further, the growth of industry's GDP has consistently remained below that of agriculture and services – a process often referred to as 'deindustrialization'. A main factor behind the reduced share of industrial GDP is the strong overvaluation of the real for most of the years since 1994. There has also occurred a significant reduction of the share of investment in GDP (until 2005), as well as a trend of larger profits at the expense of the wage share. In addition, unemployment rates have been very high, and one can further identify a tendency of increasing share of exports in GDP. The prevalence of economic stagnation in the post-Real-Plan era has gone against the predictions of many analysts that, after the elimination of very high inflation, anticipated that economic growth would be more in line with the strong rates of the 1970s.[25] However, the considerable distortions due to the overvaluation of the Real and the extremely high real interest rates, besides the stagnation of wages, have impaired the perspectives of

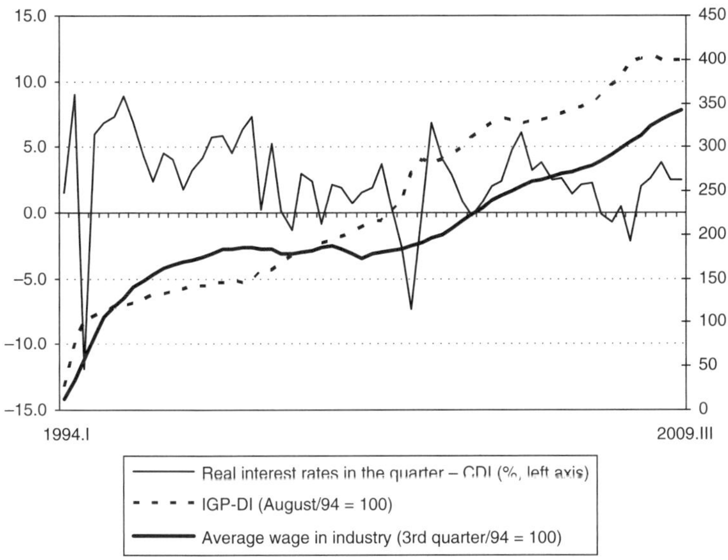

Sources: See Table 20.3.

Figure 20.2 Interest rates, prices and wages.

higher economic growth. It is also important to note that this trend is in sharp contrast with the period of record growth that followed the economic program of the 1960s – the underestimated PAEG.

Figure 20.2 contains quarterly data that illustrate some important macroeconomic trends that accompanied the stabilization process after the start of the Real Plan. It presents data for the general price index (IGP-DI), together with information for real interest rates accumulated in each quarter and an index for the average wage in industrial firms (in current values).[26] Figure 20.2 clearly illustrates the long-run trend of very high real interest rates mentioned in Section 20.3. Moreover, until 2000, the average nominal wage in the industrial sector rose above inflation, but after that period industrial wages were increasingly surpassed by the price level – in fact, during the second term of the Cardoso presidency this wage index was virtually unchanged. From the end of 2003 onwards, industrial wages grew again in nominal terms, but remained far behind the price level – that is, there were major losses in real wages in the post-Real-Plan period.[27] This latter trend was accompanied by a significant increase of trade balances – especially since the end of 2002. Therefore, the growth of domestic demand was surpassed by GDP increases, and economic growth in Brazil became increasingly dependent on external demand.

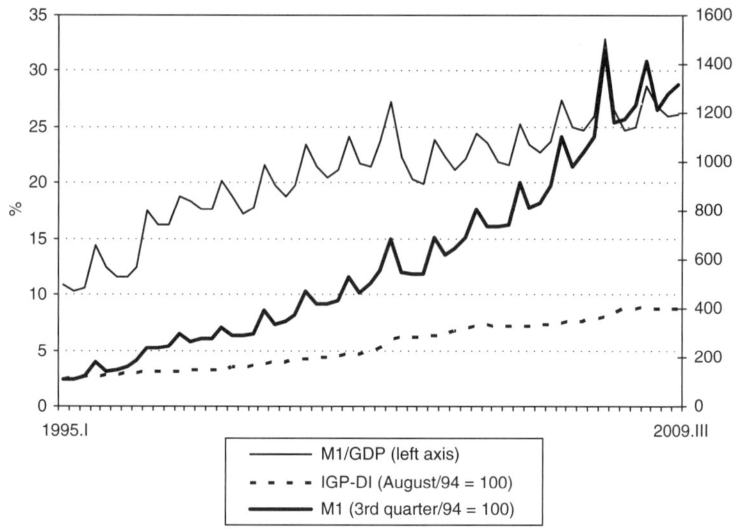

Sources: See Table 20.3.

Figure 20.3 Money and prices.

20.4.2 Loose Fiscal Policy and Fast-Growing Money Supply

Figure 20.3, in turn, contains quarterly data for the stock of money – M1, information for end of period – together with numbers for the share of M1 in GDP. To put the money supply series in perspective, data of the general price index were also included. The main conclusion that can be drawn from this figure is that money supply growth was far superior to the increase of prices. Further, the impressive expansion of M1 occurred despite the extremely high levels of real interest rates, and some important restrictions on bank credit – in particular, a 40 per cent reserve requirement on cash deposits. There are several factors behind this lack of monetary control and the most important one is the chronic fiscal disequilibrium, that is, the major budget deficits (nominal deficits) that become apparent when interest payments made by the government are taken into account. One can then conclude that the main flaw of the Real Plan, which almost two decades after its start remains unresolved, is that a consistent and sustainable fiscal equilibrium, which would be a necessary condition for the success of a stabilization program, has never been achieved. Moreover, this deficiency was aggravated by the ever present policy of extremely high real interest rates. Also, this policy, coupled with the restrictions on bank credit and the stagnation of real wages, contributed in an important way to the economic stagnation for the most part of the post-Real-Plan period.

Another factor that explains the economic stagnation of the past decade and a half is the continued and impressive increase of the tax burden in Brazil. In comparison with GDP, the total tax revenue increased from 25.3 per cent in 1993 to a level above 36 per cent at the end of the 2000s. This trend of ever increasing tax revenues results from the evaluation by Brazilian policymakers that price stability depends heavily on the capacity of the government to generate fiscal surpluses, which are necessary to keep to the financial commitments of a growing public debt. However, given the very large interest payments on this debt, there were only *primary* surpluses, while *nominal* deficits have been the rule.

20.4.3 Internationalization of Domestic Financial Markets

Many of the changes that occurred in the Brazilian economy after the Real Plan originated in the financial sector, and they are related to two major tendencies that became commonplace in many countries – the internationalization of domestic financial markets and the ever increasing role of institutional investors. Overlapping is clearly present here: institutional investors quite often are located abroad. In the Brazilian case, the first of these trends originated from two interconnected developments: the increasing participation of international commercial banks in the country's monetary system and the loosening of the restrictions on the activities of foreign investors and on international capital flows. Since the beginning of the 1990s, the entry of international banks has been encouraged by the central bank, although in an unofficial manner, since current legislation still creates barriers to the participation of foreign institutions in the domestic market (Cerqueira Lima, 1998). On the other hand, two initiatives of the government are emblematic of the unconditional support of post-Real-Plan administrations of the liberalization of capital flows: the elimination of the income tax on profits obtained by foreign investors in the treasury bond market – a measure adopted in the first term of Lula da Silva's presidency – and the removal of barriers preventing Brazilian nationals from investing in international financial markets.

The relevance of the second tendency mentioned above – that is, the increasing weight of institutional investors – can be illustrated by the growth of the portfolio of pension funds belonging to state companies, which increased from R$130.0 billion (12 per cent of GDP) in 2000 to R$274.3 billion (13 per cent of GDP) in 2005 (Dias Leite, 2007). In the case of mutual funds, the aggregate value of their portfolios grew from R$497.2 billion in December 2003 to R$892.1 billion in December 2006

– respectively, 29 per cent and 38 per cent of GDP.[28] Two major consequences of these interconnected trends, which mainly occurred between 2003 and 2007, were the spectacular inflow of financial capital and the significant expansion of Brazil's stock market.[29] Further, these developments were accompanied by the strong overvaluation of the real, especially in relation to the dollar, and this last movement contributed decisively to the macroeconomic scenario described at the beginning of this section.

The exceptional growth of stocks in the Brazilian market has led many international investors – in particular, managers of mutual funds – to invest in Brazilian companies, a movement that was especially strong in the case of initial public offers (IPOs) in the construction sector. Certainly the great number of IPOs with external financing that occurred until 2008, and especially in 2007, represents a major exception in a domestic capital market that, traditionally, does not provide the necessary long-term financing to Brazilian companies. On the other hand, Brazil's capital market has absorbed large values of treasury bonds, although the average maturity of these securities has, as a rule, remained very short.

20.5 AN ECONOMETRIC EVALUATION OF INFLATION IN BRAZIL

The starting point of this econometric analysis of inflation applied to Brazilian data is the proposition that the countless and diverse factors that affect the inflation rate can be divided into two basic sets, one linked to aggregate (nominal) demand and the other resulting from general (macroeconomic) cost factors – which is consistent with the very common analysis that distinguishes *cost* inflation from *demand* inflation.[30] The demand side of the inflation rate can be modeled through the quantitative theory of money. Considering that money velocity is a stable parameter – an assumption not too realistic in a country like Brazil, where very high inflation has gradually been replaced by more moderate rates of price change – inflation pressures result from the growth of the money stock in excess of real GDP's growth:[31]

$$\Delta p_t^D = \alpha(\Delta m_t - \Delta y_t). \tag{20.1}$$

The variables in equation (20.1) are measured in natural logarithms: p is a price index, m is the money stock in current values, and y is real GDP. In turn, the cost or supply side of inflation, which is linked to its so-called 'inertial' component, will be represented through the following equation:

$$\Delta p_t^S = \beta_1 \Delta w_t + \beta_2 \Delta e_t + \beta_3 \Delta com_t + \beta_4 \Delta agr_t. \qquad (20.2)$$

Variables on the right-hand side of equation (20.2), also measured in natural logarithms, are: the average nominal wage rate (w), the dollar exchange rate (e), a series of international commodity prices (com), and an index of domestic agricultural prices (agr). Certainly, the list included in equation (20.2) could be extended, as it could also be reduced, to fit more adequately Brazil's inflation data; these possibilities can best be dealt with empirically.

Finally, the inflation rate at a given period is the sum of both demand and cost factors, that is, $\Delta p_t = \Delta p_t^D + \Delta p_t^S$, and, in theory, the sum of the coefficients should be one ($\alpha + \beta_1 + \beta_2 + \beta_3 + \beta_4 = 1$), a condition that, if reputed necessary, could be imposed in the estimation process. The data used (quarterly data) and their sources are as follows. p: GDP deflator (2005 = 100); m: M1 stock (R\$millions); y: quarterly GDP (R\$millions of 2005); w: average wage (R\$1000); e: R\$ per dollar; com: petroleum prices (US\$ per barrel); agr: index of agricultural prices (IPA-OG; August 1994 = 100). The sources are the Brazilian Statistical Institute – IBGE (p, y); Brazil's central bank (m, e); International Monetary Fund – IMF (com); and the Getúlio Vargas Foundation (agr). The series for w was compiled by the author from data available in Brazil's input–output tables and national accounts.

Two sets of estimations were performed: one with quarterly rates of change – that is, data that include seasonality – and one with rates of change in four quarters (without seasonal patterns). As will be seen below, the strong seasonal component of quarterly inflation rates conditions the econometric results and obscures some relations that can be perceived in the data without the seasonal component. According to the augmented Dickey–Fuller test, all series can be considered stationary – in the case of data based on quarterly rates, the null hypothesis of non stationarity was rejected at a 1 per cent significance level.[32] Figure 20.4 illustrates the demand side of inflation in Brazil: it contains the quarterly data for ($\Delta m - \Delta y$) compared with Δp. It stands out in this figure the strong seasonal component of inflation, which is also present in the rates of change of money supply and average wage (not depicted).

The estimation results using ordinary least squares appear in Table 20.4. The coefficients for Δe and Δcom were not significantly different from zero and Δagr was included with a one-period lag. An important criterion for the quality of the regression is the conformity of the residuals to the hypotheses of the regression model – the so-called 'misspecification testing', or the testing of the assumptions underlying the regression model. Two types of tests are particularly important: to test

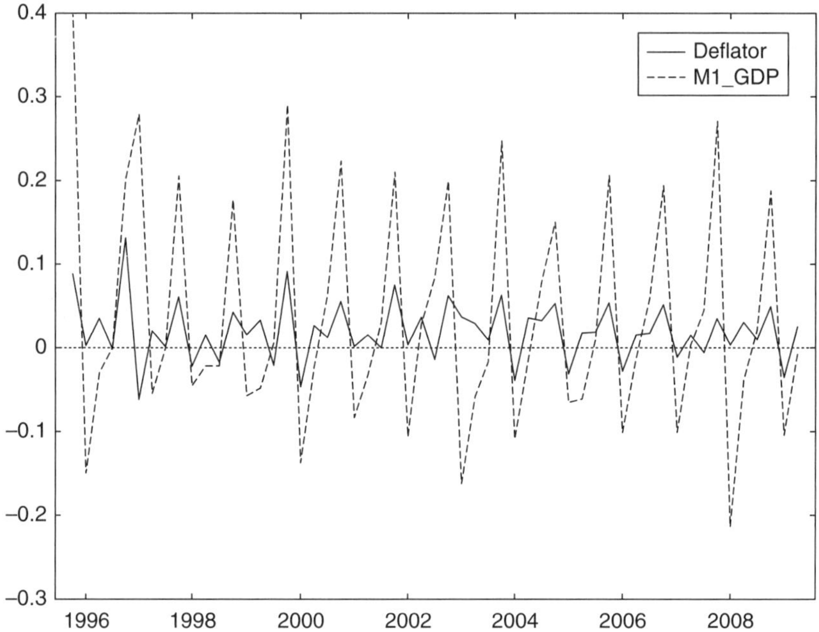

Source: See Section 20.5.

Figure 20.4 Rates of change: GDP deflator and (M1-GDP).

Table 20.4 Quarterly rates of change – estimation results

	Coefficient	Std error	*t*-stat	*p*-value
M1_GDP	0.120124	0.0235585	5.099	<0.00001
Avg wage	0.389682	0.052003	7.4934	<0.00001
IPA_OG_1	0.129673	0.0476233	2.7229	0.00884

Mean of dependent variable	0.018702	Std deviation of dependent variable	0.035428
Sum sqd residuals	0.022832	Std error of regression	0.021159
R-square	0.732677	Adjusted *R*-square	0.722194
F (3, 51)	46.59347	*p*-value (F)	1.22E–14
Log-likelihood	133.1289	Akaike information criterion	−260.2578
Schwarz B. criterion	−254.2908	Hannan–Quinn criterion	−257.9566
Rho	−0.189574	Durbin–Watson	2.282828

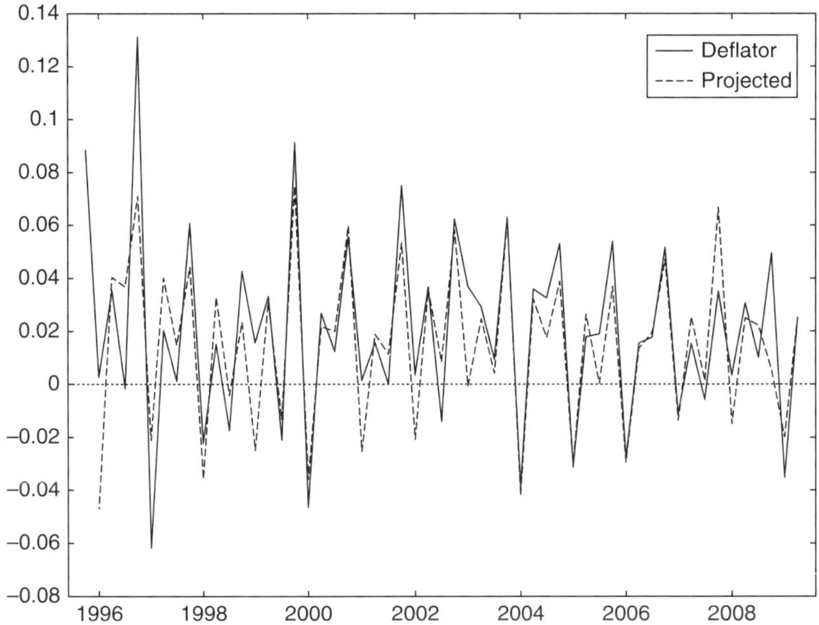

Source: Estimation made by the author.

Figure 20.5 GDP deflator (quarterly rates of change): effective and projected values.

if the residuals can be considered independent – in this case, with time series data, to test if there is no autocorrelation – and if they are normally distributed. The Durbin–Watson test indicates that there is no autocorrelation and, further, the null hypothesis of normality for the residuals could not be rejected – the p-value of the Jarque–Bera test was 0.2336. Figure 20.5 contains effective and projected values for Δp using quarterly rates of change.

The estimation using rates of change in four quarters reveals different relations, with a reduced contribution of $(\Delta m - \Delta y)$ and an increasing role of the exchange rate – although this latter relation becomes clearer through the use of a dummy variable. The initial regression results appear in Table 20.5, which shows that both the coefficients of $(\Delta m - \Delta y)$ and Δcom are not significantly different from zero. Further, to take into account the relation between the exchange rate and inflation, a dummy variable was used in which the quarters with major increases of the dollar exchange rate were set equal to one. In this way, the dummy variable captures the effect on inflation of sharp increases of the exchange rate.

Table 20.5 Rates of change in four quarters – estimation results

	Coefficient	Std error	*t*-stat	*p*-value
M1_GDP	0.0162728	0.0257013	0.6332	0.52952
Avg wage	0.772049	0.0348471	22.1554	<0.00001
Exchg	0.029649	0.0166367	1.7821	0.0808
IPA_OG	0.0572392	0.0267756	2.1377	0.03745
Petrole	0.00597143	0.00935	0.6387	0.52596

Mean of dependent variable	0.086682	Std. deviation of dependent variable	0.054578
Sum sqd residuals	0.022912	Std error of regression	0.021407
R-Square	0.960091	Adjusted *R*-square	0.956899
F (5, 50)	240.5722	p-value (F)	1.01E-33
Log-likelihood	136.0025	Akaike information criterion	−262.0051
Schwarz B. criterion	−251.9684	Hannan–Quinn criterion	−258.1238
Rho	0.334799	Durbin–Watson	1.263523

Table 20.6 Rates of change in four quarters – estimation results

	Coefficient	Std error	*t*-stat	*p*-value
Avg wage	0.778528	0.0266761	29.1844	<0.00001
IPA_OG	0.0656359	0.0201617	3.2555	0.00199
Dummy	0.0188328	0.00640116	2.9421	0.00486

Mean of dependent variable	0.086682	Std deviation of dependent variable	0.054578
Sum sqd residuals	0.02107	Std error of regression	0.02013
R-square	0.963299	Adjusted *R*-square	0.961888
F (5, 50)	454.956	*p*-value (F)	2.75E-37
Log-likelihood	138.307	Akaike information criterion	−270.614
Schwarz B. criterion	−264.592	Hannan–Quinn criterion	−268.2852
Rho	0.345937	Durbin–Watson	1.255269

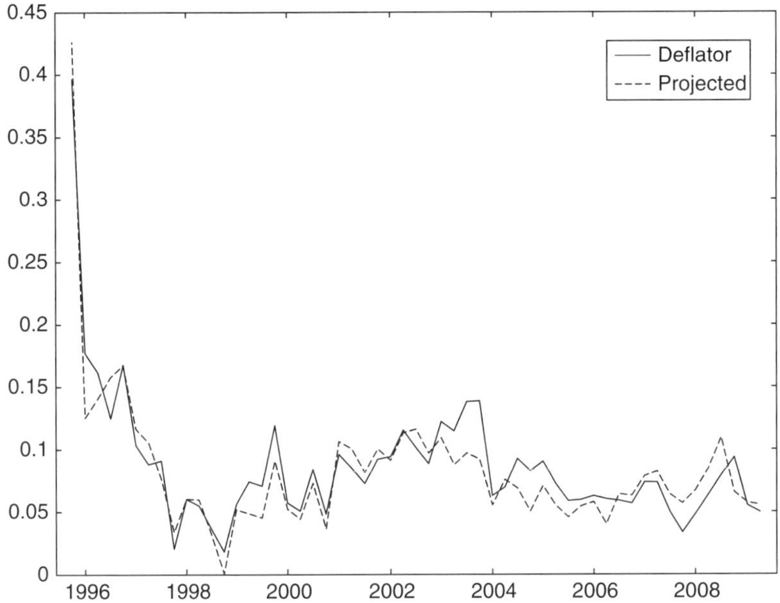

Figure 20.6 *GDP deflator (rates of change in four quarters): effective and projected values.*

Regression results appear in Table 20.6 and the effective and projected values are included in Figure 20.6. Once again, the assumption of normality for the residuals could not be discarded – the *p*-value of the Jarque–Bera test was 0.7238 although the Durbin–Watson test rejected the assumption of non-autocorrelation in the residuals.

The most important conclusion of this analysis is that the predominant variable that explains the inflation rate is the rate of change of the average wage – a conclusion that prevails in both sets of data (with and without seasonality). Also, changes in money supply (M1) in excess of real GDP displayed a strong relation with inflation (seasonal data). Further, rates of change of agricultural prices and the exchange rate also reveal significant relations with inflation – in the latter, when data without seasonality are used.

20.6 CONCLUSIONS

In historical perspective, the main cause of Brazilian inflation is the continued government drive to spend far beyond what could be financed by tax revenues, coupled with the fact that the country's capital market has been very limited and could not provide the necessary resources to finance fiscal deficits in favorable conditions – that is, with low real interest rates and long maturities. Given the deficiencies of Brazil's capital market, the financing of fiscal deficits has become a major source of additional spending, higher deficits, and stronger inflationary pressures. Moreover the major limitations of the country's capital market are undoubtedly linked to the pattern of extremely high real interest rates that has predominated since the 1980s.

The instruments of the Real Plan, in much the same way as those of its predecessors of the 1980s and 1990s, affected almost exclusively the cost components of inflation – especially the exchange rate – leaving the financial disequilibrium of the public sector not significantly different from the situation before the plan. The consequences of this disequilibrium are more clearly perceived in the monetary and capital markets, with the impressive growth of the public debt, and the growth of money supply far superior to price increases. Also to be mentioned is the firm stance of the government in pursuing, and obtaining, frequent increases in tax revenue. At its origin, the Real Plan was consolidated on a nominal anchor based on the dollar exchange rate, but after the exchange rate crisis of 1998, Brazilian authorities introduced a new stabilization strategy centered on inflation targeting, whose record is dubious. Since inflation targeting was introduced, only in 4 years was annual inflation lower than the midpoint target, and even considering a tolerance margin of 2 percentage points introduced by the central bank, inflation surpassed the target in 3 consecutive years – from 2001 to 2003 (in 2002, by more than 9 percentage points).

Many of the changes that occurred in the Brazilian economy after the Real Plan originated in the financial sector, and they are related to 2 major tendencies that became commonplace in many countries: the internationalization of domestic financial markets and the ever increasing role of institutional investors.

The most important conclusion of the empirical analysis in this chapter is that the predominant variable that explains inflation in Brazil is the rate of change of the average wage – a conclusion that prevails in sets of data with and without seasonality. Also, changes in money supply (M1) in excess of real GDP displayed a strong relation with inflation (seasonal data). Further, rates of change of agricultural prices and the exchange rate also reveal significant relations with inflation – in the latter, when data without seasonality are used. The evaluation of the Real Plan developed in previous sections has shown that it has been very successful in limiting wage increases and, especially, in keeping the exchange rate at a very low level for most of the last decade. These are, very likely, the main factors behind the relatively low rates of inflation in the post-Real-Plan period. On the other hand, given the loose fiscal policies of the last decade and a half, the supply of money has grown at a very high rate, and this has been a major source of inflationary pressures.

NOTES

1. The author is greatly indebted to Daniel Arce, Wilson Calmon, Fernando Cerqueira Lima and Rodolfo Hoffmann for valuable comments and suggestions on earlier versions. Since many of these suggestions could not be implemented for limitations of time and space, the author is solely responsible for any remaining errors.
2. Law no. 22.626 of 7 April.
3. The profound, negative effects of increasing inflation in Brazil's financial markets are acutely described in the following passage: 'Commercial banks started to reduce systematically the maturity of their credit operations, and eventually specialized in the supply of short-term credit, rarely exceeding 120 days, with commercial paper as collateral. Credit for longer periods was no longer offered by banks, and it only reappeared in the market when the Sociedades de Crédito e Financiamento introduced new securities that could side step the usury law. The supply of long-run credit was limited to a few government agencies, and the supply of private funds in this segment virtually disappeared . . . Insurance companies, for the most part, had to specialize in the most elementary branches of the business, losing their classic role as institutional investors . . . At a certain point, private savings could only be spared the losses due to inflation by the acquisition of either real estate or foreign currency . . . The stock market could have been greatly stimulated by inflation, but . . . the [Brazilian] tradition of companies controlled by a single family caused this market to remain incipient' (Chacel et al., 1970). The most important security mentioned in the passage was a private note, a *letra de câmbio*, which was sold with a discount, therefore allowing financial gains far beyond the 12 per cent limit. These funds were demanded mainly by commercial and industrial firms. The *letras de câmbio* became very popular in the early 1960s and, in the middle of the decade, the total value issued was about twice that of time deposits in banks.
4. In 1986, the government closed the BNH and transferred its operations to another public financial institution, the Caixa Econômica Federal (CEF).
5. The PAEG also included wage and price controls. For a thorough analysis of its measures, see Barbosa et al. (1989).
6. Data for December; see *Boletim do Banco Central do Brasil – Suplemento Estatístico*, September 1995. Commercial banks include the 'multiple banks', which operate more than one line of business, and the state-owned Banco do Brasil.
7. See Tullio and Ronci (1996).
8. The Constitution enacted in 1988 imposes a limit to *real* interest rates. Its art. 192, para. 3, says: 'Real interest rates . . . will not surpass twelve percent a year; to charge interest above this limit will be considered the crime of usury . . . ' However this new version of the usury law was never properly regulated, and therefore it is not considered to be in effect.
9. In the second half of the 2000s, some specific segments benefited from a greater availability of credit that, for the most part, flowed in from international markets – this trend was particularly noticeable in the financing of homes and automobiles. However, interest rates remained extremely high by international standards.
10. The major consequences of this mechanism are depicted in the following passage: 'As financial institutions could transform treasury bills into currency and vice versa without

any significant risk of capital loss . . . the public debt acquired such a degree of liquidity that it could be considered money for all practical purposes. In addition, the development of checking deposits backed by treasury bills paying daily interest and allowing instantaneous convertibility into currency became widespread' (Tullio and Ronci, 1996, p. 640).

11. See Williamson (1990).
12. These ideas are developed, for example, in Lopes (1984), and in Pereira and Nakano (1984).
13. The economic policies pursued in Brazil in the second half of the 1980s and in the 1990s, and the ideas behind them, are extensively analyzed elsewhere. See e.g. Fonseca (1995, 1998), especially ch. 7; and Baer (2001), especially ch. 7, 8 and 9.
14. In February 1990, the total amount of federal bonds in the market was $60,165 million; the following month this figure dwindled to $21,936 million. In national currency, though, this loss was less dramatic: from CR$1,843 million to CR$934 million (millions of cruzeiros reais). The confiscated bonds, and the bank deposits that backed them, were returned 18 months later, in 12 monthly installments.
15. Arida and Resende (1986). This proposal was not really original since it had been applied in Hungary immediately after World War II, with disastrous consequences. See, on this subject, Nogaro (1948).
16. Contrary to government expectations, the use of the URV in the private sector as a basis for determining price changes remained very limited.
17. The new currency, the real, was introduced on 1 July 1994.
18. For a discussion of the effects of the 1988 Constitution on inflation, see Barbosa et al. (1989).
19. Before the Real Plan, the Central Bank acted in the foreign exchange market to keep the dollar-exchange rate constant in real terms. For a long-run perspective on exchange rate policy in Brazil, see Coes (2009).
20. In the 1990s, New Zealand, Canada, the United Kingdom, Sweden, Finland, Australia and Spain adopted inflation targeting (Mishkin, 1999).
21. Since inflation targeting was introduced, based on an official price index – the *Índice de Preços ao Consumidor Amplo* (IPCA) – in only 4 years was annual inflation lower than the midpoint target. Moreover, even considering a tolerance margin of 2 percentage points introduced by the central bank, which from 2003 to 2005 was increased to 2 1/2 points, inflation surpassed the target in 3 consecutive years (from 2001 to 2003). The worst case happened in 2002 when, with the major devaluation of the real due to the election of Lula da Silva – then perceived as a radical – the midpoint target was set at 3.5 per cent and inflation rose to 12.53 per cent. After this failure, the central bank reset the target for 2003 to 8.5 per cent and the official inflation rate was 9.30 per cent.
22. This trend occurred until the second term of President Cardoso, having stabilized since then. The debt figures in Table 20.3 do not include treasury bonds kept by the central bank. In the period 2007–09, the total value of the public debt (including the share with the central bank) reached 56.2 per cent of GDP.
23. In relation to this point, a recent article examined the distributive effects of the Brazilian government's revenues and expenses, and concluded that, in comparison with the income of taxpayers, the tax burden is concentrated in the lower-income segments (Baer and Galvão Jr, 2008).
24. For a recent analysis of Brazil's stagnating performance in recent years – mostly centered on microeconomic factors – see Bezerra and Cavalcanti (2009).
25. This view clearly appears in the following passage: 'One is left with the impression that this inflation must have enormous costs for society as a whole and that a serious stabilization program should create the conditions for a very large once-and-for all jump in real GDP and higher growth thereafter' (Tullio and Ronci, 1996, p. 656).
26. In the case of the average wage in the industrial sector, the data presented are four-quarter moving averages.

27. It should be mentioned, though, that more often than not the minimum wage in Brazil had real gains that surpassed those of the average wage in the industrial sector. Therefore, there were relative changes among segments of the labor force benefiting those whose incomes depend on the official minimum wage – usually the less qualified workers.
28. Data available in www.andima.com.br
29. In the case of capital inflows, they also resulted from the very high level of interest rates, especially in treasury bonds.
30. This distinction goes back to the origins of macroeconomics, since it is included in the original contributions of Keynes and Kalecki. It has also been used in a few econometric analysis of inflation applied to Brazilian data. See, for example, Zottman (1989), Barbosa and McNelis (1990) and Tullio and Ronci (1996).
31. According to quarterly data compiled by the author, money velocity decreased rather smoothly, albeit with oscillations, from 8.3 in the last quarter of 1995 –the start of the period selected for the econometric analysis – to 3.5 in the first quarter of 2009. If the econometric analysis indicated that the assumption of stable money velocity would be too restrictive, then equation (20.1) would be replaced by $\Delta p_t^D = \alpha\,(\Delta m_t + \Delta v_t - \Delta y_t)$.
32. See e.g. Zivot and Wang (2006) and Shumway and Stoffer (2006).

REFERENCES

Arida, P. and A.L. Resende (1986), 'Inflação inercial e reforma monetária', in P. Arida (ed.), *Inflação Zero*, Rio de Janeiro: Paz e Terra, pp. 9–34.

Baer W. (2001), *The Brazilian Economy,* 6th edn, Boulder, CO: Lynne Rienner.

Baer, W. and A. Galvão Jr (2008), 'Tax burden, government expenditures and income distribution in Brazil', *Quarterly Review of Economics and Finance*, **48** (2), 345–58.

Banco Central do Brasil, *Boletim do Banco Central do Brasil*, Brasília, several issues.

Barbosa, F.H., A.S.P. Brandão and C. de Faro (1989), *Fiscal Reform and Stabilization: The Brazilian Experience*, Rio de Janeiro: Getúlio Vargas Foundation.

Barbosa, F.H. and P.D. McNelis (1989), 'Indexation and inflationary inertia: Brazil 1964–1985', *World Bank Economic Review*, **3** (3), pp. 339–58.

Bezerra, J. and T.V. de V. Cavalcanti (2009), 'Brazil's lack of growth', in Love and Baer (2009), pp. 67–89.

Cerqueira Lima, F.C.G. de (1998), *Intermediação Financeira e Internacionalização Bancária*, Texto Didático no. 1, Universidade Federal do Rio de Janeiro – ECEX: Especialização em Comércio Exterior.

Chacel, J., M.H. Simonsen and A. Wald (1970), *A Correção Monetária*, Rio de Janeiro: APEC.

Coes, D.V. (2009), 'Exchange rate policy, perceptions of risk, and external constraints under Lula', in Love and Baer (2009), pp. 115–33.

Dias Leite, A.F. de A. (2007), *Avaliação do Desempenho do Mercado de Debêntures no Brasil – 2000 a 2005,* Universidade Federal do Rio de Janeiro, Monografia de Graduação em Economia.

Fonseca, M.A.R. da (1995), *O Processo Inflacionário: Análise da Experiência Brasileira*, Petrópolis, Brazil: Vozes.

Fonseca, M.A.R. da (1998), 'Brazil's *Real* Plan', *Journal of Latin American Studies*, **30** (3), pp. 619–39.
Lopes, F. (1984), 'Inflação inercial, hiperinflação e desinflação'. *Revista da ANPEC*, **7** (8), pp. 55–71.
Love, J.L. and W. Baer (eds) (2009), *Brazil under Lula: Economic, Politics, and Society under the Worker-President*, New York: Palgrave Macmillan.
Mishkin, F.S. (1999),'International Experiences with Different Monetary Policy Regimes', NBER Working Paper no. 6965, Cambridge, MA.
Nogaro, B. (1948), 'Hungary's recent monetary crisis and its theoretical meaning', *American Economic Review*, **38** (4), pp. 526–42.
Pereira, L.C.B. and Y. Nakano, *Inflação e Recessão*, São Paulo, Brazil: Brasiliense.
Schumway, R.H. and D.S. Stoffer (2006), *Time Series Analysis and Its Applications: With R Examples*, 2nd edn, New York: Springer.
Tullio, G. and M. Ronci (1996), 'Brazilian inflation from 1980 to 1993: causes, consequences and dynamics', *Journal of Latin American Studies*, **28** (3), pp. 635–66.
Williamson, J. (1990), 'What Washington means by policy reform', in J. Williamson (ed.), *Latin American Adjustment: How Much Has Happened?*, Washington, DC.: Peterson Institute for International Economics, pp. 7–40.
Zivot, E. and J. Wang (2006), *Modeling Financial Time Series with S-PLUS*, 2nd edn, New York: Springer.
Zottman, L. (1989), 'Inflação, processo decisório governamental e a modelagem: um comentário metodológico', *Anais do XI Encontro Brasileiro de Econometria*, Fortaleza, Brazil: ANPEC.

21. Comments on part VII

Daniel G. Arce M.

The chapters by Heymann et al. and Fonseca are not what pass as traditional macroeconomics these days.[1] This means that they are data-driven policy-based and focused on economic aggregates, rather than on presenting precise results from complex models that are sensitive to potato chip elasticities and the like. In other words, the chapters are a pleasure to read and I learned something about the real world! Moreover, their judicious coverage of the 'lost decade' in Argentina and Brazil was well worth reading even though the facts are now well known. As such, my focus will be on what these chapters have to say about the Argentine and Brazilian economies of the Noughties (2000–09) and the lessons they provide for US policy during the aftermath of the financial crisis.

Both chapters are quick to point out that the improvement in each country's primary surplus (central government budget excluding debt payments) may not be what it seems. Fonseca documents the perpetual lack of fiscal correction in Brazil. Furthermore, aggressive tax increases to finance debt payments represent a transfer of income to domestic and international debt holders. In Argentina there has been an increase in domestic tax revenues as well. Again, the tax revenue increase has been accompanied by an increase in government expenditure. On the plus side, Argentina has had (until recently) an increasing trade surplus owing to favorable world prices. I would like to know to what extent international trade is in Argentina a function of demand stemming from the Brazilian and Chinese economies. Is Argentina susceptible to the fortunes of these two trading partners in the same way that the Brazilian devaluation of 1998–99 exposed the cracks in Argentina's convertibility regime? Finally, neither study examines the fiscal stance after correcting for endogenous movements and automatic stabilizers. It is therefore difficult to substantiate claims about fiscal profligacy without having a good sense of what portion of fiscal policy is actually discretionary.

The two chapters also raise important issues about what is meant by central-bank 'independence'. In Argentina the politicization of the transfer of foreign reserves from the central bank to the treasury in order to meet debt servicing is a disturbing step backwards relative to the independent charter established in the 1990s. In Brazil there is almost complete monetary–fiscal symbiosis when it comes to financing deficits. At the same time, Brazil has weathered the international financial crisis quite nicely. Might the Cardoso reforms to monetary policymaking – removing financial firms' representation on the open market committee – be part of the explanation? By contrast, the US Fed is independent in terms of the monetary–fiscal nexus but not in terms of private sector participation on the boards of regional Fed banks. To me a central bank should be independent of both private and public sectors. Monetary–fiscal independence does not ensure a central bank's credibility, as the role of the New York Federal Reserve Bank's bailout of AIG's creditors makes clear.

Another observation common to these two chapters is that inflation still has social components. What is novel about Heymann et al. is the argument that although economic conditions for a hyperinflation were present in the wake of the collapse of the convertibility plan, the Argentine citizenry apparently now understands the welfare-enhancing aspects of moderate inflation. The idea that moderate inflations seem to be both anticipated and accepted without creating an inertial component marks a significant structural change in Argentine political economy. By contrast, Fonseca finds traditional social drivers of inflation in Brazil; specifically, the predominant variable that explains Brazilian inflation is the rate of change of the average wage. I have two comments about this finding. First, to what extent is Brazilian inflation inertial? For example, Heymann et al.'s econometric analysis of Argentine inflation includes lagged values of inflation whereas Fonseca's does not. Second, much is made in Fonseca about the inflationary consequences of deficit finance, yet fiscal policy is not accounted for in the inflation regressions. Again, this is a point where the distinction between endogenous and discretionary components of fiscal policy would prove useful.

I conclude with a word about growth. After accounting for the post-convertibility recovery effect, Heymann et al. find the peak-to-peak average rate of increase of Argentine GDP to be approximately 3 per cent per annum. Their rationale for this growth is again novel – they argue that it is an impressive and unusual case of self-financed increases in production and demand without pressure on interest rates. By contrast, Fonseca sees even higher rates of growth for Brazil (3.5–3.7 per cent for 2003–09) as impaired, reflecting constraints brought on by overvaluation and high (short-term) interest rates. The difference in perspective is marked; particularly as the US aspires to such rates of growth in what might otherwise be its own lost decade.

NOTE

1. On this point see Polborn (2001) and Caballero (2010).

REFERENCES

Caballero, Ricardo (2010), 'Macroeconomics after the crisis: time to deal with the pretense of knowledge', NBER Working Paper no. 16429, Cambridge, MA.
Polborn, Mattias (2001), 'Calibrating the world and the world of calibration', Department of Economics, Working Paper, University of Western Ontario, London, ON.

PART VIII

Foreign trade and investment: past and present

22. Trade and foreign investment in Argentina: from the agro-export model to the present

Andrés López

The changing foreign trade and investment patterns observable throughout Argentina's history need to be understood in the context of the different development styles the country has adopted since the mid nineteenth century.

During the period of the so-called agro-export model, Argentina was a very open country and took advantage of the international markets for selling agricultural commodities to industrialized countries as well as of high levels of mobility of capital and of labor flows.

Things changed dramatically after the crisis of the 1930s and then with World War II, which disrupted trade and investment flows and forced the adoption of protectionist measures. After the war, protectionism was maintained in order to push industrialization, and by the end of this period Argentina was one of the more closed economies in the world, although industrial exports began to grow from the mid 1960s onwards.

In turn, Argentina was mostly hostile to foreign direct investment (FDI) under the Peronist government (1946–55), but then FDI became the pillar of the 'heavy' phase of import substitution launched by the 'desarrollista' government (1958–62). This generated concerns in intellectual and political circles, leading to restrictions on transnational corporations (TNCs) from the late 1960s onwards, and to policies favoring domestic firms.

The military dictatorship that took office in 1976 adopted a trade liberalization strategy and deregulated FDI. In 1981 a huge economic crisis emerged and in 1982 the debt crisis led to a new round of protectionism. Things changed again in the early 1890s, with the adoption of the convertibility plan and of a far-reaching program of structural reforms (inspired by Washington Consensus ideas). Growth resumption led to significant FDI inflows, and the TNC presence in Argentina's economy reached record levels. However, although both primary and industrial exports grew significantly, Argentina did not regain weight in world trade flows.

In 2001–02 the country underwent its worst economic crisis, in the context of a mega devaluation of the peso. In spite of a strong anti-Washington-Consensus social and political mood, the new governments did not reverse trade liberalization dramatically, although the use of protectionist measures gradually increased. In turn, conflicts with foreign investors emerged because of the debt default, the banking system bankruptcy and the freezing of privatized firms' tariffs, and later on because of the government's attempts to manage some domestic prices. Although no overt anti-FDI policy was adopted, the government pushed for the retirement of foreign investors in some privatized firms in order to favor the entry of local partners. In turn, in a context of a higher exchange rate and fostered by favorable international prices for commodities, Argentina's exports have recorded strong growth in the past decade and huge trade surpluses have emerged, in sharp contrast with the 1990s.

This chapter's main objective is to analyze the above-mentioned historical evolution of Argentina's integration in the world economy. Sections 22.1 to 22.4 each deal with one of the historical periods sketched above. Section 22.5 concludes and offers some reflections on the future challenges for Argentina's integration in the new world of globalization.

22.1 THE AGRO-EXPORT MODEL 1860–1930

Between 1860 and 1930 Argentina went through an institutional, technological and economic catch-up process. According to Maddison's (1995) data, Argentina ranked seventeenth in terms of GDP per capita in 1870 (over a sample of 56 countries for which GDP data for that year are available) while in 1929 it had climbed to eleventh place.

Agricultural resources played a key role in this period, since growth was mainly led by exports of a number of staples. Natural fertility and the good climate of the pampas were key factors for export success. However, technological and institutional innovations were also needed.

The rule of law was guaranteed by the gradual emergence of a modern state and the enactment of a number of laws and regulations aiming at protecting property rights and at providing the infrastructure needed for investments and exports. Regarding technology, it is important to highlight the process of genetic and technical innovations that made it possible to adapt the domestic cattle stock to the requirements of the European markets (Sesto, 2000). As a consequence of a massive process of the adoption of modern (mostly imported) machinery in agriculture, there was

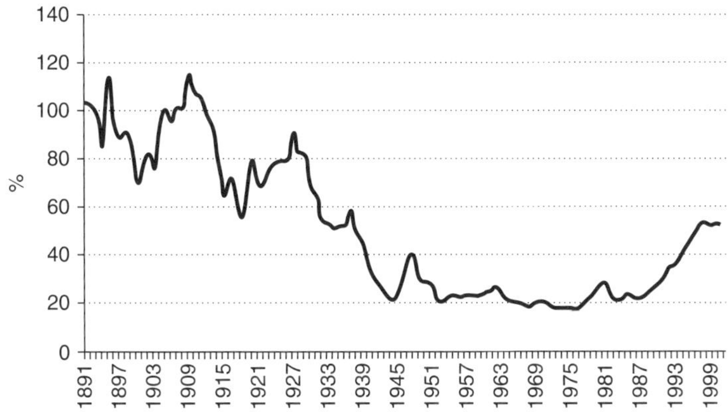

Source: Gerchunoff and Llach (2003).

Figure 22.1 Argentina's foreign trade as a percentage of domestic tradable production 1891–1999 (in 1993 constant prices).

neither a technological nor a productivity gap between the large farms in Argentina vis-à-vis those in Australia or Canada (see Villarroel, 1992).

Domestic transformations went hand in hand with the opportunities open in world markets, that is, the growing demand for primary products in industrialized countries, especially in Great Britain, and some key innovations in maritime transport and refrigeration techniques that allowed the export of chilled and canned meat to Europe.

Argentina was a very open economy during this period, as is seen in the high share of exports and imports in tradable production[1] (Figure 22.1). Although agriculture was the leading economic activity, a rapid process of industrialization took place, and a modern services sector developed.

The leading export products changed throughout time and some diversification existed within the primary sector. Until 1860 the main exports items were jerked beef, wool, fat and leather. By the 1870s, wool had become the country's first successful export staple and represented half of total exports. Later on, cereals (wheat and maize) surpassed wool, and in the new century chilled and frozen meat significantly increased their share in exports (replacing live cattle).

Between 1870 and 1913 Argentina was only surpassed by Japan and Mexico in terms of export growth rate. Although Argentina's performance declined between 1913 and 1929, it was still above the world average (Table 22.1). Hence, Argentina's share in world exports increased from 0.39 per cent in 1870 to 0.93 per cent in 1929.

Table 22.1 World exports: cumulative annual growth rates 1870–1929 (in constant 1990 prices in US$) (percentages)

	1870–1913	1913–29		1870–1913	1913–29
Germany	4.0	−0.5	United Kingdom	2.7	−1.2
Argentina	**5.1**	**2.7**	India	2.3	−0.8
Australia	4.7	0.4	Indonesia	4.1	5.9
Brazil	1.8	1.9	Italy	2.2	1.2
Canada	4.0	3.9	Japan	8.3	5.7
Chile	3.3	3.9	Mexico	5.3	2.7
China	2.5	2.4	Norway	3.1	3.1
Colombia	2.0	6.8	Peru	1.6	6.2
Korea	n.a.	12.6	Sweden	3.0	2.7
Denmark	3.6	3.6	Taiwan	–	8.0
Spain	3.4	−0.5	Thailand	4.0	1.5
United States	4.7	2.7	USSR	–	−3.8
Finland	3.8	2.9	Venezuela	–	3.8
France	2.7	2.3	**World**	**3.3**	**2.1**

Note: –: No significant information available.

Source: Author's elaboration on the basis of Maddison (1995).

Import composition also changed over time, with non-durable consumption goods declining in favor of durable, capital goods, raw materials and intermediate inputs. Imports of foreign machinery were high – imports of industrial capital goods during the 1920s were a historical record until the 1960s – not only owing to the high levels of investment in agriculture and industry, but also because high urban wage levels fostered the use of capital-intensive techniques.

It is common wisdom to state that trade policy was 'liberal' in this period (Ferrer, 1975; Ortiz, 1971; Di Tella and Zymelman, 1967). These authors argue that no protection was given to the industrial sector, mainly because of the influence of agricultural producers who feared wage competition with manufacturers and retaliations from the United Kingdom (whose exports would suffer from Argentina's protectionism). Other authors claim not only that no structural opposition existed between landlords and industrial producers, but also that many industrial branches enjoyed protection in this period (Díaz Alejandro, 1975; Guy, 1979; Hora, 2000; Rocchi, 1998). Maddison (1992), comparing tariffs in different countries between 1913 and 1925, includes Argentina among the 'strongly protectionist' ones. All authors acknowledge that protection was seldom given on the basis of structured policy strategies aimed at promoting industrialization, since it was mainly the result of political pressures.

In a context of no regulations for foreign capital, FDI had a strong weight in Argentina's economy, comparable with those observed in other recent settlement regions like Australia and Canada, and in other Asian and Latin American countries (Twomey, 1998). FDI was concentrated in export-related activities – railroads, meat-packing – as well as in import-substituting industries – food and beverages, chemicals, pharmaceuticals – and in sectors where demand was growing owing to urbanization and economic modernization – public utilities, banking. British investment was dominant. However, US investments began to grow in the twentieth century and were more oriented to manufacturing than British ones.

The predominance of FDI in natural resources was far from being an exclusive feature of Argentina, since most FDI in those years was North – South and aimed at exploiting the resources of host countries (resource-seeking). In turn, investment in manufacturing in Argentina was 'market-seeking', motivated by economic stability, domestic market growth and tariff protection in some cases. US investments were also motivated by the objective of contesting the domestic market with British firms, which dominated it through their exports.

In general, foreign affiliates operated with scales above those of local firms, and had higher productivity levels. Some spillovers took place, since FDI (specially from the US) brought new products, new production and organizational methods, which were to some extent copied by domestic entrepreneurs (Villanueva, 1972; Barbero, 2003). On the negative side, foreign affiliates adopted monopolistic or collusive behaviors in some industries (e.g. meatpacking).

In turn, immigrants played a key role in industrialization (almost all manufacturing branches were dominated by foreign entrepreneurs), since they brought in their knowledge about technologies, production methods, management and marketing. Many of the firms created by them went through a learning process in which they accumulated capabilities of competing with foreign products in the local market and also, in a number of cases, of investing abroad,[2] an infrequent phenomenon in a developing country at that time (Katz and Kosacoff, 1983).

22.2 IMPORT-SUBSTITUTION INDUSTRIALIZATION 1930–76

The crisis of the 1930s led to the end of the agro-export model and to the beginning of the import-substitution industrialization (ISI) process.

Although Argentina's growth performance during the ISI was relatively weak by international comparison, between 1964 and 1974 the economy experienced 11 years of GDP growth in a row. However, even during those years recurrent balance-of-payments and institutional crises and growing social unrest were present.

The 1930s crisis (and, later on, World War II) hit the economy severely, since the disruption of world trade led to a dramatic fall in exports. Measured in current prices, exports in 1932 were only a third of the 1928 level, and would only surpass that level in 1946. The currency shortage forced the government to restrict imports and introduce foreign exchange controls. This was a 'pragmatic' response that led to a 'market-driven' import substitution process, which basically took place in light industries, but also in activities such as machinery (where many repair shops became manufacturers) and chemicals. Hence, import substitution took place as a way to meet local demand for goods that were previously supplied from abroad.

During this transition period, there was a hot debate about the style of development that Argentina should adopt. Many intellectuals criticized the agro-export model, because of the dependence on foreign (notably British) markets, the excessive weight of foreign capital (which was also suspected of influencing the political game) and the unbalanced ('imperialist') relations with the UK. Hence, they pushed for a strong impulse to manufacturing and to local industries.

In turn, others thought that the disruptions caused by the crisis and the war were only temporary and that 'normality' would soon return, allowing the country to resume its role as an exporter of agricultural products. A sort of intermediate position was that held in the so-called 'Plan Pinedo' (after the name of the Minister of Economy), which fostered industrialization in an open economy, putting emphasis on trade relations with the US and Latin American countries, and promoted non-traditional exports (the plan was proposed in 1940, but never approved in Congress, mainly because of the opposition of the financial and agricultural sectors).

After the war, the pendulum moved towards a state-led industrialization strategy. During the Peronist government (1946–55) a strongly inward-oriented development style was adopted. This decision was due to a number of factors. First, a strong redistributionist strategy was adopted, leading to large increases in real wages, fostering consumption and making it difficult for manufacturing industry to compete abroad, given its low productivity levels. Second, Perón assumed that it would be dangerous to rely on foreign markets again. Third, as in many other countries, by that time development was equal to industrialization, and industrialization needed a state granting subsidies and protecting the local market.

Exports of agricultural products were monopolized by the state through

Table 22.2 World exports: cumulative annual growth rates 1929–70 (in constant 1990 prices in US$) (percentages)

	1929–50	1950–70		1929–50	1950–70
Germany	−4.4	13.7	United Kingdom	0.9	4.3
Argentina	**−1.8**	**3.4**	India	−1.8	2.7
Australia	1.8	6.2	Indonesia	−0.7	7.1
Brazil	1.4	5.1	Italy	0.1	12.8
Canada	2.2	7.7	Japan	−0.9	17.0
Chile	−0.7	2.7	Mexico	−2.8	4.7
China	0.1	3.0	Norway	2.2	8.0
Colombia	1.4	4.2	Peru	0.1	6.4
Korea	−10.5	22.5	Sweden	2.6	7.6
Denmark	1.3	7.6	Taiwan	−1.7	17.9
Spain	−2.3	10.1	Thailand	2.7	4.8
United States	1.6	6.9	USRR	3.8	13.8
Finland	1.0	7.9	Venezuela	6.2	4.4
France	0.1	9.1	**World**	**0.5**	**6.6**

Source: Author's elaboration on the basis of Maddison (1995).

the Instituto Argentino para la Promoción del Intercambio (IAPI), created in 1946, which also tried to regulate imports of the so-called 'essentials goods'. Bank deposits were also nationalized as well as most public utilities (see Mallon and Sourrouille, 1975). The industrial sector was favored not only by cheap credits and high tariff and non-tariff barriers, but also by transfers from the agricultural sector in the form of differential exchange rates.

Tariff protection specially favored consumption goods (whose weight in the imports structure fell from almost 40 per cent in the first half of the 1930s to 10 per cent in the first half of the 1950s). Capital goods tariffs were fluctuating and augmented when foreign currency was in shortage. This context was far from being conducive to fostering microeconomic efficiency, since protected industries did not feel the impact of foreign competition at all, while they had to pay high tariffs for importing capital goods (Díaz Alejandro, 1975; Taylor, 1994).

Industrial exports, which had been growing until 1943, were discouraged by the Peronist government. Agricultural exports were also harmed, owing to a combination of stagnating productivity and public policies that transferred part of the export rents to the industry. This led to a fall in Argentina's exports between 1929 and 1950 (Table 22.2), which in turn made the country's share in world exports decline from 0.93 to 0.55 per cent between 1929 and 1950.

Argentina also lost attractiveness for foreign investors.[3] While in 1940 FDI from the US was 60 per cent higher than that in Brazil, in 1955 Argentina only had 40 per cent of the US FDI received by Brazil (Díaz Alejandro, 1975). In turn, in 1955 foreign capital represented 5 per cent of the total capital stock of the country, against 50 per cent at the beginning of the twentieth century (ECLAC, 2001).

Owing to the growing difficulties since 1948 – growth deceleration, inflation, foreign currency crisis – a number of reforms began to be adopted from 1952 onwards, including more friendly policies for the agricultural sector and actions to attract foreign investment, but they failed to revert those problems and the Peronist government was deposed by a military coup in 1955.

The new government adopted some liberalizing measures, including the elimination of the IAPI and the relaxation of controls on FDI (especially profit remittances). Later on, President Frondizi's 'developmentalist' government that took office in 1958 launched an ambitious project aimed at 'deepening' import substitution by promoting the intermediate, consumption durables and capital goods industries. The final objective was to reduce industry's dependence on imports, eliminating what was perceived as the main obstacle to sustained growth, since local production of consumption goods had not reduced import need, but merely transformed its structure (from final to intermediate and capital goods). 'Stop-and-go' cycles characterized that period, based on a dual economy structure with an exporter sector (agriculture) and a noncompetitive sector (industry) which depended upon the currency incomes generated for importing capital and intermediate goods.

Although the growth in industrial exports from the 1960s onwards modified somewhat the cyclical context, the frequent fluctuations in economic activity and the distributive conflicts between capital and labor and between agriculture and industry were key features of this period.

The 'desarrollista' investment drive was fostered by Law 14780 on foreign direct investment and Law 14781 on industrial promotion.[4] They jointly defined the incentives regime through which significant physical investments in new plants making chemicals, petrochemicals, oil refining, motor vehicles, machinery and other metal products were made.

The call to FDI was based on two arguments: (1) the rate of domestic savings was low; (2) the industrialization process had to be fast and TNCs could rapidly contribute with the technology and capital needed. Between 1959 and 1962 authorizations for FDI amounted to US$500 million, duplicating the authorizations granted between 1954 and 1958 and 1963 and 1970. The main investor was the US, followed by Germany, France, the UK and Italy (Sourrouille et al., 1985).

In this stage FDI was mainly market-seeking and tariff-jumping. The TNCs' operations usually had negative impacts on the current-account balance, given their low export propensity and the transfers made to their headquarters through different channels – profits, royalties, etc.

Although an investment boom took place in the wake of the strategy, the 'desarrollista' project had to deal with balance-of-payments crises and huge devaluations, increasing strikes and growing discontent among the armed forces. The latter ultimately led to a military coup in 1962. Although import-substitution policies were also pursued by the subsequent governments, the project aimed at almost complete self-sufficiency was never fulfilled.

TNCs were a key agent of this stage. Between 1958 and 1963, 200 foreign companies made green-field investments. By the early 1970s, TNCs' share in industrial production reached 33 per cent (Kosacoff and Bezchinsky, 1993). Production by foreign affiliates grew at an annual rate of 8.8 per cent between 1955 and 1973 vis-à-vis 4.3 per cent in local firms, but employment in such affiliates only grew at 0.94 per cent, as against 1.2 per cent in domestic firms (Sourrouille et al., 1985).

Though many TNCs brought second-hand machinery, they also transferred modern product and process technologies, quality control and subcontracting practices to their subsidiaries (Katz and Kosacoff, 2000). This, jointly with the use of less labor-intensive techniques and their propensity to locate in capital-intensive sectors, ensured higher labor productivity levels in TNC affiliates than in local firms. In 1963 labor productivity in such affiliates was 185 per cent higher in the manufacturing sector. Between 1955 and 1973 labor productivity in foreign firms grew at an annual rate of 7.7 per cent vis-à-vis 3 per cent in domestic firms (Sourrouille et al., 1985).

The massive arrival of TNCs had a substantial impact beyond the installation of new plants. Many of those firms created engineering departments and supplier development programs. Gradually, activities such as product engineering and design, then production and methods, and, finally, organization and planning were undertaken in a systematic manner and consolidated the accumulation of an internal technological capacity. This capacity was not only specific to each firm, but also generated positive spillovers for the industrial sector. Even though TNCs did not invest in Argentina with the explicit intention of developing a local technological capacity – and their expenditures in R&D were usually very low – in practice they contributed to such development. In fact, in view of the idiosyncratic characteristics of the host country (market size, regulations, consumers' preferences, infrastructure), the affiliates often had to conduct innovative adaptive activities to apply product and process technologies developed in their respective parent companies (Cimoli and Katz, 2003).

Table 22.3 Argentine legal tariff rates 1959-97 (percentages)

	1959	1969	1976	1988	1991	1993	1997
Nondurable consumer goods	197	142	200	53	25	30	23
Durable consumer goods	198	142	149	63	21	20	19
Intermediate goods	118	102	86	44	17	20	14
Machinery	147	93	87	57	22	8	14
Transport equipment	188	124	132	57	27	9	21
Weighted average	141	107	99	48	19	17	16
Mean (unweighted average)	145	103	97	52	19	17	15
Standard deviation	56	42	41	16	5	8	5
Dispersion (%)	38	41	42	30	27	44	30

Source: Berlinski (2003).

As TNCs invested with the goal of exploiting the domestic market, exports played a marginal role in their activities. They often used product and process technologies which fell well short of international practices, and operated plants with considerable diseconomies of scale. However, a learning process took place in many affiliates, contributing over time to increased export flows, which were mostly destined for Latin America (Katz and Ablin, 1977).

The first attempt to introduce pro-efficiency measures during the ISI was applied during the military government of Onganía (1966–69). Although it preserved the ISI strategy, it also stressed the need to foster efficiency improvements in the industrial sector – an increasingly widespread concern among local economists. To attain this objective, tariffs were reduced (Table 22.3) and industrial exports were promoted. Furthermore, the new economic team favored large domestic and foreign firms in order to stimulate a new investment boom in the country.

A devaluation of the peso by 40 per cent was also implemented during Onganía's government. For traditional exports, the devaluation was almost offset by a tax, while subsidies for nontraditional exports were removed. On the import side, reductions in tariffs did not fully offset the devaluation. While agricultural producers were critical of these policies (owing to export taxes), large manufacturing and services enterprises were in favor of them. By contrast, local SMEs – almost exclusively oriented to the internal market – criticized the orientation towards large businesses and the overtures to foreign capital.

Later on, several changes took place in the military government and in the economic policy framework. Successive devaluations created a race between exchange rate and nominal wages, fuelling inflation, while measures were taken to promote exports and control imports (including technology transfer payments). The deepening of the ISI was fostered through special policy regimes that favored investments in intermediate goods. When Aldo Ferrer was appointed minister of the economy in 1970 by Onganía's successor, Levingston, several measures to favor local firms were announced, including changes in the credit system, the 'Buy National Law' and the preference in investment projects promoted by the government.[5]

The Peronist government that took office in 1973 benefited initially from the rise in world prices and took advantage of the improved balance-of-payments position to expand demand and raise real wages. The new economic policy was at odds with that implemented by Onganía, since it clearly favored local capital (and mostly SMEs) and introduced several restrictions on FDI. Strong quantitative import restrictions were reintroduced jointly with foreign exchange controls. Generous promotion schemes were put in place for nontraditional exports while traditional exports were taxed.

Growth lasted until trading conditions turned against Argentina in mid 1974. In 1975 a severe economic crisis set in and, against a huge fiscal deficit, a drastic devaluation ('Rodrigazo') was applied. This gave rise to pressures from labor unions and the outcome was an acceleration of inflation to (at the time) unknown levels. The impaired economic situation, coupled with a weak government and the violent political and social scenario, paved the way for the 1976 military coup which marked the beginning of the end of the ISI.

However, in spite of this end, and of the criticisms by many economists of the ISI, some successes were visible at that time. Industrial production grew at an annual rate of 6.1 per cent between 1962 and 1974, while the figure for labor productivity was 3.2 per cent. Industrial exports grew from US$100 million in 1969 to US$800 million in 1974, representing 20 per cent of total exports in the latter year. Total manufacturing exports (including agricultural-based products) surpassed US$2300 million in 1974, accounting for almost 60 per cent of total exports (Bisang and Kosacoff, 1995). Furthermore, by the end of the ISI period, significant technology exports were flowing to other Latin American countries – e.g. 'turnkey' plants, licenses, technical services, etc. (Katz and Ablin, 1985) – and several local firms were engaged in internationalization processes through FDI in neighboring countries (Katz and Kosacoff, 1983).

The leading sectors during this phase of the ISI were automobiles, chemicals, metallurgy and electrical machinery and equipment, while food and textiles lagged behind. Capital deepening took place in most industrial sectors, and, as shown by Katz (1972), technical progress (measured as the 'residual' of the production function) accounted for almost 70 per cent of industrial production growth in the 1960s.

However, in spite of this substantial transformation of manufacturing industry, the plants established during the ISI, including TNC affiliates, generally fell short of international competitiveness standards. A key issue was that most of them had been established to sell almost exclusively in the domestic market, which was not large enough to permit efficient operations and adequate economies of scale. The stagnation of agricultural production jointly with the lack of competitiveness and the inward market orientation of the industrial sector made Argentina's share in world exports fall to 0.29 per cent in 1970, a figure below that of 1870.

Hence, the balance of this experience shows shadows and lights. Orthodox economists mostly tend to stress the shadows, deeming the whole ISI process a big mistake, which would back the sweeping reforms adopted by the military government in 1976. However, other authors argue that, in spite of the drawbacks, a learning process had been taking place within manufacturing industry which had led to a gradual closing of the competitiveness gap with the industrialized world (Katz and Kosacoff, 1989). Llach (2002) states that by the early 1970s the manufacturing sector was ready to start a self-sustained growth process which was unfortunately frustrated by political and macroeconomic instability. In this view, reforms were certainly needed – aimed not at drastically changing the rules of the game created by the ISI but rather at improving the efficiency of the manufacturing sector through a gradual process of trade liberalization and the improvement of the institutional foundations for growth. This stance placed the emphasis on preserving the accumulated productive and technological capabilities in a large part of the manufacturing sector and on the relevance of the process of knowledge creation and diffusion that had been taking place.

22.3 STRUCTURAL REFORMS AND MACROECONOMIC VOLATILITY: THE 'GREAT ARGENTINE DEPRESSION' OF 1976–2001

Macroeconomic and institutional instability increased between 1976 and 2001. In 1990, GDP per capita in constant pesos was below that of 1965, after a fall of 23 per cent in comparison with that of 1975. In turn, GDP per capita in 2002 was 5 per cent lower than that of 1992 and 11 per cent lower than in 1974.

Table 22.4 Argentine exports 1980–2008 (current US$ million, 5-year averages)

	Total	%	Primary products	%	Manufactures of agricultural origin	%	Manufactures of industrial origin	%	Fuels and energy	%
1980–84	8,147	100	3,513	43	2,857	35	1,346	17	430	5
1985–89	8,064	100	2,399	30	3,275	41	2,112	26	279	3
1990–94	13,104	100	3,397	26	5,065	39	3,499	27	1,144	9
1995–99	24,189	100	5,617	23	8,395	35	7,379	30	2,799	12
2000–04	28,609	100	5,998	21	9,087	32	8,352	29	5,173	18
2005–08	53,233	100	11,326	21	17,876	33	16,555	31	7,476	14

Source: Author's calculations on the basis of INDEC data.

Although the bloody dictatorship that took office in 1976 did not dismantle the whole regulatory setting of the ISI (e.g. industrial promotion policies were maintained), a process of trade liberalization took place, in a context of increasing peso overvaluation (which was a tool for fighting inflation). At the same time, a new FDI law was passed, which guaranteed equal treatment of foreign and domestic investors and the free remittance of profits and principals.

The failure of the military regime's economic policy led to a major crisis in 1981, which particularly hit the industrial sector. The 1982 debt crisis further aggravated the situation and the 1980s were characterized by strong macroeconomic volatility and stagnation. In 1982 exchange controls and import restrictions were reestablished, again closing the economy to competing imports.

The only economic indicator with a positive performance during the 1980s was export trade, which expanded by almost 55 per cent between 1980 and 1990, favored by prevailing high exchange rates and the domestic recession.[6] Exports of manufactured goods (Table 22.4) benefited from various types of government subsidies and also from cross-subsidization because of high prices commanded by firms operating in concentrated and protected domestic markets (Bisang, 1990). Furthermore, a program to foster cooperation and expand bilateral trade with Brazil was launched in 1986, which also had a positive impact on exports.

In so far as imports fell more than 60 per cent between 1980 and 1990, the trade balance went from a deficit of US$2500 million in 1980 to a surplus of US$8300 million in 1990. However, this was far from being a sign of a healthy economy, considering the scenario of hyperinflation and recession in which that surplus emerged.

In turn, FDI inflows were not very high during the military regime, while the volatile and stagnating macroeconomic context of the 1980s was not very attractive for new foreign investments. Hence, TNC affiliates lost presence in Argentina's economy (their share of industrial production fell from 30.4 to 26.8 per cent between 1973 and 1984; see Azpiazu, 1992), while some large domestic conglomerates seemed to emerge as the new 'economic elite' at that time. These conglomerates, jointly with other medium and large domestic Argentine firms, made investments abroad in the 1970s and 1980s, trying to compensate for the stagnation and uncertainty of the local economy (Bisang et al., 1992).

In this scenario, deep changes in the industrial structure took place. Capital-intensive, large-scale sectors that mostly rely on natural resources (edible oils, paper and pulp, steel, petrochemicals) expanded during this period (and fostered exports growth). The machinery and equipment sector, which had accumulated significant capabilities during the ISI, as well as labor-intensive industries (e.g. textiles), were the sectors that contracted the most.

After two hyperinflationary crises, a currency board scheme (the so-called Convertibility Law) was launched in 1991. This policy succeeded in controlling inflation, but at the cost of peso overvaluation. Convertibility went along with a far-reaching program of structural reforms that had been cautiously initiated during the late 1980s.

Trade liberalization measures had already started in 1988, when the government limited the number of items subject to quantitative restrictions, and the weighted average tariff rate was reduced to 48 per cent. The new government carried out the second phase of reforms with successive rounds of tariff reductions from 1989 onwards. The weighted average tariff rate was reduced to 19 per cent by 1991 (Table 22.3). In turn, the government eliminated many specific duties and quantitative restrictions on imports of capital and durable goods. In 1993 import tariffs for capital goods were eliminated. Another instrument that favored the acquisition of foreign technology was the scheme which permitted duty-free imports of 'turnkey plants'.

In conjunction with unilateral trade liberalization, the integration process with Brazil, initiated in the mid 1980s, was deepened with the signature of the Asunción Treaty in 1991. This treaty drew Paraguay and Uruguay into the preferential trade agreements with Argentina and Brazil, thereby creating Mercosur. The four countries agreed on a schedule of automatic rounds of tariff reduction for intra-regional trade during 1991–94. After difficult negotiations, an agreement on a common external tariff structure – largely based on the Brazilian one – was reached in 1995. This transformed Mercosur into a customs union, although each country was allowed to maintain lists of exceptions to the common tariff.

Trade liberalization cum regional integration and peso overvaluation led to a significant growth in imports of manufactured goods. For the first time since 1976–81, imported goods flowed into Argentina, forcing domestic producers to compete in the local market by launching new products and production processes and increasing productivity (or, as was often the case, to close or shrink their business or sell their firms to TNCs). Import penetration ratios in the manufacturing sector rose from 5.7 per cent in 1990 to 19 per cent in 1999.

There was a strong increase in imports of capital goods, as a result of trade liberalization and the increase of domestic investment. They rose from an annual average of US$800 million between 1982 and 1990 to over US$5.8 billion between 1992 and 2000. In 1990 capital goods imports totaled US$635 million; by 1994 they were in the order of US$6 billion and in 1998 they reached the maximum level of the decade at US$8.5 billion.

Exports also grew (see Table 22.4), especially from 1994 on, favored by the regional integration in Mercosur, better international prices for commodities (until 1998), growth in agricultural output and the maturation of some large industrial and energy projects. Hence, exports in 2000 had doubled the 1993 levels. However, Argentina's share of world exports by the end of the 1990s was similar to that in the early 1980s: around 0.4 per cent according to World Bank data.[7]

Industrial exports grew substantially throughout the decade and their share of total exports rose from 27 to 30 per cent (see Table 22.4). Chemicals, petrochemicals and motor vehicles (where a sectoral promotion regime was in place), accounted for 60 per cent of the increase in manufacturing exports in the 1990s. Paper and pulp, steel and machinery and equipment contributed with 25 per cent. In contrast, exports of shoe and leather goods declined and the share of textiles in total non-agricultural-resource-based industrial exports fell from 6.3 to 3.7 per cent.

Mercosur was the main destination for industrial exports, accounting for almost 70 per cent of the increase in non-agricultural-resource-based manufacturing exports between 1990 and 2000. Mercosur's share of those exports jumped from 23 to 49 per cent over that period. The low share of developed markets as destinations reflects not only the influence of geography but also the weak competitive capabilities in many sectors and the influence of TNCs' strategies.

Regarding agriculture, the elimination of taxes and withholdings on agricultural exports, the reduction of import tariffs on inputs and capital goods and the deregulation of several markets all created the conditions for a large expansion of cereal and oilseed production (from 26 million tons in 1988–89 to over 67 million tons in 2000–01), which obviously

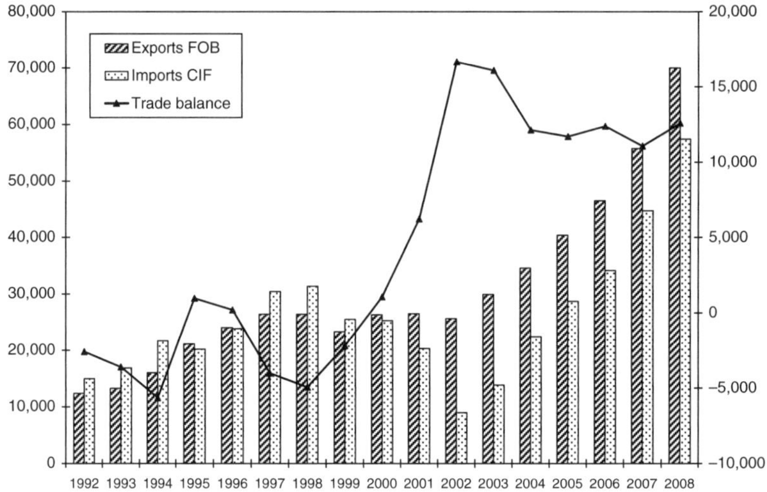

Source: Author's elaboration on the basis of INDEC data.

Figure 22.2 Argentina's Exports, imports and trade balance 1992–2008 (US$ billion).

favored a strong increase in exports. Production increases were particularly remarkable in soybeans, which soon became Argentina's leading export complex, thanks to the introduction of genetically modified seeds jointly with the adoption of no-tillage techniques.

Fuel and energy exports also grew, strongly favored by deregulation and privatization measures, while agricultural-resource-based manufactures lost share but still remained the main source of exports for Argentina.

As imports grew far more than exports, significant trade deficits appeared (Figure 22.2). Trade deficits were financed by growing inflows of foreign capital, both through portfolio capital (which turned negative from 1999 onwards) as well as through FDI (Figure 22.3).

Despite the initial commitment to liberalization, the unfavorable trade balance and the emergence of sectoral pressures amid growing unemployment induced the government to introduce certain ad hoc instruments to restrain imports. The 'statistics tax' on imports was increased from 3 per cent to 10 per cent in 1992 and the government made aggressive use of safeguards and defensive commercial legislation, such as anti-dumping and compensatory duties.

In sum, although trade policy was more liberal than in any other period since 1930, in the 1990s there were many modifications in the trade protection framework (changes in nominal tariffs, the introduction or removal

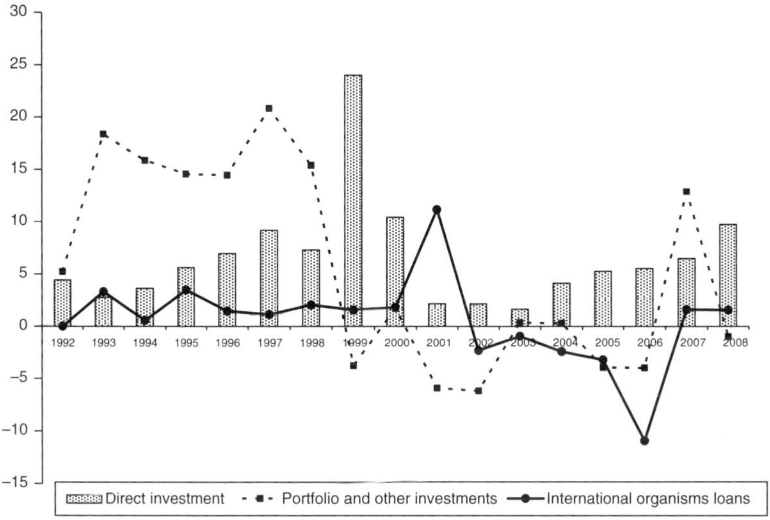

Source: Author's elaboration on the basis of Ministry of Economy data.

Figure 22.3 External capital flows to Argentina 1992–2008 (US$ billion).

of special regimes, non-tariff barriers and other charges). While sectoral pressures and short-term policy objectives (related to inflation abatement, current-account imbalances and fiscal revenues) help to explain why there were frequent changes in trade policy, those changes impaired the role of a tariff structure as a guideline for resource allocation by private agents (Bouzas and Pagnotta, 2003).

There was a similar evolution in the area of regional integration. Although intra-regional trade expanded substantially, disputes arose periodically, especially between Argentina and Brazil, and reached their peaks during economic crises in one or more of the members. The disputes were aggravated by the lack of effective institutional arrangements to deal with conflicts, and by the absence of 'deep' integration mechanisms beyond trade liberalization. Of particular importance is that Mercosur has not been able to coordinate macroeconomic policies and has never had regional competitiveness or sectoral policies aimed at taking advantage of the potential gains from integration. In this scenario, defensive or protective trade measures prevailed, while the underlying structural problems were not solved.

Regarding FDI, it had already been strongly deregulated in 1976. The Menem administration (1989–99) completed this task, removing almost all the few remaining sectoral restrictions. After these reforms, no approvals,

Table 22 5 Argentina's share in world FDI flows (percentages)

Years	Inflows	Outflows
1971–1975	0.37	n.a.
1976–1980	0.85	0.09
1981–1985	0.84	0.02
1986–1990	0.58	0.02
1991–1995	1.65	0.34
1996–2000	1.42	0.26
2001–2005	0.42	0.06
2006–2008	0.40	0.10

Note: n.a.: Not available.

Source Author's elaboration on the basis of UNCTAD's data.

formalities or registration procedures were required for FDI operations. There were neither discriminatory withholding taxes towards income nor taxes applied to the remission of profits and dividends. This investor-friendly approach was also followed by the signing of 51 bilateral investment treaties and generous concessions in the negotiations leading up to the General Agreement on Trade in Services (GATS).

In sharp contrast to the previous decade, Argentina was one of the main destinations for FDI in the developing world during the 1990s. Between 1992 and 2001 inflows amounted to more than US$76 billion[8] and Argentina's share in world FDI inflows grew significantly (Table 22.5).

Most FDI inflows were related to takeovers, initially of public firms and then of private domestic enterprises, accounting for around 60 per cent of FDI inflows in the 1990s. In turn, profit reinvestment levels were low in most years. FDI came mainly from the US and some European countries such as Germany, France, Italy, Netherlands, Spain and UK. There were also some major inflows from Chile and, to a lesser extent, from Brazil.

The oil industry attracted a third of FDI between 1992 and 2001, while manufacturing industry received around 22 per cent of those inflows. Chemicals (especially petrochemicals), automobiles (the only sector which continued to benefit from special tariff protection in the 1990s) and food and beverages attracted most manufacturing FDI. The rest went into services, in privatizations (communications, electricity and gas), banking, retail trade etc.

The main attractions were the abundance of natural resources and the size and growth of the domestic market, together with privatization, price stabilization, trade liberalization and, to a lesser extent, integration within

Table 22.6 TNCs' share among the 500 largest firms 1993–2007: Argentina (percentages)

	1993	2000	2004	2007
Number of firms	44	64	67	66
Value added	62	82	86	84
Employees	40	62	63	63
Wages	48	68	71	69
Goods exports	67	82	86	n.a.
Goods imports	76	88	87	n.a.
Gross fixed investment	75	88	89	n.a.

Note: n.a.: Not available.

Source: INDEC.

Mercosur (Chudnovsky and López, 2001). As wages in US dollars were relatively high in Argentina during the 1990s, labor costs were not an FDI determinant. The 'investor-friendly approach' was perhaps a necessary precondition but would not have had a sizable impact in the absence of the other aforementioned conditions.

In this scenario, TNC affiliates were the main 'winners' in the restructuring process of Argentina's economy during the 1990s (Chudnovsky and López, 2001). The number of TNC affiliates among the 500 Argentine leading firms increased from 219 in 1993, to 318 in 2000 and to 340 in 2004. Their share in total production value added rose from 62 per cent to 82 per cent and to 86 per cent in the respective years. Similar trends are observed in terms of foreign trade, investment, and, although at lower absolute levels, employment (Table 22.6).

FDI in Argentina was predominantly market-seeking, mainly aimed at the services sector, while resource-seeking inflows have also been important. Efficiency-seeking strategies, basically regional in scope, were facilitated by the dismantling of tariff barriers within Mercosur, which allowed TNC affiliates to specialize in lines of products to be exchanged later within the region. Trade liberalization also allowed TNC branches to complement the wares they produced locally with imported goods and to replace local suppliers with imported inputs and capital goods.

However, local branches were rarely restructured to become part of global efficiency-seeking intra-corporate strategies, the prevailing rationale being of a local/regional nature. In this regard, note must be taken of the evidence gathered in Chudnovsky and López (2001) and in Hiratuka and Sabatini (2006), who found that TNC affiliates had a preference for exporting to Mercosur and, in fact, that that preference is higher than in the case of domestic firms.

In contrast to the growing TNC presence, local conglomerates showed heterogeneous strategies and performances, although, as a whole, they lost the central role played since the late 1970s. While some of these disappeared or shrank, others strengthened their positions in the domestic market, often concentrating on their 'core business'. At the same time, successful conglomerates (such as Techint, Arcor, IMPSA) increased their presence in external markets, combining exports and FDI (Kosacoff, 1999). These investments led to an increase in the very low share of Argentina in total world FDI outflows (Table 22.5).

Given the significant role played by FDI in the 1990s, it is important to learn about its macro and microeconomic impacts on the Argentine economy (see Chudnovsky et al., 2010 for an econometric approach). Macroeconomic impacts were not significant, since the effect of FDI on GDP growth and domestic investment was neither positive nor negative. This is no surprise considering that many of the latest studies on this subject for other countries and/or regions point in the same direction. On the other hand, the microeconomic impacts of FDI seem to have been stronger though heterogeneous. TNC affiliates adopted modern organizational and production technologies that allowed them to launch new products and to increase labor productivity and trade more than domestic firms. However, no horizontal spillovers from FDI onto the productivity of domestic firms have emerged. The same applies to trade and innovation. Backward spillovers arise only in the case of innovation outputs, meaning that domestic firms need to upgrade their technological assets to become TNC suppliers.

22.4 AFTER THE WASHINGTON CONSENSUS, 2002 ONWARDS

By the end of 2001, convertibility was abandoned and soon afterwards the default on the external debt was declared. In 2002 not only did GDP record drastic fall, but there was also a banking crash, a huge peso devaluation and a sharp increase in the unemployment and poverty rates (which had emerged as severe social problems in Argentina during the 1990s).

The end of convertibility was accompanied by conflicts with foreign investors mainly in two areas: banking (owing to the post-devaluation compensations of dollar-denominated deposits and loans) and privatized enterprises (owing to the freezing in pesos of the rates originally in dollars). In the privatization area, many enterprises filed demands with the

International Center for Settlement of Investment Disputes (ICSID) and Argentina became the country with the largest number of demands filed with that organization (40 over 183 demands as of June 2005) (see Bouzas and Chudnovsky, 2004).

In 2003 the Argentine economy began its recovery. GDP in US dollars at constant 2000 prices recorded a growth of 63 per cent between 2003 and 2008. This growth trajectory parted from tradition in recent Argentine history by going hand in hand with huge trade surpluses.

The external trade adjustment started before the devaluation, owing to the reduction in imports, first with the recession and then accentuated by the crisis. Later on, the rapid growth of exports from 2003 onwards made it possible to keep a large trade surplus even when imports started to grow with the economic recovery and increasing domestic investment (see Figure 22.2).

Export growth was remarkable, as shown in Table 22.4, with the 2005–08 average almost 90 per cent higher than that of 2000–04. The growth of exports has been strongly related to the high prices for commodities in international markets. To illustrate this point, we can mention that in the first quarter of 2008 terms of trade for Argentina had improved by 50 per cent vis-à-vis 2002 and that between 2003 and 2008 export prices increased by 68 per cent.

No major changes have taken place in terms of exports composition (Table 22.4), although a fall in the share of fuels and energy is visible (due to increased local consumption and a decline in the investment in that sector), favoring a slight increase of manufactures. In 2008, 50 per cent of exports consisted of oilseeds, cereals, meat, leather and petroleum and gas. Automobiles, steel, aluminum and petrochemicals accounted for another 20 per cent. Copper, gold, dairy products, fish, and fruits and vegetables contributed with 10 per cent. Hence, Argentina's exports are concentrated in natural-resources-based products and a handful of industrial commodities, automobiles being the only exception. In this latter sector, a special trade regime regulates commerce with Brazil, while the domestic market enjoys a 35 per cent tariff protection (well above Argentina's average tariff), giving rents to the TNC affiliates operating in Argentina and allowing them to export on the basis of intra-corporate specialization schemes.

In spite of the remarkable growth in exports, the weight of Argentina in world exports stayed at levels similar to those of the previous two decades, around 0.4 per cent according to World Bank data.

Two relevant trade-related phenomena have occurred in latter years. First is the growing presence of China as a trade partner. Argentina's exports to China went from less than US$160 million in 1980 to US$6.6 billion in 2008. In turn, imports from China grew from US$30 million to

US$7.1 billion between the same years. As a consequence, China became the second export destination and the second import supplier (Brazil is still the main trade partner on both fronts). The bilateral trade pattern is clearly asymmetric. Only 5 per cent of exports to China are manufactured goods, nondependant on agricultural raw materials, while in Chinese imports this figure rises to almost 80 per cent. Soybeans and soybean oil account for more than 80 per cent of the increase in exports to China between 1995 and 2005 (López and Ramos, 2009a). In 2005, 90 per cent of Argentina's exports to China were composed by those two products (which accounted for more than 75 per cent of all exports), jointly with petroleum oil, leather and copper. In turn, in just 10 years Chinese imports went from being led by consumer goods (60 per cent in 1995) to having capital goods as their main item (over 30 per cent in 2006).

The other interesting new phenomenon is the strong increase in services exports, fostered by the fall in US-dollar-denominated wages after the devaluation. In 2008 they amounted to US$12,000 million, against US$5000 million in 2000. The share of 'other business services' in total services exports grew from 6.6 per cent in 2000 to almost 30 per cent in 2007–08. Also notable is the growth of personal, cultural and recreational services exports and the export of computer and information services, whose share went from 3 per cent in 2000 to more than 9 per cent in 2007–08. This reflects the interest of many TNCs in taking advantage of Argentina's skilled human resources in areas such as business process outsourcing, software and information services etc. However, most of these exports correspond to activities that are mostly routine and of low technological complexity, which means that Argentina is not perceived as an attractive location for exporting high-valued-added services (see López et al., 2009).

In turn, analyzing the structure of goods exports, Guerson et al. (2006) find that the current export structure in Argentina is not favorable to future growth, given that it is highly concentrated in 'low-income' goods, i.e. goods that low-income countries tend to export. This finding goes hand in hand with the low presence in Argentina's export basket of those goods whose international markets have been more dynamic in the last two decades (Mulder, 2009; Kuwayama, 2009). Moreover, Argentina has a limited participation in international production networks organized around global value chains (Kosacoff et al., 2007; Mulder, 2009). These trends may be the result of different factors, including some structural ones (e.g. geography, weaknesses in the national innovation system, the lack of deepening of local financial markets), policy-related ones (e.g. the lack of a clear strategy of integration in the world, the anti-export bias of some trade policy instruments, the existence of protectionism in some potential destination markets) and firm-related ones (e.g. the role of TNC affiliates in their corporate value chains, the lack of Argentinean TNCs which could create their own chains).

Although no major setback took place in trade liberalization (mainly because the exchange rate was high enough to grant a high level of protection), the use of protective measures was more intense than in the 1990s, especially from 2007 on, and mainly aimed at blocking imports from Asia (especially China). Brazil was also heavily affected by protectionism in recent years. It is no surprise that Brazil and China have been targets of measures, considering that in both cases Argentina runs trade deficits (since many years ago with Brazil and since 2008 with China) and that their exports harm many labor-intensive industries (see Bouzas, 2008). The protectionist trends were reinforced in 2009, in the context of the international crisis. Moreover, unlike in the 1990s, Argentina adopted a strongly defensive stance in bilateral and multilateral negotiations (e.g. the Doha Round of the WTO).

Another important aspect of Argentina's trade policy in this decade was the return of export taxes, which had been eliminated in the 1990s. These taxes (higher for primary products than for manufactures) were introduced in 2002 as a way to reduce the impact of the devaluation on domestic prices (especially those of wage goods exported by Argentina), but also to have access to fiscal resources. In so far as international agricultural commodity prices strongly increased in recent years, the government tried to raise export taxes. Although this attempt failed, in order to keep domestic prices low the government resorted to different restrictions for export of agricultural products, which have affected not only exports but also production.

Regarding FDI, in Figure 22.3 we can see a marked drop in the flows received. The annual average inflows between 2002 and 2006 amounted to US$3476 million as against US$7644 million between 1992 and 2001. This drop was in part a reflection of similar international tendencies, after the peak reached by world FDI in 2000. However, it also responded to specific local determinants. The first of these was the end of privatizations, which had contributed with a relevant part of FDI in the 1990s. Second was the 2001–02 crisis, which eroded investors' confidence. Third was the crisis and the end of convertibility, which generated a strong increase in the indebtedness of TNC affiliates as measured in dollars, in the context of a steep decline in internal demand and interrupted access to domestic and foreign borrowings (Bezchinsky et al., 2008). Fourth were the above-mentioned conflicts between the government and foreign investors. Although some investors withdrew their demands at ICSID, some enterprises left the country, selling their shareholdings to local investors or investment funds. Even some renationalizations took place, affecting foreign enterprises (the latest was the elimination in 2008 of the private retirement and pension system which had been created in the 1990s). Some banks left the country, too, but they were only a few small-magnitude operations.

Notwithstanding this context, the TNC presence in the leading businesses elite remained practically unaltered in the period under discussion (Table 22.6). Likewise, in 2007 and 2008 there was an increase in FDI inflows, with the levels attained close to the 1996–98 average (Figure 22.3), although the upturn was in part a consequence of the increase in global FDI flows.

Table 22.5 shows that beyond these ups and downs, Argentina has been losing attractiveness for FDI since 2002; in 2006–08 the country's share was the lowest since the early 1970s. The same trend is observable at the Latin American level. While Argentina's share in total FDI inflows in the region was 17 per cent in 1990–2000, it fell to 4.5 per cent between 2001 and 2007.

As to FDI origins, one of the new features of the decade since 2002 is the significant role played by Brazil, whose firms have made relevant investments in Argentina in sectors such as oil, meat-packing, steel, textiles and others (see Bianco et al., 2008; Niembro et al., 2009).

As regards participation by sectors, in the post-devaluation and public utility frozen rates context, manufacturing industry gained presence (around 40 per cent of FDI in 2002–07, against 21 per cent in 1992–2001), while services weight fell (in particular, the sectors associated with infrastructure). More generally, the sectors that have attracted more FDI have been the tradable ones (regardless of whether they are industries or services) – as seen, for instance, in the TNCs' growing interest in establishing the operation in Argentina of export services associated with the use of ICTs (from call centers to software development, shared service centers, business process outsourcing etc.) (see López and Ramos, 2008).

According to data from the Central Bank of Argentina, enterprises having FDI accumulated 87 per cent of natural-resource exports in 2007, in contrast to 64 per cent in manufacturing industry. In turn, Asia bought 43 per cent of the oilseed and cereal exports by enterprises having FDI in 2007, and the European Union another 24 per cent. Mercosur concentrated 43 per cent of the external sales of enterprises having FDI in the manufacturing sector, against 22 per cent for all other manufacturing exporters, which reflects the high degree of intra-Mercosur export specialization by manufacturing TNCs, a particularly remarkable fact in the cases of the automotive industry (60 per cent) and chemicals, rubber and plastics (58 per cent). This shows contrasting trade patterns in FDI in agriculture and industry, and that TNC affiliates in the latter sector have a limited integration in global value chains. Moreover, where Argentina is really integrated, i.e. in agriculture, this integration is limited to the first stages of the value chain (see Bisang et al., 2009).

Finally, the growth in FDI outflows observed in the 1990s was reversed after 2002, and the country lost share at the world level (Table 22.5). This reflects the fact that some Argentine firms that invested abroad in the previous decade abandoned those operations or were sold to foreign TNCs. In any case, Argentina lost presence among the emerging 'multilatinas' vis-à-vis Brazil (1 per cent in world FDI outflows), Chile (0.2 per cent) or Mexico (0.3 per cent).

22.5 CONCLUSIONS AND FUTURE CHALLENGES

The story told in this chapter may have many different interpretations. Orthodox economists would stress the fact that Argentina was never as close to the international income frontier as when it was an open country and still had not adopted 'distortive' industrialization policies, which would mark the beginning of a 'rent-seeker' era (Llach, 1997; Rodríguez, 1988).

Heterodox economists, in turn, could argue that Argentina's failure is due to the fact that the country never got to reverse its natural-resources-based specialization pattern, which was at odds with the dynamics of world markets after the end of World War II. In this view, pro-industrialization policies are to be blamed not for Argentina's 'excesses' but for its weakness and lack of continuity (Di Tella and Zymelman, 1967; Ferrer, 1975; Nochteff, 1994). The growing predominance of TNCs is also observed as a negative factor, since their objectives may systematically differ from those of host developing countries in terms of technology, investment and foreign trade decisions (the brief 'anti-dependentist' interlude of Argentina's economic policy in the early 1970s reflects the influence of these arguments at that time).

The relevant role played by trade and foreign investment issues in debates about Argentina's history illustrates their key role in the country's economy. However, we do not want to enter into this more general debate, since the analysis of Argentina's development process should incorporate many other key issues. Notwithstanding this caveat, it is indeed the case that one cannot separate the discussion of the areas covered by this chapter from the more general analysis of Argentina's development process.

During the agro-export model, the country welcomed foreign capital and labour, and took advantage of the opportunities for exporting meat and grains to the developed world. The main engine of growth was world demand. When that engine broke in 1930, the country had to resort to the domestic market. Until 1945 there were strong debates between those who foresaw the possibility of retaking the old development style and those who advocated the need of new avenues. In the context of this debate, the failed Pinedo Plan pushed not for closing the domestic economy but for a change in Argentina's main trade partners (Latin America and the US instead of Great Britain) and in its export basket (with a growing role of manufactures). However, that was not the path chosen by those who governed Argentina between 1946 and 1955, and a strongly inward-oriented development style was adopted.

In 1958 a turning point took place within the import-substitution industrialization paradigm. Although the economy was still closed to imports, a strong call was made for FDI, in order to extend substitution to heavy and capital goods industries. This call was aligned with world trends at that time, when TNCs were avid to invest in protected domestic markets ('tariff-jumping' FDI). Ten years of high growth were the result of the investment boom (and technology transfer) generated by the developmentalist government.

However, Argentina's experience with ISI was not as successful as that of other countries such as Brazil. Among other factors, the limited size of the domestic market, the continued social and political unrest, the strong conflicts on income distribution and the mistakes in the industrialization policy could help to explain that result.

Nevertheless, by the end of ISI Argentina had begun to change its export basket and for the first time manufactures had a high share in exports. Moreover, technology exports in the form of turnkey plants, FDI, technical assistance and licenses were also made. As history happens only once, we don't know what would have occurred had gradual pro-efficiency reforms been adopted in order to push for more competitiveness gains in industry, so as to leave behind the dual economic structure of the ISI period and the stop–go cycles.

From 1976 onwards, frequent dramatic policy changes were the norm and it is not possible to distinguish a clear model of economic development and integration. Between 1976 and 1981 the military dictatorship liberalized trade and FDI in a context of increasing peso overvaluation and economic unbalances, the experiment ending in a big crisis in 1981. After the debt crisis of 1982, trade liberalization was reversed for macroeconomic reasons, while the country attracted almost no FDI. In the late 1980s a new round of trade liberalization began, which was rapidly extended in the next decade, when regional integration within Mercosur was also pursued and FDI deregulation was deepened.

As a whole, the macroeconomic outcomes of this process were disappointing. However, some major changes took place in this period in the areas of trade and investment: (1) manufactures' share in total exports grew notably, pushed by exports of industrial commodities and later on automobiles (investments in these commodities had been fostered by industrial promotion policies since the 1970s and automobile exports were also promoted by public policies in the 1990s); (2) the relevance of Mercosur and especially Brazil in Argentina's foreign trade pattern strongly increased; (3) soybeans emerged as the main export complex in the 1990s; (4) Argentina became a key destination for FDI in the 1990s and TNCs' share in the domestic economy reached record levels.

The 2001–02 crisis was provoked, among other factors, by the persistence of huge external imbalances that were first financed by private foreign capital inflows (in the context of a fixed exchange rate). When a sudden stop in those flows took place (after the Asian, Brazilian and Russian crisis) these imbalances proved to be unsustainable and finally led to a mega devaluation of the peso and the default on the foreign debt. The devaluation allowed for huge external surpluses from 2003 onwards, even in the context of rapid economic growth (which fostered imports). This change was also helped by growing international prices of the commodities exported by Argentina. In turn, FDI levels fell significantly in the first years of the new decade, but later on they rose again to levels close to those of the 1990s.

Although no precise statements regarding how the current administration foresees the main lines of Argentina's development model may be found, one can think that the government is following a moderately inward-looking strategy (associated with employment and redistributionist objectives). Hence, the protection of the local market has been increasing (mainly through non-tariff measures), while agricultural exports are controlled to keep domestic prices low. Although no overt anti-FDI policies have been enacted (in spite of some restrictions introduced in the media law passed last year), the government has favored some domestic groups for access to certain business, especially formerly privatized firms.

Anyway, things are changing in the globalization scenario, and fast. The emergence of China (and to a lesser extent of India) as a major player, the rapid growth of trade in services and the new world of global value chains are key phenomena that must be taken into account in a strategy of integration in the world. Moreover, although the worst effects of the international systemic crisis seem to be over, one may expect important changes in global competition that should have strong impacts on trade and investment flows.

In this scenario, the main concern is that key trade and investment issues hardly appear on the domestic policy agenda. Nowadays, Argentina's weight in the international economy is higher in terms of GDP (0.8 per cent according to PPP-based World Bank estimates) than in terms of exports and FDI inflows (0.4 per cent) and FDI outflows (0.1 per cent). This might be to an extent a good thing for the economy when an international crisis emerges, but it also means that it is not taking advantage of the potential gains associated with integration in the world economy.

This concern is further aggravated when one looks at some qualitative aspects of the way Argentina currently participates in trade and investment international flows, including: (1) exports are concentrated in natural-resource-based commodities, while Argentina's share in the most dynamic world goods markets is very low; (2) even though Argentina has taken advantage of the export opportunities in the Chinese market, exports are concentrated in the soybean complex (75 per cent) and a handful of other commodities, while Chinese imports are growing fast, leading to a reversal of the bilateral trade balance which had been positive until 2007; (3) although exports of services grew fast in the decade to 2010, they were mostly based on low-value-added activities; (4) FDI is mostly associated with resource-seeking and market-seeking objectives, while TNC affiliates in Argentina rarely undertake strategic activities for their respective corporations; (5) even though some Argentinean domestic conglomerates internationalized through FDI in the 1990s, there was later a retraction of this movement and Argentina has only a small place in the world of emerging 'multilatinas'.

In sum, Argentina has a weak integration in the new world of global value chains (see López and Ramos, 2009b). Reversing this situation requires a clear strategy to define the desired pattern of integration in the world economy, based on the country's assets and the existing opportunities in global markets and with a view to removing the obstacles that harm the economy's competitiveness. Unfortunately, as said before, this strategy seems to be absent from the government's agenda, while good prices for international commodities foster exports and protectionism helps to preserve local employment in sectors affected by foreign competition. We hope that this short-term strategy will be abandoned, as it is far from contributing to solving the above-mentioned problems, and hence not conducive to sustained growth in Argentina.

NOTES

1. To avoid distortions in long-run comparisons, Gerchunoff and Llach (2003) – on whose data Figure 22.1 is based – use exports and imports in the numerator and tradable production in the denominator. This eliminates the bias that could come from the inclusion of services, whose share in Argentina's economy grew during the twentieth century.
2. Among the most important examples of FDI from Argentina in this stage we can

mention Alpargatas in textiles, Bunge y Born in cereals and foods and Siam Di Tella in machinery (Katz and Kosacoff, 1983).
3. Controls on profit remittances and capital repatriation were introduced by the Peronist government.
4. Industrial promotion policies granted generous subsidies as well as duty-free imports of capital goods.
5. This bet was made in a context in which the 'anti-dependentist' ideas were dominant in many academic and political circles. The anti-dependentist movement, among other things, heavily criticized the role of TNCs in developing countries, specially regarding the use of their monopolistic power in host markets, the huge volume of profit remittances often 'disguised' under concepts such as royalties, and their interference in the political game.
6. Many new industrial plants, especially in sectors such as steel and petrochemicals, began exporting because actual domestic demand was lower than that expected when the respective investment decisions were taken.
7. Figures are not comparable with those provided in the previous section because the sources are different.
8. These figures were substantially higher than their counterparts during the ISI period. Between 1959 and 1963, FDI inflows to Argentina averaged US$464 million annually (measured in constant 2001 dollars). In the 1990s, the same figure was over US$6760 million. In 1959–63, FDI inflows amounted to around 0.3 per cent of GDP.

REFERENCES

Azpiazu, D. (1992), 'Las empresas transnacionales en una economía en transición: la experiencia argentina en los años ochenta', paper presented at the Simposio de Alto Nivel sobre la Contribución de las Empresas Transnacionales al Crecimiento y el Desarrollo de América Latina y el Caribe, Santiago de Chile.

Barbero, M. (2003), 'Impacto de la inversión extranjera directa en la industria argentina en la década de 1920: estrategias empresariales y sus efectos sobre el sector productivo local', *Anais do V Congresso Brasileiro de História Econômica e 6ª Conferência Internacional de História de Empresas*, Belo Horizonte, Brazil: ABPHE – Associação Brasileira de Pesquisadores em História Econômica (Brazilian Economic History Society).

Berlinski, J. (2003), 'International trade and commercial policy', in G. Della Paolera and A. Taylor (eds), *A New Economic History of Argentina*, Cambridge: Cambridge University Press, pp. 197–232.

Bezchinsky, G., M. Dinenzon, L. Giussani, O. Caino, B. López and S. Amiel (2008), 'Inversión extranjera directa en la Argentina: crisis, reestructuración y nuevas tendencias después de la convertibilidad', in B. Kosacoff (ed.), *Crisis, Recuperación y Nuevos Dilemas. La Economía Argentina 2002–2007*, Buenos Aires: ECLAC.

Bianco, C., P. Moldovan and F. Porta (2008), 'La internacionalización de empresas brasileñas en Argentina', ECLAC Working Paper no 22, Santiago de Chile.

Bisang, R. (1990), 'Sistemas de promoción a las exportaciones industriales: la experiencia argentina en la última década', ECLAC Working Paper no. 35, Buenos Aires.

Bisang, R., G. Anlló, M. Campi and I. Albornoz (2009), 'Cadenas de valor en la agroindustria', in B. Kosacoff and R. Mercado (eds), *La Argentina ante la Nueva*

Internacionalización de la Producción: Crisis y Oportunidades, Buenos Aires: UNDP-ECLAC.

Bisang, R., M. Fuchs and B. Kosacoff (1992), 'Internacionalización de empresas industriales Argentinas', *Desarrollo Económico*, **32** (127), 323–56.

Bisang, R. and B. Kosacoff (1995), 'Tres etapas en la búsqueda de una especialización sustentable: exportaciones industriales argentinas 1974–93', in B. Kosacoff (ed.), *Hacia una Nueva Estrategia Exportadora: La Experiencia Argentina' el Marco Regional y las Reglas Multilaterales*, Buenos Aires: Universidad Nacional de Quilmas, pp. 23–94.

Bouzas, R. (2008), 'Perspectivas de la política comercial argentina: ¿Es posible sobrevivir a las buenas noticias?', *Revista Brasileira de Comercio Exterior*, no. 96, pp. 66–75.

Bouzas, R. and D. Chudnovsky (2004), 'Foreign direct investment and sustainable development: the recent Argentine experience', Universidad de San Andrés, Buenos Aires, Working Paper no. 47.

Bouzas, R. and E. Pagnotta (2003), *Dilemas de la Política Comercial Externa Argentina*, Buenos Aires: Universidad de San Andrés/Fundación OSDE.

Cimoli, M. and J. Katz (2003), 'Structural reforms, technological gaps and economic development: a Latin American perspective', *Industrial and Corporate Change*, **12** (2), 387–411.

Chudnovsky, D. and A. López (2001), *La Transnacionalización de la Economía Argentina*, Buenos Aires: Eudeba.

Chudnovsky, D., A. López and E. Orlicki (2010), 'Inequality: the Argentine experience', in R. Lucas, L. Squire and T.N. Srinivassan (eds), *Global Exchange and Poverty: Trade, Investment and Migration*, Cheltenham, UK: Edward Elgar Publishing.

Di Tella, G. and M. Zymelman (1967), *Las Etapas del Desarrollo Económico Argentino*, Buenos Aires: Paidós.

Díaz Alejandro, C. (1975), *Ensayos sobre la Historia Económica Argentina*, Buenos Aires: Amorrortu.

ECLAC (2001), *La Inversión Extranjera en América Latina y el Caribe*, Santiago de Chile: ECLAC.

Ferrer, A. (1975), *La Economía Argentina*, Buenos Aires: Fondo de Cultura Económica.

Gerchunoff, P. and L. Llach (2003), 'Ved el trono a la noble igualdad: crecimiento, equidad y política económica en la Argentina, 1880–2003', mimeo, Buenos Aires: Fundación PENT.

Guerson, A., J. Parks and M. Parra Torrado (2006), 'Export structure and growth: a detailed analysis for Argentina', World Bank Policy Research Working Paper 4237.

Guy, D. (1979), 'La política de Carlos Pellegrini en los comienzos de la industrialización Argentina,' *Desarrollo Económico*, **19** (73), 3–74.

Hiratuka, C. and R. Sabatini (2006), *Avaliacao das Mudanzas Recentes na Cupula Empresarial no MERCOSUR*, Campinas, Brazil: NEIT-UNICAMP.

Hora, R. (2000), 'Terratenientes, empresarios industriales y crecimiento industrial en la Argentina: los estancieros y el debate sobre el proteccionismo (1890–1914),' *Desarrollo Económico*, **40** (159), 465–92.

Katz, J. (1972), 'Importación de tecnología, aprendizaje local e industrialización dependiente', mimeo, Buenos Aires: Instituto Torcuato Di Tella.

Katz, J. and E. Ablin (1977), 'Tecnología y exportaciones industriales: un análisis

microeconómico de la experiencia argentina reciente', *Desarrollo Económico*, **17** (65), 89–132.
Katz, J. and B. Kosacoff (1983), 'Multinationals from Argentina', in S. Lall (ed.), *The New Multinationals: The Spread of Third World Enterprises*, London: Wiley/IRM.
Katz, J. and B. Kosacoff (1989), *El Proceso de Industrialización en la Argentina: Evolución, Retroceso y Prospectiva*, Buenos Aires: ECLAC.
Katz, J. and B. Kosacoff (2000), 'Import-substituting industrialization in Argentina, 1940–80: its achievements and shortcomings', in E. Cárdenas, J.A. Ocampo and R. Thorp (eds), *An Economic History of Twentieth-Century Latin America, vol. 3: Industrialization and the State in Latin America. The Postwar Years*, Oxford: St Antony's Series, Palgrave.
Kosacoff, B. (1999), 'El caso argentino', in D. Chudnovsky, B. Kosacoff and A. López (eds), *Las Multinacionales Latinoamericanas: Sus Estrategias en un Mundo Globalizado*, Buenos Aires: Fondo de Cultura Económica.
Kosacoff, B. and G. Bezchinsky (1993), 'De la sustitución de importaciones a la globalización: las empresas transnacionales en la industria argentina', in B. Kosacoff (ed.), *El Desafío de la Competitividad: La Industria Argentina en Transición*, Buenos Aires: ECLAC/Alianza, pp. 249–302.
Kosacoff, B., A. López and M. Pedrazzolli (2007), 'Comercio, inversión y fragmentación del comercio global: ¿Está quedando atrás América latina?', in R. Bouzas (ed.), *Después de Doha: La Agenda Emergente del Sistema de Comercio Internacional*, Madrid: Marcial Pons.
Kuwayama, M. (2009), 'Quality of Latin American and Caribbean industrialization and integration into the global economy', ECLAC Serie Comercio Internacional no. 92, Santiago de Chile.
Llach, J. (1997), *Otro Siglo, otra Argentina: Una Estrategia para el Desarrollo Económico y Social Nacida de la Convertibilidad y de su Historia*, Buenos Aires: Ariel.
Llach, J. (2002), 'La industria (1945–1983)', in *Nueva Historica de la Nacion Argentina*, Vol. 9, Buenos Aires: Planeta.
López, A. and D. Ramos (2008), 'Argentina y la industria de software y servicios informáticos', *Revista Comercio Exterior*, **58** (5), 366–84.
López, A. and D. Ramos (2009a), 'The Argentine case', in R. Jenkins and E. Dussel Peters (eds), *China and Latin America: Economic Relations in the Twenty-First Century*, Bonn, Germany: Deutsches Institut für Entwicklungspolitik/ German Development Institute.
López, A. and D. Ramos (2009b), 'Inversión extranjera directa y cadenas de valor en la industria y servicios', in B. Kosacoff and R. Mercado (eds), *La Argentina Ante la Nueva Internacionalización de la Producción. Crisis y Oportunidades*, Buenos Aires: UNDP-ECLAC.
López, A., D. Ramos and I. Torre (2009), 'Las exportaciones de servicios de América Latina y su integración en las cadenas globales de valor', ECLAC Working Paper, Buenos Aires.
Maddison, A. (1992), *La Economía Mundial en el Siglo XX*, México DF: Fondo de Cultura Económica.
Maddison, A. (1995), *Monitoring the World Economy 1820–1992*, Paris: OECD.
Mallon, R. and J. Sourrouille (1975), *La Política Económica en una Sociedad Conflictiva: el Caso Argentino*, Buenos Aires: Amorrortu.
Mulder, N. (2009), 'Weak links between exports and economic growth in Latin

America and the Caribbean', Serie Comercio Internacional no. 91, Santiago de Chile: ECLAC.
Niembro, A., D. Ramos and C. Simkievich (2009), 'El papel del MERCOSUR en la llegada de IED a Brasil y en la internacionalización de empresas brasileñas', CENIT Working Paper no. 33, Buenos Aires.
Nochteff, H. (1994), 'Los senderos perdidos del desarrollo: elite económica y restricciones al desarrollo en la Argentina', in D. Azpiazu and H. Nochteff (eds), *El Desarrollo Ausente: Restricciones al Desarrollo, Neoconservadorismo y Elite Económica en la Argentina*, Buenos Aires: FLACSO/Tesis-Norma, pp. 21–156.
Ortiz, R. (1971), *Historia Económica de la Argentina*, Buenos Aires: Plus Ultra.
Rocchi, F. (1998), 'El Imperio del pragmatismo: intereses, ideas e imágenes en la política industrial del orden conservador', *Anuario IEHS* no. 13, Buenos Aires: Instituto de Estudios Histórico-Sociales, Universidad Nacional del Centro.
Rodríguez, C. (1988), 'Estabilización versus cambio estructural: la experiencia argentina', CEMA Working Paper no. 62, Buenos Aires.
Sesto, C. (2000), 'Tecnología pecuaria y periodización: el refinamiento del vacuno en la provincia de Buenos Aires entre 1856 y 1900: un intento de re-periodizar, incorporando como factor central de análisis el empleo de una tecnología de alta productividad' (Redes), *Revista de Estudios Sociales de la Ciencia*, **7** (16), 49–85.
Sourrouille, J., B. Kosacoff and J. Lucangeli (1985), *Transnacionalización y Política Económica en la Argentina*, Buenos Aires: CEAL/CET.
Taylor, A. (1994), 'Tres fases del crecimiento económico argentino', *Revista de Historia Económica*, **12** (3), 649–83.
Twomey, M. (1998), 'Patrones de la inversión extranjera en los países del tercer mundo en el siglo XX', *Revista de Economía*, **21** (41), 9–60.
Villanueva, J. (1972), 'El origen de la industrialización argentina', *Desarrollo Económico*, **12** (47), 451–76.
Villarroel, J.C. (1992), 'Las ventajas competitivas de una estepa humedecida: la pampa, 1890–1914', *Revista Ciclos en la Historica, la Economia y la Sociedad*, **2** (3), 23–46.

23. Foreign trade and foreign investments: the Brazilian experience in the last two decades

Simão Davi Silber

23.1 INTRODUCTION

The objective of this chapter is to analyze Brazilian trade and investment policy during the two decades to 2010 and its effects on trade performance, foreign direct investment (FDI), competitiveness and growth. It was a very rich period in terms of experiences that changed the profile of Brazilian economy, and one in which a more integrated world economy opened new trade and investment opportunities. It was also a turbulent period, with recurrent crisis in Mexico, Southeast Asia, Russia, Brazil and Argentina. The benefits of trade and investment liberalization were blurred by international crisis and inconsistencies in domestic macroeconomic policies. After 2002, the world economy boomed for 5 years, with important consequences for the Brazilian foreign sector. The country's exports almost quadrupled, with important compositional and regional changes. The benefits of more trade and FDI appeared clearly and the country moved to a higher-growth-rate plateau. In a certain way, the twenty-first century resembles the nineteenth, with the most dynamic economies having a scarce endowment of natural resources and their growth irradiating to the world through increasing demand for staple, oil and mining products, and very favorable effects on Brazilian exports. This was the case with Britain in the nineteenth century and is the case with China today. This period also witnessed the resurgence of world FDI. By the end of the 1980s, FDI was less than 1 per cent of world GDP, but it rose to 3.1 per cent in the period 2006–08. In this period Brazil ranked fifteenth in world FDI stock.

During this period, Brazil implemented important economic reforms, including trade liberalization, stabilization of inflation, an aggressive privatization program and a floating-exchange-rate regime. Trade and foreign investment policies have always been of paramount importance in Brazil, given the frequent balance-of-payments crises and their restricting impacts on economic growth. In which direction did trade reform and international demand change the composition of trade? In which sectors has the country been more competitive in world markets? Which were the consequences of 'getting the fundamentals right' on trade and FDI flows? These are the some key questions to be answered.

The chapter is in five sections, including the present introduction. In Section 23.2 we examine the trade liberalization policy, a radical departure from the historical inward-looking import policies. The policy's results were impressive in terms of slashing tariffs and non-tariff controls that fostered increased competition, modernization of the industrial sector and significant productivity growth. Historically, Brazilian trade and investment policies were highly protectionist to foster inward industrialization growth. A large array of tax and credit subsidies for industrial investments, plus high tariffs and non-tariff barriers, protected the domestic market from import competition, leaving export promotion policies to mitigate the anti-export bias of trade policies. Even the liberalization attempt of the late 1980s and early 1990s were partial and not enough to change the focus in the domestic market of the Brazilian development model. By the end of the first decade of the present century, the country had an export/GDP ratio of 14 per cent and a modest share of 1.3 per cent of world trade, much like 40 years ago.

Section 23.3 is devoted to analyzing trade performance and comparing it with world trends. The composition of world exports has evolved gradually in the direction of high-technology manufactured goods, but Brazilian trade structure moved in the opposite direction during the past decade. The estimated indices of revealed comparative advantage show that at an aggregate level Brazil lost ground in the world market for most of the product categories except commodities. In particular, in agricultural trade the country became a 'big player' in several markets and the increased exports contributed to the large trade surplus during the past decade.

The role of FDI is discussed in Section 23.4. Since World War II, FDI has made an important contribution to shaping the production and trade structure of the Brazilian economy. There have been several ups and downs in FDI flows to Brazil, following the world cycle of investment and the domestic economic conditions and economic policies. There were two clear cycles of FDI inflows in the recent period: one after stabilization and the privatization program, the second after 2005. During this period there was a radical change in the composition of FDI stock: by the mid 1990s, most of the capital was allocated to the industrial sector, as a consequence still of the incentives to industrial investment originating in the period of import substitution. After the privatization program, the picture becomes completely different. On the latest figures, the largest share belongs to services, clearly a nontradable sector.

Section 23.5, the last section, sums up the findings and discusses the future challenges in terms of trade and investment policies.

23.2 TRADE LIBERALIZATION REFORM

By the end of the 1980s high tariffs and non-tariff barriers (NTB) became dysfunctional and one important impediment for investment, productivity growth and competition in the Brazilian economy. Brazil was so isolated from the world market that clearly the first move had to be a unilateral opening up of the domestic market to foreign competition. The costs of near-autarky were very high, distorting resource allocation, reducing economic welfare and hindering economic growth. Starting in 1988, a series of measures were undertaken to reduce the level and the variance of import controls. Import duties were reduced and the government agency for NTB was discontinued. Over 6 years, tariffs fell sharply, but after 1995 no additional progress was made in terms of trade liberalization, and a slight reversal occurred after the mid 1990s, as can be seen from Figure 23.1.

The opening up of the economy was implemented in three steps: between 1988 and 1989, tariff redundancy (water in the tariff) was eliminated, leaving untouched the NTB control by CACEX (the state agency responsible for administrative import controls); in the period 1990–93, the elimination took place of the 42 special import regimes, quotas and a list of 1300 forbidden import items, while CACEX was discontinued

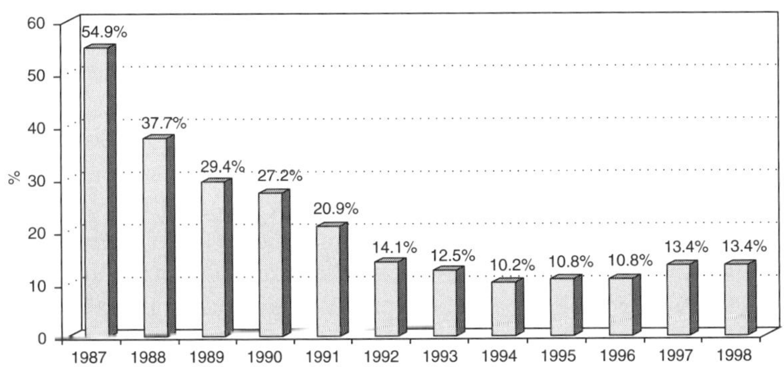

Source: Kume et al. (2003).

Figure 23.1 Brazil 1987–1998: weighted average nominal tariff.

and a new tariff law was passed, reducing import duties over a period of 4 years; finally, in 1994, after the inauguration of the Real Plan, there was one additional round of tariff reduction anticipating the tariff levels of the Ouro Preto Protocol that instituted Mercosur's common external tariff (CET). By the mid 1990s trade policy reform moved import controls to market instruments (tariffs and exchange rate) instead of using the unpredictable, informal and nontransparent bureaucratic controls of previous decades that were prone to rent-seeking activities. The results were impressive. Prior to reform, the average tariff was 55 per cent, one of the highest in the world; in 1998, the tariff was one-quarter of the earlier level, reaching 13.4 per cent and accompanied by the removal of all important NTBs.

Even though this represents one important step in trade reform, the resultant scheme still resembles the structure of the previous regime: high tariff rates by international standards and a large variation in nominal and effective protection, which discriminates against the imports of the capital goods that are essential for productivity growth (Moreira, 2009). The same sectors that had the highest protection in the peak of import substitution still receive shelter from international competition.

There is plenty of empirical evidence of the effects of the Brazilian trade reform on productivity growth and competitiveness. Hay (2001), using panel data for the period 1986–94 for large manufacturing firms, finds important total factor productivity (TFP) gains, and reductions in market share and profits. The supply shock from import liberalization forced firms to improve their efficiency. Ferreia and Rossi (2003), using panel data for 16 industrial sectors in the period 1985–97, found that trade reform increased average TFP in most sectors of Brazilian manufacturing industry but no significant change in domestic market power associated with increased import competition. Productivity growth was attributed to access to imported inputs and technologies, not to competitive pressures from abroad. Lopez-Córdoba and Moreira (2003) concluded that total factor productivity increased in the manufacturing sector of Brazil and Mexico after the unilateral and regional trade integration. To the countrary, however, Muendler (2004), using firm level statistics for the period 1986–98, found that competition in the product market had an important role in boosting TFP growth, but that access to inputs in world markets and the elimination of inefficient firms had no significant effect on productivity growth. Tyler and Gurgel (2009), using a computable general equilibrium model to simulate the effect of trade liberalization of the 1990s, came up with some favorable effects: an increase of 1.9 per cent in welfare, measured by the increase in consumption, and a 9.1 per cent real exchange rate devaluation and income redistribution in favor of Brazilian relatively abundant natural resources. The model also simulated increases in trade flows and changes in production composition in the direction of agricultural products, mineral products and light manufacturing, sectors where the country's comparative advantage lies.

But Brazilian trade liberalization is rather limited compared with the average world pattern, and the relative price of capital goods is still high. The following statistical data illustrate the challenges for future trade policy. Compared with a large sample of countries, Brazil stands as a country of high nominal tariffs. The weighted manufactures tariff of 10.9 per cent in 2006 appears in the upper quartile of the distribution, well above (27 per cent) the median tariff (UNCTAD TRAINS). It is worth mentioning that the present Brazilian tariff is above the 1994 level and that there has since then been no further effort to liberalize trade and reap the advantages of better resource allocation and productivity growth. Macroeconomic imbalances since the mid 1990s, linked with overvalued exchange rates and international financial turbulences, gave new strength to protectionist demands, and punctual tariff hikes and NTBs were implemented. The Brazilian anti-dumping and unfair trade practices agency has been very active. According to the latest DECOM (2009) report, in the decade 1998–08, 295 anti-dumping investigations were conducted, with countervailing duties imposed in 57 per cent of the cases. As pointed out by Tavares de Araujo and Miranda (2008), in 50 per cent of the cases the decisions protected domestic monopolies, in 41 per cent they protected domestic oligopolies, and in only 9 per cent of the cases where protection was granted was the number of firms greater than six. Similar results appear for unfair trade practices (subsidies) and safeguard measures, protecting domestic firms with monopoly power.

There is a large variation in nominal and effective protection, as can be seen from Figure 23.2. The nominal tariff ranges from 0 per cent for alcohol and oil to 30 per cent for trucks and passenger cars, but the great variance occurs with the effective tariff rate – it ranges from −4.6 per cent for alcohol to 180 per cent for passenger cars. The average nominal tariff in 2005 was estimated at 11.1 per cent and the effective rate at 25.8 per cent. Compared with the tariff levels of 1988, where the average nominal tariff was 38.5 per cent and the effective rate was 50.4 per cent, there was a significant reduction in tariff levels, but there is room for further trade liberalization.[1] There is no economic rationale for the present tariff structure. Why protect the car industry with an effective rate of 180 per cent and penalize the production of alcohol and oil with negative rates? The only answer is the vested interests of protected sectors consolidated in the tariff structure. But the costs for the country are high in terms of distorted resource allocation, unemployment, welfare loss and a reduced rate of growth.

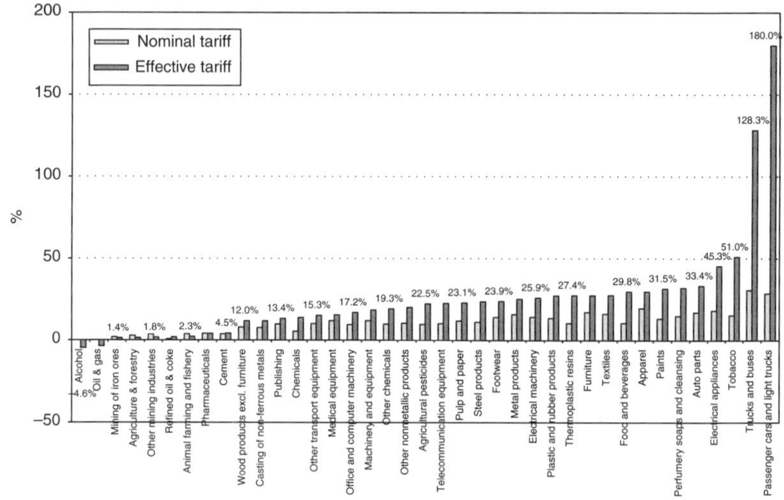

Source: Castilho et al. (2009).

Figure 23.2 Nominal and effective tariffs – 2005.

The high protection given to the machinery and equipment sectors is an important burden on investment in Brazil. There is some empirical literature showing that high relative prices of capital goods have a negative impact on a country's investment and growth rates. Using a selected sample of developing countries (WTO, 2009), we can see that the Brazilian weighted tariff applied on machinery is relatively high. The Brazilian tariff of 13.4 per cent in 2007 was the highest among representative countries of Latin America, Asia and the BRICs.[2] One stylized fact of the Brazilian economy is the low rate of investment. In the five years to 2010 the average gross investment/GDP rate was 17.5 per cent, and there is no sound economic argument for penalizing investment that is badly needed to increase productivity and growth.

Brazil was one of the last countries to embark in trade liberalization and did not go far enough from its autarkic model, taking as a yardstick the average degree of the trade openness of developing countries. After the unilateral trade reform and the Mercosur initiatives at the beginning of the 1990s, no relevant move can be pointed out in terms of trade policy liberalization. Domestic and international turbulences, contradictory domestic macroeconomic policies with recurrent exchange rate overvaluation, the strengthening of protectionist lobbies and a different government strategic view after 2003, can be invoked to explain the paralysis in trade policy reform. In particular, there was a revival of the South–South integration initiatives. The abandonment of the trade negotiations in the Western Hemisphere and with the European Union eliminated the possibility of preferential access to high-per-capita-income markets. The trade agreements with India, the Southern African Customs Union and South American countries were very limited in scope and did not increase bilateral trade flows significantly.

23.3 BRAZILIAN TRADE PERFORMANCE

It is a stylized fact that historically the degree of openness of the Brazilian economy has been small, and during the 1970s and 1980s the country followed the opposite path to the rest of the world, reducing the share in GDP of its trade. After the first oil shock in 1973 the share of imports declined steadily till the end of the 1980s. Tight import controls and an additional round of import-substitution industrialization (ISI) in intermediate goods, petrochemicals and capital goods explain the path to near autarky. Imports fell to 6 per cent of GDP, one of the lowest in the world and incompatible with any criteria of comparative advantage. Since 1990, imports have had an increased share in domestic supply, and this is explained by the opening up of the economy. With a decade lag, exports at first had a downward trajectory, then rose again in the past decade.

Exports fell from 14 per cent to 7 per cent of GDP as a consequence of the overvalued exchange rates associated with various attempts to control inflation, the discontinuity of tax subsidies to exports, and the isolation of world-class technologies embodied in imports and FDI flows. In 1999, Brazil adopted a floating exchange rate regime followed by three large devaluations of the real (1999, 2001 and 2002) and this was the first factor behind the recent export expansion. Compared with the world pattern, the Brazilian insertion in world markets is still modest, deserving additional steps in trade liberalization policies. In the last half century world economic integration advanced steadily. In the beginning of the 1960s exports accounted for 12 per cent of world GDP. With trade liberalization through multilateral and regional agreements, exports represent nowadays more than 30 per cent of world GDP. Brazil did not follow the same track. In 2008, the Brazilian export/GDP ratio was similar to the world ratio of 1973.

Taking a long-run perspective, the price competitiveness of Brazilian exports had fluctuated widely and this had been a hindrance on exports, mainly of manufactured goods. During the period 1985–98 the real effective exchange rate became highly overvalued as a consequence of various attempts to use the exchange rate as an anchor against inflation. With a 33 per cent appreciation of the real exchange rate during this period, balance-of-payment deficits increased sharply and the country was on the verge of an additional default on foreign debt in 1998. In January 1999, after an acute speculative attack against the real, the central bank had no choice but to move to a floating exchange rate regime. After that, there were three large real devaluations of the Brazilian currency but after 2004 the exchange rate appreciated again.

There are two major factors explaining the exchange rate's behavior. The first one is Brazilian sovereign risk. From the 1980s on, inconsistent macroeconomic policies led to increased foreign and government debts and risk fluctuated wildly, determining the path of the exchange rate. The huge devaluations of 1999, 2001 and 2002 are explained by risk aversion behavior with respect to Brazilian financial assets. With the consolidation of the three pillars of the present macroeconomic policy (inflation targeting, floating exchange rates, and fiscal responsibility) Brazil reached in 2008 the status of 'investment grade', while risk and the exchange rate took a consistent downward path in the 5 years to 2010. The second factor explaining lower exchange rates is the inappropriate mix of macroeconomic policy. It is a well-known result in macroeconomic models that – with flexible exchange rates and integrated financial markets – the combination of an expansionary fiscal policy with a restrictive monetary policy produces higher equilibrium interest rates, lower exchange rates and balance-of-payments deficits. Price competitiveness in world markets depends crucially on the exchange rate, and the present macroeconomic policy represents an important constraint on export performance.

The main factors behind the export recovery after 1999 were exchange rate devaluations, the rapid expansion of world demand and the sharp increase in commodity prices associated with the emergence of China as a big player in world markets. Finally, structural reforms and support policies by government agencies must be mentioned as favorable factors affecting export performance. Import liberalization and privatization were responsible for important productivity gains, increasing the competitiveness of Brazilian companies. Embraer and Vale are vivid examples of success in world markets after privatization. The role of Embrapa, the state agricultural research institute, has been key to the increased share in world agricultural markets through innovations in seed varieties and production techniques. As a consequence, the Brazilian share in world exports increased modestly. According to WTO (2010) data, in 1983 the Brazilian share in world exports was 1.19 per cent, and in 2008 reached 1.26 per cent. Increasing market share is a measure of dynamic export competitiveness and by this criterion Brazil had a dismal performance.

Table 23.1 Composition of world exports 2008 (percentages)

	Agricultural products	Fuels and mining products	Manufactures
Africa	7.1	74.1	18.8
Asia	6.1	12.7	81.2
Brazil	32.1	22.8	45.1
Europe	9.5	12.1	78.3
North America	10.9	17.8	71.3
South and Central America[a]	24.1	54.4	21.5
World	8.8	23.0	68.2

Note: [a] Excluding Brazil.

Source: WTO (2009a).

The following analysis covers the two decades to 2010, a period of import liberalization, the stabilization of inflation at low levels, change in the exchange rate regime and increased world demand for commodities. Over this period, both the product composition and trade direction of Brazil's trade have experienced considerable changes and the long-run response of exports and imports to the exchange rate has varied according to product types. The stylized facts that emerge are as follows.

The volume of world exports grew at an annual rate of 5.8 per cent and Brazilian exports at 6.6 per cent. In nominal terms world exports expanded by 9.1 per cent per year and Brazilian exports by 9.6 per cent. The composition of world exports has evolved gradually in the direction of manufactured goods but the Brazilian trade structure moved in the opposite direction during the past decade. The present structure of world exports can be depicted by the data in Table 23.1. The share of Brazilian agricultural exports is almost four times the world average; on the other hand, manufactured exports are 35 per cent below the world average pattern. There is no region of the world with a higher share of agricultural exports than Brazil. The proportion of manufactured goods exports declined over the past two decades with an increased share of primary products.

The changes in Brazilian trade are detailed in the following tables. After the 1980s, the composition of Brazilian exports changed in the direction of primary products. At the end of the 1980s the share of commodities (identified by the categories 0 to 4 of the SITC classification) was 41 per cent; in 2008 it had increased to 51 per cent. The main exports in this group are: iron ore, petroleum, meat, soybean, sugar and coffee. The opposite move was observed in manufactured goods (categories 5 to 9), the share diminishing from 59 per cent to 49 per cent. In this group the main exports are vehicles, iron and steel, aircraft, organic chemicals and machinery. With respect to imports, the opening up of the economy increased the share of manufactures substantially, from 57 per cent in 1989 to 73 per cent in 2008.

The annual growth of exports and imports shows additional characteristics of the recent trade performance. Mineral fuels presented the highest rate of growth exports during this period. Two main factors explain oil product exports: the end, in 1997, of the Petrobras production monopoly, allowing joint ventures with domestic and international private capital, and the successful biofuel (alcohol) program, which generated surplus oil and gasoline supplies sold in world markets. Next should be mentioned the growth in iron ore and soya beans and meals, which represented 80 per cent of total exports within the raw-materials category in 2008. The annual average growth of those products was, respectively, 11.7 per cent and 12.6 per cent. Of the top ten products by export revenue in 2008, at a two-digit level in SITC classification, six are agriculture or mining commodities, representing 38 per cent of the total foreign sales.

Using the UNCTAD classification for non-fuel commodities it is possible to arrange trade data according to the underlying sources of comparative advantage.[3] The non-fuel primary-commodity items include foodstuffs, beverages, tobacco, iron ore and soybean products as the main items traded in the Brazilian case. Leather, textiles, apparel, footwear, toys, wood products and nonmetallic mineral products are considered as labor or resource-intensive manufactures. Low-skill-technology manufactures include iron, steel, metal products, simple transport equipment, ships and boats. Medium-skill-technology manufactures include electrical and non-electrical machinery other than semiconductors and road motor vehicles. The last category, high-skill-technology manufactures, includes chemical and pharmaceutical products, computers and office equipment, communications equipment and semiconductors, aircraft, scientific instruments, watches and photographic equipment.

The more important changes in the composition of Brazilian trade were: on the export side, the increased share of commodities and the reduced share of labor-intensive and low-skill manufactures in export flows. At the end of the 1980s the share of non-fuel primary commodities was 44.4 per cent; in 2008 it had increased to 50.1 per cent. The opposite move was observed in manufactured goods, with its share diminishing from 55.6 per cent to 49.9 per cent. With respect to imports, the opening up of the economy increased substantially the share of manufactures, from 73.6 per cent in 1989 to 88 per cent in 2008.

In the case of commodities, increased world demand and comparative

Table 23.2 Composition of Brazilian trade (percentages)

	1989		2002		2008	
	Exports	Imports	Exports	Imports	Exports	Imports
Non-fuel primary commodities	44.4	26.4	43.9	12.6	50.1	12.0
Labour-intensive and resource-intensive manufactures	12.4	6.8	12.7	5.5	7.2	6.0
Low-skill-technology, capital- and scale-intensive manufactures	14.9	3.9	8.5	4.3	10.7	6.7
Medium-skill-technology, capital and scale-intensive manufactures	17.0	25.4	18.7	38.9	19.1	32.7
High-skill-technology, capital- and scale-intensive manufactures	11.2	37.4	16.3	38.7	13.0	42.7

Source: COMTRADE.

advantage of the Ricardian type are the factors behind the observed tendency in the past two decades. The declining share of labor-intensive and low-skill-technology manufactures are explained by the increasing competition from Asia's lower-wage countries. Medium- and high-skill technology manufactures increased slightly their share on exports. According to UNCTAD (2002), primary products and resource-based manufactures have been losing their share in world exports over several decades and are in those sectors in which Brazil had an increased export concentration. For the developing countries as a whole, the fastest-growing exports were in the high-technology sectors, where Brazil had a minor share. The UNCTAD study considered a 'winner' in world markets to be any country that increased its share in world trade of manufactured goods. The striking result for the period 1985–2000 is that Brazil does not appear once among the top 20 'winning' countries for any category of manufacturing industry. With respect to the composition of imports after trade

Table 23.3 Brazil: revealed comparative advantage indices

	1989	2002	2008	% change 1989–2008
Non-fuel primary commodities	7.4	31.8	36.9	399.5
Labour-intensive and resource-intensive manufactures	2.3	7.4	1.2	−49.5
Low-skill-technology, capital- and scale-intensive manufactures	4.5	4.3	3.8	−14.8
Medium-skill-technology, capital- and scale-intensive manufactures	−3.4	−20.6	−13.2	−482.9
High-skill-technology, capital- and scale-intensive manufactures	−10.7	−22.9	−28.7	−367.3

Source: COMTRADE.

liberalization, we should note the significant increase in medium- and high-skill technology manufactures imports, that nowadays represent 75 per cent of total imports. Total imports grew at a higher annual rate than exports.

Comparative advantage changed in the past two decades, as trade evolved. Table 23.3 shows the Lafay index of revealed comparative advantage (RCA) for the years 1989, 2002 and 2008.[4] At an aggregate level, Brazil lost ground in world markets for most of the product categories, except commodities. Of the five categories, three Brazilian RCA indices were positive and four declined over time (last column in Table 23.3). For medium- and high-skill-technology manufactures the results suggest deterioration in trade performance, owing to increased import penetration and Brazilian exports being uncompetitive in those dynamic world high-tech product markets. Brazil now shows a higher export performance only for commodities, for which during the past two decades the level of the RCA index increased by 400 per cent, contrasting with the sharp reduction of RCA indices for medium- and high-skill-technology manufactures of 483 per cent and 367 per cent.

A more detailed picture of the competitiveness of Brazilian exports

Table 23.4 Brazil: highest RCA indices

	1989
Iron and steel	5.8
Feeding stuff for animals (not including unmilled cereals)	3.4
Coffee tea cocoa spices and manufactures thereof	3.3
Road vehicles	2.3
Metalliferous ores and metal scrap	2.2
Footwear	1.8
Oil seeds and oleaginous fruit	1.7
Vegetables and fruit	1.1
Non-ferrous metals	1.0
Textile yarn fabrics made-up articles and related products	0.8
	2008
Metalliferous ores and metal scrap	10.9
Meat and preparations	8.4
Oil seeds and oleaginous fruit	6.5
Iron and steel	5.1
Sugar sugar preparations and honey	3.4
Coffee tea cocoa spices and manufactures thereof	3.0
Feeding stuff for animals (not including unmilled cereals)	2.6
Other transport equipment	2.2
Pulp and waste paper	2.1
Tobacco and tobacco manufactures	1.6

can be obtained at the two-digit level of the SITC classification, through the top ten exporters in 1989 and 2008, ranked by RCA indices. In 1989 Brazil exhibited an RCA for a larger array of manufactured products ranging from footwear (labor-intensive goods) to road vehicles (medium-skill-technology goods). Twenty years later the outlook had changed substantially (Table 23.4). Brazil then displayed a higher RCA in more traditional products, those that had gained importance being iron ore, meat, sugar and tobacco. The only exception was the category 'other transport equipments', owing to aircraft exports (high-tech manufacture). The changes in comparative advantage are striking. For example: in 1989 road vehicles were ranked at 4 on the RCA index; in 2008 the country lay at 41, with a negative RCA. The opposite movement was observed with 'meat and preparations' exports: ranked at 24 in 1989, Brazil was at number 2 in 2008.

The positive results for commodities are associated with the rapid growth of trade during the past decade, especially the rapid growth of China's imports of food and raw materials, and domestic supply factors such as the rapid increase in productivity associated with import liberalization, privatization (Embraer and Vale) and new agricultural technologies developed by Embrapa.

Brazil has not been able to change its comparative advantage towards the new technological sectors. To increase competition of manufactured goods it is necessary to reduce the level of import protection to enhance modernization and efficiency gains, in particular to diminish tariffs on imported capital goods. Another important task is the elimination of the domestic tax burden on exports. Brazil has a complex tax system with a high tax burden (36 per cent of GDP in 2008), imposing large administrative costs and indirect taxation on exports, and is a significant constraint on Brazilian firms' competitiveness in world markets. The current policy of rebates for state and federal value added tax is not enough to eliminate taxes levied on exports being part of the so-called 'Brazilian cost' (an overvalued exchange rate, a high tax burden and interest rates, and a costly infrastructure). It is also fundamental to control government current expenditure and to commit higher government resources to the investment in education, research and infrastructure that is essential to the competitiveness of the industrial sector in the long run. Brazil has one of the more diversified industrial bases of the developing countries but is not able to reap its advantage in world markets owing to the heavy burden of inappropriate government policies.

There are two final topics regarding trade issues, namely regional market diversification and the outstanding agribusiness performance. One distinctive feature of recent export performance has been the increasing sales to new markets (Bonelli and Pinheiro, 2007). All developing regions increased their purchases from Brazil, as can be seen in Table 23.5. The share of Latin America doubled between 1989 and 2008, as a consequence of preferential regional agreements and the lower transport costs associated with shorter distances and infrastructure improvements.[5] The developed countries declined in importance as major trade partners, the USA in particular. In 1989, 65.3 per cent of Brazilian exports went to the European Union, the US and Japan, and this share fell to 41.4 per cent, in 2008. Brazil is a 'global trader'. Brazilian exports are distributed among all the regions of the world. This is does not come as a surprise. Given the size of the country, its different climates (ranging from tropical to temperate), its large endowment of natural resources and labor and its highly diversified industry all influence the composition and regional distribution of Brazilian exports.

Another distinctive characteristic of the present Brazilian trade profile is the regional specialization of exports. Manufactured exports are dominant in only two regions: Africa and Latin America. With the exception of Mercosur, in all other markets the countries' exports follow the uniform pattern of reduced importance of manufactured goods.

Table 23.5 *Destinations of Brazilian exports 1989 and 2008 (percentages)*

	1989				2008			
	Basic	Semi-manu-factured	Manu-factured	% total exports	Basic	Semi-manu-factured	Manu-factured	% total exports
Africa	16.5	13.8	69.7	2.8	22.1	13.2	64.7	5.3
Aladi excluding Mercosur	6.4	6.5	87.1	6.4	18.4	4.7	76.9	11.1
Mercosur	14.2	4.0	81.8	4.0	4.9	3.0	92.1	11.3
China	11.7	27.5	60.8	1.8	77.5	15.8	6.7	8.5
Japan	40.4	34.6	24.9	7.2	65.1	22.2	12.7	3.2
USA	10.7	11.6	77.7	24.2	22.9	18.0	59.0	14.2
Eastern Europe	63.7	23.6	22.8	1.6	61.1	22.0	16.9	2.9
Middle East	26.7	11.1	62.2	3.3	57.12	15.4	27.4	4.2
European Union	46.9	15.4	37.8	33.9	47.0	14.8	38.2	24.0
Russia	0.0	0.0	0.0	0.0	61.1	25.3	13.5	2.4
Others	22.6	29.8	47.6	14.6	40.6	18.8	40.8	13.2
Total	28.1	17.1	54.8		37.9	14.0	48.1	

Source: Ministry of Development, Industry and Trade statistics.

This is the result of an important pitfall of the Brazilian trade strategy. When multilateral trade negotiations waned, the country moved to South–South agreements, with minor effects on trade flows. The international trade specialization with developing countries is limited by market size and similarity in factor endowments. A smaller market does not allow the exploitation of the comparative advantage of a larger array of manufactured products and the benefits of economies of scale. Similar factor endowments impose very high adjustment costs for a full-blown free-trade agreement. The adjustment costs of a bilateral agreement with India or China would not be trivial in labor-intensive industries. On the other hand, the absence of preferential access to developed countries's markets explains the falling share of Brazilian exports in those markets. Developed countries have been very active in regional trade agreements; NAFTA, the European Union enlargement and their agreements with Latin American countries explain, at least partially, the eroded Brazilian position in developed countries' markets. The competition in the manufactured goods world market has increased sharply in the past three decades with the entry of new and large players. China with its aggressive trade and exchange rate policies is the great novelty, becoming in one generation the second-largest exporter in the world. This is one of the challenges facing Brazil in the near future: how to increase market access in a world segmented by regional agreements, new competitive players and laggardly multilateral trade negotiations to open agricultural markets.

One distinctive aspect of Brazil's position in world trade is the outstanding performance of agriculture in the past decade. From the early 1960s the share of agriculture among total exports fell steadily as a consequence of the import substitution policy and government export incentives for manufactured goods exports. In 1990, agricultural exports were reduced to 28 per cent of total exports and remained at this level up to 2005; three years later it had increased to 31 per cent (2008). Agriculture has always been an export-oriented sector and at present its share in exports is five times its share in GDP. There are several factors behind the recent export growth: the high growth rate of world demand; the price increases of commodities in world markets; the increased competitiveness of Brazilian agriculture; the regional diversification of exports; and the elimination of the anti-export bias in Brazil's trade policy after import liberalization.

Agricultural exports had two basic characteristics in the two decades to 2010: the changed composition of exported products and regional diversification in the direction of developing countries' markets.

With the increased importance of meat and sugar, agricultural exports are nowadays diversified within tropical products, temperate products and meat. During the past decade there was a relative decline of exports to

Table 23.6 Brazil in world agricultural markets 2008–09

	Exports		Production		% Production exported
	% of World	Ranking	% of World	Ranking	
Orange juice	85.0	1	55.8	1	98.4
Centrifugal sugar	46.5	1	23.3	1	66.7
Poultry	40.1	1	15.5	3	29.3
Coffee	27.2	1	34.1	1	55.4
Beef and veal	26.0	1	16.5	2	20.1
Soybeans	29.8	2	25.7	2	36.9
Soybean meal	22.4	2	15.5	4	49.6
Soybean oil	16.0	2	16.3	4	24.8
Corn	10.6	2	6.4	4	17.7
Pork	12.5	4	3.2	4	21.5
Cotton	5.9	4	5.4	5	36.0

Source: United States Department of Agriculture (USDA).

developed countries and the developing countries' markets were becoming increasingly important. Within the developed countries, the reduction was across the board: a diminishing share in every relevant market; for the developing countries, China appears to be the most dynamic market for agricultural exports. There is no one unique factor to explain regional diversification, but clearly rapid growth per capita in Southeast Asia and highly protected markets in the developed countries are two key factors explaining the observed tendency in agricultural trade.

One stylized fact of the world economy after World War II was the diminishing share of agriculture in world production and trade. The opposite movement happened in the case of Brazilian agriculture. In 1990, Brazil had 2.4 per cent of the world agriculture trade; by 2008, the Brazilian share was almost the double, 4.6 per cent. Brazil is the third-largest agricultural exporter in the world, after the European Union and the United States. Brazil is now a big player in several markets, ranking as the largest exporter of orange juice, sugar, poultry, coffee and beef, and is in second place in soybean products and corn. The degree of openness of the agricultural sector to exports is the largest in the country. According to FIESP data for 2010, Brazilian industry exported 22 per cent of its production in 2008, a figure clearly inferior to those for the agriculture sector that appear in Table 23.6.

The increased competitiveness of Brazilian agriculture is due to a series of factors. The most important in explaining the expansion of output is productivity growth. There are several empirical studies showing that total factor productivity (TFP) growth was impressive. Avila and Evenson (2005) data show that TFP in Brazilian agriculture in the period 1981–2001 grew on average by 3.2 per cent per year, the highest figure in a developing country. Gasques (2006) estimated that between 1975 and 2005 total farm productivity doubled. Productivity growth was linked to government policy decisions to invest in Embrapa's research in new agricultural technologies, and also to investment in human capital. Public universities turned out the large numbers of forestry engineers and veterinarians necessary for high-tech production in agriculture. The main competitors in agriculture world markets are the developed countries, and their exports depend on subsidies, modern agricultural technologies and large-scale production. As the world's third-largest exporter, Brazil was able to overcome unfair trade practices and become a big player in the world agricultural market.

Trade liberalization also had a positive impact in agricultural export performance. In the period of import substitution, the agriculture sector was penalized by trade policies through overvalued exchange rates, tariffs on final products and imported inputs, quotas, licensing and domestic taxation of exports. Trade reform during 1987–2004 eliminated export licensing and quotas, and reduced tariffs and non-tariff barriers for agricultural imports; in 1996 came abolition of value added tax on exports of agricultural and semimanufactured goods. During this period the domestic government program of credit subsidies and price support was phased out, forcing the agricultural sector to compete in the environment of an open world market.

Finally, the rapid international increase in demand should be mentioned in explaining the success of agricultural trade.

The results were impressive, and the agribusiness sector was responsible for changing the Brazilian trade balance. In 1989, the agribusiness trade surplus reached US$11 billions, or 67 per cent of total trade surplus; in 2008, with a trade surplus of US$60 billions, the agribusiness sector was the only sector with a trade surplus, compensating for the trade deficits of the manufactured and service sectors.

To sum up Brazilian trade performance, the country continues as a global trader, with an increasing relative share of new developing markets, a decreasing share of manufactured goods exports and an increasing share of agribusiness and mining. The main factors to explain export performance are productivity growth, economic reforms, the diversification of markets and natural resources. Brazil experienced an export boom in the 2000s, with two main characteristics: new markets and changes in the composition of exports.

23.4 FOREIGN DIRECT INVESTMENT

Since World War II, FDI has made an important contribution to shaping the production and trade structure of the Brazilian economy. Among the factors that attracted FDI was the size of the Brazilian market, one of the largest in a developing country, a domestic market sheltered from international competition and stable legislation on foreign capital. FDI had the role of financing current-account deficits, given the low level of domestic savings. There were several ups and downs in FDI flows to Brazil, following domestic economic conditions and world cycles in investment. Particularly during the 1980s, the inflow of FDI almost disappeared as a consequence of macroeconomic uncertainties associated with threats of hyperinflation, low GDP growth and economic plans that violated contracts by freezing prices and financial assets. One additional and important legal restriction on FDI appeared with the 1988 Constitution, through the distinction between companies on the basis of resident and nonresident ownership of capital. The Constitution also maintained the state monopoly of oil and gas and restricted to domestically owned companies any participation in infrastructure sectors like electricity, transportation and mining.

Trade liberalization was the first reform to stimulate foreign investment, since MNCs have a higher propensity to import and export than have domestic firms. This is due first of all to the high proportion of intra-firm trade that is enhanced by trade liberalization. Second, the larger size of MNCs gives them advantages of scale, efficiency and product differentiation. The stabilization of the economy, higher GDP growth rates and the large masses of low-income consumers in the domestic market are all additional factors. Two institutional reforms were also relevant: in 2005, an amendment to the Constitution abolished the distinction between resident and non-resident ownership of capital, ending the discrimination against foreign investment in infrastructure. In 1996 came the abolition of the state monopoly in oil and gas and telecommunications. Second, an ambitious privatization program and a new concession law opened new opportunities for heavy foreign investment in infrastructure and in the banking sectors. State investment in infrastructure in Brazil had been faltering since the 1980s owing to the public sector fiscal crisis, and sectors like telecommunications were experiencing a period of rapid technological change throughout the world. Investment in infrastructure had to come from domestic and foreign private companies, given the government's budget constraint. The results can be seen in the statistics which follow. During the 15 years to 2010, Brazil attracted an increasing share of world FDI. The peak of interest coincided with the privatization period of 1996–2002, when 3 per cent of total world FDI, almost a fourfold increase, was

Table 23.7 Brazilian share in FDI flows

	1989–95	1996–2002	2003–08
World	0.8	3.0	1.9
Developing countries	3.0	11.1	5.8
Latin America	11.0	28.5	23.2

Source: UNCTAD FDI database.

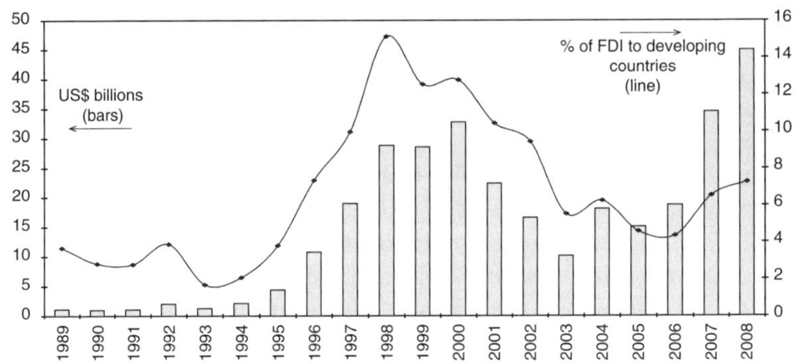

Source: UNCTAD FDI database.

Figure 23.3 FDI – US$ billions and percentages of FDI flows to developing countries.

invested in Brazil (Table 23.7). This is in sharp contrast with the 1989–95 period, when MNCs had a minor strategic interest in the country. In more recent years, Brazil has held an intermediate position between the two previous periods. Even so, it continues to attract a fairly high level of FDI: in 2008, Brazil ranked third among the developing countries, behind China and Russia, with an inflow of US$45 billion.

There are two clear cycles of FDI inflows in the recent period: one after stabilization and the privatization program and the second one after 2005. The intensity of the first period appears to be the stronger, as can be seen in Figure 23.3. Taking as a yardstick the Brazilian share in inward FDI to developing countries, the country was able to attract 15 per cent of the total in 1998 and only 7 per cent in 2008.

The stock of FDI, in nominal terms, grew from US$42 billion in 1995 to US$262 billion in 2008, with an annual rate of growth of 15 per cent, slightly above that for developing countries (13 per cent) and the world 13.3 per cent. During this period, there was a radical change in

Table 23.8 Brazil: FDI by sector – percentages of total stock

	1995	2000	2005	2008[a]
Agriculture	0.6	0.4	0.5	1.0
Mining	1.6	2.0	3.1	8.5
Industry	66.9	33.7	33.1	33.9
Services	30.9	64.0	63.3	56.7
Total (US$ thousand)	41,696	103,015	162,474	262,296

Note: [a] 2005 stocks plus 2006–08 flows.

Source: Banco Central do Brasil FDI Census.

the composition of FDI stock: by the mid 1990s, most of the capital was allocated to the industrial sector, as a consequence still of the incentives to industrial investment from the period of import substitution. In 1995, 67 per cent of the stock of FDI was in the industrial sector. After the privatization program, the picture became completely different. On the latest figures, industrial FDI represents 34 per cent of the total stock and the largest share belongs to services – clearly a nontradable sector, as can be seen in Table 23.8. Within each sector the concentration of FDI is very high. According to the 2005 central bank census, 73 per cent of total FDI was invested in five industrial sectors: chemical, auto, food, electronic/telecommunication equipment and machinery. A similar picture is found in the service sector: telecommunication, services for business, banking, wholesale/retail trade and electricity account for 78 per cent of the total stock of FDI in Brazil.

Using the standard classification for FDI it is possible to identify which motives attracted FDI to Brazil. A small fraction is resource-seeking FDI – in agriculture and mining – reaching 9.5 per cent of the total stock in 2008. FDI in services (the sector with a high nontradable share) is basically market-seeking and is dominant in Brazil now. In the manufacturing sector, a blend of efficiency-seeking and market-seeking motives can be pointed out to explain FDI inflows. The international empirical evidence suggests that resource-seeking and efficiency-seeking FDI are export-oriented and generate strong increases in foreign exchange earnings. Market-seeking FDI will not be export-oriented, especially if protection for sales in the domestic market discriminates against exports.

There is a rather limited empirical literature in Brazil about the determinants of FDI and its impact on competitiveness and foreign trade in Brazil. Bonelli (1999) estimated empirically the links between competitiveness and the increased presence of FDI in Brazilian manufactured sectors during the period 1991–96. According to theory, one should expect a positive association between competitiveness and MNC investments. Competitiveness was measured by changes in unit labor costs and export growth. The results showed a partial and weak relation between either reduction in unit labor costs or higher export growth with FDI stock growth. De Negri (2003), using panel data for the period 1996–2000, analyzed the impact of MNCs on trade performance. MNCs have some advantages as compared with domestic firms: easier access to international markets through their own distribution networks, large scale, technology and productivity, and specialization in sectors with growing shares in international trade. There is no dispute that MNCs have a higher propensity to engage in foreign trade operations. With a large sample of domestic and foreign firms, two equations were estimated: with fixed effects, the FDI coefficient was not significant statistically in the export equation but is significant in the import equation; with random effects, both coefficients were significant but the coefficient for the import equation is bigger than for the export equation. These results were similar to previous studies: MNCs did not improve the trade balance. Rothmuller (2003) used a gravity model for the period 1996–2002 to test the direct effect of FDI on exports and imports of manufactured goods and came up with similar empirical findings. MNCs were more interested in supplying the domestic market than exporting. The main result for ten manufacturing sectors was that: FDI had a positive impact on imports, but no effect on exports. De Negri (2003), using panel data for the period 1996–2000, estimated with a model of multivariate logistic regression the relative probability of a firm in the manufacturing sector exporting or importing according to the origin of capital. The general conclusion was that an exporting firm had a five times higher probability of being an MNC, and an importing firm a seven times higher probability of being foreign-owned. Fernandes and Campos (2008) divided foreign-owned companies into two categories: those with a propensity to export (exports/net operating revenue) above the average and below the average. The data covered the period 1995–2000 and the methodology chosen was multivariate discriminant analysis. In the estimated function, the stock of FDI was unable to discriminate between the two groups, or in other words FDI was not related to better export performance. On this scant empirical base, there are indications in the Brazilian case that FDI is mainly domestic-market-oriented. The UNCTAD (2002) study shows the same feature in a different way: of those developing economies that increased their share in world manufactures markets, several depended on MNC exports, but Brazil was not one of the successful cases of export competitiveness through foreign affiliates.

23.5 CONCLUDING REMARKS

Brazil implemented an ambitious trade and investment reform during the 1990s. Tariff and non-tariff barriers were removed, new opportunities were opened for foreign direct investment and the country became better integrated in the world economy. A more open economy was able to reap the advantages of international specialization and it is well documented empirically what the gains in efficiency, productivity and competitiveness were in the Brazilian case. The structure of foreign trade moved in the direction of an increasing share of commodities in exports and one of high-skill-technology goods in the import side, reflecting the existing comparative advantage. Some 20 years after the beginning of the economic reforms, Brazil still faces important unsettled trade issues.

The first challenge for policymakers is to choose the appropriate mix of macroeconomic policy. Price competitiveness in world markets depends crucially on the exchange rate. The present combination of an expansionary fiscal policy with a restrictive monetary policy produces higher equilibrium interest rates, lower exchange rates and balance of payments deficits. A more restrictive fiscal policy and an expansionary monetary policy will be suitable for promoting exports through a devalued exchange rate and lower interest rates without jeopardizing inflation control. It is also fundamental to control government current expenditure and to commit higher government resources to the investment in education, in research and in infrastructure that is essential to competitiveness in the long run. The small amount of resources devoted to these sectors has been an important constraint on export performance during the past two decades, and is one important part of the 'Brazilian cost'. One further effect of a sound fiscal policy is to improve the business environment for investment, attracting both the domestic and the foreign capital essential for brighter growth prospects. Higher domestic savings are fundamental to avoiding the recurrent balance-of-payments crisis that constrained Brazilian growth in the period after World War II.

Even though nominal and effective tariffs were reduced, by international standards they remain comparatively high and with a large variance. There is no economic rationale for the present tariff structure. Nominal tariff rates range from zero to 35 per cent and the effective exchange rate goes from −4.6 per cent to 180 per cent. The only explanation for this is the strength of special-interest groups, consolidated in the tariff structure. High tariffs on capital goods penalize investments that are badly needed in a country where the investment rate is low. The costs of the present tariff structure for the country are high in terms of distorted resource allocation, less employment, welfare loss and reduced rate of growth. The direction of tariff reform is clear: reduce the level and the variance of the present tariff schedule. Ideally, a Chilean type of homogeneous tariff will eliminate the privileges and the rent-seeking activities. An additional advantage of a reduced tariff rate is to increase the demand for imports, contributing to the devaluation of the exchange rate, reinforcing the results of the previous proposal. It should be noted that the proposed round of trade liberalization is a completely different case from that at the opening of the 1990s. Then, the country was so isolated from the world market that the first task depended only on domestic will and the move towards more trade was unilateral. Now, market access is of paramount importance. This leads to the last challenge: market access at the regional level.

During the past decade Brazil moved to South–South agreements with minor effects on trade flows. The international trade specialization with developing countries is desirable, but is limited by market size and similarity in factor endowments. On the other hand, the absence of preferential access to developed countries' markets explains the falling share of Brazilian manufactured exports to those markets. Developed countries have been very active in regional trade agreements. NAFTA, the European Union enlargement, and their agreements with Latin American countries eroded Brazilian positions in developed countries' markets. This is one of the challenges facing Brazil in the near future: how to increase market access in a world segmented by regional agreements, where there are new competitive players and where multilateral trade negotiations to open agricultural markets are slow and hesitant.

NOTES

1. According to Kume's (1996) calculations for 1988.
2. For capital goods without substitutable national equivalents, there is the possibility of reducing the tax burden by a bureaucratic and nontransparent import regime called 'ex-tarifário'.
3. The UNCTAD commodity classification can be found in Mayer et al. (2002) (see Table 23.2).
4. The Lafay index of revealed comparative advantage (RCA) is defined as:

$$RCA_{ij} = \frac{1000}{GDP_j}\left[(X_i - M_i)_j - \left(\frac{(X_i + M_i)}{(X + M)} \times (X - M)\right)j\right],$$

   where:
   $RCA_{i,j}$ is the index of revealed comparative advantage of product i, for country j;
   X_i and M_i are the exports and imports of the product i; and X and M are the total exports and imports of country j. A positive index indicates revealed comparative advantage, a negative comparative disadvantage. For details see Nonnenberg (1995) and Pasteels (1998).
5. Mercosur signed trade agreements with Chile and Bolivia (1996), the Andean Community

(2003), India (2004) and Southern African Customs Union (2008), the last one pending on Congress's approval of individual countries. Brazil and Mexico (2002) signed a bilateral agreement within the LAIA initiative granting free-trade status for 800 tariff lines, even though trade is heavily concentrated in autos and auto parts.

REFERENCES

Avila, A.F.D. and R.E. Evenson (2005),'Total factor productivity growth in agriculture: the role of technological capital', available at: http://www.earthinstitute.columbia.edu/cgsd/events/documents/evenson.pdf/

Bonelli, R. (1999),'A note on foreign direct investment and industrial competitiveness in Brazil', *Oxford Development Studies*, **27** (3), available at: http://ideas.repec.org/a/taf/oxdevs/v27y1999i3p305-327.html

Bonelli, R. and Pinheiro, A.C. (2007),'New export activities in Brazil: comparative advantage, policy or self-discovery?', IPEA Texto Para Discussão no. 1269a, available at: http://www.ipea.gov.br/sites/000/2/publicacoes/tds/td_1269a.pdf

Banco Central do Brasil (BCB), http://www.bcb.gov.br/default.asp?id=boletimhist&ano=1996/.

Banco Central do Brasil (BCB),'*Censos de capital estrangeiro*' – 1995/2000/2005, available at: http://www.bcb.gov.br/?CAMBIO/

Castilho, M.F., A.R. Ruiz and M. Melo (2009), 'Evolução da proteção efetiva no Brasil, 2000–2005', paper presented at the XXXVII Encontro Nacional de Economia, Foz do Iguaçu, Brazil, available at: http://www.anpec.org.br/encontro2009/inscricao.on/arquivos/000-e604cef117775b4e016615ed3c92b7c6.pdf

Comtrade – United Nations Commodity Trade Statistics Database, available at: http://comtrade.un.org/db/

De Negri, F. (2003),'Desempenho comercial das empresas estrangeiras no Brasil na década de noventa: uma análise dos dados em painel', paper presented at the XXXI Encontro Nacional de Economia, Porto Seguro, Brazil, available at: http://www.anpec.org.br/encontro_2003.htm

Fernandes, E.A. and A.C. Campos (2008), 'Investimento direto estrangeiro e o desempenho das exportações brasileiras', *Revista de Economia Política*, **28** (3), 490–509, available at: http://www.scielo.br/pdf/rep/v28n3/a08v28n3.pdf/

Ferreira, P.C. and J.L. Rossi (2003), 'New evidence from Brazil on trade liberalization and productivity growth', *International Economic Review*, **44** (4), 1383–405, available at: http://www.fgv.br/professor/ferreira/FerreiraIGuillen.pdf

Gasques, J.G., E.T. Bastos and M.R.P. Bacchi (2006), *Produtividade e Fontes de Crescimento da Agricultura Brasileira*, available at: http://www.ipea.gov.br/sites/000/2/livros/inovacaotecnologica/capitulo11.pdf/

Hay, D.A (2001), 'The post-1990 Brazilian trade liberalization and the performance of large manufacturing firms: productivity, market share and profits', *Economic Journal*, **111** (473), 620–41, available at: http://www.jstor.org/stable/2667950?cookieSet=1/

Kume, H., G. Piani and C.F.B Souza (2003), *A Política Brasileira de Importação no Período 1987–1998: Descrição e Avaliação*,available at: http://www.ipea.gov.br/sites/000/2/livros/aberturacomercial_/Capitulo%201_politica.pdf/

Lopez-Cordoba, E. and M.M. Moreira (2003), 'Regional integration and productivity: the experiences of Brazil and México', INTAL ITD-STA Working Paper no. 14, available at: http://www.iadb.org/intal/aplicaciones/uploads/publicaciones/i_INTALITDSTA_WP_14_2003_Cordova_Moreira.pdf

Mayer, J., A. Butkevicius and A. Kadri (2002), 'Dynamic products in world exports', UNCTAD Discussion Paper no. 159, available at: http://ideas.repec.org/p/unc/dispap/159.html

Ministério do Desenvolvimento, Indústria e Comércio Exterior, Departamento de Defesa Comercial (DECOM) (2009), *Relatório do Decom – 2008*, available at: http://www.desenvolvimento.gov.br/arquivos/dwnl_1242396716.pdf

Ministry of Development, Industry and Trade statistics, available at: http://www.desenvolvimento.gov.br/sitio/interna/interna.php?area=5&menu=576

Moreira, M.M (2009), 'Brazil's trade policy: old and new issues', in L. Brainard and L. Martinez-Diaz (eds), *Brazil as an Economic Superpower?*, Washington, DC: Brookings Institution Press, pp.137–58.

Muendler, M. (2004), 'Trade, technology and productivity: a study on Brazilian manufactures, 1986-1998', CESifo Working Paper no. 1148, available at: http://www.cesifo-group.de/portal/page/portal/ifoHome/

Nonnenberg, M. (1995), 'Vantagens comparativas reveladas, custo relativo dos fatores e intensidade de recursos naturais: resultados para o Brasil – 1980–1988', *Pesquisa e Planejamento Econômico*, **25** (2), 373–404, available at: http://ppe.ipea.gov.br/index.php/ppe/article/viewFile/783/723/

Pasteels, J.M. (1998), '*Foreign Trade Statistics – a Guide to Their Use in Market Research*', International Trade Centre, UNCTAD/WTO, available at: http://www.intracen.org/countries/statguid/statguid.pdf/

Rothmuller, L. (2003), 'Does FDI matter for trade in Brazil? An application of the gravity model', paper presented at the XXXI Encontro Nacional de Economia, Porto Seguro, Bahia, Brazil, available at: http://www.anpec.org.br/encontro_2003.htm.

Tavares de Araujo, J. and Miranda, P. (2008), 'Antidumping and antitruste: peculiaridades do caso brasileiro', Série Breves Cindes no. 8, Rio de Janeto: CINDES.

Tyler, W. and A.C. Gurgel (2009), 'Brazilian trade policies: some observed and estimated effects of the 1990s liberalization', *Estudos Economicos* (São Paulo), **39** (1), 59–88, available at: http//www.estecon.fea.usp.br/index.php/estecon/article/view/390/376/

UNCTAD (2002), '*World Investment Report 2002 Transnational Corporations and Export Competitiveness*', Geneva, also available at: http://www.unctad.org/en/docs/wir2002_en.pdf/

UNCTAD, Foreign Direct Investment Database, available at: http://stats.unctad.org/FDI/TableViewer/tableView.aspx?ReportId=3084

UNCTAD TRAINS, *Most Favoured Nation Average Applied Import Tariff Rates on Non-agricultural and Non-fuel Products,* available at: http://stats.unctad.org/Handbook/TableViewer/tableView.aspx?ReportId=1912

United States Department of Agriculture (USDA), Foreign Agricultural Service, http://www.ers.usda.gov/Browse/view.aspx?subject=TradeInternationalMarketsCommodityTrade/

Valor Econômico, Data on EMBI+, available at: http://www.valoronline.com.br/Busca.aspx?termo=embi&searchTerm=embi

World Trade Organization (WTO) (2009a), *International Trade Statistics 2009*, available at: http://www.wto.org/english/res_e/statis_e/its2009_e/its09_toc_e.htm
World Trade Organization (WTO) (2009b), *World Tariff Profiles 2009*, Geneva, available at: http://www.wto.org/english/res_e/publications_e/world_tariff_profiles09_e.htm

24. Comments on part VIII

Donald N. Coes

Beginning with the nineteenth century, Andrés López looks over a grand sweep of Argentine economic history. Given this long time period, the chapter is remarkably successful in portraying the large ups and sometimes even larger downs of an economy whose experience has few parallels in its variability.

López notes Argentina's rapid progress between 1870 and 1930, when the world depression put an end to export-led growth. He notes that the common characterization of trade policy as 'liberal' or laissez-faire is inaccurate, with significant departures from free trade in a number of sectors, even if such policies were the result of ad hoc political pressures rather than structured policies.

Argentina in the pre-1930 period was 'liberal', however, in capital account policy. Foreign investment was virtually unfettered, making the country one of the major destinations for FDI. But what Lopez's historically sweeping account makes clear is that the large swings in international direct investment in Argentina over a century and a half may not be the result of Argentine policy changes. The military dictatorship that took over in the 1970s also followed an almost 'classical' or pre-1930s foreign investment model, but had little to show for it. One can indeed read Lopez's lengthy account of Argentina's rise and fall in favor with international investors as a combination of world financial market trends and the constraints imposed by Argentine domestic macroeconomic policies.

López is cautious in drawing any sweeping conclusions from the wealth of data he surveys. But it is clear that the reduction in Argentina's openness to trade and foreign investment after the breakdown of international markets in the 1930s imposed a high cost on several generations of Argentines. The gradual reversal of these trends, beginning in a serious way only in recent decades, is now well established. López's account of the ups and downs of more than a century of Argentine interaction with the world economy are a reminder of how long and bumpy a road has been traveled.

In contrast to the lengthy time span of López's survey, Simão Silber concentrates on the 20-year span of Brazilian trade and capital account history during and after the economic reforms of the early 1990s. His chapter is an informative and thoughtful examination of the international economic experience and policies of one of the world's important participants in both trade and capital markets. Brazil's experience since 1990 raises a number of questions about its international economic objectives, and Silber provides tentative answers to some of the most significant ones.

If we look back more than half a century, Brazil's movement toward greater trade openness that began in the 1990s was long overdue. What is intriguing is why it took so long for policy-makers to realize this and to act upon it. Much as we economists like to think that our arguments may be responsible for sensible policy changes, we probably should not flatter ourselves. Silber makes it clear that a good part of the change was forced upon Brazil by a combination of international market pressures and by domestic macroeconomic disasters.

Given the success of Brazil's macroeconomic stabilization after the Plano Real in 1994, one of the most interesting issues that Silber's chapter raises is why the move toward trade liberalization appears to have stagnated since then, with the level of protection by several measures now higher than it was in the mid 1990s. An indirect answer to this is provided by his analysis of the capital account in the same period. One consequence of Brazilian success in attaining 'investment grade' status in international capital markets was an increase in capital inflows to Brazil. The consequent real appreciation of the real removed some of the pressure for continued trade reform.

Silber is entirely right in measuring Brazilian trade performance by a comparison not with the country's own past but with other large economies today. By this standard, Brazil is still not anywhere nearly as open an economy as it might have become, had trade policy reform not become a rather neglected objective after 1994. Compared with countries as diverse as the US, China, or even Russia, Brazilian manufacturing in the past decade has enjoyed significantly higher levels of protection. Much of this may derive from the effect of high levels of protection activities in areas such as automobiles, continuing Brazilian traditions in trade policy of more than half a century. As Silber points out, other productive activities, such as in alcohol or petroleum, may actually have negative effective rates.

One interesting point Silber makes is that international markets have put Brazil in a position parallel to its role in the nineteenth century, with exports of primary products among the most dynamic items on its export list. Although one can perhaps push the parallel too far, there is no question that the trading relations of a resource-scarce manufacturing power like Great Britain in the nineteenth century have their echo in twenty-first-century China's position relative to Brazil. Even though Brazil has benefited from the rapid growth of this emerging economy, its own participation in the world economy has lagged well behind these markets, with Brazil's share of world markets no higher than it was half a century ago.

A simple interpretation of Silber's message is that Brazil's foreign trade and investment patterns probably rate little more than a passing grade in a contemporary world context. This may be surprising for observers focused either on Brazil's success in eliminating high inflation or on the performance of Brazilian capital markets. But the numbers are telling a more down-to-earth story: had Brazil maintained the trends in trade opening that appeared to be operating in the early part of the period he considers, the country might be an even larger participant in the international economy.

Index

Entries for Argentina and Brazil can mainly be found under specific subject headings, principally the following: agricultural sector; foreign trade and investment; income distribution; industrialization; inflation and stabilization; privatization; regional development; service sector.